Leaving Certificate Maths

Text & Tests

Higher Level Maths

4

O.D. Morris • Paul Cooke • Frances O'Regan

The Celtic Press

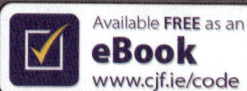

Acknowledgements
The authors would like to thank Paul Behan and Frances O'Regan for their valuable contributions to the original texts.
We also wish to express our deep gratitude to Aidan Roantree, a highly experienced and well-regarded Maths teacher and fellow author, for his thorough reading of the text and for his insightful suggestions, many of which helped to shape this new edition.

First Published in April 2018 by
The Celtic Press
Ground Floor – Block B
Liffey Valley Office Campus
Dublin 22

This reprint April 2021

ISBN: 978-0-7144-2464-4

Contents

Preface

This substantially revised book is the first of two volumes that amalgamate the previous editions of **Text & Tests 4, 5, 6** and **7** into two books for the Higher Level Leaving Certificate Project Maths course. **Text & Tests 4** encompasses more than 55% of the course.

As a Fifth-Year book, it introduces students to all five strands of the course and fully reflects the overall approach to the teaching of Maths as stated in the learning outcomes for Project Maths. It encourages the development of not only the students' knowledge and skills but also the understanding necessary to apply these skills.

The extensive range of imaginatively written and probing questions on each topic will help students understand the concepts involved and develop their problem-solving skills. Every attempt has been made to grade the questions in order of difficulty.

At the beginning of each chapter, there is a list of Key Words that students are expected to know and understand when the chapter is completed.

Each chapter concludes with a three-part revision exercise section consisting of (a) Core, (b) Advanced, and (c) Extended Response questions.

The Higher Level course will be completed by the new edition of **Text & Tests 5**.

O. D. Morris, Paul Cooke
February 2018

Algebra 1

Key words

polynomial   expression   equation   variable   linear   quadratic   cubic
expanding   degree   factors   identity   in terms of   simultaneous

Section 1.1 Polynomial expressions

Polynomial expressions are formed from the addition
of **many** algebraic terms with **positive integer powers.**

> A **binomial** expression
> contains two terms.
>
> A **trinomial** expression
> contains three terms.

$5x^3 - 3x^2 + 4x - 6$ is a polynomial expression.

This expression consists of four **terms**;
$5x^3, -3x^2, 4x$ and -6.

The **degree** of a polynomial is given by the highest
power of x.

(a) $4x - 6$ is a **linear** polynomial since the highest power (degree) of x is 1.
(b) $-3x^2 + 4x - 6$ is a **quadratic** polynomial of degree 2.
(c) $5x^3 - 3x^2 + 4x - 6$ is a **cubic** polynomial of degree 3.

Each polynomial is written in order of (i) decreasing powers of x, e.g. $5x^3 - 3x^2 + 4x - 6$,
or (ii) increasing powers of x, e.g. $9 + 3x - 4x^2$.

The **coefficient** of x^3 is the number before x^3 in the expression.

In $4x^3 - 2x^2 + 5x - 6$, the coefficient of x^3 is 4, the coefficient of x^2 is -2, the coefficient of x
is 5, and -6 is the **constant term**.

1. Addition and subtraction of polynomial expressions

Each term in a polynomial represents a different quantity, e.g. $8, 6x, 4x^2$.

When simplifying an expression, all like terms should be combined into a single term.

Example 1

Expand and simplify each of the following expressions.

(i) $7(x^3 + 2x^2 - 5x) - 2(2 + 3x + 4x^2 - 2x^3)$
(ii) $3x^2(4x^2 - 5x + 6) + 4x(8x^3 - 2x - 3)$

(i) $7(x^3 + 2x^2 - 5x) - 2(2 + 3x + 4x^2 - 2x^3) = 7x^3 + 14x^2 - 35x - 4 - 6x - 8x^2 + 4x^3$
$$= 11x^3 + 6x^2 - 41x - 4$$

(ii) $3x^2(4x^2 - 5x + 6) + 4x(8x^3 - 2x - 3) = 12x^4 - 15x^3 + 18x^2 + 32x^4 - 8x^2 - 12x$
$$= 44x^4 - 15x^3 + 10x^2 - 12x$$

2. Multiplying polynomial expressions

To multiply algebraic expressions, we use the distributive law, i.e. $a(b + c) = ab + ac$.

Example 2

Simplify the following: $(x - 5)(2x^2 - 3x + 6)$

$$(x - 5)(2x^2 - 3x + 6) = x(2x^2 - 3x + 6) - 5(2x^2 - 3x + 6)$$
$$= 2x^3 - 3x^2 + 6x - 10x^2 + 15x - 30$$
$$= 2x^3 - 13x^2 + 21x - 30$$

Note: Multiplying polynomial expressions is often called **expanding**.

3. Perfect squares

Any polynomial of the form $(x + a)^2$ is called a perfect square.

$$(x + a)^2 = (x + a)(x + a)$$
$$= (x)(x + a) + (a)(x + a)$$
$$= x^2 + ax + ax + a^2$$
$$= x^2 + 2ax + a^2$$

$$(x + a)^2 = x^2 + 2ax + a^2$$
$$(x - a)^2 = x^2 - 2ax + a^2$$

Similarly, $(x - a)^2 = x^2 - 2ax + a^2$.

For example, $(2x - 3)^2 = (2x)^2 - 2(2x)(3) + (3)^2 = 4x^2 - 12x + 9$

Example 3

Given that $25x^2 + px + 16$ is a perfect square and $p > 0$, find the value of p.

Since $25x^2 = (5x)^2$ and $16 = (4)^2$, $\quad \therefore \quad 25x^2 + px + 16 = (5x + 4)^2$
$$\therefore \quad 2(5x)(4) = px$$
$$\therefore \quad 40x = px \quad \Rightarrow p = 40.$$

(**Note:** $16 = (-4)^2 \quad \therefore \quad 2(5x)(-4) = px \quad \Rightarrow p = -40$, which is not valid
because $p > 0$)

4. Expanding $(x - a)(x + a)$

The expansion of $(x - a)(x + a) = x^2 + ax - ax - a^2$
$$= x^2 - a^2$$

$$(x - a)(x + a) = x^2 - a^2$$

Similarly, $(a - 5b)(a + 5b) = a^2 - 5ab + 5ab - (5b)^2 = \mathbf{a^2 - (5b)^2}$
$$= a^2 - 25b^2$$

This expansion results in a binomial expression called the **difference of two squares.**

This result is important when we need to factorise an expression of the form $a^2 - b^2$ as we will see later on in the chapter.

5. Dividing algebraic expressions

Algebraic quotients take many different forms. Some may be simplified as in the following cases.

Case 1. The denominator is a factor of each term of the numerator.

(i) $\dfrac{6x^3 - 8x^2y + 4xy^2 + 2x^2}{2x} = \dfrac{6x^3}{2x} - \dfrac{8x^2y}{2x} + \dfrac{4xy^2}{2x} + \dfrac{2x^2}{2x} = 3x^2 - 4xy + 2y^2 + x$

Case 2. The denominator is one of the factors of the numerator.

(ii) $\dfrac{6x^2 + 5xy + y^2}{(2x + y)} = \dfrac{(3x + y)(2x + y)}{(2x + y)} = 3x + y$

Case 3. The denominator divides into the numerator using long division.

(iii) $\dfrac{2x^3 - 9x^2 + 10x - 3}{(x - 3)} = 2x^2 - 3x + 1$ using long division.

Long Division

$$
\begin{array}{r}
2x^2 - 3x + 1 \\
x - 3 \overline{)2x^3 - 9x^2 + 10x - 3} \\
\underline{2x^3 - 6x^2} \quad \text{(subtract)} \\
-3x^2 + 10x - 3 \\
\underline{-3x^2 + 9x} \quad \text{(subtract)} \\
x - 3 \\
\underline{x - 3} \quad \text{(subtract)}
\end{array}
$$

... divide $2x^3$ by x to get $2x^2$

... multiply $2x^2$ by denominator

... divide $-3x^2$ by x to get $-3x$

... multiply $-3x$ by denominator

... divide x by x to get 1

Hence, $\dfrac{2x^3 - 9x^2 + 10x - 3}{(x - 3)} = 2x^2 - 3x + 1.$

3

Example 4

Divide $(2x^3 - 11x + 6)$ by $(2x^2 + 4x - 3)$.

Since this cubic polynomial has no power of x^2, it is good practice to rewrite the polynomial leaving space for the x^2 coefficients as follows;

$$
\begin{array}{r}
x - 2 \\
2x^2 + 4x - 3 \overline{)\,2x^3 \qquad\quad - 11x + 6} \\
\underline{2x^3 + 4x^2 - 3x} \\
-4x^2 - 8x + 6 \\
\underline{-4x^2 - 8x + 6}
\end{array}
$$

... divide $2x^2$ into $2x^3$ to get x
... multiply x by $2x^2 + 4x - 3$ and then subtract
... divide $2x^2$ into $-4x^2$ to get -2
... multiply -2 by $2x^2 + 4x - 3$ and then subtract

$\therefore \quad (2x^3 - 11x + 6) \div (2x^2 + 4x - 3) = x - 2$

Note also that when we divide $2x^3 - 11x + 6$ by $x - 2$ we get $2x^2 + 4x - 3$.

The factors of the polynomial $2x^3 - 11x + 6$ are $(x - 2)$ and $(2x^2 + 4x - 3)$,

i.e. $2x^3 - 11x + 6 = (x - 2)(2x^2 + 4x - 3)$.

We will use this property more fully in the chapter on factorisation.

$$
\begin{array}{r}
2x^2 + 4x - 3 \\
x - 2 \overline{)\,2x^3 \qquad\quad - 11x + 6} \\
\underline{2x^3 - 4x^2} \\
4x^2 - 11x + 6 \\
\underline{4x^2 - 8x} \\
-3x + 6 \\
\underline{-3x + 6}
\end{array}
$$

Exercise 1.1

1. Given the polynomial $4x^3 + 3x^2 - 9x + 5$, write down
   (i) the coefficient of x^2
   (ii) the coefficient of x
   (iii) the term independent of x (the constant term).

2. State the degree of each of the following polynomial expressions.
   (i) $-3x^2 + 5x - 1$ (ii) $4x^3 - 4x^2 + 9x + 3$ (iii) $7 + 3x - 3x^3 - 6x^4$

3. Give two reasons why $3x^2 - \dfrac{4}{x} + x^{\frac{3}{2}}$ is not a polynomial.

4. Simplify each of the following.
   (i) $3x^2 - 6x + 7 + 5x^2 + 2x - 9$ (ii) $x^3 - 4x^2 - 5x + 3x^3 + 6x^2 - x$
   (iii) $x(x + 4) + 3x(2x - 3)$ (iv) $3(x^2 - 7) + 2x(3x - 1) - 7x + 2$

5. Simplify each of the following.
   (i) $3x^2(4x + 2) + 5x^2(2x - 5)$ (ii) $x^3(x - 2) + 4x^3(2x - 6)$
   (iii) $x(x^3 + 4x^2 - 7x) + 3x^2(2x^2 - 3x + 4)$ (iv) $3x(x^2 - 7x + 1) + 2x^2(6x - 5)$

6. Expand each of the following.

    (i) $(x + 4)(2x + 5)$ (ii) $(2x + 3)(x - 2)$ (iii) $(3x - 2)(x + 3)$
    (iv) $(3x - 2)(4x - 1)$ (v) $(3x - 1)(2x + 5)$ (vi) $(4x + 1)(2x - 6)$
    (vii) $(x - 2)(x + 2)$ (viii) $(2x + 5)(2x - 5)$ (ix) $(ax - by)(ax + by)$

7. Expand each of the following perfect squares.

    (i) $(x + 2)^2$ (ii) $(x - 3)^2$ (iii) $(x + 5)^2$
    (iv) $(a + b)^2$ (v) $(x - y)^2$ (vi) $(a + 2b)^2$
    (vii) $(3x - y)^2$ (viii) $(x - 5y)^2$ (ix) $(2x + 3y)^2$

8. Express each of the following in the form $ax^2 + bx + c$.

    (i) $(x + \frac{1}{2})^2$ (ii) $8(x - \frac{1}{4})^2$ (iii) $-(1 - x)^2$

9. Which of the following are perfect squares? Explain your answers.

    (i) $x^2 + 5x + 25$ (ii) $9x^2 - 6x - 1$ (iii) $4 + 12x + 9x^2$

10. If $px^2 + 4x + 1$ is a perfect square for all values of x, find the value of p.

11. If $25x^2 + tx + 4$ is a perfect square for all values of x, find the value of t.

12. If $9x^2 + 24x + s$ is a perfect square for all values of x, find the value of s.

13. Expand and simplify each of the following.

    (i) $(x + 2)(x^2 + 2x + 6)$ (ii) $(x - 4)(2x^2 + 3x - 1)$
    (iii) $(2x + 3)(x^2 - 3x + 2)$ (iv) $(3x - 2)(2x^2 - 4x + 2)$

14. Show that $(x + y)(x^2 - xy + y^2) = x^3 + y^3$.

15. Verify that $(x - y)(x^2 + xy + y^2) = x^3 - y^3$.

16. Find the coefficient of x in the expansion of $(2x - 3)(3x^2 - 2x + 4)$.

17. Expand fully and simplify $(x + 3)(x - 4)(2x + 1)$.

18. Expand fully and simplify $(x^2 - 3x - 2)(2x^2 - 4x + 1)$.

19. Find the coefficient of x^2 in the expansion of $(3x^2 + 5x - 1)(2x^2 - 6x - 5)$.

20. Simplify each of the following quotients:

    (i) $\dfrac{3x + 6}{3}$ √(ii) $\dfrac{x^2 + 2x}{x}$ (iii) $\dfrac{3x^3 - 6x^2}{3x}$ √(iv) $\dfrac{15x^2y - 10xy^2}{5xy}$

21. Simplify each of the following quotients:

    √(i) $\dfrac{6x^2y + 9xy^2 - 3xy}{3xy}$ √(ii) $\dfrac{6x^4 - 9x^3 + 12x^2}{3x^2}$

22. Simplify each of the following:

   (i) $\dfrac{12a^2b}{3ab}$
   (ii) $\dfrac{12a^2bc}{3ac}$
   (iii) $\dfrac{4xy^2z}{2xy}$
   (iv) $\dfrac{3xy}{2} \times \dfrac{4}{6x^2}$

23. Simplify each of the following:

   ✓(i) $\dfrac{2x^2 + 5x - 3}{2x - 1}$
   ✓(ii) $\dfrac{2x^2 - 2x - 12}{x - 3}$
   (iii) $\dfrac{8x^2 + 8x - 6}{4x - 2}$

24. Divide each of the following:

   ✓(i) $x^3 - 8x^2 + 19x - 12 \div (x - 1)$
   (ii) $2x^3 - x^2 - 2x + 1 \div (2x - 1)$
   (iii) $3x^3 - 4x^2 - 3x + 4 \div (3x - 4)$
   (iv) $4x^3 - 7x^2 - 21x + 18 \div (x - 3)$
   (v) $x^3 - 22x + 15 \div (x + 5)$
   (vi) $2x^3 - x^2 - 12 \div (x - 2)$

25. Perform the following operations:

   ✓(i) $x^3 - 2x^2 + 2x - 4 \div (x^2 + 2)$
   (ii) $x^3 - 9x^2 + 27x - 27 \div (x^2 - 6x + 9)$
   (iii) $3x^3 + 2x^2 - 7x + 2 \div (x^2 + x - 2)$
   (iv) $5x^3 + 14x^2 + 7x - 2 \div (5x^2 + 4x - 1)$

26. Divide each of these:

   (i) $x^3 - 8 \div (x - 2)$
   (ii) $8x^3 - 27y^3 \div (2x - 3y)$

Section 1.2 Polynomial functions, an introduction ——————

Polynomial functions arise as we try to solve day-to-day problems.

Let x cm be the length of a rectangle.

If the width of the rectangle is 5 cm shorter than the length, then $(x - 5)$ cm is the width.

$(x - 5)$ cm

x cm

The area, A, of the rectangle depends on the length and width and by extension depends on x.

The symbol for the area depending on x is written as $A(x)$.

Therefore, $A(x) = x(x - 5) = x^2 - 5x$. As x varies, the area A varies.

x is called the **independent variable** and $A(x)$ the **dependent variable**.

$A(x)$ is the quadratic polynomial $x^2 - 5x$ of degree 2.

We note that if $x = 10$ cm, then $A(10) = (10)^2 - 5(10) = 50$ cm^2.

We also note that the width is $(x - 5) \Rightarrow x - 5 > 0$

$\Rightarrow x > 5$ cm

Example 1

The length of a rectangle is $(2x + 3)$ cm. If the area of the rectangle is given by the polynomial function $A(x) = 2x^2 + 7x + 6$, find

(a) an expression for the width of the rectangle
(b) an expression for the perimeter, $P(x)$, of the rectangle
(c) the minimum value of x.

Let w be the width of the rectangle.

(a) Area $A(x) = 2x^2 + 7x + 6 = w(2x + 3)$

$$\therefore \quad w = \frac{2x^2 + 7x + 6}{(2x + 3)} = \frac{(2x + 3)(x + 2)}{(2x + 3)} = (x + 2).$$

(b) The perimeter $P(x) = 2(2x + 3) + 2(x + 2) = 4x + 6 + 2x + 4 = 6x + 10$.

(c) Since $(2x + 3)$ is the length of the rectangle,
$$\Rightarrow (2x + 3) > 0$$
$$\Rightarrow x > -1.5$$

Note 1: $A(x)$ must be understood as a single concept and does not imply that A is multiplied by x.
It simply tells us that the quantity A depends on a variable x.

Note 2: Polynomial functions can be added and subtracted as before by collecting like terms and simplifying.

Example 2

Given $f(x) = 3x^3 - 4x^2 - 3x + 4$ and $g(x) = 5x^3 + 14x^2 + 7x - 2$, find

(a) $2f(x) - g(x)$ and state its degree
(b) $f(x) + 2g(x)$ and state its degree.

(a) $2f(x) - g(x) = 2(3x^3 - 4x^2 - 3x + 4) - (5x^3 + 14x^2 + 7x - 2)$
$\qquad\qquad\qquad = 6x^3 - 8x^2 - 6x + 8 - 5x^3 - 14x^2 - 7x + 2$
$\qquad\qquad\qquad = x^3 - 22x^2 - 13x + 10$ which is of degree 3.

(b) $f(x) + 2g(x) = (3x^3 - 4x^2 - 3x + 4) + 2(5x^3 + 14x^2 + 7x - 2)$
$\qquad\qquad\qquad = 3x^3 - 4x^2 - 3x + 4 + 10x^3 + 28x^2 + 14x - 4$
$\qquad\qquad\qquad = 13x^3 + 24x^2 + 11x$ which is of degree 3.

Evaluating polynomial functions

The value of a polynomial function is obtained by substituting a given value for the independent variable and simplifying.

If $p(x) = 2x^2 - 5x + 6$, then $p(1) = 2(1)^2 - 5(1) + 6 = 3$

and $p(-3) = 2(-3)^2 - 5(-3) + 6 = 39$.

A new variable can also be introduced in a similar way.

Given that $p(x) = 2x^2 - 5x + 6$,

$$p(t) = 2t^2 - 5t + 6.$$

Also $\quad p(t^2) = 2(t^2)^2 - 5(t^2) + 6 = 2t^4 - 5t^2 + 6$

Example 3

A paint manufacturer knows that the daily cost (€C) of producing x litres of paint is given by the formula $C(x) = 0.001x^2 + 0.1x + 5$.

(a) State the degree of $C(x)$.
(b) Find the daily cost of producing   (i) 100 ℓ of paint   (ii) 400 ℓ of paint.

(a) The degree of $C(x)$ is 2.
(b) (i) $C(100) = 0.001(100)^2 + 0.1(100) + 5 = €25$
    (ii) $C(400) = 0.001(400)^2 + 0.1(400) + 5 = €205$.

Example 4

An open box has dimensions $x + 3, x + 1$ and x, where x is the height (in cms) of the box. Find an expression for the external surface area of the box, $S(x)$, and hence find $S(5)$.

Area of the sides $= 2(x)(x + 3) + 2(x)(x + 1)$
$$= 2x^2 + 6x + 2x^2 + 2x = 4x^2 + 8x$$

Area of the base $= (x + 3)(x + 1) = x^2 + 4x + 3$

Total surface area $S(x) = x^2 + 4x + 3 + 4x^2 + 8x$
$$= (5x^2 + 12x + 3)\,\text{cm}^2$$

$S(5) = 5(5)^2 + 12(5) + 3 = 188\,\text{cm}^2$

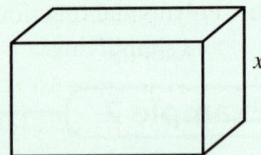

Example 5

Given the function $f(x) = 2x - 4$ for all $x \in R$, find

(a) $f(3), f(-2), f(t)$
(b) for what values of t is $f(t) = t$.

(a) $f(x) = 2x - 4 \Rightarrow f(3) = 2(3) - 4 = 2$
$$f(-2) = 2(-2) - 4 = -8$$
$$f(t) = 2(t) - 4 = 2t - 4$$

(b) $f(t) = t \Rightarrow 2t - 4 = t$
$$t - 4 = 0$$
$$t = 4$$

Note: Polynomial functions with more than one independent variable occur regularly.

The volume of a cylinder $V = \pi . r^2 . h$, where r is the radius of the base and h the height of the cylinder.

In function terms: $V(r, h) = \pi . r^2 . h$,

that is, the volume of the cylinder depends on both the radius, r, and the height, h.

The volume V depends on two independent variables, r, h.

The degree of this polynomial is 2, the highest power (index) of either variable.

Exercise 1.2

1. A rectangle has one side 4 cm longer than the other.
   Let x be the length of the smaller side.

   Find (i) an expression for $A(x)$, the area of the rectangle
   (ii) an expression for $P(x)$, the perimeter of the rectangle.

2. The area of a rectangle, $A(x)$, is $6x^2 + 4x - 2$.
   If the length is given by $(3x - 1)$, find

   (i) an expression for the width of the rectangle
   (ii) an expression for the perimeter, $P(x)$, of the rectangle.

3. The dimensions (in cm) of an open rectangular box are given in the diagram. Find

   (a) an expression for the volume, $V(x)$, of the box
   (b) an expression for the external surface area, $S(x)$, of the box
   (c) the value of
   (i) $V(x)$ and (ii) $S(x)$ when $x = 5$.

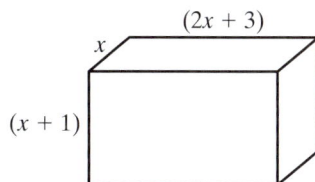

4. If $f(x) = 2x^3 - x^2 - 5x - 4$, find

   (a) $f(0)$ (b) $f(1)$ (c) $f(-2)$ (d) $f(3a)$

5. If $f(x) = x^2 - 3x + 6$, find

   (a) $f(0)$ (b) $f(-5)$ (c) $f\left(-\frac{1}{2}\right)$ (d) $f\left(\frac{a}{4}\right)$

6. A rectangle has length $(x - y)$ and width $(2x + 3y)$.
   Find, in terms of x and y, an expression for the

   (a) area   (b) perimeter   of the rectangle.

7. The width of an open rectangular box is 5 cm shorter than its length and the height of the box is twice the length.
   By letting the length of the box be x cm, find
   (a) an expression for the volume, $V(x)$, of the box
   (b) an expression for the total surface area, $S(x)$ (internal and external), of the box.

8. The number of diagonals, d, in an n-sided polygon is given by the polynomial

$$d(n) = \frac{n^2}{2} - \frac{3n}{2}.$$

Explain what is meant by (i) $d(4)$ (ii) $d(5)$ and find values for $d(4), d(5), d(6)$.

Copy each polygon below and verify your answer in each case.

Explain why $d(3) = 0$.

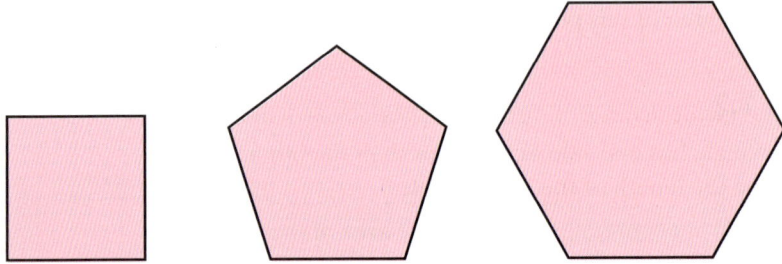

9. If $f(x) = x + 5$, find, in terms of a, $f(a^2) - 3f(a) + 2$.

10. Given $f(x) = x^2 - 3x + 6$, find

(i) $f(-2t)$ (ii) $f(t^2)$ (iii) $f(t - 2)$

State the degree of each of the polynomial functions in t.

11. The volume of a cone, $V(r, h)$, is given by the formula $V(r, h) = \frac{1}{3}\pi r^2 h$, where r is the radius and h is the perpendicular height of the cone. Find

(i)   the volume, in terms of π, of a cone with height 21 cm and radius 14 cm
(ii) the volume of a cone, in terms of r and π, if the cone has the same height as the radius r
(iii) the volume of a cone, in terms of h and π, if the radius of the base is twice the height h.

12. A rectangular piece of cardboard has dimensions 18 cm by 24 cm. Four squares each x cm by x cm are cut from the corners. An open box is formed by folding up the flaps.

Find a function for V, which gives the volume of the box in terms of x.

If $a < x < b$, find a and b.

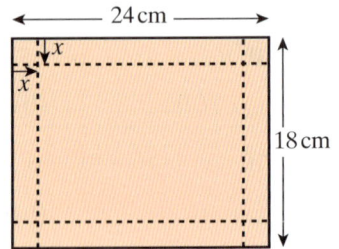

13. Use the formula $T = 2\pi\sqrt{\dfrac{l}{g}}$ to find the value of l, in terms of π, if $T = 4\,\text{s}$ and $g = 10\,\text{m s}^{-2}$.

14. Use the formula $V = \frac{4}{3}\pi r^3$ to find the value of r if $V = \frac{792}{7}\,\text{m}^3$ and $\pi = \frac{22}{7}$.

15. In the morning, every student in a classroom shakes hands with every other student as a greeting. The number of handshakes, H, between x students is given by the expression $H(x) = \frac{x}{2}(x - 1)$.

Using this formula, find

   (i) the number of handshakes between 5 students

  (ii) the number of handshakes between 6 students

 (iii) the number of handshakes between 10 students.

Using a pattern created by the above, or otherwise, find, if on a particular morning 136 handshakes were given, the number of students in the room.

Section 1.3 Factorising algebraic expressions

An algebraic **factor** divides evenly into a polynomial leaving no remainder.

$(x - 3)$ is a factor of $2x^3 - 9x^2 + 10x - 3$
because $(2x^3 - 9x^2 + 10x - 3) \div (x - 3) = (2x^2 - 3x + 1)$.

$(x - 4)$ and $(x + 3)$ are both factors of $x^2 - x - 12$ because

(i) $(x^2 - x - 12) \div (x - 4) = (x + 3)$ and also   (ii) $(x^2 - x - 12) \div (x + 3) = (x - 4)$.

To solve algebraic equations, we first need to be able to factorise different algebraic expressions.

Several different techniques can be used for factorising expressions and these are shown below.

1. Finding the highest common factor by inspection

   (i) $3x^2 - 9xy = 3x(x - 3y) \Rightarrow$ the factors are $3x$ and $(x - 3y)$

  (ii) $2a^2b - 4ab^2 + 12\,abc = 2ab(a - 2b + 6c) \Rightarrow$ the factors are $2ab$ and $(a - 2ab + 6c)$.

2. Grouping terms

$$6x^2y + 3xy^2 - 12x - 6y = 3xy(2x + y) - 6(2x + y)$$
$$= (2x + y)(3xy - 6)$$
$$\Rightarrow \text{the factors are } (2x + y) \text{ and } (3xy - 6)$$

3. Difference of two squares

Since $(x + y)(x - y) = x^2 - y^2$, the factors of $x^2 - y^2$ are $(x + y)$ and $(x - y)$.

Note: When simplifying quotients, it is important to be able to factorise fully expressions containing the difference of two squares.

(i) $c^2 - d^2$ $= (c - d)(c + d)$

(ii) $x^2 - 9y^2 = x^2 - (3y)^2$ $= (x - 3y)(x + 3y)$

(iii) $x^2 - 8y^2 = x^2 - (\sqrt{8}y)^2 = (x - \sqrt{8}y)(x + \sqrt{8}y)$

(iv) $x - 9 = (\sqrt{x})^2 - 3^2$ $= (\sqrt{x} - 3)(\sqrt{x} + 3)$

Example 1

Factorise fully   (i) $x^4 - y^4$ (ii) $12x^2 - 75y^2$

(i) $x^4 - y^4 = (x^2)^2 - (y^2)^2$ … write as the difference of two squares
$\qquad\quad = (x^2 - y^2)(x^2 + y^2)$ … another difference of two squares occurs
$\qquad\quad = (x - y)(x + y)(x^2 + y^2)$

(ii) $12x^2 - 75y^2 = 3(4x^2 - 25y^2)$ … find the highest common factor by inspection
$\qquad\qquad\quad = 3[(2x)^2 - (5y)^2]$ … write as the difference of two squares
$\qquad\qquad\quad = 3(2x - 5y)(2x + 5y)$

Example 2

Simplify $\dfrac{x^2 - 9y^2}{3x + 9y}$

$$\frac{x^2 - 9y^2}{3x + 9y} = \frac{(x - 3y)(x + 3y)}{3(x + 3y)} = \frac{x - 3y}{3}$$

4. Factorising quadratic expressions

We can factorise quadratic expressions of the form $ax^2 + bx + c$ using either

(i) trial and error   **or**
(ii) when the coefficients are large or irrational, the quadratic formula.

(i) $x^2 + 3x - 18 = (x \pm ?)(x \pm ?)$ … checking all the factor pairs of -18
$\qquad\qquad\quad = (x + 6)(x - 3)$ … $(\pm 1, \pm 18), (\pm 2, \pm 9), (\pm 3, \pm 6) \dots (+6, -3)$ is the factor pair
$\qquad\qquad\qquad\qquad\qquad\qquad$ which, when added, produces $+3$ for the middle term.

(ii) $3x^2 - 17x + 20 = ax^2 + bx + c \rightarrow a = 3, b = -17, c = 20.$

Using $x = \dfrac{-b \pm \sqrt{b^2 - 4ac}}{2a}$,

> If $ax^2 + bx + c = 0,$
>
> then $x = \dfrac{-b \pm \sqrt{b^2 - 4ac}}{2a}$

$x = \dfrac{17 \pm \sqrt{(-17)^2 - 4.3.20}}{2.3} = \dfrac{17 \pm \sqrt{289 - 240}}{6}$

$\Rightarrow x = \dfrac{17 \pm 7}{6} = \left(\dfrac{24}{6} \text{ or } \dfrac{10}{6}\right) = \left(4 \text{ or } \dfrac{5}{3}\right)$

If $x = 4,$ then $(x - 4)$ is the factor.

And if $x = \dfrac{5}{3} \Rightarrow 3x = 5,$ therefore the second factor is $(3x - 5).$

$\therefore \quad 3x^2 - 17x + 20 = (3x - 5)(x - 4).$

Example 3

Factorise (i) $3x^2 + 10x + 8$ (ii) $x^2 - 2\sqrt{2}x - 6$

(i) $3x^2 + 10x + 8 = (3x \pm ?)(x \pm ?)$ ... the factor pairs of 8 are $(\pm 1, \pm 8), (\pm 2, \pm 4)$

$\qquad\qquad\qquad = (3x + 4)(x + 2)$ ... producing a middle term of $+10x$

(ii) $x^2 - 2\sqrt{2}x - 6 = ax^2 + bx + c \rightarrow a = 1, b = -2\sqrt{2}, c = -6$

$$x = \frac{-b \pm \sqrt{b^2 - 4ac}}{2a} \rightarrow x = \frac{2\sqrt{2} \pm \sqrt{(-2\sqrt{2})^2 - 4(1)(-6)}}{2.1} = \frac{2\sqrt{2} \pm \sqrt{32}}{2}$$

Therefore, $x = \dfrac{2\sqrt{2} \pm 4\sqrt{2}}{2} = \sqrt{2} \pm 2\sqrt{2} = 3\sqrt{2}$ or $(-\sqrt{2})$.

The factors are $(x + \sqrt{2})$ and $(x - 3\sqrt{2})$.

5. Factorising expressions of the form $x^3 - y^3$ and $x^3 + y^3$

We can show by long division that $(x - y)$ is a factor of $x^3 - y^3$, creating a second factor $x^2 + xy + y^2$.

Therefore, we can write
$x^3 - y^3 = (x - y)(x^2 + xy + y^2)$.

Similarly, we have that
$x^3 + y^3 = (x + y)(x^2 - xy + y^2)$.

If we can write a polynomial in one of these forms, we can use these factor pairs as templates to find its factors.

For example, we can write
   (i) $27x^3 + y^3 = (3x)^3 + y^3$
   (ii) $64x^3 - 125y^3 = (4x)^3 - (5y)^3$.

$$
\begin{array}{r}
x^2 + xy + y^2 \\
x - y \overline{)x^3 \qquad\qquad\quad - y^3} \\
x^3 - x^2y \\
\overline{+ x^2y \qquad\quad - y^3} \\
+ x^2y - xy^2 \\
\overline{+ xy^2 - y^3} \\
+ xy^2 - y^3 \\
\overline{}
\end{array}
$$

$\boxed{\begin{array}{l} x^3 - y^3 = (x - y)(x^2 + xy + y^2) \\ x^3 + y^3 = (x + y)(x^2 - xy + y^2) \end{array}}$ Also $\boxed{\begin{array}{l} (ax)^3 - (by)^3 = (ax - by)(a^2x^2 + abxy + b^2y^2) \\ (ax)^3 + (by)^3 = (ax + by)(a^2x^2 - abxy + b^2y^2) \end{array}}$

Example 4

Factorise   (i) $a^3 + 8b^3$ (ii) $64c^3 - 125d^3$

(i) $a^3 + 8b^3 = a^3 + (2b)^3$ ... note: let $x = a$ and $y = 2b$ in the box on previous page
$$= (a + 2b)(a^2 - 2ab + 4b^2)$$

(ii) $64c^3 - 125d^3 = (4c)^3 - (5d)^3$ ... note: let $x = 4c$ and $y = 5d$
$$= (4c - 5d)[(4c)^2 + (4c)(5d) + (5d)^2]$$
$$= (4c - 5d)(16c^2 + 20cd + 25d^2)$$

Exercise 1.3

Using the highest common factor, factorise each of the following:

1. $5x^2 - 10x$

2. $6ab - 12bc$

3. $3x^2 - 6xy$

4. $2x^2y - 6x^2z$

5. $2a^3 - 4a^2 + 8a$

6. $5xy^2 - 20x^2y$

7. $2a^2b - 4ab^2 + 12abc$

8. $3x^2y - 9xy^2 + 15xyz$

9. $4\pi r^2 + 6\pi rh$

Factorise each of the following by grouping terms.

10. $3a(2b - c) - 4(2b - c)$

11. $x^2 - ax + 3x - 3a$

12. $2c^2 - 4cd + c - 2d$

13. $8ax + 4ay - 6bx - 3by$

14. $7y^2 - 21by + 2ay - 6ab$

15. $6xy + 12yz - 8xz - 9y^2$

16. $6x^2 - 3y(3x - 2a) - 4ax$

17. $3ax^2 - 3ay^2 - 4bx^2 + 4by^2$

Using the difference of two squares, factorise the following:

18. $a^2 - b^2$

19. $x^2 - 4y^2$

20. $9x^2 - y^2$

21. $16x^2 - 25y^2$

22. $36x^2 - 25$

23. $1 - 36x^2$

24. $49a^2 - 4b^2$

$\sqrt{}$**25.** $x^2y^2 - 1$

$\sqrt{}$**26.** $4a^2b^2 - 16c^2$

27. $3x^2 - 27y^2$

28. $45 - 5x^2$

29. $45a^2 - 20$

30. $(2x + y)^2 - 4$

31. $(3a - 2b)^2 - 9$

32. $a^4 - b^4$

Factorise each of the following quadratic expressions:

33. $x^2 + 9x + 14$

34. $2x^2 + 7x + 3$

35. $2x^2 + 11x + 14$

36. $x^2 - 9x + 14$

37. $x^2 - 11x + 28$

38. $2x^2 - 7x + 3$

39. $3x^2 - 17x + 20$

40. $7x^2 - 18x + 8$

41. $2x^2 - 7x - 15$

42. $3x^2 + 11x - 20$

43. $12x^2 - 11x - 5$

44. $6x^2 + x - 15$

$\sqrt{}$**45.** $3x^2 + 13x - 10$

46. $6x^2 - 11x + 3$

47. $36x^2 - 7x - 4$

$\sqrt{}$**48.** $15x^2 - 14x - 8$

49. $6y^2 + 11y - 35$

50. $12x^2 + 17xy - 5y^2$

51. Using the quadratic formula, factorise each of the following:

    (i) $x^2 + 3\sqrt{3}x + 6$ (ii) $x^2 + 2\sqrt{5}x - 15$ (iii) $2x^2 - 5\sqrt{2}x - 6$

52. Using both the sum and the difference of two cubes, factorise the following:

    (i) $a^3 + b^3$ (ii) $a^3 - b^3$ (iii) $8x^3 + y^3$

Factorise each of the expressions in numbers (53–55):

53. (i) $27x^3 - y^3$ (ii) $x^3 - 64$ (iii) $8x^3 - 27y^3$

54. (i) $8 + 27k^3$ (ii) $64 - 125a^3$ (iii) $27a^3 + 64b^3$

55. (i) $a^3 - 8b^3c^3$ (ii) $5x^3 + 40y^3$ (iii) $(x + y)^3 - z^3$

Section 1.4 Simplifying algebraic fractions

Algebraic fractions are added, subtracted, multiplied and divided in the same way as numerical fractions.

Revision:

(i) $\frac{2}{5} + \frac{3}{7} = \frac{14}{35} + \frac{15}{35} = \frac{29}{35}$ (fractions can only be added or subtracted when they have the same denominator.)

(ii) $\frac{2}{5} \times \frac{3}{7} = \frac{6}{35}$ (fractions are multiplied by multiplying the numerators and denominators separately.)

(iii) $\frac{2}{5} \div \frac{3}{7} = \frac{2}{5} \times \frac{7}{3} = \frac{14}{15}$ (fractions are divided by changing the division into a product.)

Note: $\dfrac{\overset{2}{\cancel{6}} \times 12}{\underset{1}{\cancel{3}}} = 24$ $\dfrac{\overset{2}{\cancel{6}} + \overset{4}{\cancel{12}}}{\underset{1}{\cancel{3}}} = 6$

Similarly with algebraic terms;

(i) $\dfrac{2}{x + 1} - \dfrac{2x}{2x + 3} = \dfrac{2(2x + 3)}{(x + 1)(2x + 3)} - \dfrac{2x(x + 1)}{(x + 1)(2x + 3)}$ ... getting a common denominator

                    $= \dfrac{4x + 6 - 2x^2 - 2x}{(x + 1)(2x + 3)} = \dfrac{-2x^2 + 2x + 6}{(x + 1)(2x + 3)}$ ... simplifying the numerator

(ii) $\dfrac{2}{x + 1} \times \dfrac{2x}{2x + 3} = \dfrac{4x}{(x + 1)(2x + 3)}$ ... multiplying numerators and multiplying denominators

(iii) $\dfrac{2}{x + 1} \div \dfrac{2x}{2x + 3} = \dfrac{2}{x + 1} \times \dfrac{2x + 3}{2x} = \dfrac{2(2x + 3)}{2x(x + 1)} = \dfrac{(2x + 3)}{x(x + 1)}$ ... changing division to multiplication and then dividing above and below by a common factor

So, in general when dealing with algebraic fractions;

    (i)   A common denominator is needed to add or subtract fractions.

    (ii) A fraction can be reduced (simplified) only if the numerator and denominator have a common factor.

    (iii) If the denominator or numerator contain fractions added or subtracted, they must be reduced into a single fraction first before proceeding.

    (iv) To divide fractions, we multiply by the denominator inverted.

Example 1

Simplify   (i) $\dfrac{5ax}{15a + 10a^2}$ (ii) $\dfrac{t^2 + 3t - 4}{t^2 - 16}$ (iii) $\dfrac{\frac{5}{8} + y}{\frac{1}{8}}$

(i) $\dfrac{5ax}{15a + 10a^2} = \dfrac{(\overset{1}{\cancel{5a}})x}{(\underset{1}{\cancel{5a}})(3 + 2a)} = \dfrac{x}{3 + 2a}$

(ii) $\dfrac{t^2 + 3t - 4}{t^2 - 16} = \dfrac{(\overset{1}{\cancel{t + 4}})(t - 1)}{(t - 4)(\underset{1}{\cancel{t + 4}})} = \dfrac{t - 1}{t - 4}$

(iii) $\dfrac{\frac{5}{8} + y}{\frac{1}{8}} = \left(\frac{5}{8} + y\right).8 = 5 + 8y$

Example 2

Simplify each of the following

(i) $\dfrac{6y}{x(x + 4y)} - \dfrac{3}{2x}$ (ii) $\dfrac{x - 4}{x^2 - x - 2} - \dfrac{x - 3}{x^2 - 4}$

(i) $\dfrac{6y}{x(x + 4y)} - \dfrac{3}{2x} = \dfrac{2(6y)}{2x(x + 4y)} - \dfrac{3(x + 4y)}{2x(x + 4y)}$

$= \dfrac{2(6y) - 3(x + 4y)}{2x(x + 4y)} = \dfrac{12y - 3x - 12y}{2x(x + 4y)}$

$= \dfrac{-3x}{2x(x + 4y)} = \dfrac{-3}{2(x + 4y)}$

(ii) $\dfrac{x-4}{x^2-x-2} - \dfrac{x-3}{x^2-4} = \dfrac{x-4}{(x-2)(x+1)} - \dfrac{x-3}{(x-2)(x+2)}$

$$= \dfrac{(x-4)(x+2) - (x-3)(x+1)}{(x-2)(x+1)(x+2)}$$

$$= \dfrac{x^2 - 4x + 2x - 8 - x^2 + 3x - x + 3}{(x-2)(x+1)(x+2)}$$

$$= \dfrac{-5}{(x-2)(x+1)(x+2)} = \dfrac{-5}{(x^2-4)(x+1)}$$

Example 3

Simplify $\dfrac{y - \dfrac{x^2+y^2}{y}}{\dfrac{1}{x} - \dfrac{1}{y}}$.

$$\dfrac{y - \dfrac{x^2+y^2}{y}}{\dfrac{1}{x} - \dfrac{1}{y}} = \dfrac{\dfrac{y^2 - (x^2+y^2)}{y}}{\dfrac{(y-x)}{xy}} = \dfrac{\dfrac{-x^2}{y}}{\dfrac{(y-x)}{xy}} = \dfrac{-x^2}{y} \times \dfrac{xy}{(y-x)}$$

$$= \dfrac{-x^3 y}{y(y-x)} = \dfrac{-x^3}{y-x}$$

Exercise 1.4

1. Simplify each of the following fractions:

   (i) $\dfrac{8y}{2y^3}$ (ii) $\dfrac{7a^6 b^3}{14a^5 b^4}$ (iii) $\dfrac{(2x)^2}{4x}$ (iv) $\dfrac{7y + 2y^2}{7y}$ (v) $\dfrac{5ax}{15a + 10a^2}$

2. Express each of the following as a single fraction:

   (a) $\dfrac{2x}{5} + \dfrac{4x}{3}$ (b) $\dfrac{3x}{5} - \dfrac{x}{2}$ (c) $\dfrac{2x+3}{4} + \dfrac{x}{3}$

   (d) $\dfrac{x+1}{4} + \dfrac{2x-1}{5}$ (e) $\dfrac{3x-4}{6} - \dfrac{2x+1}{3}$ (f) $\dfrac{3x-2}{6} - \dfrac{x-3}{4}$

(g) $\dfrac{5x-1}{4} - \dfrac{2x-4}{5}$

(h) $\dfrac{3x+5}{6} - \dfrac{2x+3}{4} - \dfrac{1}{12}$

(i) $\dfrac{3x-2}{4} + \dfrac{3}{5} - \dfrac{2x-1}{10}$

(j) $\dfrac{1}{3x} + \dfrac{1}{5x}$

(k) $\dfrac{3}{4x} - \dfrac{5}{8x}$

(l) $\dfrac{1}{x} + \dfrac{1}{x+3}$

(m) $\dfrac{2}{x+2} + \dfrac{3}{x+4}$

(n) $\dfrac{2}{x-2} + \dfrac{3}{2x-1}$

(o) $\dfrac{5}{3x-1} - \dfrac{2}{x+3}$

(p) $\dfrac{3}{2x-7} - \dfrac{1}{5x+2}$

(q) $\dfrac{2}{3x-5} - \dfrac{1}{4}$

(r) $\dfrac{5}{2x-1} - \dfrac{3}{x-2}$

(s) $\dfrac{x}{x-y} - \dfrac{y}{x+y}$

(t) $\dfrac{3}{x} + \dfrac{4}{3y} - \dfrac{2}{3xy}$

(u) $\dfrac{3}{x} - \dfrac{2}{x-1} - \dfrac{4}{x(x-1)}$

$$(x^2 - a^2) = (x-a)(x+a)$$

3. By factorising the numerator and the denominator fully, simplify each of the following.

(i) $\dfrac{2z^2 - 4z}{2z^2 - 10z}$

(ii) $\dfrac{y^2 + 7y + 10}{y^2 - 25}$

(iii) $\dfrac{t^2 + 3t - 4}{t^2 - 3t + 2}$

(iv) $\dfrac{x}{x^2 - 4} - \dfrac{1}{x+2}$

(v) $\dfrac{2}{a+3} - \dfrac{a+2}{a^2 - 9}$

(vi) $\dfrac{x-1}{x^2 - 4} + \dfrac{1}{x-2}$

4. By factorising the denominator, simplify each of the following:

(i) $\dfrac{10}{2x^2 - 3x - 2} - \dfrac{2}{x-2}$

(ii) $\dfrac{x+2}{2x^2 - x - 1} - \dfrac{1}{x-1}$

5. Simplify the following:

(i) $\dfrac{1}{x^2 - 9} - \dfrac{2}{x^2 - x - 6}$

(ii) $\dfrac{3}{x^2 + x - 2} - \dfrac{2}{x^2 + 3x + 2}$

(iii) $\dfrac{2}{6x^2 - 5x - 4} - \dfrac{3}{9x^2 - 16}$

(iv) $\dfrac{1}{xy - x^2} - \dfrac{1}{y^2 - xy}$

6. Simplify each of the following complex fractions:

(i) $\dfrac{\frac{1}{2} + \frac{3}{4}}{\frac{1}{4}}$

(ii) $\dfrac{\frac{2}{3} + \frac{5}{6}}{\frac{3}{8}}$

(iii) $\dfrac{x - \frac{1}{x}}{1 + \frac{1}{x}}$

7. Simplify each of these:

(i) $\dfrac{\frac{1}{x} + 1}{\frac{1}{x} - 1}$

(ii) $\dfrac{\frac{1}{x^2} - 4}{\frac{1}{x} - 2}$

(iii) $\dfrac{x + y}{\frac{1}{x} + \frac{1}{y}}$

8. By expressing the numerator as a single fraction, simplify the following fractions:

(i) $\dfrac{4y - \dfrac{3}{2}}{2}$ 　　(ii) $\dfrac{2 - \dfrac{1}{x}}{2}$ 　　(iii) $\dfrac{3x + \dfrac{1}{x}}{2}$ 　　(iv) $\dfrac{y + \dfrac{1}{4}}{\dfrac{1}{2}}$

9. By expressing the numerator and the denominator as single fractions, write the following fractions in their simplest forms.

(i) $\dfrac{z - \dfrac{1}{3}}{z - \dfrac{1}{2}}$ 　　(ii) $\dfrac{2x + \dfrac{1}{2}}{x + \dfrac{1}{4}}$ 　　(iii) $\dfrac{z - \dfrac{1}{2z}}{z - \dfrac{1}{3z}}$ 　　(iv) $\dfrac{x - \dfrac{1}{x + 1}}{x - 1}$

10. Simplify each of the following.

(i) $\dfrac{1 + \dfrac{2}{x}}{\dfrac{x + 2}{x - 2}}$ 　　(ii) $\dfrac{2 + \dfrac{1}{x}}{2x^2 + x}$ 　　(iii) $\dfrac{x + \dfrac{2x}{x - 2}}{1 + \dfrac{4}{(x + 2)(x - 2)}}$

11. Simplify each of the following.

(i) $\dfrac{\dfrac{a + b}{a - b} - \dfrac{a - b}{a + b}}{1 + \dfrac{a - b}{a + b}}$ 　　(ii) $\dfrac{x + \dfrac{3}{x}}{x - \dfrac{9}{x^3}}$ 　　(iii) $\dfrac{9 - \dfrac{1}{y^2}}{9 + \dfrac{6}{y} + \dfrac{1}{y^2}}$

12. Show that $\dfrac{3x - 5}{x - 2} + \dfrac{1}{2 - x}$ simplifies to a constant when $x \neq 2$.

Section 1.5 Binomial Expansions

We expand $(a + b)^2$ as $a^2 + 2ab + b^2$.

Also $(a + b)^3 = (a + b)(a + b)^2 = (a + b)(a^2 + 2ab + b^2)$

$$= a^3 + 2a^2b + ab^2 + a^2b + 2ab^2 + b^3$$

$$= a^3 + 3a^2b + 3ab^2 + b^3$$

However with higher powers this method is too time consuming.

Examining a number of expansions the following patterns are noted:

$(a + b)^2 = \mathbf{1}a^2 + \mathbf{2}ab + 1b^2$

$(a + b)^3 = \mathbf{1}a^3 + \mathbf{3}a^2b + \mathbf{3}ab^2 + 1b^3$

$(a + b)^4 = \mathbf{1}a^4 + \mathbf{4}a^3b + \mathbf{6}a^2b^2 + \mathbf{4}ab^3 + 1b^4$

$(a + b)^5 = \mathbf{1}a^5 + \mathbf{5}a^4b + \mathbf{10}a^3b^2 + \mathbf{10}a^2b^3 + \mathbf{5}ab^4 + \mathbf{1}b^5$

1. The powers of a decrease by 1 from term to term, a^5, a^4, a^3, a^2, a.
2. The powers of b increase by 1 from term to term b, b^2, b^3, b^4, b^5
3. The sum of the powers of a and b for each term is 5, a^4b^1, a^3b^2, a^2b^3, a^1b^4.
4. The number of terms in each expansion is 1 greater than the power.
   i.e. $(a + b)^3$ has 4 terms, $(a + b)^4$ has 5 terms, $(a + b)^5$ has 6 terms etc.
5. The coefficients form Pascal's triangle.

$$
\begin{array}{ccccccc}
 & & & 1 & & & & \binom{0}{0} & & & & & \text{..Row 1} \\
 & & 1 & & 1 & & & & \binom{1}{0} & \binom{1}{1} & & & \text{..Row 1} \\
 & 1 & & 2 & & 1 & & & \binom{2}{0} & \binom{2}{1} & \binom{2}{2} & & \text{..Row 2} \\
1 & & 3 & & 3 & & 1 & & \binom{3}{0} & \binom{3}{1} & \binom{3}{2} & \binom{3}{3} & \text{..Row 3}
\end{array}
$$

$\binom{0}{0}$ ..Row 1
$\binom{1}{0}$ $\binom{1}{1}$ ..Row 1
$\binom{2}{0}$ $\binom{2}{1}$ $\binom{2}{2}$ ..Row 2
$\binom{3}{0}$ $\binom{3}{1}$ $\binom{3}{2}$ $\binom{3}{3}$ ..Row 3
$\binom{4}{0}$ $\binom{4}{1}$ $\binom{4}{2}$ $\binom{4}{3}$ $\binom{4}{4}$ ..Row 4
$\binom{5}{0}$ $\binom{5}{1}$ $\binom{5}{2}$ $\binom{5}{3}$ $\binom{5}{4}$ $\binom{5}{5}$ ..Row 5

```
          1
        1   1
      1   2   1
    1   3   3   1
  1   4   6   4   1
1   5  10  10   5   1
```

The coefficients can be expressed in terms of combinations (see Chapter 5 - Probability) where $\binom{n}{r}$ stands for the number of ways of choosing r objects from n different objects.

So $(a + b)^5 = \binom{5}{0}a^5 + \binom{5}{1}a^4b + \binom{5}{2}a^3b^2 + \binom{5}{3}a^2b^3 + \binom{5}{4}ab^4 + \binom{5}{5}b^5$

All of the coefficients can be quickly evaluated using a calculator with an **nCr** function.

For example $\binom{5}{4}$, press $\boxed{5}\boxed{nCr}\boxed{4}\boxed{=}$ 5 and $\binom{9}{3}$, press $\boxed{9}\boxed{nCr}\boxed{3}\boxed{=}$ 84

In general we can write,

$(a + b)^n = \binom{n}{0}a^n + \binom{n}{1}a^{n-1}b + \binom{n}{2}a^{n-2}b^2 + \binom{n}{3}a^{n-3}b^3 + \dots$ where the *general term* of this expansion is written as, $\binom{n}{r}a^{n-r}b^r$.

Example 1

Expand fully   (i) $(p + q)^6$ (ii) $(2x - 3y)^4$

(i) $(p + q)^6 = \binom{6}{0}p^6 + \binom{6}{1}p^5q + \binom{6}{2}p^4q^2 + \binom{6}{3}p^3q^3 + \binom{6}{4}p^2q^4 + \binom{6}{5}pq^5 + \binom{6}{6}q^6$

$= p^6 + 6p^5q + 15p^4q^2 + 20p^3q^3 + 15p^2q^4 + 6pq^5 + q^6$

(ii) $(2x - 3y)^4$ by comparison with a general expansion we let $a = 2x$, $b = -3y$ and $n = 4$.

$\therefore$ $(2x - 3y)^4 =$

$\binom{4}{0}(2x)^4 + \binom{4}{1}(2x)^3(-3y) + \binom{4}{2}(2x)^2(-3y)^2 + \binom{4}{1}(2x)^1(-3y)^3 + \binom{4}{4}(-3y)^4$

$= 16x^4 - 96x^3y + 216x^2y^2 - 216xy^3 + 81y^4$

When calculating binomial coefficients we note that:

1. $\binom{n}{0} = \binom{n}{n} = 1$, for all values of $n \in N$

2. $\binom{n}{1} = n$, for all values of $n \in N$

3. $\binom{n}{r} = \binom{n}{n-r}$ for all values of $n \in N$ i.e. $\binom{6}{4} = \binom{6}{2}$ and $\binom{8}{7} = \binom{8}{1}$

4. Since the binomial coefficients start with $\binom{n}{0}$, the 3rd coefficient is given by $\binom{n}{2}$

The binomial theorem gives a quick and efficient way to expand any binomial to a given power.

The formula for the theorem is given on page 20 of the *Formulae and Tables* booklet.

Binomial Theorem

$$(x + y)^n = \binom{n}{0}x^n + \binom{n}{1}x^{n-1}y + \binom{n}{2}x^{n-2}y^2 + \dots \binom{n}{r}x^{n-r}y^r + \dots \binom{n}{n}y^n$$

Binomial coefficients

$$\binom{n}{r} = {}^nC_r$$

Example 2

(i) Find the first 3 terms of the expansion of $(1 - 5y)^8$
(ii) Find the fourth term of the expansion of $(3a + b)^7$

(i) Comparing $(1 - 5y)^8$ with $(x + y)^n$,
we let $x = 1$, $y = -5y$ and $n = 8$ in the general Binomial Expansion.

$$\therefore \quad (1 - 3y)^8 = \binom{8}{0} + \binom{8}{1}(-5y) + \binom{8}{2}(-5y)^2 + \dots$$
$$= 1 - 40y + 700y^2 + \dots$$

(ii) In the expansion of $(3a + b)^7$ we let $x = 3a$, $y = b$, $n = 7$
and for the fourth term let $r = 3$ in the general term. (since $r = 0, 1, 2, 3, \dots$)

$$\binom{n}{r}a^{n-r}b^r = \binom{7}{3}(3a)^4b^3 = 2835a^4b^3$$

Exercise 1.5

1. Using a calculator evaluate each of the following:

(i) $\binom{7}{4}$ (ii) $\binom{6}{2}$ (iii) $\binom{6}{4}$ (iv) $\binom{15}{4}$ (v) $\binom{10}{9}$

2. Without using a calculator evaluate each of the following:

(i) $\binom{9}{0}$ (ii) $\binom{10}{1}$ (iii) $\binom{13}{13}$ (iv) $\binom{30}{0}$ (v) $\binom{18}{17}$

3. If $\binom{12}{k} = \binom{12}{3}$, find the value of k, $k \in N$, $k \neq 3$.

4. If $\binom{16}{k} = \binom{16}{12}$, find the value of k, $k \in N$, $k \neq 12$.

5. Expand fully $(a + 2b)^4$.

6. Using Pascal's triangle write out the coefficients of $(x + y)^6$.

7. Using Pascal's triangle find the coefficient of the 4th term in the expansion of $(1 + 2x)^5$

8. Use the Binomial Theorem to expand each of the following:

    (i) $(a - 2b)^4$ (ii) $(2x - y)^3$ (iii) $(p + 3q)^4$ (iv) $(1 + 2y)^5$

9. Expand fully each of the following:

    (i) $(2 + 3p)^6$ (ii) $(1 - b)^7$ (iii) $(p - 4q)^5$.

10. If the numbers, 1 6 15 20 15 6 1, form the 6th row of Pascal's triangle write down the numbers for the 7th row.

11. Find the 5th term in the expansion of $(x + y)^8$.

12. Find the 4th term in the expansion of $(x - y)^9$.

13. Find the 6th term in the expansion of $(2x + y)^{10}$.

14. How many terms are in the expansion of $(p + 2q)^6$?
    Hence find the coefficient of the middle term of this expansion.

15. Expand fully each of the following

    (i) $(2x - y)^8$ (ii) $(a + 2b)^9$.

16. Using, $\binom{n}{r}x^{n-r}y^r$ as the general term of $(x + y)^n$, find the 3rd term of the expansion of $(5x + 1)^{10}$.

17. Find the coefficient of the 4th term of the expansion of $\left(x - \frac{3y}{2} \right)^9$.

Section 1.6 Algebraic identities

The word identity occurs in many different areas of mathematics. It is used in trigonometry, in sets, in functions and in algebra.

> In an **identity,** all coefficients of like powers are equal.
>
> An identity must be true **for all values** of the independent variable.

If $3x + 7 = ax + b$ **for all values of x**, this is called an **algebraic identity**.

We can conclude that for this to be true, then $a = 3$ and $b = 7$.

When two expressions are equal **for all values of x**, then the resulting equation is an identity.

All coefficients of like powers of x in an identity are equal.

Generally, if $ax^3 + bx^2 + cx + d = px^3 + qx^2 + rx + s$ for all values of x,

then $a = p, b = q, c = r, d = s$.

Also, if $ax^3 + bx^2 + cx + d = qx^2 + s$ for all values of x,

then $a = c = 0$ and $b = q, d = s$.

This property is used to find unknown coefficients in certain equations.

Example 1

Find the values of a and b given that $(2x + a)^2 = 4x^2 + 12x + b$, **for all values of x.**

Given $(2x + a)^2 = 4x^2 + 12x + b$ for all values of x,

$$4x^2 + 4ax + a^2 = 4x^2 + 12x + b$$

$4a = 12$ (comparing like powers of x) $\therefore$ $a = 3$

and $a^2 = b$ (comparing the constant terms) $\therefore$ $3^2 = 9 = b$.

Example 2

If $3t^2x - 3px + c - 2t^3 = 0$ **for all values of x**, find c in terms of p.

Given $3t^2x - 3px + c - 2t^3 = 0$ for all values of x,

$\therefore$ $(3t^2 - 3p)x + c - 2t^3 = (0)x + (0)$ ... writing both sides as polynomials in x

$\therefore$ $3t^2 - 3p = 0$ (comparing like powers of x) $\therefore$ $t = \sqrt{p}$

and $c - 2t^3 = 0$ (comparing the constant terms) $\therefore$ $c = 2t^3$

$$\therefore \ c = 2(\sqrt{p})^3 = 2p^{\frac{3}{2}}$$

Algebraic identities can also be used to create **partial fractions** from a given fraction.

For example, $\dfrac{1}{(x + 1)(x - 2)} = \dfrac{A}{(x + 1)} + \dfrac{B}{(x - 2)}$ where A and $B \in Q$.

Example 3

Given $\dfrac{1}{(x + 1)(x - 2)} = \dfrac{A}{(x + 1)} + \dfrac{B}{(x - 2)}$ for all values of x, find the values of A and B.

$$\dfrac{1}{(x + 1)(x - 2)} = \dfrac{A}{(x + 1)} + \dfrac{B}{(x - 2)} = \dfrac{A(x - 2) + B(x + 1)}{(x + 1)(x - 2)}$$

$\therefore$ $1 = A(x - 2) + B(x + 1)$ for all values of x.

We can find values of A and B using two different methods.

Method 1: Since this equation must be true for all values of x, by picking two suitable values of x, A and B can be easily evaluated.

Since $\qquad 1 = A(x - 2) + B(x + 1)$

Let $x = 2 \quad \therefore \quad 1 = A(0) + B(2 + 1) \qquad \therefore \quad B = \frac{1}{3}$

Let $x = -1 \quad \therefore \quad 1 = A(-1 - 2) + B(0) \qquad \therefore \quad 1 = -3A \Rightarrow A = -\frac{1}{3}$

Method 2: Equating coefficients of like powers and then solve using simultaneous equations.

$$1 = A(x - 2) + B(x + 1)$$
$$1 = Ax - 2A + Bx + B$$
$$1 = Ax + Bx - 2A + B$$
$$1 = x(A + B) - 2A + B$$
$$x(0) + 1 = x(A + B) - 2A + B \text{ for all values of } x.$$

$\therefore \quad 0 = A + B$ and $1 = -2A + B$ ... equating like powers of x and constant terms

$\therefore \quad A = -B$ and using substitution, $1 = -2(-B) + B = 3B$.

$\therefore \quad B = \frac{1}{3}$ and $A = -\frac{1}{3}$

$$\therefore \quad \frac{1}{(x + 1)(x - 2)} = \frac{A}{(x + 1)} + \frac{B}{(x - 2)} = \frac{-1}{3(x + 1)} + \frac{1}{3(x - 2)}$$

Algebraic identities and factors

If $x^2 - ax + b$ is a factor of $x^3 + 2ax^2 + 4bx + c$,
using **algebraic identities** we can find a relationship between the coefficients a, b and c.

It is important to realise that when a factor is divided into an expression, there can be no remainder by definition of a factor.

$$\begin{array}{r} x + 3a \\ x^2 - ax + b \overline{) x^3 + 2ax^2 + 4bx + c} \\ \underline{x^3 - ax^2 + bx} \\ 3ax^2 + 3bx + c \\ \underline{3ax^2 - 3a^2x + 3ab} \\ \end{array}$$
$$\text{Remainder} = x(3b + 3a^2) + c - 3ab$$

Since there can be no remainder, we can conclude that **for all values of x,**

(i) $3b + 3a^2 = 0$, i.e. $b = -a^2$ and

(ii) $c - 3ab = 0$, i.e. $c = 3ab$

The same results can be obtained by letting the missing factor $= (x + k)$.

$\therefore \quad (x + k)(x^2 - ax + b) = x^3 + 2ax^2 + 4bx + c$

Expanding the left-hand side we get,

$$x^3 - ax^2 + bx + kx^2 - akx + bk = x^3 + 2ax^2 + 4bx + c \quad \textbf{... for all values of } x.$$
$$\therefore \quad x^3 + (k - a)x^2 + (b - ak)x + bk = x^3 + 2ax^2 + 4bx + c \quad \text{... grouping like terms.}$$

Comparing coefficients of x^2: $(k - a) = 2a$, hence $k = 3a$ as above.

Comparing coefficients of x: $(b - ak) = 4b$
$(b - 3a^2) = 4b$, hence $3b = -3a^2$, i.e. $b = -a^2$ as above.

Finally, comparing constant terms: $bk = c$
$\therefore$ $3ab = c$, again the same as above.

Example 4

Given that $(x - t)^2$ is a factor of $x^3 + 3px + c$, show that $p = -t^2$ and $c = 2t^3$.

$(x - t)^2 = x^2 - 2xt + t^2$ and using long division we get;

$$
\begin{array}{r}
x + 2t \\
x^2 - 2xt + t^2 \overline{\smash{)}\,x^3 \qquad\ + 3px + c} \qquad \text{(note: there is no } x^2 \text{ term)}\\
\underline{x^3 - 2tx^2 + t^2x} \\
2tx^2 - t^2x + 3px + c
\end{array}
$$

(rewriting this line as) ... $2tx^2 + (3p - t^2)x + c$ ... (factorising, x, from the previous line)

$$
\begin{array}{r}
\underline{2tx^2 - 4t^2x + 2t^3} \\
(3p + 3t^2)x + c - 2t^3 \quad (= \text{remainder})
\end{array}
$$

Since we should get no remainder, $(3p + 3t^2)x + c - 2t^2 = 0$ **for all values of x.**

$\therefore$ $(3p + 3t^2)x + c - 2t^3 = (0)x + 0$ for all values of x.

$\therefore$ $3p + 3t^2 = 0 \rightarrow p = -t^2$

and $+c - 2t^3 = 0 \rightarrow c = 2t^3$.

(Note: The factors of $x^3 + 3px + c$ are $x^2 - 2xt + t^2$ and $x + 2t$.)

Example 5

$2x - \sqrt{3}$ is a factor of $4x^2 - 2(1 + \sqrt{3})x + \sqrt{3}$; find the second factor.

Let the second factor take the form $(ax + b)$.
(Note: a needs to be introduced because the coefficient of x^2 is 4; it should be clear that $a = 2$)

Then $(2x - \sqrt{3})(ax + b) = 4x^2 - 2(1 + \sqrt{3})x + \sqrt{3}$

$2ax^2 + 2bx - \sqrt{3}ax - \sqrt{3}b = 4x^2 - 2(1 + \sqrt{3})x + \sqrt{3}$

$2ax^2 + (2b - \sqrt{3}a)x - \sqrt{3}b = 4x^2 - 2(1 + \sqrt{3})x + \sqrt{3}$

Equating coefficients of like powers,

(i) $(x^2) \ldots 2a = 4 \Rightarrow a = 2$

(ii) $(x) \ldots + (2b - \sqrt{3}a) = -2(1 + \sqrt{3})$
   since $a = 2$, $\Rightarrow 2b - 2\sqrt{3} = -2 - 2\sqrt{3}$
   $\therefore \quad b = -1$

(iii) (comparing the constants) $\ldots -\sqrt{3}b = \sqrt{3}$, verifying that $b = -1$.

   Therefore the second factor is $2x - 1$.

Exercise 1.6

1. If $ax^2 + bx + c = (2x - 3)(3x + 4)$ for all values of x, find the values of a, b and c.

2. If $(3x - 2)(x + 5) = 3x^2 + px + q$ for all values of x, find the values of p and q.

3. If $x^2 + 6x + 16 = (x + a)^2 + b$ for all values of x, find the values of a and b.

4. Find the real numbers a and b such that $x^2 + 4x - 6 = (x + a)^2 + b$ for all $x \in R$.

5. If $2x^2 + 5x + 6 = p(x + q)^2 + r$ for all values of x, find the values of p, q and r.

6. Find the values of a and b if $(2x + a)^2 = 4x^2 + 12x + b$, for all x.

7. If $x^2 - 4x - 5 = (x - n)^2 - m$ for all x, find the values of m and n.

8. The volume of this closed box, V, is given by the function $V(x) = ax^3 + bx^2 + cx + d$, where a, b, c and $d \in Z$.

   (i) Find the values for a, b, c and d.

   The external surface area, $S(x)$, is given by the equation $S(x) = px^2 + qx + r$, where p, q and $r \in Z$.

   (ii) Find the values of p, q and r.

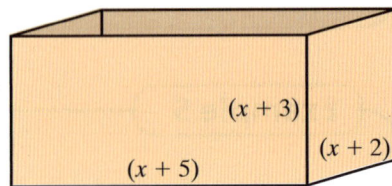

   $(x + 3)$

   $(x + 2)$

   $(x + 5)$

9. If $3(x - p)^2 + q = 3x^2 - 12x + 7$ for all x, find the values of p and q.

10. The volume of a solid box is given by $V(x) = x^3 + 12x^2 + bx + 30$.

   If the top of the box has an area of $x^2 + cx + 4$ and the height is $x + a$, find the values of a, b and c.

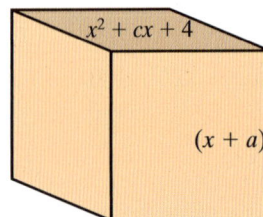

   $x^2 + cx + 4$

   $(x + a)$

11. If $(x - 4)^3 = x^3 + px^2 + qx - 64$ for all x, find the values of the constants p and q.

12. If $(x + a)(x^2 + bx + 2) = x^3 - 2x^2 - x - 6$ for all x, find the values of the constants a and b.

13. Find the values of b and c given that $(x - 2)(x^2 + bx + c) = x^3 + 2x^2 - 5x - 6$ for all values of x.

14. Given that $(5a - b)x + b + 2c = 0$ for all values of x, find a in terms of c.

15. If $(4x + r)(x^2 + s) = 4x^3 + px^2 + qx + 2$ for all x, find a value for pq.

16. $(x + s)(x - s)(ax + t) = ax^3 + bx^2 + cx + d$ for all values of x.
Using this identify, show that $bc = ad$.

17. If $\dfrac{1}{(x + 1)(x - 1)} = \dfrac{A}{(x + 1)} + \dfrac{B}{(x - 1)}$ for all x, find values for A and B.

18. If $\dfrac{1}{(x + 2)(x - 3)} = \dfrac{C}{(x + 2)} + \dfrac{D}{(x - 3)}$ for all x, find values for C and D.

19. Write $\dfrac{1}{(x + 1)(x + 4)}$ as the partial fractions $\dfrac{A}{(x + 1)} + \dfrac{B}{(x + 4)}$.

20. If $(x - 3)^2$ is a factor of $x^3 + ax + b$, find the value of a and the value of b.

21. If $(x - 2)^2$ is a factor of $x^3 + px + q$, find the value of p and the value of q.

22. Given that $(x^2 - 4)$ is a factor of $x^3 + cx^2 + dx - 12$, find the values of the coefficients c and d.
Hence factorise the cubic polynomial fully.

23. If $(x^2 + b)$ is a factor of $x^3 - 3x^2 + bx - 15$, find the value of b.

24. If $x^2 - px + 9$ is a factor of $x^3 + ax + b$, express (i) a (ii) b in terms of p.
Hence find the values of p for which $a + b = 17$.

25. If $x^2 - kx + 1$ is a factor of $ax^3 + bx + c$, show that $c^2 = a(a - b)$.

26. If $(x - a)^2$ is a factor of $x^3 + 3px + c$, show that (i) $p = -a^2$ (ii) $c = 2a^3$.

27. If $x^2 + ax + b$ is a factor of $x^3 - k$, show that (i) $a^3 = k$ (ii) $b^3 = k^2$.

28. Show by long division that $2x - \sqrt{3}$ is a factor of $4x^2 - 2(1 + \sqrt{3})x + \sqrt{3}$ and hence find the second factor.

29. Find the values of A, B and C such that
$$5x + 3 = Ax(x + 3) + Bx(x - 1) + C(x - 1)(x + 3) \text{ for all values of } x.$$

Section 1.7 Manipulating formulae

The area of a disc is given by the formula $A = \pi r^2$.

A is said to be defined **in terms of** r (r is the independent variable).

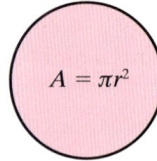

$A = \pi r^2$

If we know r, we can find A.

For example, if $r = 3$, then $A = 9\pi$; if $r = 8$, then $A = 64\pi$, etc..

In some cases we may need to find r in terms A, i.e. make r the **subject** of the equation.

$$\therefore \quad \pi r^2 = A \Rightarrow r^2 = \frac{A}{\pi} \Rightarrow r = \sqrt{\frac{A}{\pi}} \ \dots \ r \text{ is now defined in terms of } A.$$

Thus, if we know the area of the circle, we can find the radius.

For example, if $A = 9\pi$, then $r = \sqrt{\frac{A}{\pi}} \Rightarrow r = \sqrt{\frac{9\pi}{\pi}} = \sqrt{9} = 3$.

Example 1

(i) If $v^2 = u^2 + 2as$, express a in terms of v, u and s.

(ii) If $\sqrt{\dfrac{x + y}{x - y}} = \dfrac{1}{2}$, express y in terms of x. Hence find the value of y when $x = 5$.

(i)
$$v^2 = u^2 + 2as$$
$$u^2 + 2as = v^2$$
$$2as = v^2 - u^2$$
$$\therefore a = \frac{v^2 - u^2}{2s}$$

(ii) $\sqrt{\dfrac{x + y}{x - y}} = \dfrac{1}{2}$

$\dfrac{x + y}{x - y} = \dfrac{1}{4}$ ... squaring both sides

$4(x + y) = x - y$ ... multiplying both sides by $4(x - y)$

$4x + 4y = x - y$ ... expanding the left-hand side

$y + 4y = x - 4x$ ... gathering only y terms on the left-hand side

$5y = -3x$

$y = \dfrac{-3x}{5}$ ... finding y in terms of x

When $x = 5$, $y = \dfrac{-3(5)}{5} = -3$.

Example 2

A container in the shape of an inverted cone is used to hold liquid.

Given $\tan \theta = \dfrac{r}{h}$, express the volume, V, in terms of the depth, h, of the liquid and the angle θ.

Volume of a cone, $V = \frac{1}{3}\pi r^2 h$

But $\tan \theta = \dfrac{r}{h} \Rightarrow h \tan \theta = r$

$$V = \tfrac{1}{3}\pi r^2 h = \tfrac{\pi}{3}(h \tan \theta)^2 h = \tfrac{\pi}{3}h^3 \tan^2 \theta$$

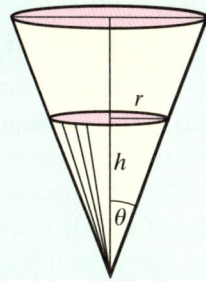

Example 3

Given $x = \dfrac{t + 4}{3t + 1}$, find t in terms of x.

$$x = \dfrac{t + 4}{3t + 1}$$

$x(3t + 1) = t + 4$ ... multiplying both sides by $3t + 1$

$3tx + x = t + 4$ ... expanding the left-hand side

$3tx - t = 4 - x$ ... gathering only t terms on the left-hand side

$t(3x - 1) = 4 - x$ ... factorising

$$t = \dfrac{4 - x}{3x - 1}$$ ... dividing both sides by $3x - 1$

Exercise 1.7

1. In each of the following, express x in terms of the other variables.

   (i) $3x - 2y = 4$

   (ii) $2x - b = 4c$

   (iii) $5x - 4 = \dfrac{y}{2}$

   (iv) $5(x - 3) = 2y$

   (v) $3y = \dfrac{x}{3} - 2$

   (vi) $xy = xz + yz$

2. Express x in terms of the other variables in each of the following:

   (i) $2x - \dfrac{y}{3} = \dfrac{1}{3}$

   (ii) $z = \dfrac{y - 2x}{3}$

   (iii) $\dfrac{a}{x} - b = c$

3. (a) The volume of a cylinder is given by $V = \pi r^2 h$.
   Find the radius r in terms of V and h.

   (b) The curved surface area of a cylinder is given by $A = 2\pi r h$.
   Find the radius r in terms of A and h.

   (c) Hence show that $A^2 = 4\pi h V$.

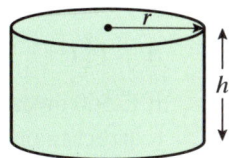

4. A circle of radius r is drawn inside a square as shown.

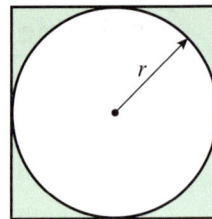

(a) Find the area of the circle, A.

(b) Find the area of the square in terms of r.

(c) Hence find an expression for the area of the shaded corners in terms of r.

(d) If the side of the square is doubled while the radius of the circle is halved, find an expression for the shaded area in terms of r.

(e) If a circle is circumscribed around the original square, prove that the area of the outer disc is twice the area of the inner disc.

5. A speed camera measures the change in frequency of waves from f to f', caused by a moving car, using the formula $f' = \dfrac{fc}{c - u}$, where c is the speed of the waves and u the speed of the car. Find

(i) the speed of the car, u, in terms of the other variables f', f and c.

(ii) the speed of the waves, c, in terms of the other variables f', f and u.

6. The time taken for one complete cycle of a pendulum is given by $T = 2\pi\sqrt{\dfrac{l}{g}}$, where l is the length of the pendulum and g the acceleration due to gravity.

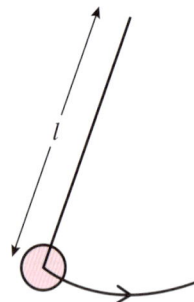

(i) Find l in terms of the other variables.

(ii) Given that $T = 3\,\text{s}$ and $g = 10\,\text{m s}^{-2}$, calculate the length of the pendulum correct to one decimal place.

7. In each of the following, express a in terms of the other variables:

(i) $\dfrac{x}{y} = \dfrac{a + b}{a - b}$

(ii) $bc - ac = ac$.

8. Express v in terms of the other variables in each of the following:

(i) $y = \dfrac{3(u - v)}{4}$

(ii) $S = \dfrac{t}{2}(u + v)$

9. The final value of €P, invested for 3 years at $i\%$, is given by the formula $A = P\left(1 + \dfrac{i}{100}\right)^3$. Find i in terms of P and A.

If €2500 invested 3 years ago has a present value of €2650, find the rate of interest, i (correct to one place of decimals).

10. Write c in terms of the other variables in each of the following.

    (i) $d = \sqrt{\dfrac{a - b}{ac}}$ (ii) $b = \dfrac{2c - 1}{c - 1}$

11. A cone has a radius r cm and a vertical height h cm.
If the slant height $l = 15$ cm, and using Pythagoras' theorem:

    (i)   Express h in terms of r.

    (ii)   Hence find the value of h when $r = 5$ cm.

    (iii)   At what value of h will the radius r be equal
to half the slant height l?
Give your answer correct to the nearest cm.

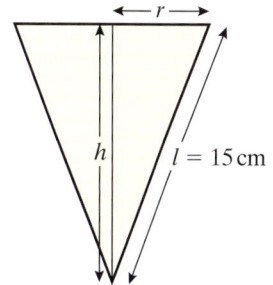

12. A farmer has 300 metres of fencing and wants
to make a rectangular paddock against an existing
wall, as shown, using all of this fencing.

    (i)   Find the length (L) of the paddock in
terms of the width (W).

    (ii)   Hence find the area of the paddock
(A) in terms of the width only.

    (iii)   Find the dimensions of the paddock
if the maximum allowable area is 10,000 m².

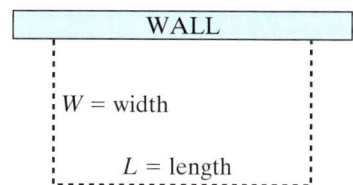

Section 1.8 **Algebraic patterns, an introduction**

1. Linear   Each polynomial function creates a pattern
which can be studied both numerically
and graphically.

Patterns such as $0, 3, 6, 9, \ldots$ can be described by
the function

     $f(x) = (y) = 3x$, where $x \geqslant 0, x \in N$.

Patterns such as $1, 4, 7, 10, \ldots$ can be described by
the function

     $f(x) = (y) = 3x + 1$, where $x \geqslant 0, x \in N$.

Patterns such as $2, -2, -6, -10 \ldots$ can be described by
the function

     $f(x) = (y) = 2 - 4x$, where $x \geqslant 0, x \in N$.

Each of these number patterns has a constant amount
added or subtracted between terms and each, when
graphed, produces a straight line as shown.

Functions of the form $f(x) = y = mx + c$ are
called **linear** functions.

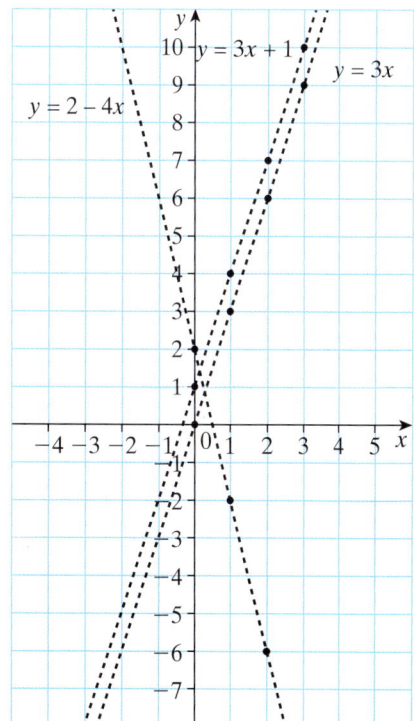

In a linear pattern, the difference between consecutive terms (called the 1st difference) gives *m*, the slope of the line.

						$y = mx + c$
Pattern	0	3	6	9	12	$f(x) = (y) = 3x$
1st Difference		3	3	3	3	
Pattern	1	4	7	10	13	$f(x) = (y) = 3x + 1$
1st Difference		3	3	3	3	
Pattern	2	-2	-6	-10	-14	$f(x) = (y) = 2 - 4x$
1st Difference		-4	-4	-4	-4	

The starting point of each pattern determines *c*, the constant term. We note that when $x = 0$, geometrically, we get the *y*-axis intercept, *c*.

2. Quadratic   Patterns such as 0, 1, 4, 9, 16 … do not have a constant amount added or subtracted between terms.

Studying the 1st differences between terms, we get 1, 3, 5, 7, … .

The **2nd difference** $(3 - 1)$, $(5 - 3)$, … however is a constant, 2.

Such patterns can be represented by the function $f(x) = (y) = x^2$ for $x \geqslant 0$.

Functions of the form $f(x) = x^2 + b$ create similar patterns.

Pattern	0	1	4	9	16	25	$f(x) = (y) = x^2$
1st Difference		1	3	5	7	9	
2nd Difference			2	2	2	2	
Pattern	2	3	6	11	18	27	$f(x) = (y) = x^2 + 2$
1st Difference		1	3	5	7	9	
2nd Difference			2	2	2	2	
Pattern	-3	-2	1	6	13	22	$f(x) = (y) = x^2 - 3$
1st Difference		1	3	5	7	9	
2nd Difference			2	2	2	2	
Pattern	2	1	-2	-7	-14	-23	$f(x) = (y) = 2 - x^2$
1st Difference		-1	-3	-5	-7	-9	
2nd Difference			-2	-2	-2	-2	

As can be seen from the graphs, the curves are symmetrical about the line $x = 0$ (y-axis).

Patterns of the form $f(x) = x^2 + b$ are $\cup$-shaped.

Patterns of the form $f(x) = b - x^2$ are $\cap$-shaped.

Consider the following pattern.

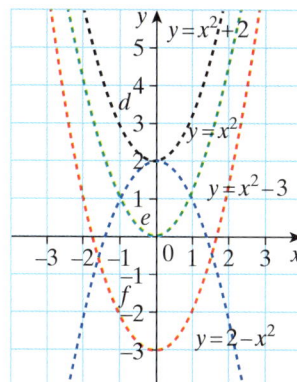

Pattern	4	7	16	31	52	79
1st Difference		3	9	15	21	27
2nd Difference			6	6	6	6

Because the 2nd difference is a constant, we know this is a quadratic pattern of the form
$ax^2 + bx + c, x \geqslant 0, x \in N.$

When $x = 0, ax^2 + bx + c = 4, \therefore c = 4$

When $x = 1, ax^2 + bx + 4 = 7, \therefore a + b + 4 = 7$

When $x = 2, ax^2 + bx + 4 = 16, \therefore 4a + 2b + 4 = 16$

Solving we find $a = 3, b = 0$

> If $f(x) = ax^2 + bx + c,$
> the second difference $= 2a.$

Thus the pattern can be represented by the polynomial function $f(x) = 3x^2 + 4.$

Example 1

Examine each of the following patterns of numbers and determine if there is a linear or quadratic relationship between the terms.

Write an algebraic expression for each set of numbers:
  (a) $-2, 1, 4, 7, \ldots$ (b) $3, 5, 11, 21, \ldots$

Pattern	-2	1	4	7
1st Difference		3	3	3

(a) Since the first difference is a constant, this indicates a linear relationship $f(x) = ax + b.$
$a = 3$ and $b = -2,$
$\therefore f(x) = 3x - 2, x \geqslant 0.$

Pattern	3	5	11	21
1st Difference		2	6	10
2nd Difference			4	4

(b) Since the second difference is a constant, this indicates a quadratic relationship
$f(x) = ax^2 + b.$
$4 = 2a \Rightarrow a = 2$ and $b = 3,$
$\therefore f(x) = 2x^2 + 3, x \geqslant 0.$

More complex quadratic patterns of the form $ax^2 + bx + c$ can be formed in two stages; first to identify the quadratic element x^2, then subtracting this from the pattern to form the linear element $bx + c.$

Example 2

Single matchsticks were used to form a sequence of patterns as shown. Find an algebraic quadratic expression for the number of matchsticks needed for each pattern. How many matchsticks are needed for the 10th pattern?

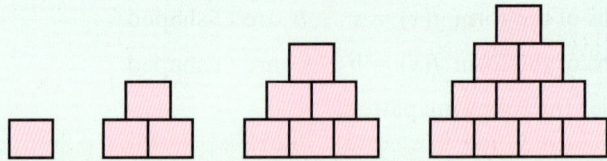

Counting the matchsticks needed for the first four patterns, we get the number pattern $4, 10, 18, 28, \ldots$

Pattern	4	10	18	28
1st Difference		6	8	10
2nd Difference			2	2

The 2nd difference produces $2, 2, 2, \ldots$ etc.

So there is a quadratic element (x^2) to this pattern.

Letting $f(x) = ax^2 + bx + c$, when $x = 0$, $f(0) = c = 4$.

Also the 2nd difference $= 2a = 2, \therefore a = 1$

When $x = 1$, $f(1) = a + b + c = 10$

$\qquad\qquad\qquad = 1 + b + 4 = 10 \therefore b = 5$

$\therefore \quad f(x) = x^2 + 5x + 4$ for $x \geqslant 0$

To get the 10th pattern, we let $x = 9$ (since pattern starts with $x = 0$)

$\therefore \quad f(9) = 9^2 + 5(9) + 4 = 130$ matchsticks needed.

Note: Linear and quadratic patterns of numbers are studied in greater depth in chapter 9.

Exercise 1.8

1. Examine each of the following patterns of numbers and determine if the pattern has a linear or quadratic relationship.

   (a) $4, 7, 10, 13, 16, \ldots$
   (b) $-2, 2, 6, 10, 14, \ldots$
   (c) $-4, -3, 0, 5, 12, \ldots$
   (d) $2, 1, -2, -7, -14, -23, \ldots$
   (e) $2, 7, 22, 47, \ldots$
   (f) $3, 1, -5, -15, -29, \ldots$
   (g) $1, -4, -19, -44, -79, \ldots$
   (h) $3, -2, -7, -12, -17, \ldots$
   (i) $0, 3, 12, 27, 48, \ldots$
   (j) $5, 17, 37, 65, 101, \ldots$

2. Write an algebraic expression to represent each of the followings number patterns.

   (a) $-1, 3, 15, 35, 63, \ldots$
   (b) $4, 3, 0, -5, -12, -21, -32, \ldots$

3. Each of the following number patterns can be written in the form $f(x) = ax + b$, $x \geqslant 0$. Find the values of a and b.

   (i) $2, 7, 12, 17, 22, \ldots$ (ii) $-6, -2, 2, 6, 10, \ldots$
   (iii) $3, 2, 1, 0, -1, -2, \ldots$ (iv) $-2, -7, -12, -17, -22, -27, \ldots$
   (v) $3, 3.5, 4, 4.5, 5, \ldots$ (vi) $-1, -0.8, -0.6, -0.4, -0.2, \ldots$

4. If $x \geqslant 3$, find an algebraic linear expression for the pattern $11, 13, 15, 17, 19, \ldots$

5. If $x \geqslant -2$, find a and b such that $f(x) = ax + b$ represents the number pattern $1, 3, 5, 7, 9, \ldots$

6. Convert each of the following designs to number patterns. By finding an algebraic linear expression for the number of matchsticks needed for each design, find the number of matchsticks needed to make the 15th element of each design.

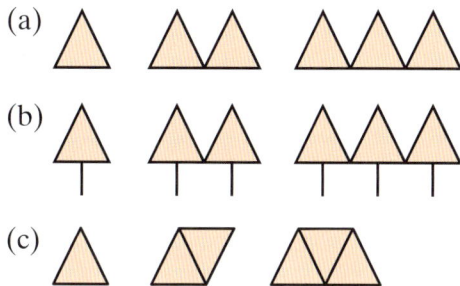

(a)

(b)

(c)

7. A company offers two different billing plans for the purchase of a TV over a number of months. Plan A where the repayments are €35.00 per month with a down-payment of €70.00, or Plan B with repayments of €24.00 per month with a down-payment of €125.00. If x represents the number of months of the plan, write an expression for each billing plan. Write a number sequence representing the cost per month of each plan (A and B) for the first four months. After how many months would both plans have repaid the same amount?

8. A biologist counted the number of bacteria cells growing in a culture every hour. The pattern $4, 7, 14, 25, 40, \ldots$ was recorded for the first four hours, with 4 being the initial number present. Show that this sequence contains both a linear and a quadratic element. Find an expression for the number of bacteria after t hours, i.e. find $f(t)$. Using your expression for $f(t)$, and trial and error, find in which hour the colony will have reached 529.

Section 1.9 Solving equations

To solve an equation, we need to find the values of the given variable that satisfy the equation.

If $4x - 12 = 0$, then $x = 3$ is the only solution of this equation.
If $x^2 - 5x + 6 = 0$, then $x = 2$ and $x = 3$ are both solutions of this equation.
If $y = 4x - 12$, then $(x, y) = (4, 4)$ is one of the many values of (x, y) that satisfy this equation.

Given $f(x) = 4x - 12$,
then $x = 3$ is the value that makes $f(x) = 0$.

Therefore, $(x, y) = (3, 0)$ is the solution
of $y = 4x - 12$.

Similarly, $(2, 0)$ and $(3, 0)$ are solutions
of $y = x^2 - 5x + 6$.

The values of x that make $y = 0$
are called the **roots** of an equation.

If a graph of the function is plotted, the roots
are those points where the graph crosses the x-axis.

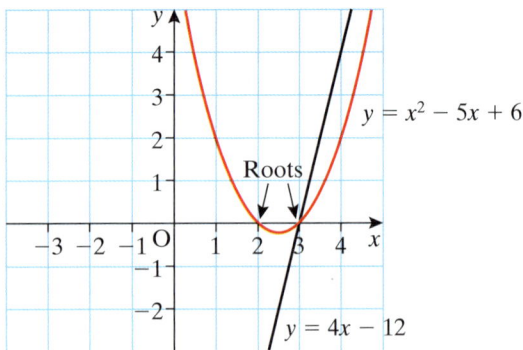

Solving linear equations

Any equation of the form $y = ax + b$, when plotted, creates a straight line.

Such equations are called **linear equations**.

To solve the equation $2x + 1 = 0$, we need to find the value of x that makes $y = 0$, i.e. where
the line crosses the x-axis.

$$2x + 1 = 0$$
$$\Rightarrow \quad x = \frac{-1}{2} = -0.5$$

Similarly, to solve the equation $2x + 1 = 2$, we have
to find the value of x that makes $y = 2$, i.e. where the
line crosses the line $y = 2$.

$$2x + 1 = 2$$
$$\Rightarrow \quad x = \frac{1}{2} = 0.5$$

In each case, there is only one value of x (one root)
produced.

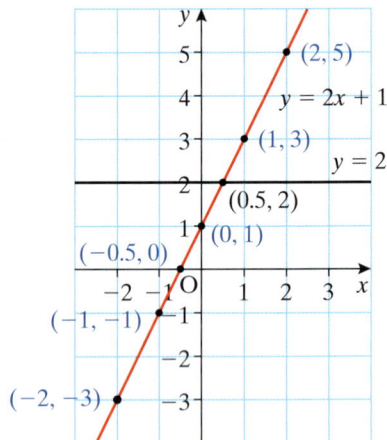

Example 1

Solve the linear equation $\dfrac{2t - 3}{5} + \dfrac{1}{20} = \dfrac{t - 1}{4}$.

$$\frac{2t - 3}{5} + \frac{1}{20} = \frac{t - 1}{4}$$

$$\frac{4(2t - 3)}{20} + \frac{1}{20} = \frac{5(t - 1)}{20} \quad \text{... finding the lowest common denominator}$$

$$4(2t - 3) + 1 = 5(t - 1)$$
$$8t - 12 + 1 = 5t - 5 \quad \text{... expanding}$$
$$3t = 6$$
$$t = 2$$

Exercise 1.9

1. Explain why each of the following is a **non-linear** equation.

   (i) $y = 2x^2 + 2x - 1$

   (ii) $y = \dfrac{2}{(x-1)} = 2(x-1)^{-1}$

   (iii) $y^2 = 3x + 4$

2. Solve each of the following equations.

   (i) $5x - 3 = 32$ (ii) $3x + 2 = x + 8$ (iii) $2 - 5x = 8 - 3x$

3. Solve each of these equations.

   (i) $2(x - 3) + 5(x - 1) = 3$ (ii) $2(4x - 1) - 3(x - 2) = 14$

   (iii) $3(x - 1) - 4(x - 2) = 6(2x + 3)$ (iv) $3(x + 5) + 2(x + 1) - 3x = 22$

4. Solve each of the following equations:

   (i) $\dfrac{2x + 1}{5} = 1$ (ii) $\dfrac{3x - 1}{4} = 8$ (iii) $\dfrac{x - 3}{4} = \dfrac{x - 2}{5}$

5. Find the value of the unknown in each of the following equations:

   (i) $\dfrac{2a}{3} - \dfrac{a}{4} = \dfrac{5}{6}$ (ii) $\dfrac{b + 2}{4} - \dfrac{b - 3}{3} = \dfrac{1}{2}$ (iii) $\dfrac{3c - 1}{6} - \dfrac{c - 3}{4} = \dfrac{4}{3}$

6. Find the value of the unknown in each of the following equations:

   (i) $\dfrac{x - 2}{5} + \dfrac{2x - 3}{10} = \dfrac{1}{2}$ (ii) $\dfrac{3y - 12}{5} + 3 = \dfrac{3(y - 5)}{2}$

   (iii) $\dfrac{3p - 2}{6} - \dfrac{3p + 1}{4} = \dfrac{2}{3}$ (iv) $\dfrac{3r - 2}{5} - \dfrac{2r - 3}{4} = \dfrac{1}{2}$

7. Solve each of the following:

   (i) $\frac{3}{4}(2x - 1) - \frac{2}{3}(4 - x) = 2$ (ii) $\frac{2}{3}(x - 1) - \frac{1}{5}(x - 3) = x + 1$

Section 1.10 Solving simultaneous linear equations

1. Solving simultaneous linear equations with two variables

The linear equation $y = \frac{2}{3}x - 3$ can be rearranged as follows:

$$y = \tfrac{2}{3}x - 3$$

$$3y = 2x - 9$$

$2x - 3y - 9 = 0$ is the equation of the same line, expressed in standard form.

> Standard form of the equation of a line:
>
> $$ax + by + c = 0$$

This equation has two variables (x, y) for which there are many solutions.

However, if we have two equations in x and y, they are either

(a) parallel, with no point of intersection or
(b) they intersect at a point (x_1, y_1), common to both lines.

In this diagram, the lines $2x - y + 1 = 0$ and $3x + y - 4 = 0$ are plotted.

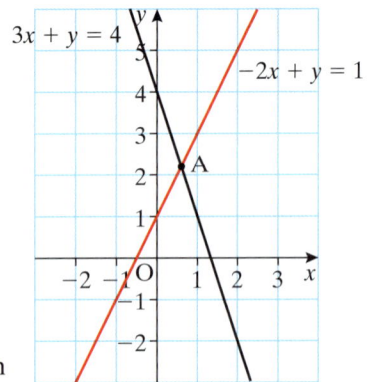

They have a point of intersection $A(x, y) = \left(\frac{3}{5}, \frac{11}{5}\right)$ which satisfies both equations at the same time, i.e. simultaneously.

We can solve two linear equations (i.e. find their point of intersection) by:

(i) substitution

(ii) elimination

(iii) graphically (as above).

Example 1

Solve the equations $3x - y = 1$ and $x - 2y = -8$.

Take $x - 2y = -8$ and rearrange the terms, finding **x in terms of y**,
$$\rightarrow x = -8 + 2y$$

Substitute this expression for x into the second linear equation.

$$3x - y = 1 \text{ becomes } 3(-8 + 2y) - y = 1$$
$$-24 + 6y - y = 1 \text{ ... expanding}$$
$$5y = 25$$
$$y = 5$$

If $y = 5$, then $x = -8 + 2y$ becomes $x = -8 + 2(5) = 2$

Therefore $(x, y) = (2, 5)$ is the point of intersection.

[Note: Since $3(2) - (5) = 1$ and $(2) - 2(5) = -8$, the point $(2, 5)$ is on both lines.]

Note 1: The technique for solving equations by substitution will be used later to find the point(s) of intersection of a line and a curve.

Note 2: Either variable can be substituted.
(Always choose the variable that is easiest to isolate.)

Example 2

Solve the equations $2x - 5y = 9$ and $3x + 2y = 4$.

Let A be $2x - 5y = 9$
Let B be $3x + 2y = 4$

$\therefore$ 3A: $6x - 15y = 27$
and 2B: $\underline{6x + 4y = 8}$
$\qquad\qquad -19y = 19$ ... Subtracting to eliminate x
$\qquad\qquad\quad y = -1$

Now substituting $y = -1$ into A, we get $2x - 5(-1) = 9$
$$2x = 4$$
$$x = 2$$

The point of intersection is $(x, y) = (2, -1)$.

[Note: $2(2) - 5(-1) = 9$ and $3(2) + 2(-1) = 4$ and so this point is on both lines.]

2. Solving simultaneous equations with three variables

$x + y + z = 6$ is an equation with three variables (three dimensions).

To plot this equation we need three axes, x, y and z-axes, at right angles to one another.

When plotted, this equation represents a plane of points.

If three planes are plotted on the same axes, there will be one point of intersection $(x, y, z,)$ provided none of the planes are parallel.

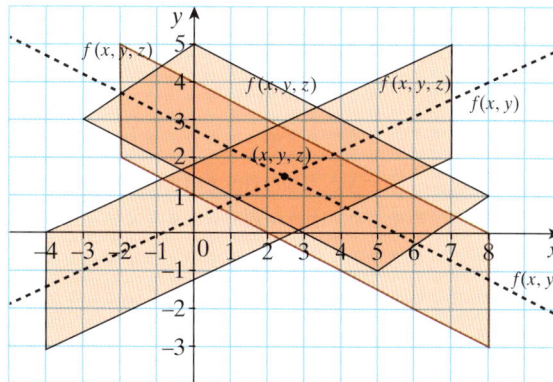

To solve an equation with three unknowns,

(i) reduce the three equations to two by eliminating one of the unknowns
(ii) choose an unknown that is easy to isolate
(iii) eliminate this unknown from all three equations, taking them two at a time
(iv) solve these two equations as before
(v) use your values for these unknowns in one of the original equations to solve for the third unknown
(vi) check your solutions in all equations.

Example 3

Solve the simultaneous equations:　　A: $x + y + z = 6$
　　　　　　　　　　　　　　　　　　B: $2x + y - z = 1$
　　　　　　　　　　　　　　　　　　C: $4x - 3y + 2z = 4$

Eliminating z from all three equations we get,

A: $\underline{x + y + z = 6}$　　　　　　　　　2B: $4x + 2y - 2z = 2$
B: $\underline{2x + y - z = 1}$　　　　　　　　　　　　C: $\underline{4x - 3y + 2z = 4}$
D: $3x + 2y = 7$　… adding A and B　　E: $8x - y = 6$　… adding 2B and C

D: $3x + 2y = 7$
2E: $\underline{16x - 2y = 12}$
　　$19x = 19$　… adding D and 2E

　　　　$x = 1$　　　　　　　　　　$\therefore$　Using D:　$3(1) + 2y = 7$
　　　　　　　　　　　　　　　　　　　　　　　　　　　　$2y = 4$
　　　　　　　　　　　　　　　　　　　　　　　　　　　　$y = 2$

Finally, using A:　$(1) + (2) + z = 6$
　　　　　　　　　　　　　　$z = 3$　　$\therefore$　the point of intersection is
　　　　　　　　　　　　　　　　　　　　　　$(x, y, z) = (1, 2, 3)$

[**Note:**　A: $(1) + (2) + (3) = 6$, and
　　　　　B: $2(1) + (2) - (3) = 1$, and
　　　　　C: $4(1) - 3(2) + 2(3) = 4$　and so this point satisfies all three equations]

3. Simultaneous equations in context

Example 4

An opera was attended by 240 people. Two ticket prices, €31 and €16, were available. If the total takings on the night were €5595, find using this data

(i)　two linear equations connecting the two types of tickets sold
(ii)　the number of €31 tickets sold
(iii)　the number of €16 tickets sold.

Let x represent the number of €16 tickets sold and y represent the number of €31 tickets sold.

(i)　Since 240 people attended altogether, then　A: $x + y = 240$
　　　If the receipts were €5595, then　　　　　　　B: $16x + 31y = 5595$

(ii) Solving, we get 16A: $16x + 16y = 3840$

 B: $16x + 31y = 5595$

 $-15y = -1755$ (subtracting)

 $y = 117$, i.e. 117 €31 tickets were sold

(iii)   Using $y = 117$: $x + (117) = 240$

 $x = 123$, i.e. 123 €16 tickets were sold.

Example 5

Fifty, twenty and ten cent coins are collected from a coin machine and counted. The total value of the coins is €32. When counting, the cashier noted that twice the number of twenty cent coins, added to the number of ten cent coins, equalled three times the number of fifty cent coins. She then noticed that four times the number of fifty cent coins, added to the number of ten cent coins, equalled six times the number of twenty cent coins.
Find the number of each type of coin in the machine.

Let x = the number of 50 cent coins
Let y = the number of 20 cent coins
Let z = the number of 10 cent coins.

(i) $50x + 20y + 10z = 3200$ ... €32 = 3200c
(ii) $2y + z = 3x$
(iii) $4x + z = 6y$

Rearranging the equations into standard form, we get   A: $50x + 20y + 10z = 3200$

 B: $3x - 2y - z = 0$

 C: $4x - 6y + z = 0$

Adding B and C eliminates z $\therefore$ B + C $\Rightarrow 7x - 8y = 0$.

Adding A and 10B also eliminates z (and y in this case) $\therefore$ A: $50x + 20y + 10z = 3200$

 10B: $30x - 20y - 10z = 0$

 A + 10B $\Rightarrow 80x = 3200$

 $\therefore$ $x = 40$

Since $7x - 8y = 0 \Rightarrow 7(40) - 8y = 0$

 $\Rightarrow 280 - 8y = 0$

 $\Rightarrow y = 35$

Also, $3x - 2y - z = 0 \Rightarrow 3(40) - 2(35) - z = 0$ $\therefore z = 120 - 70 = 50$.

$\therefore (x, y, z) = (40, 35, 50)$.

There are forty 50c coins, thirty-five 20c coins and fifty 10c coins in the machine.

Exercise 1.10

1. Find the point of intersection of each of the following pairs of lines.

   (i) $3x - 2y = 8$
   $x + y = 6$

   (ii) $3x - y = 1$
   $x - 2y = -8$

   (iii) $2x - 5y = 1$
   $4x - 3y - 9 = 0$

2. Solve each of the following pairs of simultaneous equations.

   (i) $4x - 5y = 22$
   $7x + 3y - 15 = 0$

   (ii) $\dfrac{x}{2} - \dfrac{y}{6} = \dfrac{1}{6}$
   $x - 2y = -8$

   (iii) $\dfrac{4x - 2}{5} = \dfrac{8y}{10}$
   $18x - 20y = 4$

3. Solve for x and y given that $\dfrac{2x - 5}{3} + \dfrac{y}{5} = 6$ and $\dfrac{3x}{10} + 2 = \dfrac{3y - 5}{2}$.

4. Given that $y = 3x - 23$ and $y = \dfrac{x}{2} + 2$, find the values of y and x.

5. Solve the following equations with three unknowns.

   (i) $2x + y + z = 8$
   $5x - 3y + 2z = 3$
   $7x + y + 3z = 20$

   (ii) $2x - y - z = 6$
   $3x + 2y + 3z = 3$
   $4x + y - 2z = 3$

   (iii) $2x + y - z = 9$
   $x + 2y + z = 6$
   $3x - y + 2z = 17$

6. Find the point of intersection of each of the following sets of planes.

   (i) $2a + b + c = 8$
   $5a - 3b + 2c = -3$
   $7a - 3b + 3c = 1$

   (ii) $x + y + 2z = 3$
   $4x + 2y + z = 13$
   $2x + y - 2z = 9$

   (iii) $x + y + z = 2$
   $2x + 3y + z = 7$
   $\dfrac{x}{2} - \dfrac{y}{6} + \dfrac{z}{3} = \dfrac{2}{3}$

7. Find the solution (x, y, z) for

   $6x + 4y - 2z - 5 = 3x - 2y + 4z + 10 = 5x - 2y + 6z + 13 = 0$.

8. The curve $f(x) = y = ax^2 + bx + c$ passes through the three points $(1, 2)$, $(2, 4)$ and $(3, 8)$. Use these points to find three equations in a, b and c and hence solve to find $f(x)$.

9. A curve of the form $f(x) = y = ax^2 + bx + c$ is drawn as shown.
   By using any three points on the curve, form three equations connecting the coefficients a, b and c and hence solve to find $f(x)$.

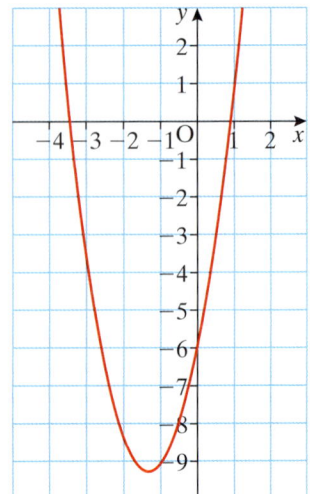

10. 44 000 people attended a match in Croke Park. The two ticket prices on the day were €30 and €20. The total receipts for the game came to €1.2 million.
How many people paid the higher ticket price?

11. Three years from now, Callum will be twice as old as Lydia was five years ago.
At the moment, half their combined ages is 16. Find their ages.

12. Find the equation of the line AB in the form, $y = ax + b$, by forming two simultaneous equations in a and b using the two given points on the line.
Verify that your line passes through a selected point between A and B.

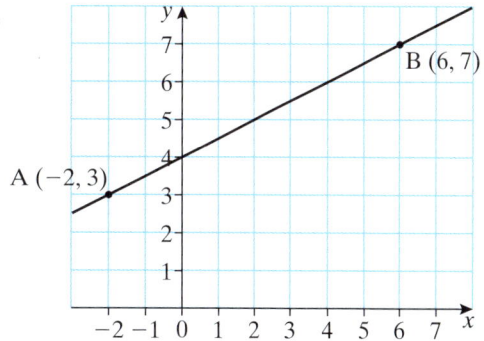

13. Two forces, N_1 and N_2, act on a hemisphere at rest.
If $\frac{1}{4}N_1 - N_2 = 0$ and $N_1 + \frac{1}{2}N_2 - 99 = 0$,
find the values of N_1 and N_2.

14. If $\dfrac{a}{x - 2} + \dfrac{b}{x + 2} = \dfrac{4}{(x - 2)(x + 2)}$ for all values of x,

using algebraic identities, write down two equations in terms of a and b only.
Hence solve for a and b.
Verify your answers using the original equation.

15. If $\dfrac{c}{z - 3} + \dfrac{d}{z + 2} = \dfrac{4}{(z - 3)(z + 2)}$ for all values of z, solve for c and d.

Verify your answers by substitution.

16. How many litres of 70% alcohol need to be added to 50 litres of 40% alcohol to make a 50% solution?

17. The sum of two numbers is 26.
If five times the smaller number is taken from four times the larger number, the result is 5.
Let x be the bigger number and y the smaller number.
   (i) Write down two equations in x and y.
   (ii) Solve these equations for x and y.
   (iii) Verify your answers by substitution.

18. A student studied a car rolling down an inclined plane and took measurements of its speed at two different times.
    After 7 seconds, it had a speed of 2 m/sec and after 13 seconds, the speed increased to 5 m/sec.
    Using the equation $v = u + at$, where v is the speed and t is the time, write down two linear equations in u and a.
    Solve these equations to find values for u and a.

19. A farmer builds a long narrow pen for sheep using 60 m of fencing.
    If he doubles the width and halves the length, he only needs to use 42 m of fencing.
    Find the dimensions of the two pens.

    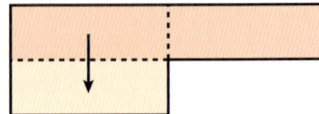

    (As can be seen from the diagram, the areas of the two pens remain the same. Explain why less fencing is needed in the second pen.)

20. The curve $y = ax^2 + bx + c$ contains the points $(0, 1)$, $(2, 9)$ and $(4, 41)$.

    (i) Using these points, write three simultaneous equations in a, b and c.
    (ii) Hence solve the equations to find the values of a, b and c.

21. Solve the simultaneous equations.

    (i) $y - z = 3$

    $x - 2y + z = -4$

    $x + 2y = 11$

    (ii) $\dfrac{x}{3} + \dfrac{y}{2} - z = 7$

    $\dfrac{x}{4} - \dfrac{3y}{2} + \dfrac{z}{2} = -6$

    $\dfrac{x}{6} - \dfrac{y}{4} - \dfrac{z}{3} = 1$

22. The circle $x^2 + y^2 + ax + by + c = 0$ passes through the points $(1, 0)$, $(1, 2)$ and $(2, 1)$. Find the values of a, b, and c.

23. The school tuck shop sold a small bag of popcorn for €3.00, a medium bag for €5.00 and a large bag for €7.00. During break-time they sold 15 bags of popcorn earning a total of €77.00. If they sold 2 more medium bags than small bags, how many bags of each size did the shop sell?

24. Aileen invested her savings of €10 500.00 in three different savings schemes.
    Fund A, a mutual fund paid 11% interest for the first year.
    Fund B, a government bond paid 7% interest
    Fund C, her local bank paid 5% interest.
    She invested twice as much in the mutual fund as she did in the bank. If her total interest for the first year was €825.00, find out how much she invested in each fund.

25. In making a bracelet a jeweller used white, blue and green beads. The number of blue beads was four less than the number of white and green beads. He used the same number of green beads as blue and white beads and he used twice as many blue beads as white beads. How many beads of each colour did he use in each bracelet?

Revision Exercise 1 (Core)

1. Simplify each of the following algebraic expressions.

   (i) $\dfrac{12m^2n^3}{(6m^4n^5)^2}$

   (ii) $\dfrac{3 + \dfrac{1}{x}}{\dfrac{5}{x} + 4}$

   (iii) $\dfrac{2 + \dfrac{x}{2}}{x^2 - 16}$

2. Solve for x and y:

   (i) $y = x + 4$
   $5y + 2x = 6$

   (ii) $3x + y = 7$
   $x^2 + y^2 = 13$

3. Using long division, find $x^3 - x^2 - 7x + 3 \div x - 3$.

4. Divide $3x^4 - 9x^2 + 27x - 66$ by $x - 2$.

5. Solve the equations.

   (i) $x^4 - 9x^2 = 0$

   (ii) $(2x - 1)^3(2 - x) = 0$

6. Given that $4x^2 + 20x + k$ is a perfect square, find k.

7. Expand (i) $(2x + 3)^5$ (ii) $(x - 2)^6$

8. Factorise $x^3 - 27$.

9. If $p(x - q)^2 + r = 2x^2 - 12x + 5$ for all values of x, find the values of p, q and r.

10. Solve the simultaneous equations
    $3x + 5y - z = -3$
    $2x + y - 3z = -9$
    $x + 3y + 2z = 7$.

11. Simplify $(b + 1)^3 - (b - 1)^3$.

12. Find the rule (i.e. the nth term) for each of the following quadratic patterns.
    (i) $3, 12, 27, 48, 75 \ldots$ (ii) $5, 20, 45, 80, 125 \ldots$ (iii) $0.5, 2, 4.5, 8, 12.5 \ldots$

13. Find the rule for the pattern $6, 12, 20, 30, 42$ using first and second differences.
    Hence find the 100th term of this pattern.

14. Three times the width of a certain rectangle exceeds twice the length by 3 cm.
    Four times the length is 12 cm more than its perimeter.
    Find the dimensions of the rectangle.

15. The formula for a spherical mirror of radius r cm is given by $\dfrac{1}{u} + \dfrac{1}{v} = \dfrac{2}{r}$, where u cm is the object distance and v cm is the image distance to the mirror.

    The magnification in the mirror is given by $m = \dfrac{v - r}{r - u}$.

    (i) Find r in terms of u and v.
    (ii) Find m in terms of v and u only.

Revision Exercise 1 (Advanced)

1. By converting the number of squares in the following designs into a number pattern, write down a rule for the pattern. Use the rule to find out how many bricks are needed to build the 49th design.

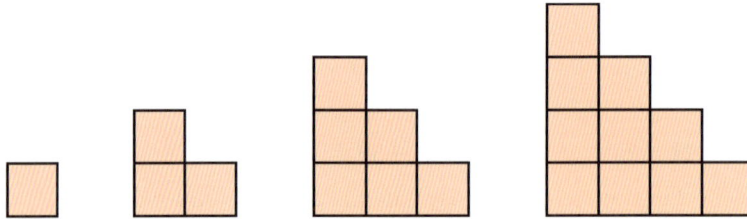

2. How much soil containing 55% sand needs to be added to $1\,m^3$ of soil containing 25% sand to make soil containing 35% sand?

   Hint: let $x\,m^3$ be the amount of soil needed.

3. A metallurgist needs to make 8.4 kg of an alloy containing 50% gold. He is going to melt two metal alloys, one containing 60% gold with a second metal alloy that contains 40% gold.

   (i) Let x kg and y kg be the amounts needed of each metal alloy. Write two equations linking the unknowns x and y.
   (ii) Solve the equations to find the amount of each metal needed.

4. If, for all values of x, $(3p - 2t)x + r - 4t^2 = 0$, show that $r = 9p^2$.

5. Simplify the equation $\dfrac{x + y^2}{x^2} + \dfrac{x - 1}{x} = -1$ and hence find the ratio of x^2 to y^2.

6. In a chemistry class, a group of students need a 15% acid solution to complete a test. The lab only has 10% acid solution and 30% acid solution.
   The students decide to mix the two solutions to get the 15% solution they require. If the students need 10 litres of the new solution, find

   (i) the number of litres of the 10% solution they require
   (ii) the number of litres of the 30% solution they require.

7. At a concert a ticket for a seat in section A cost €75, while a ticket for a seat in section B cost €55. A standing ticket cost €30. There were three times as many seats sold in section B as compared to section A. If 23 000 tickets in total were sold for a total revenue of €870 000, how many of each type of ticket were sold?

8. Brian and Luke race over 50 metres. Brian runs so that it takes him a seconds to run 1 metre. Luke runs so that it takes him b seconds to run 1 metre. Luke wins the race by 1 second. The next day, they race again over 50 metres (and again at the same speeds) but Luke gives Brian a 3-metre start so that Brian only runs 47 metres. Luke wins this race by 0.1 seconds. Find

   (i) the values of a and b
   (ii) Luke's speed.

9.   (i) Find the sixth term in the expansion of $\left(2 - \frac{1}{3}x\right)^9$.

    (ii) Find the eight term in the expansion of $(3x + 1)^{12}$.

10. Using, $\binom{n}{r}x^{n-r}y^r$ as the general term of $(x + y)^n$, find the 6th term of the expansion of $(3x - 1)^{11}$.

11. Find the coefficient of x^{10} in the expansion of $(2x - 3)^{14}$.

Revision Exercise 1 (Extended-Response Questions)

1. A football club wanted to organise a family day as a fund-raiser.
They decided to pre-sell tickets at €5.00 for adults and €2.50 for children aged 6 years or younger.
Last year, when they held a similar event 13 000 attended.
Last year they had only one ticket-price.
The organisers wanted to estimate the expected revenue for the day. They decided to use the information obtained from the pre-sold tickets to arrive at this estimate.
However, the members selling the tickets did not record the numbers of adult and children separately. It was known however that 548 tickets in total were sold and that €2460 was collected.

  (a) By setting up suitable equations, find
      (i) the number of adult tickets pre-sold
     (ii) the number of children tickets pre-sold
    (iii) the proportion of adult tickets sold.

  (b) Based on the same attendance for this year, estimate the revenue expected for the coming fund-raiser.

2. A factory makes two types of sofa. The standard sofa requires 2 hours of work in the manufacturing section and 1 hour in the finishing section.
The deluxe sofa requires 2.5 hours in the manufacturing section and 1.5 hours of finishing work.
Each day, there is a maximum of 48 hours of worker-time available in the manufacturing section and a maximum of 26 hours available in the finishing section.

  (i) If x standard sofas and y deluxe sofas are made per day, and the manufacturing section is worked to its capacity, explain why $2x + 2.5y = 48$.
  (ii) Find a second equation in x and y if the finishing section is also used to its capacity.
  (iii) How many of each sofa can be produced if each section is used to its capacity?

3. A closed rectangular box has a square base of length x cm and height h cm.
The volume of the box is $40\,cm^3$.

  (i) Write an expression for h in terms of x.
  (ii) Show that the surface area, $S\,cm^2$, of this box is given by

$$S = 2x^2 + \frac{160}{x}.$$

  (iii) Sketch a graph of S against x, for $0 \leqslant x \leqslant 10$.
  (iv) Estimate from the graph the possible values of x and h for which this box has a surface area of $72\,cm^2$.

4. A game made by a company sells for €11.50. The cost of production consists of an initial cost of €3500 and then €10.50 for each game produced.
   Let x be the number of games produced.

   (i) If $C(x)$ is the cost of producing x games, find an expression for $C(x)$ in terms of x.
   (ii) If $I(x)$ represents the income received for selling x games, find an expression for $I(x)$ in terms of x.
   (iii) Plot the graphs of $I(x)$ and $C(x)$ on the same axes. (Scale the x-axis in units of 500 and the y-axis in units of 10,000.)
   (iv) How many games need to be sold to recoup the production costs?
   (v) Let $P = I - C$. What does P represent?
   (vi) How many games need to be sold to make a profit of €2000?

5. Celine completed a quilt for a sale of work in exactly 15days. She can sew blue squares in the quilt at a rate of 4 squares per day and white squares at a rate of 7 squares per day. The finished quilt had 96 squares. The blue fabric cost €0.80 per square and the white fabric cost €1.20 per square.

   (a) Find the cost of the quilt.
   (b) The 96 squares are used to form a rectangle whose length and width are to be in the ratio $3:2$.
      Celine decides to have a rectangle of blue squares in the centre of the quilt surrounded by white squares.
      Draw an arrangement of blue and white squares that creates a symmetrical design.

6. A small company manufactures wheelbarrows for the garden-supply market.
   The company has overheads of €30 000 per year.
   It costs €40 to manufacture each wheelbarrow.

   (i) Write a rule which determines the total cost, €C, of manufacturing x wheelbarrows per year.
   (ii) If the average production is 6000 wheelbarrows per year, what is the overall cost per wheelbarrow?
   (iii) How many wheelbarrows must be made so that the average cost is €46 per wheelbarrow?
   (iv) The wheelbarrows are sold to retailers at €80 each. Write a rule which determines the revenue, €R, from the sale of x wheelbarrows to the retailers.
   (v) Plot the graphs for C and R on the same axes, with the number of wheelbarrows, x, on the horizontal axis.
   (vi) What is the minimum number of wheelbarrows that have to be sold to make a profit each year?
   (vii) Write a rule that determines the profit, €P, from the manufacture and sale of x wheelbarrows.

Algebra 2

Key words

substitution   discriminant   completing the square   real and distinct

imaginary   rational   vertex   parabola   maximum   minimum   surd

irrational   rationalising the denominator

Section 2.1 Quadratic equations

As mentioned already, when the highest power of a variable in a polynomial is two, the resulting expression is called a quadratic expression.
The following are examples of quadratic equations:

(i) $3x^2 + 4x - 5 = 0$ (ii) $6 = 3t + 8t^2$ (iii) $A = 2\pi rh + 2\pi r^2$

Each quadratic equation has two solutions (or roots).

Solving quadratic equations

Techniques for solving quadratic equations include

(i) factorising   (ii) quadratic formula   (iii) graphical methods   (iv) substitution.

(i) Factorising methods (as in Chapter 1)

If an equation which equates to zero can be factorised, then at least one of its factors must equal zero.

If $(a)(b) = 0$, then $a = 0$ or $b = 0$.

Example 1

Use factors to solve   (i) $x^2 - 5x - 6 = 0$ (ii) $y^2 - 5y = 0$ (iii) $4t^2 - 100 = 0$

(i) $x^2 - 5x - 6 = 0$
$(x - 6)(x + 1) = 0$
$\therefore\ x - 6 = 0 \rightarrow x = 6$
or $x + 1 = 0 \rightarrow x = -1$

(ii) $y^2 - 5y = 0$
$y(y - 5) = 0$
$\therefore\ y = 0$
or $y - 5 = 0 \rightarrow y = +5$

(iii) $4t^2 - 100 = 0$
$4(t^2 - 25) = 0$
$4(t - 5)(t + 5) = 0$
$\therefore\ t - 5 = 0 \rightarrow t = +5$
or $t + 5 = 0 \rightarrow t = -5$

Solutions (roots)   (i) $x = \{6, -1\}$ (ii) $y = \{0, 5\}$ (iii) $t = \{5, -5\}$

(ii) Quadratic formula

The quadratic formula $x = \dfrac{-b \pm \sqrt{b^2 - 4ac}}{2a}$ can be
used to solve any quadratic equation of the form
$ax^2 + bx + c = 0$.

If $\quad ax^2 + bx + c = 0,$

then $\quad x = \dfrac{-b \pm \sqrt{b^2 - 4ac}}{2a}$

It is good practice to write out the coefficients a, b, and c separately before applying
the formula.

Example 2

Solve $x - 6 = \dfrac{3}{x}$. (Note: It is not always obvious that we are dealing with an
equation of the form $ax^2 + bx + c = 0$.)

$$x - 6 = \frac{3}{x}$$

Rearranging $\;\to\; x^2 - 6x = 3 \;\Rightarrow\; x^2 - 6x - 3 = 0$

$\therefore\;\; a = 1,\, b = -6,\, c = -3,\;$ hence $x = \dfrac{-b \pm \sqrt{b^2 - 4ac}}{2a} = \dfrac{6 \pm \sqrt{(-6)^2 - 4(1)(-3)}}{2(1)}$

$$x = \frac{6 \pm \sqrt{48}}{2} = \frac{6 \pm 4\sqrt{3}}{2} = 3 \pm 2\sqrt{3}$$

$\therefore\;\; x = 3 + 2\sqrt{3}$ or $x = 3 - 2\sqrt{3}$ are the roots (solutions) of the equation.

(iii) Graphical methods

Graphing the expression $y = x^2 - 5x + 1, 0 \leqslant x \leqslant 5$,
we get the points
$(0, 1), (1, -3), (2, -5), (3, -5), (4, -3), (5, 1)$,
which, when plotted, produce the familiar
$\cup$-shaped curve.

To solve $y = x^2 - 5x + 1 = 0$ graphically,
we must find the points on the curve
where $y = 0$, i.e. the points $G(0.2, 0)$ and $H(4.8, 0)$.

$\therefore\;\;$ The roots are 0.2 and 4.8.

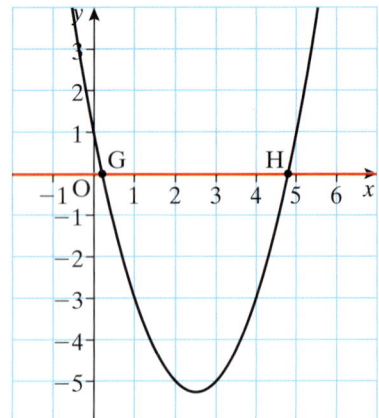

When the expression $y = -x^2 - 3x + 2$ is plotted, a ∩-shaped graph results.

Again, the roots of the equation $-x^2 - 3x + 2 = 0$ occur where the curve intersects the x-axis (i.e. where $y = 0$), i.e. the points $G(-3.6, 0)$ and $H(0.6, 0)$.

Graphical methods can only give approximate values for the roots of an equation.

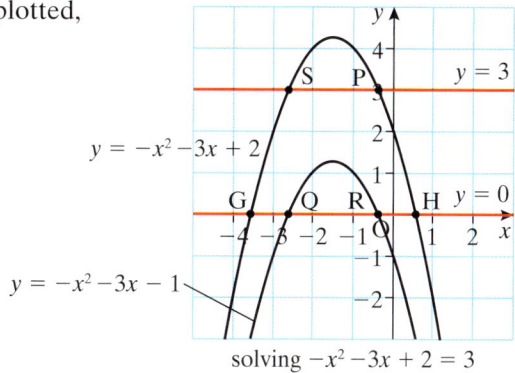

$y = -x^2 - 3x + 2$

$y = 3$

$y = 0$

$y = -x^2 - 3x - 1$

solving $-x^2 - 3x + 2 = 3$

To solve the equation $-x^2 - 3x + 2 = 3$, we can consider two approaches;

(i) To find the points on the curve $y = -x^2 - 3x + 2$ where $y = 3$ (i.e. S, P) **or**

(ii) To create the new curve $y = -x^2 - 3x + 2 - 3 = -x^2 - 3x - 1$ and solve $-x^2 - 3x - 1 = 0$.

Both are different curves but with the same solutions (roots) for Q and S, $x \cong -2.6$ and for P and R, $x \cong 0.4$.

(iv) Substitution

The following types of equations can be solved by choosing a suitable substitution which creates a new quadratic equation in standard form.

(i) $\left(t - \dfrac{6}{t}\right)^2 - 6\left(t - \dfrac{6}{t}\right) + 5 = 0$ let $u = \left(t - \dfrac{6}{t}\right)$,   then $u^2 - 6u + 5 = 0$

(ii) $x^4 + x^2 - 6 = 0$ let $u = x^2$,   then $u^2 + u - 6 = 0$

(iii) $2x + 3\sqrt{x} = 5$ let $u = \sqrt{x}$,   then $2u^2 + 3u - 5 = 0$

Once the values for u have been found, the values for x can then be obtained.

Example 3

Solve $x^4 + x^2 - 6 = 0$ for $x \in R$.

Let $u = x^2$, $\Rightarrow u^2 = x^4$.

$$x^4 + x^2 - 6 = 0 \Rightarrow u^2 + u - 6 = 0$$
$$\Rightarrow (u + 3)(u - 2) = 0$$
$$u + 3 = 0 \Rightarrow u = -3 \Rightarrow x^2 = -3 \Rightarrow x = \pm\sqrt{(-3)}$$
$$\textbf{or} \quad u - 2 = 0 \Rightarrow u = 2 \Rightarrow x^2 = 2 \Rightarrow x = \pm\sqrt{(2)}$$

$x = \pm\sqrt{(-3)}$, two imaginary roots which are not required.

$\therefore \quad x = +\sqrt{(2)}, -\sqrt{(2)}$ are the solutions.

[Note: $(+\sqrt{(2)})^4 + (+\sqrt{(2)})^2 - 6 = 0$ and $(-\sqrt{(2)})^4 + (-\sqrt{(2)})^2 - 6 = 0$]

Example 4

Solve $2x + 3\sqrt{x} = 5$ for $x \in R$.

Let $u = \sqrt{x} \Rightarrow u^2 = x$

$\therefore \quad 2x + 3\sqrt{x} = 5 \Rightarrow 2u^2 + 3u - 5 = 0$

$\Rightarrow (u - 1)(2u + 5) = 0$

$\Rightarrow u = 1$ or $u = \dfrac{-5}{2}$

$\therefore \quad \sqrt{x} = 1$ or $\sqrt{x} = \dfrac{-5}{2}$

Remember:
The $\sqrt{b}$, where $b \geqslant 0$, is the non-negative square root of b.
e.g $\sqrt{25} = 5$.

But $\sqrt{x}$ must be a non-negative number.

$\therefore \quad \sqrt{x} = 1, x = 1$

Validating the solution; $x = 1 \Rightarrow 2x + 3\sqrt{x} = 2(1) + 3(\sqrt{1}) = 5$

Exercise 2.1

1. Use factors to solve the following equations:
   (a) (i) $(x - 4)(x + 5) = 0$ (ii) $x^2 - 7x + 12 = 0$ (iii) $x^2 - 4x - 5 = 0$
   (b) (i) $x^2 - 2x - 15 = 0$ (ii) $2x^2 + 7x - 15 = 0$ (iii) $3x^2 - 13x - 10 = 0$
   (c) (i) $5x^2 - 13x - 6 = 0$ (ii) $9x^2 + 3x - 20 = 0$ (iii) $8x^2 - 2x - 15 = 0$
   (d) (i) $x^2 - 9 = 0$ (ii) $3x^2 - 10x = 0$ (iii) $5x^2 - 8x = 0$
   (e) (i) $15 - 7x - 2x^2 = 0$ (ii) $10 + x - 3x^2 = 0$ (iii) $12 - 6x - 6x^2 = 0$
   (f) (i) $(x + 5)(x^2 - 16)$ (ii) $(x - 3)(4x^2 - 4) = 0$
   (g) (i) $(x^2 - 4)(3x + 4) = 0$ (ii) $(2x + 8)(x^2 - 2x - 15) = 0$

2. Use the quadratic formula to solve each of the following, giving your answers correct to one place of decimals:
   (a) (i) $x^2 - 2x - 2 = 0$ (ii) $x^2 + 3x - 2 = 0$ (iii) $2x^2 - 6x + 3 = 0$
   (b) (i) $x^2 - 6x + 3 = 0$ (ii) $3x^2 - 8x + 1 = 0$ (iii) $2x^2 + 4x - 5 = 0$

3. Use the quadratic formula to solve each of the following, leaving your answers in surd form:
   (a) (i) $3x^2 + 4x - 5 = 0$ (ii) $2x^2 - 12x - 5 = 0$ (iii) $(2x - 3)^2 = 8$
   (b) (i) $x^2 + 4x - 8 = 0$ (ii) $5x^2 + 4x - 2 = 0$ (iii) $x^2 - x - 1 = 0$

4. Solve the following equations:
   (a) (i) $\dfrac{x + 7}{3} + \dfrac{2}{x} = 4$ (ii) $\dfrac{1}{x - 1} + \dfrac{4}{x} = 3$ (iii) $\dfrac{3}{x - 1} - \dfrac{2}{x + 1} = 1$

   (b) (i) $\dfrac{1}{x} + \dfrac{2}{x - 2} = 3$ (ii) $\dfrac{x + 2}{x - 4} = \dfrac{2x + 1}{x - 2}$ (iii) $\dfrac{2}{x - 2} + \dfrac{3}{x} = \dfrac{5}{x - 4}$

5. By finding a suitable substitution, solve each of the following:

(a) (i) $x^4 - 7x^2 + 10 = 0, x \in R$ (ii) $(x+1)^2 + 3(x + 1) - 2 = 0$
    (iii) $x^4 - 2x^2 - 2 = 0$ (iv) $2(k - 2)^2 - 3(k - 2) - 4 = 0$

(b) (i) $(2y - 1)^2 - 3(2y - 1) - 28 = 0$ (ii) $(2y - 3)^2 - 1 = 0$

(c) $\left(y + \dfrac{4}{y}\right)^2 - 9\left(y + \dfrac{4}{y}\right) + 20 = 0$

(d) $\left(2t - \dfrac{5}{t}\right)^2 - 12\left(2t - \dfrac{5}{t}\right) + 27 = 0$

6. Solve $2x^2 - \sqrt{3}x - 3 = 0$.

7. Using the graphs, find *approximate* solutions to each of the following equations.

(a) $x^2 + 3x - 5 = 0$ (b) $-x^2 - x + 1 = -2$ (c) $p(x) = 0$ (d) $g(x) > 0$
(e) $-x^2 - x + 1 = 0$ (f) $g(x) = f(x)$ (g) $h(x) = 5$ (h) $p(x) > h(x)$

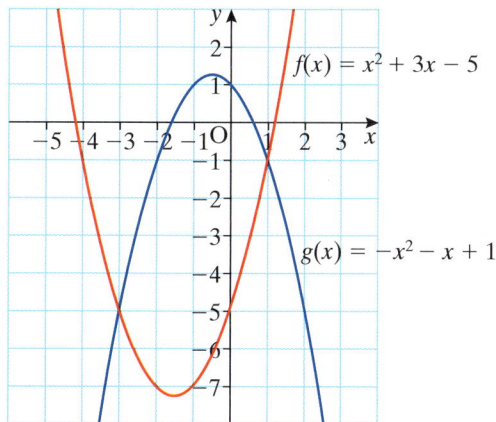

$f(x) = x^2 + 3x - 5$

$g(x) = -x^2 - x + 1$

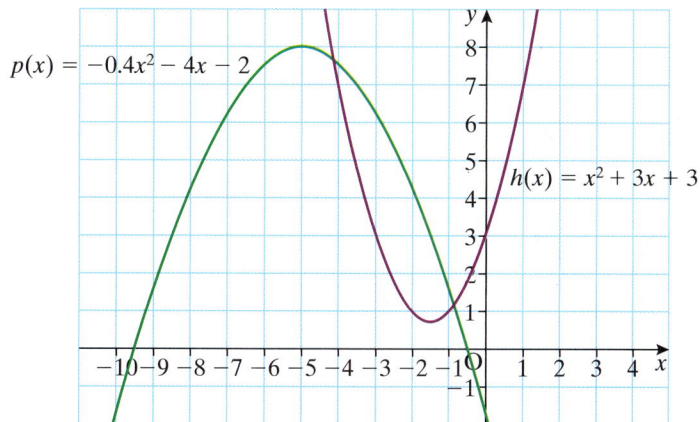

$p(x) = -0.4x^2 - 4x - 2$

$h(x) = x^2 + 3x + 3$

8. Using the graphs above, explain why $x^2 + 3x + 3 = 0$ has no real solutions.

9. If x_1 and x_2 are the roots of the equation $f(x) = 0.2x^2 + 5x + 9 = 0$ and $x_1 > x_2$, using the graph, find an approximate value for

   (a) $(x_2 - x_1)$
   (b) $(x_2 + x_1)$

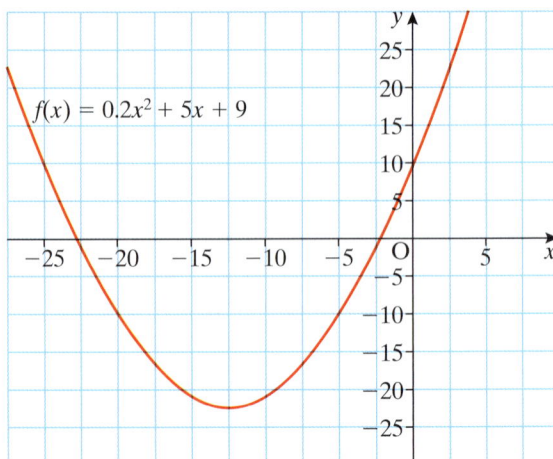

$f(x) = 0.2x^2 + 5x + 9$

10. The graphs of the functions

    $f(x) = 2x^2 - 3x - 2$ and $g(x) = \dfrac{4x + 3}{5}$

    are drawn as shown. Using the graphs, estimate the solutions of the following equations

    (a) $f(x) = 0$
    (b) $g(x) = 0$
    (c) $f(x) = g(x)$.

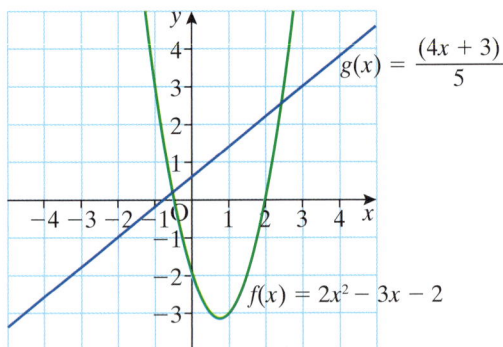

$g(x) = \dfrac{(4x + 3)}{5}$

$f(x) = 2x^2 - 3x - 2$

11. By using the substitution $u = \sqrt{x}$, solve each of the following equations. Explain why there is only one solution for each equation.

    (i) $2x + 3\sqrt{x} = 5$ (ii) $x - 3\sqrt{x} - 4 = 0$

12. Solve each of the following equations, giving your answers in surd form.

    (i) $x^2 - \sqrt{7}x - 14 = 0$ (ii) $2x^2 + 7\sqrt{5}x + 15 = 0$

Section 2.2 Nature of quadratic roots

1. The discriminant

We have used the formula $x = \dfrac{-b \pm \sqrt{b^2 - 4ac}}{2a}$ to solve quadratic equations of

the form $ax^2 + bx + c = 0$, where $a, b, c \in R$.

The value of the expression $(b^2 - 4ac)$ will determine the nature of the roots of this equation and is called the **discriminant** of the equation.

$(b^2 - 4ac) = \text{discriminant}$

2. Real and distinct roots

Real distinct roots occur when $(b^2 - 4ac) > 0$.

e.g. $3x^2 + 5x - 2 = 0$; $a = 3, b = 5, c = -2$;

$\therefore (b^2 - 4ac) = [5^2 - 4(3)(-2)] = 49 > 0$.

$$x = \frac{-b \pm \sqrt{b^2 - 4ac}}{2a} \rightarrow x = \frac{-5 \pm \sqrt{49}}{6}$$

$$\rightarrow x = \frac{-5 + 7}{6}, \frac{-5 - 7}{6} = (0.33, -2)$$

In this case, the graph crosses the x-axis at two distinct places, $(-2, 0)$ and $(0.33, 0)$.

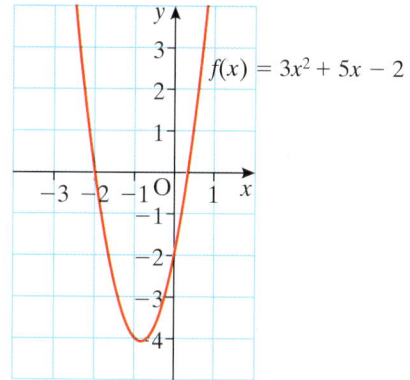

$f(x) = 3x^2 + 5x - 2$

$b^2 - 4ac > 0$

3. Real and equal roots

Real and equal roots occur when $(b^2 - 4ac) = 0$.

e.g. $4x^2 - 12x + 9 = 0$; $a = 4, b = -12, c = 9$;

$\therefore (b^2 - 4ac) = [144 - 4(4)(9)] = 0$.

$$x = \frac{-b \pm \sqrt{b^2 - 4ac}}{2a} \rightarrow x = \frac{12 \pm \sqrt{(0)}}{2.4}$$

$$= \frac{12}{8} = \frac{3}{2}$$

Only one solution occurs and the graph touches the x-axis at this point, $A\left(\frac{3}{2}, 0\right)$.

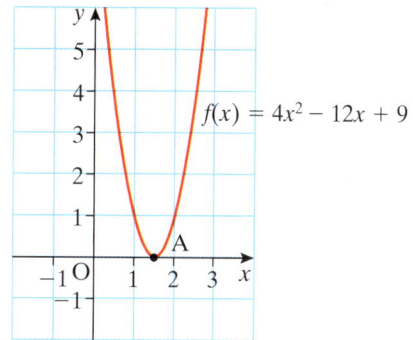

$f(x) = 4x^2 - 12x + 9$

$b^2 - 4ac = 0$

4. Complex roots

Imaginary roots occur when $(b^2 - 4ac) < 0$.

e.g. $x^2 - 4x + 5 = 0$; $a = 1, b = -4, c = 5$;

$\therefore (b^2 - 4ac) = [16 - 4(1)(5)] = -4 < 0$.

$$x = \frac{-b \pm \sqrt{b^2 - 4ac}}{2a} \rightarrow x = \frac{4 \pm \sqrt{(-4)}}{2.1}$$

$$\rightarrow x = \frac{4 + \sqrt{-4}}{2}, \frac{4 - \sqrt{-4}}{2}$$

If we let $\sqrt{-1} = i$, then we can rewrite the solutions as follows:

$$x = \frac{4 + 2i}{2}, \frac{4 - 2i}{2} = 2 + i, 2 - i$$

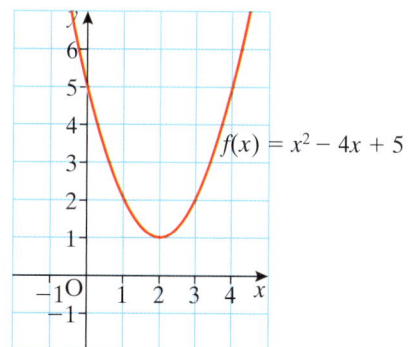

$f(x) = x^2 - 4x + 5$

$b^2 - 4ac < 0$

These points cannot be represented on the real plane. (We will study these types of numbers further in Complex Numbers book 5.)

We note that the curve does not cut (cross) the x-axis.

5. Rational roots

If $(b^2 - 4ac)$ is a perfect square then $\sqrt{(b^2 - 4ac)}$ is a rational number and this means that the equation has rational roots.

(Perfect squares are 1, 4, 9, 16, ... or $\frac{16}{9}, \frac{4}{25}$ ... etc.)

e.g. $3x^2 + 5x + 2 = 0$; $a = 3, b = 5, c = 2$;

$\therefore (b^2 - 4ac) = [25 - 4(3)(2)] = 1$ which is a perfect square.

$f(x) = 3x^2 + 5x + 2$

$$x = \frac{-b \pm \sqrt{b^2 - 4ac}}{2a} \Rightarrow x = \frac{-5 \pm \sqrt{(25 - 24)}}{2.3}$$

$$\Rightarrow x = \frac{-5 \pm 1}{6} = \frac{-6}{6}, \frac{-4}{6} = -1, -\frac{2}{3}$$

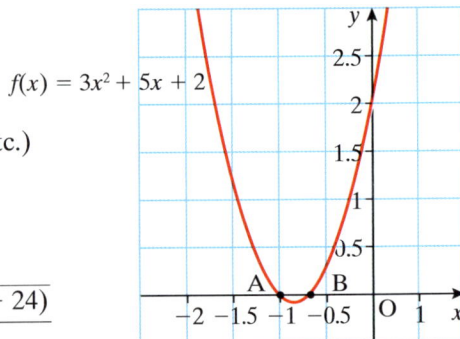

In summary

1. If $(b^2 - 4ac) > 0 \Rightarrow$ two different (distinct) real roots
2. If $(b^2 - 4ac) = 0 \Rightarrow$ two equal real roots
3. If $(b^2 - 4ac) < 0 \Rightarrow$ two imaginary roots
4. If $(b^2 - 4ac)$ is a perfect square $\rightarrow$ rational roots

Note: When the phrase "has **real roots**" is used in questions, then this must be taken to mean "has *either* two real distinct roots *or* two equal (repeated) roots".

Roots are **real** if $(b^2 - 4ac) \geqslant 0$

Example 1

Evaluate the discriminant of each of the following, stating whether the equation has

(i) two distinct real roots   (ii) two identical real roots   (iii) no real roots.

(a) $3x^2 + 5x - 1 = 0$ (b) $49x^2 + 42x + 9 = 0$
(c) $2x^2 + 8x + 9 = 0$ (d) $2x^2 + 7x + 4 = 0$

(a) $3x^2 + 5x - 1 = 0 \rightarrow a = 3, b = 5, c = -1$.
  $\therefore (b^2 - 4ac) = 25 - 4(3)(-1) = 37 > 0$ $\therefore$ two distinct real roots.

(b) $49x^2 + 42x + 9 = 0 \rightarrow a = 49, b = 42, c = 9$.
  $\therefore (b^2 - 4ac) = 1764 - 4(49)(9) = 0$ $\therefore$ two identical real roots.

(c) $2x^2 + 8x + 9 = 0 \rightarrow a = 2, b = 8, c = 9$.
  $\therefore (b^2 - 4ac) = 64 - 4(2)(9) = -8 < 0$ $\therefore$ no real roots.

(d) $2x^2 + 7x + 4 = 0 \rightarrow a = 2, b = 7, c = 4$.
  $\therefore (b^2 - 4ac) = 49 - 4(2)(4) = 17 > 0$ $\therefore$ two distinct real roots.

Example 2

Find the values of k so that $-8 + kx - 2x^2 = 0$ has equal roots.

$$-8 + kx - 2x^2 = 0 \Rightarrow a = -2, b = k, c = -8.$$

For equal roots, we have that $(b^2 - 4ac) = 0$

$\therefore \quad (b^2 - 4ac) = [k^2 - 4(-2)(-8)]$

$\therefore \quad k^2 - 64 = 0 \qquad \therefore \quad k = \pm 8$

Example 3

Given the equation $px^2 + (p + q)x + q = 0$.
(i) Show that the roots are real for all values of p and $q \in R$.
(ii) Show that the roots are rational.
(iii) Hence find
    (a) the roots, in terms of p and q
    (b) the factors, in terms of p and q.

$$px^2 + (p + q)x + q = 0 \rightarrow a = p, b = (p + q), c = q.$$

(i) For real roots, we need to show that $(b^2 - 4ac) \geqslant 0$.

$\begin{aligned}
\therefore \quad (b^2 - 4ac) &= (p + q)^2 - 4(p)(q) \\
&= p^2 + 2pq + q^2 - 4pq \\
&= p^2 - 2pq + q^2 = (p - q)^2
\end{aligned}$

Since (any real quantity)^2 cannot be negative $\Rightarrow (p - q)^2 \geqslant 0$.

$\therefore \quad (b^2 - 4ac) \geqslant 0$

$\therefore \quad$ the roots are real.

(ii) For rational roots, $(b^2 - 4ac)$ must be a perfect square.

Since $(b^2 - 4ac) = (p - q)^2$, i.e. a perfect square,

$\therefore \quad$ the roots are also rational.

(iii) (a) The roots are $x = \dfrac{-b \pm \sqrt{b^2 - 4ac}}{2a} = \dfrac{-(p + q) \pm \sqrt{(p - q)^2}}{2p}$

$$= \dfrac{-(p + q) \pm (p - q)}{2p}$$

$$\therefore \quad x = \dfrac{-2q}{2p}, \dfrac{-2p}{2p} = \dfrac{-q}{p}, -1$$

(b) Since $x = -\dfrac{q}{p} \Rightarrow px + q = 0$

Also $x = -1 \Rightarrow x + 1 = 0$

$\therefore$ the factors of $px^2 + (p + q)x + q$ are $px + q$ and $x + 1$

Exercise 2.2

1. By inspection, state which of the curves – f, g and h – have

   (i) real and distinct roots
   (ii) real and equal roots
   (iii) imaginary roots.
   (iv) In the case of real roots, estimate from the graph the roots of each equation.

   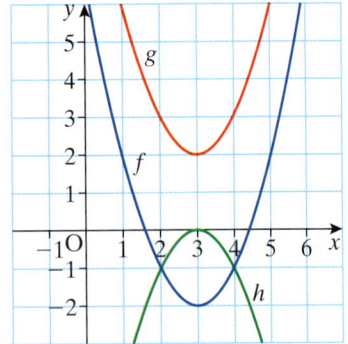

2. The curve shown has equation of the form
   $$ax^2 + bx + c = 0.$$

   Find, in terms of a, b, and c, the coordinates of the points A and B.

   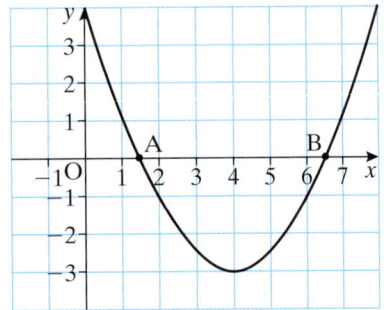

3. Find the discriminant of each of the following equations and state if the roots are
       (a) real and different   (b) real and equal   (c) imaginary.

   (i) $2x^2 + x + 5 = 0$ (ii) $-2x^2 + 3x + 1 = 0$ (iii) $3x^2 + 2x - 1 = 0$
   (iv) $-3 + 2x - x^2 = 0$ (v) $x^2 + 8x + 16 = 0$ (vi) $25 - 10x + x^2 = 0$

4. Draw a sketch of any quadratic curve that is positive for all values of x.
   Given that $3x^2 - kx + 12$ is positive for all values of x, find the range of possible values of k.

5. For what value(s) of k does each of the following equations have equal roots?
   (i) $x^2 - 10x + k = 0$ (ii) $4x^2 + kx + 9 = 0$ (iii) $x^2 - x(2k + 2) + 5k + 1 = 0$

6. Find the values of k if the equation $k^2x^2 + 2(k + 1)x + 4 = 0$ has equal roots.

7. Given that (any real number)$^2 \geqslant 0$, prove that the following equations have real roots for all values of $k \in R$.
   (i) $x^2 - 3kx - k^2 = 0$ (ii) $kx^2 + 2x + (2 - k) = 0$

8. Show that the roots of the equation $x^2 - 3x + 2 - c^2 = 0$ are real for all values of $c \in R$.

9. Prove that the equation $(k - 2)x^2 + 2x - k = 0$ has real roots, whatever the value of k.

10. Find the value of k for which the equation $(k - 2)x^2 + x(2k + 1) + k = 0$ has equal roots.

11. Show that the equation $(m + 3)x^2 + (6 - 2m)x + m - 1 = 0$ has equal roots if $m = \frac{3}{2}$.

12. If the equation $ax^2 + bx + 1 = 0$ has equal roots, express a in terms of b.

Hence write down the root of the equation in terms of b.

13. Show that the equation $x^2 - 2px + 3p^2 + q^2 = 0$ cannot have real roots for $p, q \in R$.

Section 2.3 Solving quadratic and linear equations

To find the point(s) of intersection between a line and a curve, we use the technique of **substitution**. We have used this method already when solving simultaneous linear equations.

We note that in this case, the line may
  (i)   intersect the curve at two points
 (ii)   intersect at one point
(iii)   or not intersect the curve at all.

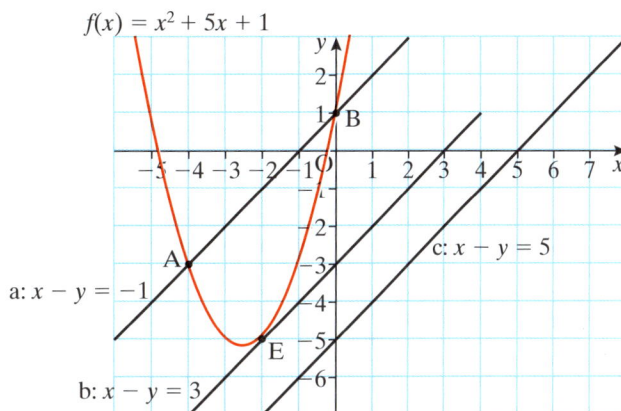

If there is just one point of intersection, the line is said to be a **tangent** to the curve.

The line $x - y = -1$ intersects the curve $y = x^2 + 5x + 1$ at two points, A$(-4, -3)$ and B$(0, 1)$.

The line $x - y = 3$ is a tangent to the curve $y = x^2 + 5x + 1$ at the point E$(-2, -5)$.

The line $x - y = 5$ does not intersect the curve.

Example 1

Find the point(s) of intersection between
  (i) $x - y = -1$ (ii) $x - y = 3$ and the curve $y = x^2 + 5x + 1$.

(i) Since $x - y = -1$ $\qquad$ Substituting $y = (1 + x)$ into $y = x^2 + 5x + 1$,
$\qquad \to -y = -1 - x \qquad$ we get $(1 + x) = x^2 + 5x + 1$.
$\qquad \to y = (1 + x) \qquad \therefore \quad 0 = x^2 + 5x + 1 - 1 - x = x^2 + 4x$.
$\qquad\qquad\qquad \therefore \quad 0 = x(x + 4)$
$\qquad\qquad\qquad \therefore \quad (x + 4) = 0$ or $x = 0$, i.e. $x = -4$ or 0.
$\qquad\qquad\qquad \therefore \quad y = 1 - 4 = -3 \to (x, y) = (-4, -3)$
$\qquad\qquad\qquad$ and $y = 1 - 0 = 1 \to (x, y) = (0, 1)$
$\therefore$ the points of intersection for $x - y = -1$ are $(-4, -3)$ and $(0, 1)$.

(ii) $x - y = 3$

$\rightarrow -y = 3 - x$

$\rightarrow y = (-3 + x)$

Substituting $y = (-3 + x)$ into $y = x^2 + 5x + 1$,

$\therefore$ $(-3 + x) = x^2 + 5x + 1$

$0 = x^2 + 5x + 1 + 3 - x = x^2 + 4x + 4$

$\therefore$ $(x + 2)(x + 2) = 0$

$\therefore$ $x = -2$ (a repeated solution)

$\therefore$ $y = -3 - 2 = -5 \rightarrow (x, y) = (-2, -5)$

$\therefore$ the point of intersection for $x - y = 3$ is $(-2, -5)$.

$\therefore$ $x - y = 3$ is a **tangent** to the curve $y = x^2 + 5x + 1$ at the point $(-2, -5)$.

In summary, to find the point(s) of intersection between a line and a curve,

(i) isolate one of the variables in the equation of the line, e.g. $y = ax + b$.

(ii) Substitute this expression for y into the equation for the curve $y = cx^2 + dx + e$,
i.e. $ax + b = cx^2 + dx + e$ and simplify.

(iii) Solve the resulting quadratic equation.

Example 2

Show that there are no point(s) of intersection between the line $x - y = 5$ and the curve $y = x^2 + 5x + 1$.

$x - y = 5$

$\rightarrow -y = 5 - x$

$\rightarrow y = (-5 + x)$

Substituting $y = (-5 + x)$ into $y = x^2 + 5x + 1$,
we get $(-5 + x) = x^2 + 5x + 1$.

$\therefore$ $0 = x^2 + 5x + 1 + 5 - x$

$0 = x^2 + 4x + 6$.

If there are no points of intersection, this implies that $0 = x^2 + 4x + 6$ has no real roots.

$\therefore$ $(b^2 - 4ac) < 0$

$0 = x^2 + 4x + 6 \rightarrow a = +1, b = +4, c = +6$.

$\therefore$ $(b^2 - 4ac) = [4^2 - 4(1)(6)] = (16 - 24) = -8 < 0$.

$\therefore$ the line $x - y = 5$ does not intersect the curve $y = x^2 + 5x + 1$.

Exercise 2.3

Solve the following pairs of simultaneous equations, one linear and one quadratic.

1. $y = x^2$
$2x + y = 3$

2. $x^2 + y^2 = 5$
$x - y + 1 = 0$

3. $4x^2 - y = 0$
$2x + y = 2$

4. $y = x^2 - 6x + 5$
$x + y - 1 = 0$

5. $x^2 + y^2 = 25$
$x + y = 7$

6. $3x^2 - y^2 = 3$
$2x - y = 1$

7. $y = x^2 - 4x + 6$
$y = 3x - 4$

8. $x^2 + y^2 - 4x + 2 = 0$
$x + y - 4 = 0$

9. $x^2 + 4y^2 = 4$
$x + 2y - 2 = 0$

10. $xy = 4$
$2x - y + 2 = 0$

11. $y^2 + xy = 2$
$2x + y = 3$

12. $x^2 + y^2 + 2x - 4y + 3 = 0$
$x - y + 3 = 0$

13. $s = 2t - 1$
$3t^2 - 2ts + s^2 = 9$

14. $2s^2 = t^2 + 1$
$2s = t - 3$

15. $2t - 3s = 1$
$t^2 + ts - 4s^2 = 2$

Section 2.4 Quadratic and linear equations in context —

Algebraic methods can be used to solve many real-life problems.
If we can represent an unknown or variable with a symbol, and write the relationship
between the variables in the form of a linear or quadratic equation, then the resulting
equations can be solved using the techniques discussed earlier.

Example 1

A right-angled triangle is to be made from a rope
24 m long. If the hypotenuse of the triangle, AB,
has to be 10 m, find

(i) an equation in terms of x and y for the
perimeter of the triangle

(ii) an equation in terms of x and y for the
hypotenuse of the triangle.

(iii) Solve the equations to find possible
lengths of the base (x) and height (y)
of the triangle.

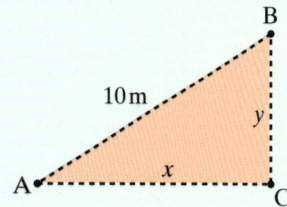

(i) The perimeter of the triangle $= x + y + 10$.
$\Rightarrow x + y + 10 = 24 \Rightarrow x + y = 14$.

(ii) The (hypotenuse)$^2 = x^2 + y^2 = 10^2$.

(iii) Since $x + y = 14 \Rightarrow x = 14 - y$.

$\therefore \quad (14 - y)^2 + y^2 = 10^2$

$\therefore \quad 196 - 28y + y^2 + y^2 = 10^2$

$\therefore \quad 2y^2 - 28y + 96 = 0$

$\therefore \quad y^2 - 14y + 48 = 0$

$\quad (y - 6)(y - 8) = 0$

$\therefore \quad y = 6 \text{ or } y = 8$

When $y = 6$
$\Rightarrow x = 14 - y = 14 - 6 = 8$.

Also, if $y = 8$
$\Rightarrow x = 14 - y = 14 - 8 = 6$.

$\therefore$ if the base is 8 m, the height is 6 m, or vice versa.

A satellite is on a fact-finding
mission to the moons of Pluto.
The equation $x - y = 3$
represents its path. A comet is
discovered moving in a curve in
the same plane as the satellite.
If the path of the comet is determined
to be $x^2 + y^2 - 36x + 224 = 0$,
decide if their paths will cross.

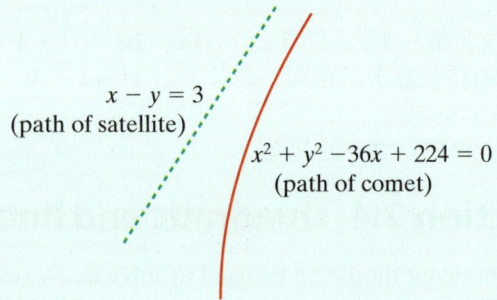

$x - y = 3$
(path of satellite)

$x^2 + y^2 - 36x + 224 = 0$
(path of comet)

If the paths are to collide, then the intersection of the two equations must
have real solution(s).

i.e. $b^2 - 4ac \geqslant 0$.

If $x - y = 3$,

then $y = x - 3$. Substituting into $x^2 + y^2 - 36x + 224 = 0$,

we get $x^2 + (x - 3)^2 - 36x + 224 = 0$

$\therefore \quad 2x^2 - 42x + 233 = 0$ ... must have real solutions.

$\therefore \quad a = 2, b = -42, c = 233$.

$\therefore \quad b^2 - 4ac = [(-42)^2 - 4(2)(233)] = -100 < 0$

$\therefore$ There are no real solutions and the paths do not cross.

Exercise 2.4

1. Find the values of two consecutive numbers, the sum of the squares of which equals 61.

2. Find two consecutive **even** numbers, the sum of the squares of which equals 52.

3. 62 m of fencing is used to form a rectangular pen of
   area 198 m^2.

   (i) Find two equations linking the length and width
   of the rectangle.

   (ii) Solve the equations to find the dimensions of the
   rectangle.

   perimeter = 62 m
   area = 198 m^2

4. A right-angled triangle is to be made using three
   consecutive integer numbers as sides.

   Find the length of the perimeter of the triangle.

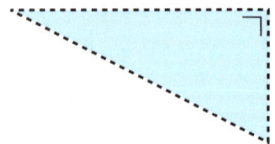

5. The distance s travelled by a car is given by the formula $s = 12t - t^2$.
   Find the two times at which the car passes a point 25 m away, giving your answers
   correct to two places of decimals.

6. The square of a number is reduced by 15. The resulting value is twice the original number. Find the number(s).

7. A football is kicked up into the air. The height of the ball can be modelled by the equation $h = -16t^2 + 24t + 1$, where h = the height in metres and t = time in seconds.
   At what times will the ball be at a height of 6 m?

8. One side of a right-angled triangle is 4 cm longer than the other side. The hypotenuse is 20 cm long. Find the shortest side of the triangle.

9. The product of two consecutive odd integers is 1 less than four times their sum. Find the two integers.

10. The hypotenuse of a right-angled triangle is 6 cm longer than the shortest side. The third side is 3 cm longer than the shortest side. Find the length of the shortest side.

11. The length of a rectangular garden is 4 metres longer than its width. If the area of the garden is 60 m^2, find the dimensions of the garden.

12. Find three consecutive integers such that three times their sum equals the product of the larger two.

13. A circular swimming pool with a diameter of 28 metres has a wooden deck around its edge.
    If the deck has an area of 60π m^2, find the width of the deck.

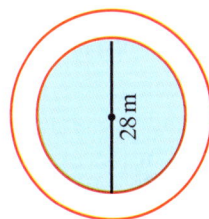

14. If one side of a square is doubled and the adjacent side is decreased by 2 cm, the resulting rectangle has an area that is 96 cm^2 larger than the original square. Find the dimensions of the rectangle.

15. A skateboard ramp is in the shape of a curve with equation $h = 0.1x^2 - x + 2.5$. Two platforms represent the starting and finishing points as shown.

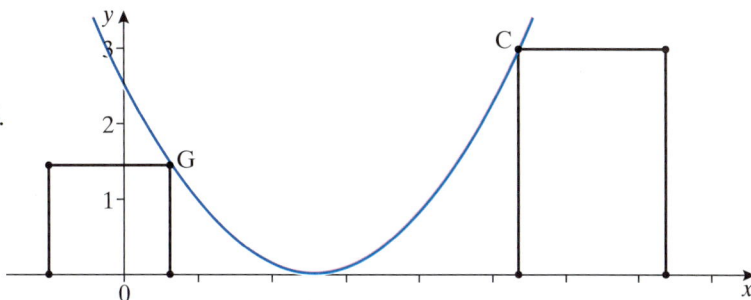

If the starting point C is at a height of 3 m and G, the finishing point, is at a height of 1.5 m, calculate the distance between the bases of the two platforms, correct to two places of decimals.

16. A rocket travels along a path given by the equation $3t - s = 4$, where t represents time and s represents distance from the ground.

A comet is travelling along a path represented by the equation $2t^2 + s^2 = 43$.

Determine the point where the paths cross.

Suggest a reason why there is only one solution, i.e. one point of intersection.

17. A plane is travelling along a path given by the equation $x + 3y = 5$.

A weather front is reported in the path of the plane.

If the front is modelled using the equation $x^2 + 6y^2 = 40$, determine if the plane will cross this front.

If the path of the plane is given by $x + 3y = k$, find the minimum value of k so that the plane will avoid the weather front.

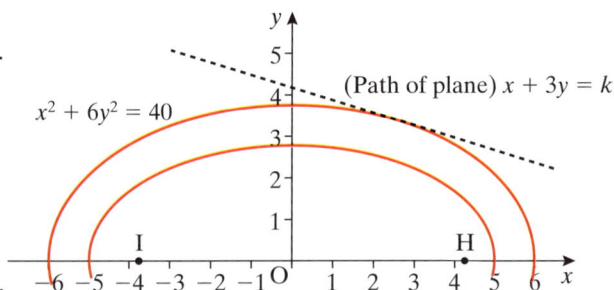

Section 2.5 Forming quadratic equations from their roots

If we know the roots of an equation, we can find the equation by

  (i) finding the factors of the equation

  (ii) multiplying the factors to get the equation.

Generally, if we let $x = r_1$ and $x = r_2$ be the roots of a quadratic equation,

  then $(x - r_1)$ and $(x - r_2)$ are the factors

  and $(x - r_1)(x - r_2) = 0$ is the equation.

    i.e. $x^2 - xr_2 - xr_1 + r_1r_2 = 0$

        $x^2 - x(r_2 + r_1) + r_1r_2 = 0.$

> Given r_1, r_2 as the roots of an equation, then the equation is
>
> $$x^2 - x(r_1 + r_2) + r_1r_2 = 0,$$
>
> i.e. $x^2 - x \text{ (sum of the roots)} + \text{product of the roots} = 0.$

Example 1

Write the equation of a curve whose roots are 7 and -5.

Since the equation has only two roots, it must be a quadratic equation.

$\therefore \quad x^2 - x \text{ (sum of the roots)} + \text{product of the roots} = 0$

$\therefore \quad x^2 - x [7 + (-5)] + [(7)(-5)] = 0$ is the equation.

$\therefore \quad x^2 - x(2) - 35 = 0$

The equation is $x^2 - 2x - 35 = 0$.

Example 2

If $x = \sqrt{3}$ and $x = \dfrac{-\sqrt{3}}{2}$ are the roots of a quadratic equation $ax^2 + bx + c = 0$, find possible values for a, b and c.

We have that $x^2 - x$ (sum of the roots) + product of the roots = 0.

$$\Rightarrow x^2 - x\left(\sqrt{3} + \frac{-\sqrt{3}}{2}\right) + \sqrt{3}\left(\frac{-\sqrt{3}}{2}\right) = 0 \text{ is the equation.}$$

$$\Rightarrow x^2 - x\left(\frac{2\sqrt{3}}{2} - \frac{\sqrt{3}}{2}\right) - \frac{3}{2} = 0$$

$$\Rightarrow x^2 - x\left(\frac{\sqrt{3}}{2}\right) - \frac{3}{2} = 0$$

$$2x^2 - \sqrt{3}x - 3 = 0 \text{ ... multiplying both sides of the equation by 2}$$

$$\therefore \quad a = 2, b = -\sqrt{3} \text{ and } c = -3.$$

Note: If $a = 4$, $b = -2\sqrt{3}$ and $c = -6$ we would have a different quadratic function but with the same roots.

Exercise 2.5

1. State (i) the sum and (ii) the product of the roots of each of the following quadratic equations.

   (a) $x^2 + 9x + 4 = 0$ (b) $x^2 - 2x - 5 = 0$

   (c) $x^2 - 7x + 2 = 0$ (d) $x^2 - 9x - 3 = 0$

   (e) $2x^2 - 7x + 1 = 0$ (f) $7x^2 + x - 1 = 0$

   (g) $3x^2 + 10x - 2 = 0$ (h) $5x^2 + 10x + 1 = 0$

   (i) $3 - 2x - x^2 = 0$ (j) $-5 + 3x - 4x^2 = 0$

2. In the following table, you are given both the sum and the product of the roots of quadratic equations. In each case, find the quadratic equation in the form $ax^2 + bx + c = 0$, with a, b and c taking integer values.

	(a)	(b)	(c)	(d)	(e)	(f)	(g)	(h)
Sum	-3	6	7	$-\frac{2}{3}$	$-\frac{5}{2}$	$-\frac{3}{2}$	$-\frac{1}{4}$	$-1\frac{2}{3}$
Product	-1	-4	-5	$-\frac{7}{3}$	-2	-5	$-\frac{1}{3}$	$\frac{1}{2}$

3. Find the quadratic equations that have the following pairs of roots $\{r_1, r_2\}$.

   (i) $\{4, 6\}$ (ii) $\{2, -3\}$ (iii) $\{-5, -1\}$ (iv) $\{\sqrt{5}, 4\}$

   (v) $\{a, 3a\}$ (vi) $\left\{\frac{2}{5}, \frac{3}{5}\right\}$ (vii) $\left\{\frac{2}{b}, \frac{3}{b}\right\}$ (viii) $\left\{\frac{5}{2}, \frac{3}{5}\right\}$

Section 2.6 Max and Min of Quadratic graphs

The quadratic expression $x^2 - 6x + 11$ can be rewritten as

$$x^2 - 6x + 9 - 9 + 11$$
$$= (x - 3)(x - 3) - 9 + 11 = (x - 3)^2 + 2.$$
$$\therefore \quad x^2 - 6x + 11 = (x - 3)^2 + 2.$$

This is called **completing the square**.

This form of a quadratic expression can give us very useful information about the behaviour of the quadratic function.

(i) **Maximum or minimum values.**
   At $x = 3$, $(x - 3) = 0$.
   $\therefore (x - 3)^2 + 2 = 2$ is the minimum value of this expression.

(ii) **Real or complex roots.**
   Let $(x - 3)^2 + 2 = 0$ to find the roots.
   Then $(x - 3)^2 = -2$
   $x - 3 = \pm \sqrt{-2}$
   $x = 3 \pm \sqrt{-2} \Rightarrow$ Complex roots.

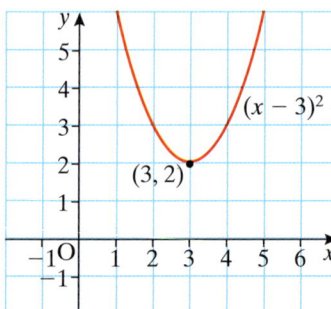

$(x - 3)^2 + 2 = x^2 - 6x + 11$

$(3, 2)$

(iii) **Values of x which make the function positive or negative.**
   $(x - 3)^2$ is positive for all $x \in R$.
   $\therefore (x - 3)^2 + 2$ is positive for all $x \in R$.

(iv) Each graph has a **turning point** which is the maximum or minimum point of the graph.

(v) Each graph has an **axis of symmetry** parallel to the y-axis through this point.

(vi) The graph of a quadratic function is called a **parabola.**

Example 1

Complete the square on each of the following quadratic expressions.
Hence find the minimum value of each expression.

   (i) $x^2 - 8x + 10$ (ii) $4x^2 + 4x + 2$

(i) $x^2 - 8x + 10$

$= x^2 - 8x + 16 - 16 + 10$

$= (x - 4)(x - 4) - 6$

$= (x - 4)^2 - 6$

Minimum value $= -6$

(ii) $4x^2 + 4x + 2$

$= 4(x^2 + x + \frac{1}{2})$

$= 4(x^2 + x + \frac{1}{4} - \frac{1}{4} + \frac{1}{2})$

$= 4[(x + \frac{1}{2})^2 + \frac{1}{4}]$

$= 4(x + \frac{1}{2})^2 + 1$

Minimum value $= +1$

Generally, to complete the square of expressions of the form $x^2 + bx + c$, **add and subtract (half the coefficient of x)^2** to the expression and isolate the perfect square portion.

$$x^2 + bx + c = \left(x + \frac{b}{2}\right)^2 - \left(\frac{b}{2}\right)^2 + c$$

i.e. $x^2 + bx + c = x^2 + bx + \left(\frac{b}{2}\right)^2 - \left(\frac{b}{2}\right)^2 + c = \left(x + \frac{b}{2}\right)^2 - \left(\frac{b}{2}\right)^2 + c$

Note: If the coefficient of x^2 is not 1, the x^2 coefficient must be factored out before proceeding, e.g.,

(i) $\begin{aligned}[t] x^2 + 2x + 5 &= x^2 + 2x + 1 - 1 + 5 \\ &= (x + 1)^2 + 4 \end{aligned}$

(ii) $\begin{aligned}[t] 4 - 2x - x^2 &= 4 - (x^2 + 2x) = 4 - (x^2 + 2x + 1 - 1) = 4 - [(x + 1)^2 - 1] \\ &= 5 - (x + 1)^2 \end{aligned}$

(iii) $\begin{aligned}[t] 3x^2 - 3x + 2 &= 3\left(x^2 - x + \frac{2}{3}\right) = 3\left(x^2 - x + \frac{1}{4} - \frac{1}{4} + \frac{2}{3}\right) \\ &= 3\left[\left(x - \frac{1}{2}\right)^2 + \frac{5}{12}\right] = 3\left(x - \frac{1}{2}\right)^2 + \frac{5}{4} \end{aligned}$

All quadratic expressions ($ax^2 + bx + c$) can be written in the form of

$a(x - p)^2 + q$, a $\cup$-shaped graph

or $q - a(x - p)^2$, a $\cap$-shaped graph.

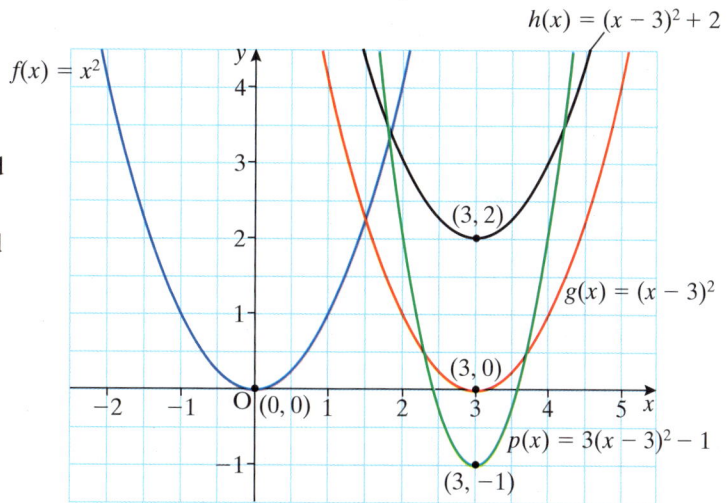

$h(x) = (x - 3)^2 + 2$

$f(x) = x^2$

$g(x) = (x - 3)^2$

$p(x) = 3(x - 3)^2 - 1$

ICT: Using a graphics calculator or computer software (e.g. Geogebra), sketches of the following curves can be compared, identifying the minimum points and the axes of symmetry for each.

	Min
$f(x) = x^2 = (x - 0)^2 + 0$	$(0, 0)$
$g(x) = x^2 - 6x + 9 = (x - 3)^2 + 0$	$(3, 0)$
$h(x) = x^2 - 6x + 11 = (x - 3)^2 + 2$	$(3, 2)$
$p(x) = 3x^2 - 18x + 26 = 3(x - 3)^2 - 1$	$(3, -1)$

The point (p, q) is the **minimum point** of the curve $a(x - p)^2 + q$.

At $x = p, (x - p) = 0$.

$\Rightarrow a(x - p)^2 + q = 0 + q = q$, the minimum value.

Similarly, a quadratic equation in the form $q - a(x - p)^2$ has a **maximum point** at (p, q) and a maximum value q at the point $x = p$.

When quadratic expressions can be written as $a(x - p)^2 + q$, there is a **minimum** point (p, q). When quadratic expressions can be written as $q - a(x - p)^2$, there is a **maximum** point (p, q).

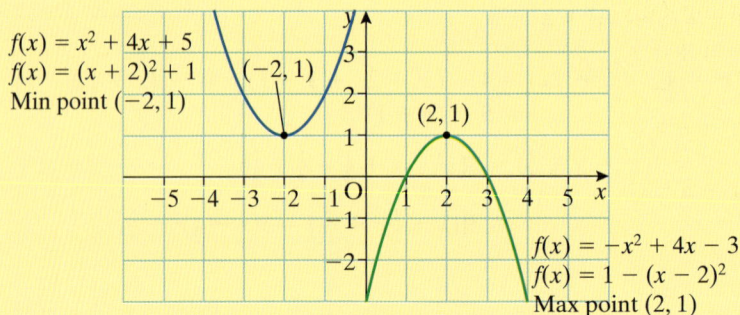

$f(x) = x^2 + 4x + 5$
$f(x) = (x + 2)^2 + 1$
Min point $(-2, 1)$

$(-2, 1)$

$(2, 1)$

$f(x) = -x^2 + 4x - 3$
$f(x) = 1 - (x - 2)^2$
Max point $(2, 1)$

Example 2

Write the quadratic equation $x^2 + 4x + 1$ in the form $(x - p)^2 + q$ and hence,

(i) find the minimum point and minimum value of $x^2 + 4x + 1$
(ii) solve the equation $x^2 + 4x + 1 = 0$, leaving your answer in surd form.

(i) $x^2 + 4x + 1 = x^2 + 4x + \mathbf{4} - \mathbf{4} + 1$
$\qquad\qquad\quad\; = (x + 2)^2 - 3$

$\qquad\qquad \Rightarrow$ the minimum point is $(-2, -3)$
$\qquad\qquad \Rightarrow$ the minimum value of the expression is -3.

(ii) Solving $x^2 + 4x + 1 = 0$,
$\qquad \Rightarrow (x + 2)^2 - 3 = 0$
$\qquad \Rightarrow (x + 2)^2 = 3$
$\qquad \Rightarrow x + 2 = \pm \sqrt{3}$
$\qquad \Rightarrow x = -2 \pm \sqrt{3}.$

(**Note:** It should be verified that the same result is obtained using the quadratic formula.)

Example 3

(i) Write the equation of the graph provided in the form $y = q - a(x - p)^2$, where (p, q) is the maximum point of the curve and a is a constant.

(ii) By choosing any suitable point on the curve, find a.

(iii) Hence write the equation in the form $y = ax^2 + bx + c$.

(i) The maximum point $= (-1, 3) = (p, q)$.

$$y = q - a(x - p)^2$$
$$\therefore \quad y = 3 - a(x + 1)^2$$

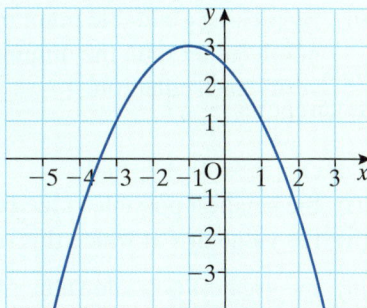

(ii) Selecting $(x, y) = (1, 1)$,

$$\Rightarrow 1 = 3 - a(1 + 1)^2$$
$$= 3 - 4a$$
$$\Rightarrow a = \tfrac{1}{2}$$

(iii) $\therefore \quad y = 3 - \left(\tfrac{1}{2}\right)(x + 1)^2$

$$\therefore \quad y = 3 - \frac{x^2}{2} - x - \tfrac{1}{2}$$
$$= -\frac{x^2}{2} - x + 2\tfrac{1}{2}$$

Exercise 2.6

1. Find the value of c that completes the square in each of the following:

   (i) $a^2 + 28a + c$ (ii) $x^2 - 6x + c$ (iii) $y^2 - 5y + c$

2. Complete the square in each of the following:

   (i) $x^2 - 8x - 3 = 0$ (ii) $x^2 - 2x - 5 = 0$ (iii) $x^2 - 2x + 1 = 0$

3. Write each of the following in the form $(x - p)^2 + q = 0$.

   (i) $x^2 + 4x - 6 = 0$ (ii) $x^2 + 9x + 4 = 0$ (iii) $x^2 - 7x - 3 = 0$

4. The graph of $y = a(x - p)^2 + q$ has a minimum point (p, q).
   By completing the square, find the minimum point of each of the following quadratic equations:

   (i) $2x^2 + 4x - 5 = 0$ (ii) $3x^2 - 6x - 1 = 0$ (iii) $4x^2 + x + 3 = 0$

5. Complete the square of the expression $x^2 - 6x + k$.
   Find the minimum value of k such that $x^2 - 6x + k$ is positive for all values of x.

6. Express $2x^2 - 12x + 7$ in the form $a(x - b)^2 + c$.

7. Given that $g(x) = x^2 + 8x + 20$, show that $g(x) \geqslant 4$ for all values of x.

8. (i) Write down the coordinates (p, q) of the
minimum point of each of these
graphs.

  (ii) Write the equation of each graph in
the form
  (a) $y = (x - p)^2 + q$
  (b) $y = ax^2 + bx + c$.

  (iii) By picking a suitable point on each
graph (other than the minimum point),
verify each equation.

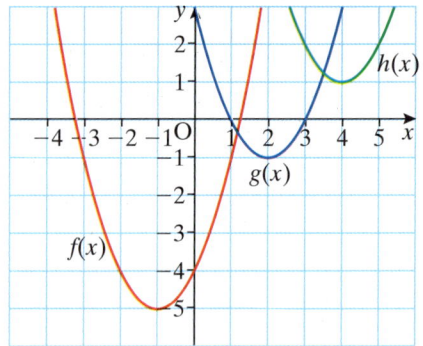

9. If $f(x) = x^2 + 4x + 7$, find
  (i) the smallest possible value of $f(x)$
  (ii) the value of x at which this smallest value occurs
  (iii) the greatest possible value of $\dfrac{1}{(x^2 + 4x + 7)}$.

10. The path of a golf ball is given by the equation $y = -x^2 + 6x$.
By completing the square, find the maximum point of the path and hence the greatest
height reached. Sketch the curve in the domain $0 < x < 6$ to validate your result.

11. Identify the graphs of the equations
  (i) $y = x^2 - 6x + 8$
  (ii) $y = x^2 - 6x + 9$
  (iii) $y = x^2 - 6x + 10$.

  Express each equation in the form
  $y = a(x - p)^2 + q$.

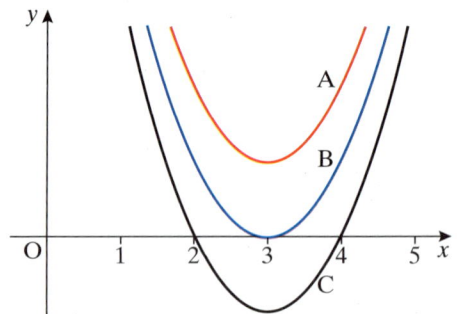

12. Each of the curves C and D can be
represented by equations in the form

  $p - a(x - q)^2$.

  Find the values of p, a and q for each curve.

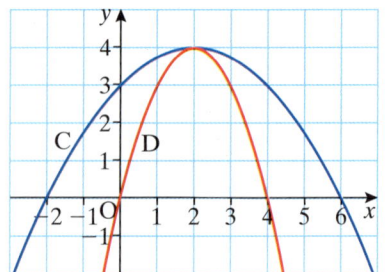

13. A parabola has x-axis intercepts of 6 and -3 and passes through the point $(1, 10)$.
Find the equation of the parabola.

14. A parabola has a minimum vertex with coordinates $(-1, 3)$ and y-axis intercept 4.
Find the equation of the parabola.

15. The path of a golf ball is given below.
  (i) Using the maximum point of the path (p, q), complete the equation
      $f(x) = q - 0.1(x - p)^2$ for this curve.
  (ii) Solve the equation $f(x) = 0$ to find the point from which the ball started, and the
       point where the ball finished on level ground (leaving your answer in square root
       form).
  (iii) Hence find the horizontal distance travelled by the ball, giving your answer in
        the form $a\sqrt{b}$.

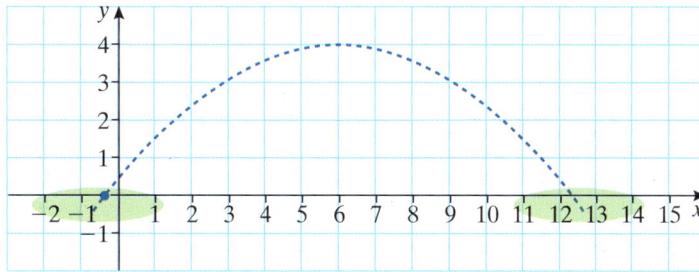

16. A trapezium has a base of 20 and a
    height of $2x$ as shown in the diagram.
    (i) Show that the area of this
        trapezium can be given by
        $x^2 + 20x$.
    (ii) If the area of the trapezium is to
         be 400, by completing the square
         show that $x = 10(\sqrt{5} - 1)$

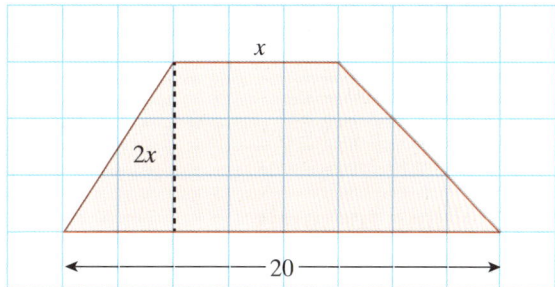

17. Probes used to record the temperature of a patient indicated that their temperature
    changed according to the equation $T(°C) = 36 + 4t - t^2$, where t was measured in hours.

    By writing this quadratic in the form $a(t - p)^2 + q$, find the maximum temperature
    of the patient and use it to determine how long (in hours) it will be before their
    temperature returns back to normal (36°C).

Section 2.7 Surds

A surd is a **square root** which cannot be reduced to a whole number, e.g. $\sqrt{2}, \sqrt{3}, \sqrt{5}, \sqrt{6}, \sqrt{7}, \ldots$

If $x^2 = 2$, then $x = \sqrt{2} = 1.414213562\ldots$
A surd is therefore an irrational number,
a number which cannot be expressed as
a fraction.

> **Remember:**
> The $\sqrt{x}$, where $x \geqslant 0$, is the non-negative
> square root of x. e.g. $\sqrt{25} = 5$.

$\sqrt{1}, \sqrt{9}, \sqrt{\frac{25}{16}} \ldots$ are not surds since $1, 9, \frac{25}{16}$ etc.,
are perfect squares and have square roots.

Note: $x = \sqrt{2}$ is an exact answer.

   $x = 1.414213562\ldots$ is an approximate or corrected answer and should be only
   given when asked for.

1. Reducing surds to their lowest form

$\sqrt{5}, \sqrt{6}, \sqrt{7}$ cannot be simplified further,

but $\sqrt{8} = \sqrt{4 \times 2} = \sqrt{4} \times \sqrt{2} = 2\sqrt{2}$,

since 8 has a factor that is a perfect square.

$$\sqrt{ab} = \sqrt{a} \times \sqrt{b}$$

2. Simplifying surd quotients

$$\sqrt{\frac{50}{64}} = \frac{\sqrt{50}}{\sqrt{64}} = \frac{\sqrt{25} \times \sqrt{2}}{8} = \frac{5\sqrt{2}}{8}$$

$$\sqrt{\frac{a}{b}} = \frac{\sqrt{a}}{\sqrt{b}}$$

3. Adding or subtracting surds

$2\sqrt{3} + 4\sqrt{3} = 6\sqrt{3}$.

$\sqrt{27} - \sqrt{12} = \sqrt{9 \times 3} - \sqrt{4 \times 3} = 3\sqrt{3} - 2\sqrt{3} = \sqrt{3}$.

$$a\sqrt{b} \pm c\sqrt{b} = (a \pm c)\sqrt{b}$$

4. Multiplying surds

$\sqrt{4} \times \sqrt{4} = (\sqrt{4})^2 = 4$.

$\sqrt{5} \times \sqrt{6} = \sqrt{30}$.

$(7 - \sqrt{2})(7 + \sqrt{2}) = 49 + 7\sqrt{2} - 7\sqrt{2} - 2 = 47$.

$$\sqrt{a} \times \sqrt{b} = \sqrt{ab}$$

5. Dividing by surds

It is normal practice not to leave a surd (an irrational number) in the denominator of a quotient, hence the practice of "**rationalising the denominator**".

$$\frac{5}{\sqrt{3}} = \frac{5}{\sqrt{3}} \cdot \frac{\sqrt{3}}{\sqrt{3}} = \frac{5\sqrt{3}}{3} \quad \left(\textbf{Note: } \text{Multiplying by } \frac{\sqrt{3}}{\sqrt{3}} \text{ is equivalent to multiplying by 1.}\right)$$

$$\frac{1}{7 - \sqrt{2}} = \frac{1}{7 - \sqrt{2}} \cdot \frac{7 + \sqrt{2}}{7 + \sqrt{2}}$$

$$= \frac{7 + \sqrt{2}}{7^2 - \sqrt{2}^2} = \frac{7 + \sqrt{2}}{47}$$

To rationalise the denominator:

$$\frac{1}{a - \sqrt{b}} = \frac{1}{a - \sqrt{b}} \cdot \frac{a + \sqrt{b}}{a + \sqrt{b}}$$

Example 1

(i) Express $\sqrt{80}$ in the form $a\sqrt{5}$, where a is an integer.

(ii) Express $(4 - \sqrt{5})^2$ in the form $b + c\sqrt{5}$, where b and c are integers.

(i) $\sqrt{80} = \sqrt{16 \times 5} = 4\sqrt{5}$

(ii) $(4 - \sqrt{5})^2 = (4 - \sqrt{5})(4 - \sqrt{5}) = 16 - 8\sqrt{5} + 5 = 21 - 8\sqrt{5}$

Example 2

Simplify (i) $\dfrac{\sqrt{12}}{5\sqrt{3} - \sqrt{27}}$ (ii) $\dfrac{7}{\sqrt{13} - \sqrt{11}}$

(i) $\dfrac{\sqrt{12}}{5\sqrt{3} - \sqrt{27}} = \dfrac{\sqrt{4 \times 3}}{5\sqrt{3} - \sqrt{9 \times 3}} = \dfrac{2\sqrt{3}}{5\sqrt{3} - 3\sqrt{3}} = \dfrac{2\sqrt{3}}{2\sqrt{3}} = 1$

(ii) $\dfrac{7}{\sqrt{13} - \sqrt{11}} = \dfrac{7}{\sqrt{13} - \sqrt{11}} \cdot \dfrac{\sqrt{13} + \sqrt{11}}{\sqrt{13} + \sqrt{11}} = \dfrac{7(\sqrt{13} + \sqrt{11})}{13 - 11} = \dfrac{7(\sqrt{13} + \sqrt{11})}{2}$

Exercise 2.7

1. Simplify each of the following:

   (i) $\sqrt{8}$ (ii) $\sqrt{27}$ (iii) $\sqrt{45}$ (iv) $\sqrt{200}$ (v) $3\sqrt{18}$

2. Express each of the following in its simplest form:

   (i) $2\sqrt{2} + 6\sqrt{2} - 3\sqrt{2}$ (ii) $2\sqrt{2} + \sqrt{18}$ (iii) $\sqrt{32} + \sqrt{18}$
   (iv) $\sqrt{27} + \sqrt{48} - 2\sqrt{3}$ (v) $\sqrt{8} + \sqrt{200} - \sqrt{18}$ (vi) $7\sqrt{5} + 2\sqrt{20} - \sqrt{80}$

3. In each of the following quotients, rationalise the denominator.

   (i) $\dfrac{1}{\sqrt{3}}$ (ii) $\dfrac{2}{\sqrt{8}}$ (iii) $\dfrac{2}{5\sqrt{2}}$ (iv) $\dfrac{20}{\sqrt{50}}$ (v) $\dfrac{8}{\sqrt{128}}$

4. Simplify each of the following:

   (i) $\sqrt{8} \times \sqrt{12}$ (ii) $3\sqrt{2} \times 5\sqrt{2}$ (iii) $\sqrt{2}(\sqrt{6} + 3\sqrt{2})$
   (iv) $(5 - \sqrt{3})(5 + \sqrt{3})$ (v) $(\sqrt{7} + \sqrt{5})(\sqrt{7} - \sqrt{5})$ (vi) $(a + 2\sqrt{b})(a - 2\sqrt{b})$

5. By rationalising the denominator, express each of the following in its simplest form.

   (i) $\dfrac{4}{\sqrt{5} + 1}$ (ii) $\dfrac{12}{3 - \sqrt{2}}$ (iii) $\dfrac{2 - \sqrt{5}}{2 + \sqrt{5}}$ (iv) $\dfrac{1}{\sqrt{8} - \sqrt{2}}$

6. Simplify each of the following.

   (i) $\dfrac{1}{\sqrt{2} - 1} - \dfrac{1}{\sqrt{2} + 1}$ (ii) $\dfrac{1}{2 + \sqrt{3}} + \dfrac{1}{2 - \sqrt{3}}$

7. Simplify

   (i) $(2\sqrt{3} - \sqrt{5})(2\sqrt{3} + \sqrt{5})$ (ii) $\dfrac{4}{2 - \sqrt{5}} + \dfrac{2}{2 + \sqrt{5}}$

8. Letting $X = \dfrac{4 + \sqrt{3}}{\sqrt{2}}$ and $Y = \dfrac{4 - \sqrt{3}}{\sqrt{2}}$, find in its simplest form:

    (i) $X + Y$ (ii) $X - Y$ (iii) XY (iv) $\dfrac{X}{Y}$

9. Show that $(2\sqrt{5} - 3\sqrt{2})(2\sqrt{5} + 3\sqrt{2}) = 2$.

10. Simplify $\dfrac{5}{2 + \sqrt{3}}$.

11. Simplify $\dfrac{(2 + \sqrt{2})(3 + \sqrt{5})(\sqrt{5} - 2)}{(\sqrt{5} - 1)(1 + \sqrt{2})}$.

12. Show that $\dfrac{-1 + \sqrt{3}}{1 + \sqrt{3}} = 2 - \sqrt{3}$.

13. Express $\dfrac{\sqrt{3}}{1 - \sqrt{3}} - \dfrac{1}{\sqrt{3}}$ as a single fraction and simplify by rationalising the denominator.

Section 2.8 Algebraic surd equations

Expressions such as $\sqrt{2x + 1}$ occur often in algebra.

To solve the equation $\sqrt{2x + 1} = 5$, we proceed as follows.

$$(\sqrt{2x + 1})^2 = 5^2 \quad \text{… squaring both sides to remove the square root}$$
$$2x + 1 = 25$$
$$2x = 24$$
$$\Rightarrow \quad x = 12$$

Note: With surds, it is important to check all solutions in the original equation as some may result in complex (non-real) solutions.

At $x = 12$, $\sqrt{2x + 1} = \sqrt{2.12 + 1} = \sqrt{25} = 5$, which is correct.

Example 1

Solve $x = \sqrt{x + 6}$

$x = \sqrt{x + 6}$

$\therefore \quad x^2 = x + 6 \quad \text{… (squaring both sides)}$

$\therefore \quad x^2 - x - 6 = 0$

$\therefore \quad (x - 3)(x + 2) = 0$

$\therefore \quad x = 3 \text{ or } x = -2$

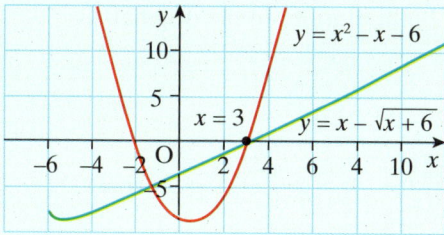

Note: If we look at these curves graphically we can see why there is only one valid solution.

Validating both solutions (in original equation) we find

(i) at $x = 3$: $\quad 3 = \sqrt{3 + 6} = 3$ (*True*)

(ii) at $x = -2$: $\quad -2 = \sqrt{-2 + 6} = 2$ (False)

- If there is **only one surd**, isolate it on one side and then square both sides and solve.
- If there are **two surds**, move one to each side of the equation. Square both sides and isolate any remaining surds. Square both sides again to remove any remaining surd.
- Solve the resulting equation.
- Check your answers in the original equation.

Example 2

Solve $\sqrt{5x + 6} - \sqrt{2x} = 2$.

$$\sqrt{5x + 6} - \sqrt{2x} = 2$$
$$\sqrt{5x + 6} = \sqrt{2x} + 2 \qquad \text{... place one surd on each side}$$
$$(\sqrt{5x + 6})^2 = (\sqrt{2x} + 2)^2 \quad \text{... square both sides}$$
$$5x + 6 = 2x + 4\sqrt{2x} + 4$$
$$3x + 2 = 4\sqrt{2x} \qquad \text{... isolate the surd on one side of the equation}$$
$$(3x + 2)^2 = (4\sqrt{2x})^2 \qquad \text{... square both sides again}$$
$$9x^2 + 12x + 4 = (16)2x$$
$$9x^2 - 20x + 4 = 0$$
$$(9x - 2)(x - 2) = 0.$$
$$\therefore \quad x = 2 \text{ or } x = \frac{2}{9}$$

Note: It is important to check the validity of both solutions in the original equation

i.e. (i) at $x = 2 : \sqrt{5(2) + 6} - \sqrt{2(2)} = 4 - 2 = 2$ (*True*)

(ii) at $x = \frac{2}{9} : \sqrt{5\left(\frac{2}{9}\right) + 6} - \sqrt{2\left(\frac{2}{9}\right)} = \sqrt{\left(\frac{64}{9}\right)} - \sqrt{\left(\frac{4}{9}\right)} = \frac{8}{3} - \frac{2}{3} = 2$ (*True*)

Exercise 2.8

1. One side of a rectangular park is $(x + 2)$ m long and the other $(x - 2)$ m wide. Find an expression for the length of the diagonal, leaving your answer in surd form.

2. (a) Find the length of the diagonal [AC] of the rectangular field ABCD.

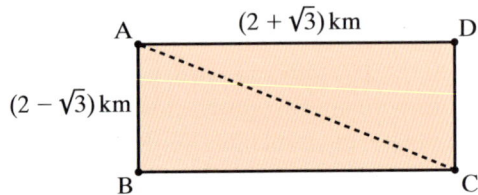

   (b) One runner completes a full circuit ABCDA on a path, at a rate of $1.5\,\text{ms}^{-1}$.

   A second runner runs from A to C and then back to A across the field at a rate of $1.4\,\text{ms}^{-1}$.

   (i) Express, in surd form, the difference in the distances travelled by the two runners.

   (ii) Calculate the time difference between the two runners, correct to the nearest second.

3. Martin starts at G and walks along a path towards a point F. At F, he takes the perpendicular path to E. He then takes the path EK, which is the same length as [EF] and is at right angles to [EG]. From K, he returns directly to G. Find exactly, in surd form, the distance travelled by Martin.

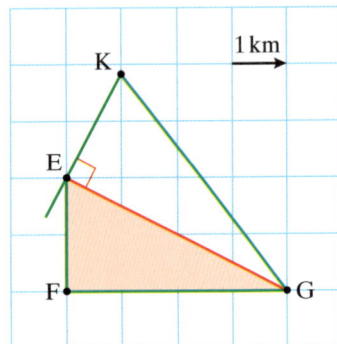

4. If $x = \sqrt{a} + \frac{1}{\sqrt{a}}$ and $y = \sqrt{a} - \frac{1}{\sqrt{a}}$ and $a > 0$, find (i) $x + y$ (ii) $x - y$.

   Hence find the value of $\sqrt{x^2 - y^2}$.

5. Solve the following equations and check your solutions in each case:

   (i) $\sqrt{2x + 1} = 3$ (ii) $\sqrt{3x + 10} = x$ (iii) $\sqrt{2x - 1} = \sqrt{x + 8}$

   (iv) $\sqrt{3x - 5} = x - 1$ (v) $\sqrt{2x + 5} = x + 1$ (vi) $\sqrt{2x^2 - 7} = x + 3$

6. Solve each of these equations and check each solution:

    (i) $\sqrt{x+5} = 5 - \sqrt{x}$ (ii) $\sqrt{5x+6} = \sqrt{2x} + 2$

    (iii) $\sqrt{x+7} + \sqrt{x} = 7$ (iv) $\sqrt{3x-2} = \sqrt{x-2} + 2$

7. If $\dfrac{1}{\sqrt{x+2}} - \dfrac{1}{\sqrt{4x+8}} = \dfrac{a}{b\sqrt{x+2}}$, find the values of a and b.

    Hence solve $\dfrac{1}{\sqrt{x+2}} - \dfrac{1}{\sqrt{4x+8}} = 2$.

8. Solve $x = \sqrt{4x+5}$

9. If $x = \sqrt{a} + \dfrac{1}{\sqrt{a}} + 1$ where $a > 0$, express $x^2 - 2x$ in terms of a.

10. Given that $(a + \sqrt{3})(b - \sqrt{3}) = 7 + 3\sqrt{3}$, and that a and b are positive integers, find the values of a and b.

11. The length of an open rectangular box is 2 m longer than its height.
The width is 2 m shorter than its height.
Let x be the height in metres and find an expression for
  (i) the diagonal [IC]
  (ii) the diagonal [ID].
If $|ID| = \sqrt{56}$, find x.

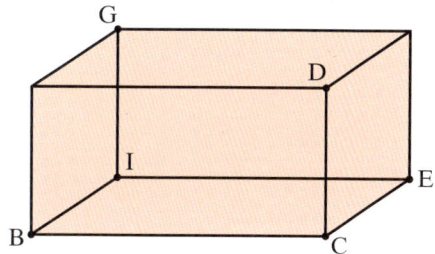

Section 2.9 The factor theorem

In Chapter 1 we revised techniques for factorising algebraic expressions.
The factor theorem is a more general technique that can be applied to expressions of higher orders.
Using long division, we can divide $f(x) = x^3 + 3x^2 - 4x - 12$ by $x + 3$ as before.

$$
\begin{array}{r}
x^2 - 4 \\
x+3 \,\overline{)\, x^3 + 3x^2 - 4x - 12} \\
x^3 + 3x^2 \\
\hline
-4x - 12 \\
-4x - 12 \\
\hline
\text{no remainder}
\end{array}
$$

$\therefore\ f(x) = x^3 + 3x^2 - 4x - 12 = (x^2 - 4)(x + 3)$.

$\therefore\ $ the factors of $f(x)$ are $(x^2 - 4)$ and $(x + 3)$.

$\therefore\ $ the roots of $f(x)$ are $(x + 3) = 0 \Rightarrow x = -3$
and $(x^2 - 4) = 0 \Rightarrow x = \pm 2$.

Evaluating the function at $x = -3, +2, -2$;

$f(-3) = (-3)^3 + 3(-3)^2 - 4(-3) - 12 = 0$
$f(-2) = (-2)^3 + 3(-2)^2 - 4(-2) - 12 = 0$
$f(2) = (2)^3 + 3(2)^2 - 4(2) - 12 = 0$, as we would expect of every root.

Generalising this for every polynomial $f(x)$; if $f(k) = 0$, then $x - k$ is a factor.

Conversely, if $x - k$ is a factor, then $f(k) = 0$.

The Factor Theorem:

If $f(k) = 0$, then $(x - k)$ is a factor.

Conversely, if $(x - k)$ is a factor, then $f(k) = 0$.

Also, if $(ax - k)$ is a factor, then $f\left(\dfrac{k}{a}\right) = 0$.

Example 1

Show that $(2x - 3)$ is a factor of $2x^3 - 5x^2 + 5x - 3$.

Given $(2x - 3)$ is a factor, then $(2x - 3) = 0$ is a root, i.e. $x = \frac{3}{2}$ is a root.

If $(2x - 3)$ is a factor, then $f(\frac{3}{2})$ must equal 0.

$$f(x) = 2x^3 - 5x^2 + 5x - 3$$
$$f(\tfrac{3}{2}) = 2(\tfrac{3}{2})^3 - 5(\tfrac{3}{2})^2 + 5(\tfrac{3}{2}) + 3 = (\tfrac{27}{4}) - (\tfrac{45}{4}) + (\tfrac{15}{2}) - 3 = 0.$$

$\therefore$ $(2x - 3)$ is a factor of $f(x) = 2x^3 - 5x^2 + 5x - 3$.

Example 2

If $(x - 2)$ and $(x + 1)$ are both factors of $ax^3 + 3x^2 - 9x + b$, find the values a and b.

If $(x - 2)$ is a factor, then $f(2) = 0$.
If $(x + 1)$ is a factor, then $f(-1) = 0$.

(i) $f(2) = a(2)^3 + 3(2)^2 - 9(2) + b = 0$

$\Rightarrow a.8 + 3.4 - 18 + b = 0$

$\Rightarrow 8a + 12 - 18 + b = 0$

$\Rightarrow 8a + b = 6$

Using simultaneous equations,

$\Rightarrow 8a + b = 6$

$ a - b = 12$

$\overline{ 9a = 18}$

$ a = 2$ $\therefore$ $a = 2$ and $b = -10$.

(ii) $f(-1) = a(-1)^3 + 3(-1)^2 - 9(-1) + b = 0$

$\Rightarrow a(-1) + 3.1 + 9 + b = 0$

$\Rightarrow -a + 3 + 9 + b = 0$

$\Rightarrow -a + b = -12$

$\Rightarrow a - b = 12$

1. Factorising cubic expressions

We can now use the **factor theorem** to factorise higher-order polynomials, e.g. cubic polynomials of the form $f(x) = ax^3 + bx^2 + cx + d$ that have at least one integer root.

Using trial and error, we evaluate $f(0), f(1), f(-1), f(2), f(-2), f(3)$ ... etc., until we get a value of zero.

This is the integer root.

> If $f(-2) = 0,$ then $(x + 2)$ is a factor.
> If $f(3) = 0,$ then $(x - 3)$ is a factor.

Dividing by this factor produces a quadratic expression which can be factorised separately using factor pairs or using the quadratic formula.

Example 3

Factorise $f(x) = 2x^3 + x^2 - 13x + 6.$

$f(x) = 2x^3 + x^2 - 13x + 6$

$f(0) = 0 + 0 - 0 + 6 = 6 \neq 0$

$f(1) = 2(1)^3 + (1)^2 - 13(1) + 6 = -4 \neq 0$

$f(-1) = 2(-1)^3 + (-1)^2 - 13(-1) + 6$
$\qquad = +18 \neq 0$

$f(2) = 2(2)^3 + (2)^2 - 13(2) + 6 = 0$

$\therefore \quad (x - 2)$ is a factor.

Dividing $2x^3 + x^2 - 13x + 6$ by $(x - 2),$

$$
\begin{array}{r}
2x^2 + 5x - 3 \\
x - 2 \overline{)2x^3 + x^2 - 13x + 6} \\
\underline{2x^3 - 4x^2} \\
5x^2 - 13x + 6 \\
\underline{5x^2 - 10x} \\
-3x + 6 \\
\underline{-3x + 6} \\
0 + 0
\end{array}
$$

$\Rightarrow$ the factors of $f(x)$ are $(x - 2)(2x^2 + 5x - 3)$

$\Rightarrow$ the factors of $f(x)$ are $(x - 2)(x + 3)(2x - 1).$

---

2. Solving cubic equations

To solve cubic equations of the form $f(x) = ax^3 + bx^2 + cx + d = 0,$ we first find the factors as in the above example and then equate each factor to zero to find the roots(solutions).

Example 4

Solve the equation $2x^3 - 4x^2 - 22x + 24 = 0$.

Let $f(x) = 2x^3 - 4x^2 - 22x + 24$

$\Rightarrow f(0) = 2(0)^3 - 4(0)^2 - 22(0) + 24 = 24$

$\Rightarrow f(1) = 2(1)^3 - 4(1)^2 - 22(1) + 24 = 0$

$\Rightarrow (x - 1)$ is a factor.

The factors are $(x - 1)(2x^2 - 2x - 24)$

Factorising further ; $(x - 1)(2x + 6)(x - 4)$

Dividing we get,

$$\begin{array}{r}
2x^2 - 2x - 24 \\
x - 1 \overline{)2x^3 - 4x^2 - 22x + 24} \\
\underline{2x^3 - 2x^2} \\
-2x^2 - 22x + 24 \\
\underline{-2x^2 + 2x} \\
-24x + 24 \\
\underline{-24x + 24}
\end{array}$$

$\therefore \ f(x) = 0 \Rightarrow (x - 1) = 0 \Rightarrow x = 1$.

Also, $(2x + 6) = 0 \Rightarrow x = -3$

and $(x - 4) = 0 \Rightarrow x = 4$.

The solutions are $\{1, -3, 4\}$

Exercise 2.9

1. Show that $(x - 3)$ is a factor of $x^2 - 8x + 15$.

2. Show that $(x - 1)$ is a factor of $x^3 - x^2 - 9x + 9$.

3. Show that $(x + 2)$ is a factor of $x^3 + 6x^2 + 11x + 6$.

4. Show that $(x - 2)$ is a factor of $2x^3 - 3x^2 - 12x + 20$.

5. Investigate if $(x - 2)$ is a factor of $x^3 - 5x^2 + 8x - 4$.

6. Show that $(2x - 1)$ is a factor of $2x^3 + 7x^2 + 2x - 3$.

7. Investigate if $(2x + 1)$ is a factor of $2x^3 - x^2 - 5x - 2$.

8. If $(x - 1)$ is a factor of $x^3 + kx^2 - x - 8$, find the value of k.

9. Find p if $(x + 2)$ is a factor of $x^3 + 6x^2 + px + 6$.

10. Show that $(x - 3)$ is a factor of $x^3 - 2x^2 - 5x + 6$ and find the other two factors.

11. Show that $(x + 3)$ is a factor of $x^3 - 2x^2 - 9x + 18$ and find the other two factors.

12. Use the *factor theorem* to factorise fully each of the following:

   (i) $x^3 - 4x^2 - x + 4$ (ii) $x^3 - 8x^2 + 19x - 12$

   (iii) $x^3 + 6x^2 - x - 30$ (iv) $3x^3 - 4x^2 - 3x + 4$

   (v) $2x^3 - 3x^2 - 8x - 3$ (vi) $2x^3 - 3x^2 - 12x + 20$.

13. Given $f(x) = 2x^3 + 13x^2 + 13x - 10$.

Show that $f(-2) = 0$ and hence find the three factors of $f(x)$.

14. If $(x + 2)$ is a factor of $x^3 + ax^2 - x - 2$, find a and hence find the other two factors.

15. Factorise fully $x^3 - x^2 - 14x + 24$.

Hence solve the equation $x^3 - x^2 - 14x + 24 = 0$.

16. Show that $x = 1$ is a root of the equation $x^3 + 5x^2 + 2x - 8 = 0$ and find the other two roots.

17. Solve each of the following equations

(i) $x^3 - 4x^2 - x + 4 = 0$ (ii) $x^3 + 2x^2 - 11x - 12 = 0$
(iii) $3x^3 - 4x^2 - 3x + 4 = 0$ (iv) $x^3 - 7x - 6 = 0$

18. If $(x + 1)$ and $(x + 3)$ are both factors of $2x^3 + ax^2 + bx - 3$, find the values of a and b.

Find the third factor and hence solve the equation $2x^3 + ax^2 + bx - 3 = 0$.

19. If $(x + 1)$ is a factor of $x^3 + 5x^2 + kx - 12$, find the value of k and the other two factors of the cubic expression.

20. If $(x + 2)$ and $(x - 3)$ are both factors of $2x^3 + ax^2 - 17x + b$, find the values of a and b.

Hence find the third factor.

21. Given that the expression $ax^3 + 8x^2 + bx + 6$ is exactly divisible by $x^2 - 2x - 3$, find the values of a and b.

Hence solve the equation $ax^3 + 8x^2 + bx + 6 = 0$.

22. Solve the following equations for x:

(i) $ax^3 - b = c$ (ii) $a(x + b)^3 = c$

Section 2.10 Graphs of cubic (and higher order) polynomials

The coefficients of a cubic polynomial $f(x) = ax^3 + bx^2 + cx + d$ determine the final shape of each graph. Some important features need to be noted and emphasised.

ICT: *Input* each of the following functions using a graphics calculator or computer software (e.g. Geogebra). Examine the effect of changing coefficients on the shape of each graph.

Note: The factor form of each function is very suitable in some cases.

1. Three real roots

$f(x) = 2x^3 - 4x^2 - 22x + 24$

$f(x) = (x - 1)(2x + 6)(x - 4)$

This graph has three real roots, $-3, 1, 4$.

As the graph passes through a root, the value of the function changes from $(-)^{ve}$ to $(+)^{ve}$ or $(+)^{ve}$ to $(-)^{ve}$.

The graph has two turning points, a local maximum and a local minimum.

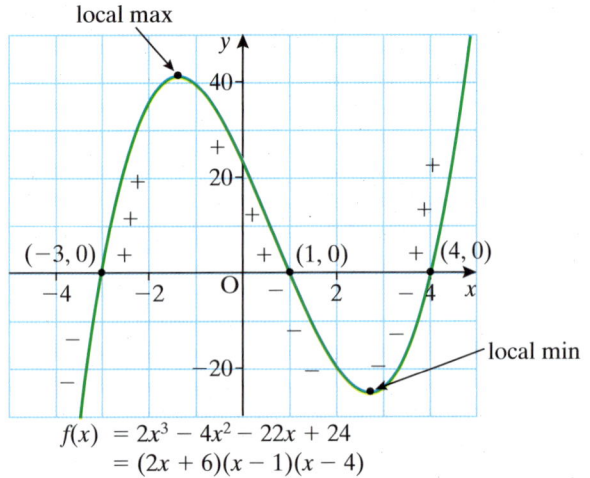

local max

$(-3, 0)$ $(1, 0)$ $(4, 0)$

local min

$$f(x) = 2x^3 - 4x^2 - 22x + 24$$
$$= (2x + 6)(x - 1)(x - 4)$$

2. Three real roots, two of which repeat

$f(x) = x^3 - x^2 - 8x + 12$
$\quad = (x + 3)(x - 2)^2$

This graph again has three real roots, $-3, 2, 2$, but one of the roots is repeated.

This graph only crosses the x-axis once because of the repeated root.

The graph has two turning points.

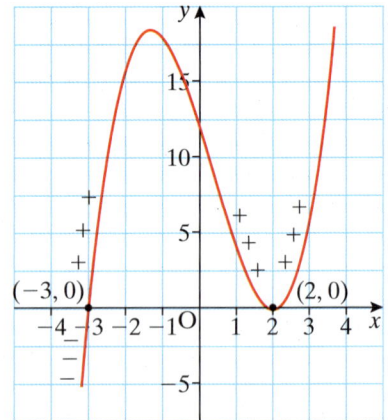

$(-3, 0)$ $(2, 0)$

$$f(x) = x^3 - x^2 - 8x + 12$$
$$= (x + 3)(x - 2)(x - 2)$$
$$= (x + 3)(x - 2)^2$$

3. One real, two non-real roots

$f(x) = x^3 - 2x - 4$
$\quad = (x - 2)(x^2 + 2x + 2)$
$\quad = (x - 2)(x + 1 - \sqrt{-1})(x + 1 + \sqrt{-1})$ ... using the quadratic formula

This polynomial has only one real root but two non-real (complex) roots.

It crosses the x- axis once and has two turning points.

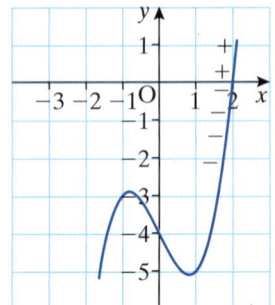

$$f(x) = x^3 - 2x - 4$$
$$= (x - 2)(x^2 + 2x + 2)$$

4. Comparing $f(x) = x^3 - 3x^2 + 2x$ and $g(x) = 2x^3 - 6x^2 + 4x = 2f(x)$

Both polynomials have the same roots, $x = 0, 1, 2$.
∴ the polynomials have common factors (x), $(x - 1)$ and $(x - 2)$.

But $g(x)$ has an integer factor 2 as well that multiplies each value of the curve, except where the value is zero at the roots.

This integer factor acts as an amplification factor.

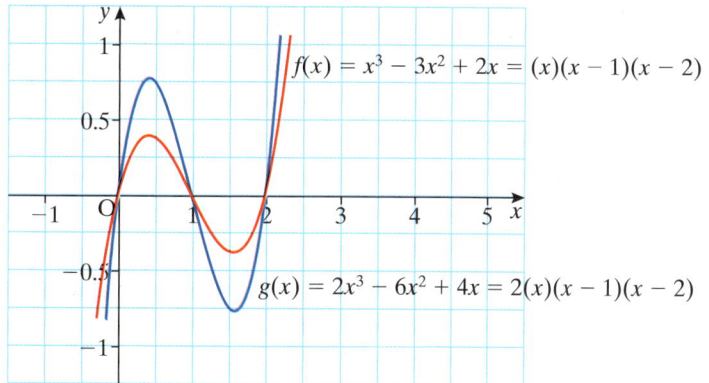

$f(x) = x^3 - 3x^2 + 2x = (x)(x - 1)(x - 2)$

$g(x) = 2x^3 - 6x^2 + 4x = 2(x)(x - 1)(x - 2)$

5. Comparing $f(x) = x^3 - 3x^2 + 2x$ and $g(x) = -x^3 + 3x^2 - 2x = -f(x)$

Again, both polynomials have the same roots and hence common factors. The graphs are symmetrical across the x-axis.

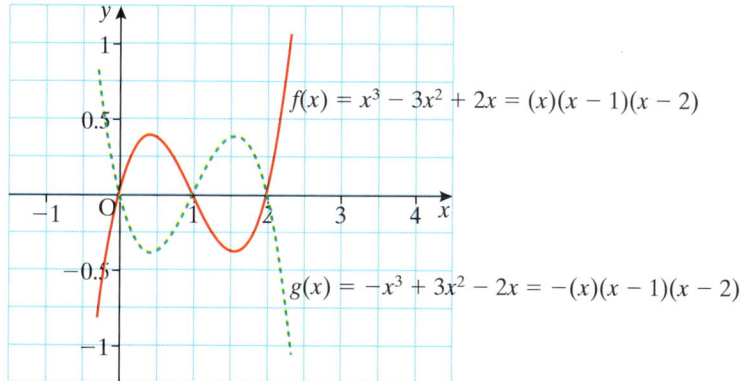

$f(x) = x^3 - 3x^2 + 2x = (x)(x - 1)(x - 2)$

$g(x) = -x^3 + 3x^2 - 2x = -(x)(x - 1)(x - 2)$

$g(x) = -x^3 + 3x^2 - 2x = -(x^3 - 3x^2 + 2x) = -f(x)$.

Multiplying by a minus inverts the graph.

6. The graphs of $f(x) = ax^3$

All the graphs pass through $(0, 0)$.
For $a > 0$, the graphs are all increasing, and as a increases, the graphs rise more steeply.
For $a < 0$, the graphs are decreasing.

Note:
(i) If $f(x) = 3x^3$ and $g(x) = -3x^3$,
   $\Rightarrow f(x) = -g(x)$, i.e. $f(x)$ is the reflection of $g(x)$ in the x-axis.
(ii) $f(-x) = g(x)$, i.e. $f(x)$ and $g(x)$ reflect each other in the y-axis.

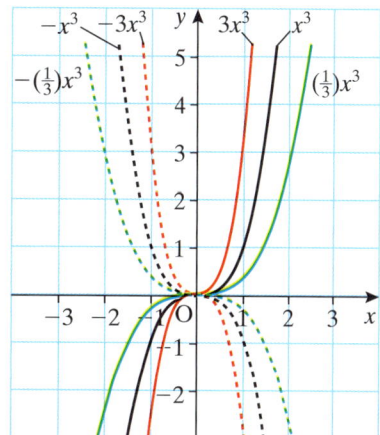

Note: There are no local maximum or minimum points as in the previous graphs.

Summary:

  (i) Every cubic polynomial crosses the x-axis at least once, i.e. has one real root.

 (ii) Each root produces a factor of the polynomial.

(iii) If a polynomial has a repeated root with an even power e.g. $(x - 2)^2$, $(x - 3)^4$ etc., then the graph touches, but does cross, the x-axis at these points.

(iv) If the coefficient of x^3 is positive, the graph starts below the x-axis, i.e. starts with a negative y-value and increases with increasing x-values.

 (v) If the coefficient of x^3 is negative, the graph starts above the x-axis, i.e. starts with a positive y-value and decreases with increasing x-values.

(vi) Some cubic graphs have local maximum and minimum turning points.

(vii) When forming a polynomial from its roots, check for an integer factor.

Example 1

By examining the graph, find an expression for this cubic polynomial.

  (i) The graph crosses the x-axis at $x = -2$.

 (ii) $\Rightarrow x = -2$ is a root
    $\Rightarrow (x + 2)$ is a factor.

(iii) The graph touches the x-axis at $x = 1$.
    $\Rightarrow x = 1$ is a repeated root
    $\Rightarrow (x - 1)^2$ is a factor.

(iv) The graph may contain an integer factor,
    i.e. $f(x) = a(x + 2)(x - 1)^2$.

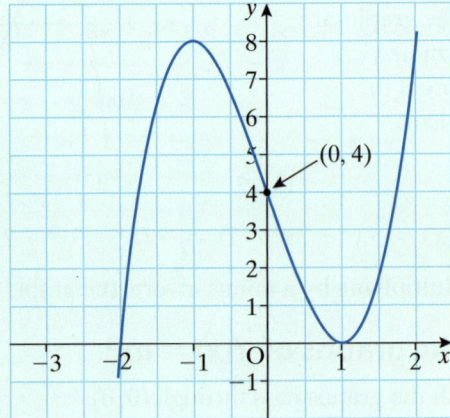

From the sketch of this graph, when $x = 0$, $f(x) = 4$.

$\therefore \quad 4 = a(2)(1)^2 = 2a$

$\therefore \quad a = 2$.

$\therefore \quad f(x) = 2(x + 2)(x - 1)^2 = 2x^3 - 6x + 4.$

7. Higher-order polynomials

Example 2

The graph of the polynomial $f(x) = a(x + b)(x + c)(x + d)(x + d)$ is given in the diagram. Find the values of a, b, c and d.

From the diagram, the roots are $x = -2, -1, 3$.

A double root occurs at $x = 3$.

Hence the factors are $(x + 2), (x + 1), (x - 3)$ and $(x - 3)$.

$\therefore \quad f(x) = a(x + 2)(x + 1)(x - 3)(x - 3)$.

At $x = 0$, $f(x) = 18$.

$\therefore \quad 18 = a(0 + 2)(0 + 1)(0 - 3)(0 - 3) = 18a$

$\therefore \quad a = 1$

$\therefore \quad a = 1, b = 2, c = 1, d = -3$.

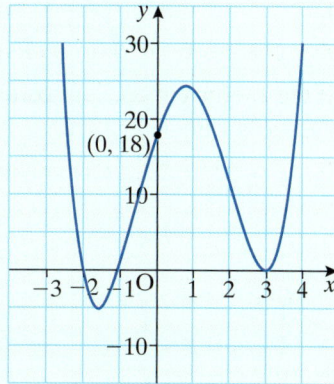

Exercise 2.10

1. Find a cubic expression for each of the following graphs, giving your answers in the form $f(x) = ax^3 + bx^2 + cx + d$.

(i)

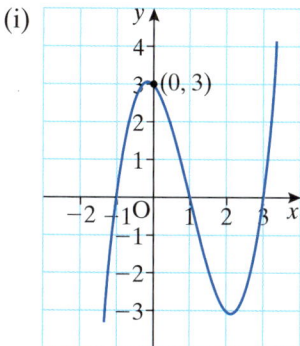

(ii)

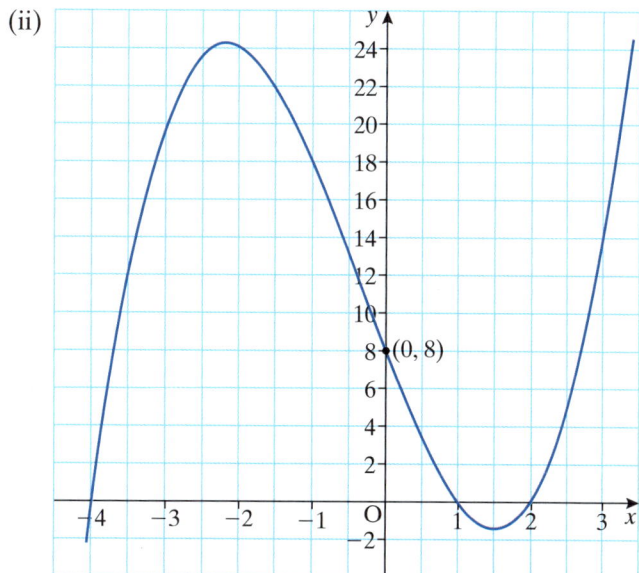

2. Write a polynomial expression for each of the following cubic graphs.

(i)

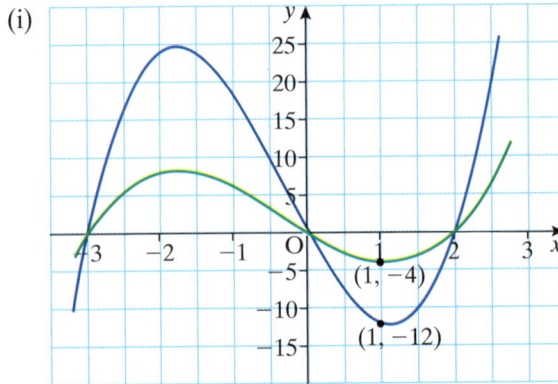

(ii)

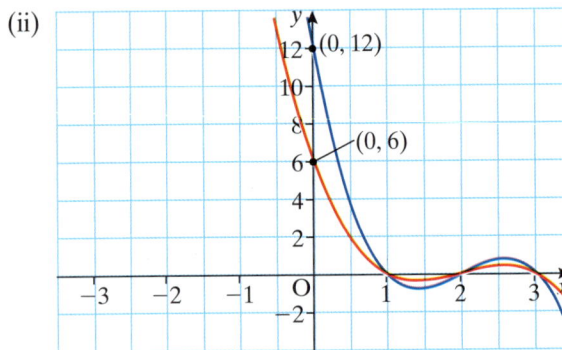

3. The graph of $y = f(x) = ax^3 + bx^2 + cx + d$ crosses the x-axis at $x = 1, x = -2$ and $x = \frac{1}{2}$. It also crosses the y-axis at the point $(0, 6)$.

Find the coefficients a, b, c and d.

4. The factors of a given polynomial $f(x)$ are $(x - 3), (x + 1)$ and $(x + 2)$.

If $f(x) = x^3 + ax^2 + bx + c$, find the values of a, b and c.

5. Identify the graphs of the three polynomial expressions,
   (i) $x^3 + 2$
   (ii) x^3
   (iii) $2x^3$, given in this diagram.

Find the coordinates of the point A.

ICT: Note that several answers in this exercise can be verified using a graphing calculator or computer software (e.g. Geogebra).

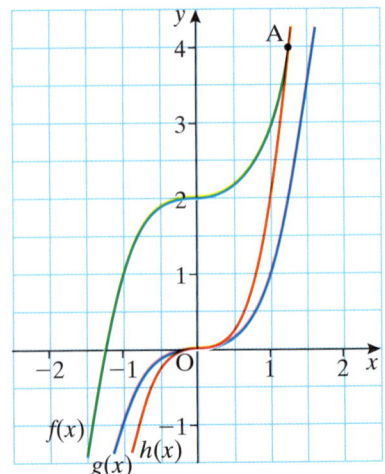

6. Given that $f(x) = (x)(x - 4)(x - 6)$, find the values of $f(2)$ and $f(5)$.
Hence draw a rough sketch of the curve.

7. Given $f(x) = (x + 2)(x - 1)(x - 3)$, find the values of $f(0), f(\frac{1}{2})$ and $f(2)$.
Hence draw a rough sketch of the curve.

8. The graph of a polynomial
$f(x) = ax^4 + bx^3 + cx^2 + dx + e$
is given in the diagram.

   (i) Find the factors of the expression.
   (ii) Hence find the values of a, b, c, d and e.

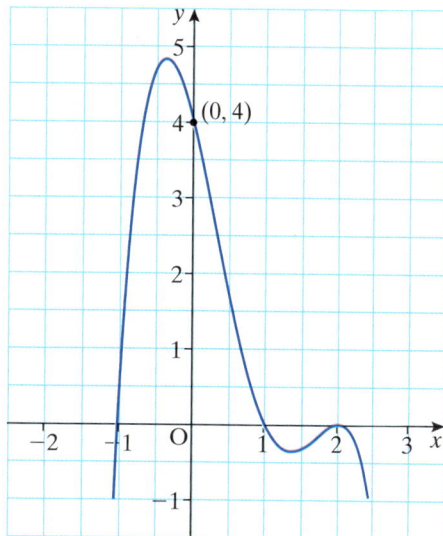

9. The graphs of two functions $f(x)$ and $g(x)$
are given in the following diagram.

  If $f(x) = ag(x)$,

   (i) find the value of a
   (ii) find equations for $f(x)$ and $g(x)$.

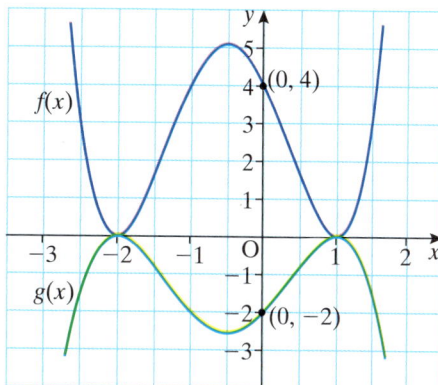

10. Write, in the form $ax^3 + bx^2 + cx + d = 0$, a cubic equation with the following roots:

  (i) $-1, 2, 5$ (ii) $-3, -1, 0$ (iii) $-2, \frac{1}{4}, 3$ (iv) $\frac{1}{2}, 2, 4$.

11. Find a cubic expression for each of the following curves.

(i)

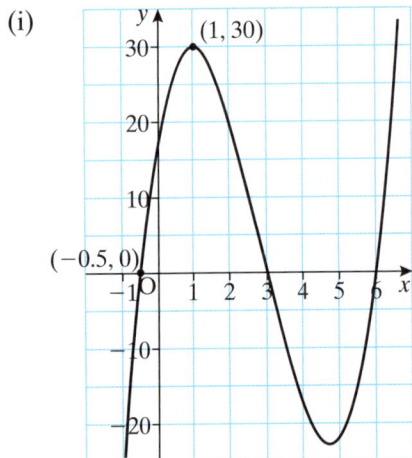

(ii)

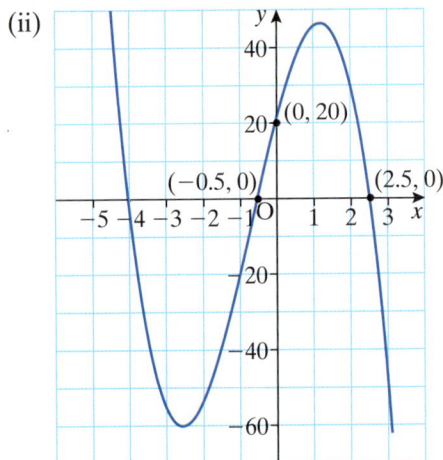

12. The diagram shows a graph of the function
$f(x) = -3x^3 + 17x^2 + bx - 8$.

The graph crosses the x-axis at the points a, 2 and 4.

Find the values of a and b.

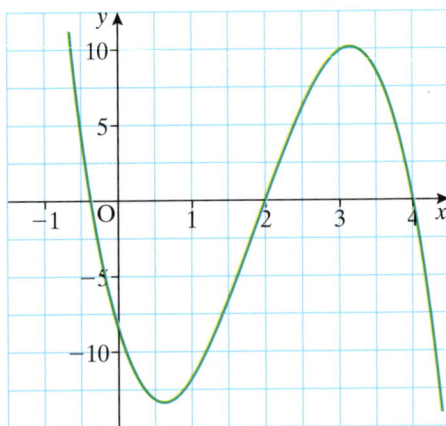

13. The diagram shows a graph of $f(x) = x^3 - x^2 - 2x$ and $g(x) = x$.
Use the graph to solve

   (i) $f(x) = 0$

   (ii) $f(x) = g(x)$.

   (iii) By solving the equations, correct to one place of decimals, check the accuracy of your answers.

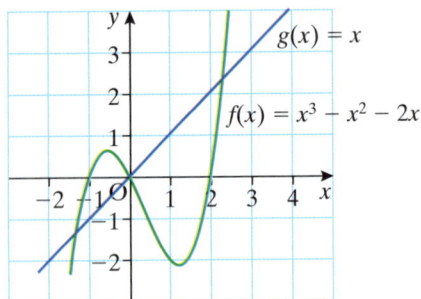

14. A box has dimensions x cm, $(x + 1)$ cm and $(x - 1)$ cm, as shown.

   (i) Find the volume of the box in terms of x.

   (ii) If the volume of the box is 24 cm³, and using the *factor theorem*, find the value of x.

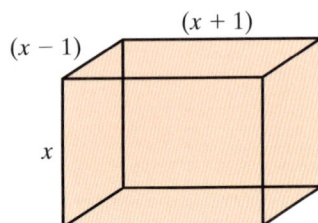

15. The volume of a cylinder is given by $V = \pi r^2 h$, where r is the radius and h is the height.

Given that the diameter is equal to the height, show that the volume can be written as

$$V = ah^3.$$

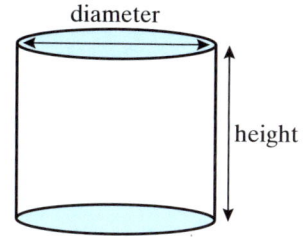
diameter
height

Taking $\pi = 3.14$, find the value of a correct to two places of decimals.

Using this function, calculate the volume of a cylinder with a diameter of 11 cm.

Find the diameter of a cylinder whose volume is $215.58\,\text{cm}^3$, correct to one place of decimals.

16. The contents of a spherical container of radius 3 cm completely fill a cube of side x cm.

If the volume of a sphere is given by the formula $V = \frac{4}{3}\pi x^3 \simeq 4.19x^3$, where x is the radius, using the cubic graphs, find an approximate value for x, the length of the side of the cube.

At what approximate value of x would the volume of a sphere be 150 cm³ greater than the volume of the cube, given that the broken line represents $(V - 150)\,\text{cm}^3$?

[i.e. $(4.19x^3 - 150)\,\text{cm}^3$]

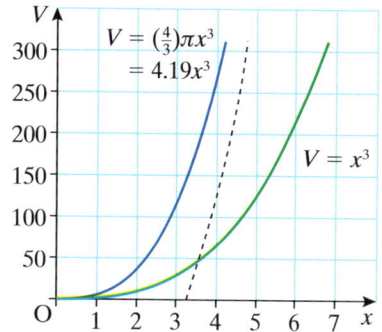

Revision Exercise 2 (Core)

1. Solve the equation $x^2 - 6x + 5 = 0$.

Hence solve fully the equation

$$\left(t - \frac{6}{t}\right)^2 - 6\left(t - \frac{6}{t}\right) + 5 = 0.$$

2. Find the roots of the equation $2(x + 1)(x - 4) - (x - 2)^2 = 0$, leaving your answer in surd form.

3. Find the range of values of p for which $px^2 + 2x + 1 = 0$ has no solutions.

4. Show that the roots of the equation $x^2 - (a + d)x + (ad - b^2) = 0$ are real.

5. Given that $(x + 1)$ and $(x - 2)$ are factors of $6x^4 - x^3 + ax^2 - 6x + b$, find the values of a and b.

6. Using trial and error, find

    (i) a root of the polynomial $f(x) = x^3 - 4x^2 - 11x + 30$
    (ii) the factors of $f(x)$, and
    (iii) hence solve the equation $x^3 - 4x^2 - 11x + 30 = 0$.

7. By using the discriminant, determine the nature of the roots of each of the following:

  (i) $x^2 - 2x - 5 = 0$ (ii) $x^2 - 4x + 6 = 0$ (iii) $-6 + 4x - x^2 = 0$

8. Using the substitution $y = 3^x$, write the equation $3^{2x} - 12(3^x) + 27 = 0$ in terms of y. Hence solve the equation for x.

Revision Exercise 2 (Advanced)

1. Express $2x^2 - 4x - 5$ in the form $a(x + h)^2 + k$ and hence,

  (i) solve the equation $2x^2 - 4x - 5 = 0$
  (ii) find the minimum point of this curve.

2. Expand $(2\sqrt{2} - \sqrt{3})^2$.

3. Simplify and then rationalise the denominator of $\dfrac{\sqrt{7} + \sqrt{5}}{\sqrt{80} + \sqrt{5}}$.

4. Solve $\sqrt{x + 2} = x - 4$.

5. The motion of a car is given by the equation $8t^2 + 4t = s$, where s is the distance travelled in metres.

  (i) By inspection, *estimate* the time, t, taken for the car to pass a point 10 metres away.
  (ii) Find, correct to two places of decimals, the time taken and explain why there is only one such time.
  (iii) Calculate the percentage error in correcting the answer to two places of decimals.

6. The standard error, of the proportion p of a population is given by the formula

$$\sigma = \sqrt{\dfrac{p(1 - p)}{n}}, \text{ where } p \text{ is the proportion and } n \text{ the number in the sample.}$$

  Using the quadratic formula, find p, the proportion, in terms of σ and n.

7. Complete the table by stating whether each quantity is positive $(+)^{ve}$ or negative $(-)^{ve}$.

	$k < 0$	$0 < k < \frac{1}{4}$	$k > \frac{1}{4}$
k	*Negative*		*Positive*
$4k$			
$4k - 1$			
$k(4k - 1)$			

  Using this table, find the range of values of k so that the quadratic expression $x^2 + 4kx + k$ is positive for all values of x.

8. a, b, and c are positive constants and the roots of $ax^2 + 2bx + c$ and $bx^2 + 2cx + a$ are all real and unequal (unique). Show that the roots of $cx^2 + 2ax + b = 0$ are not real.

9. Given $f(x) = -x^2 + 5x + 3$ and $g(x) = x^2 + 5x - 1$.

Find the coordinates of the points A and B, leaving your answers in surd form.

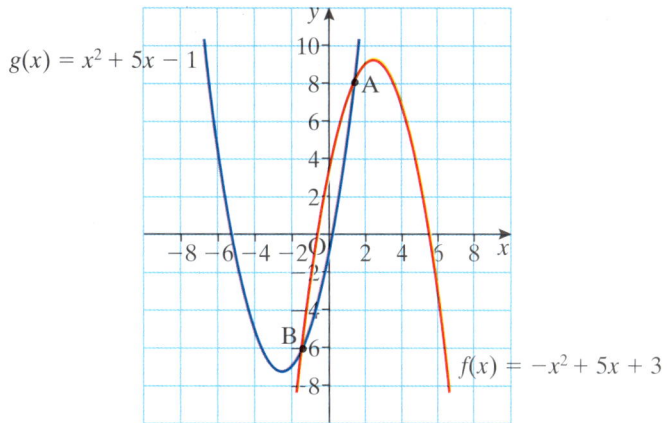

$g(x) = x^2 + 5x - 1$

$f(x) = -x^2 + 5x + 3$

10. Find the values of k so that $kx^2 - 2kx - 3k - 12 = 0$ has real and equal roots.

11. If r_1 and r_2 are the roots of the equation $x^2 - \sqrt{3}x - 6 = 0$, evaluate $r_1 r_2$.

12. Solve the simultaneous equations $3x + y = -1$ and $x^2 + y^2 = 53$.

13. If the length of a rectangular kitchen is half the square of its width and its perimeter is 48 m, find the dimensions of the kitchen.

14. If x is real, find the set of possible values of the function $y = \dfrac{x^2}{x + 1}$.

15. Find the equation of the quadratic curve that passes through the points $(-2, -1), (1, 2), (3, -16)$.

16. (i) State what you understand by the "*Factor Theorem*".
    (ii) Given that $f(x) = x^3 - 6x^2 + 11x - 6$, find the values of $f(0), f(1), f(2), f(3), f(4)$ and hence, solve the equation $x^3 - 6x^2 + 11x - 6 = 0$.
    (iii) Sketch the curve, $y = f(x)$.

17. A section of the graph of a polynomial
$$f(x) = ax^3 + bx^2 + cx + d$$
is drawn in this diagram.
    (i) Find the roots of the equation $f(x) = 0$.
    (ii) Write an expression for $f(x)$ in terms of the factors of this polynomial.
    (iii) Find the values of a, b, c and d.
    (iv) Find an expression for the reflected image of this curve in the x-axis.
    (v) Find an expression for the reflected image of this curve in the y-axis.

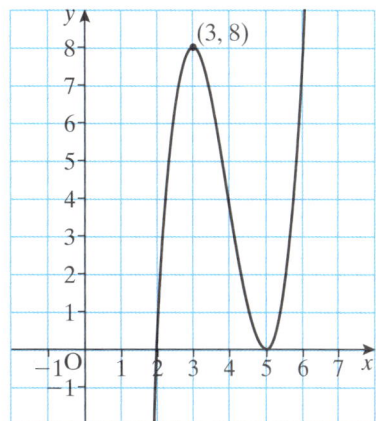

(3, 8)

Revision Exercise 2 (Extended-Response Questions)

1. A person who contracts a particular disease requires treatment with a certain drug. The concentration C of that drug in the bloodstream, t hours after taking a dose of the drug, is given by the equation $C(t) = 0.02t - at^3$. The concentration C is measured as 0.075, five hours after taking the first dose.

   (i) Find the value of the constant a.
   (ii) For how many hours is some of the drug still in the bloodstream?
   (iii) Explain why the graph of $C(t)$ is approximately linear up to $t = 10$ hours.

2. A large rectangular poster is subdivided into 6 purple squares of side x m, with dividing strips y m wide as shown.

   (i) Find the area of the full poster in terms of x and y.
   (ii) If the area of the dividing strips can be written in the form $kxy + 2y^2$, find k.
   (iii) If the total area of the purple is 1.5 m², and the area of the dividing strips is 1 m², find x and hence find an equation for y and solve it.

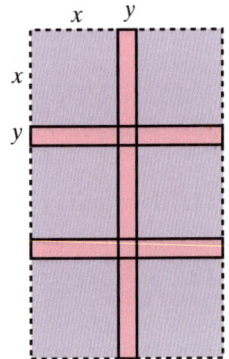

3. A TY project consists of making a reinforced box, as shown in diagram. The plan for the box is as follows:

   • Squares of side x cm are cut from the four corners of a rectangular piece of cardboard that measures 48 cm by 96 cm.
   • The fold lines are indicated by dotted lines.
   • Two flaps are then folded with a double thickness of card at each end.

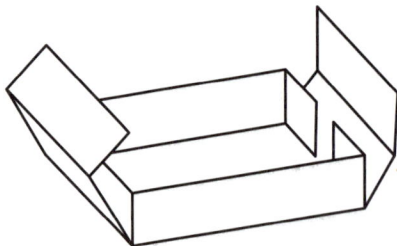

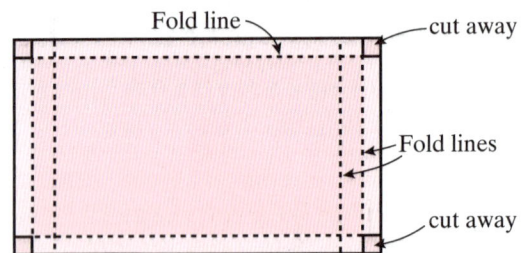

   (a) Find an expression for the volume V of the open box.
   (b) A section of the graph of this expression is given in the diagram shown.

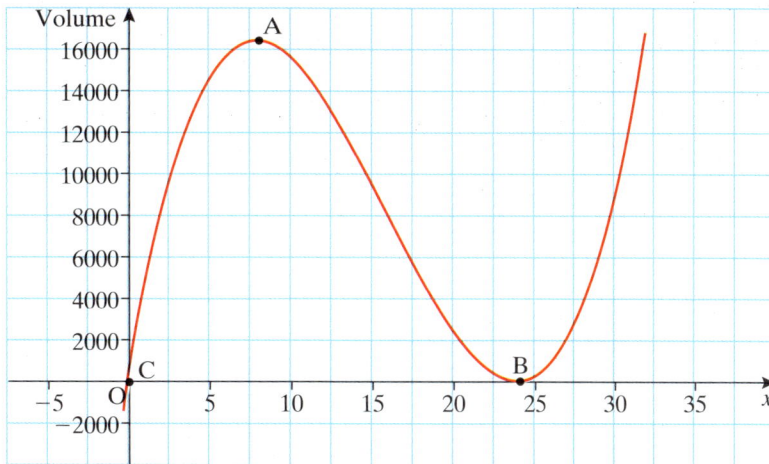

    (i) What domain set of values of x are valid for making this box?

   (ii) Explain the significance of the points A, B and C.

  (iii) Estimate from the graph the maximum volume of the box and the value of x at which this occurs.

  (iv) Find the volume of the box when $x = 10$ cm.

   (v) It is decided that $0 < x < 5$ cm. Find the maximum volume possible.

  (vi) If $5 \leqslant x \leqslant 15$ cm, what is the minimum volume of the box?

(c) The external surface area of the box can be given by the formula

     $A = a(b - x)(c + x)$; find the values of a, b and c.

4. Riding stables need temporary additional paddock space for an upcoming horse show. There is sufficient funding to rent 120 m of temporary chain-link fencing. The plan is to form two paddocks with a shared fence running down the middle.

    (i) Show that the area of the paddocks can be represented by the quadratic equation $A = -\frac{3}{2}w^2 + 60w$, where A stands for the area and w for the width of the paddock.

   (ii) Find the roots of this equation and hence draw a rough sketch of the curve.

  (iii) By completing the square of the equation for the area A, find the maximum area of the paddock, and

  (iv) the value of w at which this maximum area occurs.

   (v) Hence find the dimensions of each of the paddocks.

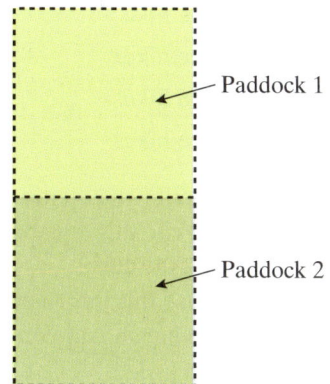

Paddock 1

Paddock 2

5. A golf ball is hit from the top of a 2 m-high tee. If the height of the ball, h, above ground level is given by the equation $h = 2 + 4t - t^2$, where t is the time measured in seconds,

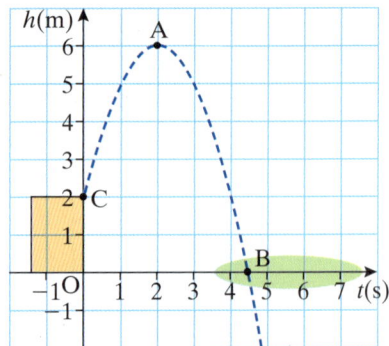

(a) estimate from the graph:

    (i) the times, t, at which the ball is 5 m above ground level,

    (ii) the time the ball takes to land on the ground.

(b) Find, correct to two places of decimals, the time taken by the ball to reach the ground.

(c) The equation $h = 2 + 4t - t^2$ can be written in the form $q - (t - p)^2$ for all values of t, where q is the highest point of the ball above ground, at time p. Find (p, q).

6. You have managed a bike-rental scheme in a seaside holiday resort for the summer. You found that if you charged €12.00 per bike per day, then on average you did 36 rentals per day.

For every 50 cent increase in the rental price, the average number of rentals decreased by 2 rentals per day.

Complete the following table.

No. of price hikes	Price per rental	Number of rentals	Total income (*I*)
	€12	36	
1 price hike			
2 price hikes			
3 price hikes			
x price hikes			

    (i) Write an equation in terms of x for the income I.

    (ii) Write this equation in the form $q - (x - p)^2$, where (p, q) is the maximum point of the curve.

    (iii) Use this information to find the maximum income.

    (iv) What should you change to increase income?

7. The plan of a garden against a wall is shown. The rectangle GCED is of length y m and width x m. The garden is to have two borders, each a quarter circle, at each end. The radius of the circle is x m. A fence is to be erected along BCEF.

(a) Write an expression for the area A of the garden in terms of x and y.

(b) If the length of the fence is to be 100 m, find

    (i) y in terms of x

    (ii) A in terms of x

    (iii) the maximum domain for the values of x for the area A in (ii).

(c) Find, correct to one place of decimals, the values of x for a garden of area $1000\,m^2$.

(d) It is decided to build the garden up to a height of $\frac{x}{50}\,m$. If the length of the fence is $100\,m$, find correct to one place of decimals,

    (i) the volume $V\,m^3$ of soil needed in terms of x,

    (ii) the volume of soil needed for a garden of area $1000\,m^2$,

    (iii) the value(s) of x for which $500\,m^3$ of soil is required.

8. Examine the graph supplied.

(a) Using the information contained in the graph, find the coordinates of the points $A(x_1, y_1)$ and $B(x_2, y_2)$, giving your answers in surd form.

(b) Write an expression for the "vertical distance", d, between the graphs, in terms of x.

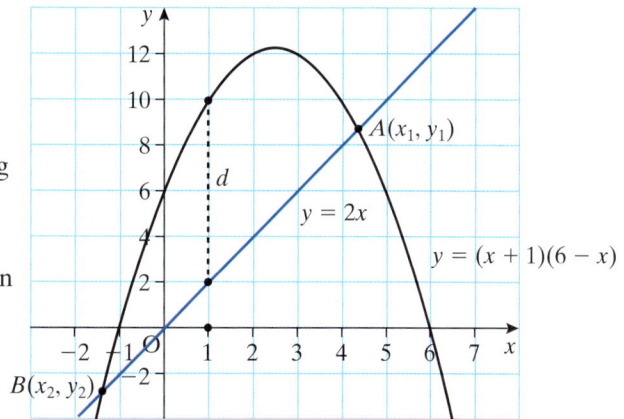

(c) On separate axes, draw a sketch of the distance $d(x)$ between the two graphs.

(d) Write the equation for $d(x)$ in the form $y = q - a(x - p)^2$ by completing the square.

(e) Write down the coordinates of the maximum point (p, q) of this graph and interpret the meaning of the coordinates (p, q).

(f) Find the range of values of $d(x)$.

9. Examine the curve $y = \sqrt{x - b} + c$.

    (i) Show that if the line $y = x$ intersects this curve at the point (a, a), then $a^2 - a(2c + 1) + c^2 + b = 0$.

    (ii) If the line is a tangent to the curve, show that $c = \dfrac{4b - 1}{4}$.

    (iii) Sketch the graph $y = \sqrt{x} - \frac{1}{4}$ for the domain $0 \leqslant x \leqslant 4$, indicating the x and y intercepts.

    (iv) Find the coordinates at which the line $y = x$ is a tangent to $y = \sqrt{x} - \frac{1}{4}$.

    (v) Find the values of k for which $y = x + k$ meets the curve $y = \sqrt{x} - \frac{1}{4}$:

        (a) twice   (b) once   (c) not at all.

Trigonometry 1

Key words

radian measure   arc   sector   trigonometric function   unit circle
quadrant   sine rule   cosine rule   three dimensional   angle of elevation
angle of depression   period   range   periodic   asymptote   general solution

Section 3.1 Radian measure

In your study of geometry and trigonometry so far, you will have worked with angles which were measured in degrees. One complete revolution is 360°. However, in more advanced trigonometry and calculus, angles are almost always measured in **radians**.

The diagram on the right shows an arc AB equal in length to the radius, r.

The measure of $\angle AOB$ is said to be 1 radian.

If the length of the arc AB was $2r$, then $|\angle AOB|$ would be 2 radians.

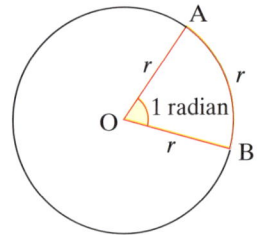

Radian   A radian is the measure of the angle at the centre of a circle subtended by an arc equal in length to the radius.

Since the circumference of a circle is $2\pi r$, i.e., 2π times the radius, then there are 2π radians in one complete revolution.

$$\Rightarrow \quad 2\pi \text{ radians} = 360°$$
$$\Rightarrow \quad \pi \text{ radians} = 180°$$

Frequently used angles are given in degrees and radians in the box below:

Degrees	0°	30°	45°	60°	90°	180°	270°	360°
Radians	0	$\dfrac{\pi}{6}$	$\dfrac{\pi}{4}$	$\dfrac{\pi}{3}$	$\dfrac{\pi}{2}$	π	$\dfrac{3\pi}{2}$	2π

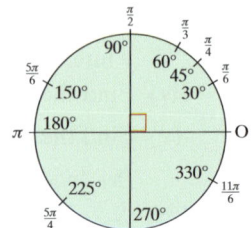

Since π radians $= 180°$ $\Rightarrow$ 1 radian $= \dfrac{180°}{\pi} = 57.3°$

Length of arc – Area of sector

If l is the length of an arc of a circle of radius r, then the angle θ at the centre of the circle is given by

$$\theta \text{ radians} = \frac{l}{r}$$

$$\Rightarrow \quad l = r\theta$$

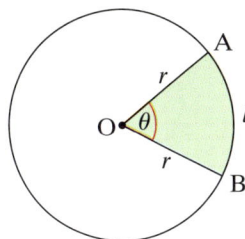

Also since area of the circle is πr^2, the area of the sector AOB is

$$\text{Area} = \frac{\theta}{2\pi} \times \pi r^2 \quad \Rightarrow \quad \text{Area} = \frac{\theta r^2}{2} = \frac{1}{2} r^2 \theta$$

> Arc length $l = r\theta$
> Area of sector $= \frac{1}{2} r^2 \theta$

Example 1

Express (i) $\frac{2\pi}{5}$ radians in degrees

(ii) $210°$ in radians.

(i) $\frac{2\pi}{5}$ radians $= \frac{2 \times 180°}{5} = \frac{360°}{5} = 72°$

(ii) $210°$ to radians

$$180° = \pi \text{ radians}$$

$$\Rightarrow \quad 1° = \frac{\pi}{180} \text{ radians}$$

$$\Rightarrow \quad 210° = \frac{\pi}{180} \times \frac{210}{1} \text{ radians} = \frac{21\pi}{18}$$

$$= \frac{7\pi}{6} \text{ radians}$$

Example 2

The radius of a circle is $8\,cm$. Find
  (i) the angle at the centre of the circle subtended by an arc of length $10\,cm$
  (ii) the length of the arc if the angle subtended at the centre of the circle is $\frac{\pi}{4}$.

(i) Length of arc $l = r\theta \quad \Rightarrow \quad \theta = \frac{l}{r} = \frac{10}{8} \quad \Rightarrow \quad \theta = \frac{5}{4} \text{ radians}.$

(ii) Length of arc $= r\theta$

$$= 8 \times \frac{\pi}{4}$$

$$= 2\pi \,cm$$

Exercise 3.1

1. Express each of the following angles in radians, giving your answers in terms of π:
   (i) $30°$ (ii) $45°$ (iii) $150°$ (iv) $135°$ (v) $36°$ (vi) $240°$ (vii) $390°$

2. Express each of the following angles in degrees:

    (i) π (ii) $\dfrac{\pi}{2}$ (iii) $\dfrac{\pi}{6}$ (iv) $\dfrac{5\pi}{6}$ (v) $\dfrac{4\pi}{9}$ (vi) $\dfrac{11\pi}{6}$ (vii) $\dfrac{5\pi}{12}$

3. Find the length of the arc of a circle of radius 4 cm if the angle subtended at the centre is

    (i) 2 radians   (ii) 4 radians   (iii) $2\frac{1}{2}$ radians   (iv) $\frac{5}{4}$ radians

4. Find, in radians, the measure of the angle subtended at the centre of a circle of radius 6 cm by an arc of length

    (i) 6 cm   (ii) 12 cm   (iii) 3 cm   (iv) 9 cm   (v) $7\frac{1}{2}$ cm

5. An arc of length 15 cm subtends an angle of 2 radians at the centre of a circle. Find the length of the radius.

6. The radius of a circle is 5 cm.
Find the area of the sector if the length of the arc is 6 cm.

7. The area of a sector of a circle of radius 8 cm is 40 cm².
Find, in radians, the measure of the angle in this sector.

8. The circumference of a circle is 12π cm.
Find the angle in a sector of this circle if the area of the sector is 3π cm².

9. The area of a sector of a circle is 27 cm².
The length of the radius of the circle is 6 cm.
Find, in radians, the measure of the angle in the sector.

10. Find the area of the shaded section ABCD created by an angle of rotation of $\dfrac{\pi}{4}$ radians about the centre O.

    Give your answer in terms of π.

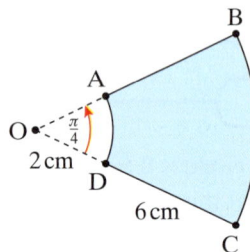

11. The length of an arc of a circle is 10 cm. The radius of the circle is 4 cm.
The measure of the angle at the centre of the circle subtended by the arc is θ.
    (i) Find θ in radians.
    (ii) Find θ in degrees, correct to the nearest degree.

12. In the given figure, OABC is a square and the radius of the circle is 2 cm.
Find the area of the shaded region in terms of π.

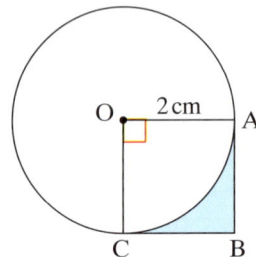

13. The diagram shows a line segment [AB] and arcs of two
quarter circles, both with the same radius length.
One circle has its centre at O, the midpoint of [AB].
Find the area of the shaded figure.

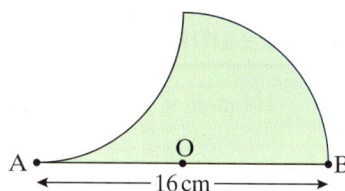

14. The diagram shows two arcs AB and BC.
C is the centre of the arc AB and A is the centre of
the arc BC and |AC| = 6 cm.
   (i)   Show that |∠ABC| = 60°.
   (ii) Find the length of the arc AB.
   (iii) Find the area of the shaded region.

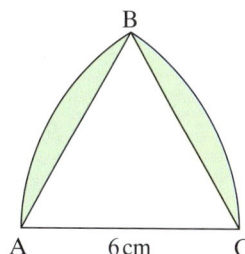

15. A piece of wire 40 cm long is bent into the shape of a sector
AOB with radius r.
If the area of the sector is 100 cm², find
   (i)   an expression for the sector angle $θ$ in terms of r
   (ii) the value of r
   (iii) the value of $θ$.

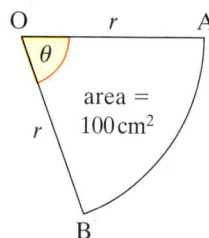

Section 3.2 Trigonometric ratios

In your study of trigonometry so far you will have used the theorem of Pythagoras and
trigonometric ratios to find the missing sides or angles of a right-angled triangle.

The three basic trigonometric ratios are given below:

$$\sin A = \frac{\text{opposite side}}{\text{hypotenuse}}$$

$$\cos A = \frac{\text{adjacent side}}{\text{hypotenuse}}$$

$$\tan A = \frac{\text{opposite side}}{\text{adjacent side}}$$

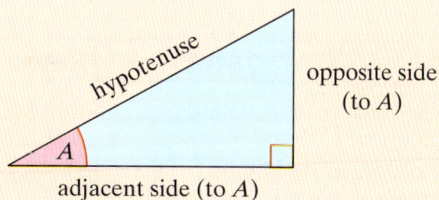

Example 1

If $\tan B = \dfrac{\sqrt{5}}{2}$, find the value of $\sin B$ and $\cos B$.

$\tan B = \dfrac{\sqrt{5}}{2} \Rightarrow$ opposite side to B is $\sqrt{5}$ and adjacent side is 2.

Now draw a rough sketch of a right-angled triangle.
Let x be the length of the hypotenuse.

$x^2 = 2^2 + (\sqrt{5})^2 \ldots (\sqrt{5})^2 = 5$

$x^2 = 4 + 5$

$x^2 = 9 \Rightarrow x = 3$

From the triangle: $\sin B = \dfrac{\sqrt{5}}{3}$ and $\cos B = \dfrac{2}{3}$.

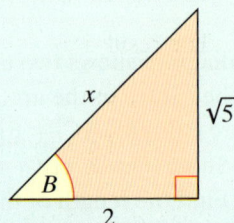

Using a calculator

We use the $\boxed{\sin}$, $\boxed{\cos}$ and $\boxed{\tan}$ keys on an electronic calculator to find the sine, cosine and tangent of any angle.

To find $\sin 35°$, key in $\boxed{\sin}$ 35 $\boxed{=}$.

The result is $0.573576\ldots = 0.5736$, correct to 4 decimal places.

Parts of a degree

A degree can be divided into 60 parts.

$1° = 60'$

Each part is called 1 **minute**, written $1'$.

Thus $34.5° = 34°30'$.

To find $\tan 34.5°$ or $34°30'$ on your calculator, you may use either of these methods:

1. For $\tan 34.5°$

key in $\boxed{\tan}$ 34.5 $\boxed{=}$

Result $= 0.6873$

2. For $\tan 34°30'$

key in $\boxed{\tan}$ 34 $\boxed{°\,{}_{,,,}}$ 30 $\boxed{°\,{}_{,,,}}$ $\boxed{=}$

Result $= 0.6873$

Using the $\boxed{\sin^{-1}}$ $\boxed{\cos^{-1}}$ and $\boxed{\tan^{-1}}$ keys

If we are given that $\sin A = 0.8661$, we can find the angle A by using the $\boxed{\sin^{-1}}$ key.

The $\boxed{\sin^{-1}}$ key is got by keying in $\boxed{\text{SHIFT}}$ $\boxed{\sin}$.

Thus if $\sin A = 0.8661$, we find A by keying in $\boxed{\text{SHIFT}}$ $\boxed{\sin}$ 0.8661 $\boxed{=}$.

The result is $60.008° = 60°$.

Similarly, if $\tan B = 1.2734$, we find the angle B by keying in $\boxed{\text{SHIFT}}$ $\boxed{\tan}$ 1.2734 $\boxed{=}$.

The result is $51.86°\ldots$ correct to 2 decimal places.

Example 2

(i) Find cos 72°18′, correct to 4 decimal places.

(ii) If sin A = 0.5216, find A correct to the nearest degree.

(i) To find cos 72°18′, key in $\boxed{\cos}$ 72 $\boxed{\text{°,,,}}$ 18 $\boxed{\text{°,,,}}$ $\boxed{=}$

Notice that the $\boxed{\text{°,,,}}$ key is used twice.

The result is 0.3040.

$$\text{Or } 18' = \frac{18^\circ}{60} = 0.3^\circ \Rightarrow 72°18' = 72.3^\circ$$

Thus to find 72.3°, key in $\boxed{\cos}$ 72.3 $\boxed{=}$

(ii) If sin A = 0.5216, we find A by keying in

$\boxed{\text{SHIFT}}$ $\boxed{\sin}$ 0.5216 $\boxed{=}$

The result is 31.44°. $\Rightarrow$ $A = 31°$, to the nearest degree.

Note: If you are given sin $A = \frac{4}{7}$, you can find the angle A by keying in

$\boxed{\text{SHIFT}}$ $\boxed{\sin}$ $\boxed{(}$ 4 $\boxed{\div}$ 7 $\boxed{)}$ $\boxed{=}$

The result is 34.8°.

The angles 30°, 45° and 60°

The angles 30°, 45° and 60° are used very frequently and we will use triangles to express the sine, cosine and tangent ratios of these angles as fractions or surds.

The triangle on the right is isosceles where the equal sides are 1 unit in length.

The hypotenuse is $\sqrt{2}$ units in length.

The sine, cosine and tangent ratios can be read from the triangle.

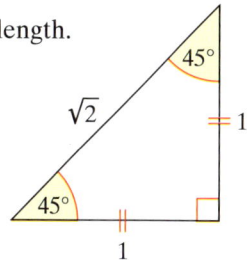

$$\sin 45^\circ = \frac{1}{\sqrt{2}} \qquad \cos 45^\circ = \frac{1}{\sqrt{2}} \qquad \tan 45^\circ = 1$$

The given right-angled triangle has angles of 60° and 30°.

We can use this triangle to write down the trigonometric ratios of these two angles.

$$\sin 60^\circ = \frac{\sqrt{3}}{2} \qquad \cos 60^\circ = \frac{1}{2} \qquad \tan 60^\circ = \sqrt{3}$$

$$\sin 30^\circ = \frac{1}{2} \qquad \cos 30^\circ = \frac{\sqrt{3}}{2} \qquad \tan 30^\circ = \frac{1}{\sqrt{3}}$$

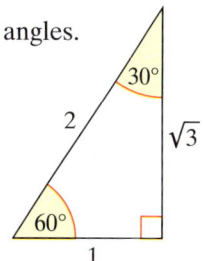

Note: The sine, cosine and tangent ratios for 30°, 45° and 60° are given on page 13 of *Formulae and Tables*.

Exercise 3.2

1. Use your calculator to find the value of each of the following ratios, correct to four decimal places:
   (i) $\sin 48°$ (ii) $\cos 74°$ (iii) $\tan 28.4°$ (iv) $\cos 43°24'$ (v) $\tan 30°36'$

2. Use your calculator to find the measure of each of these angles, correct to the nearest degree:
   (i) $\sin A = 0.7453$ (ii) $\cos B = 0.3521$ (iii) $\tan C = 1.4538$
   (iv) $\cos A = 0.2154$ (v) $\tan B = 0.8923$ (vi) $\sin C = 0.2132$

3. Find the measure of the angle θ, correct to the nearest degree in each of the following:
   (i) $\sin \theta = \frac{2}{3}$ (ii) $\cos \theta = \frac{3}{5}$ (iii) $\tan \theta = \frac{7}{8}$ (iv) $\sin \theta = \frac{2}{5}$

4. Use the given triangles to show that
   (i) $\sin^2 45° + \cos^2 45° = 1$
   (ii) $\sin 60° \cos 30° + \cos 60° \sin 30° = 1$
   (iii) $\cos^2 60° + \cos 60° \sin 30° = \frac{1}{2}$

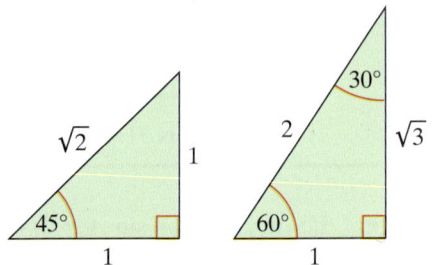

5. Show that $\sin^2 \frac{\pi}{6} + \sin^2 \frac{\pi}{4} + \sin^2 \frac{\pi}{3} = \frac{3}{2}$.

6. Find the perimeter of the triangle XYZ in the form $a + b\sqrt{c}$, where a, b and c are integers.

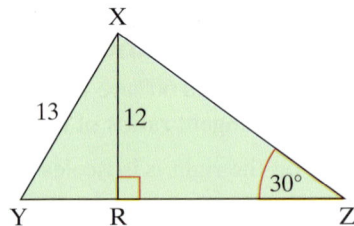

7. In the given triangle, find
   (i) x, correct to 1 decimal place
   (ii) the angle A, correct to the nearest degree.

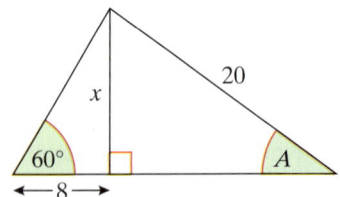

8. In the given triangle, $RT \perp PQ$, $|PR| = \sqrt{8}$, $|\angle RPT| = 30°$ and $|\angle RQT| = 45°$.
   Express in its simplest surd form
   (i) $|RT|$ (ii) $|PT|$.
   Hence find the area of $\triangle RPQ$, giving your answer in the form $a + \sqrt{b}$, where $a, b \in \mathbb{N}$.

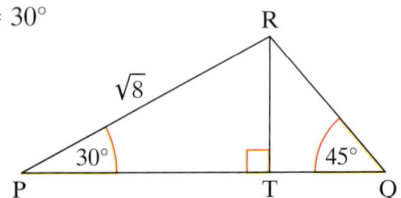

Section 3.3 Trigonometric functions

In this section we will deal with angles from 0° to 360° and show how to find the sine, cosine or tangent of these angles.

Angles are measured from the positive *x*-axis.

Positive angles are measured in an anti-clockwise direction.

Negative angles are measured in a clockwise direction.

The diagrams below illustrate two positive and two negative angles.

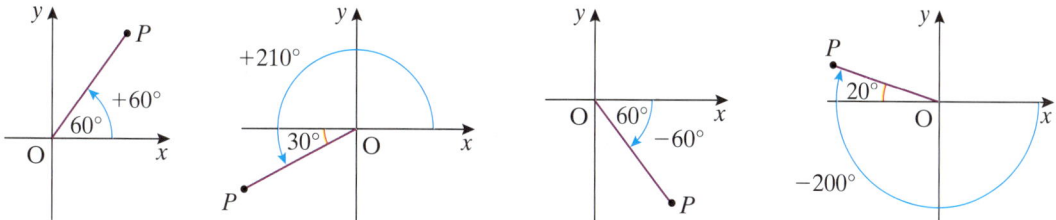

1. The Unit Circle

The circle on the right has centre at $(0, 0)$ and radius 1 unit in length.
It is generally referred to as the unit circle.

Let P(x, y) be any point on the circle, as shown.

From the triangle OPC,

$$\frac{x}{1} = \cos \theta \qquad x = \frac{y}{1} = \sin \theta$$
$$\Rightarrow \quad x = \cos \theta \qquad \Rightarrow \quad y = \sin \theta$$

$\therefore$ the coordinates of P are **($\cos \theta$, $\sin \theta$)**

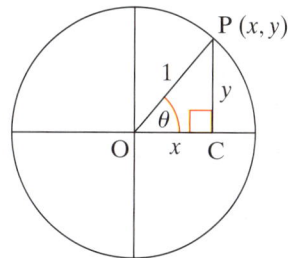

> The coordinates of any point on the unit circle are **($\cos \theta$, $\sin \theta$)**.

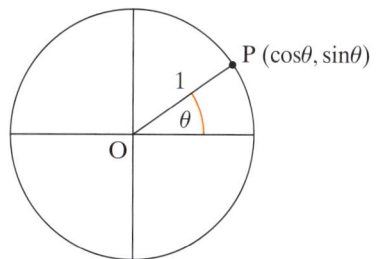

2. The Four Quadrants

The *x*-axis and *y*-axis divide a full rotation of 360° into 4 quadrants, as shown on the right.

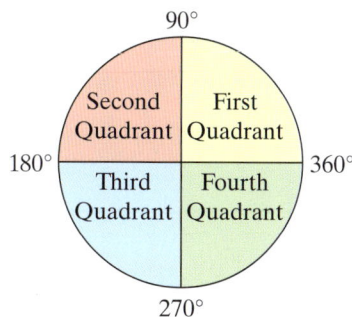

The unit circle on the right shows an angle, θ, in each of the four quadrants. The signs shown in each triangle determine whether a ratio is positive or negative.

The positive ratios in the four quadrants are shown in the highlighted section below.

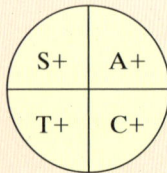

(i) In the 1st quadrant, all (A) positive
(ii) In the 2nd quadrant, sin(S) only positive
(iii) In the 3rd quadrant, tan(T) only positive
(iv) In the 4th quadrant, cos(C) only positive

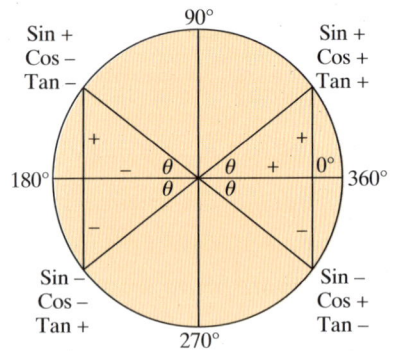

The **reference angle**, of any angle A, is always the smallest (acute) angle to the horizontal x-axis.

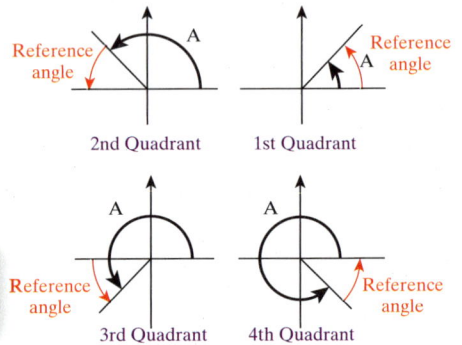

Example 1

Find in surd form   (i) sin 120°   (ii) cos 225°

(i) sin 120°:
   120° is in the second quadrant
   ⇒ the sine ratio is positive
   The reference angle is 180° − 120° = 60°.
   Using page 13 of *Formulae and Tables*,
   $\sin 60° = \dfrac{\sqrt{3}}{2}$ ⇒ $\sin 120° = \dfrac{\sqrt{3}}{2}$

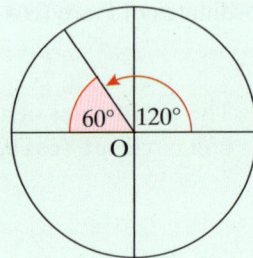

(ii) cos 225°:
   225° is in the third quadrant
   ⇒ the cosine ratio is negative
   The reference angle is 225° − 180° = 45°.
   $\cos 45° = \dfrac{1}{\sqrt{2}}$ ⇒ $\cos 225° = -\dfrac{1}{\sqrt{2}}$.

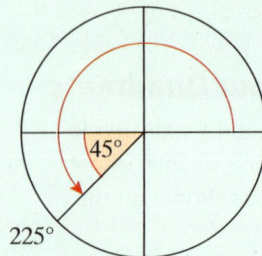

(i) Express in surd form, $\cos(-135°)$.

(ii) If $\sin x = -\dfrac{\sqrt{3}}{2}$, find two values for x if $0° \leqslant x \leqslant 360°$.

(i) $\cos(-135°) = \cos 45°$ in the 3rd quadrant

$\qquad = -\cos 45°$ ... cosine negative in 3rd quadrant

$\qquad = -\dfrac{1}{\sqrt{2}}$

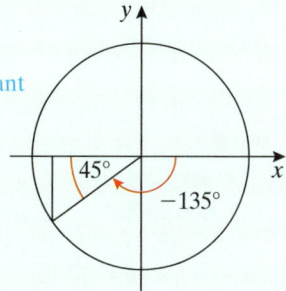

(ii) $\sin x = -\dfrac{\sqrt{3}}{2}$

$\Rightarrow \quad x = 60°$ in the 3rd or 4th quadrants

$\Rightarrow \quad x = (180° + 60°)$ or $x = (360° - 60°)$

$\Rightarrow \quad x = 240° \quad$ or $\quad x = 300°$

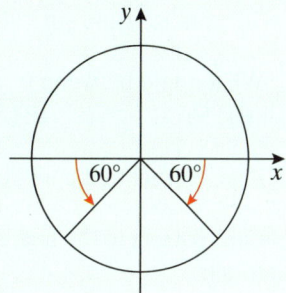

The diagram on the right shows an acute angle θ in each of the four quadrants.

CAST shows the positive ratios in these quadrants.

The diagram shows that $\sin(180° + \theta) = -\sin\theta$ as the sine is negative in the 3rd quadrant.

The results for sine, cosine and tangent are given below:

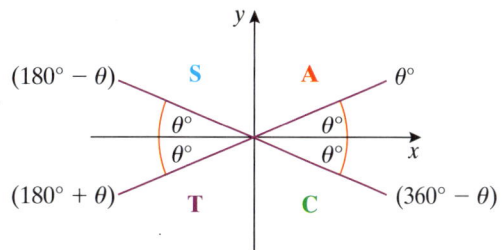

$\sin(180° - \theta) = \sin\theta$	$\cos(180° - \theta) = -\cos\theta$	$\tan(180° - \theta) = -\tan\theta$
$\sin(180° + \theta) = -\sin\theta$	$\cos(180° + \theta) = -\cos\theta$	$\tan(180° + \theta) = \tan\theta$
$\sin(360° - \theta) = -\sin\theta$	$\cos(360° - \theta) = \cos\theta$	$\tan(360° - \theta) = -\tan\theta$

Exercise 3.3

1. Use the unit circle on the right to write down the value of
   (i) $\sin 50°$ (ii) $\cos 220°$
   (iii) $\cos 50°$ (iv) $\sin 220°$
   (v) $\sin(-55°)$ (vi) $\cos(305°)$

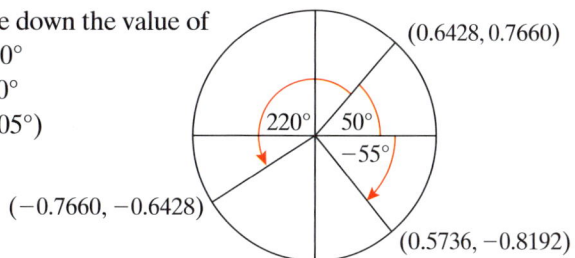

2. Use a calculator to write down, correct to four decimal places, the value of each of these ratios:
    (i) $\sin 138°$
    (ii) $\cos 212°$
    (iii) $\tan 318°$
    (iv) $\cos 159°$

3. If $\cos 120° = -\cos 60°$, copy and complete the following in the same way:
    (i) $\sin 130° = ...$
    (ii) $\cos 115° = ...$
    (iii) $\tan 160° = ...$
    (iv) $\cos 220° = ...$
    (v) $\sin 250° = ...$
    (vi) $\tan 300° = ...$

4. Use your *Formulae and Tables* book to express each of the following as a fraction or as a surd:
    (i) $\sin 120°$
    (ii) $\cos 135°$
    (iii) $\sin 240°$
    (iv) $\sin 210°$
    (v) $\cos 330°$
    (vi) $\tan 225°$
    (vii) $\cos 150°$
    (viii) $\sin 300°$

5. In which quadrant is
    (i) $\cos < 0$ and $\tan > 0$
    (ii) $\cos > 0$ and $\sin > 0$
    (iii) $\tan < 0$ and $\sin > 0$
    (iv) $\tan > 0$ and $\cos > 0$?

6. What angle between $0°$ and $360°$ has exactly the same sine as each of these angles?
    (i) $56°$
    (ii) $112°$
    (iii) $300°$
    (iv) $195°$
    (v) $105°$

7. Find, correct to the nearest degree, the two values of A if $\sin A = 0.2167$ and $0° \leqslant A \leqslant 360°$.

8. Find, correct to the nearest degree, the two values for each of these angles in the range $0°$ to $360°$.
    (i) $\cos A = -0.8428$
    (ii) $\sin B = -0.6947$
    (iii) $\tan C = 0.9325$

9. If $\sin \theta = \frac{1}{2}$, find 2 values for θ, if $0° \leqslant \theta \leqslant 360°$.

10. If $\cos \theta = \frac{1}{\sqrt{2}}$, find 2 values for $\tan \theta$, if $0° \leqslant \theta \leqslant 360°$.

11. If $\tan A = \frac{1}{\sqrt{3}}$, find 2 values for $\cos A$, if $0° \leqslant A \leqslant 360°$.

12. If $\sin \theta = -\frac{\sqrt{3}}{2}$, find two values for $\cos \theta$ without using a calculator if $0° \leqslant \theta \leqslant 360°$.

13. Find A, correct to the nearest degree, if $\sin A = -\frac{4}{5}$ and $\cos A = -\frac{3}{5}$ for $A \leqslant 360°$.

14. If $\sin B = \frac{3}{5}$ and $\cos B = -\frac{4}{5}$, find the value of $\tan B$ without using a calculator if $0° \leqslant B \leqslant 360°$.

15. If $\tan B = \frac{1}{\sqrt{3}}$ and $\sin B = -\frac{1}{2}$, express $\cos B$ as a surd.

16. If $\tan A = \frac{1}{2}$ and $180° < A < 270°$, find $\sin A$ in surd form.

17. Find, in surd or fraction form, each of these:
    (i) $\sin 420°$
    (ii) $\cos 495°$
    (iii) $\tan (-120°)$

Section 3.4 Sine Rule – Area of a triangle

In this section dealing with the sides and angles of any triangle, we will use the usual notation A, B and C to denote the angles and a, b and c to denote the sides opposite these angles.

In your study of trigonometry so far, you will have used the Theorem of Pythagoras to find sides and angles of a right-angled triangle.

In order to deal with any triangle, we will establish the first of two very important relationships between the angles and sides of the triangle.
This rule is known as the **sine rule**.

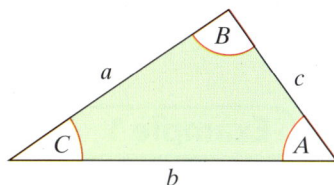

1. The Sine Rule: $\dfrac{a}{\sin A} = \dfrac{b}{\sin B} = \dfrac{c}{\sin C}$

To prove the Sine rule $\dfrac{a}{\sin A} = \dfrac{b}{\sin B}$

Mandatory Proof

Proof (i) Acute angled triangle

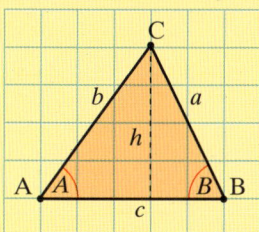

i) $\dfrac{h}{b} = \sin A \implies h = b \sin A$

ii) $\dfrac{h}{a} = \sin B \implies h = a \sin B$

$\therefore a \sin B = b \sin A$

(ii) Obtuse angled triangle

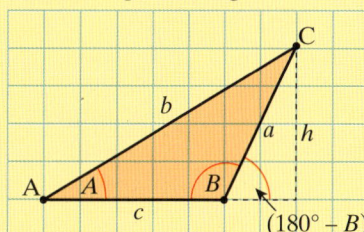

i) $\dfrac{h}{b} = \sin A \implies h = b \sin A$

ii) $\dfrac{h}{a} = \sin(180° - B) \implies h = a \sin(180° - B)$

$\implies h = a \sin B$

$\therefore a \sin B = b \sin A$

(since $(180° - B)$ is in the 2nd quadrant with reference angle B and sine is (+)ve in the 2nd quadrant)

In both cases if we divide by $\sin A \sin B$ we get

$$\frac{a}{\sin A} = \frac{b}{\sin B}$$

Similarly it may be shown that $\dfrac{b}{\sin B} = \dfrac{c}{\sin C}$

$$\therefore \frac{a}{\sin A} = \frac{b}{\sin B} = \frac{c}{\sin C}$$

Sine Rule $\quad \dfrac{a}{\sin A} = \dfrac{b}{\sin B} = \dfrac{c}{\sin C} \quad$ or $\quad \dfrac{\sin A}{a} = \dfrac{\sin B}{b} = \dfrac{\sin C}{c}$

Note: If we need to find an unknown angle using the sine rule, then $\dfrac{\sin A}{a} = \dfrac{\sin B}{b}$ is a more suitable form of the rule.

Using the sine rule

> To use the sine rule to solve a triangle, we need to know one side and the angle opposite this side as well as one other angle or side.

Example 1

In the triangle ABC, $|AB| = 8\,cm$, $|\angle BAC| = 30°$ and $|\angle BCA| = 40°$.
Find $|BC|$.

A sketch of the triangle is shown opposite.

> Always draw a diagram of the triangle and add the information given.

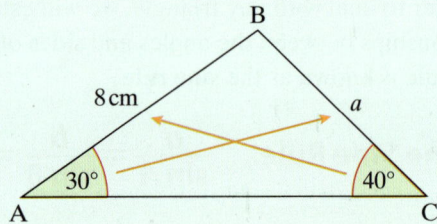

From the triangle, $|AB| = 8$, $A = 30°$ and $C = 40°$.

$$\frac{a}{\sin 30°} = \frac{8}{\sin 40°}$$

$\Rightarrow \quad a \sin 40° = 8 \sin 30°$

$\Rightarrow \qquad a = \dfrac{8 \sin 30°}{\sin 40°}$

$\Rightarrow \qquad a = 6.22\,cm$

$\Rightarrow \quad |BC| = 6.22\,cm$

Example 2

In the $\triangle ABC$, $|AB| = 3.8\,cm$, $|BC| = 5.2\,cm$ and $|\angle BAC| = 35°$. Find $|\angle ACB|$.

In the triangle ABC
$A = 35°$, $a = 5.2\,cm$ and $c = 3.8\,cm$

$$\frac{\sin C}{3.8} = \frac{\sin 35°}{5.2}$$

$\Rightarrow \qquad \sin C = \dfrac{3.8 \sin 35°}{5.2}$

$\qquad\qquad\quad = 0.4192$

$\Rightarrow \qquad\quad C = \sin^{-1}(0.4192)$

$\Rightarrow \qquad\quad C = 24.8°$

$\Rightarrow \quad |\angle ACB| = 24.8°$

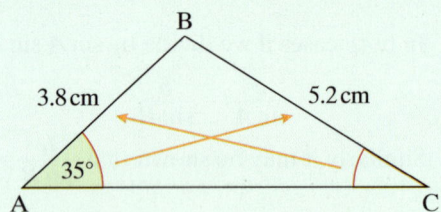

Caution!

In a $\triangle ABC$, $|AC| = 4\,cm$, $|BC| = 6\,cm$ and $|\angle ABC| = 30°$.

If we construct this triangle with ruler and compass, we get the diagram shown below.

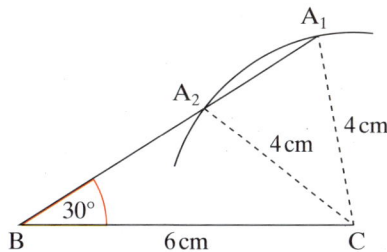

There are two possible positions for vertex A, namely A_1 and A_2.

This situation arises when we are given two sides and a non-included angle.

When two possible triangles can be drawn, it is generally referred to as the **ambiguous case**.

In the triangle above, $|\angle BA_1C| = 48.6°$ and $|\angle BA_2C| = 180° - 48.6°$
$$= 131.4°$$

Example 3

In a triangle ABC, $|AB| = 4\,cm$, $|AC| = 3\,cm$ and $|\angle ABC| = 44°$.
  (i) Draw a sketch of the two possible triangles to satisfy this information.
  (ii) Find the two possible values of $\angle ACB$.

  (i) The two possible triangles ABC_1 and ABC_2
      are shown on the right.

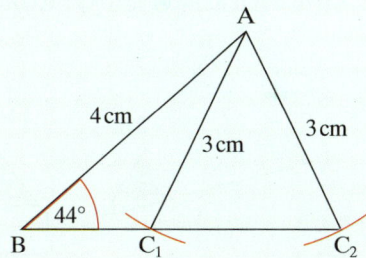

  (ii) $\dfrac{\sin C}{4} = \dfrac{\sin 44°}{3}$

   $\Rightarrow \quad \sin C = \dfrac{4 \times \sin 44°}{3} = 0.9262$

   $\Rightarrow \quad\quad C = \sin^{-1}(0.9262)$

   $\Rightarrow \quad\quad C = 67.9°$ or $180° - 67.9°$

   $\Rightarrow \quad |\angle ACB| = 67.9°$ or $112.1°$

2. The area of a triangle

In the given triangle, h is the perpendicular distance from A to [BC].

Area of $\triangle ABC = \frac{1}{2}$ base $\times$ perpendicular height

$\qquad\qquad = \frac{1}{2}a \times h$

$\qquad\qquad = \frac{1}{2}ah$

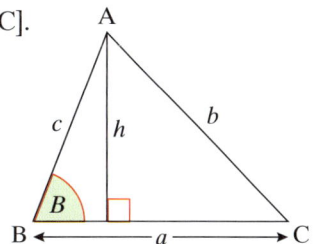

But $\dfrac{h}{c} = \sin B \quad \Rightarrow \quad h = c \sin B$

$\Rightarrow \quad$ area of $\triangle ABC = \frac{1}{2}ac \sin B$

By using different perpendicular heights,

area of $\triangle ABC = \frac{1}{2}ab \sin C$ or $\frac{1}{2}ac \sin B$ or $\frac{1}{2}bc \sin A$

> Area of $\triangle ABC = \frac{1}{2}ab \sin C$ or $\frac{1}{2}ac \sin B$ or $\frac{1}{2}bc \sin A$
>
> In words, area = half the product of any two sides multiplied by the sine of the angle between them.

Example 4

If the area of the given triangle is 12 cm², find the measure of the acute angle A, correct to the nearest degree.

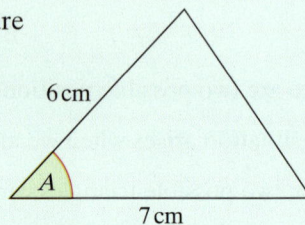

Area of $\triangle = \frac{1}{2}(6)(7) \sin A$

$\Rightarrow \quad \frac{1}{2}(6)(7) \sin A = 12$

$\Rightarrow \quad \sin A = \frac{12}{21} = 0.5714$

$\Rightarrow \quad A = \sin^{-1}(0.5714)$

$\Rightarrow \quad A = 34.8° = 35°$, to the nearest degree

Exercise 3.4

1. Find the length of the side marked with a letter in each of these triangles. Give each answer correct to one decimal place.

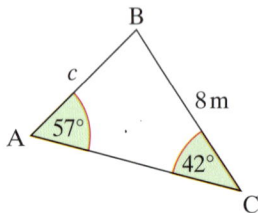
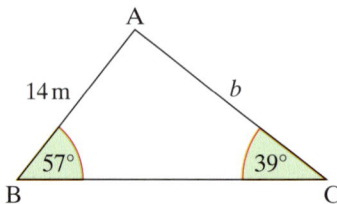
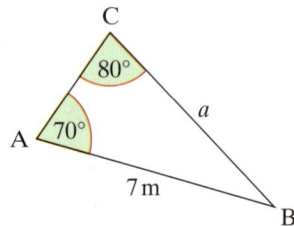

2. In each of the following triangles, find the value of the angle x, correct to the nearest degree:

(i)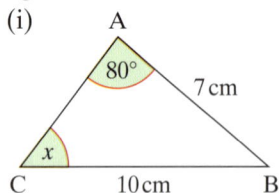
(ii)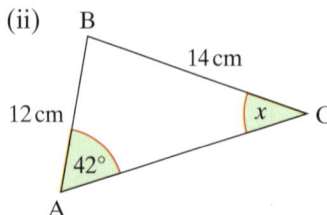
(iii)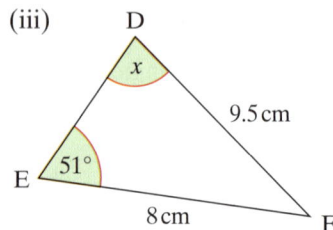

3. In the given triangle ABC, $|AC| = 8$, $|BC| = 10$ and $|\angle ABC| = 48°$.
   Find (i) $|\angle BAC|$ (ii) $|AB|$, correct to 1 decimal place
   (iii) area of $\triangle ABC$, correct to the nearest whole number.

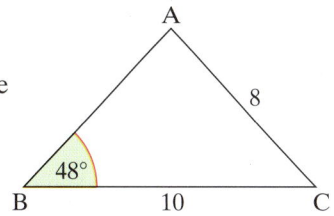

4. Find the area of each of these triangles in cm², correct to one decimal place:

   (i)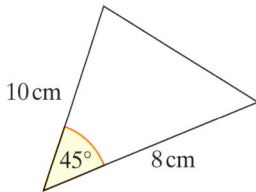

   (ii)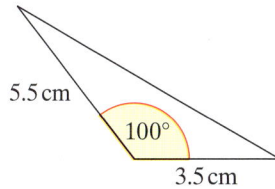

   (iii)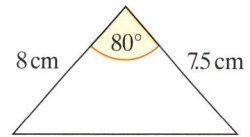

5. Find the acute angle marked with a letter in each of the following triangles.
   Give each answer correct to the nearest degree.

   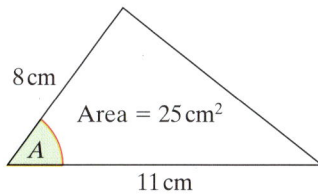

   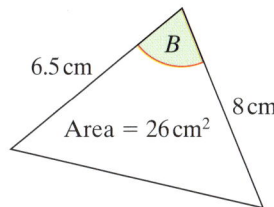

   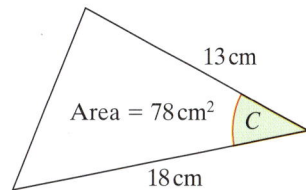

6. In the given triangle, $|AB| = 22$ cm, $|\angle ABC| = 46°$ and $|\angle BAC| = 71°$.
   Find correct to the nearest integer
   (i) $|BC|$
   (ii) area of $\triangle ABC$.

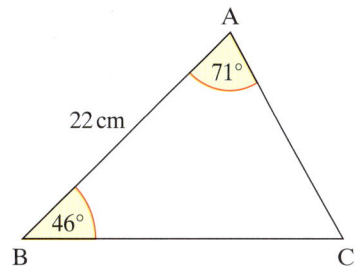

7. In the given triangle, $|PR| = \sqrt{8}$ m, $|\angle RPQ| = 30°$ and $|\angle RQP| = 45°$.
   (i) Find $|RQ|$.
   (ii) Hence show that the area of $\triangle PQR$ is 2.7 m², correct to one decimal place.

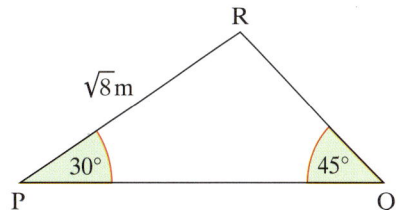

8. In the triangle ABC, shown right, $BC = (x + 2)$ cm, $AC = x$ cm and $|\angle BCA| = 150°$.
   Given that the area of the triangle is 6 cm², find the value of x.

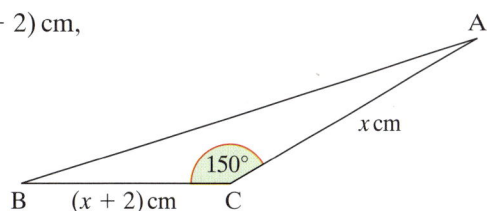

9. The diagram shows two possible triangles with
$|AB| = 5.4$ cm, $|\angle BAC| = 32°$ and $|BC| = 3$ cm.
Find the two possible values of the angle C, correct
to one decimal place.

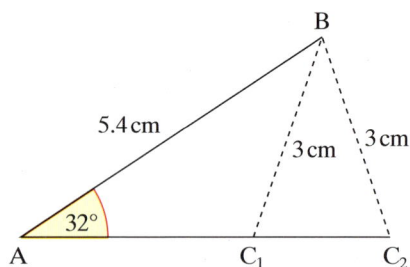

10. In the given diagram, $|AD| = |DB| = 5$ cm,
$|\angle ABC| = 43°$ and $|\angle ACB| = 72°$.
Find (i) $|AB|$ (ii) $|CD|$.
Give each answer correct to one decimal place.

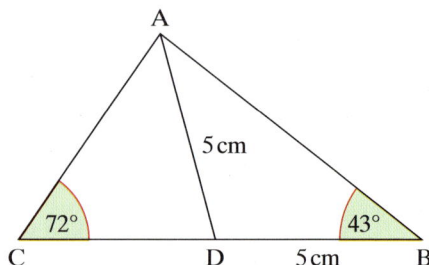

11. From a point A on the same level
as the base of a radio mast, the
angle of elevation of the top of the
mast is 25°.
From a point B, 20 metres closer to
the mast, and on the same level, the
angle of elevation is 32°.
Find the height of the radio mast
in metres, correct to one decimal
place.

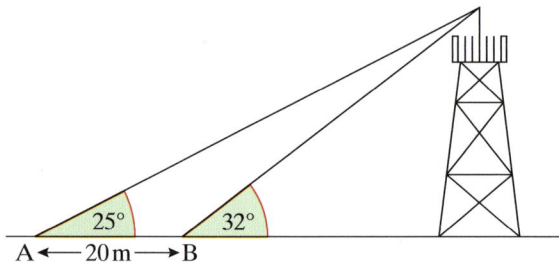

12. A lighthouse, L, is 40 km due north of a harbour, H.
A speedboat leaves H and travels in a direction N 53° E
from the harbour H until it reaches a point P.
The point, P, lies N 75° E from L.
Calculate the distance travelled by the speedboat,
correct to the nearest km.

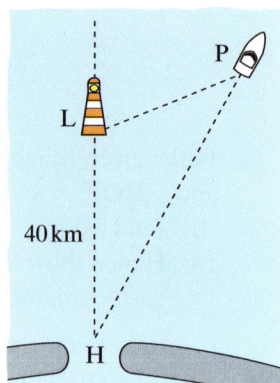

13. Barry and Colin swim across a parallel
sided river to a point A. Barry starts at
the point B and Colin starts at the point C
800 m up river. Calculate the distance each
has to swim to the nearest metre.

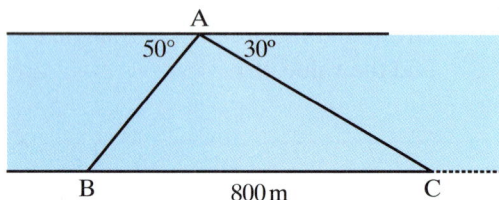

14. Lighthouses A and B stand on the coast. A trawler at a point C is 5km from lighthouse A.

If the trawler has a bearing of 130° from A and 20° from B as shown, calculate the distance between the two lighthouses. (Diagram not drawn to scale)

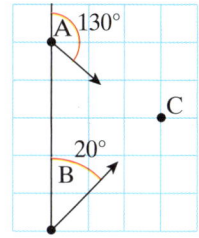

Section 3.5 The Cosine rule

In the given triangle, we are given the lengths of the three sides but no angle. We cannot use the sine rule here to find the angle A.

Instead we use another rule for solving triangles.

It is called the **cosine rule**.

The cosine rule states that for any triangle,

$$a^2 = b^2 + c^2 - 2bc \cos A.$$

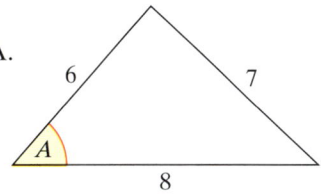

The Cosine Rule: $a^2 = b^2 + c^2 - 2bc \cos A$

Mandatory Proof

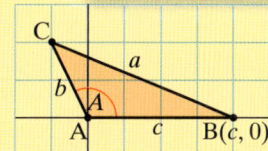

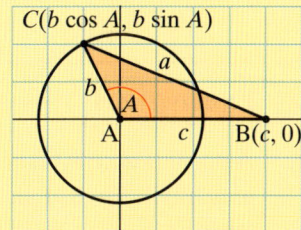

To prove the Cosine Rule $a^2 = b^2 + c^2 - 2bc \cos A$
Draw triangle with vertex A at the origin, $B(c, 0)$ and point C making an obtuse angle with A.

Draw a circle of radius length b with centre at A.

Since the coordinates of any point on a unit circle can be written as $(\cos \theta, \sin \theta)$, the coordinates of C can now be written as $C(b \cos A, b \sin A)$.
$|BC| = a$ and $|BC|$ is the distance from $(c, 0)$ to $(b \cos A, b \sin A)$
$\Rightarrow a^2 = (c - b \cos A)^2 + (0 - b \sin A)^2$
$\Rightarrow a^2 = c^2 - 2bc \cos A + b^2 \cos^2 A + b^2 \sin^2 A$
$\quad = c^2 - 2bc \cos A + b^2 (\cos^2 A + \sin^2 A)$
$\quad = c^2 - 2bc \cos A + b^2 \quad (\cos^2 A + \sin^2 A = 1)$
$\Rightarrow a^2 = b^2 + c^2 - 2bc \cos A$

Similarly it may be proved that
$b^2 = a^2 + c^2 - 2ac \cos B$ and $c^2 = a^2 + b^2 - 2ab \cos C$.

The cosine rule is generally used:
  (i) to find the third side of a triangle when the other two sides and the included angle are given.
  (ii) to solve a triangle when the lengths of the three sides are given.

$a^2 = b^2 + c^2 - 2bc \cos A$	$b^2 = a^2 + c^2 - 2ac \cos B$	$c^2 = a^2 + b^2 - 2ab \cos C$
or	or	or
$\cos A = \dfrac{b^2 + c^2 - a^2}{2bc}$	$\cos B = \dfrac{a^2 + c^2 - b^2}{2ac}$	$\cos C = \dfrac{a^2 + b^2 - c^2}{2ab}$

Example 1

In the triangle ABC, $|AB| = 8$, $|AC| = 10$ and $|\angle BAC| = 50°$.
Find $|CB|$.

Let $|CB| = a$.
Using
$$a^2 = b^2 + c^2 - 2bc \cos A$$
$$a^2 = 10^2 + 8^2 - 2(10)(8) \cos 50°$$
$$= 100 + 64 - 160\,(0.6428)$$
$$a^2 = 61.15$$
$$\Rightarrow \quad a = \sqrt{61.15} = 7.8, \text{ correct to one decimal place}$$
$$\Rightarrow \quad |CB| = 7.8$$

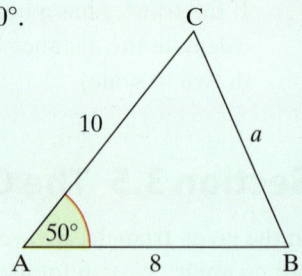

Example 2

In the given triangle PQR, $|PR| = 7\,cm$, $|PQ| = 6.8\,cm$
and $|RQ| = 9\,cm$.
Find $|\angle RPQ|$.

We require the angle P, so we start with cos P.
$$\cos P = \frac{q^2 + r^2 - p^2}{2qr}$$
$$= \frac{7^2 + (6.8)^2 - 9^2}{2(7)(6.8)}$$
$$\Rightarrow \quad \cos P = 0.1495$$
$$\Rightarrow \quad P = \cos^{-1}(0.1495)$$
$$\Rightarrow \quad |\angle RPQ| = 81.4°$$

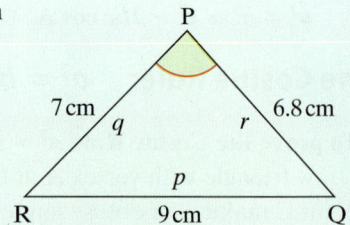

Example 3

A vertical pole AC stands
on a hill inclined at an
angle of 8°.
Down the hill, 20m from
the base C, a support wire
is attached to the ground at B.
If the wire makes an angle of 12° with the hill, calculate the
 (i) height of the pole h, correct to 2 decimal places
(ii) the length of the wire AB

Draw horizontal lines through B and A.
$\angle CBD = 8°$ ...(corresponding angles)
$\therefore \angle ABD = 20°$

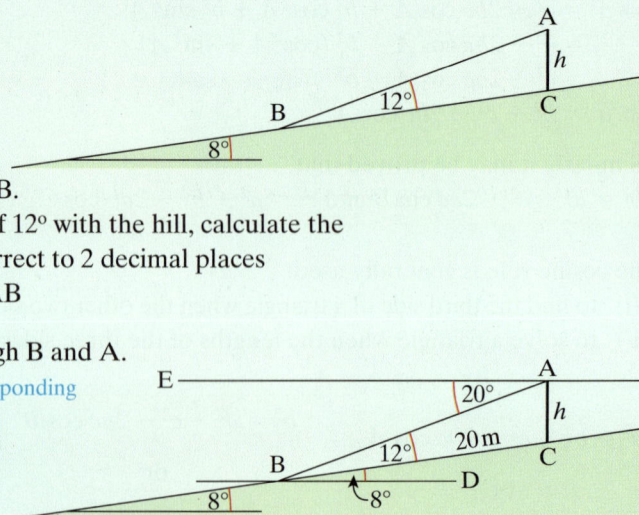

$\therefore \angle EAB = 20^\circ$ ...(alternate angles)
$\therefore \angle BAC = 70^\circ$
Also $\angle ACB = 98^\circ$ ...$(180^\circ - 12^\circ - 70^\circ)$

(i) $\dfrac{h}{\sin 12} = \dfrac{20}{\sin 70} \Rightarrow h = \dfrac{20 \times \sin 12}{\sin 70} = 4.43\,\text{m}$

(ii) $|AB|^2 = 20^2 + 4.43^2 - 2 \times 20 \times 4.43 \times \cos(98) = 444.286$

$\therefore |AB| = 21.07\,\text{m}$

Exercise 3.5

1. Calculate the length of the side marked x in each of these triangles.
    Give your answers correct to 1 decimal place.

    (i)   (ii)   (iii)

    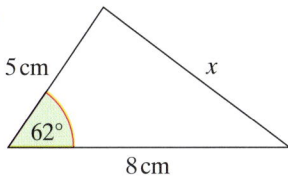   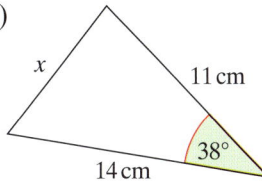   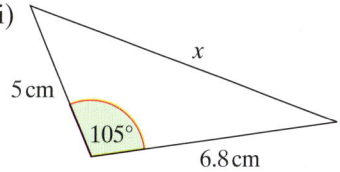

2. Find, correct to the nearest degree, the measure of the angle marked with a letter in
    each of these triangles:

    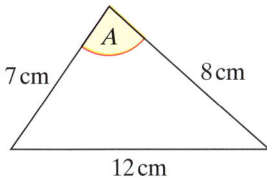   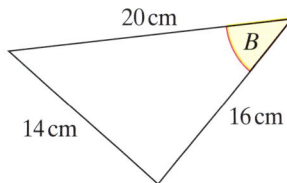   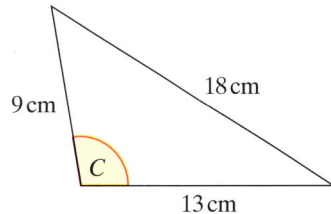

3. If the lengths of the sides of a triangle are 3 cm, 5 cm and 7 cm, show that the largest angle
    is 120°.

4. Find, correct to one decimal place, the area of a triangle whose sides are 4, 8 and 10 units in
    length.

5. In the given figure, $|PQ| = 3.5$, $|QR| = 2$, $|PS| = 6.5$,
    $|\angle QSR| = 30^\circ$ and $|\angle SQR| = 52^\circ$.
    Find   (i) $|QS|$, correct to 1 decimal place
            (ii) $|\angle PQS|$.

    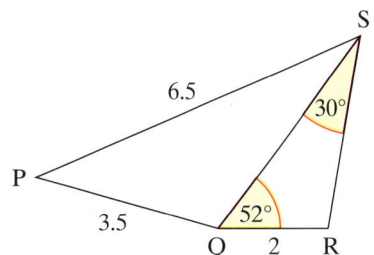

6. A builder ropes off a triangular plot of ground, PQR.
    The length of [PQ] = 42 m and the length of [PR] = 50 m.
    $|\angle QPR| = 72°$.
    Calculate the length of rope needed by the builder.
    Give your answer correct to one decimal place.

7. In a triangle ABC, $|AC| = 15$ cm, $|AB| = 12$ cm and the area of $\triangle ABC$ is 65 cm². Find
    (i) $|\angle BAC|$, correct to the nearest degree (ii) $|BC|$ in cm, correct to one decimal place.

8. The lengths of the sides of a triangle are 4 cm, 5 cm and 6 cm.
    The largest angle of the triangle is θ.
    (i) Find the value of cos θ as a fraction.
    (ii) Hence show that $\sin \theta = \dfrac{a\sqrt{7}}{b}$, where a and b are integers, and write down their values.

9. In a triangle, the longest side has length 2 cm and one of the other sides has length $\sqrt{2}$ cm.
    Given that the area of the triangle is 1 cm², show that the triangle is right-angled and
    isosceles.

10. The area of $\triangle ABC$ is 10 cm².
    $|AB| = 3.2$ cm and $|BC| = 8.4$ cm.
    Find the perimeter of the triangle ABC in cm,
    correct to one decimal place.

    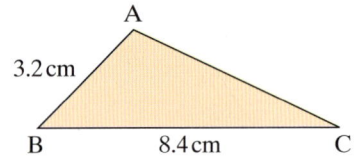

11. The longest side of a triangle has length $(2x - 1)$ cm.
    The other sides have lengths $(x - 1)$ cm and $(x + 1)$ cm.
    Given that the largest angle is 120°, find
    (i) the value of x (ii) the area of the triangle in surd form.

12. The diagram below shows part of the wooden framework of the roof of a shed.

    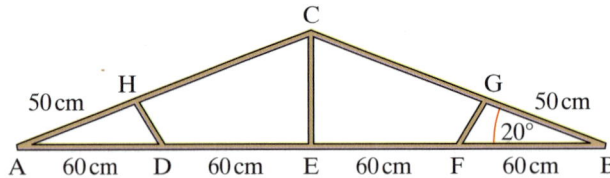

    In the triangle ABC, $|AC| = |BC|$ and $|AD| = |DE| = |EF| = |FB| = 60$ cm.
    $|\angle ABC| = 20°$ and $|AH| = |BG| = 50$ cm.
    Find (i) the length of [FG], correct to one decimal place.
          (ii) the total length of wood required to make the framework shown in the diagram.

13. The diagram shows a cube of side 10 cm from which one
    corner has been cut.
    Calculate the angle PQR, correct to the nearest degree.

    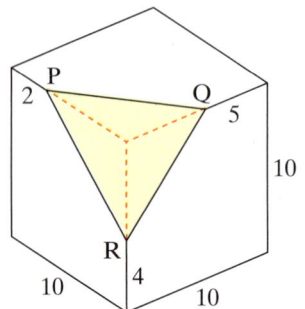

14. Sinead draws a circle, centre A, radius 2 cm.
She then draws a chord CB of length 3 cm and joins B to A.
Calculate the size of the angle ∠CAB correct to 1 place
of decimals.

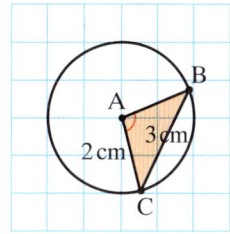

15. The diagram shows a quadrilateral ABCD containing
∠ADC = 56°.
Using the information in the diagram find:
  (i) the size of the angle ∠ABC and hence
  (ii) the area of the quadrilateral.

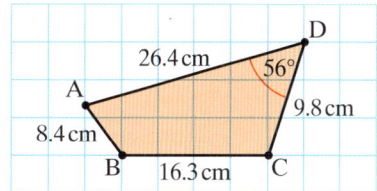

16. A 6 m ladder rests on an inclined slope
1.2 m from the base of a vertical wall.
If the ladder reaches up the wall a
distance of 5.5 m, find the angle of
inclination of the slope, A.

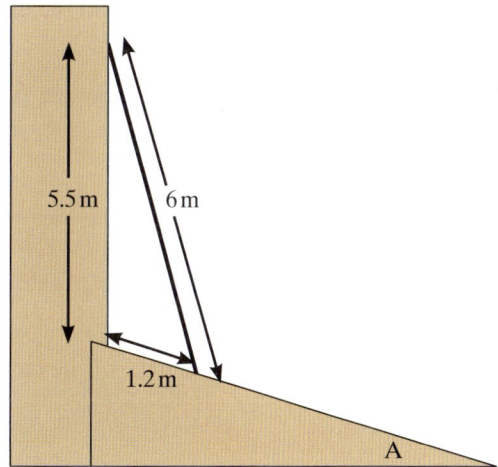

17. An aircraft traffic station at an airport measures the angle between two approaching
aircraft as 49°.
If the station measures the range of each approaching aircraft to be 50 km and 72 km
respectively, calculate the distance between the aircraft correct to 1 place of decimals.

18. A trawler leaves port at 1 pm and travels due North at a speed of
30 km/h. At 3 pm the trawler adjusts its course and travels 20°
east of North.
  (i) How far will the trawler be from port at 4 pm.
  (ii) If the trawler has enough diesel to travel 270 km, what is the latest
       time the trawler should turn and return directly to port.
       (Assume the trawler travels at the same speed for the whole
       round trip)

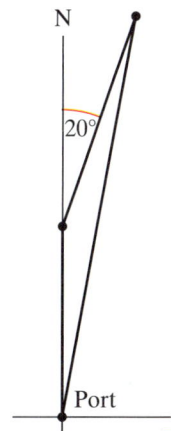

Section 3.6 Problems in three dimensions

In this section you will deal with trigonometric problems in three dimensions.

One of the first things you are required to do is to identify which angles or which lengths you need to calculate. For this reason it is of the utmost importance that you sketch good diagrams.

Most problems in three dimensions consist of a series of connected triangles. It is important to identify right-angled triangles in particular. If we require an angle or length in a particular triangle, it simplifies the work if the triangle is drawn separately. From this point on you can work from a two-dimensional figure, just as you have been doing so far in this chapter.

In this cube there are many connected right-angled triangles.

The triangle HED can be used to find the length of the side [HD].

The side [HD] can be used in the triangle AHD to find |AD| and |∠ADH|.

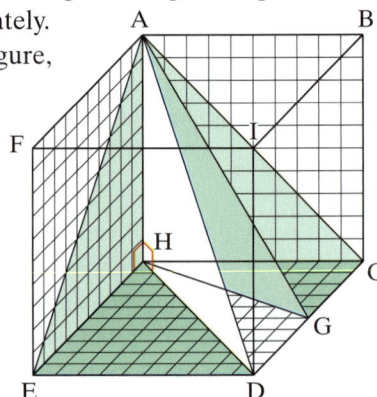

Example 1

The given figure shows a cube of side 5 cm.

Find the measure of the angle between the diagonal [AD] and the base of the cube.

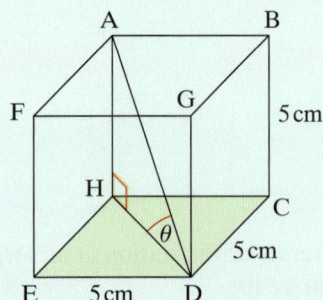

(i) Redraw △HED

$$|HD|^2 = 5^2 + 5^2$$
$$= 50$$
$$\Rightarrow \quad |HD| = \sqrt{50}$$

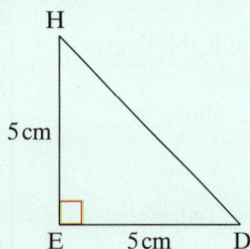

(ii) Redraw △AHD

$$\tan \theta = \frac{5}{\sqrt{50}}$$
$$\Rightarrow \quad \theta = \tan^{-1}\left(\frac{5}{\sqrt{50}}\right)$$
$$\Rightarrow \quad \theta = 35.26°$$

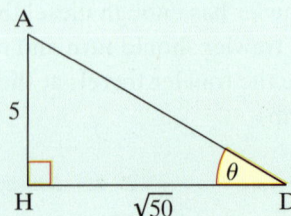

Example 2

The pyramid shown has a square base of side 4 m and a vertical height of 3 m.

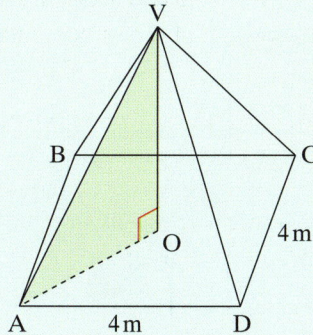

(i) Calculate the length of the edge [AV].

(ii) Hence calculate, correct to the nearest whole number, the total area of the four triangular faces.

(i) Using the base ABCD:

$$|AC|^2 = 4^2 + 4^2$$
$$|AC|^2 = 32$$
$$\Rightarrow \quad |AC| = \sqrt{32}$$
$$|AO| = \frac{1}{2}|AC| = \frac{\sqrt{32}}{2}\,m$$

Using $\triangle$AVO:

$$|AV|^2 = 3^2 + \left(\frac{\sqrt{32}}{2}\right)^2$$
$$= 9 + \frac{32}{4}$$
$$= 17$$
$$\Rightarrow \quad |AV| = \sqrt{17}\,m$$

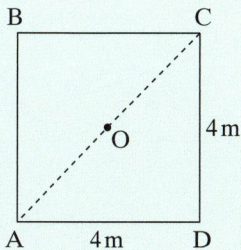

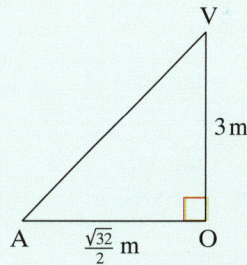

(ii) Area of face AVD:

$$h^2 + 2^2 = (\sqrt{17})^2$$
$$h^2 + 4 = 17$$
$$h^2 = 13 \quad \Rightarrow \quad h = \sqrt{13}\,m$$

Area of $\triangle$AVD $= \frac{1}{2}(4\,cm)(\sqrt{13})$

$$= 2\sqrt{13}\,m^2$$

Area of 4 faces $= 4(2\sqrt{13})\,m^2$

$$= 28.84\,m^2$$

$$= 29\,m^2, \text{ correct to the nearest whole number.}$$

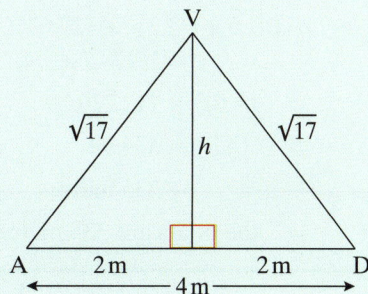

Note: If a triangle is not right-angled, we use the sine rule or the cosine rule to find an unknown angle or unknown side.

Example 3

From the top of a vertical cliff 100 m high, a boat A lies in a direction S 30° E and a boat B lies due east.

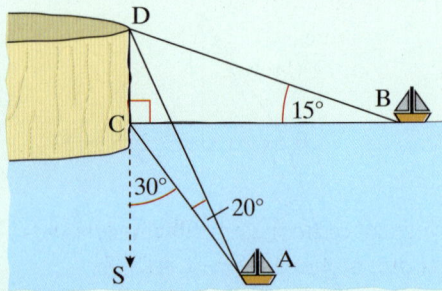

The angle of elevation of the top of the cliff from boat A is 20° and the angle of elevation from boat B is 15°. Calculate how far the boats are apart.
Give your answer correct to the nearest metre.

(i) Using △ADC:

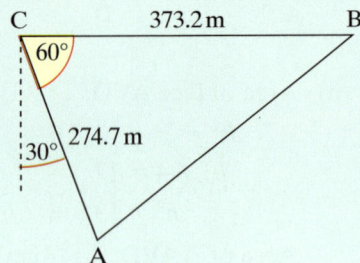

$$\frac{100}{|CA|} = \tan 20°$$

$$\Rightarrow \quad |CA| \tan 20° = 100$$

$$\Rightarrow \quad |CA| = \frac{100}{\tan 20°} = \frac{100}{0.364}$$

$$\Rightarrow \quad |CA| = 274.7 \text{ m}$$

(ii) Using △BCD:

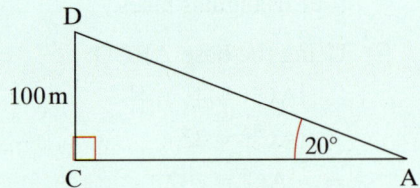

$$\frac{100}{|CB|} = \tan 15°$$

$$\Rightarrow \quad |CB| = \frac{100}{\tan 15°}$$

$$\Rightarrow \quad |CB| = 373.2 \text{ m}$$

(iii) Using △ACB:

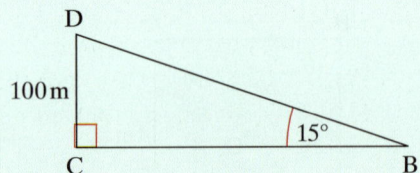

Here we use the cosine rule to find |AB|.

$$|AB|^2 = (373.2)^2 + (274.7)^2$$
$$- 2(373.2)(274.7) \cos 60°$$

$$\Rightarrow \quad |AB|^2 = 112\,220.29$$

$$\Rightarrow \quad |AB| = 334.99$$

$$= 335 \text{ metres}$$

$$\Rightarrow \quad \text{the boats are 335 metres apart.}$$

Exercise 3.6

1. An open rectangular box has dimensions
   10 cm by 5 cm by 4 cm, as shown.
   (i) Find the length of the diagonal [GH].
   (ii) Find the measure of the angle
        between GH and the base of the box.

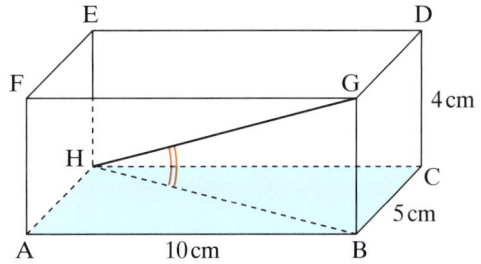

2. The diagram shows a vertical radio mast [BT] which stands
   at the corner of a horizontal rectangular plot ABCD.
   The mast is 12 m in height and |BC| = 15 m.
   The angle of elevation of the top of the mast from A is 25°.
   (i) Find the length of [AB].
   (ii) Calculate the angle of elevation of the top of
        the mast from C.
   (iii) Find |DB|.
   (iv) Calculate the angle of elevation of the top
        of the mast from D.
   Give each answer correct to one decimal place.

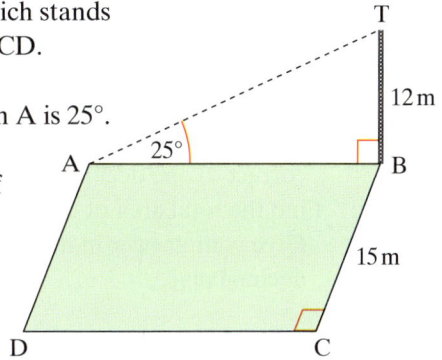

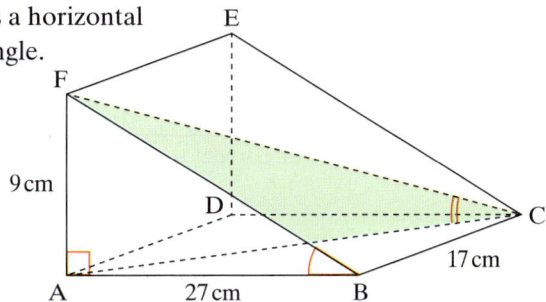

3. A balloon X is 200 metres vertically above a point Y on level ground.
   Two points P and Q are also on level ground.
   The angle of elevation of X from P is 48°.
   The angle of elevation of X from Q is 34°.
   (i) Find |PY| and |QY| correct to the nearest metre.
   (ii) If |∠PYQ| = 84°, find |PQ| correct to the nearest metre.

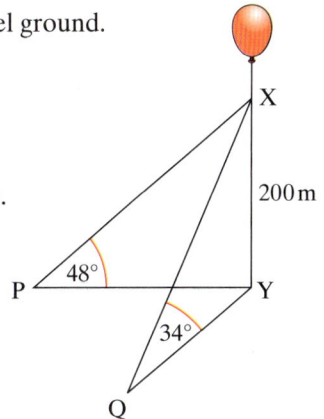

4. In the given model of a ramp, ABCD is a horizontal
   rectangle and ADEF is a vertical rectangle.
   Find   (i) |∠ABF|
          (ii) |AC|
          (iii) |∠ACF|.
   Give each answer correct to one
   decimal place.

5. P, Q and R are points on a horizontal plane.
[PD] is a vertical mast.
The angle of elevation of D from R is 60°.
If |PQ| = 5 m, |QR| = 3 m and ∠PQR = 120°,
find
  (i) |PR|
  (ii) |DQ|, corect to the nearest metre.

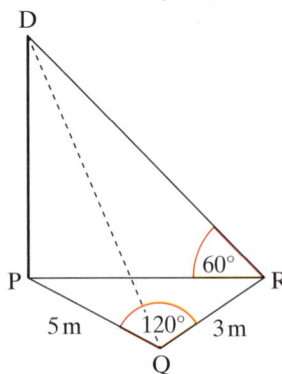

6. A tent in the shape of a pyramid has a square base of side
3 metres and a central vertical pole of height 2.5 m.
  (i) Calculate the length of the slanted edge [AE],
      correct to one decimal place.
  (ii) Find the total area of the four triangular faces.
      Give your answer in m², correct to one
      decimal place.

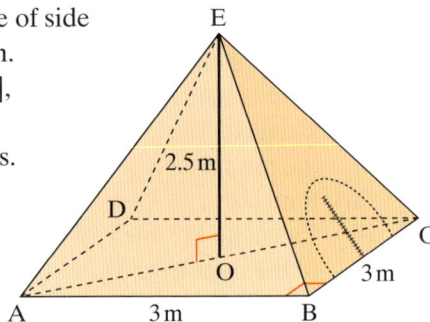

7. A river flows due east and a vertical tower [CD] stands
on its left-hand bank.
From a point A upstream and on the same bank as the tower,
the angle of elevation of the top of the tower is 60°.
From a point B on the other bank directly across from A,
the angle of elevation is 45°.
If the height of the tower is 36 metres, find the width
of the river, correct to the nearest metre.

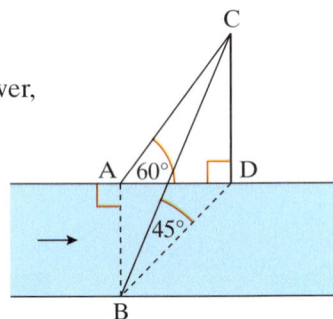

8. In the solid figure shown, ABCD is a horizontal
rectangle and ABFE is a vertical rectangle.
M is the midpoint of [CD].
Given that |AD| = 7 cm, |AE| = 5 cm and
|EF| = 12 cm, find
  (i) |DF| (ii) |∠BDF| (iii) |∠FMB|.
Give each answer correct to one decimal place.

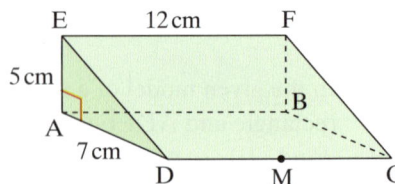

9. The diagram represents a right pyramid.
The base is a square of side $2x$ cm.
The length of each of the slant edges is $8\sqrt{3}$ cm.
The height of the pyramid is x cm.
Calculate the value of x.

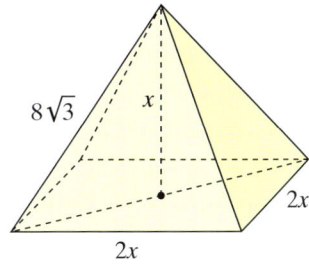

10. The given diagram shows two walls of length 10 metres and 5 metres meeting at right angles. The height of each wall is 4 metres.

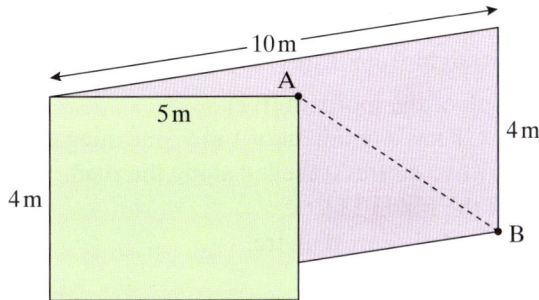

Calculate the distance between the points A and B on the walls.
Give your answer in metres, correct to one decimal place.

11. The given figure shows a vertical wall TUVS four metres in height.
From a point O on level ground, the angle of elevation from O to U is 60° and the angle of elevation of T from O is 30°.
If $|\angle SOV| = 60°$, find the length of the wall [SV] in metres, correct to 1 place of decimals.

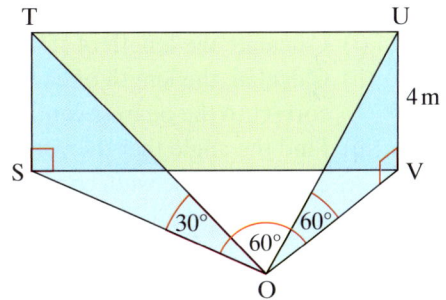

12. The given figure shows three vertical poles supporting a triangular roof RST.
$|AB| = |AC| = 10$ metres, $|AR| = 6$ m,
$|SB| = |TC| = 4$ m and $|BC| = 6$ m.
  (i) Find the area of the shelter ABC.
  (ii) Find the area of the roof RST.

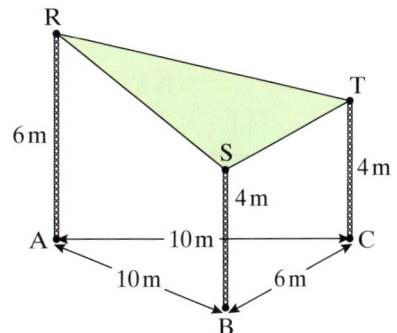

13. The diagram shows a plane hillside, which slopes at an angle of 41° to the horizontal. The vertical height of the hill is 105 m. A straight horizontal road ABC runs along the bottom of the hill. A funicular railway AT runs straight up the hillside.

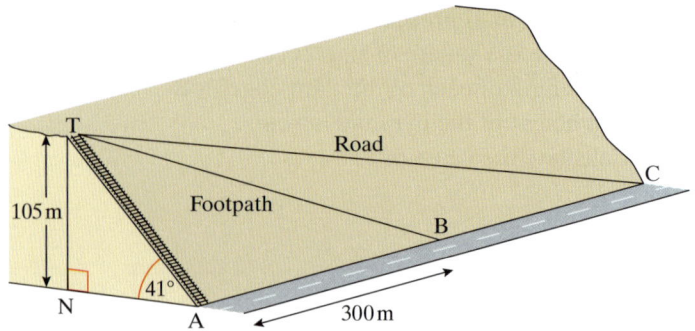

(i) Calculate the length of the railway [AT], correct to the nearest metre.

A footpath goes straight from B to T, where |AB| = 300 m

(ii) Calculate the length of the footpath [BT].

The straight road CT has a 'gradient of 1 in 5', meaning that it rises one metre vertically for every five metres travelled **along the road**.

(iii) Find the length of the road [CT].

(iv) Find |BC|, correct to the nearest metre.

14. In the given diagram, a pole [EA] supports an inn sign.

The pole is perpendicular to a vertical wall and is supported by two wires [AB] and [AC]. The hooks at B and C are in a horizontal line and D is 120 cm vertically above E.

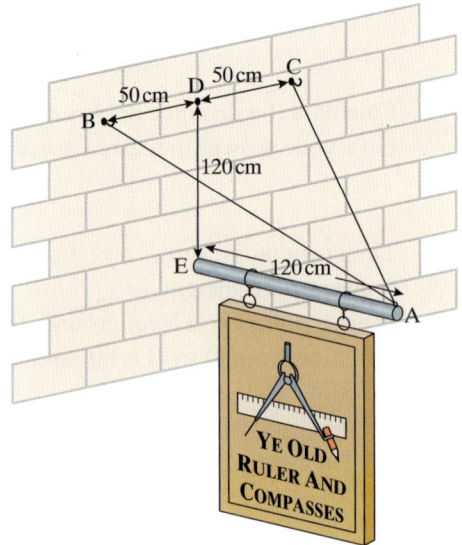

(i) Calculate the length of [DA].

(ii) Calculate the length of each wire, correct to the nearest centimetre.

(iii) Find the angle that the wire AB makes with the wall, correct to the nearest degree.

Section 3.7 Graphs of trigonometric functions

Graph of $y = \sin x$

Consider a point A on a unit circle.

The y-coordinate of this point is the length of the *opposite* side of a right-angled triangle.

The sine ratio (at this point) is

$$\sin x = \frac{Opposite}{Hypotenuse} = \frac{Opposite}{1}$$

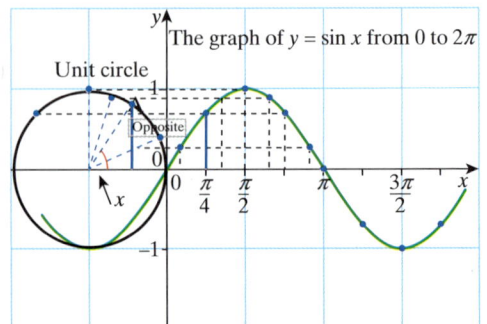

The graph of $y = \sin x$ from 0 to 2π

As the point moves around the circle, the angle increases from 0 to 2π radians (0° to 360°).

At the same time the y-coordinate of A changes from 0 to 1 to 0 to -1 to 0.

By measuring the length of the opposite (y) and the angle (x) contained, a set of ordered pairs (x, y) is created. When plotted these points all lie on a smooth curve, $y = \sin x$.

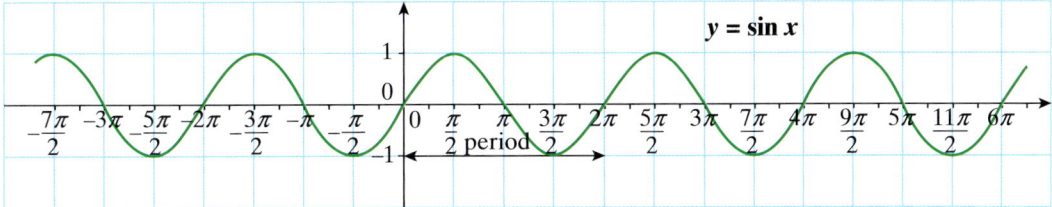

It is also clear that the point can continue to rotate making larger angles but the y-value continues to repeat within a **range** of values $[-1, 1]$.

This function, $y = \sin x$, is therefore said to be **periodic**.

The shortest measurement along the x-axis after which it repeats is the **period** of the function.

The period of $y = \sin x$ is 360° or 2π radians.

> The **period** of a function, f, is a positive number a such that $f(x + a) = f(x)$.
> The period of $\sin(x)$ is 2π as $\sin(x + 2\pi) = \sin(x)$.

Graph of $y = \cos x$

The cosine function, $\cos x = \dfrac{Adjacent}{Hypotenuse} = \dfrac{Adjacent}{1}$, is also a periodic function.

When the angle $x = 0°$, the $Adjacent$ side $= 1$

As x increases to 90°, the $Adjacent$ side decreases to 0.

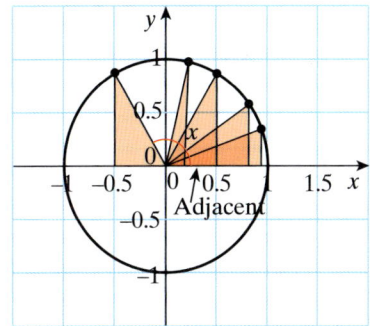

As x increases further (past 90°), the adjacent side becomes negative and decreases in value to -1.

The cosine graph repeats after 2π.

The period of $\cos x$ is 2π radians and its range is $[-1, 1]$.

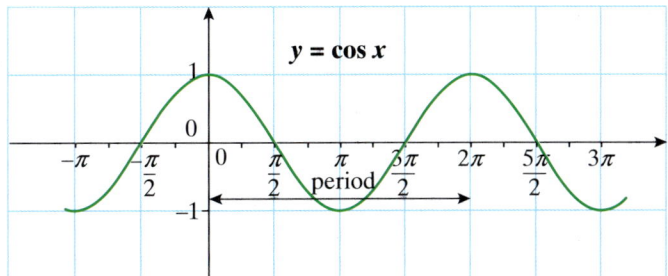

Graph of $y = \tan x$

Since $\tan x = \dfrac{opposite}{adjacent}$,

at $x = 0$, the opposite is zero
$\therefore \tan 0 = 0$.

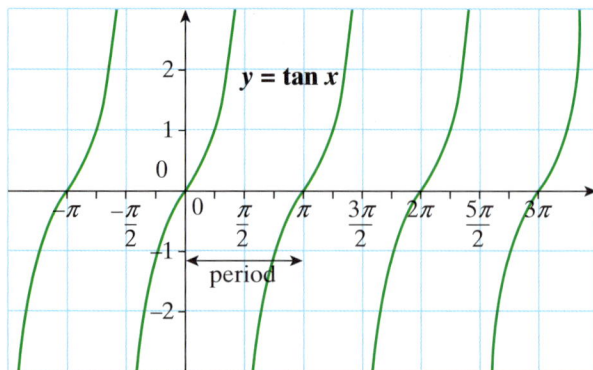

As the angle x increases the opposite side
increases as the adjacent decreases.

At $x = \dfrac{\pi}{4}$, the opposite and adjacent sides
have the same length $\therefore \tan \dfrac{\pi}{4} = 1$

However as x approaches $90°$ $\left(\dfrac{\pi}{2} \text{ radians}\right)$, the opposite approaches 1 while the adjacent

approaches zero and so $\tan \dfrac{\pi}{2} = \dfrac{opposite}{adjacent}$, is undefined.

We cannot get a value for $\tan x$ when $x = \pm 90°, \pm 270°, \ldots$

Note: $\tan(89°) \approx \dfrac{1}{0.02} \approx 57.3$ (try to imagine the position of the point $(89°, 57.3)$
on the $y = \tan x$ graph above)

The curve gets closer and closer to the $x = \dfrac{\pi}{2}$ line but never touches it.

The lines $x = \dfrac{\pi}{2}, \dfrac{3\pi}{2}, \dfrac{5\pi}{2} \ldots$ and $x = \dfrac{-\pi}{2}, \dfrac{-3\pi}{2}, \dfrac{-5\pi}{2} \ldots$ are **asymptotes** to the curve.

As can be seen from the graph, $\tan x$ has a period of π radians ($180°$).

Its range is R, the set of real numbers.

Function	Domain	Range	Period
$y = \sin x$	$\mathbb{R}$	$[-1, 1]$	$360°$ (2π radians)
$y = \cos x$	$\mathbb{R}$	$[-1, 1]$	$360°$ (2π radians)
$y = \tan x$	$\mathbb{R}\backslash\{\pm 90°, \pm 270°, \ldots\}$	$\mathbb{R}$	$180°$ (π radians)

Example 1

Draw a graph of $y = \cos x$ in
the domain $-360° \leqslant x \leqslant 360°$.
Show on the graph that
there are four angles in
this domain that satisfy
the equation $\cos x = \dfrac{1}{2}$.

A sketch of the graph
is shown below.

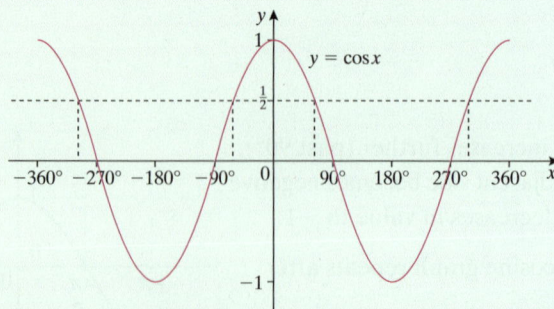

The line $y = \dfrac{1}{2}$ $\left(\text{i.e. } \cos x = \dfrac{1}{2}\right)$ intersects the graph at four points.

The points where the vertical lines from these intersections meet the x-axis give the
values of the four angles.

Exercise 3.7

1. Draw a graph of $y = \sin x$ in the domain $-360° \le x \le 360°$.
   From your graph find out the number of angles that satisfy $\sin x = \frac{1}{2}$ i.e. $y = \frac{1}{2}$

2. (i) Copy and complete the table below.

x	0°	45°	90°	135°	180°	225°	270°	315°	360°	405°	450°	495⁰	540°
$\sin x$													

   (ii) Plot these points on a graph and use the graph to estimate values of x for which $\sin x = -0.5$

3. Sketch the graph of $y = \cos x$ in the domain $-\pi \le x \le 2\pi$
   Find the coordinates of the maximum point of this curve in this domain.

4. Write an equation and a domain for each of the following curves.

   (i)

   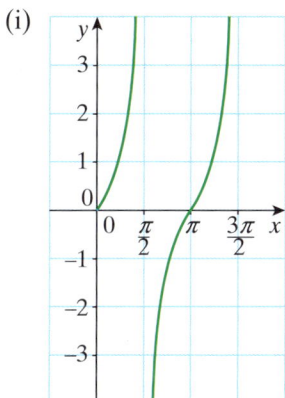

   (ii)

   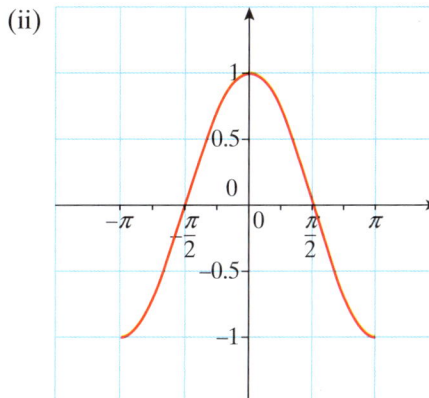

5. Draw a graph of $y = \cos x$ in the domain $-90° \le x \le 540°$ and use the graph to estimate values of x for which $\cos x = 0.9$ in this domain.

6. (i) Using a protractor mark points on the circumference of a (large) unit circle at 0°, 10°, 20°, 30°... 80°, 85° (D, 30° is shown in the diagram).
   (ii) Draw a line perpendicular to the x-axis at G using a setsquare.
   (iii) Then using a ruler extend AD to H.
   Measure $|GH|$
   (iv) Complete the following
   $$\tan 30° = \frac{|DC|}{|AC|} = \frac{|\ \ |}{1} =$$

   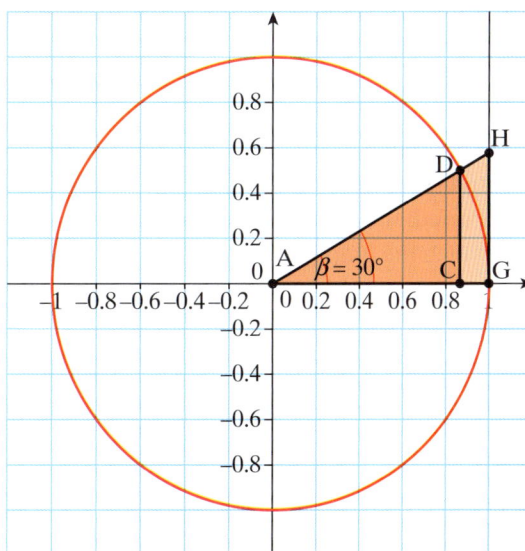

127

(v) Join A to each point on the circumference and using (iii) and (iv) copy and complete the following table.

x	0°	10°	20°	30°	40°	50°	60°	70°	80°	85°
$\tan x$										

(vi) Scaling the x-axis from 0° to 90° and the y-axis from 0 to 12 draw a graph of $y = \tan x$ using the values from the table.

(vii) Estimate from your graph the tan 65°.

(viii) Using a calculator find a value for tan 65° and calculate a percentage error on your estimate.

7. A graph of $\sin x$, $\cos x$ and $\tan x$ in the domain $0 \le x \le 2\pi$ is given. From this graph find values of x for which:
   (i) $\cos x = \sin x$
   (ii) $\tan x = \sin x$
   (iii) $\sin x > \cos x$
   (iv) $\tan x > \sin x > 0$

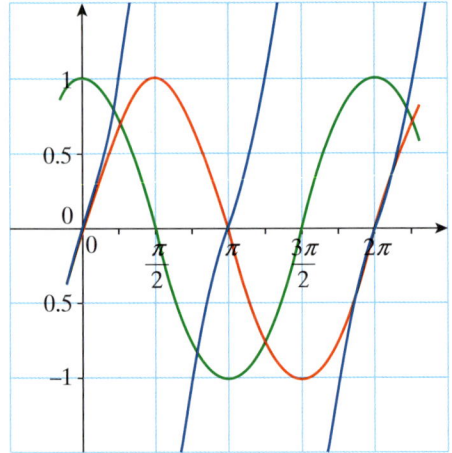

Section 3.8 Related trigonometric graphs

The main features of trigonometric graphs are:
(a) **Range:** the interval on the y-axis from the lowest to the highest value.
(b) **Midline:** a horizontal line which lies halfway between the highest and lowest points.
(c) **Amplitude:** the distance between the midline and the maximum or minimum values of the graph.
(d) **Period:** the shortest distance along the x-axis after which the graph repeats itself.

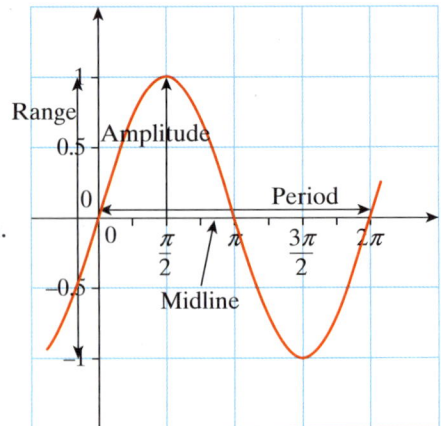

1. Changes to the amplitude, $y = b \sin x$

For $y = 2 \sin x$ every value of $\sin x$ is multiplied by 2, the graph stretches in the y direction by a factor of 2. The amplitude is now 2.

The **amplitude** of $y = b \sin x$ is $|b|$.

The period does not change, however, the range changes from $[-1, 1]$ to $[-2, 2]$.

The range of $y = \sin x$ is $[-1, 1]$

The range of $y = b \sin x$ is $[-|b|, |b|]$

Similarly $y = b \cos x$ has an amplitude of $|b|$ and a range of $[-|b|, |b|]$

If $b = -1$ then the graphs, $y = -\sin x$ and $y = -\cos x$ are reflections in the x-axis of $y = \sin x$ and $y = \cos x$ repectively.
(Note; the amplitude remains $|-1| = 1$)

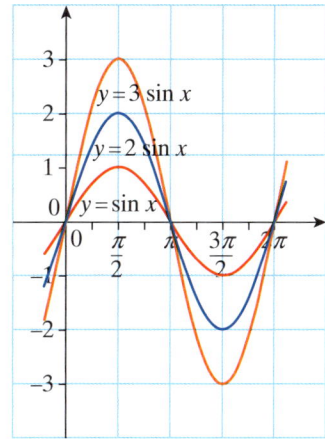

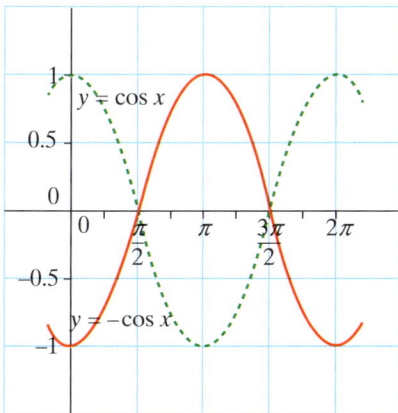

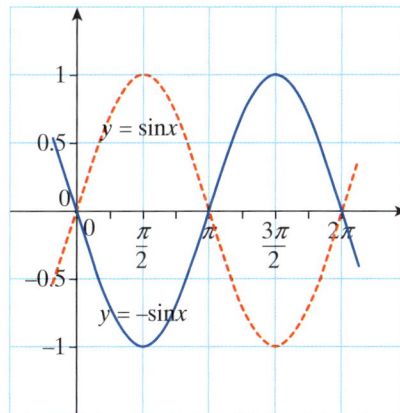

2. Changes to the period $y = \sin(cx)$

x	0°	45°	90°	135°	180°	225°	270°	315°	360°
$2x$	0°	90°	180°	270°	360°	450°	540°	630°	720°
$\sin 2x$	0	1	0	−1	0	1	0	−1	0

The graph of $y = \sin 2x$ has the same overall shape as $y = \sin x$ but the period has decreased to 180° (π radians).
In other words **two** sine curves fit into the domain 0° to 360°.

$\therefore$ for $\sin 2x$, the period is $\dfrac{360°}{2} = 180°$

In general for $y = \sin nx$, n sine waves fit into the domain 0° to 360°.

$\therefore y = \sin nx$ has a period of $\dfrac{360°}{n} = \dfrac{2\pi}{n}$.

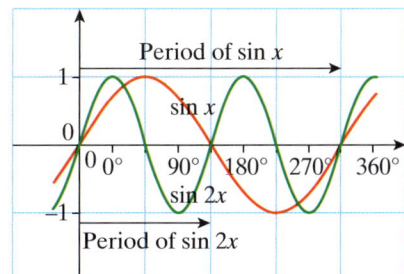

129

e.g., $y = \sin 3x$ has a period of $\dfrac{2\pi}{3}$

$\quad y = \sin\dfrac{x}{4}$ has a period of $\dfrac{2\pi}{\frac{1}{4}} = 8\pi$

Similarly $y = \cos nx$ has a period of $\dfrac{2\pi}{n}$.

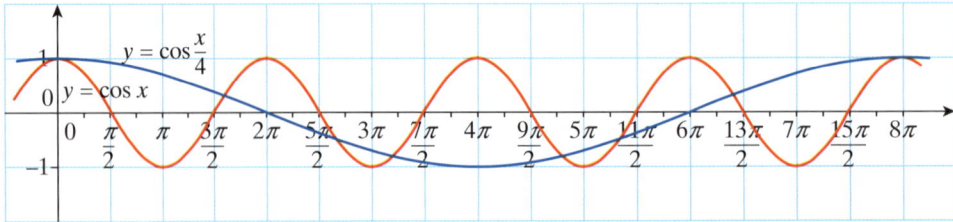

3. Graphs of the form, $y = a + b \sin (cx)$ and $y = a + b \cos (cx)$

The graph of $y = 1 + \cos x$ is obtained from the graph of $y = \cos x$ by a translation of 1 unit in the positive direction of the y-axis.

Adding 1 unit to $y = \cos x$ does not change the period or the amplitude of the function.

Adding 1 unit does change the maximum and minimum values of the function and so changes the range.

It therefore changes the mid-line as well.

The mid-line of $y = 1 + \cos x$ is $y = 1$

The range of $y = \cos x$ is $[-1, 1]$
The range of $y = 1 + \cos x$ is $[0, 2]$
The range of $y = -1 + \cos x$ is $[-2, 0]$

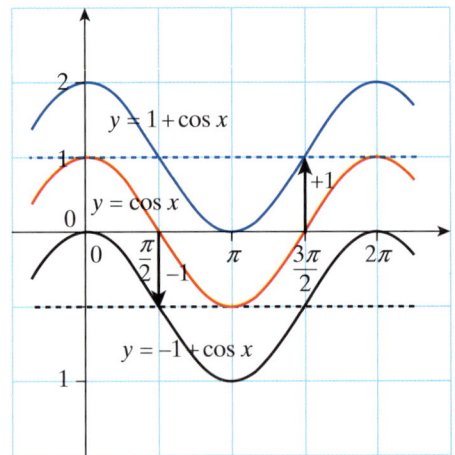

In general for graphs of the form,
$y = a + b \sin (cx)$ and $y = a + b \cos (cx)$
  (i) $y = a$ is the the mid-line
  (ii) the amplitude is $|b|$
  (iii) $y = a + |b|$ is the maximum value of
      the curve
      $y = a - |b|$ is the minimum value of
      the curve
  (iv) The range is $[a - |b|, a + |b|]$
  (v) The period is $\left(\dfrac{2\pi}{c}\right)$ radians or $\left(\dfrac{360°}{c}\right)$

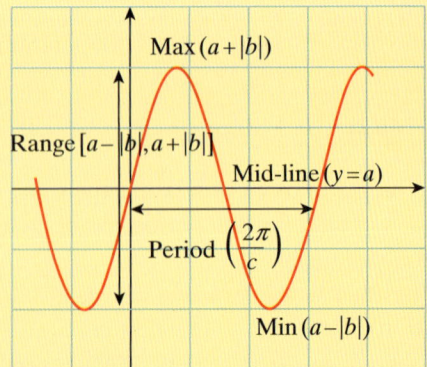

Example 1

Find the (a) amplitude (b) mid-line equation (c) range (d) maximum value
(e) minimum value (f) period of each of the following functions in terms of π.

(i) $y = 3 + 2\cos 2x$ (ii) $y = 4 - \sin 6x$ (iii) $y = -1 + 4\cos\frac{x}{2}$

(i) $y = 3 + 2\cos 2x$
   (a) amplitude = 2
   (b) mid-line equation, $y = 3$
   (c) range = $[3 - 2, 3 + 2] = [1, 5]$
   (d) max value = 5
   (e) min value = 1
   (f) period = $\frac{2\pi}{2} = \pi$ radians

(ii) $y = 4 - \sin 6x$
   (a) amplitude = 1
   (b) mid-line equation, $y = 4$
   (c) range = $[4 - 1, 4 + 1] = [3, 5]$
   (d) max value = 5
   (e) min value = 3
   (f) period = $\frac{2\pi}{6} = \frac{\pi}{3}$ radians

(iii) $y = -1 + 4\cos\frac{x}{2}$
   (a) amplitude = 4
   (b) mid-line equation, $y = -1$
   (c) range = $[-1 - 4, -1 + 4] = [-5, 3]$
   (d) max value = 3
   (e) min value = -5
   (f) period = $\frac{2\pi}{\frac{1}{2}} = 4\pi$ radians

Example 2

Part of a sine graph is shown, find
(i) the mid-line value (ii) the amplitude (iii) the period.

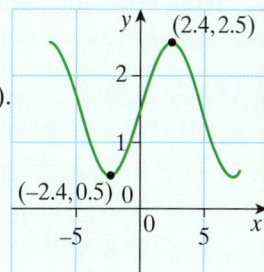

Write an equation for the graph in the form $y = a + b\sin(cx)$.

(i) the mid-line value is $y = \frac{2.5 + 0.5}{2} = 1.5 = a$

(ii) the amplitude is $(2.5 - 1.5) = 1 = |b|$
   Note: since $|b| = 1, \therefore b = \pm 1$.
   From the orientation of the graph we see that $b = 1$
   i.e. not inverted.

(iii) the x-distance between the max and min points = $\left(\frac{\text{period}}{2}\right) = 2.4 - (-2.4) = 4.8$

$$\therefore \text{ period} = 4.8 \times 2 = 9.6 = \frac{360°}{c}$$

$$\Rightarrow c = \frac{360°}{9.6} = 37.5°$$

The equation of the curve $y = 1.5 + \sin(37.5°x)$.

Example 3

A water wave represented by $y = 3 + 4 \sin (2t)$ approaches a bank represented by the y-axis.
(t measured in seconds)
  (i) Find the coordinates of the points A, C, E on the y-axis.
  (ii) Find the period of the graph and hence
  (iii) Find the coordinates of the maximum and minimum points H and I.

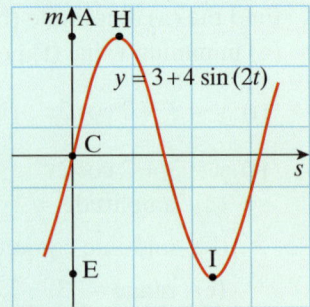

  (i) The midline of $y = 3 + 4 \sin (2t)$ is $y = 3$ ∴ C has coordinates $(0, 3)$
       The amplitude of $y = 3 + 4 \sin (2t)$ is 4 ∴ A has coordinates $(0, 7)$ and E $(0, -1)$
  (ii) The period of $y = 3 + 4 \sin (2t)$ is $\dfrac{2\pi}{2} = \pi$ seconds
  (iii) H is $\dfrac{1}{4}$ of a wave from the bank ∴ maximum has coordinates $\left(\dfrac{\pi}{4}, 7\right) = (0.79s, 7m)$

       I is $\dfrac{3}{4}$ of a wave from the bank, ∴ minimum has coordinates $\left(\dfrac{3\pi}{4}, -1\right)$

       $= (2.36s, -1m)$

Exercise 3.8

1. Find the amplitude and period of each of the following graphs:
   (i) $y = 3 \sin x$ (ii) $y = -2 \cos x$ (iii) $y = 4 \sin 4x$ (iv) $y = \dfrac{1}{4} \cos 2x$

2. Write down the period of the following graphs in radians
   (i) $y = 3 \cos 2x$ (ii) $y = -4 \sin 3x$ (iii) $y = 5 \cos \dfrac{x}{4}$ (iv) $y = \dfrac{1}{4} \cos 6x$

3. Find the range of each of the following graphs
   (i) $y = 2 \sin 4x$ (ii) $y = -5 \cos 2x$ (iii) $y = 8 \sin \dfrac{x}{8}$ (iv) $y = 6 \cos x$

4. Given $y = a \sin bx$, find possible values of a and b if
   (i) the graph has a period of π and a range of $[-3, 3]$
   (ii) the graph has a period of 4π and an amplitude of 4.

5. The diagram on the right shows the graph of the function $y = a \sin bx$.
   Write down the values of a and b.

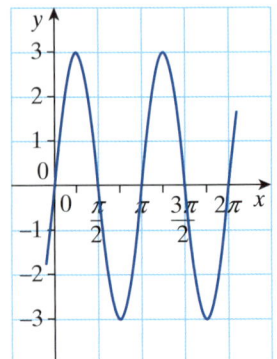

6. Write down the period and range of each of the following curves.
Hence write down the function.

(i)

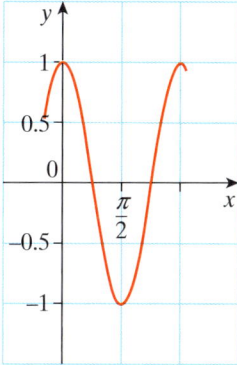

(ii)

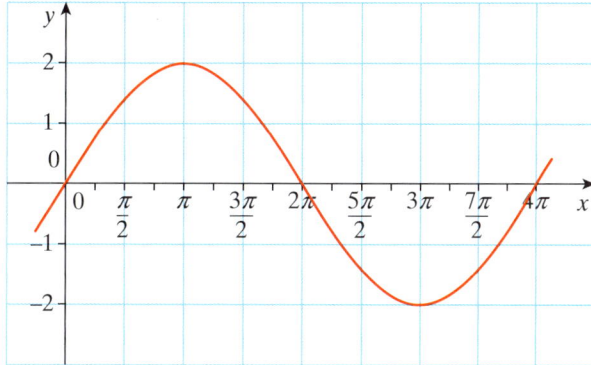

(iii)

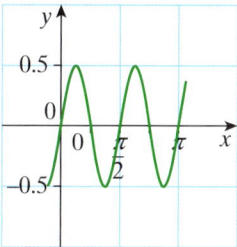

(iv)

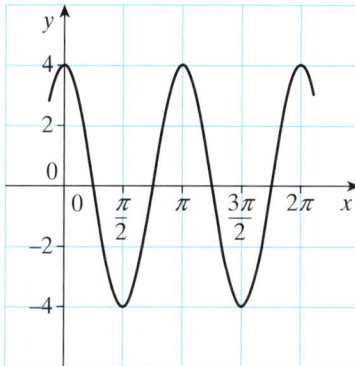

7. The graphs of three functions are shown in the diagram below. The scales on the axes are not labelled. The three functions are:

$x \rightarrow \cos 3x$

$x \rightarrow 2 \cos 3x$

$x \rightarrow 3 \cos 2x$

  (i) Identify the functions $f(x)$, $g(x)$, $h(x)$

  (ii) Write down the coordinates of
     A, B, C and D in terms of π.

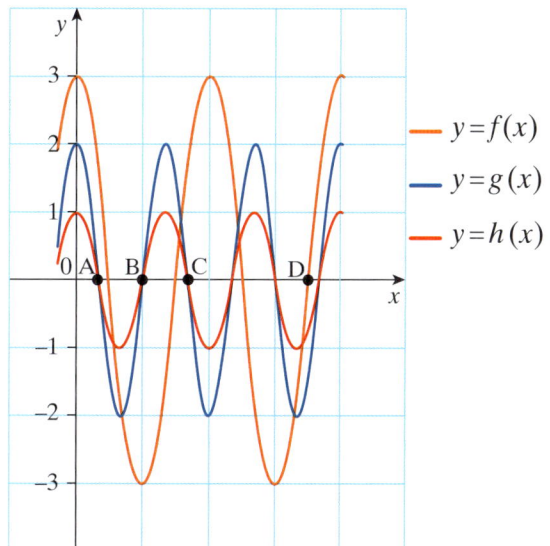

$y = f(x)$

$y = g(x)$

$y = h(x)$

133

8. Find (a) the mid-line equation (b) the range (c) the period of each of the following:

(i) $y = 4 + 2 \sin x$ (ii) $y = -1 + 2 \cos 3x$ (iii) $y = -2 - \cos 4x$ (iv) $y = 2 + 5 \cos \dfrac{x}{4}$

9. Write down (a) the mid-line equation (b) the period for each of the following curves.

(i)

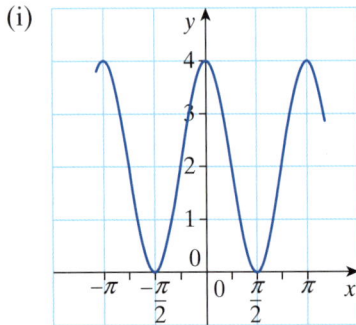

(ii)

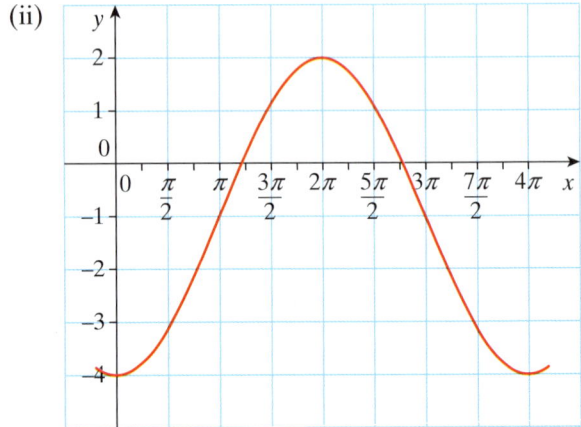

(iii)

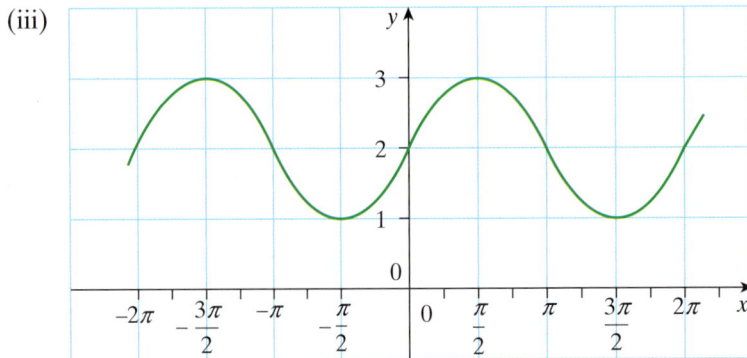

(iv)

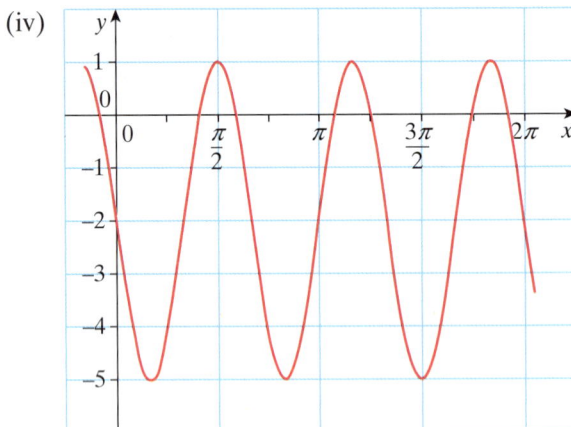

Use your answers to (a) and (b) to find a possible equation for each curve.

10. A function is defined by (i) $f(x) = 3 \cos x$ (ii) $g(x) = -2 \cos x$. Using the same axes draw a graph of both functions in the domain $0 \le x \le 360°$.

11. A function is defined by (i) $f(x) = 2 \sin 2x$ (ii) $g(x) = \cos 4x$. Using the same axes draw a graph of both functions in the domain $-360° \le x \le 360°$.

12. Write an equation for each of the curves in this graph. The curves have a common maximum after π radians. At what point will the maxima next coincide.

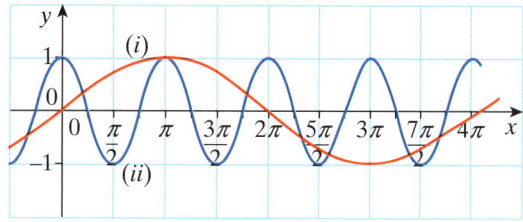

13. A scientist claims that the size of a population of rabbits on a local hillside can be modelled by the equation $N = a + b\cos ct$, where N is measured in thousands and t is measured in months and a, b and c are constants.

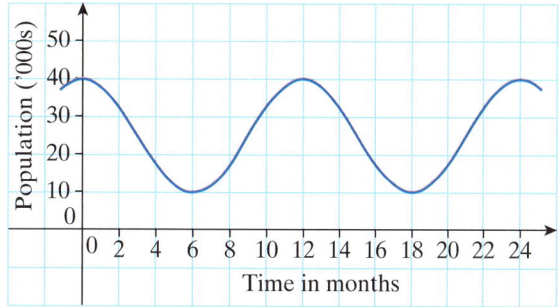

   (i) Using the graph of the function find the values of a, b and c.
   (ii) Over a three year period how many times will the population be exactly 25 000.
   (iii) From the graph estimate for how many months each year the population is below 17 500.

14. The depth of water at the entrance to a harbour, d metres, can be modelled by the equation $d = 4 + 2\sin\dfrac{\pi t}{5}$, where t is the number of hours after midnight.

   (i) Find the depth of the water at low and high tides.
   (ii) By completing the table below, sketch the graph of d over a 25 h period.
       i.e. $0 \leq t \leq 25$

t	0	2.5	5	7.5	10	12.5	15	17.5	20	22.5	25
d											

   (iii) A boat wants to enter the harbour at 2 p.m. What is the depth of the water at this time? Give your answer correct to 2 places of decimals.
   (iv) Ideally the depth of the water should be 5 m for the boat to pass safely. Estimate the times of the day it be best for the boat to pass into the harbour.

Section 3.9 General solutions of trigonometric equations

In Section 3.3 we solved equations such as $\sin x = \dfrac{\sqrt{3}}{2}$ for angles in the range $0 \leq x \leq 360°$ (or $0 \leq x \leq 2\pi$).

This generally gave us two values for the angle x.

Consider again the equation $\cos\theta = \frac{1}{2}$.

A calculator in degree mode gives an answer of $60°$.

But recall that this is only the principal value.

Check that $\theta = 300°$ and $\theta = 420°$ also work.

The equation $\cos\theta = \frac{1}{2}$ has no restriction on the set of values of θ that are solutions.

The graph below shows the function $y = \cos\theta$ and the function $y = \frac{1}{2}$.

The graph shows that there is an infinite number of solutions to the equation $\cos\theta = \frac{1}{2}$ as the graph of $y = \cos\theta$ repeats itself indefinitely.

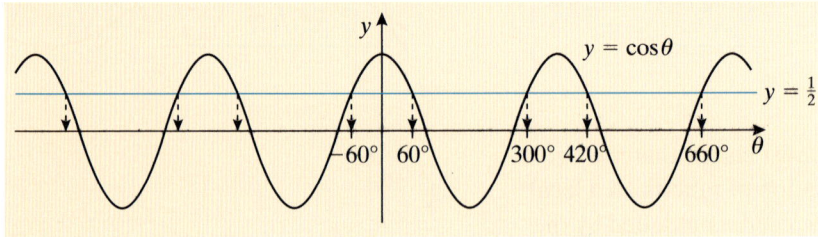

In the range $0° \leqslant \theta \leqslant 360°$, there are two values of θ for which $\cos\theta = \frac{1}{2}$.

These value are 60° and 300°.

Notice that the value $\theta = 420°$ is $60° + 360°$ and $\theta = 660°$ is $300° + 360°$.

Thus further solutions of the equation are found by repeatedly adding 360° to the angles 60° and 300°.

So the solutions to the equation $\cos\theta = \frac{1}{2}$ are

$\theta = 60° + n360°$ or $\theta = 300° + n360°$, where n is an integer.

This is called the **general solution** of the equation.

We can find the general solution of any trigonometric equation in the form $\sin\theta = k$ or $\cos\theta = k$ in the same way.

This method is given below.

Remember

> To find the general solution of $\sin x = k$ or $\cos x = k$, you find the two solutions in the interval $0° \leqslant \theta \leqslant 360°$ and then add $n360°$ to each of the solutions.

Example 1

Find the general solution of the equation $\cos\theta = -\dfrac{\sqrt{3}}{2}$, θ in radians.

$\cos\theta = \dfrac{\sqrt{3}}{2} \Rightarrow \theta = \cos^{-1}\left(\dfrac{\sqrt{3}}{2}\right) = \dfrac{\pi}{6}\ (30°) \dots$ the reference angle

cosine is negative in the 2nd and 3rd quadrants.

$\cos\theta = -\dfrac{\sqrt{3}}{2} \Rightarrow \theta = \dfrac{\pi}{6}$ in the 2nd and 3rd quadrants

$\Rightarrow \theta = \dfrac{5\pi}{6}$ or $\dfrac{7\pi}{6}$

The general solution is $2n\pi + \dfrac{5\pi}{6}$ or $2n\pi + \dfrac{7\pi}{6}$, $n \in Z$

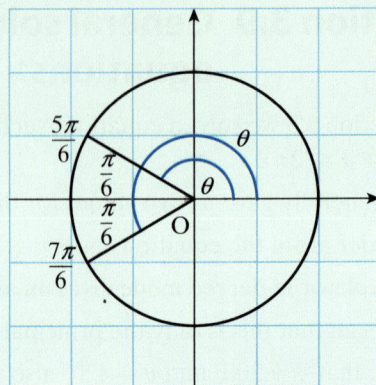

Example 2

Solve the equation $\sin 3\theta = \frac{1}{2}$, for $\theta \in R$, θ in radians.

$\sin 3\theta = \frac{1}{2} \Rightarrow 3\theta = \sin^{-1}\left(\frac{1}{2}\right) = \frac{\pi}{6}$

$\Rightarrow 3\theta = \frac{\pi}{6}$ or $\frac{5\pi}{6}$ ... sine is positive in the 1st and 2nd quadrants

All the solutions for 3θ (i.e. the general solution) are

$3\theta = 2n\pi + \frac{\pi}{6}$ or $2n\pi + \frac{5\pi}{6}$

$\Rightarrow \theta = \frac{2n\pi}{3} + \frac{\pi}{18}$ or $\frac{2n\pi}{3} + \frac{5\pi}{18}, n \in Z$

> The full general solution should be found for 3θ before dividing by 3 to find the general values for θ.

Note: The following example illustrates how we use the general solution of an equation to find all the solutions in a given interval.

Example 3

Find all the solutions for $\cos 2\theta = -\frac{1}{2}$ for $0° \leq \theta \leq 360°$.

$\cos 2\theta = -\frac{1}{2} \Rightarrow 2\theta = \cos^{-1}(-\frac{1}{2})$

$\Rightarrow 2\theta = 60°$ ... the reference angle

cosine is negative in the 2nd and 3rd quadrants.

$\Rightarrow 2\theta = 120°$ or $240°$

To find all the solutions we add $n(360°)$
to each angle.

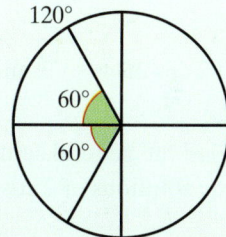

$\Rightarrow 2\theta = 120° + n(360°)$ or $2\theta = 240° + n(360°)$

$\Rightarrow \theta = 60° + n(180°)$ or $\theta = 120° + n(180°)$

To find the values of θ in the range $0° \leq \theta \leq 360°$,
we let $n = 0, 1, 2, 3, ...$

$n = 0 \Rightarrow \theta = 60°$ or $120°$

$n = 1 \Rightarrow \theta = 240°$ or $300°$

$n = 2 \Rightarrow \theta = 420°$ or $480°$

Since $420°$ and $480°$ are outside the range $0°$ to $360°$, we disregard these values.

Thus the values of θ are $60°, 120°, 240°, 300°$.

Exercise 3.9

1. Find the the two values of x for which $\sin x = \frac{1}{2}, 0 \leqslant x \leqslant 360°$.

2. Find the two solutions of the equation $\cos x = \frac{\sqrt{3}}{2}$ for $0 \leqslant x \leqslant 2\pi$.

3. If $\tan \theta = 1$, find the two solutions of the equation $y = \tan \theta$ for $0 \leqslant \theta \leqslant 2\pi$.

4. Find **all** the solutions of the equation $\sin 2\theta = \frac{1}{2}$, for $\theta \in \mathbb{R}$ and θ in radians.

5. Find the general solution of the equation $\cos 3\theta = \frac{\sqrt{3}}{2}$, for $\theta \in \mathbb{R}$ and θ in degrees.

6. Find all the solutions of the equation $\sin 3\theta = -\frac{\sqrt{3}}{2}$, for $\theta \in \mathbb{R}$ and θ in radians.

7. Find the general solution of the equation $2 \cos 4\theta = 1$, θ in radians.

8. Find the general solution of the equation $\cos 2x = -\frac{\sqrt{3}}{2}$.

   Use your answer to find all the solutions of $\cos 2x = -\frac{\sqrt{3}}{2}$, in the domain $0 \leqslant x \leqslant 4\pi$.

9. Find all the solutions of the equation $\sin 3x = -\frac{1}{\sqrt{2}}$, for $0° \leqslant x \leqslant 360°$.

10. If $2 \cos 2\theta = -\sqrt{3}$, find all the values of θ which satisfy this equation, for $0° \leqslant \theta \leqslant 360°$.

11. Find the general solution of the equation $2 \cos 3x - \sqrt{2} = 0$. Use your answer to find all the solutions of $2 \cos 3x - \sqrt{2} = 0$, in the domain $0 \leqslant x \leqslant \pi$.

12. Find the general solution of the equation $2 \cos 4\theta = \sqrt{3}$, $\theta \in \mathbb{R}$ and θ in radians.

13. Find all the solutions of the equation $\cos 3\theta = -\frac{1}{2}$, for $0° \leqslant \theta \leqslant 360°$.

14. Find, correct to the nearest degree, all the solutions of the equation $\sin 3\theta = 0.78$ for $0° \leqslant \theta \leqslant 360°$.

1. In the given triangle ABC, $|AB| = 9\,\text{cm}$, $|AC| = 8\,\text{cm}$ and $|\angle CAB| = 40°$.
   Find the area of $\triangle ABC$, in cm^2, correct to one decimal place.

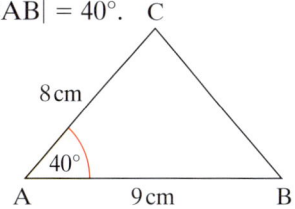

2. Find the values of θ for which $\tan\theta = -\dfrac{1}{\sqrt{3}}$, $0° \leqslant \theta \leqslant 360°$.

3. The area of the sector AOB is $240\,\text{cm}^2$.
   (i) Express θ in radians.
   (ii) Find the length of the arc AB.

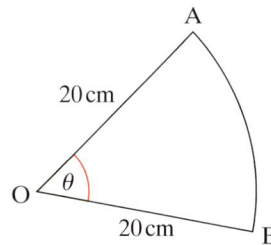

4. If $\tan\theta = \frac{3}{4}$, find the area of the given triangle without using a calculator.

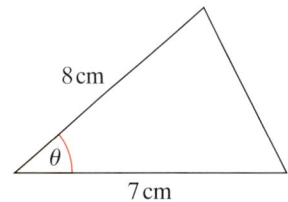

5. (i) Write down the period and range of the function graphed on the right.
   (ii) If the function is
   $$y = a \sin bx,$$
   find the values of a and b.

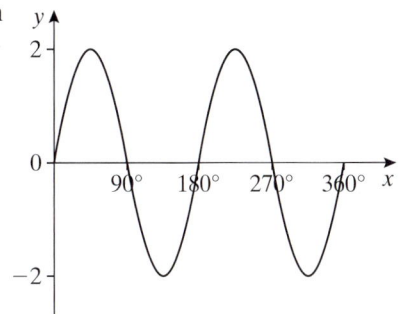

6. A square is inscribed in a circle, as shown.
   If the area of the circle is π square units,
   find the area of the square.

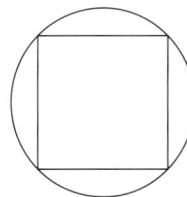

7. If $\sin\theta = -\frac{3}{5}$ and $\cos\theta = \frac{4}{5}$, find the value of $\tan\theta$ in the domain $0° \leqslant x \leqslant 360°$, without using a calculator.

8. The area of a triangle PQR is $20\,\text{cm}^2$. $|PQ| = 10\,\text{cm}$ and $|PR| = 8\,\text{cm}$.

   Find the two possible values of $|\angle QPR|$.

9. Find the values of θ for which $4\sin\theta = 3$, $0 \leqslant \theta \leqslant 360°$.
   Give each answer correct to the nearest degree.

10. If the area of the given triangle is $14\sqrt{3}$ square units,
    find the value of $\cos\theta$, giving your answer as a fraction.

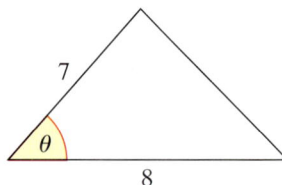

    7

    θ

    8

11. Draw a graph of the function $y = 3\sin 2x$ in the domain $0° \leqslant x \leqslant 360°$. Write down
    the period and range of the function.

Revision Exercise 3 (Advanced)

1. The lengths of the sides of a triangle are $17\,\text{cm}$, $12\,\text{cm}$ and $8\,\text{cm}$.
   (i) Find the largest angle of the triangle, correct to the nearest degree.
   (ii) Hence calculate the area of the triangle in cm^2, correct to one decimal place.

2. (i) Find all the solutions to the equation

   $$\cos 2\theta = -\frac{\sqrt{3}}{2}, \theta \in R \text{ and } \theta \text{ in radians.}$$

   (ii) AOB is a sector of a circle of centre O and radius length $4\,\text{cm}$.
        If the area of AOB is $12\,\text{cm}^2$, express θ in radians.

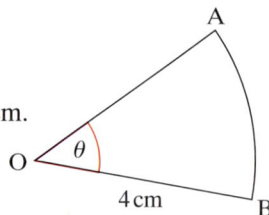

   A

   O θ

   4 cm

   B

3. The diagram represents a car bonnet, [AB], hinged at A
   and propped open by a stay, [CD].
   $|AC| = 23\,\text{cm}$, $|AB| = 47\,\text{cm}$, $|AD| = 18\,\text{cm}$ and $|CD| = 20\,\text{cm}$.
   (i) Calculate the size of angle CAD, correct to
       the nearest degree.
   (ii) Find the height of B above the level of AC, giving
        your answer correct to the nearest centimetre.

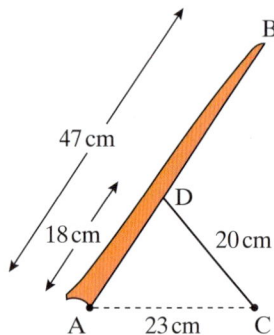

   B

   47 cm

   18 cm   D   20 cm

   A   23 cm   C

4. The diagram shows two sightings, made
   from a point O, of a helicopter flying at a height of
   1600 metres. At the first sighting, the helicopter
   was due East of O and the angle of elevation
   was 58°. One minute later it was still due
   east of O, but the angle of elevation was 45°.
   Calculate the speed of the helicopter in
   kilometres per hour, correct to the nearest
   whole number.

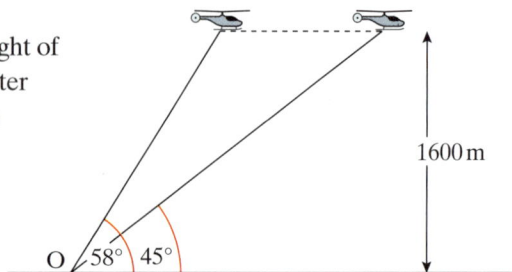

   1600 m

   O 58° 45°

5. In $\triangle ABC$, $|AB| = 10\,\text{cm}$, $|BC| = a\sqrt{3}\,\text{cm}$, $|AC| = 5\sqrt{13}\,\text{cm}$ and $|\angle ABC| = 150°$.
   Find   (i)   the value of a.   (ii)   the exact area of $\triangle ABC$.

6. The diagram shows a symmetrical drawbridge.
   When lowered, the roads [AX] and [BY] just meet in the middle.
   Calculate the length [XY], in metres, correct to one decimal place.

   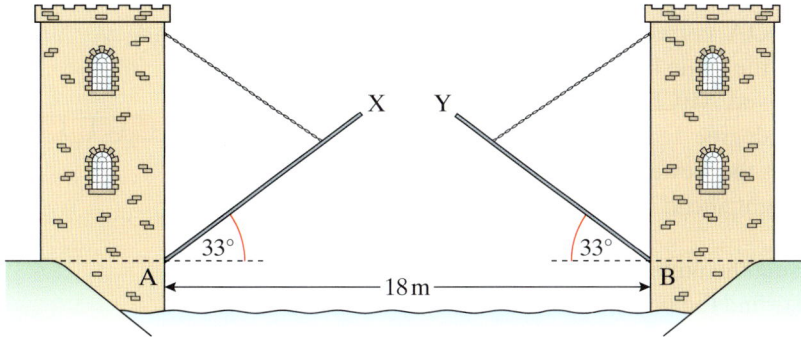

7. Two trigonometric functions f(x) and g(x) are graphed below:

   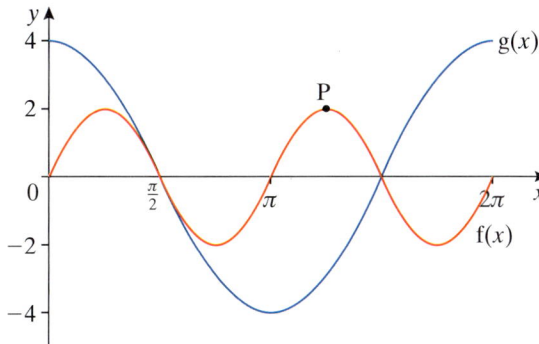

   (i)   What is the range of g(x)?   (ii)   What is the period of f(x)?
   (iii) Write down the value of g(π)   (iv)   Write down the equation of each function
   (v)   Write down the coordinates
         of the point P.

8. A rectangular paving stone 3 m by 1 m rests against a
   vertical wall as shown.
   What is the height of the highest point of the stone above
   the ground?
   Give your answer in metres, correct to two decimal places.

   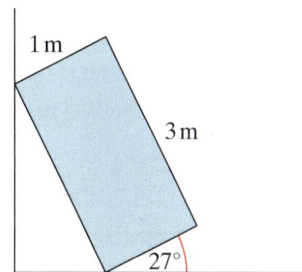

9. This viewer, as shown in the diagram, is sitting directly in front of the bottom left-hand corner of the screen. Satisfactory viewing in a cinema requires the eyes to rise through no more than 30° from the bottom to the top of the screen.

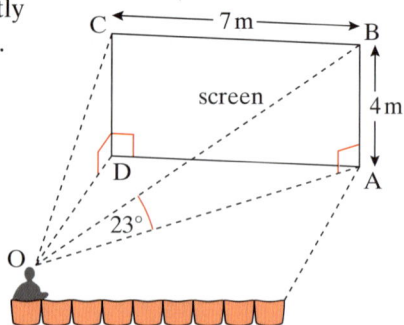

    (i) Calculate:

        (a) OA, correct to one decimal place

        (b) the angle between the two planes OAB and ABCD, correct to the nearest degree

   (ii) Does the viewer have 'satisfactory viewing' straight ahead?

10. (i) Using the dimensions shown on the given diagram,

        (a) find the perimeter of the shaded region when $\theta = 0.8$ radians

        (b) the value of θ when the perimeter of the shaded region is 14 cm.

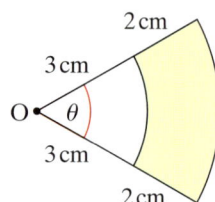

   (ii) The diagram shows two concentric circles with centre O and radii 4 cm and 6 cm. The areas of the two shaded regions are equal.

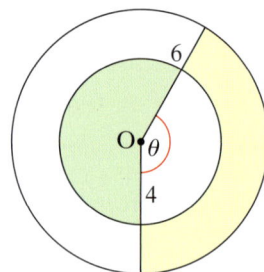

       Show that $\theta = \dfrac{8\pi}{9}$ radians.

11. Sally (S) and Kate (K) stand some distance away from a building which is 10 m high.
Sally measures the angle of elevation of the top of the building to be 35°.
From Kate's position, the angle of elevation of the top of the building is 50°.
If $|\angle SOK|$ between Sally, Kate and the bottom of the building is 60°, find the distance between Sally and Kate, correct to the nearest metre.

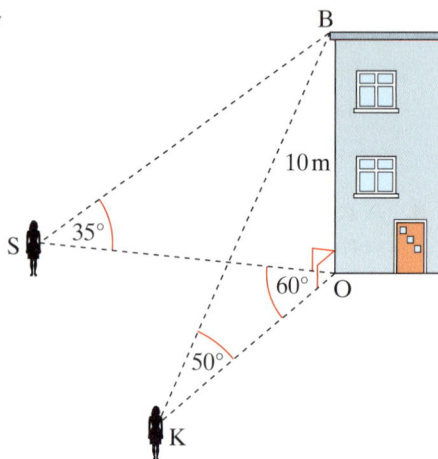

12. The two circles shown both have radius 4 cm.
The centre of each circle lies on the circumference
of the other.
Find the *exact* area which is common to both circles

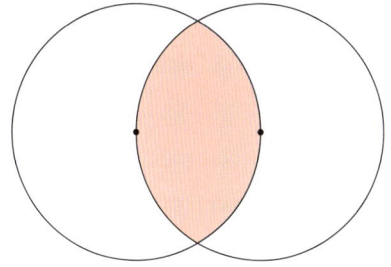

13. (i) The diagram below shows the graph of $y = 4 \cos 3x$.
Write down the coordinates of the points marked a, b, c, d, e and f.
Give the angles in radians.

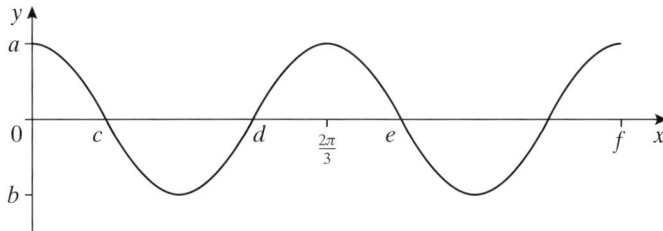

(ii) A vertical pole [PB] is erected on a sloping
piece of ground, as shown.
The ground is inclined at an angle of 15°.
At a point A on the slope and 20 metres
from the base of the pole, the angle of
elevation of the top of the pole is 38°.
Find the height of the pole, in metres,
correct to one decimal place.

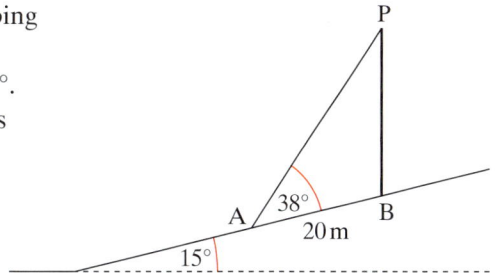

14. (i) Find the general solution to the equation $\cos 2\theta = \dfrac{\sqrt{3}}{2}$, $\theta \in R$ and θ in radians and hence

(ii) Find all the solutions to the equation $\cos 2\theta = \dfrac{\sqrt{3}}{2}$, for $0 \leqslant \theta \leqslant 2\pi$.

15. A vertical wall ABCD of
height h metres stands on
level ground. The angle
of elevation of B from the
point S is 2θ and the angle
of elevation of the point C
from S is θ, find a value for
$\tan \theta$ in the form of $\dfrac{\sqrt{a}}{b}$,
$a, b \in N$.

Given that $|SD| = 5|SA|$, find θ.

$\left[\text{Hint: } \tan 2\theta = \dfrac{2 \tan \theta}{1 - \tan^2 \theta} \right]$

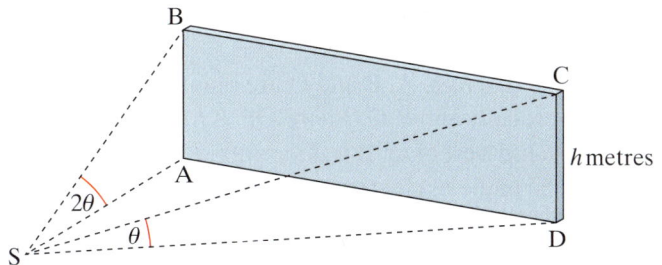

143

Revision Exercise 3 (Extended-Response Questions)

1. A ramp ADFE is made against a vertical wall BCFE.
   ADFE and BCFE are both rectangles.
   $|AB| = 20\,m$, $|AD| = 10\,m$ and $|\angle FDC| = 18°$.
   Calculate each of the following correct to
   one decimal place:
   (i) $|CF|$　　　　　　(ii) $|DF|$
   (iii) $|\angle CAD|$　　　　(iv) $|AF|$
   (v) $|\angle FAC|$

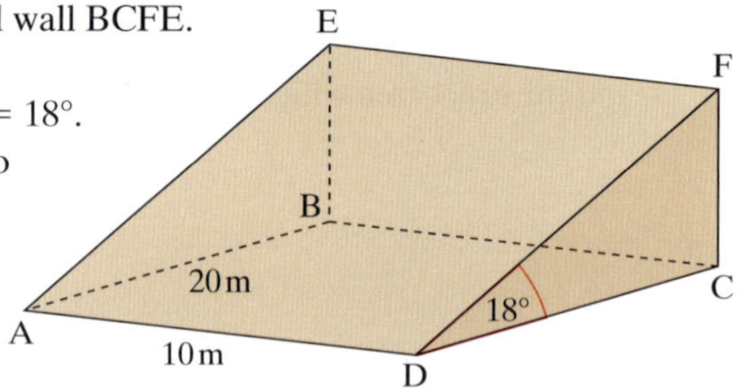

2. The figure on the right shows a rectangle ABCD
   where $|AB| = 4\,m$ and $|BC| = k$ metres.
   $$|\angle APB| = |\angle CQD| = \theta.$$
   (i) Express $|PQ|$ in terms of k and $\tan \theta$.
   (ii) If $k = 12\,m$ and $|PQ| = (12 - 4\sqrt{3})\,m$,
   find θ correct to the nearest degree.

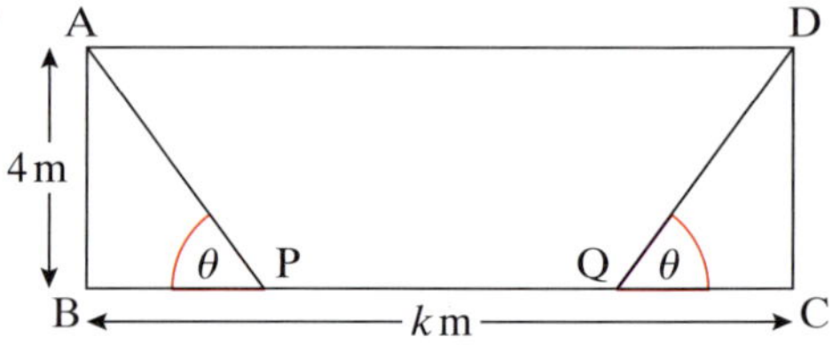

3. A, B and C are the centres of the circles k_1, k_2
   and k_3, as shown.
   The three circles touch externally and $AB \perp AC$.
   k_2 and k_3 each have radius $2\sqrt{2}$ cm.
   (i) Find, in surd form, the length of the
   radius of k_1.
   (ii) Find the area of the shaded region
   in terms of π.
   (iii) If k_1 is replaced with a circle of radius $2\sqrt{2}$ cm
   find the area of the shaded region in terms of π.

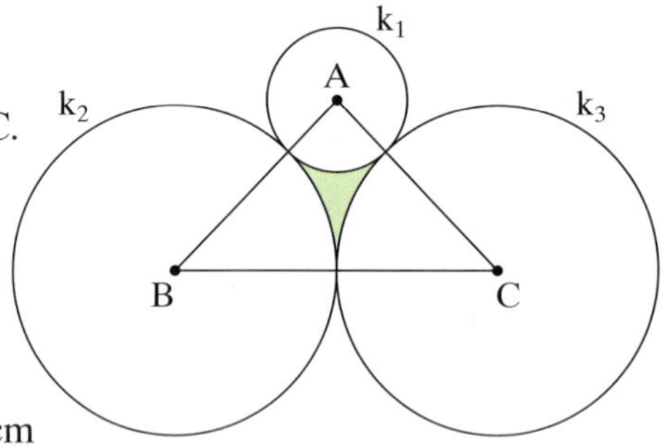

4. A triangle has sides of length a, b and c.
   The angle opposite the side of length a is A.
   (i) Prove that $a^2 = b^2 + c^2 - 2bc \cos A$
   (ii) If a, b and c are consecutive whole numbers, show that
   $$\cos A = \frac{a + 5}{2a + 4}$$

5. In the diagram, A, B and O are points in a horizontal plane and P
   is vertically above O, where $OP = h$ m.
   A is due west of O, B is due south of O and $AB = 60\,m$.
   The angle of elevation of P from A is $25°$ and the angle of
   elevation of P from B is $33°$.
   (i) Find the length [AO] in terms of h.
   (ii) Find the length [BO] in terms of h.
   (iii) Find the value of h, in metres, correct to one decimal place.

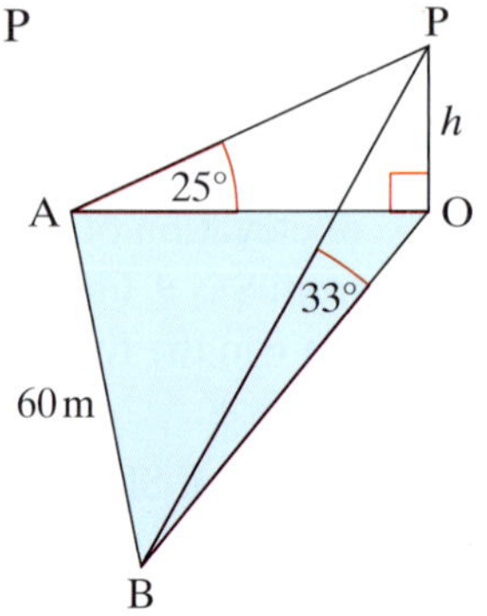

6. The depth of water at the entrance to a harbour t hours after high tide is given by the equation, $D = p + q \cos (rt)°$, where D is measured in metres and p, q and r are constants. At high tide the depth is 8 m; at low tide, 9 hours later the depth is 2 m
    (i)   Show that $r = 20$ and find the values of p and q.
    (ii) By completing the table below sketch the graph of D in the domain $0 \le t \le 18$.

t(hours)	0	4.5	9	13.5	18
D					

    (iii) Find how soon after *low tide* a ship can enter the harbour if it requires at least a depth of 3.5 m.

7. A particle moves in a straight line, OX, and its distance s(metres) from O at time t(s) is given by $s = 6 + 3 \sin(3t)$.
    *(where the angle $(3t)$ is measured in radians)
    (i)   (a) Find the greatest distance (b) the least distance from O.
    (ii) Find the first time it is at (a) the greatest distance (b) the least distance from O.
    (iii) Find the (a) amplitude (b) range of the equation.
    (iv) Find the period (in radians) correct to one place of decimals.
    (v)   Using the information in (iii) and (iv) draw a sketch of the curve for $0 \le t \le 9$.
    (vi) Find the times, correct to three places of decimals, at which the particle is 9 m from O for $0 \le t \le 9$.
    (vii) Describe the motion of the particle.

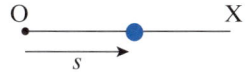

8. At 8 a.m. in the morning a computer starts collecting data from two sensors one inside and the other outside the glasshouse. On a particular day the temperature inside is given by $T_1(°C) = 22 + 3 \sin \left(\frac{\pi t}{12} \right)$ while the temperature outside is given by $T_2(°C) = 19 + 8 \sin \left(\frac{\pi t}{12} \right)$ where $t = 0$ corresponds to 8 a.m.
    (i)   Find the temperature inside and outside the glasshouse at 10 a.m.
    (ii) Find the temperature outside the glasshouse when the temperature inside is at its highest.
    (iii) Draw a sketch T_1 and T_2 on the same axes in the domain $0 \le t \le 24$.
    (iv) Find the times on this day when the temperatures inside and outside are equal.

Coordinate Geometry: The Line

Key words

equation   origin   perpendicular   parallel   intercept   translation

area   collinear   slope-intercept   internal division   ratio   centroid

circumcentre   orthocentre   linear relationship

Section 4.1 Revision of formulae

In this section we will deal with some coordinate geometry formulae that you will have met in the course of your work for the Junior Certificate. The main formulae dealing with coordinates are given below:

1. Distance between two points

The distance between $A(x_1, y_1)$ and $B(x_2, y_2)$ is $|AB| = \sqrt{(x_2 - x_1)^2 + (y_2 - y_1)^2}$

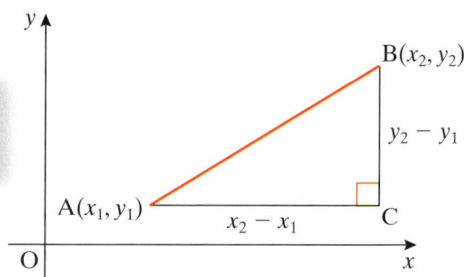

2. The midpoint of a line segment

The midpoint M of the line segment joining $A(x_1, y_1)$ and $B(x_2, y_2)$ is
$$\left(\frac{x_1 + x_2}{2}, \quad \frac{y_1 + y_2}{2}\right)$$

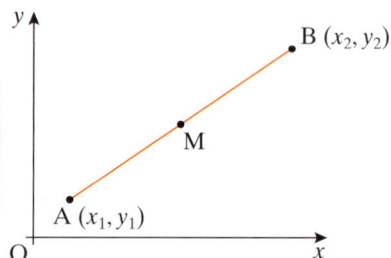

3. The slope of a line

In the diagram on the right, the slope, m, of AB is found by getting the value of

$$\frac{\text{vertical change}}{\text{horizontal change}} = \frac{y_2 - y_1}{x_2 - x_1}$$

The slope, m, of the line passing through (x_1, y_1) and (x_2, y_2) is

$$m = \frac{y_2 - y_1}{x_2 - x_1}$$

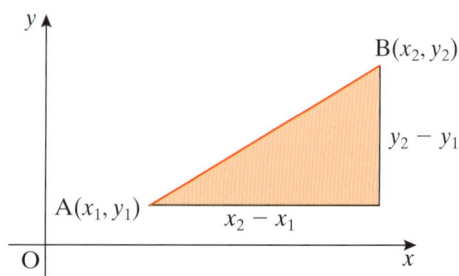

4. Positive and negative slopes

As we go from left to right, the slope is positive if the line is rising and the slope is negative if the line is falling.

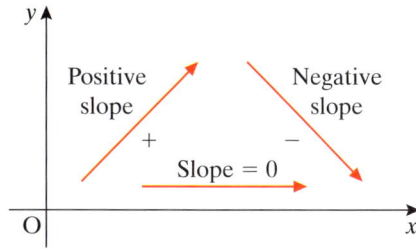

The slope of a horizontal line is zero.

5. Parallel lines

The lines a and b in the given diagram both have the slope $\frac{3}{2}$.

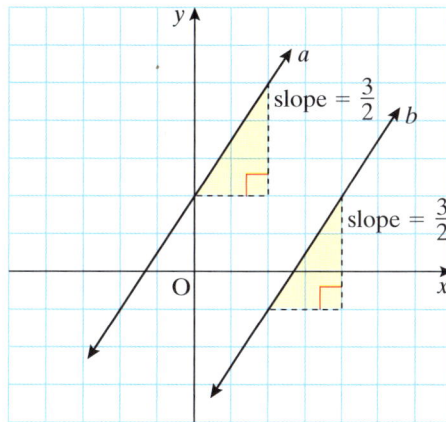

These lines are parallel.

Parallel lines have equal slopes.

6. Perpendicular lines

The given lines a and b are perpendicular.

The slope of a is $\frac{3}{2}$.

The slope of $b = -\frac{2}{3}$.

Notice that one slope is the reciprocal of the other with the sign changed.

Notice also that the product of the two slopes is -1, i.e.,

$$-\frac{2}{3} \times \frac{3}{2} = -1$$

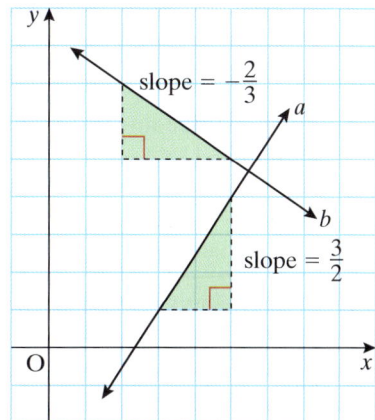

If two lines are perpendicular, the product of their slopes is -1, i.e.,
$$m_1 \times m_2 = -1$$

147

Example 1

A(3, 1), B(2, −3) and C(−1, k) are three points in the plane.
If AB ⊥ AC, find the value of k.

A(3, 1) and B(2, −3)

Slope of AB $= \dfrac{y_2 - y_1}{x_2 - x_1}$

$= \dfrac{-3 - 1}{2 - 3}$

$= \dfrac{-4}{-1} = 4$

A(3, 1) and C(−1, k)

Slope of AC $= \dfrac{k - 1}{-1 - 3}$

$= \dfrac{k - 1}{-4}$

If AB ⊥ AC, then the product of the slopes equals −1.

$\Rightarrow \quad 4 \times \dfrac{k - 1}{-4} = -1$

$\Rightarrow \quad \dfrac{4(k - 1)}{-4} = -1$

$\Rightarrow \quad \dfrac{4(k - 1)}{4} = 1 \quad \Rightarrow \quad k - 1 = 1$

$\Rightarrow \qquad\qquad k = 2$

Exercise 4.1

1. Given three points A(−1, 3), B(3, −2) and C(5, 2).
   Find   (i) |AB| (ii) |BC| (iii) the slope of AC   (iv) the midpoint of [BC].

2. Find M, the midpoint of the line segment joining A(1, −6) and B(−3, 4).
   Hence show that |AM| = |MB|.

3. The slope of a line ℓ is $\frac{3}{4}$.
   (i) What is the slope of any line parallel to ℓ?
   (ii) What is the slope of any line perpendicular to ℓ?

4. A(2, 3), B(−2, 1), C(−1, −2) and D(5, 1) are four points in the plane.
   Show that AB is parallel to CD.

5. Show that the line through A(−1, 1) and B(1, 3) is perpendicular to the line through C(6, 2) and D(4, 4).

6. If the line through (−2, 0) and (4, 3) is parallel to the line through (1, −1) and (k, 1), find the value of k.

7. The straight line passing through the points A(−1, 1) and B(−P, 13) has slope 2.
   Find the value of P.

8. The coordinates of the points A, B and C are (−2, 3), (2, 5) and (4, 1) respectively.
   (i) Find the gradients of the lines AB, BC and CA.
   (ii) Hence or otherwise show that triangle ABC is a right-angled triangle.

9. The diagram shows four lines a, b, c and d.

   (i) Which lines have positive slopes?

   (ii) Which lines have negative slopes?

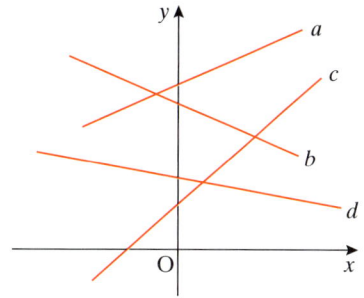

10. Three line segments [AB], [CD] and [EF] are drawn on the grids below.

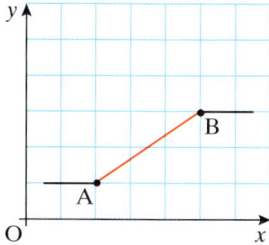

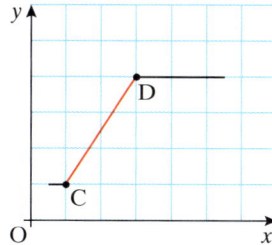

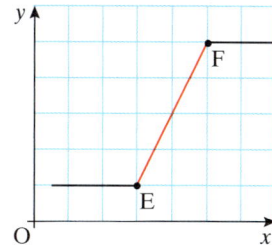

Write down the slope of each line segment.

11. Why is the slope of the given line negative?
Use the grid to work out the slope of the line.

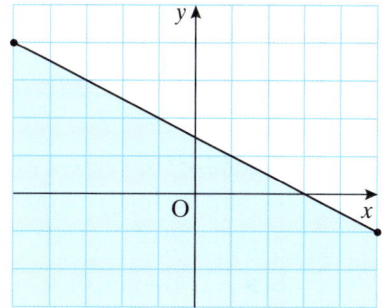

12. P$(a, 4)$, Q$(2, 3)$, R$(3, -1)$ and S$(-2, 4)$ are four points.
If $|PQ| = |RS|$, find the possible values of a.

13. P$(5, 6)$, Q$(k, 2)$ and R$(9, -1)$ are three points such that PQ is perpendicular to QR.
Find the two values of k.

14. The points A$(-1, -2)$, B$(7, 2)$ and C$(k, 4)$, where k is a constant, are the vertices of a triangle ABC. The angle ABC is a right angle.

   (i) Find the slope of AB.

   (ii) Find the slope of BC and hence find the value of k.

   (iii) Show that the length of [AB] may be written in the form $p\sqrt{5}$, where p is an integer to be found.

   (iv) Given that the area of a triangle is half the length of the base multiplied by the perpendicular height, find the exact value of the area of $\triangle$ABC.

15. A triangle has vertices P$(-2, 2)$, Q$(q, 0)$ and R$(5, 3)$.

   (i) The side PQ is twice as long as side QR. Find the possible values of q.

   (ii) Show that triangle PQR is right-angled when $q = 4$.

Section 4.2 The area of a triangle

The area of the triangle with vertices $(0, 0)$, (x_1, y_1) and (x_2, y_2) is

$$\text{Area} = \tfrac{1}{2}|x_1 y_2 - x_2 y_1|$$

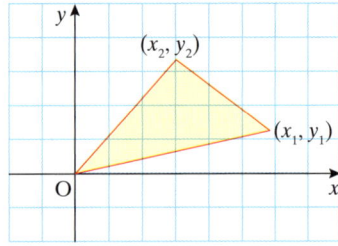

Example 1

Find the area of the triangle with vertices $(0, 0)$, $(-2, 1)$ and $(3, 4)$.

$$\begin{aligned}
\text{Area} &= \tfrac{1}{2}|x_1 y_2 - x_2 y_1| \\
&= \tfrac{1}{2}|(-2)(4) - (3)(1)| \\
&= \tfrac{1}{2}|-8 - 3| \\
&= \tfrac{1}{2}|-11| \\
&= 5\tfrac{1}{2} \text{ square units}
\end{aligned}$$

$(x_1, y_1) \qquad (x_2, y_2)$
$\downarrow \qquad\qquad \downarrow$
$(-2, 1) \qquad (3, 4)$

The modulus symbol $|\,|$ indicates that we take the positive value of the answer.

Note: If none of the vertices of the triangle is at the origin, we find the image of the triangle under a translation so that one of the vertices is $(0, 0)$.

Let $(2, 4) \rightarrow (0, 0)$
$(7, 3) \rightarrow (5, -1)$
$(4, 1) \rightarrow (2, -3)$

Here we take 2 from each x-value and 4 from each y-value for each of the points.

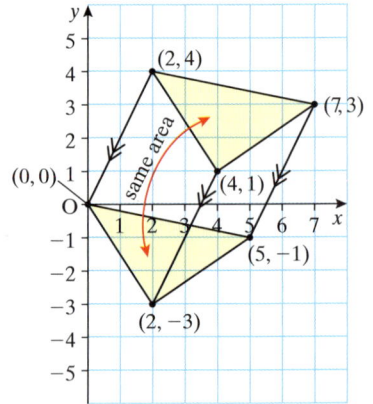

Example 2

Find the area of the triangle with vertices $(1, 5)$, $(-3, 1)$ and $(3, -5)$.

Let $(1, 5) \quad \rightarrow (0, 0)$
$(-3, 1) \rightarrow (-4, -4)$
$(3, -5) \rightarrow (2, -10)$

Here we take 1 from each x-value and 5 from each y-value.

$$\text{Area of triangle} = \tfrac{1}{2}|x_1 y_2 - x_2 y_1|$$

$$= \tfrac{1}{2}|(-4)(-10) - (2)(-4)|$$

$$= \tfrac{1}{2}|40 + 8|$$

$$= \tfrac{1}{2}|48|$$

$$= 24 \text{ square units}$$

$$
\begin{array}{cc}
(x_1, y_1) & (x_2, y_2) \\
\downarrow & \downarrow \\
(-4, -4) & (2, -10)
\end{array}
$$

Note: To find the area of a quadrilateral, divide it into two triangles.

Exercise 4.2

1. Find the area of the triangle whose vertices are
   (i) $(0, 0)$, $(2, 1)$, $(3, 4)$ (iii) $(0, 0)$, $(-2, 3)$, $(1, -4)$
   (ii) $(0, 0)$, $(5, 1)$, $(3, 6)$ (iv) $(0, 0)$, $(3, 4)$, $(-2, -6)$

2. $A(2, 3)$, $B(-5, 1)$ and $C(3, 1)$ are the vertices of a triangle.
   By using the translation $A(2, 3) \to (0, 0)$, find the images of B and C under this translation. Hence find the area of the triangle ABC.

3. By translating one of the vertices to $(0, 0)$, find the area of each of the triangles whose vertices are
   (i) $(2, 3)$, $(5, 1)$ and $(2, 0)$ (ii) $(-2, 3)$, $(4, 0)$ and $(1, -4)$

4. $A(0, 0)$, $B(4, -1)$, $C(2, 3)$ and $D(-2, 4)$ are the vertices of a quadrilateral.
   Find the area of the quadrilateral by dividing it into the two triangles ABC and ACD.

5. $A(0, 0)$, $B(1, 6)$ and $C(-1, k + 1)$ are the vertices of a triangle.
   If the area of the triangle ABC is 7 square units, find two values for k.

6. $A(4, 1)$, $B(-1, -3)$ and $C(3, k)$ are the vertices of a triangle.
   If the area of the triangle ABC is 12 square units, find the two values of k.

7. Find the values of k if the area of the given triangle is 7 square units.

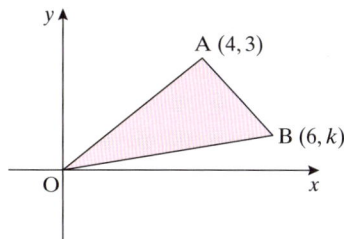

8. Find the area of the triangle whose vertices are $(0, 0)$, $(1, 3)$ and $(2, 6)$.
   What conclusion can you draw from your answer?

9. The area of the triangle with vertices $(-2, -1)$, $(1, 2)$ and $(k, 13)$ is 6. Find the values of k.

10. A triangle has coordinates $A(2, 1)$, $B(b, 3)$ and $C(5, 5)$, where $b > 3$.
    If $|\angle ABC| = 90°$, find the value of b. Hence find the area of the triangle ABC.

11. The points P(2, −1), Q(8, k) and R(11, 2) are three collinear points. By finding the area of the 'triangle' PQR, or otherwise, find the value of k.

> Collinear points lie on the same straight line.

12. The diagram shows a triangle whose vertices are A(−2, 1), B(1, 7) and C(3, 1). The point L is the foot of the perpendicular from A to BC, and M is the foot of the perpendicular from B to AC.

    (i) Using [AC] as base, write down the area of △ABC.

    (ii) Find |BC|.

    (iii) Using your answers to part (i) and (ii), find the length of [AL].

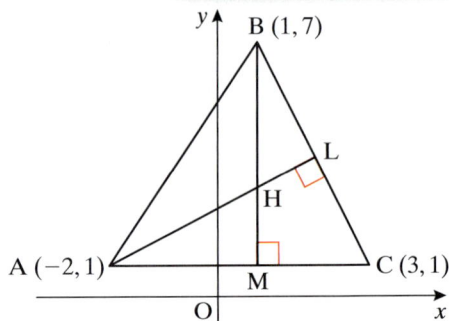

Section 4.3 The equation of a line

The equation of a line is generally given in the form **$ax + by + c = 0$**, e.g., $2x + 3y − 12 = 0$. This may be described as the **general form of the equation of a line**.

To find the equation of a line, we generally need to know
(i) a **point** on the line
(ii) the **slope** of the line.

If (x_1, y_1) is a point on the line and m is the slope, we then use $y − y_1 = m(x − x_1)$ to find the equation of the line.

> The equation of a line with slope m and containing the point (x_1, y_1) is
> $$y − y_1 = m(x − x_1)$$

The equation $y = mx + c$

If the equation of a line is in the form

    $y = mx + c$, then

(i) the slope is m
(ii) the line intersects the y-axis at $(0, c)$.

c is the value of y at the point where the line crosses the y-axis and is called the y intercept.

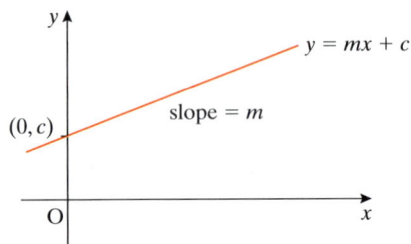

The equation $y = mx + c$ is generally referred to as the **slope-intercept** form of the equation of a line.

If the equation of a line is in the form $2x + 3y − 7 = 0$, we express it in the form $y = mx + c$. The slope is m.

For example, if $3x − 4y + 3 = 0$, then

$$−4y = −3x − 3$$
$$\Rightarrow 4y = 3x + 3 \Rightarrow y = \frac{3}{4}x + \frac{3}{4} \Rightarrow m = \frac{3}{4}$$

Note: The slope of a line is defined as the tangent of the angle which the line makes with the **positive** direction of the x-axis.

1. If the angle is less than $90°$, the slope is positive.

2. If the angle is between $90°$ and $180°$, the slope is negative.

3. $\tan 45° = 1$; $\tan 135° = -1$

Example 1

Find the equation of the line through the point $(-2, 3)$ which is perpendicular to the line $2x - y + 5 = 0$.

To find the slope of $2x - y + 5 = 0$, we express it in the form $y = mx + c$.

$$2x - y + 5 = 0$$
$$\Rightarrow \quad -y = -2x - 5$$
$$\Rightarrow \quad y = 2x + 5... \qquad \text{multiply each term by } -1$$
$$\Rightarrow \quad \text{the slope is 2.}$$

The slope of the line perpendicular to this line is $-\dfrac{1}{2}$.

Equation of line through $(-2, 3)$ with slope $-\dfrac{1}{2}$ is:

$$y - y_1 = m(x - x_1) \qquad (x_1, y_1) = (-2, 3)$$
$$y - 3 = -\frac{1}{2}(x + 2) \qquad m = -\frac{1}{2}$$
$$y - 3 = \frac{-x}{2} - 1$$
$$\Rightarrow \quad 2y - 6 = -x - 2... \qquad \text{multiply each term by 2}$$
$$\Rightarrow \quad x + 2y - 4 = 0 \text{ is the required equation.}$$

More difficult problems

To find the equation of a line (or lines) we generally require two pieces of information.

From the information given it may not be possible to find a point on the line and the slope of the line immediately. When dealing with more difficult problems, the following approaches should prove useful.

1. The equation of any line through the point $(3, 4)$, for example, is $y - \mathbf{4} = m(x - \mathbf{3})$,
   i.e. $mx - y - 3m + 4 = 0$.
   A second condition should enable us to find the value or values of m.

2. The equation of any line parallel to $\mathbf{2x - 3y + 8 = 0}$ is $2x - 3y + c = 0$.
   The equation of any line perpendicular to $2x - 3y + 8 = 0$ is $3x + 2y + k = 0$.

> The equation of any line parallel to $ax + by + c = 0$ is $ax + by + k = 0$.
> The equation of any line perpendicular to $ax + by + c = 0$ is $bx - ay + k = 0$.

To find where a line intersects the axes

To find the point of intersection of a line and
(i) the x-axis, let $y = 0$ and find the x-value
(ii) the y-axis, let $x = 0$ and find the y-value.

Example 2

Find the value of k if the lines $2x + ky + 5 = 0$ and $(k + 6)x + 2y - 9 = 0$ are perpendicular to each other.

$2x + ky + 5 = 0 \Rightarrow$ the slope $m_1 = \dfrac{-2}{k}$

$(k + 6)x + 2y - 9 = 0 \Rightarrow$ the slope $m_2 = \dfrac{-(k + 6)}{2}$

Since the lines are perpendicular, $m_1 \times m_2 = -1$.

$\Rightarrow \quad \dfrac{-(k + 6)}{2}\left(\dfrac{-2}{k}\right) = -1$

$\Rightarrow \quad \dfrac{2(k + 6)}{2k} = -1$

$\Rightarrow \quad k + 6 = -k$

$\Rightarrow \quad 2k = -6$

$\Rightarrow \quad k = -3$

Example 3

Find the equations of the line l through the point $(4, 2)$ so that the area of the triangle formed by l and the positive x and y-axes is 25 square units.

Equation of any line through $(4, 2)$ is
$\qquad y - 2 = m(x - 4)$
i.e. $mx - y + 2 - 4m = 0$
l intersects the x-axis at $y = 0$

$y = 0 \Rightarrow x = \dfrac{4m - 2}{m}$

$x = 0 \Rightarrow y = 2 - 4m$

Area of shaded $\triangle = \dfrac{1}{2}\left(\dfrac{4m - 2}{m}\right)(2 - 4m)$

Area $= 25 \Rightarrow \dfrac{1}{2}\left(\dfrac{4m - 2}{m}\right)(2 - 4m) = 25$

$\Rightarrow (4m - 2)(2 - 4m) \quad = 50m$

$\Rightarrow 8m - 16m^2 - 4 + 8m = 50m$

$\Rightarrow 16m^2 + 34m + 4 \quad = 0$

$\Rightarrow (16m + 2)(m + 2) \quad = 0$

$\Rightarrow m = -\dfrac{1}{8}$ or $m \quad = -2$

$\therefore$ the equations of the line l are

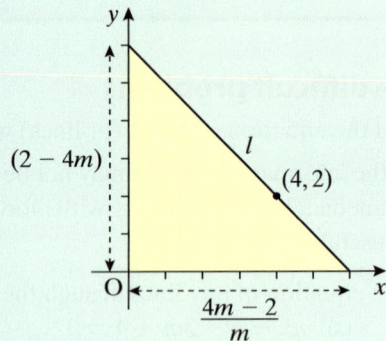

(i) $y - 2 = -\dfrac{1}{8}(x - 4)$ or   (ii) $y - 2 = -2(x - 4)$

$\Rightarrow 8y - 16 = -x + 4$ $\Rightarrow y - 2 = -2x + 8$

$\Rightarrow x + 8y - 20 = 0$ $\Rightarrow 2x + y - 10 = 0$

$\therefore$ the two equations are $x + 8y - 20 = 0$ and $2x + y - 10 = 0$

Note: To verify that a point is on a given line, we substitute the coordinates of x and y into the equation of the line. If the coordinates satisfy the equation, then the point is on the line.

For example, the point $(-3, 2) \in 2x - 4y + 14 = 0$, because
$$2(-3) - 4(2) + 14 = -6 - 8 + 14$$
$$= 0$$

Exercise 4.3

1. Find the equation of the line through

   (i) $(4, -1)$ with slope 3   (ii) $(-5, -2)$ with slope -2.

2. Find the equation of the line through $(-3, 1)$ with slope $\frac{2}{3}$.

3. l is the line $x - 3y + 4 = 0$

   (i) Write down the slope of l.
   (ii) Find the equation of the line through $(3, -4)$ parallel to l.

4. $A(3, -1)$, $B(4, 5)$ and $C(-2, 1)$ are three points in the plane.
   Find   (i)   the slope of AB
              (ii)   the equation of the line through C perpendicular to AB.

5. If the line $2x - 3y + 5 = 0$ is perpendicular to $3x + ky - 8 = 0$, find the value of k.

6. Find the value of t if the lines $3x + 4y = 7$ and $2y - tx - 6 = 0$ are perpendicular.

7. Find the value of k if the line $2x + ky - 8 = 0$ contains the point $(3, 1)$.

8. Write down the coordinates of the points where the line $x - 3y - 6 = 0$ intersects the x-axis and y-axis.

9. The line h contains the points $(6, -2)$ and $(-4, 10)$.
   The equation of the line k is $ax + 6y + 12 = 0$ and k is perpendicular to h.
   Find the value of the real number a.

10. The line $2x - 3y + 6 = 0$ intersects the x-axis at the point C.
    (i) Find the coordinates of C.
    (ii) Now find the equation of the line which contains the point C and which is perpendicular to $2x - 3y + 6 = 0$.

11. (a) Write down the slope of the line k in the given diagram.
Now find the equation of the line k in the form $ax + by + c = 0$.

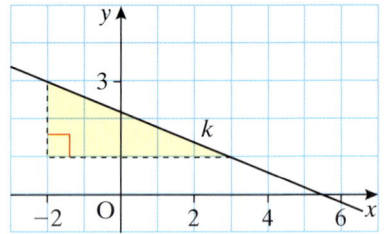

(b) Hence find the coordinates of the x and y axis intercepts.

12. By finding the slopes of the following points of lines, state whether they are parallel, perpendicular or neither.

(i) $y = 3x$ $x = 3y$
(ii) $2x + y = 1$ $x - 2y = 1$
(iii) $2x + 3y = 4$ $2y = 3x - 2$
(iv) $x + 2y - 1 = 0$ $x + 2y + 1 = 0$
(v) $y = 2x - 1$ $2x - y + 3 = 0$
(vi) $x + 3y - 2 = 0$ $y = 3x + 2$

13. Use simultaneous equations to find the point of intersection of the lines $x + 2y = 1$ and $2x + 3y = 4$.

14. Find the point of intersection of the lines $x + y = 5$ and $2x - y = 1$.
Now find the equation of the line which contains this point of intersection and has slope $\frac{2}{3}$.

15. Find the equation of the line that is parallel to the line $3x - y + 4 = 0$ and which contains the point of intersection of the lines $2x + 3y = 12$ and $3x - 4y = 1$.

16. (i) Verify that $(2, 6)$ is on the line $x - 2y + 10 = 0$.

(ii) If the line $2x + ky - 12 = 0$ contains the point $(3, 2)$, find the value of k.

17. The line $\ell_1: 3x - 2y + 7 = 0$ and the line $\ell_2: 5x + y + 3 = 0$ intersect at the point P. Find the equation of the line through P perpendicular to ℓ_2.

18. Find in terms of k the coordinates of the points where the line $3x + 4y = k$ cuts the x-axis and y-axis.
If the area of the triangle formed by $3x + 4y = k$ and the positive x and y axes is 24 square units, find the value of k.

19. Write down the equation of any line parallel to $2x - 3y + 8 = 0$.
If a particular parallel line contains the point $(4, 2)$, find its equation.

20. Write down the equation of any line parallel to $\ell: 4x + y = 6$.
Hence find the equation of the line parallel to ℓ which forms a triangle of area 18 square units in the first quadrant.

21. An aircraft flight-path takes a plane directly over a beacon B(36, −4) heading to the airport at A(4, −75).
There is a proposal to build a school at C(20, −36).

(a) Check if the flight path [BA] passes over the school.

(b) If not, find out how far (directly) east or west of C, the aircraft would be, if flown along this flight path, give your answer correct to 2 places of decimals.

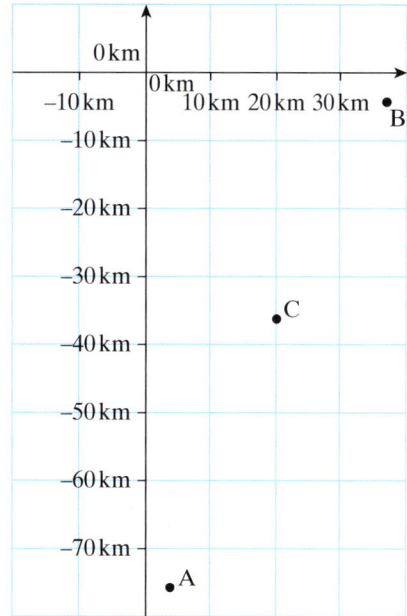

Section 4.4 Dividing a line segment in a given ratio

Internal division

In the given diagram, the point C divides the line segment [PQ] in the ratio $a : b$.
The coordinates of C are given by the formula,

$$C = \left(\frac{bx_1 + ax_2}{b + a}, \frac{by_1 + ay_2}{b + a} \right)$$

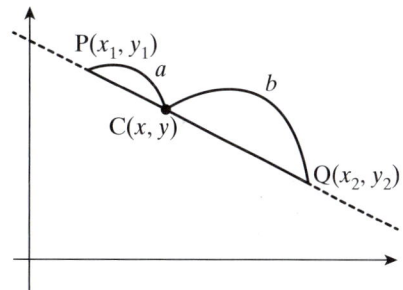

Example 1

Find the coordinates of the point which divides the line segment A(−1, 3) and B(4, −2) in the ratio $h : k = 2 : 1$.

$$A(−1, 3) \qquad B(4, −2) \qquad h : k = 2 : 1$$

$$(x_1, y_1) \qquad \quad (x_2, y_2)$$

$$\text{Internal divisor} = \left(\frac{hx_2 + kx_1}{h + k}, \frac{hy_2 + ky_1}{h + k} \right)$$

$$= \left(\frac{(2)(4) + (1)(−1)}{2 + 1}, \frac{(2)(−2) + (1)(3)}{2 + 1} \right)$$

$$= \left(\frac{7}{3}, −\frac{1}{3} \right)$$

Exercise 4.4

1. Find the coordinates of the point which divides the line segment A$(-3, 4)$ and B$(5, -4)$ in the ratio $4:1$.

2. Find the coordinates of the point P which divides the line segment X$(-5, 8)$ and Y$(3, -8)$ in the ratio $3:1$.

3. Find the coordinates of the point which divides the line segment joining $(2, -3)$ and $(4, 6)$ in the ratio $5:2$.

4. A line segment joins A$(5, 0)$ and B$(1, -2)$.
    Find the coordinates of the point which divides [AB] in the ratio $3:2$.

5. The extremities of a line segment are A$(2, 3)$ and B$(5, 7)$.
    Find the point (x, y) which divides [AB] in the ratio $3:1$.

6. The line segment A$(-2, -1)$ and B$(3, 4)$ is produced to C such that $|AC|:|CB| = 4:1$.
    Find the coordinates of C.

7. A$(2, -3)$ and B(x, y) are two points in the plane.
    The point P$(6, 1)$ divides [AB] in the ratio $2:1$.
    Find the values of x and y. By plotting the points $(2, -3)$, $(6, 1)$ and (x, y) show how the same result can be obtained by translation.

8. The point P$(-6, y)$ divides the line segment A$(-10, 7)$ and B$(x, -5)$ in the ratio $1:3$.
    Find the values of x and y.

9. A$(x, 0)$ and B$(0, y)$ are two points in the plane.
    The point C$(9, -8)$ divides [AB] in the ratio $4:3$.
    Find the values of x and y.

10. A$(4, -3)$ and B$(-2, 0)$ are the end points of a line segment.
    The point P$(2, -2)$ divides [AB] in the ratio $h:k$.
    Find the ratio $h:k$.

Section 4.5 Concurrencies of a triangle

The line which joins a vertex of a triangle to the midpoint of the opposite side is called a **median**.

In the given triangle [AM] is the median.

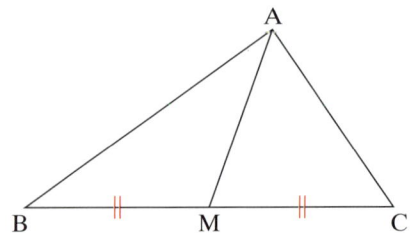

1. The Centroid

The given diagram shows the three medians [AE], [BF] and [CD] intersecting at the point G.

G is called the **centroid** of the triangle.

The medians of a triangle divide each other in the ratio $2:1$.

In the given triangle,

$|AG|:|GE| = 2:1$; $|BG|:|GF| = 2:1$ and

$|CG|:|GD| = 2:1$.

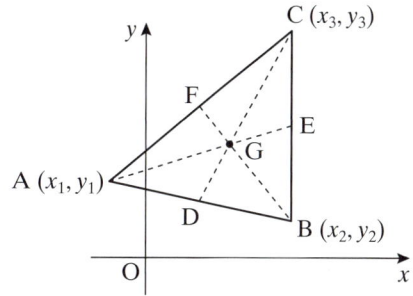

> If $A(x_1, y_1)$, $B(x_2, y_2)$ and $C(x_3, y_3)$ are the coordinates of the vertices of a triangle, then the coordinates of the centroid, G, are
> $$G = \left(\frac{x_1 + x_2 + x_3}{3}, \frac{y_1 + y_2 + y_3}{3} \right)$$

2. The circumcentre

The circumcentre of a triangle is the point of intersection of the **mediators** (the perpendicular bisectors of the sides) of a triangle.

The line segment from a vertex of a triangle to the circumcentre is the radius of the circumcircle. This is shown here as r.

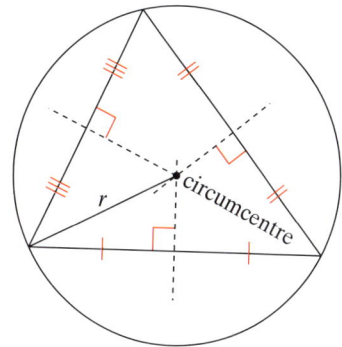

3. The orthocentre

The orthocentre of a triangle is the point of intersection of the perpendiculars from the vertices to the opposite sides.

In the given triangle, H is the orthocentre.

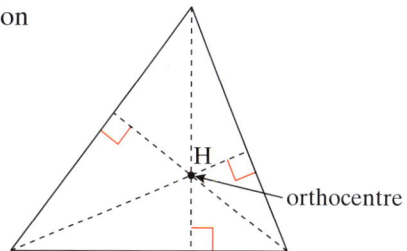

Example 1

The vertices of a triangle are $A(-4, 3)$, $B(0, -5)$ and $C(3, 4)$.
Find the coordinates of
(i) the centroid   (ii) the orthocentre of the triangle.

(i) Centroid $= \left(\dfrac{x_1 + x_2 + x_3}{3}, \dfrac{y_1 + y_2 + y_3}{3}\right)$

$= \left(\dfrac{-4 + 3 + 0}{3}, \dfrac{3 + 4 + (-5)}{3}\right)$

$= \left(-\dfrac{1}{3}, \dfrac{2}{3}\right)$

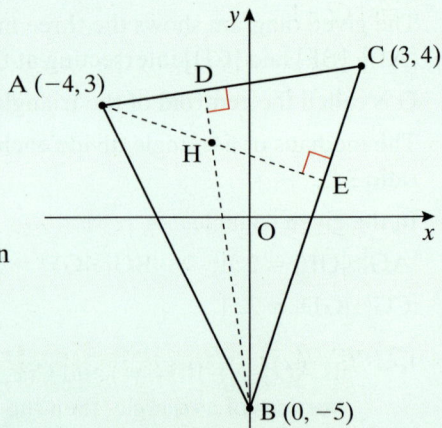

(ii) The orthocentre is the point of intersection of the perpendiculars from the vertices to the opposite sides, as shown.
(Two perpendiculars are sufficient.)

Slope of BC $= \dfrac{4 + 5}{3 - 0} = \dfrac{9}{3} = 3$

$\Rightarrow$ slope of AE $= -\dfrac{1}{3}$

Equation of AE: $\quad y - y_1 = m(x - x_1)$ $\qquad (x, y_1) = (-4, 3)$

$y - 3 = -\dfrac{1}{3}(x + 4)$

$\Rightarrow \quad 3y - 9 = -x - 4$

$\Rightarrow \quad x + 3y - 5 = 0 \dots \text{①}$

Slope of AC: $\dfrac{4 - 3}{3 + 4} = \dfrac{1}{7}$

$\Rightarrow \qquad$ slope of BD $= -7$

Equation of BD: $\quad y + 5 = -7(x - 0)$ $\qquad B = (0, -5)$

$\Rightarrow \quad 7x + y + 5 = 0 \dots \text{②}$

Solving equations ① and ②: $\quad x + 3y = 5 \dots \text{①}$
$\qquad\qquad\qquad\qquad\qquad\quad 7x + y = -5 \dots \text{②}$

① $\qquad\qquad x + 3y = 5$
② $\times 3$: $\qquad 21x + 3y = -15$
$\qquad\qquad \overline{-20x \qquad\quad = 20} \Rightarrow x = -1$ and $y = 2$

$\therefore$ the coordinates of the orthocentre are $(-1, 2)$

Exercise 4.5

1. Find the coordinates of the centroid of the triangle whose vertices are
    (i) $(2, -3), (4, 0)$ and $(-3, 9)$
    (ii) $(1, 3), (6, 2)$ and $(5, -2)$.

2. Find the coordinates of the circumcentre of the triangle with vertices $(0, 0), (4, 0)$ and $(1, 3)$.
    (Draw a sketch to simplify your work.)

3. Find the coordinates of the circumcentre of the triangle with vertices $(8, -2), (6, 2)$ and $(3, -7)$.

4. Find the coordinates of the orthocentre of the triangle with vertices A(4, 2), B(−2, 5) and C(−1, −3).

5. Find the coordinates of the orthocentre of the triangle with vertices O(0, 0), A(4, −2) and B(4, 4).

6. Show that the circumcentre of the triangle with vertices (−2, 2), (−4, −2) and (5, −5) is (1, −2).

7. A(4, 6), B(−2, 7) and C(k, −4) are the vertices of a triangle.
   If the coordinates of the centroid of the triangle are (−1, 3), find the value of k.

Section 4.6 Perpendicular distance from a point to a line

The perpendicular distance, d, from the point (x_1, y_1) to the line $ax + by + c = 0$ is given by the formula

$$d = \frac{|ax_1 + by_1 + c|}{\sqrt{a^2 + b^2}}$$

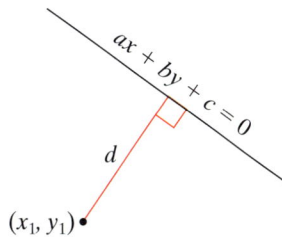

Example 1

(i) Find the perpendicular distance from the point (1, −4) to the line $3x − y − 2 = 0$.

(ii) Find the distance between the parallel lines $3x − 4y + 12 = 0$ and $3x − 4y − 1 = 0$.

(i) Perpendicular distance $= \dfrac{|ax_1 + by_1 + c|}{\sqrt{a^2 + b^2}}$ ... $\left\{ \begin{array}{l} ax + by + c = 3x − y − 2 \\ (x_1, y_1) = (1, −4) \end{array} \right\}$

$$= \frac{|3(1) + (−1)(−4) + (−2)|}{\sqrt{3^2 + 1^2}}$$

$$= \frac{5}{\sqrt{10}} = \frac{5\sqrt{10}}{10} = \frac{\sqrt{10}}{2}$$

(ii) To find the distance between two parallel lines, we find a point on one of the lines and then find the distance from that point to the other line.
A point on the line $3x − 4y + 12 = 0$ is (0, 3).

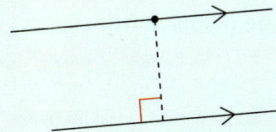

Perpendicular distance from (0, 3) to $3x − 4y − 1 = 0$ is

$$d = \frac{|3(0) + (−4)(3) − 1|}{\sqrt{3^2 + 4^2}} = \frac{|−12 − 1|}{\sqrt{25}}$$

$$= \frac{|−13|}{5} = \frac{13}{5} = 2\frac{3}{5}$$

Points in relation to a given line

The sign of the expression inside the modulus signs can be very useful when we are investigating whether points are on the same side or opposite sides of a given line.

> **1.** Perpendiculars to a line from points on the same side of the line have the same sign.
> **2.** Perpendiculars from points on opposite sides of a line have different signs.

Example 2

Investigate whether the points $(5, -2)$ and $(3, -3)$ lie on the same side of the line $5x - 4y - 30 = 0$.

The perpendicular distance from $(5, -2)$ to the line $5x - 4y - 30 = 0$ is:

$$\text{Distance} = \frac{ax_1 + by_1 + c}{\sqrt{a^2 + b^2}}$$

$$= \frac{5(5) + (-4)(-2) - 30}{\sqrt{5^2 + 4^2}}$$

$$= \frac{25 + 8 - 30}{\sqrt{41}} = \frac{3}{\sqrt{41}} \dots \text{positive}$$

> Here we do not use the modulus bars $||$ as we require a positive or negative answer.

The perpendicular distance from $(3, -3)$ to the line $5x - 4y - 30 = 0$ is:

$$\text{Distance} = \frac{5(3) + (-4)(-3) - 30}{\sqrt{5^2 + 4^2}}$$

$$= \frac{15 + 12 - 30}{\sqrt{41}} = \frac{-3}{\sqrt{41}} \dots \text{negative}$$

Since the perpendicular distances are opposite in sign, the points are on opposite sides of the line.

Example 3

Find the equations of the two lines which are parallel to the line $3x - 4y - 1 = 0$ and 3 units from it.

The equation of any line parallel to $3x - 4y - 1 = 0$ has the form $3x - 4y + k = 0$.
$(0, -\frac{1}{4})$ is a point on the line $3x - 4y - 1 = 0$.

The distance from $(0, -\frac{1}{4})$ to $3x - 4y + k = 0$ is 3 units.

$$\Rightarrow \frac{|3(0) - 4(-\frac{1}{4}) + k|}{\sqrt{3^2 + 4^2}} = 3$$

$$\Rightarrow \frac{|1 + k|}{5} = 3$$

$$\Rightarrow \frac{1 + k}{5} = \pm 3 \Rightarrow 1 + k = 15 \text{ or } 1 + k = -15$$

$$\Rightarrow k = 14 \text{ or } k = -16$$

> $|x| = 3$
> $\Rightarrow x = \pm 3$

The equations of the lines are
$$3x - 4y + 14 = 0 \quad \text{or} \quad 3x - 4y - 16 = 0.$$

Exercise 4.6

1. Find the perpendicular distance from $(2, -4)$ to $3x - 4y - 17 = 0$.

2. Show that the point $(1, 1)$ is equidistant from the lines $3x + 4y - 12 = 0$ and $5x - 12y + 20 = 0$.

3. Show that the perpendicular distance from the point $(6, 2)$ to the line $5x - 3y + 10 = 0$ is $\sqrt{34}$.

4. Verify that $(5, -5)$ is equidistant from the lines $x - 2y + 10 = 0$ and $2x + y - 30 = 0$.

5. Find the values of c if the perpendicular distance from $(3, 1)$ to the line $4x + 3y + c = 0$ is 5.

6. Verify that the line $3x - y - 4 = 0$ contains the point $(2, 2)$.
   Hence find the shortest distance between the parallel lines $3x - y - 4 = 0$ and $6x - 2y + 7 = 0$.

7. Investigate if the point $(1, 1)$ is equidistant from the lines $x + 7y - 3 = 0$ and $x - y + 1 = 0$.

8. Find the values of a if the perpendicular distance from the point $(-2, 3)$ to the line $ax + y - 7 = 0$ is $\sqrt{10}$.

9. If the point $(-2, a)$ is equidistant from the lines $4x + 3y - 3 = 0$ and $12x + 5y - 13 = 0$, find the value of a, $a \in Z$.

10. Show that $(-2, 6)$ lies on the same side of the line $3x + 2y - 7 = 0$ as the origin.

11. Show that the points $(3, 4)$ and $(9, 3)$ lie on opposite sides of the line $3x + 4y - 36 = 0$.

12. Investigate if the points $(-3, 1)$ and $(3, -4)$ are on the same side of the line $2x - 3y + 7 = 0$.

13. Write down the equation of any line parallel to $4x + 3y + 1 = 0$.
    Hence find the equations of the two lines which are parallel to the line $4x + 3y + 1 = 0$ and two units from it.

14. Write down the equation of any line that is perpendicular to the line $3x - 4y + 5 = 0$.
    Now find the equations of the two lines which are perpendicular to the line $3x - 4y + 5 = 0$, if the perpendicular distance from the point $(1, 1)$ to each line is 4 units.

15. Write down the equation of any line through the point $(-4, 2)$.
    Hence find the equations of the two lines through the point $(-4, 2)$ whose perpendicular distance from the origin is 2.

16. The length of the perpendicular to a line from the origin is 5 units.
    The line passes through the point $(3, 5)$.
    Find the equations of two such lines.

17. The vertices of a triangle are the points
    A(1, 2), B(3, 1) and C(−1, −2).
    (i) Find the length of the perpendicular
        from A to BC, i.e., find |AN|.
    (ii) Hence find the area of the triangle ABC.

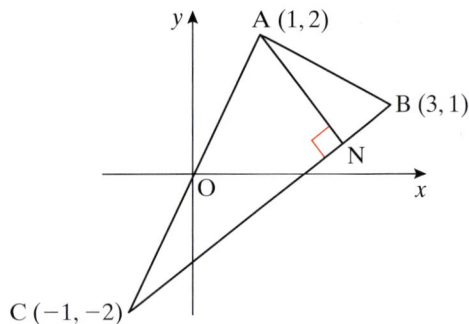

18. Two aircraft approach an airport along
    parallel flight paths, one red and one blue,
    as shown.
    (a) Find an equation for each flight path.
    (b) Calculate the shortest possible distance
        between two aircraft travelling along
        these paths at the same time.

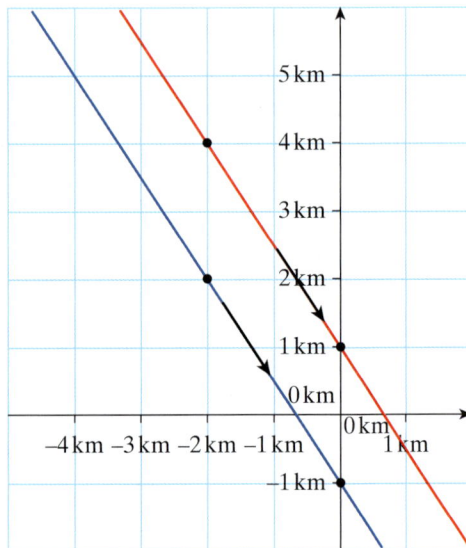

19. A river flows through a town and its path can be approximated by the line $4x - 5y = -6$.
    Two friends live at coordinates $(-5, -3)$ and $(4, 4)$ respectively. Investigate if they both
    live on the same side of the river.

20. The council has two waste pipes travelling along
    the lines $4x - 5y = -2$ and $4x - 5y = -1$
    as shown in diagram.
    They want to place a third pipe in the centre, parallel
    to the existing pipes.
    (a) Find the equation of the line of the third pipe.
    (b) What is the shortest between the centres of the
        original pipes.

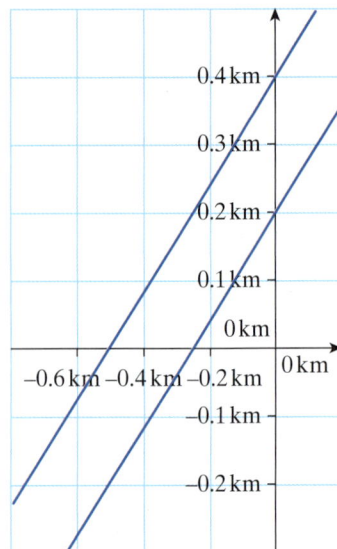

Section 4.7 The angle between two lines

The diagram shows two lines l_1 and l_2.

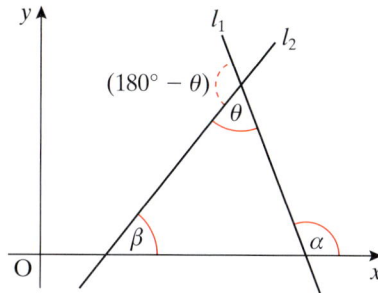

Let the slope of l_1 be m_1.

$\Rightarrow m_1 = \tan \alpha$

The angle, θ, between the lines is given by

$\theta = \alpha - \beta$

$\tan \theta = \tan(\alpha - \beta)$

$\qquad = \dfrac{\tan \alpha - \tan \beta}{1 + \tan \alpha \tan \beta}$

$\Rightarrow \tan \theta = \dfrac{m_1 - m_2}{1 + m_1 m_2}$

Let the slope of l_2 be m_2.

$\Rightarrow m_2 = \tan \beta$

The second angle between l_1 and and l_2 is $(180° - \theta)$.

$\tan(180° - \theta) = -\tan \theta$

$\qquad\qquad = -\dfrac{m_1 - m_2}{1 + m_1 m_2}$

Since the angle between l, and l_2 may be acute or obtuse, we generally define the angle as shown on the right.

$$\tan \theta = \pm \dfrac{m_1 - m_2}{1 + m_1 m_2}$$

Note: In practice we generally use $\tan \theta = \left| \dfrac{m_1 - m_2}{1 + m_1 m_2} \right|$ to find the acute angle, θ, between two lines.

The obtuse angle is obtained by finding $180° - \theta$.

Example 1

Find the acute angle between the lines $y = 2x + 5$ and $3x + y = 7$.

Let the slope of $y = 2x + 5$ be $m_1 \Rightarrow m_1 = 2$
Let the slope of $3x + y = 7$ be $m_2 \Rightarrow m_2 = -3$
Let θ be the angle between the lines.

$$\tan \theta = \left| \dfrac{m_1 - m_2}{1 + m_1 m_2} \right| = \left| \dfrac{2 - (-3)}{1 + 2(-3)} \right| = \left| \dfrac{2 + 3}{1 - 6} \right| = \left| \dfrac{5}{-5} \right| = |-1| = 1$$

$\tan \theta = 1 \Rightarrow \theta = 45°$ is the acute angle.

Note: the obtuse angle is $180° - 45° = 135°$.

More difficult problems

A particular type of problem in coordinate geometry involves finding the equations of two lines through a given point and which make angles of 45°, for example, with a given line.

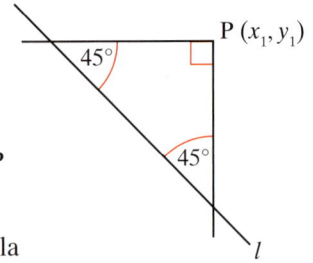

From the given diagram we can see that there are 2 lines through P which make angles of 45° with the line l.

To find the equations of the required lines, we start with the formula

$$\tan \theta = \pm \frac{m_1 - m_2}{1 + m_1 m_2},$$

where θ is the angle between the line required and the given line and m_1 is the slope of the given line.

By solving the equation using the $\pm$ signs, we get two values for m_2.

Example 2

Find the equations of the two lines through the point $(2, 3)$ which make angles of 45° with the line $x - 2y = 1$.

Let m_1 be the slope of the given line $x - 2y = 1$.

$$\Rightarrow m_1 = \tfrac{1}{2}$$

Let m_2 be the slope of the required line.

The angle between the two lines is 45°.

Using the formula $\tan \theta = \pm \dfrac{m_1 - m_2}{1 + m_1 m_2}$, we have

$$\tan 45° = \pm \frac{m_1 - m_2}{1 + m_1 m_2}$$

$$\Rightarrow \quad 1 = \pm \frac{\tfrac{1}{2} - m_2}{1 + \left(\tfrac{1}{2}\right)m_2} \qquad \Rightarrow \qquad 1 = \pm \frac{1 - 2m_2}{2 + m_2}$$

$$\Rightarrow \quad 2 + m_2 = \pm(1 - 2m_2)$$

$$\Rightarrow \quad 2 + m_2 = 1 - 2m_2 \quad \text{or} \quad 2 + m_2 = -(1 - 2m_2)$$

$$\Rightarrow \quad 3m_2 = -1 \qquad\qquad \text{or} \quad 2 + m_2 = -1 + 2m_2$$

$$\Rightarrow \quad m_2 = -\tfrac{1}{3} \qquad\qquad\qquad \Rightarrow \quad m_2 = 3$$

Taking these two values of the slope and the point $(2, 3)$ we get these equations

$\boldsymbol{m_2 = -\tfrac{1}{3}}$:
$$y - y_1 = m(x - x_1)$$
$$y - 3 = -\tfrac{1}{3}(x - 2)$$
$$3y - 9 = -x + 2$$
i.e. $\quad x + 3y - 11 = 0$

$\boldsymbol{m_2 = 3}$:
$$y - y_1 = m(x - x_1)$$
$$y - 3 = 3(x - 2)$$
i.e $\quad 3x - y - 3 = 0$

$\therefore \quad x + 3y - 11 = 0 \quad$ and $\quad 3x - y - 3 = 0$ are the required lines.

---

1. Find the value of the tangent of the acute angle between each of the following pairs of lines:
   (i) $x + 2y + 4 = 0$ and $x - 3y + 2 = 0$
   (ii) $2x + 3y - 1 = 0$ and $x - 2y + 3 = 0$
   (iii) $2x + y - 6 = 0$ and $2x - 3y + 5 = 0$.

2. Find the acute angle between the lines $y = 2x + 5$ and $3x + y = 7$.

3. Find the obtuse angle between the lines $x - 2y - 1 = 0$ and $3x - y + 2 = 0$.

4. Find, correct to the nearest degree, the smaller angle between the lines $x - 3y + 4 = 0$ and $2x + y - 5 = 0$.

5. Find the measure of the obtuse angle between the lines $x - 2y + 7 = 0$ and $3x - y + 2 = 0$.

6. Find the measure of the acute angle between the lines $x - \sqrt{3}y + 4 = 0$ and $\sqrt{3}x - y - 7 = 0$.

7. Find the slopes of the lines which make an angle measuring $45°$ with the line $2x - 3y + 1 = 0$.

8. Find the equations of the two lines through the origin which make angles of $45°$ with the line $2x + 3y - 4 = 0$.

9. Find the equations of the two lines through the point $(-1, 1)$ which make angles of $45°$ with the line $2x + y - 2 = 0$.

10. Find the equations of the two lines through the point $(4, 2)$ which make angles of $\tan^{-1}\left(\frac{2}{3}\right)$ with the line $x + y - 2 = 0$.

11. Find the equation of the line such that the x-axis bisects the angle between it and the line $2x - 3y - 6 = 0$.

12. ℓ is the line $tx + y - 7 = 0$.
    (i) Write down the slope of ℓ.
    (ii) If the angle between the line ℓ and the line $y = 2x + 5$ is $45°$, find two possible values of t.

Section 4.8 Using linear relationships to solve problems

In this section we will illustrate the importance of the straight line when the relationship between two variables is plotted on a graph. In many scientific experiments when the relationship between two sets of data is displayed graphically, the points often lie on, or very close to, a straight line.

This line is generally referred to as the **line of best fit**.
We will deal more fully with this line in another part of our course.

In this section we will deal only with straight-line graphs and show how useful they can be in the world of science and business.

Example 1

A spring has an unstretched length of 10 cm. When it is hung with a load of 80 g attached, the stretch length is 28 cm. Assuming that the extension of the spring is proportional to the load,

(i)   draw a graph of extension E against load L.
       (Put load L on the horizontal axis.)
(ii) find the equation of the line you have drawn in terms of L and E.
(iii) use your graph to find the load required to extend the spring to a length of 20 cm.

This particular spring passes its elastic limit when it is stretched to four times its original length. (This means that if it is stretched more than that it will not return to its original length.)

(iv) Find the load which would cause this to happen.

(i)   Two points on the line are (0, 10) and (80, 28).

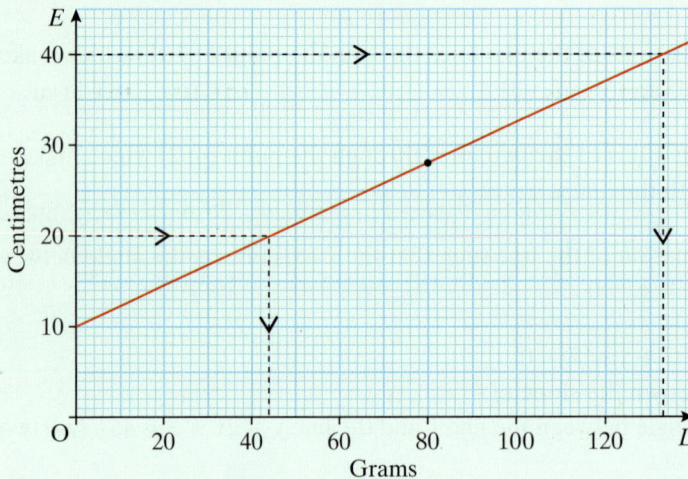

(ii) The line contains the points (0, 10) and (80, 28)

$$\text{Slope} = \frac{28 - 10}{80 - 0} = \frac{18}{80} = \frac{9}{40}$$

Equation of line: $y - y_1 = m(x - x_1)$ Here L replaces x and E replaces y.

$$E - 10 = \frac{9}{40}(L - 0)$$

$$\Rightarrow \quad 40E - 400 = 9L$$

$$\Rightarrow \quad 9L - 40E + 400 = 0 \text{ is the required equation}$$

(iii) From the graph it can be seen that a load of 44 grams is required to extend the spring to a length of 20 cm.

(iv) A load of 133 grams is required for the elastic limit of 40 cm to be reached.

Exercise 4.8

1. The linear graph below shows the relationship between degrees Celsius and degrees Fahrenheit.

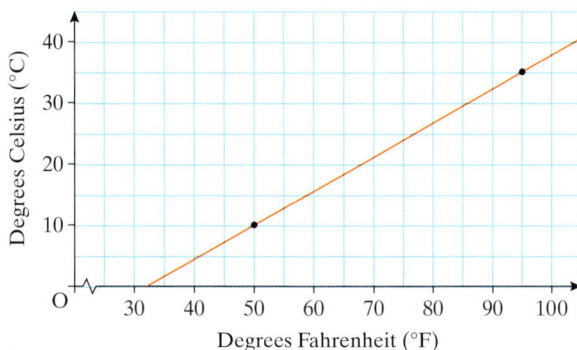

(i) Use the graph to convert approximately
   (a) 35°C to Fahrenheit
   (b) 15°C to Fahrenheit
   (c) 50°F to Celsius
   (d) 100°F to Celsius.

(ii) Use the two marked points on the graph to find the equation of the line in the form $ax + by + c = 0$.

(iii) Use the equation you have found to convert 95°C to degrees Fahrenheit.

2. When a carpet cleaner visits a house to clean carpets, his charge €C is based on the formula

$$C = €(20 + 4M),$$

where M is the number of square metres of carpets cleaned.
Draw a straight-line graph of this relation, plotting M on the horizontal axis for $0 \leqslant M \leqslant 80$.
Use your graph to find
   (i) the cost of cleaning 75 m² of carpet
   (ii) the number of square metres of carpet that can be cleaned for €200.
Use the formula to find
   (iii) the cost of cleaning 105 m² of carpet.

3. A sum of €5000 is invested and simple interest is paid at the rate of 8%.
   (i) Calculate the interest received after 1, 2 and 3 years, and hence draw a sketch of the graph of interest (I) against time (T), putting time on the horizontal axis.

(ii) Find the equation of the line you have drawn using the variables I and T, where I = interest and T = time.

(iii) Use the equation to find the length of time for which the money must be invested for the total interest to reach €3500.

Adding the interest to the sum invested gives the amount of the investment after a period of time.

(iv) Find the linear equation of amount against time, using A and T as variables.

4. A firm manufacturing jackets finds that it is capable of producing 100 jackets per day, but it can only sell all of these if the charge to the wholesalers is no more than €60 per jacket. On the other hand, at the current price of €100 per jacket, only 50 can be sold per day.

Assuming that the graph of price, P, against the number sold per day, N, is a straight line,

(i) draw a sketch of the graph, putting the number sold per day on the vertical axis

(ii) find the equation of the line you have drawn using the variables P and N.

Use the equation to find

(iii) the price at which 88 jackets a day could be sold

(iv) the number of jackets that should be manufactured if they were to be sold at €72 each.

5. Two rival taxi firms have the following fare structures:

Firm A: fixed charge of €5 plus €2 per kilometre

Firm B: no fixed charge and €2.20 per kilometre

(i) Sketch the graph of price (vertical axis) against distance travelled (horizontal axis) for each firm (on the same axes).

(ii) Find the equation of each line using P for price and D for distance travelled.

(iii) Use your graph to find the distance for which both firms charge the same amount.

(iv) Which firm would you use for a distance of 12 km?

6. When the market price €p of an article sold in a free market varies, so does the number demanded, D, and the number supplied, S.

In a particular month, $D = 20 + 0.2p$ and $S = -12 + p$.

(i) Sketch both of these lines on the same graph.

The market reaches a state of equilibrium when the number demanded equals the number supplied.

(ii) Find the equilibrium price and the number bought and sold in equilibrium.

Revision Exercise 4 (Core)

1. The equation of the line ℓ is $3x - 2y + 6 = 0$.

Find the equation of the line perpendicular to ℓ that contains the point $(-1, 4)$.

2. Find the area of the triangle with vertices $(0, 0)$, $(3, -2)$ and $(-2, 4)$.

3. The line ℓ contains the points $(3, -2)$ and $(1, 6)$.
   If the line $2x + ay + 7 = 0$ is perpendicular to ℓ find the value of a.

4. The line joining the points $(6, a)$ and $(-3, 6)$ has a slope of $\frac{1}{3}$.
   What is the value of a?

5. The line $y = \frac{3}{2}x - 2$ crosses the x-axis at the point P and the y-axis at the point Q.
   (i) Write down the slope of the line.
   (ii) Find the coordinates of P and Q.
   (iii) Calculate the area of the triangle OPQ, where O is the origin.

6. Write down the slope of the given line l.
   Hence find the equation of l.

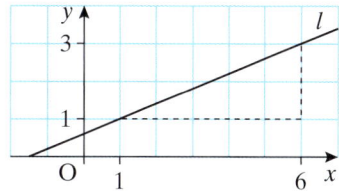

7. The straight lines $y = k^2x + 12$ and $2ky = 4x + 5$ are perpendicular, $k \neq 0$.
   (i) Find the value of k.
   (ii) Find the point of intersection of the two lines.

8. Determine which of the following pairs of lines are perpendicular.
   (a) $2x + y = 3$ and $x - 2y + 4 = 0$
   (b) $y = 3x + 2$ and $x + 3y - 2 = 0$
   (c) $y + 2x + 1 = 0$ and $x = 2y - 4$
   (d) $x + 3y = 6$ and $3x + y + 2 = 0$

9. Find the equation of the line through the point $(5, 2)$ and which is perpendicular to the line $x + 2y - 3 = 0$.

10. The perpendicular bisector of the line joining the points $(1, 2)$ and $(5, 4)$ meets the y-axis at the point $(0, k)$.
    Find k.

Revision Exercise 4 (Advanced)

1. (i) Calculate the perpendicular distance from the point $(-1, -5)$ to the line $3x - 4y - 2 = 0$.
   (ii) The point $(-1, -5)$ is equidistant from the lines $3x - 4y - 2 = 0$ and $3x - 4y + k = 0$, where $k \neq -2$. Find the value of k.

2. (i) $A(-7, 3)$ and $B(8, -2)$ are two points.
      Find the coordinates of the point that divides $[AB]$ in the ratio $2 : 3$.
   (ii) ℓ is the line $2x + ky = 6$.
      (a) Find, in terms of k, the points where ℓ intersects the x-axis and y-axis.
      (b) If the area of the triangle formed by ℓ, the x-axis and the y-axis is k square units, find the value of k.

3. (i) Find the equation of the line which is parallel to the line $2x + y = 5$ and which passes through the point $(2, 5)$.
   (ii) (a) Find the equation of the line ℓ which is perpendicular to the line $2x + y = 5$ and which passes through the point $(1, k)$, where k is constant.
   (b) Hence find the value of k for which the line ℓ passes through the origin.

4. The vertices of a triangle are $A(4, 2)$, $B(-1, 7)$ and $C(h, k)$.
   If the coordinates of the centroid of the triangle ABC are $(2, 4)$, find the values of h and k.

5. Find the coordinates of the orthocentre of the triangle with vertices $(1, 8)$, $(1, -2)$ and $(7, 1)$.

6. The line k passes through the point $(-4, 6)$ and has slope m, where $m > 0$.
   (i) Write down the equation of k in terms of m.
   (ii) Find, in terms of m, the coordinates of the points where k intersects the axes.
   (iii) The area of the triangle formed by k, the x-axis and the y-axis is 54 square units. Find the possible values of m.

7. (i) Find the value of k if the distance from the point $(3, k)$ to the line $3x - 4y + 7 = 0$ is 6 units and $k < 0$.
   (ii) Use this value for k to find the equation of the line through $(3, k)$ which is parallel to the line $3x - 4y + 7 = 0$.

8. Find the equations of the two lines parallel to $4x - 3y + 8 = 0$ if the perpendicular distance from the origin to each line is 4.

9. Find the equations of the lines through the point $(2, 4)$ which make angles of $45°$ with the line $x - 2y - 6 = 0$.

10. ℓ is the line $4x + 3y - 5 = 0$.
    (i) Verify that $(2, -1) \in \ell$.
    (ii) Write down the equation of any line parallel to ℓ.
    (iii) Hence find the equations of the two lines parallel to ℓ and 2 units from it.

Revision Exercise 4 (Extended-Response)

1. To clean the upstairs window on the side of a house, it is necessary to position the ladder so that it just touches the edge of the lean-to shed as shown in the diagram. The coordinates represent distances from O in metres, in the x and y directions shown.
   (i) Find the equation of the line of the ladder.
   (ii) Find the height of the point A reached by the top of the ladder.
   (iii) Find the length of the ladder, correct to the nearest centimetre.

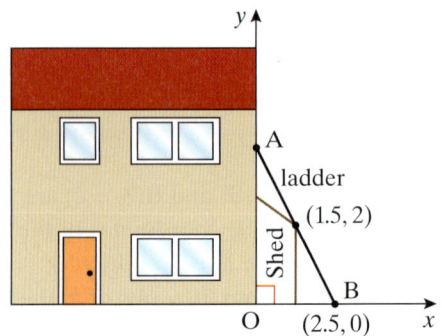

2. A line ℓ contains the point $(2, 5)$ and has slope m.
   (i) Find the equation of ℓ in terms of m.
   (ii) Find, in terms of m, the coordinates of the points where ℓ intersects the x-axis and y-axis.
   (iii) Find the values of m if the area of the triangle formed by ℓ and the positive x and y-axes is 36 square units.

3. ABCD is a rectangle, where A, B and C are the points $(3, 4)$, $(1, k)$ and $(4, -3)$ respectively.
   (i) Find the gradient of the line AB, giving your answer in terms of k.
   (ii) Determine the two possible value of k.
   (iii) Find the area of the rectangle ABCD for the case in which k is positive.

4. (i) The line k has a positive slope and passes through the point P $(2, -9)$.
   k intersects the x-axis at Q and the y-axis at R and $|PQ| : |PR| = 3 : 1$.
   Find the coordinates of Q and the coordinates of R.
   (ii) The line $3x + 2y = c$ intersects the x-axis at P and the y-axis at Q.
   If the area of the triangle OPQ is 24 square units, find the values of c.

5. The vertices of a triangle are $(0, -9)$, $(-3, 6)$ and $(8, 3)$.
   (i) Find the coordinates of the circumcentre of the triangle.
   (ii) Find the length of the radius of the circumcircle.
   (iii) Find the area of the circle in terms of π.

6. In the parallelogram OABC where O is the origin, B is the point $(2, 3)$. The equation of OA is $x = 4y$ and the slope of OC is -1.
   (i) Draw a rough sketch of the parallelogram and then find the equation of BC.
   (ii) Find the coordinates of the points A and C.

7. RSTU is a quadrilateral where R $= (-1, -5)$ and S $= (13, 9)$.
   Q$(3, -1)$ lies on the line RS.

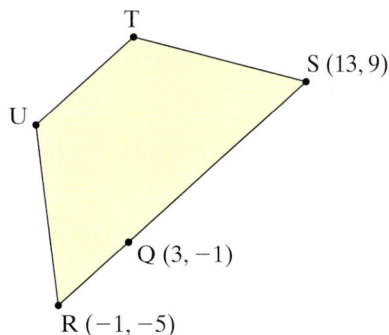

T

S $(13, 9)$

U

Q $(3, -1)$

R $(-1, -5)$

   (i) The coordinates of U are $(-2k, 3k)$, where $k \in R$ and $k > 0$.
   The area of the triangle RQU is 28 square units.
   Find the value of k.
   (ii) The slope of TS is $-\frac{3}{11}$ and SR is parallel to TU.
   Find the coordinates of T.

8. When the interest rate for deposits is 7%, a small building society attracts €35 million of savings. When the rate is increased to 8.5%, the savings increase by €2 million. Assuming that the graph of savings against interest rates is linear for interest rates between 5% and 12%,
    (i) sketch the graph of savings (in € million) against interest rates (%) in this interval, with interest rates on the horizontal axis
    (ii) find the equation of the line.

    Use the equation you have found to
    (iii) find the value of savings attracted by a rate of 11.5%
    (iv) find the interest rate needed to attract savings of €40 million.

9. A line containing the point $(2, -4)$ has slope m, where $m \neq 0$.
    The line intercepts the x-axis at $(x_1, 0)$ and the y-axis at $(0, y_1)$.
    If $x_1 + y_1 = -4$, find the slopes of the two lines that satisfy this condition.
    Hence find the tangent of the acute angle between these two lines.

10. ℓ is the line $tx + (t + 2)y - 11 = 0$, where $t \in R$.
    (i) Write down the slope of ℓ in terms of t.
    (ii) If the angle between ℓ and the line $x - 2y - 1 = 0$ is 45°, find the two possible values of t.

11. In the given diagram $\angle ABC = 90°$.
    D lies on the perpendicular bisector of AB.
    The coordinates of A and B are $(7, 2)$ and $(2, 5)$ respectively.
    The equation of the line AD is $y = 4x - 26$.
    (i) Find the equation of the perpendicular bisector of the line segment AB.
    (ii) Find the coordinates of the point D.
    (iii) Find the slope of the line BC.
    (iv) If C has coordinates $(8, c)$, find the value of c.
    (v) Find the area of the quadrilateral ABCD.

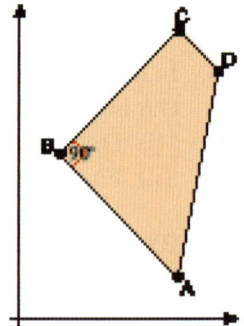

Probability 1

chapter 5

Key words

the fundamental principle of counting   permutations   factorial
combinations   relative frequency   expected frequency   addition rule
mutually exclusive   exhaustive events   Venn diagrams
independent events   multiplication rule   conditional probability

Section 5.1 Permutations

1. The fundamental principle of counting

The diagram below shows three towns A, B and C.
There are 2 roads from A to B and 3 roads from B to C.

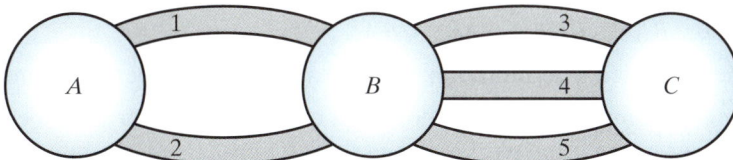

The number of ways a person can travel from A to C is 6. These are listed as follows:

$(1, 3), (1, 4), (1, 5), (2, 3), (2, 4), (2, 5)$.

This illustrates that there are 2 ways of going from A to B and for **each** way of going from A to B, there are 3 ways of going from B to C.
Thus there are $3 \times 2 = 6$ ways of going from A to C.

Similarly, if a car manufacturer produces 5 different models of a car and each model comes in 4 different colours, then a customer has 5×4 i.e. 20 different ways in which he can select a car.

These examples illustrate what is generally referred to as the **Fundamental Principle of Counting** which can be stated as follows:

Fundamental Principle of Counting

If one task can be accomplished in m ways **and** following this a second task can be accomplished in n ways, then the first task followed by the second task can be accomplished in $m \times n$ ways.

Example 1

From the given number of names and surnames, determine how many different name–surname pairs are possible.

Name	Surname
Mary	Mooney
Jennifer	Byrne
Cormac	O'Brien
Kate	Lawiski
Barry	
Shane	McCarthy

There are 6 names and for each of these, there are 5 surnames.

Number of possible different pairs = 6×5
$= 30$

Note: The *Fundamental Principle of Counting* can be extended to any number of tasks. For example, if there are 3 roads from A to B, 2 roads from B to C and 4 roads from C to D, then there are

$3 \times 2 \times 4$ i.e. 24 ways of going from A to D.

2. Permutations

A permutation is an arrangement of a number of objects in a certain order.

If the letters A, B and C are written in a row, one after another, there are 6 possible arrangements as follows:

ABC ACB BAC BCA CAB CBA

Each arrangement is called a **permutation**; so there are 6 different permutations possible.

When calculating the number of permutations that can be made from a number of items, it is convenient to use "boxes", and working from the left, write down the number of ways in which each box can be filled.

Again, returning to the permutations of the letters A, B and C.
The first letter can be selected in 3 different ways.
Once the first place has been filled, there are only two letters left to choose from.
Thus the second place can be filled in 2 ways.
Similarly the third place can be filled in 1 way only.
Thus the letters A, B and C can be arranged in

$\boxed{3}\,\boxed{2}\,\boxed{1} = 3 \times 2 \times 1 = 6$ ways

3. Factorial notation

To represent $3 \times 2 \times 1$, we write $3!$, pronounced "three factorial".
Similarly, $8 \times 7 \times 6 \times 5 \times 4 \times 3 \times 2 \times 1 = 8!$

In general, the product of all natural numbers from any number, n, down to 1 is called n **factorial**, and written as $n!$.

Definition

> $n!$ is the number of permutations of n different objects when all the objects are included in each arrangement.

Thus (i) 5 different objects can be arranged in 5! i.e. 120 ways

(ii) 8 different objects can be arranged in 8! i.e. 40320 ways.

Example 2

There are 6 different books, including a science book, on a shelf.
  (i) In how many different ways can the 6 books be arranged on the shelf?
  (ii) In how many ways can the 6 books be arranged if the science book is always on the extreme left?

(i) The number of permutations of 6 different books is 6!

$$6! = 6 \times 5 \times 4 \times 3 \times 2 \times 1 = 720$$

(ii) If we use "boxes", it is clear that the box on the extreme left can be filled in 1 way only (i.e. with the science book).

| 1 | 5 | 4 | 3 | 2 | 1 |

The next box can be filled in 5 ways, the next in 4 ways and so on.

∴ the number of permutations is $1 \times 5 \times 4 \times 3 \times 2 \times 1$

$$= 120 \text{ ways}$$

Example 3

In how many ways can the letters of the word SCOTLAND be arranged in a line?
  (i) In how many of these arrangements do the two vowels come together?
  (ii) How many of the arrangements begin with S and end with the two vowels?

The letters of the word SCOTLAND can be arranged in 8! ways.

$$8! = 8 \times 7 \times 6 \times 5 \times 4 \times 3 \times 2 \times 1 = 40320 \text{ ways}$$

(i) If the two vowels come together, we treat them as one 'unit'.

| | | | A | O | | | |

There are now seven 'units' (or boxes) and these can be arranged in 7! ways, i.e., 5040 ways. For each arrangement of these seven boxes, the box containing AO can be arranged in 2! ways.

∴ the number of arrangements is $7! \times 2!$

$$= 5040 \times 2 = 10080 \text{ ways}$$

(ii) Arrangements beginning with S and ending with AO or OA:

| S | | | | | AO |

The S is fixed and we treat AO as one 'unit' and that is also fixed.

The remaining 5 letters can be arranged in 5! ways.

For each of these arrangements, AO can be arranged in 2! ways.

∴ the number of arrangements is $5! \times 2!$

$$= 120 \times 2 = 240$$

Example 4

How many four-digit numbers can be formed using the digits 0, 2, 5, 7, 8 if a digit cannot be used more than once in any number?
(i) How many of these numbers are greater than 5000?
(ii) How many of these numbers are odd?

Using boxes for the digits, the first box can be filled in 4 ways as 0 cannot be used as a first digit.

$$\boxed{4}\,\boxed{4}\,\boxed{3}\,\boxed{2}$$

The second box can also be filled in 4 ways as one digit is used but the zero can now be used.
The third box can be filled in 3 ways and the fourth in 2 ways.
∴ the number of numbers is $4 \times 4 \times 3 \times 2 = 96$

(i) If a number is greater than 5000, the first digit must be either 5, 7 or 8.
Therefore the first box can be filled in 3 ways.

$$\boxed{3}\,\boxed{4}\,\boxed{3}\,\boxed{2}$$

The remaining boxes can be filled in 4, 3 and 2 ways.
∴ the number of numbers is $3 \times 4 \times 3 \times 2 = 72$

(ii) If one of these numbers is odd, it must end with 5 or 7.
Therefore the last box can be filled in 2 ways only.

$$\boxed{3}\,\boxed{3}\,\boxed{2}\,\boxed{2}$$

We then go to the first box and, as either 5 or 7 is used and zero cannot be used, this box can be filled in 3 ways.
The zero can now be used and 2 digits are already used, so the second and third boxes can be filled in 3 and 2 ways.
∴ the number of 4-digit odd numbers is $3 \times 3 \times 2 \times 2 = 36$

4. Permutations of n different objects taking r of them at a time

To find the number of ways the five letters A, B, C, D, E can be arranged in a line when taking 3 at a time, we could use boxes as follows:

$$\boxed{5}\,\boxed{4}\,\boxed{3} = 5 \times 4 \times 3 = 60 \text{ ways.}$$

The first box can be filled in 5 ways, the second in 4 ways and the third in 3 ways.

Notice that $5 \times 4 \times 3 = \dfrac{5 \times 4 \times 3 \times 2 \times 1}{2 \times 1} = \dfrac{5!}{2!} = \dfrac{5!}{(5-3)!}$

We use the notation $^5P_3$ to denote the number of permutations of 5 objects, taking them 3 at a time.

$^5P_3 = 5 \times 4 \times 3$ ... starting at 5 and going down 3 numbers

Similarly, $^8P_4 = 8 \times 7 \times 6 \times 5 \left(\text{or } \dfrac{8!}{(8-4)!} \right)$

In general, the number of arrangements of n objects, taking r at a time, is given on the right.

$$^nP_r = \dfrac{n!}{(n-r)!}$$

Example 5

(i) Evaluate $^{10}P_3$ (ii) Find n if $7[^nP_3] = 6[^{n+1}P_3]$

(i) $^{10}P_3 = 10 \times 9 \times 8 = 720$

(ii) $7[^nP_3] = 6[^{n+1}P_3] \Rightarrow 7n(n-1)(n-2) = 6(n+1)(n)(n-1)$
$\Rightarrow 7(n-2) = 6(n+1)$
$\Rightarrow 7n - 14 = 6n + 6$
$\Rightarrow n = 20$

Example 6

How many different four-letter arrangements can be made from the letters of the word THURSDAY if a letter cannot be repeated in an arrangement?
How many of the arrangements begin with the letter D and end with a vowel?

There are 8 letters in THURSDAY.
The number of four-letter arrangements $= {}^8P_4 = 8 \times 7 \times 6 \times 5$
$= 1680$

To find the number of arrangements that begin with D and end with a vowel, we will use 'boxes'.

$\boxed{\text{D}}\boxed{6}\boxed{5}\boxed{2}$

The first box can be filled in one way only, i.e. with D.
The last box can be filled in 2 ways, i.e., U or A.

Having used two letters, the remaining two boxes can be filled in 6 and 5 ways.
∴ the number of arrangements $= 1 \times 6 \times 5 \times 2$
$= 60$ ways

Exercise 5.1

1. A three-course lunch menu consists of four starters, three main courses and five desserts. In how many ways can a three-course lunch be chosen?

2. There are six nominations for the post of Chairman and seven nominations for the post of Secretary of a committee.
   In how many ways can a Chairman and Secretary be elected?

3. A code consists of a letter of the alphabet followed by two digits from 1 to 9, e.g. A34. How many different codes are possible if a digit cannot be repeated in the same code?

4. Jack has 10 shirts, 6 pairs of shoes and 4 pairs of trousers.
   In how many different ways can he dress himself?

5. In how many ways can six books be arranged on a shelf?

6. In how many ways can seven children sit on a bench?
   In how many of these arrangements are the two oldest always together?

7. In how many ways can the letters A, B, C, D and E be arranged in a row?
   In how many of these arrangements
   (i)   is D always first?
   (ii) is A first and E last?

8. How many different arrangements can be made from the letters of the word PROBLEM?
   (i)   How many of these arrangements begin with a vowel?
   (ii) In how many of these arrangements do the two vowels come together?

9. How many different arrangements can be made from the letters of the word PRINCE if
   (i)   the first letter must be a consonant
   (ii) the last letter must be a vowel
   (iii) the letters P and R must be together?

10. In how many ways can the letters of the word LEAVING be arranged if
    (i)   L is always at the beginning
    (ii) the letters E and A are always together?

11. In how many ways can the letters of the word IRELAND be arranged if each letter is used exactly once in each arrangement?
    In how many of these arrangements do the three vowels come together?

12. Three girls and four boys are to sit in a row of seven chairs.
    How many different arrangements are possible
    (i)   if the girls sit beside one another
    (ii) if no two boys may sit beside each other?

13. In how many ways can 7 books be arranged on a shelf, taking 4 at a time?

14. In how many ways can the letters of the word BRIDGE be arranged in a row taking 4 at a time?

15. There are eight horses in a race.
    In how many ways can the first three places be filled if there are no dead-heats?

16. A code consists of two vowels followed by two of the digits 1 to 9, e.g. AE29.
    How many different codes are possible if no repetition is allowed in a code?

17. How many three-digit numbers can be formed using the digits
    (i) 1 to 9   (ii) 0 to 9
    if a digit cannot be repeated in the same number?

18. How many 4-digit numbers can be made from the digits 4, 5, 6, 7 if no digit is repeated in the same number?
    (i)   How many of these numbers are greater than 7000?
    (ii) How many of these numbers end in 7?
    (iii) How many of these numbers are less than 6000?

19. How many four-digit numbers can be formed from the digits 0, 1, 2, 3, ..., 9, if no digit is repeated in a number?
    How many of these numbers
    (i) are greater than 8000   (ii) are divisible by 10?

20. How many different four-digit numbers greater than 5000 can be formed from the digits 2, 4, 5, 8, 9 if each digit can be used only once in any given number?
    How many of these numbers are odd?

21. How many different three-digit numbers can be formed with the digits 0, 1, 4, 6, 7, 8 if each digit can be used once only in a number?
    (i) How many of these numbers are greater than 600?
    (ii) How many of the numbers begin with 1?

22. A security lock requires a four-digit code to be keyed in before it can be released.
    The digits can be 0, 1, 2, 3, 4 or 5 but the four-digit code cannot start with the digit 0.
    How many different codes are there if
    (i) all the digits are different
    (ii) the first digit is 5 and no digit is repeated?

23. A code consists of any permutation of the letters A, B and C followed by any permutation of the numbers 1, 2, 3.
    How many different codes can be made if no letter or number can be repeated in a code?

24. A woman has 10 ornaments, including a clock, of which only 7 will fit on the mantelpiece. If the clock must go in the centre, how many different arrangements can be made with the ornaments?

25. Seven children, including one set of twins, are arranged in a line.
How many different arrangements can be made?
In how many of these arrangements are the twins
(i) always together   (ii) always apart?

26. A competition has a first prize, a second prize and a third prize. 10 competitors enter this competition and the 3 prizes are awarded in order of merit.
  (i) Find the number of different ways in which these prizes could be won.

Smith and Jones are 2 of the 10 competitors. Find the number of different ways in which the prizes could be won if
(ii) neither Smith nor Jones wins a prize
(iii) each of Smith and Jones wins a prize.

Section 5.2 Combinations

A **combination** is a selection of objects chosen from a given set.
When we select, for example, three letters from A, B, C, D and E, then the combination ABC is the same as the combination BCA.
Thus in combinations, unlike permutations, the order is not important.

We use the notation $\binom{7}{3}$ to denote the number of ways in which three objects can be chosen from seven different objects.

The value of $\binom{7}{3} = \dfrac{7 \times 6 \times 5}{3 \times 2 \times 1}$ ... start at 7 and go down 3 factors
... start at 3 and go down to 1

$$= \frac{210}{6} = 35$$

Similarly (i) $\binom{8}{4} = \dfrac{8 \times 7 \times 6 \times 5}{4 \times 3 \times 2 \times 1} = 70$

    (ii) $\binom{10}{3} = \dfrac{10 \times 9 \times 8}{3 \times 2 \times 1} = 120$

In general, $\binom{n}{r} = \dfrac{n(n-1)(n-2) \ldots (n-r+1)}{r!} = \dfrac{n!}{r!(n-r)!}$

Combinations

> The number of combinations of *r* objects, chosen from a set of *n* different objects, is denoted by $\binom{n}{r}$ where
> $$\binom{n}{r} = \frac{n(n-1)(n-2) \ldots (n-r+1)}{r!} = \frac{n!}{r!(n-r)!}$$

Again $\binom{10}{6} = \dfrac{10 \times 9 \times 8 \times 7 \times 6 \times 5}{6 \times 5 \times 4 \times 3 \times 2 \times 1}$ → start at 10 and go down 6 factors
→ start at 6 and go down to 1.

$$= 210$$

Also $\binom{10}{4} = \dfrac{10 \times 9 \times 8 \times 7}{4 \times 3 \times 2 \times 1} = 210$

This shows that $\binom{10}{6} = \binom{10}{4}$ i.e. $\binom{10}{6} = \binom{10}{10-6}$

In general, it can be shown that $\binom{n}{r} = \binom{n}{n-r}$ as follows:

$$\binom{n}{r} = \frac{n!}{r!(n-r)!} \text{ and } \binom{n}{n-r} = \frac{n!}{(n-r)![n-(n-r)]!}$$

$$= \frac{n!}{(n-r)!r!} = \frac{n!}{r!(n-r)!}$$

$$\Rightarrow \qquad \boxed{\binom{n}{r} = \binom{n}{n-r}}$$

Also since $\binom{n}{r} = \binom{n}{n-r} \Rightarrow \binom{n}{n} = \binom{n}{n-n} = \binom{n}{0} = 1$ $\qquad \boxed{0! = 1}$

$$\Rightarrow \qquad \boxed{\binom{n}{n} = \binom{n}{0} = 1}$$

The fact that $\binom{n}{r} = \binom{n}{n-r}$ is very useful for shortening the calculation involved in

evaluating $\binom{16}{12}$, for example.

$$\binom{16}{12} = \binom{16}{16-12} = \binom{16}{4} = \frac{16 \times 15 \times 14 \times 13}{4 \times 3 \times 2 \times 1} = 1820$$

Note: $\binom{n}{r}$ may also be written as ^nC_r.

The notation nCr is generally used on calculators.

To find $\binom{16}{12}$ on your calculator, key in

$\boxed{16}\ \boxed{\text{Shift}}\ \boxed{nCr}\ \boxed{12}\ \boxed{=}$ The result is 1820.

Example 1

(i) In how many ways can a team of 5 players be chosen from 9 players?
(ii) In how many ways can this be done if a certain player must be selected in each team?

(i) 5 players can be selected from 9 players in $\binom{9}{5}$ ways.

$$\binom{9}{5} = \binom{9}{4} = \frac{9 \times 8 \times 7 \times 6}{4 \times 3 \times 2 \times 1} = 126$$

(ii) If a certain player must be included, this results in 4 players being selected from the remaining 8.

4 players can be selected from 8 in $\binom{8}{4}$ ways.

$$\binom{8}{4} = \frac{8 \times 7 \times 6 \times 5}{4 \times 3 \times 2 \times 1} = 70$$

Example 2

In how many ways can a group of five be selected from ten people?
In how many ways can this group be selected if two particular people cannot both be selected for the group.

Five people can be selected from ten in $\binom{10}{5}$ ways.

$$= \frac{10 \times 9 \times 8 \times 7 \times 6}{5 \times 4 \times 3 \times 2 \times 1} = 252 \text{ ways}$$

If two particular people cannot be in the same group, we find
 (i) the total number of ways 5 people can be selected from 10, i.e., 252, from above
(ii) the number of ways the group can be selected if the two people are **always** included.

If the 2 people are in each group, the number of ways is

$$\binom{8}{3} = \frac{8 \times 7 \times 6}{3 \times 2 \times 1} = 56 \ldots \text{ select 3 from 8}$$

Therefore the number of ways the group can be selected if the two people cannot be in the same group is (i) less (ii).
∴ the number is $252 - 56 = 196$ ways

Combinations from two different sets

If we have two different sets, one containing m different things and the other containing n different things, the number of combinations which can be made containing r of the first and s of the second is,

$$\binom{m}{r} \times \binom{n}{s}$$

The selections of $\binom{m}{r}$ and $\binom{n}{s}$ are **multiplied** because for each selection from $\binom{m}{r}$ we can

associate every selection from $\binom{n}{s}$.

Example 3

Find the number of ways in which a panel of four men and three women can be chosen from seven men and five women.

4 men can be selected from 7 men in $\binom{7}{4}$ ways.

3 women can be selected from 5 women in $\binom{5}{3}$ ways.

With each of the $\binom{7}{4}$ selections, we may associate one of the $\binom{5}{3}$ selections.

$\Rightarrow$ the panel can be selected in $\binom{7}{4} \times \binom{5}{3}$ ways

$$= 35 \times 10$$
$$= 350 \text{ ways}$$

Example 4

In how many ways can a committee of six be formed from 5 teachers and 8 students if there are to be more teachers than students on each committee?

If there are more teachers than students on each committee, the committee will consist of either of the following combinations:
 (i) 4 teachers and 2 students
(ii) 5 teachers and 1 student

 (i) 4 teachers and 2 students can be selected in $\binom{5}{4} \times \binom{8}{2}$ ways

$$= 5 \times 28 = 140 \text{ ways}$$

(ii) 5 teachers and 1 student can be selected in $\binom{5}{5} \times \binom{8}{1}$ ways

$$= 1 \times 8 = 8 \text{ ways}$$

The total number of possible committees is $140 + 8$

$$= 148 \text{ committees}$$

Note: In example 4 above, the committee could consist of combinations (i) **or** (ii). Notice that these results were **added**.

In general, when dealing with problems involving permutations, combinations or probability, the word **or** indicates that results are **added**.

Exercise 5.2

1. Evaluate each of the following:

   (i) $\binom{6}{2}$ (ii) $\binom{7}{3}$ (iii) $\binom{10}{2}$ (iv) $\binom{12}{10}$ (v) $\binom{18}{16}$

2. Show that   (i) $\binom{12}{9} + \binom{12}{8} = \binom{13}{9}$ (ii) $8\binom{10}{2} = 3\binom{10}{3}$

3. In how many ways can a committee of 5 be selected from 8 people?

4. In how many ways can a team consisting of 11 players be selected from a panel of 14 players?
If the 14 players include only one goalkeeper, how many different teams can be selected if the goalkeeper is included in each team?

5. How many different selections of 5 letters can be made from the letters of the word CHEMISTRY?
  (i) How many 5-letter selections can be made if the letter C is included in each selection?
  (ii) How many 5-letter selections can be made if the letter C is always included and Y is always excluded?

6. An examination paper consists of 9 questions.
In how many ways can 5 questions be selected?
If Question 1 is compulsory, in how many ways can 5 questions then be selected?

7. From a pack of 52 cards, how many different hands of 3 cards can be selected?
How many different hands of 3 spades can be chosen from the 52 cards?

8. In how many different ways may 5 colours be selected from 10 different colours including red, blue and green,
  (i) if blue and green are always included
  (ii) if red is always excluded
  (iii) if red and blue are always included but green excluded?

9. In how many ways can a committee of six persons be chosen from five men and four women if each committee is to consist of 3 men and 3 women?

10. A school council consists of 10 teachers and 12 students.
In how many ways can a group of 6 be selected if the group consists of
  (i) 3 teachers and 3 students
  (ii) 2 teachers and 4 students?

11. How many subsets, each containing three letters, can be made from the set $\{a, b, c, d, e, f\}$?
How many such subsets can be formed if
  (i) each subset contains one vowel and two consonants
  (ii) each subset contains at least one vowel?

12. In how many ways can a jury of 6 persons be chosen from 4 men and 4 women?
In how many of these ways will all the women have been chosen?

13. A board of six persons is to be chosen from five men and three women.
In how many ways can this be done
  (i) when there are 4 men on each board
  (ii) when there is a majority of men on each board?

14. There are 3 goalkeepers, 6 backs and 4 forwards available for selection on a 6-man team. How many different teams can be selected if each team has a goalkeeper, three backs and two forwards?

15. There are eight people, including Mr. and Mrs. Jones, on a committee.
How many subcommittees of four can be selected
  (i) if all members are eligible for the subcommittee
  (ii) if Mr. and Mrs. Jones are included on each subcommittee
  (iii) if neither Mr. nor Mrs. Jones can be included on the subcommittee?

16. Five points are marked on a plane. No three of them are collinear.
How many different triangles can be formed using these points as vertices?
Two of the five points are labelled X and Y respectively.
How many of the above triangles have [XY] as a side?

17. Six points A, B, C, D, E, F are marked on a sheet and no three of them are collinear.
  (i) How many different quadrilaterals can be formed using these points?
  (ii) How many of these quadrilaterals have A and B as one side?

18. Nine friends, including Ann and Barry, wish to go to a show but only five tickets are available.
In how many ways can the group of five be selected if
  (i) both Ann and Barry are included
  (ii) either Ann or Barry is included, but not both?
Another member of the group is named Claire.
  (iii) In how many ways can the group of five be selected, given that at least one of Ann, Barry and Claire must be included?

19. An examination paper consists of 12 questions, 5 in Section A and the remainder in Section B. A candidate must attempt 5 questions, at least 2 of which must be from each section. In how many different ways may the candidate select the 5 questions?

20. A registration system consists of the four letters A, B, C, D and the four digits 2, 4, 6, 8. Find the maximum number of registrations the system can have if each registration consists of 2 letters followed by 3 digits, none of which may be repeated in a registration.

21. Find the value of $n \in N$ in each of the following:
  (i) $\binom{n}{2} = 10$ (ii) $\binom{n}{2} = 45$ (iii) $\binom{n+1}{2} = 28$

Section 5.3 **Elementary probability** ——————————

Probability uses numbers to tell us how likely something is to happen.
The **probability** or **chance** of something happening can be described by using words such as:

  Impossible   **Unlikely**   **Even Chance**   **Likely**   **Certain**

An event which is **certain to happen** has a **probability of 1**.

An event which **cannot happen** has a **probability of 0**.

All other probabilities will be a number greater than 0 and less than 1.

The more likely an event is to happen, the closer the probability is to 1.

The line shown below is called a **probability scale**.

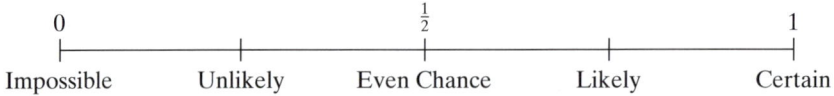

Before you start a certain game, you must throw a die and get a 6.
The act of throwing a die is called a **trial**.
The numbers 1, 2, 3, 4, 5 and 6 are all the possible **outcomes** of the trial.
The required result is called an **event**.

If you require an even number when throwing a die, then the
event or **successful outcomes** are the numbers 2, 4 and 6.

> The result we want
> is called an **event**.

The chance of getting a red with this spinner is the same as the chance
of getting a blue. Getting a red and getting a blue are **equally likely**.

In general, if E represents an event, the probability
of E occurring, denoted by $P(E)$, is given below:

$$P(E) = \frac{\text{number of successful outcomes in } E}{\text{number of possible outcomes}}$$

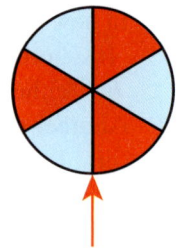

Note: 1. The probability of any event E cannot be less than 0 or greater than 1, i.e.,
$0 \leqslant P(E) \leqslant 1$.
2. The probability of a certainty is 1.
3. The probability of an impossibility is 0.
4. If E is an event, then the probability that E does not occur is 1 minus the
probability that E occurs.
This is written as **$P(E$ not occurring$) = 1 - P(E)$**.

> If A is an event, it will happen or not happen.
>
> $P(A$ happening$) = 1 - P(A$ not happening$)$.
>
> $$P(A) = 1 - P(A')$$

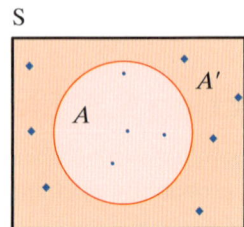

Example 1

If a card is drawn from a pack of 52, find the probability that it is
(i) an ace   (ii) a diamond   (iii) a red card.

(i) There are 4 aces in the pack $\Rightarrow P(\text{ace}) = \frac{4}{52} = \frac{1}{13}$

(ii) There are 13 diamonds in the pack $\Rightarrow P(\text{diamond}) = \frac{13}{52} = \frac{1}{4}$

(iii) There are 26 red cards in the pack $\Rightarrow P(\text{red card}) = \frac{26}{52} = \frac{1}{2}$

Example 2

A letter is selected at random from the letters of the word STATISTICS.
Find the probability that the letter is
(i) C   (ii) S   (iii) S or T   (iv) a vowel.

There are 10 letters in the word STATISTICS.

(i) There is just one C.   (ii) There are 3 Ss.
$\Rightarrow P(C) = \frac{1}{10}$ $\Rightarrow P(S) = \frac{3}{10}$

(iii) There are 3 Ss and 3 Ts, i.e. 6 altogether
$\Rightarrow P(\text{S or T}) = \frac{6}{10} = \frac{3}{5}$

(iv) There is one A and two Is in the word, i.e., 3 vowels.
$\Rightarrow P(\text{vowel}) = \frac{3}{10}$

Two events – use of sample spaces

When two coins are tossed, the set of possible outcomes is

$\{HH, HT, TH, TT\}$, where H = head and T = tail.

This set of possible outcomes is called a **sample space**.

By using this sample space, we can write down the probability of getting 2 heads, for example.

$P(HH) = \frac{1}{4}$ and $P(\text{one head and one tail}) = \frac{2}{4} = \frac{1}{2}$

In an experiment such as throwing two dice, for example, the construction of a sample space showing all the possible outcomes can assist in finding the probability of a given event.

Example 3

If two dice are thrown and the scores are added, set out a sample space giving all the possible outcomes. Find the probability that
   (i)   the total is exactly 7   (ii)   the total is 4 or less
   (iii)   the total is 11 or more   (iv)   the total is a multiple of 5.

The sample space is set out on the right.
There are 36 outcomes.
   (i)   There are 6 totals of 7.
         $\Rightarrow P(7) = \frac{6}{36} = \frac{1}{6}$
   (ii)   There are 6 totals of 4 or less.
         $\Rightarrow P(4 \text{ or less}) = \frac{6}{36} = \frac{1}{6}$
   (iii)   There are 3 totals of 11 or more.
         $\Rightarrow P(11 \text{ or more}) = \frac{3}{36} = \frac{1}{12}$
   (iv)   The multiples of 5 are 5 and 10.
         There are 7 totals of 5 or 10.
         $\Rightarrow P(\text{multiple of 5}) = \frac{7}{36}$

	1	2	3	4	5	6
1	2	3	4	5	6	7
2	3	4	5	6	7	8
3	4	5	6	7	8	9
4	5	6	7	8	9	10
5	6	7	8	9	10	11
6	7	8	9	10	11	12

Exercise 5.3

1.   There are seven labels on the probability scale below:

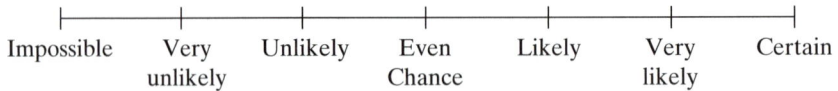

Impossible   Very unlikely   Unlikely   Even Chance   Likely   Very likely   Certain

Which of these labels best describes the likelihood of each of these events occurring?
   (i)   You will score 10 in a single throw of a normal die.
   (ii)   It will rain in Ireland sometime in the next week.
   (iii)   You will win a prize in the club lottery with a single ticket.
   (iv)   You will live to be 100 years old.
   (v)   If I toss a coin, it will show tails.
   (vi)   A day of the week ending with the letter Y.
   (vii)   You will draw an even number from these cards.

   3   2   7   9   6   5

2.   Yoghurt is sold in packs of 12.
   Robbie is going to take one without looking.

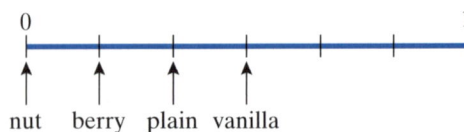

   0 ——————————— 1
   nut   berry   plain   vanilla

   Use the probability scale to work out how many of these flavours are in a pack:
   (i) vanilla   (ii) plain   (iii) nut   (iv) berry.

3.

0 ————————————————— 1

Yellow   Red   Blue

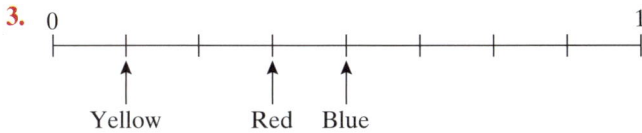

In a game, Todd spins an arrow. The arrow stops on one of sixteen equal sectors of a circle. Each sector of the circle is coloured. The probability scale shows how likely it is for the arrow to stop on any one colour. How many sectors are

(i) coloured red   (ii) coloured blue   (iii) coloured yellow?

4. A fair die is rolled.

What is the probability of getting

  (i) a 5   (ii) a 1 or a 2   (iii) 4 or more

(iv) an odd number   (v) less than 3   (vi) a prime number?

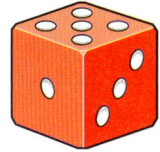

5. If one card is selected at random from a pack of 52 cards, what is the probability of getting

  (i) a king   (ii) a diamond   (iii) a picture card

(iv) a black queen   (v) an even number on the card?

6. Tickets numbered 1 to 17 are placed in a box.

If one ticket is drawn at random, what is the probability that it has

  (i) an odd number   (ii) a 2-digit number

(iii) a multiple of 3   (iv) a perfect square?

7. A letter is selected at random from the word ADDITION.

Find the probability that the letter is

(i) T   (ii) I   (iii) T or D   (iv) a vowel.

8. A counter is drawn from a box containing 15 red, 10 black and 5 green counters.

Find the probability that the counter is

(i) red   (ii) green   (iii) red or green   (iv) not red.

9. Two unbiased dice are thrown. Using the sample space given in Example 3 of this section, find the probability that

  (i) the total is 10   (ii) both numbers are odd

(iii) the total is 4 or less (iv) the total is odd and greater than 6.

10. Two dice are thrown simultaneously. The scores are to be multiplied.

If $P(n)$ is the probability that the number n is obtained, find

(i) $P(9)$ (ii) $P(4)$ (iii) $P(12)$.

11. There are 6 counters in a box.

The probability of taking a green counter out of the box is $\frac{1}{2}$.

A green counter is taken out of the box and put to one side.

Gerry now takes a counter from the box at random.

What is the probability it is green?

12. There are some yellow and purple blocks in a toddlers toy bin.
The probability of getting a yellow block, if you take a block at random out of the bin, is $\frac{2}{5}$.
   (i) What is the probability the block will be purple?
   (ii) Karl takes one block out of the bin.
   It is yellow.
   What is the smallest number of purple blocks there could be in the bin?
   (iii) Karl then takes another block out of the bin and it is also yellow.
   What is the smallest number of purple blocks there could be in the bin?

13. You play a game with two spinners, as shown.
They are spun at the same time and the scores are added.
Make out a sample space for the possible results and
write down the probability of getting a total of
(i) 6   (ii) 10   (iii) an even number.
Which score do you get most often?
Hence write down the probability of getting this score.

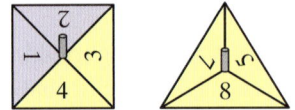

14. In a particular game, a player throws two fair dice together.
If their total is 7 or 11 he wins.
If their total is 2, 3 or 12 he loses.
For any other total, he neither wins nor loses.
   (i) Find the probability of winning.
   (ii) Find the probability of losing.

15. Three coins are tossed, each toss resulting in a head (H) or a tail (T).
Make out a sample space for the possible results and write down the probability that
the coins show
(i) *HHH*   (ii) *HTH* in that order   (iii) 2 heads and 1 tail in any order.

16. This two-way table shows the
numbers of males and females
in a group of 50 who wear or
do not wear glasses.

	Male	Female	Total
Wearing glasses	16	18	34
Not wearing glasses	9	7	16
Total	25	25	50

Work out the probability that
a person chosen at random is:
(i) female   (ii) not wearing glasses   (iii) a male who wears glasses.
If a male is chosen at random, find the probability that he wears glasses.

17. The pie chart gives information about how some
students travelled to school one day.
One of these students is chosen at random.
Use the information in the pie chart to work
out the probability that the student:
   (i) travelled to school by bus
   (ii) walked to school.

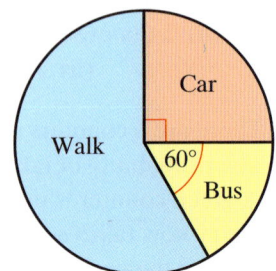

18. Consider a full deck of playing cards:
   (i)   In how many ways can 3 clubs be selected from 13 clubs
   (ii) In how many ways can 3 cards be selected from a full deck of cards.
   (iii) What is the probability of selecting 3 clubs from a full deck of cards.

19. This two way table results from a
survey of coffee drinking in a cafe.
   (i)   Complete the table.
   (ii) Complete the second table
         converting the data from
         the first table into
         probabilities.
   (iii) Using the probability table find:
         (a) the probability of a man
             not ordering coffee.
         (b) the probability of a
             customer not ordering coffee.

Data	Men	Women	Total
Orders Coffee		20	30
Does not order coffee	15		
Total			50

Probability	Male	Female	Total
Orders Coffee	0.2		
Does not order coffee			
Total		0.5	1

20. At an NCT garage it is found that 5 out of 15 trucks belonging to a company do not
meet emission standards.

If four of the trucks were chosen at random what is the probability that all of them
would have met the emission standards.

21. (i) Find the probability of rolling a total of "7" when tossing a pair of dice.
    (ii) Find the probability of rolling at least two 7's in four tosses of a pair of dice.

22. A debating team of 4 is chosen at random from 5 girls and 6 boys.
   (i) In how many ways can the team be chosen if
        (a) there are no restrictions
        (b) there must be more boys than girls.
   (ii) Find the probability that the team contains only one boy.

Section 5.4 Experimental probability
– Relative frequency

In the previous section, we calculated probabilities on the basis that all outcomes are equally
likely to happen. However in real-life situations, events are not always equally likely. For
example, the probability of a football team winning a game, or the probability that the next
car that passes the school gate will be coloured red, can only be estimated by analysing
previous results or carrying out an experiment or survey.

Experiment

John suspects that a coin is biased. In an experiment, he tossed the coin 200 times and
recorded the number of heads after 10, 50, 100, 150 and 200 tosses.

The results are shown in the table on the right:

As the number of tosses increase, the number of heads divided by the number of tosses gets closer to 0.5, i.e., $\frac{1}{2}$.

This value is called **relative frequency** and it gives an **estimate of the probability** that the event will happen.

Number of tosses	Number of heads	Heads ÷ tosses
10	7	0.7
50	28	0.56
100	53	0.53
150	78	0.52
200	103	0.515

Thus an estimate of the probability that an event will occur, by carrying out a survey or experiment, is given by

$$\text{Relative frequency} = \frac{\text{Number of successful trials}}{\text{Total number of trials}}$$

In general, as the number of trials or experiments increases, the value of the relative frequency gets closer to the true or theoretical probability.

Example 1

Dara collected data on the colours of cars passing the school gate.
His results are shown on the table below.

Colour	White	Red	Black	Blue	Green	Other
Frequency	24	32	14	16	10	4

(i)   How many cars did Dara survey?
(ii) What was the relative frequency of blue cars?
(iii) What was the relative frequency of red cars?
      Give your answer as a decimal.
(iv) Write down an estimate of the probability that the next car passing the school gate will be green.
(v)   How can the estimate for the probability of green cars be made more reliable?

(i)   The number of cars in the survey is the sum of the frequencies. This is 100 cars.

(ii) Relative frequency of blue cars $= \frac{16}{100} = \frac{4}{25}$

(iii) Relative frequency of red cars $= \frac{32}{100} = 0.32$

(iv) Probability of next car green = relative frequency of green cars
      $$= \frac{10}{100} = \frac{1}{10}$$

(v)   The estimate for the probability of green cars can be made more reliable by increasing the number of cars observed. Five hundred cars would give a very accurate estimate of the true probability.

Expected frequency

A bag contains 3 red discs and 2 blue discs.

A disc is chosen at random from the bag and replaced.

The probability of getting a blue disc is $\frac{2}{5}$.

This means that, on average, you expect 2 blue discs
in every 5 chosen or 20 blue discs in every 50 chosen.

To find the expected number of blue discs when you choose a disc 100 times,

(i) Work out the probability that the event happens once.
(ii) Multiply this probability by the number of times the experiment is carried out.
     Thus the expected number of blue discs is

$$\frac{2}{5} \times \frac{100}{1} = 40.$$

> Expected frequency is
> probability $\times$ number of trials.

Example 2

This spinner is biased.
The probability that the spinner will land on each of
the numbers 1 to 4 is given in the table below.

Number	1	2	3	4	5
Probability	0.35	0.1	0.25	0.15	k

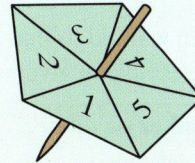

The spinner is spun once.
(i)   Work out the probability, k, that the spinner will land on 5.
(ii) Write down the number on which the spinner is most likely to land.
(iii) If the spinner is spun 200 times, how many times would you expect it to land
      on 3?

(i) The sum of the probabilities is 1.
     $\therefore \ 0.35 + 0.1 + 0.25 + 0.15 + k = 1$
     $\Rightarrow 0.85 + k = 1$
     $\Rightarrow k = 1 - 0.85 \Rightarrow k = 0.15$

(ii) The spinner is most likely to land on 1 as it has the highest probability.

(iii) $P(3) = 0.25$
      Expected frequency of $3 = P(3) \times$ number of trials
      $\qquad\qquad\qquad\qquad = 0.25 \times 200$
      $\qquad\qquad\qquad\qquad = 50$
      You would expect to land on a three 50 times.

Exercise 5.4

1. A fair die is thrown 900 times.
   - (i) How many twos would you expect to get?
   - (ii) How many sixes would you expect to get?
   - (iii) How many twos or sixes would you expect to get?

2. One ball is selected at random from the bag
   shown and then replaced. This procedure
   is performed 400 times.
   - (i) What is the probability of getting a red ball?
   - (ii) How many times would you expect to select
     - (a) a red ball   (b) a white ball?

3. Ben tosses a coin 100 times.
   His results are shown on the right.
   - (i) Find the relative frequency of getting a head.
   - (ii) Is the coin fair? Explain your answer.

Outcome	Frequency
Head	34
Tail	66

4. Helen wanted to find out if a die was biased. She threw the die 300 times.
   Her results are given in the table below.

Number on dice	1	2	3	4	5	6
Frequency	30	40	55	65	50	60

   - (i) For this die, calculate the experimental probability of obtaining
     - (a) a 6   (b) a 2.
   - (ii) For a fair die, calculate the probability of scoring
     - (a) a 6   (b) a 2.
   - (iii) Do your answers suggest that this die is fair?
     Give your reasons.

5. The sectors of a 3-sided spinner are each coloured red or orange or green.
   The table gives the results when the spinner is spun 300 times.

Colour	Red	Orange	Green
Frequency	154	56	90

   - (i) Use the information in the table to find an estimate for getting red.
   - (ii) Is this a fair spinner? Give a reason for your answer.

6. A spinner has 10 equal sectors, 5 red and 5 green.
   Dave carries out an experiment.
   He spins the spinner 300 times.
   The spinner lands on red 120 times.
   Is the spinner fair? Explain your answer.

7. The probability that a biased dice will land on each of the numbers 1 to 6 is given in the table below:

Number	1	2	3	4	5	6
Probability	x	0.2	0.1	0.3	0.1	0.2

   (i)   Calculate the value of x.
   (ii) If the dice is thrown once, find the probability that the dice will show a number higher than 3.
   (iii) If the dice is thrown 1000 times, estimate the number of times it will show a 6.

8. Gemma keeps a record of her chess games with Helen.
   Out of the first 10 games, Gemma wins 6.
   Out of the first 30 games, Gemma wins 21.
   Based on these results, estimate the probability that Gemma will win her next game of chess with Helen.

9. Paula records the number of 6s she gets when she rolls a dice 10, 100 and 1000 times. The table below shows her results.

Number of rolls	10	100	1000
Number of 6s	1	15	165

   Use this information to work out the best estimate for getting a 6 on Paula's dice.
   Give a reason for your answer.

10. Four friends are using a spinner for a game and they wonder if it is perfectly fair.
   They each spin the spinner many times and record the results.

Name	Number of spins	Results		
		0	1	2
Alan	30	12	12	6
Keith	100	31	49	20
Bill	300	99	133	68
Ann	150	45	73	32

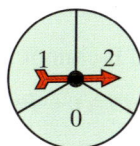

   (i)   Whose results are most likely to give the best estimate of the probability of getting each number?
   (ii) Make a table by adding together all the results.
         Use the table to decide whether you think the spinner is biased or unbiased.
   (iii) Use the results to work out the probability of the spinner getting a '2'.
   (iv) If the spinner is spun 1000 times, use the table in (ii) to write down the number of zeros you could expect.

11. (i) Sarah takes a cube and writes these numbers on its six faces: 1, 1, 2, 2, 2, 3.
        She then rolls the cube.
        What is the probability that the number 1 is uppermost?
    (ii) David writes numbers on the faces of a different cube.
        He rolls the cube many times and makes this record of how it lands.

Number uppermost	1	2	3	4
Frequency	42	79	85	34

        What numbers do you think he wrote on the six faces of the cube?

12. Mark is the captain of the basketball team.
Based on last year's results it is noted that the team won 90% of their home games when Mark played and 70% when he was injured and did not play. The team lost 15% of its away games when Mark played and 30 % when he did not.
This season it is expected that the team will play 10 games away and 10 games at home.
How many games would they expect to win if:
  (i)   Mark plays all the games
  (ii) Mark plays none of the games.

13. In a town the probability that it will rain on an April day is 0.4, the probability that in April a day in which it rains is followed by a day in which it rains is 0.7 and the probability that in April a day in which it does not rain is followed by a day in which it rains is 0.2. What are the probabilities that on three consecutive days in April it will:
  (i)   rain on each day,
  (ii) not rain on the first day and rain on the next two days?
What is the probability that it will
  (iii) rain, rain, not rain, rain on four consecutive days in April?

Section 5.5 Mutually exclusive events
– The addition rule

Consider the following two events when drawing a card from a pack of 52 playing cards:

  A = drawing an ace   B = drawing a king.

These two events are said to be **mutually exclusive** as they cannot occur together.

If the events A and B cannot happen together, then

  $P(A \text{ or } B) = P(A) + P(B)$

This is called the **addition law** for mutually exclusive events.

> Events are mutually exclusive if they cannot happen at the same time.

So $P(\text{draw an ace } \textbf{or} \text{ king}) = P(\text{ace}) + P(\text{king})$
$$= \frac{4}{52} + \frac{4}{52}$$
$$= \frac{8}{52} = \frac{2}{13}$$

When events are not mutually exclusive

We will now consider events which may occur at the same time.
If A is the event: selecting an ace from a pack of cards and
  B is the event: selecting a heart from a pack of cards
  then $P(A) = \frac{4}{52}$ and $P(B) = \frac{13}{52}$

In this situation, both events may occur at the same time since the *ace of hearts* is common to both.

In general, when two events A and B can occur at the same time,

$$P(A \text{ or } B) = P(A) + P(B) - P(A \text{ and } B)$$

Thus in the example given above,

$$P(\text{ace or heart}) = P(\text{ace}) + P(\text{heart}) - P(\text{ace and heart})$$
$$= \tfrac{4}{52} + \tfrac{13}{52} - \tfrac{1}{52}$$
$$= \tfrac{16}{52}$$

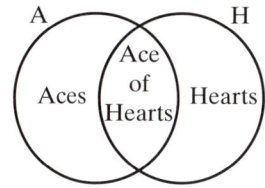

This result can be verified as there are 4 aces and 13 hearts in a pack of cards. Since one of the aces is the ace of hearts, there are 16 aces or hearts in the pack.

i.e. $P(\text{ace or a heart}) = \tfrac{16}{52}$, as already found.

Example 1

A card is drawn at random from a pack of 52.
What is the probability that the card is
  (i) a club   (ii) a king   (iii) a club or a king
 (iv) a red card   (v) a queen   (vi) a red card or a queen

  (i) $P(\text{club}) = \tfrac{13}{52} = \tfrac{1}{4}$

 (ii) $P(\text{king}) = \tfrac{4}{52} = \tfrac{1}{13}$

(iii) $P(\text{a club or a king}) = P(\text{club}) + P(\text{king}) - P(\text{club and king})$
$$= \tfrac{13}{52} + \tfrac{4}{52} - \tfrac{1}{52}$$
$$= \tfrac{16}{52} = \tfrac{4}{13}$$

 (iv) $P(\text{red card}) = \tfrac{26}{52} = \tfrac{1}{2}$

  (v) $P(\text{queen}) = \tfrac{4}{52} = \tfrac{1}{13}$

 (vi) $P(\text{a red card or a queen}) = P(\text{red card}) + P(\text{queen}) - P(\text{red card and queen})$
$$= \tfrac{26}{52} + \tfrac{4}{52} - \tfrac{2}{52}$$
$$= \tfrac{28}{52} = \tfrac{7}{13}$$

Venn diagrams for mutually exclusive events

(i) Mutually exclusive

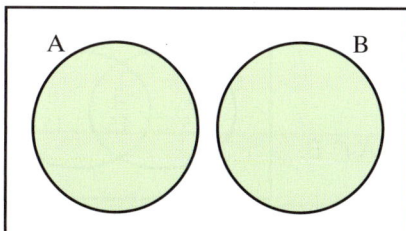

$P(\text{A or B}) = P(\text{A}) + P(\text{B})$
$P(\text{A} \cup \text{B}) = P(\text{A}) + P(\text{B})$

(ii) Non-mutually exclusive

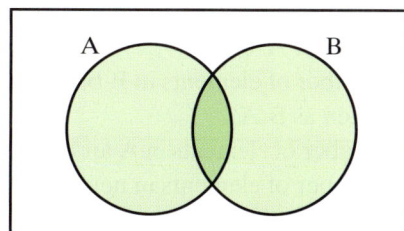

$P(\text{A or B}) = P(\text{A}) + P(\text{B}) - P(\text{A} \cap \text{B})$
$P(\text{A} \cup \text{B}) = P(\text{A}) + P(\text{B}) - P(\text{A} \cap \text{B})$

Example 2

A and B are two events such that $P(A) = \frac{19}{30}$, $P(B) = \frac{2}{5}$ and $P(A \cup B) = \frac{4}{5}$.
Find $P(A \cap B)$.

Using $P(A \cup B) = P(A) + P(B) - P(A \cap B)$

$$\frac{4}{5} = \frac{19}{30} + \frac{2}{5} - P(A \cap B)$$

$$P(A \cap B) = \frac{19}{30} + \frac{2}{5} - \frac{4}{5}$$

$$= \frac{19}{30} + \frac{12}{30} - \frac{24}{30}$$

$$= \frac{7}{30}$$

Exhaustive events

Consider these events when throwing a dice:

A: Getting an odd number
B: Getting an even number

These two events contain all the possible outcomes
when a dice is thrown.

These events are said to be **exhaustive**.

If A and B are exhaustive events, then

$$P(A) + P(B) = 1.$$

> A set of events is exhaustive if the set contains all possible outcomes.

Venn diagrams

A Venn diagram is a useful way to represent data or probabilities.
Each region of a Venn diagram represents a different set of data.

The Venn diagram on the right shows two sets, A and B,
in the sample space S.

The number of elements in each region is also shown.

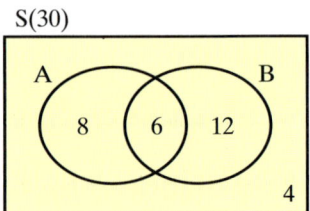

S(30)

A   8 (6) 12   B

4

8 is the number of elements in A but not in B.
This is written as A/B.
12 is the number of elements in B but not in A.
This is written as B/A.
6 is the number of elements in A and B. This is written as A ∩ B.
4 is the number of elements in neither A nor B.
This is written as (A ∪ B)'.

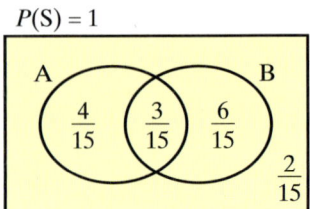

$P(S) = 1$

A $\frac{4}{15}$ ($\frac{3}{15}$) $\frac{6}{15}$ B

$\frac{2}{15}$

If information is presented in the form of a Venn diagram, it is easy to write down the
probability of different events occurring.

In the diagram on the previous page, the probability of either A or B is given by $P(A \cup B)$.

$$P(A \cup B) = \frac{8 + 6 + 12}{8 + 6 + 12 + 4} = \frac{26}{30} = \frac{13}{15}$$

Example 3

The given Venn diagram represents the subjects taken by a group of 50 pupils.
  (i) Find the value of x.

Now find the probability that a person chosen at random takes
  (ii) both subjects
  (iii) neither subject
  (iv) Science but not Maths
  (v) Maths or Science or both.

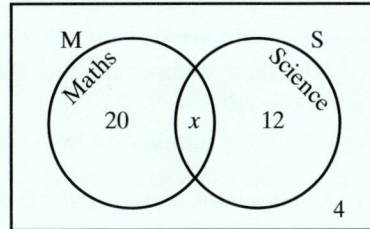

  (i) $x = 50 - (20 + 12 + 4)$ i.e. $x = 14$

  (ii) $P(\text{both}) = \frac{x}{50} = \frac{14}{50} = \frac{7}{25}$

  (iii) $P(\text{neither}) = P(M \cup S)' = \frac{4}{50} = \frac{2}{25}$

  (iv) $P(\text{Science but not Maths}) = \frac{12}{50} = \frac{6}{25}$

  (v) $P(\text{Science or Maths or both}) = \frac{20 + 14 + 12}{50} = \frac{46}{50} = \frac{23}{25}$

Exercise 5.5

1. A box contains discs numbered 1 to 16.
    If a disc is selected at random, what is the probability that it is
    (i) an odd number   (ii) a multiple of 4
    (iii) an odd number or a multiple of 4?

2. A card is selected at random from a pack of 52 playing cards.
    What is the probability that it is
    (i) a spade   (ii) a red picture card
    (iii) a spade or a red picture card?

3. A number is selected at random from the integers 1 to 30 inclusive.
    Find the probability that the number is
    (i) a multiple of 3   (ii) a multiple of 5
    Explain why events (i) and (ii) are not mutually exclusive.
    Now find the probability that a multiple of 3 or 5 is selected.

4. A number is selected at random from the integers 1 to 12 inclusive.
   Find the probability that the number is
   (i) even   (ii) a multiple of 3   (iii) even or a multiple of 3.

5. A card is drawn at random from a pack of 52.
   What is the probability that the card is
   (i) a club   (ii) a king   (iii) a club or a king
   (iv) a red card   (v) a queen   (vi) a red card or a queen?

6. If two fair dice are thrown, what is the probability of getting
   (i) the same number on both dice
   (ii) a total of 8
   (iii) the same number on both dice or a total of 8?

7. In a small school, a class consists of children of a variety of ages as given in the table.

5-year-old girls	5-year-old boys	6-year-old girls	6-year-old boys	7-year-old girls	7-year-old boys
3	4	6	8	5	2

   A pupil is selected at random.
   What is the probability that the pupil is
   (i) a girl   (ii) not 5 years old
   (iii) a boy and 6 years old   (iv) a girl or 6 years old
   (v) 6 or 7 years old   (vi) 6 and 7 years old?

8. The results of a traffic survey of colour and type of car are given in the table shown.

   One car is selected at random from this group.
   Find the probability that the car selected is
   (i) a green estate car
   (ii) a saloon car
   (iii) a black car or an estate car.

	Saloon	Estate
White	68	62
Green	26	32
Black	6	6

9. In a fairground game, players each choose a number on this board.
   An electronic device lights up and turns off the numbers
   in a random way. When it stops, one number is lit up.
   What is the probability that the lit-up number is
   (i) in the first row
   (ii) in the first column
   (iii) either in the first row or the first column
   (iv) on the edge of the board
   (v) on the diagonal from top left to bottom right
   (vi) either on the edge or on the diagonal from top left to bottom right
   (vii) either a square number or an odd number?

1	2	3	4
5	6	7	8
9	10	11	12
13	14	15	16

10. A bag contained 8 red, 12 blue and an unknown number of green beads.
    In a random draw, the probability of drawing a green bead was $\frac{1}{5}$.
    How many green beads were in the bag at the start?

11. Of 100 tickets sold in a raffle, 40 were red, 30 were blue and 30 were green.
If the winning ticket was drawn at random, find the probability that it was

   (i) red   (ii) not blue.

Every red ticket is even-numbered and every blue ticket is odd-numbered.
Of the green tickets, 20 are even-numbered and 10 are odd-numbered.
Find the probability that the winning ticket was

(iii) green or even-numbered.

12. Of one hundred people in a sports club, 40% are male. A recent survey showed that
10% of the males and 15% of the females play tennis.

   (i) Find the probability that a person chosen at random from the group is male and plays
tennis.

  (ii) Find the probability that a person chosen at random from the group plays tennis.

(iii) Find the probability that the person chosen is female **or** plays tennis.

13. These cards are turned over and shuffled.

A card is picked at random.

| 20 | 21 | 22 | 23 | 24 | 25 | 26 | 27 | 28 | 29 |

      The event A is 'The number picked is less than 24'.
      The event B is 'The number picked is a multiple of 5'.
      The event C is 'The number picked is prime'.
      The event D is 'The number picked is a multiple of 3'.

   (i) Are these pairs of events mutually exclusive?

      (a) A, B   (b) A, C   (c) A, D   (d) B, C   (e) B, D

  (ii) What is the probability that the number picked is either prime or a multiple of 3?

(iii) Jeff said:

     'The probability of picking a number less than 24 is $\frac{4}{10}$.

     The probability of picking an even number is $\frac{5}{10}$.

     So the probability of picking either a number less than 24 or an even number is $\frac{9}{10}$.'

     Is he right? If not, why not?

14. The Venn diagram on the right shows the number
of elements in each region.

Write down   (i) $P(A)$ (ii) $P(B)$ (iii) $P(A \cup B)$.
Now verify that $P(A \cup B) = P(A) + P(B) - P(A \cap B)$.

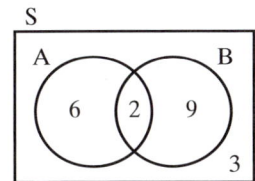

15. The given Venn diagram shows the probabilities
of events C and D in the universal set S.

Find   (i) $P(C)$ (ii) $P(D)$
     (iii) $P(C \cup D)$ (iv) $P(C \cap D)$
Verify that $P(C \cup D) = P(C) + P(D) - P(C \cap D)$

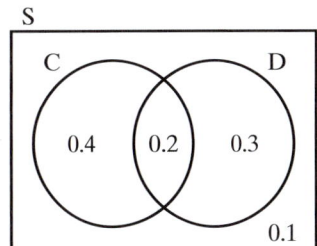

16. The given Venn diagram shows the languages taken by a group of 50 students.

    (i) Find the value of x.

If a student is selected at random, find the probability that the student takes

    (ii) French

    (iii) both French and Spanish

    (iv) French or Spanish

    (v) one of these languages only.

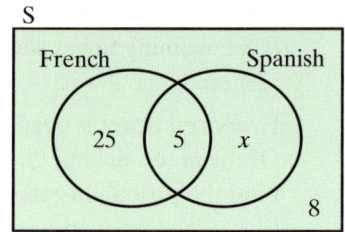

17. The Venn diagram shows the hobbies of a group of girls.

    (i) Write down the total number of girls.

    (ii) A girl is chosen at random.
        Find the probability that she does both Drama and Art.

    (iii) A girl is chosen at random. She does Drama.
        Find the probability that she does Art.

    (iv) A girl is chosen at random. She does Sport.
        Find the probability that she does Drama.

    (v) A girl is chosen at random. She does both Drama and Art.
        Find the probability that she does all three.

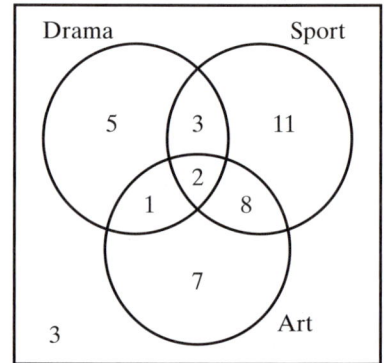

18. A town council gets a grant to build two sports centres. During the first year the centres were open, it was found that 36% of the population had been to centre A, 22% had been to centre B and 10% had been to both.

    (i) Draw a Venn diagram to represent this data.

    (ii) What percentage of the population had been to neither centre?

    (iii) What percentage had been to centre A only?

19. For events A and B, it is known that $P(A) = \frac{2}{3}$, $P(A \cup B) = \frac{3}{4}$ and $P(A \cap B) = \frac{5}{12}$. Find $P(B)$.

20. For events X and Y, it is known that $P(X) = \frac{1}{2}$, $P(Y) = \frac{3}{5}$ and $P(X \cup Y) = \frac{9}{10}$. Find $P(X \cap Y)$.

21. For events C and D, $P(C) = 0.7$, $P(C \cup D) = 0.9$ and $P(C \cap D) = 0.3$. Find $P(D)$.

22. A and B are two events such that $P(A) = 0.8$, $P(B) = 0.5$ and $P(A \cap B) = 0.3$.

    (i) Find $P(A \cup B)$.

    (ii) Verify that $P(A \cup B) = P(A) + P(B) - P(A \cap B)$.

23. A and B are two events such that $P(A) = \frac{8}{15}$, $P(B) = \frac{2}{3}$ and $P(A \cap B) = \frac{1}{3}$.

    (i) Find $P(A \cup B)$.

    (ii) Are A and B mutually exclusive? Explain your answer.

24. A and B are mutually exclusive events.
    If $P(A) = \frac{3}{7}$ and $P(B) = \frac{1}{5}$, find $P(A \cup B)$.

25. In a survey, 50 teenagers were asked if they went out to the cinema(A) or they watched movies at home(B) or both, over the weekend. The following data was collected:

(i) B ∩ A = 25

(ii) A ∩ B′ = 10

(iii) A′ ∩ B′ = 10

(a) Using this data, copy and complete the Venn diagram for this survey.

(b) Describe the set of students A′ ∩ B′.

(c) Using the data redraw the Venn diagram inputting the probabilities for regions 1, 2, 3 and 4.

(d) Using the Venn diagram find the probability of choosing a student who went to the cinema but who did not watch movies at home over the weekend.

(e) Find also (i) $P(A)$ (ii) $P(B)$

S = ( )

A( )   B( )

( )   ()   ( )

$P(S) = 1$

A   B

1   2   3

4

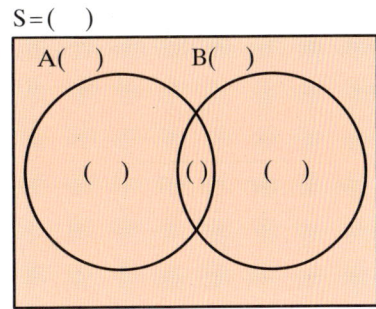

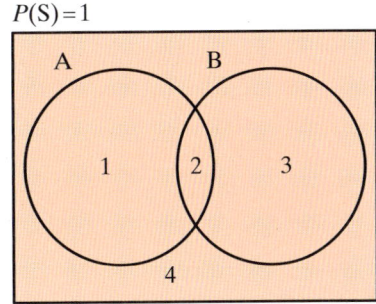

Section 5.6 The multiplication law for independent events

Paul spins a coin and rolls a dice.

His results are shown on the right.

The coin and the die do not affect each other, so their outcomes are **independent**.

There are 12 equally likely outcomes of the coin and die, as shown in the diagram on the right.

From the sample space, we can see that the probability of a head and a 5 is $\frac{1}{12}$.

Dice		
6	H, 6	T, 6
5	H, 5	T, 5
4	H, 4	T, 4
3	H, 3	T, 3
2	H, 2	T, 2
1	H, 1	T, 1
	H(ead)	T(ail)
	Coin	

The probability of each outcome can also be found by multiplying the separate probabilities i.e. $P(H) = \frac{1}{2}$, $P(5) = \frac{1}{6}$ ∴ $P(H$ and $5) = \frac{1}{2} \times \frac{1}{6} = \frac{1}{12}$

This illustrates the **multiplication law** of probability which states that for independent events A and B,

$P(A$ and B$) = P(A) \times P(B)$

This law is sometimes called the AND Rule.

The multiplication law applies to any number of independent events. If the events are A, B, C, ..., then

$P(A$ and B and C ...$) = P(A) \times P(B) \times P(C) \times ...$

The multiplication law is particularly useful when dealing with problems where one event is followed by another event such as throwing two dice or selecting two or more cards from a pack. The use of the multiplication law eliminates the need to construct a sample space and so significantly reduces the work involved in solving certain problems.

Example 1

When two dice are thrown, what is the probability of getting
(i) two sixes   (ii) 4 or more on each die?

(i) The probability of getting 6 on the first die is $\frac{1}{6}$.

The probability of getting 6 on the second die is also $\frac{1}{6}$.

$\therefore P(6, 6) = \frac{1}{6} \times \frac{1}{6} = \frac{1}{36}$

(ii) The probability of getting 4 or more on any die is $\frac{1}{2}$.

$\therefore P(4 \text{ or more on each die}) = \frac{1}{2} \times \frac{1}{2} = \frac{1}{4}$

(Both of these answers could be found by using the sample space for throwing two dice.)

Example 2

These two spinners are spun.
What is the probability that
(i) spinner A shows red
(ii) spinner B shows red
(iii) both spinners show red
(iv) A shows red and B shows blue
(v) both show blue
(vi) both show white
(vii) neither shows white?

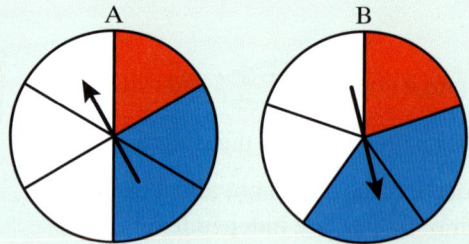

(i) $P(\text{A shows red}) = \frac{1}{6}$

(ii) $P(\text{B shows red}) = \frac{1}{5}$

(iii) $P(\text{both show red}) = P(\text{A red}) \times P(\text{B red})$

$= \frac{1}{6} \times \frac{1}{5} = \frac{1}{30}$

(iv) $P(\text{A red and B blue}) = P(\text{A red}) \times P(\text{B blue})$

$= \frac{1}{6} \times \frac{2}{5} = \frac{2}{30} = \frac{1}{15}$

(v) $P(\text{both blue}) = P(\text{A blue}) \times P(\text{B blue})$

$= \frac{2}{6} \times \frac{2}{5} = \frac{4}{30} = \frac{2}{15}$

(vi) $P(\text{both white}) = P(A \text{ white}) \times P(B \text{ white})$

$$= \tfrac{1}{2} \times \tfrac{2}{5} = \tfrac{2}{10} = \tfrac{1}{5}$$

(vii) $P(\text{neither shows white}) = P(A \text{ not white}) \times P(B \text{ not white})$

$$= \tfrac{1}{2} \times \tfrac{3}{5} = \tfrac{3}{10}$$

Example 3

A gambler must throw a 6 with a single dice to win a prize.
Find the probability that he wins at his third attempt.

To win at his third attempt, he must fail at the first, fail at the second and win at the third attempt.

$P(\text{not throwing a 6 at his first attempt}) = \tfrac{5}{6}$

$P(\text{not throwing a 6 at his second attempt}) = \tfrac{5}{6}$

$P(\text{throwing a 6 at his third attempt}) = \tfrac{1}{6}$

$\Rightarrow P(\text{winning at his third attempt}) = \tfrac{5}{6} \times \tfrac{5}{6} \times \tfrac{1}{6} = \tfrac{25}{216}$

Example 4

Three pupils A, B and C have their birthdays in the same week.
What is the probability that the three birthdays
  (i) fall on a Monday
  (ii) fall on the same day
  (iii) fall on three different days?

  (i) $P(A\text{'s birthday falls on a Monday}) = \tfrac{1}{7}$

  $P(\text{all three on Monday}) = \tfrac{1}{7} \times \tfrac{1}{7} \times \tfrac{1}{7} = \tfrac{1}{343}$

  (ii) $P(A \text{ has birthday on some day of week}) = 1 \ldots$ a certainty

  $P(B \text{ has birthday on the same day}) = \tfrac{1}{7}$

  $P(C \text{ has birthday on the same day}) = \tfrac{1}{7}$

  $\therefore P(\text{all have birthday on the same day}) = 1 \times \tfrac{1}{7} \times \tfrac{1}{7} = \tfrac{1}{49}$

  (iii) $P(A \text{ has birthday on some day of the week}) = 1 \ldots$ a certainty

  $P(B \text{ has birthday on a different day}) = \tfrac{6}{7}$

  $P(C \text{ has birthday on different day from } A \text{ and } B) = \tfrac{5}{7}$

  $\Rightarrow P(\text{all have birthday on different days}) = 1 \times \tfrac{6}{7} \times \tfrac{5}{7} = \tfrac{30}{49}$

Exercise 5.6

1. This spinner is spun twice.
   Find the probability of getting
   - (i) 2 reds
   - (ii) 2 greens
   - (iii) 2 yellows
   - (iv) a red and a green in that order.

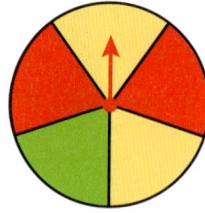

2. A dice is thrown twice. What is the probability of getting
   - (i) two sixes
   - (ii) a six on the first throw and an even number on the second
   - (iii) an odd number on the first throw and a multiple of 3 on the second?

3. A coin is tossed and a dice is thrown. Find the probability of obtaining
   - (i) a head and a six
   - (ii) a head and an even number.

4. A card is drawn from a pack of 52 and then replaced. A second card is then drawn.
   What is the probability that
   - (i) both cards are black
   - (ii) both cards are kings
   - (iii) the first card is a black ace and the second card is a diamond?

5. A bag contains 4 red discs and 6 blue discs. A disc is drawn at random and then
   replaced. A second disc is then drawn. Find the probability that
   - (i) both discs are red
   - (ii) the first is blue and the second is red
   - (iii) the first is red and the second is blue
   - (iv) both discs are blue
   - (v) both discs are of the same colour.

6. The probability that it will rain tomorrow is $\frac{2}{3}$.
   The probability that Jean will forget her umbrella tomorrow is $\frac{3}{4}$.
   Work out the probability that it will rain tomorrow and Jean will forget her umbrella.

7. A card is taken at random from each of two ordinary packs of cards, pack A and pack B.
   Work out the probability of getting:
   - (i) a red card from pack A and a red card from pack B
   - (ii) a diamond from pack A and a club from pack B
   - (iii) a King from pack A and a picture card (King, Queen, Jack) from pack B
   - (iv) a 10 from pack A and the 10 of clubs from pack B
   - (v) an ace of hearts from each pack.

8. A fruit machine has three independent reels and pays out a Jackpot of €50 when three
   raspberries are obtained. Each reel has 12 pictures. The first reel has four raspberries,
   the second has three raspberries and the third has two raspberries.
   Find the probability of winning the Jackpot.

9. An archer shoots at a target. The probability of hitting the gold area is 0.2.
   He fires two shots at the target.
   (i)   What is the probability that both arrows hit the gold area?
   (ii) What is the probability that exactly one arrow hits the gold area?

10. Three children take a test. The probability that Chris passes is 0.8, the probability that Georgie passes is 0.9 and the probability that Phil passes is 0.7.
    (i)   What is the probability that all three pass?
    (ii) What is the probability that all three fail?
    (iii) What is the probability that at least one passes?

11. Two men, Alan and Shane, each have one shot at a target. The probability that Alan hits the target is $\frac{1}{2}$ and the probability that Shane hits the target is $\frac{2}{3}$.
    Find the probability that
    (i)   both men hit the target
    (ii) neither hits the target
    (iii) only one of them hits the target.

12. John drives to work and passes three sets of traffic lights.
    The probability that he has to stop at the first is 0.6.
    The probability that he has to stop at the second is 0.7.
    The probability that he has to stop at the third is 0.8.
    (i)   Calculate the probability that he stops at all three sets of traffic lights.

    He arrives late if he has to stop at any two sets of traffic lights.
    (ii) Calculate the probability that he is late.

13. A fair dice is thrown 3 times. Find the probability that there will be
    (i) no sixes   (ii) at least one six   (iii) exactly one six.
    Find also the probability that the three throws all show the same number.

14. The birthdays of Jack and Jill fall on the same week. Find the probability that
    (i)   both have their birthdays on Monday
    (ii) both have their birthdays on the same day
    (iii) they have their birthdays on different days
    (iv) Monday is the birthday of one or both.

15. Three people were selected at random and asked on which day of the week their next birthday was falling.
    What is the probability that
    (i)   none of the birthdays falls on a Sunday
    (ii) only one of the birthdays falls on a Sunday
    (iii) at least one of the birthdays falls on a Sunday?

Section 5.7 Conditional probability

A box contains 2 red counters and 4 yellow counters, as shown.

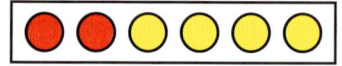

One counter is picked at random.

$P(\text{red}) = \frac{2}{6}$ and $P(\text{yellow}) = \frac{4}{6}$

Suppose the counter is **not** put back in the box.

The contents of the box will be different, depending on whether the counter taken out was red or yellow.

If it was red, the box would now contain 1 red and 4 yellow counters, as shown.

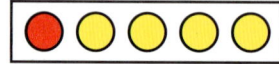

If another counter is now taken out at random, the probability that it is red is **dependent** on the colour of the first counter.

This is called **conditional probability**.

Returning to the second box above, $P(\text{red})$ is now $\frac{1}{5}$.

This probability is calculated on the assumption that a red was got on the first draw.

The box and counters discussed above is an example of a situation where the probability of the second event depends on the outcome of the first event.

If A and B are two events, the **conditional probability** that A occurs, **given that B has already occurred**, is written $P(A \,|\, B)$.

$P(A \,|\, B)$ is read as "the probability of A given B".

The conditional probability $(A \,|\, B)$ is illustrated in the given Venn diagram.

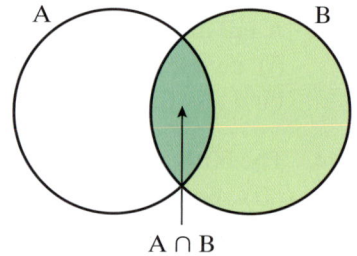

To find $P(A \,|\, B)$, the sample space is reduced to B only, since B has already occurred.

Thus $P(A \,|\, B) = \dfrac{\#(A \cap B)}{\#B} = \dfrac{P(A \cap B)}{P(B)}$.

The part of B in which A also occurs is the part denoted by $A \cap B$.

Thus $P(A \,|\, B) = \dfrac{\#(A \cap B)}{\#B} = \dfrac{P(A \cap B)}{P(B)}$

Note:

This result should be memorised as it will be used later in our study of probability.

This result can be described in words as follows:

"The probability of A given B is the probability of A and B divided by the probability of B".

A rule known as "*The General Multiplication Law*" which we will use in book 5.

The result $P(A \mid B) = \dfrac{P(A \cap B)}{P(B)}$ can be written as

$$P(A \cap B) = P(A \mid B) \times P(B) \dots \text{multiplying both sides by } P(B).$$
$$\therefore \quad P(B \cap A) = P(B \mid A) \times P(A) = P(A) \times P(B \mid A)$$
$$\therefore \quad \mathbf{P(A \cap B) = P(A) \times P(B \mid A)} \dots \text{since } P(A \cap B) = P(B \cap A).$$

Example 1

The numbers 1 to 9 are written on cards and placed in a box.
A card is drawn at random from the box.
Find the probability that the number is prime, given that the number is odd.

The prime numbers up to 9 are   2, 3, 5, 7.

$$P(\text{prime, given odd number}) = \frac{\text{number of odd primes}}{\text{number of odd numbers}}$$

$$= \frac{3}{5}$$

Example 2

A bag contains 6 red and 4 blue discs. A disc is drawn from the bag and not replaced. A second disc is then drawn.
Find the probability that
  (i) the first two discs are blue
 (ii) the second disc drawn is red
(iii) one disc is red and the other disc is blue
(iv) both discs are the same colour.

[The notation $P(R, B)$ represents the probability of red first and blue second.]

  (i) $P(\text{1st disc is blue}) = \frac{4}{10}$

   $P(\text{2nd disc is blue}) = \frac{3}{9}$

   $\Rightarrow P(B, B) = \frac{4}{10} \times \frac{3}{9} = \frac{12}{90} = \frac{2}{15}$

 (ii) For the 2nd disc to be red, we could have
    (a) 1st red and 2nd red   **or**   (b) 1st blue and 2nd red

   $P(\text{1st red and 2nd red}) = \frac{6}{10} \times \frac{5}{9} = \frac{30}{90}$

   $P(\text{1st blue and 2nd red}) = \frac{4}{10} \times \frac{6}{90} = \frac{24}{90}$

$\Rightarrow$ P(2nd disc red) = sum of probabilities $\frac{30}{90}$ and $\frac{24}{90}$

$$\frac{30}{90} + \frac{24}{90} = \frac{54}{90} = \frac{6}{10} = \frac{3}{5}$$

(iii) P(one disc is red and the other blue) is

P(1st red and 2nd blue or 1st blue and 2nd red)

$= P(R, B) + P(B, R)$

$= \left(\frac{6}{10} \times \frac{4}{9}\right) + \left(\frac{4}{10} \times \frac{6}{9}\right)$

$= \frac{24}{90} + \frac{24}{90} = \frac{48}{90} = \frac{8}{15}$

$\therefore$ P(one red, one blue) $= \frac{8}{15}$

(iv) P(both discs the same colour) = P(R, R) + P(B, B)

$P(R, R) = \frac{6}{10} \times \frac{5}{9} = \frac{30}{90}$

$P(B, B) = \frac{2}{15}$ ... from (i) above

$\Rightarrow$ P(both discs the same colour) $= \frac{30}{90} + \frac{2}{15} = \frac{7}{15}$

Example 3

Use the given Venn diagram to write down
(i) $P(A|B)$ (ii) $P(B|A)$

(i) $P(A|B) = \dfrac{P(A \cap B)}{P(B)} = \dfrac{0.1}{0.4} = 0.25$

(ii) $P(B|A) = \dfrac{P(B \cap A)}{P(A)} = \dfrac{0.1}{0.5} = 0.2$

[These probabilities could be written
down directly from the Venn diagram.]

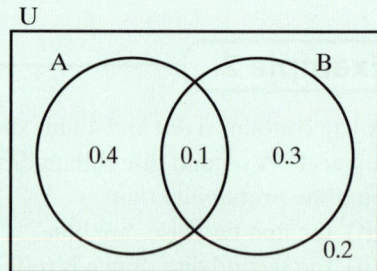

Example 4

Two events A and B are such that $P(A) = 0.7$, $P(B) = 0.4$ and $P(A|B) = 0.3$.
Determine the probability that neither A nor B occurs.

The shaded region is the part of the diagram
where **neither A nor B** occurs.

We use the formula $P(A|B) = \dfrac{P(A \cap B)}{P(B)}$

to find the probability of $A \cap B$.

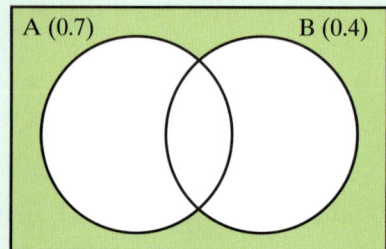

$$P(A \mid B) = \frac{P(A \cap B)}{P(B)} \Rightarrow 0.3 = \frac{P(A \cap B)}{0.4}$$

$$\Rightarrow P(A \cap B) = 0.3 \times 0.4 = 0.12$$

We now fill in the other probabilities in the Venn diagram.

$P(\text{neither } A \text{ nor } B) = 1 - P(A \cup B)$
$\qquad\qquad\qquad\quad = 1 - [0.58 + 0.12 + 0.28]$
$\qquad\qquad\qquad\quad = 1 - 0.98 = 0.02$

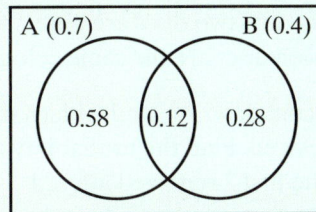

Exercise 5.7

1. A card is drawn at random from a pack of 52 playing cards.
   (i) Given that the card is black, find the probability that it is a spade.
   (ii) Given that the card is red, find the probability that it is a queen.
   (iii) Given that the card is a picture card, find the probability that it is a king.

2. The table shows information about a group of adults.

	Can drive	Cannot drive
Male	32	8
Female	38	12

   (i) A person is chosen at random from the group.
   What is the probability that the person can drive?
   (ii) A man in the group is chosen at random.
   What is the probability that he can drive?
   (iii) Find the probability that a person chosen at random can drive, given that the person is a female.

3. Two fair dice are thrown and the product of the numbers showing is recorded. Given that one dice shows a 2, find the probability that the product of the two numbers showing is
   (i) exactly 6   (ii) 6 or more.

4. A school enters 120 pupils for the Junior Certificate maths exam.
   The given table shows the details of the entries.

	Ordinary	Higher
Girls	20	35
Boys	25	40

   (i) Write down the probability that a pupil chosen at random is entered for Ordinary level.
   (ii) A pupil is chosen at random. This pupil is a girl.
   Find the probability that the girl was entered for Higher level.
   (iii) A pupil is chosen at random. The pupil was entered for Ordinary level.
   Find the probability that the pupil was a boy.

5. A bag contains 5 red discs and 3 blue discs.

A disc is taken from the bag and not replaced. A second disc is then taken from the bag.

Find the probability that

(i) the first disc is red

(ii) the first 2 discs are red

(iii) the first two discs are blue

(iv) both discs are the same colour.

6. A bag contains 5 red and 6 black marbles. The marbles are removed, one at a time, and not replaced. Find the probability that

(i) the first 2 removed are red

(ii) the first is red and the second is black

(iii) the first 2 removed are black

(iv) the first 2 removed are of the same colour

(v) the second marble removed is red.

7. Five cards, labelled E, V, E, N, T, are thoroughly shuffled and then dealt out, face upwards, on a table.

Find the probability that

(i) the first two cards to appear are labelled T, N, in that order

(ii) the first two cards to appear are labelled E, V, in that order

(iii) the second card to appear is labelled E.

8. If two letters are selected at random from the word SWIMMING, what is the probability that both letters are the same?

9. This table gives information about the children in a primary school class.

	Left-handed	Right-handed
Girls	5	15
Boys	4	9

(i) One of the children is picked at random from the class.

What is the probability that the child is a girl?

(ii) One of the boys in the class is picked at random.

What is the probability that he is left-handed?

(iii) A boy in the class is picked at random, and a girl is picked at random.

What is the probability that they are both left-handed?

(iv) One of the right-handed children is picked at random.

What is the probability that the child is a boy?

10. In a TV game show, contestants are given two tasks.

In each task, they either succeed or fail.

The probability of succeeding in the first task is 0.8.

If a contestant succeeds in the first task, the probability of succeeding in the second is 0.6.

If a contestant fails in the first task, the probability of succeeding in the second is 0.3.

What is the probability that a contestant

(i) succeeds in both tasks   (ii) fails in at least one task?

11. Josie takes a card at random from this pack and keeps it. Then she takes a second card at random. Find the probability that she takes one odd number and one even number (in either order).

12. Based on the probabilities shown in the given Venn diagram, find each of the following:

(i) $P(A)$
(ii) $P(A \cap B)$
(iii) $P(A \cup B)$
(iv) $P(A \mid B)$
(v) $P(B \mid A)$.

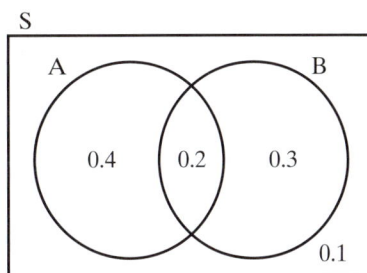

13. The given Venn diagram shows the numbers of elements in the sets A, B and the universal set S. Use the diagram to write down

(i) $P(A)$
(ii) $P(A \cap B)$
(iii) $P(A \cup B)$
(iv) $P(A \mid B)$.

Is $P(A \mid B) = P(B \mid A)$?

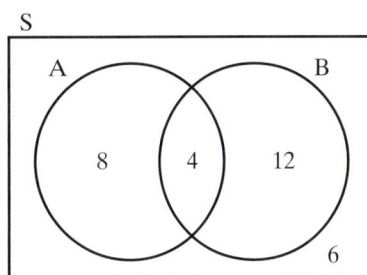

14. X and Y are two events such that $P(X) = 0.2$, $P(Y) = 0.25$ and $P(X \cap Y) = 0.1$. Illustrate this information on a Venn diagram. Use the diagram to find
(i) $P(X \cup Y)$ (ii) $P(X \mid Y)$ (iii) $P(Y \mid X)$.

15. Use the given Venn diagram to find these probabilities:

(i) $P(A)$ (ii) $P(A \cup B)$
(iii) $P(A')$ (iv) $P(A \cup B)'$
(v) $P(A' \cap B)$ (vi) $P(B \mid A)$.

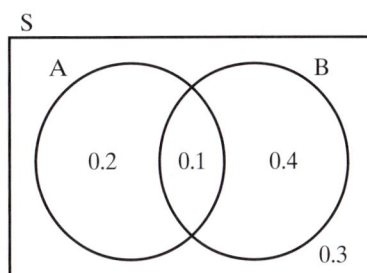

16. Two events A and B are such that
$P(A) = 0.2$, $P(A \cap B) = 0.15$ and $P(A' \cap B) = 0.6$.

(i) Copy and complete this Venn diagram.
(ii) Find the probability that neither A nor B occurs.
(iii) Find $P(A \mid B)$.
(iv) Is $P(A \mid B) = P(B \mid A)$?

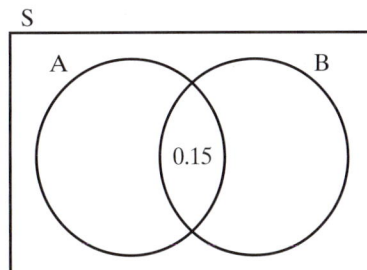

17. In a group of 100 people, 40 own a cat, 25 own a dog and 15 own a cat and a dog.
Draw a Venn diagram to illustrate this information.
Now write down the probability that a person chosen at random
  (i)   owns a dog or a cat
  (ii) owns a dog or a cat but not both
  (iii) owns a dog, given that (s)he owns a cat
  (iv) does not own a cat, given that (s)he owns a dog.

18. A and B are two events such that P(A) = 0.6, P(B) = 0.5 and P(A ∩ B) = 0.4.
Represent this information on a Venn diagram.
Use the diagram to find
  (i) $P(A \cup B)$ (iii) $P(A|B)$
  (ii) $P(B|A)$ (iv) $P(B \cap A')$.

19. A and B are two events such that $P(A) = \frac{1}{3}$, $P(B) = \frac{1}{4}$ and $P(A|B) = \frac{1}{5}$.
Draw a Venn diagram to show the probability of each region.
Use the diagram to find
  (i) $P(A \cap B)$
  (ii) $P(B|A)$.

20. The probabilities of events A, B and C are
shown in the given Venn diagram.

Use the Venn diagram to find
  (i) $P(B)$
  (ii) $P(A \cap C)$
  (iii) $P(A|B)$
  (iv) $P(C|B)$
  (v) $P(A \cap C')$
  (vi) $P(B|A \cap C)$.

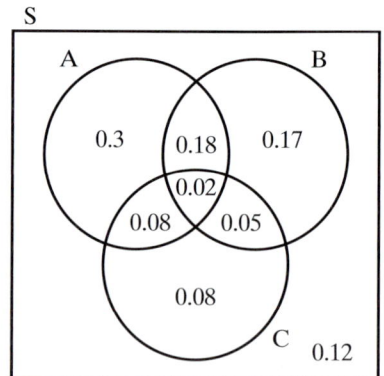

Revision Exercise 5 (Core)

1. How many different 3-digit numbers can be formed using the digits 1, 2, 3, 4, 5 if no
digit is repeated in the number?
  (i)   How many of these numbers begin with 3?
  (ii) How many of these numbers are greater than 300?

2. (i)   How many different groups of four can be selected from five boys and six girls?
     (ii) How many of these groups consist of two boys and two girls?

3. A pair of dice are thrown and the numbers are added. What is the probability of getting
  (i)   a total of 12
  (ii) the same number on both dice
  (iii) a total of 12 or the same number on both dice?

4. This spinner is biased.
   The probability that the spinner will land on each of the
   numbers 1 to 4 is given in the table below.

Number	1	2	3	4	5
Probability	0.35	0.1	0.25	0.15	

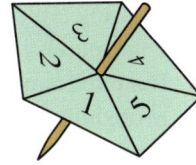

   The spinner is spun once.
      (i)   Work out the probability that the spinner will land on 5.
     (ii)   Write down the number on which the spinner is most likely to land.
    (iii) If the spinner is spun 200 times, how many times would you expect it to land on 3?

5. Six people, including Mary and John, sit in a row.
      (i)   How many different arrangements of the six people are possible?
     (ii)   In how many of these arrangements are Mary and John next to each other?

6. Thirty students were asked to state the activities
   they enjoyed from swimming (S), tennis (T) and
   hockey (H).
   The numbers in each set are shown.
   One student is randomly selected.
      (i)   Which of these pairs of events are mutually
   exclusive?
         (a) 'selecting a student from S', 'selecting a student from H'
         (b) 'selecting a student from S', 'selecting a student from T'
     (ii)   What is the probability of selecting a student who enjoyed either hockey
   or tennis?

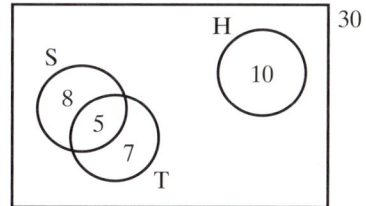

7. A dice has the numbers 1, 1, 1, 2, 2, 3 on its faces.
      (i)   What is the probability of scoring 2?

   The dice is thrown three times.
     (ii)   What is the probability of getting a 2 on each of the first two throws?
    (iii) What is the probability of getting the first 2 on the third throw?

8. There are thirteen tickets in a draw. Six of the tickets are blue, four are red and three
   are green. Three tickets are drawn at random, one at a time, without replacement.
   Find the probability that the first ticket drawn is blue, the second is red and the third is
   red or green.

9. A **possibility space** consists of integers from 1 to 20 inclusive.

   A is the event: The number is a multiple of 3
   B is the event: The number is a multiple of 4.

   If an integer is picked at random, find
      (i) $P(A)$
     (ii) $P(A \cup B)$
    (iii) $P(A \cap B)'$.

10. The following table gives the age and gender of twenty five pupils in a class.

	Boys	Girls
16-year-olds	5	7
17-year-olds	7	6

   (i) If a pupil is picked at random, what is the probability that the pupil picked is a girl aged seventeen or a boy aged sixteen?
   (ii) Find the probability of selecting a pupil aged 16, given that the pupil chosen was a girl.
   (iii) If two pupils are picked at random, find the probability that both are 16-year-old boys.

Revision Exercise 5 (Advanced)

1. To start a game, a player has to throw a 6 with a dice.
   Find the probability that a player starts at
   (i) his first throw   (ii) his second throw
   (iii) either his first or his second throw.

2. Four delegates are to be chosen from eight members of a club.
   (i) How many choices are possible?
   (ii) How many contain a certain member A?
   (iii) How many contain A or B but not both?

3. (i) How many arrangements can be made with the letters of the word SOLDIER if all the letters are taken at a time?
   (ii) How many of these arrangements begin with the letters SO in that order?
   (iii) How many of the arrangements begin and end with a consonant?

4. A game is played by spinning each of 3 arrows which are freely pivoted at the centres of 3 circles as shown below. Each arrow may score either 2 or 3 points according to the sector to which it points on stopping, and it is equally likely to face in either direction. The sectors scoring 2 points are of 240°, 180° and 240° respectively.

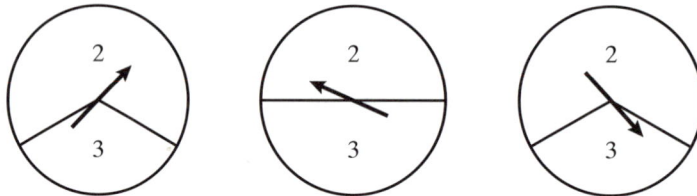

   Given that the game score is the sum of the points scored by the 3 arrows, calculate the probability of getting a game score of
   (i) 6   (ii) 9   (iii) 7.

5. (i) Give an equation involving probabilities which represents the statement 'the events L and M are mutually exclusive'. Explain what is meant by 'mutually exclusive events'.
   (ii) Janelle's mathematics class has 22 students.
      Four students are selected at random to enter a mathematics competition.
      (a) In how many ways can the four students be selected?
      (b) In how many of the selections is Janelle included?
      (c) Now find the probability that Janelle is included to enter the competition.

6. Karen has two 5c and four 10c coins in her purse. At random, she takes out one coin and then a second coin (without replacing the first). Find the probability that
    (i)   the first coin is a 10c and the second coin a 5c
    (ii) the two coins are worth 15c
    (iii) the two coins are worth 20c.

7. Use the given Venn diagram to answer these questions.

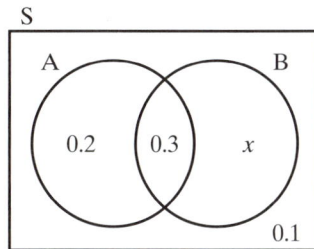

    (i)   Find the value of x (ii) Find $P(A)$
    (iii) Find $P(A \cup B)$ (iv) Find $P(A|B)$
    (v)   Verify that $P(A|B) = \dfrac{P(A \cap B)}{P(B)}$

8. There are 15 male and 20 female passengers on a train.
    10 of the males and 16 of the females are over 25 years old.
    A ticket inspector selects one of the passengers at random.

    A is the event: The person selected is female
    B is the event: The person selected is over 25 years old.

    Write down each of these:
    (i) $P(A)$ (ii) $P(B)$ (iii) $P(A|B)$ (iv) $P(A \cap B)$ (v) $P(A \cup B)$.
    Hence verify that $P(A \cap B) = P(B) . P(A|B)$
    Why is it not possible to apply the result $P(A \cup B) = P(A) + P(B)$ in this case?

9. A box contains 4 white discs, 2 red discs and x green discs.
    Two discs are picked at random, without replacement, from the box.
    (i)   Write down an expression in x for the probability that the two discs are green.

    If it is known that the probability of picking two green discs is $\frac{4}{13}$,
    (ii) how many discs are in the box?
    (iii) what is the probability that neither of the two discs picked is green?

10. In a multiple-choice test, each question offers a choice of 5 answers, only one of which is correct. The probability that a student knows the correct answer is $\frac{5}{8}$. If he does not know which answer is correct, he selects one of the 5 answers at random.
    Find the probability that he selects the correct answer to a question.

Revision Exercise 5 (Extended Response Questions)

1. A bag contains 5 red and 4 green discs, identical in all but colour.
   Three discs are drawn at random from the bag without replacement.
   Find the probability that
   (i) they are all the same colour
   (ii) at least one is red
   (iii) at most one is green.

2. 8% of a population is known to have a certain virus which can be detected by a medical test. However this test is only 90% effective, meaning that it gives a correct reading only 90% of the time. If Sam is tested for the virus, what is the probability that
   (i) he has the virus but it is not detected
   (ii) he has the virus and it is detected
   (iii) he does not have the virus but it is falsely detected?

3. (i) What do you call outcomes that have the same chance of happening?
   (ii) Explain conditional probability.
   Complete the following formula: $P(A|B) = \dfrac{P...}{P...}$
   (iii) Two events C and D are such that $P(C) = \frac{8}{15}$, $P(D) = \frac{1}{3}$ and $P(C|D) = \frac{1}{5}$.
   Find   (a) $P(C \cap D)$ (b) $P(C \cup D)$ (c) $P[(C \cup D)']$

4. The probability that a person has blue eyes is $\frac{2}{5}$ and the probability that a person is left-handed is $\frac{1}{5}$.
   Find the probability that a person
   (i) is not left-handed
   (ii) has blue eyes and is left-handed.

   Given that two people are chosen at random, find the probability that one of them has blue eyes and is left-handed and the other has blue eyes and is not left-handed.

5. To drive legally on Irish roads, all drivers are required to have both a driving licence and an insurance disc. At a checkpoint, a garda officer found that 14% had no insurance, 8% had no driving licence and 2% had neither a driving licence nor insurance.
   (i) Represent this information on a Venn diagram.
   (ii) Find the probability, as a fraction, that a driver checked in this survey was driving illegally.
   (iii) The following day, 300 drivers were stopped and checked.
   How many of these drivers can the gardaí expect to find who have a driving licence but no insurance?

6. A game is played using a regular 12-sided spinner numbered 1 to 12, a coin and a simple board with 9 rectangles, as shown in the diagram below.

L								R

Initially the coin is placed on the shaded rectangle.

The game consists of spinning the spinner and then moving the coin one rectangle towards L or R. If the outcome is a prime number (2, 3, 5, 7 or 11), the move is towards R; otherwise it is towards L.

The game stops when the coin reaches either L or R.

Find, correct to three decimal places, the probability that the game
  (i)   ends on the fourth move at R
  (ii) ends on the fourth move
  (iii) ends on the fifth move.

7.

SWEET SIXTEEN

START	1	2	3	
	8	7		5
counter	9		11	12
	16	15	14	13

'Sweet Sixteen' is a game for any number of players. To play the game, players take it in turns to throw a fair dice and then move their counter the number of places shown uppermost on the dice. If a player lands on one of the shaded squares, the player must start again. The first player to finish on square 16 is the winner. If a player would move past square 16 on a throw, the player is not allowed to move and misses that turn.
  (i)   What is the probability that a player lands on a shaded square on the first throw?
  (ii) A player moves to square 3 on the first throw. What is the probability that the player lands on a shaded square on the second throw?
  (iii) (a) A player is on square 12 after three throws.
            Write, in the order thrown, three scores the player could have had.
        (b) In how many different ways could a player have reached square 12 with three throws? Show your working to support your answer.
  (iv) (a) What is the minimum number of throws necessary to complete the game?
        (b) What is the probability of this happening?

8. The given Venn diagram shows the probabilities of the events A, B and C happening.
  (i)   Given that $P(B) = 0.4$ and $P(C) = 0.35$, find the values of x, y and z.

Now find each of these probabilities
  (ii) $P(A|B)$ (iv) $P[(A \cup B)']$
  (iii) $P(B|C)$ (v) $P(A \cup B \cup C)$

Now show that $P(A|B) = \dfrac{P(A \cap B)}{P(B)}$

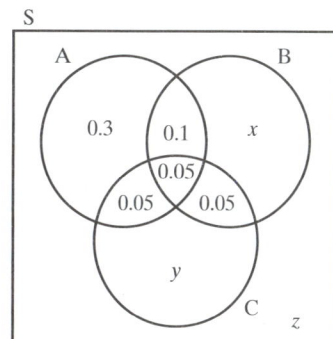

9. Two dice are thrown. Find the probability that
   (i) there is at least one 6
   (ii) the sum is 8
   (iii) there is at least one 6 *and* the total score is 8
   (iv) there is at least one 6 *or* the total score is 8 (or both)
   (v) there is at least one 6, given that the total score is 8.

10. A high-jumper training for the Olympic games estimates the probabilities that she will be able to clear the bar at various heights, based on her experience in training. These probabilities are given in the table below:

Height	Probability of success at each attempt
1.60 m	1
1.65 m	0.6
1.70 m	0.2
1.75 m	0

In a competition, she is allowed up to three attempts to clear the bar at each height. If she succeeds, the bar is raised by 5 cm and she is allowed three attempts at the new height, and so on.
If it is assumed that the result of each attempt is independent of all her previous results,
   (i) show that the probability that she will be successful at 1.65 m is 0.936.
   (ii) calculate the probability that if she is successful at 1.65 m, she will not be successful at 1.70 m.

Hence find the probabilities that, in the competition, the height she jumps will be recorded as
   (iii) 1.60 m   (iv) 1.65 m.

11. At a charity fundraiser a circular wheel of fortune is divided into n sectors, each of which makes an angle of 6° at the centre of the wheel. Each of the n sectors has a number printed on it. When the wheel is spun a player chooses five numbers to bet on for that spin. If the pointer at the top of the wheel lands on any one of the five chosen numbers the player wins.
   (i) Find the value of n.
   (ii) What is the probability that a player wins on a single spin of the wheel?
   (iii) What is the probability that the player will win at least once on two consecutive spins.
   (iv) It costs €2.00 to play and you receive €20.00 if you win.
       (a) If Tom plays 36 times, how many games would he expect to win?
       (b) How much would Tom expect to collect in winnings?
       (c) How much money would Tom expect to win/lose?
       (d) What fraction of the money bet on this game is kept by the charity?
       (e) Based on past experience the organisers know that the game will be played 300 times during the day. If they hope to make a profit of €400.00 for the day how much should they charge for each play.

Geometry 1

chapter 6

Key words

isosceles   equilateral   corresponding   alternate   axiom   theorem
converse   corollary   ratio   transversal   segment   similar triangles
tangent   chord   point of contact

Section 6.1 Angles, triangles and parallelograms

The diagrams shown below will help you recall some of the results you have encountered in your earlier study of geometry.

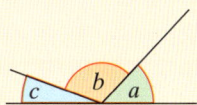

$a + b + c = 180°$

Angles which meet at a point on a straight line add up to 180°.

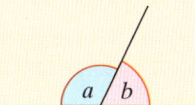

$a + b = 180°$

A pair of angles that add together to make 180° are called **supplementary angles**.

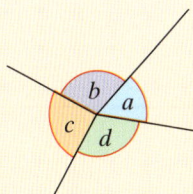

$a + b + c + d = 360°$

Angles which meet at a point add up to 360°.

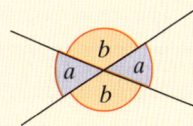

When two lines intersect, **vertically opposite angles** are equal in measure.

Angles formed when a straight line crosses a pair of parallel lines have the following properties:

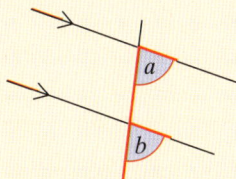

Corresponding angles are equal.
So $a = b$.
You can find them by looking for an F shape.

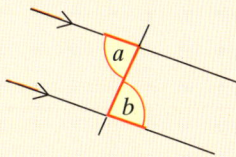

Alternate angles are equal.
So $a = b$.
Look for a Z shape.

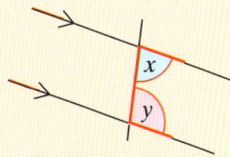

The **interior angles** x and y sum to 180°.
$x + y = 180°$.

223

Triangles and their properties

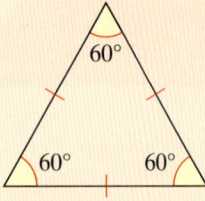

An equilateral triangle has:
- 3 sides equal
- 3 interior angles equal (60°)

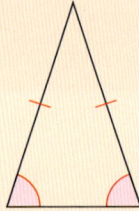

An isosceles triangle has:
- 2 sides equal
- base angles equal

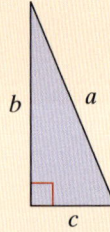

A right-angled triangle has:
- 1 angle of 90°
  $a^2 = b^2 + c^2$

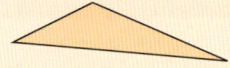

Triangles with no equal angles and no equal sides are called scalene triangles.

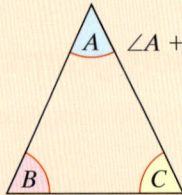

$\angle A + \angle B + \angle C = 180°$

The angles of a triangle sum to 180°.

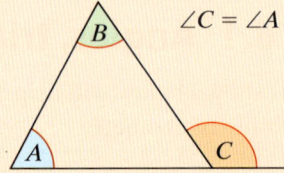

$\angle C = \angle A + \angle B$

The **exterior angle** of a triangle is equal to the sum of the interior opposite angles.

Example 1

In the given triangle, $|AB| = |BC|$, and $|\angle ABE| = 56°$.
Find (i) $|\angle ACB|$ (ii) $|\angle ACD|$.

(i) $|\angle ABC| = 180° - 56° = 124°$
$|\angle BAC| = |\angle BCA|$ ... isosceles triangle
But $|\angle BAC| + |\angle ACB| = 180° - 124° = 56°$
$\Rightarrow \quad |\angle ACB| = 28°$

(ii) $|\angle ACB| + |\angle ACD| = 180°$ ... straight line
$\Rightarrow \quad |\angle ACD| = 180° - |\angle ACB|$
$= 180° - 28°$
$\Rightarrow \quad |\angle ACD| = 152°$

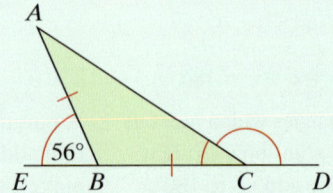

Theorem of Pythagoras

Pythagoras was a Greek mathematician and philosopher who lived during the sixth century BC. The theorem that carries his name, the Theorem of Pythagoras, is probably the best known and widely-used theorem in mathematics.

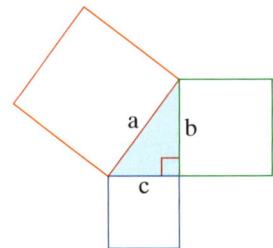

$a^2 = b^2 + c^2$

> **Theorem of Pythagoras**
> In a right-angled triangle, the area of the square drawn on the hypotenuse
> is equal to the sum of the areas of the squares on the other two sides.

Example 2

Calculate the lengths marked x and y.

$$x^2 = 3^2 + 4^2$$
$$= 9 + 16$$
$$x = \sqrt{25}$$
$$x = 5 \text{ cm}$$

$$y^2 + x^2 = 13^2$$
$$y^2 + 5^2 = 13^2$$
$$y^2 + 25 = 169$$
$$y^2 = 169 - 25$$
$$y = \sqrt{144}$$
$$y = 12 \text{ cm}$$

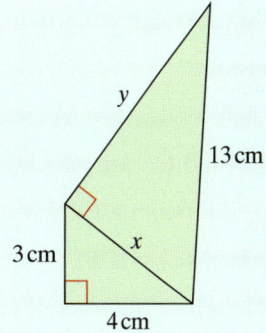

Congruent triangles

Two triangles are **congruent** to one another if they are equal in all respects i.e. all corresponding sides are equal and all corresponding angles are equal.
It follows that congruent triangles have the same area.
(Note, congruent triangles fit exactly on top of one another)

Triangles are congruent if one of these conditions is true:

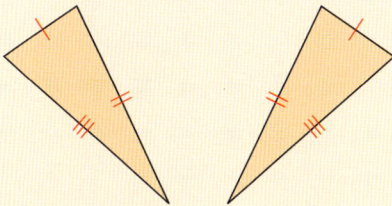

Three pairs of sides are equal (**SSS**).

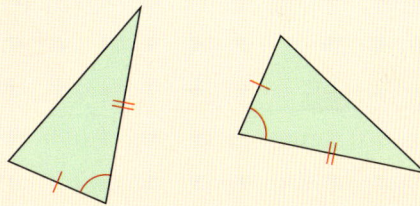

Two pairs of sides are equal and the angles between them (the included angle) are equal (**SAS**).

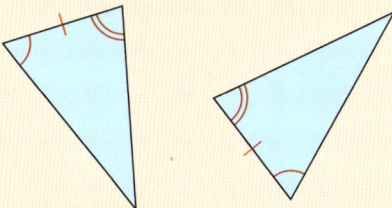

Two pairs of angles are equal and the sides between them are equal (**ASA**).

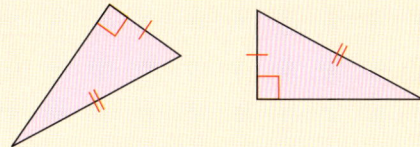

Both triangles have a right angle, the hypotenuses are equal and one pair of corresponding sides is equal (**RHS**).

Example 3

ABC is a triangle with $|AB| = |AC|$. The bisectors of the angles B and C meet the opposite sides in D and E respectively. Prove that $|BD| = |CE|$.

(*It is always advisable to draw a sketch of the information given*)

To prove that $|BD| = |EC|$ we need to prove that $\triangle BCE$ is congruent to $\triangle CBD$

Proof:

$|AB| = |AC|$(given) $\Rightarrow \angle EBC = \angle DCB$ (A)

BD and CE are bisectors of $\angle EBC$ and $\angle DCB$ (given)

$\Rightarrow \angle DBC = \angle ECB$ (A)

Also $|BC| = |CB|$ (S)

Therefore the triangles $\triangle BCE$ and $\triangle CBD$ are congruent (ASA)

Therefore the corresponding sides BD and CE have the same length i.e. $|BD| = |CE|$.

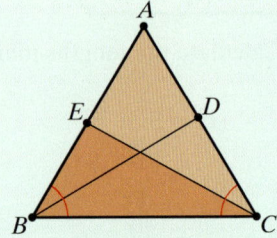

Exercise 6.1

1. Write down the size of the angles marked with letters in each of the following diagrams where arrows indicate parallel lines.

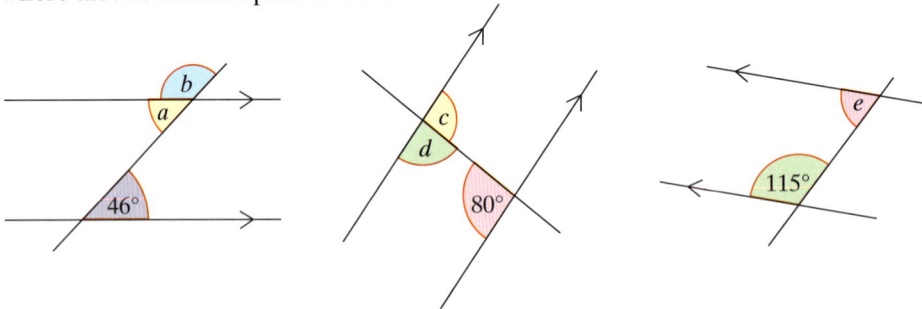

2. Find the size of the angle marked with a letter in each of the following triangles where equal sides are marked:

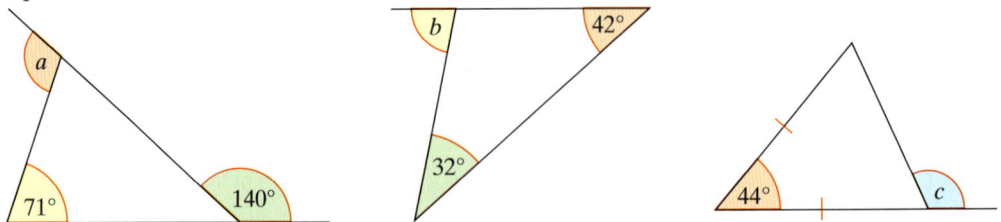

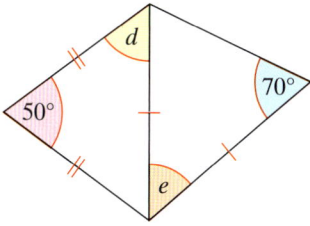

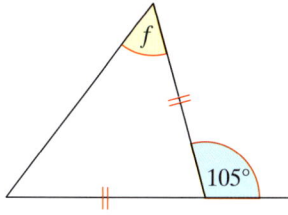

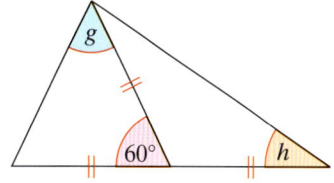

3. Find the values of *a*, *b*, *c* and *d* in the following triangles where equal sides are marked:

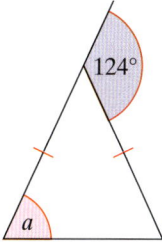

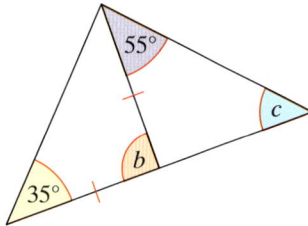

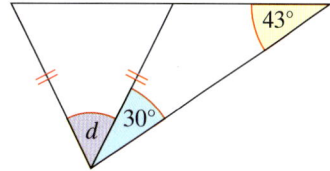

4. Find the values of *x* and *y* in the following triangles, where the arrows indicate parallel lines:

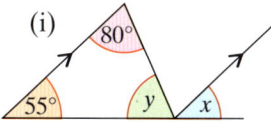

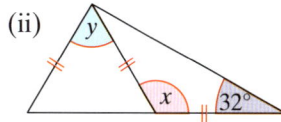

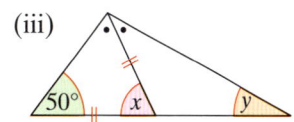

(i)

(ii)

(iii)

5. Find the length of the side marked *x* in each of the following right-angled triangles:

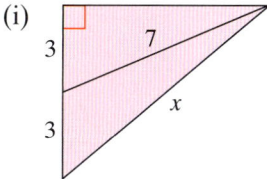

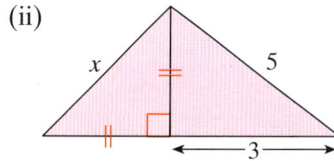

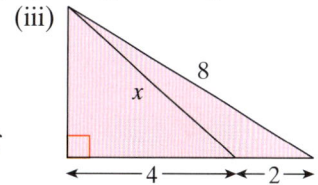

(i)

(ii)

(iii)

6. In the given figure, $|\angle ACB| = |\angle CDB| = 90°$.
Find the lengths of the sides marked *x* and *y*.

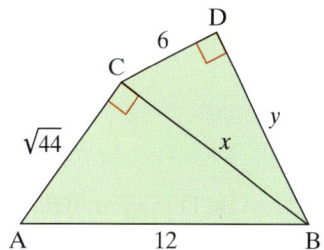

7. In the given diagram, $|AC| = |AD|$
and $|BD| = |CE|$.
Prove that the triangles ABC
and ADE are congruent.

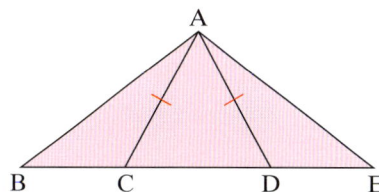

8. ABCD is a parallelogram and M is the midpoint of [AB].
   C, B and P are collinear.
   (i) Explain why $|\angle DAM| = |\angle MBP|$.
   (ii) Now show that the triangles AMD and MBP are congruent.
   (iii) Hence show that B is the midpoint of [CP].

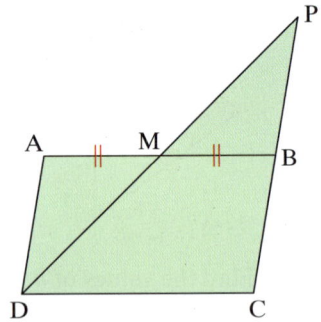

9. (i) Triangle ABC has angles 90°, 50° and 40°.
      Triangle XYZ also has angles 90°, 50° and 40°.
      The triangles are not congruent.
      Can you explain why?
   (ii) In the diagram on the right, PQ is equal and parallel to RS.
      The lines PS and QR intersect at T.
      Prove that triangles PTQ and STR are *congruent*.

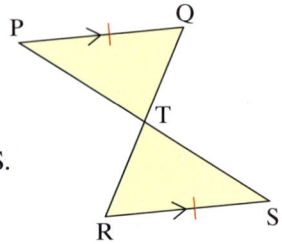

10. ABCD and BEFG are identical squares.
    (i) Explain why $|\angle ABG| = |\angle CBE|$.
    (ii) Show that $|AG| = |CE|$ by proving that
       the triangles ABG and CBE are congruent.

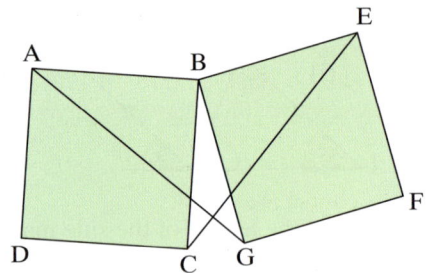

11. The outline of a rectangular solid is shown.
    $|CD| = 8$, $|CE| = 4$ and $|HE| = 5$.
    Find the length of the longer diagonal [HD],
    marked x.
    Leave your answer in $\sqrt{}$ form.

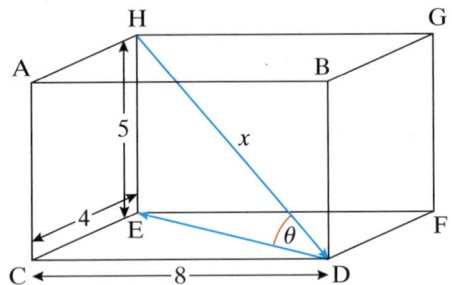

12. ABCD is a parallelogram.
    Copy the diagram on the right in which
    DE bisects $\angle ADC$.
    Mark in another angle equal to $|\angle ADE|$.
    Now prove that $|AE| = |BC|$.

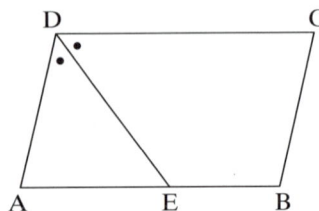

13. In the diagram
$|DX| = |CX|$, $|DF| = |CE|$
and AB is parallel to CD.
Prove that $\triangle BCF$ and $\triangle ADE$ are congruent.

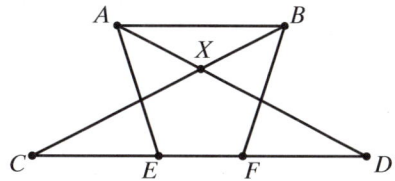

Section 6.2 Theorems involving triangles and parallelograms

Proofs of theorems

Geometry results or **theorems** are proved in a formal or structured way by using previously established results and axioms to explain the steps that we take. This method of proving geometric results was first used by a Greek mathematician named Euclid about 300 BC.

> An **axiom** is a statement accepted without proof. The angles in a straight line add to 180° is an example of an axiom.

The proofs of numerous theorems are contained in his famous book on geometry called *Elements*. Today, over 2000 years later, we still use Euclid's approach to solve many problems in geometry.

> A **theorem** is a statement that can be shown to be true through the use of axioms and logical argument.

In this section formal proofs of the theorems on your course are given.

These theorems are numberd as in the official syllabus.

You may be asked to reproduce the proofs of theorems **11**, **12** and **13** only.

> A Corollary is a statement attached to a theorem which has been proven and follows obviously from it.

Note 1. When we are asked to prove something in geometry it is important to give a reason for each deduction made. In a formal proof you must also provide the standard headings of "To prove", "Given", "Construction", "Proof"

Note 2. A **converse** is where we check if the proposition and conclusion are switched is the statement true.

e.g. In a right-angled triangle, $a^2 + b^2 = c^2$ (where a, b and c are the lengths of the sides and c is the longest side(hypotenuse).

***Converse*:** If $a^2 + b^2 = c^2$ (where a, b and c are the lengths of the sides and c is the longest side (hypotenuse) is the triangle a right-angled triangle? Answer: Yes (the converse is true).

e.g. If it is raining outside then the grass will be wet.

***Converse*:** If the grass is wet is it raining outside? Answer: Not necessarily.

Angles and sides

The triangle ABC on the right is drawn to scale.

Notice (i) the largest angle is opposite the longest side
        (ii) the smallest angle is opposite the shortest side.

These properties will hold for all triangles and are stated in the theorem below.

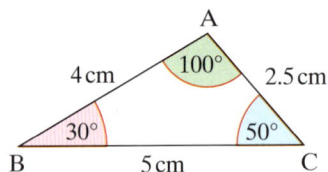

> ### Theorem 7
> The angle opposite the greater of two sides is greater than the angle opposite the lesser side.

In the triangle on the right, we are given the measures of the three angles.

The converse of the theorem above states that [BC] is the longest side because it is opposite the greatest angle and [AB] is the shortest side because it is opposite the smallest angle.

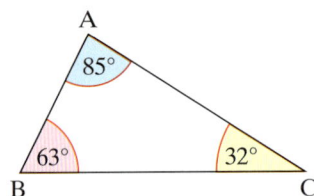

> ### Converse of theorem 7
> The side opposite the greater of two angles is longer than the side opposite the lesser angle.

Triangle inequality

The shortest distance between two points is the line that joins these points.

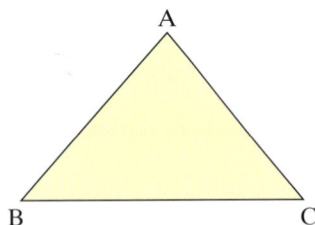

It follows from this that
$$|BA| + |AC| > |BC|$$
Similarly $\quad |AB| + |BC| > |AC|$
and $\quad |BC| + |CA| > |AB|$.

> ### Theorem 8
> Two sides of a triangle are together greater than the third side.

Areas of triangles and parallelograms

The diagrams below show two identical triangles.

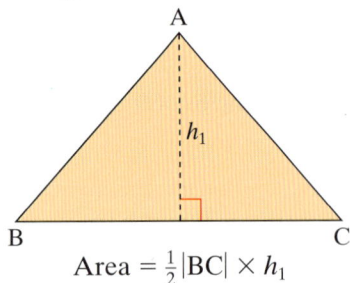

> Area of a triangle is $\frac{1}{2}$ base $\times \perp$ height

Area $= \frac{1}{2}|BC| \times h_1$

Area $= \frac{1}{2}|AB| \times h_2$

In this triangle, the base is [BC] and the perpendicular height is h_1.

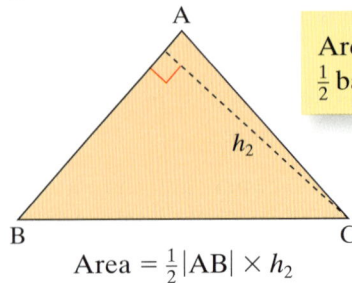

In this triangle, the base is [AB] and the perpendicular height is h_2.

Since both triangles are identical, their areas are equal.

The areas were found by using different bases and different perpendicular heights.

This illustrates an important theorem about the area of a triangle, as given on the right.

> **Theorem 16**
> For any triangle, base times height does not depend on the choice of the base.

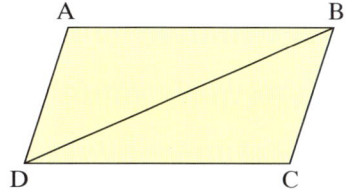

Area of a parallelogram

The figure on the right shows a parallelogram ABCD.

In a parallelogram, the opposite sides are parallel and equal in length.

The diagonal [DB] divides the parallelogram into two triangles, ABD and BCD.

These triangles are congruent because the three sides in △ABD are equal in length to the three sides in △BCD.

> **Theorem 17**
> A diagonal of a parallelogram bisects the area.

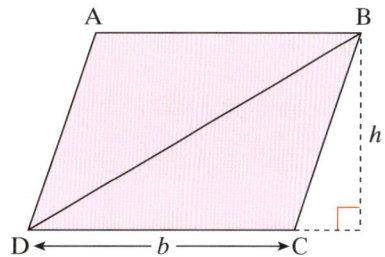

Since the triangles are congruent, they are equal in area.

This shows that the diagonal [DB] bisects the area of the parallelogram ABCD.

In the given parallelogram,

$$\text{area of } \triangle DCB = \tfrac{1}{2} \times \text{base} \times \text{height}$$
$$= \tfrac{1}{2} \times |DC| \times h$$
$$= \tfrac{1}{2}b \times h$$

Area of ABCD = twice area of △DCB.

$$\therefore \text{ Area of ABCD} = 2\left[\tfrac{1}{2}b \times h\right]$$
$$= b \times h$$

> **Theorem 18**
> Area of a parallelogram is the base multiplied by the perpendicular height.

Example 1

(i) Find the area of the given parallelogram ABCD.

(ii) If |BC| = 9 cm, find the perpendicular height, h, from A to [BC].

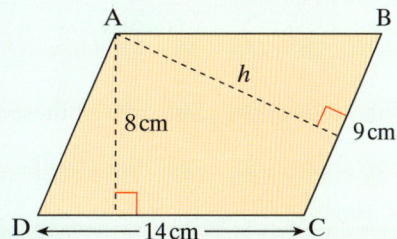

(i) Area of ABCD = base × perpendicular height
$$= 14 \times 8$$
$$= 112 \text{ cm}^2$$

(ii) Area of ABCD is also $|BC| \times h$

$$= 9\,\text{cm} \times h$$
$$= 9h\ \text{cm}^2$$

But area of ABCD $= 112\,\text{cm}^2$ ... from (i) above

$\therefore \qquad 9h = 112$

$$h = \tfrac{112}{9}\ \text{cm}$$

Problems involving area

The triangles ABC and ABD on the right are equal in area because they have the same base [AB] and they are between the same parallel lines.

The area of each triangle is $\tfrac{1}{2}|AB| \times h$.

Similarly, the parallelograms ABCD and ABEF are equal in area as they have the same base [AB] and they are between the same parallel lines.

Parallelograms (or triangles) with the same base and between the same parallel lines are equal in area.

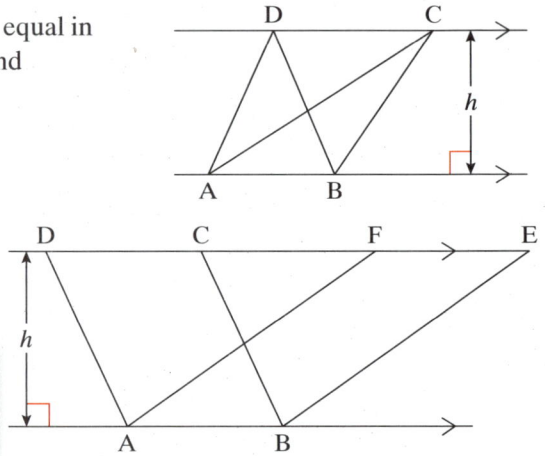

Exercise 6.2

1. In the given triangle, $|AB| = 9\,\text{cm}$, $|BC| = 12\,\text{cm}$ and the perpendicular height from C to [AB] is 8 cm.
   Find   (i)   the area of the triangle ABC
          (ii) the perpendicular distance from A to [BC].

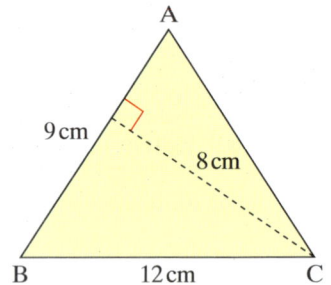

2. Find the value of h in each of these triangles:

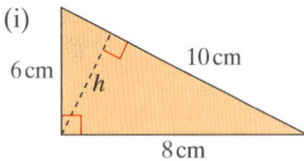

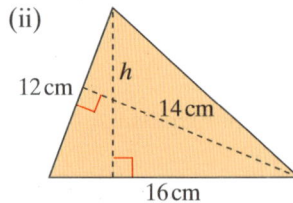

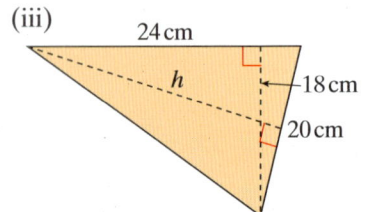

(i)   6 cm   10 cm h 8 cm

(ii)   12 cm h 14 cm   16 cm

(iii)   24 cm h 18 cm   20 cm

3. Find the area of each of these parallelograms:

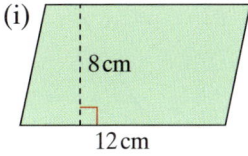

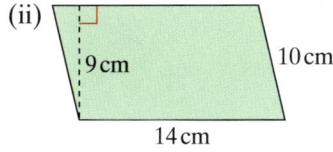

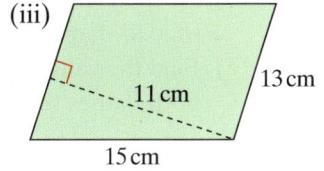

(i)

8 cm
12 cm

(ii)
9 cm
10 cm
14 cm

(iii)
11 cm
13 cm
15 cm

4. Find the area of the given parallelogram ABCD.
Now find the length of the side [BC].

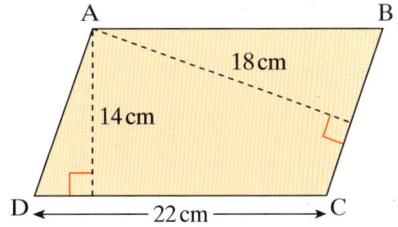

A   B
18 cm
14 cm
D ←—— 22 cm ——→ C

5. (i) Name the largest and smallest angle in △ABC.
Give reasons for your answers.

(ii) If [AB] and [BC] are fixed at 5 cm and 10 cm
respectively, what is the range of possible
lengths of [AC]?

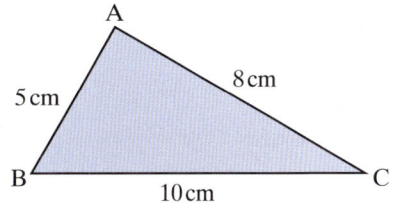

A
5 cm   8 cm
B
10 cm
C

6. In the given parallelogram, DE ⊥ AC and
BF ⊥ AC.
The area of ABCD is 80 cm².
(i) If |AC| = 16 cm, find |DE|.
(ii) Explain why |DE| = |BF|.
(iii) If |AB| = 10 cm, find the length of the
perpendicular height, h.

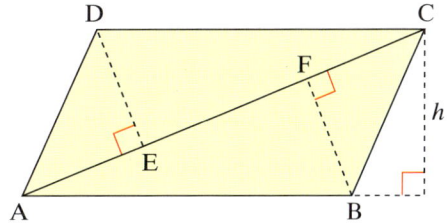

D   C
F
E
h
A   B

7. ABCD and ADBE are both parallelograms.
If the area of the triangle DCB = 15 cm², find
(i) area of parallelogram ABCD
(ii) area of parallelogram ADBE
(iii) area of the figure ADCE
(iv) the perpendicular height from A to [DC],
if |DC| = 7.5 cm.

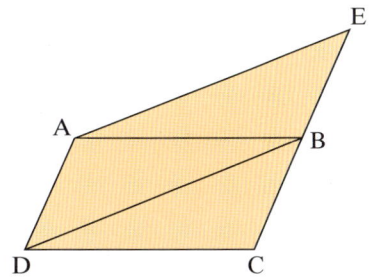

E
A   B
D   C

8. In the diagram on the right, ABCF,
ABFE and ACDE are parallelograms.
The area of triangle AFE is 30 square units.
(i) State clearly why the area of
the triangle AFB is also
30 square units.
(ii) Find the area of the figure
ABCDE.

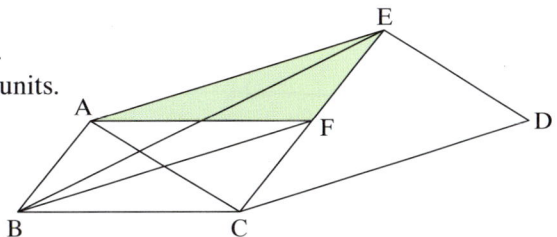

E
A
F
D
B   C

9. (i) Find and simplify an expression for the area of each of these shaded shapes.

(ii) Find the value of a that gives both shapes the same area.

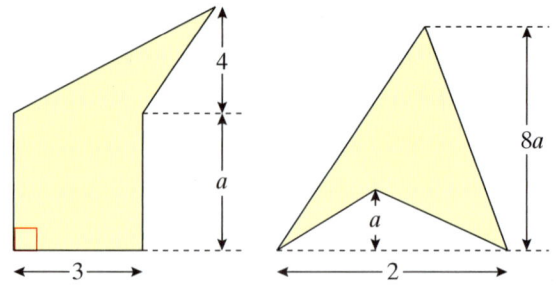

10. (i) Find and simplify an expression for the area of each of these shaded shapes.

(ii) Find the value of x that gives both shapes the same area.

(Arrows indicate parallel lines.)

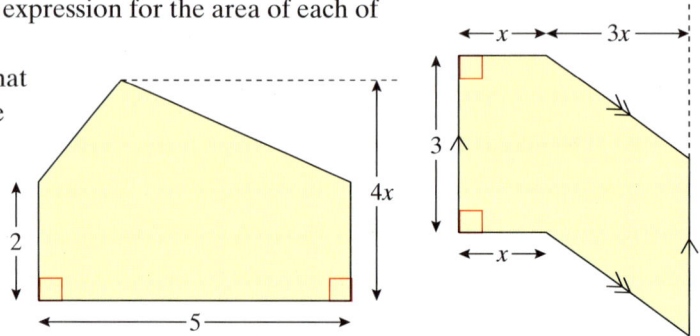

11. Calculate the area of the given shaded figure where the arrows indicate that the lines are parallel.

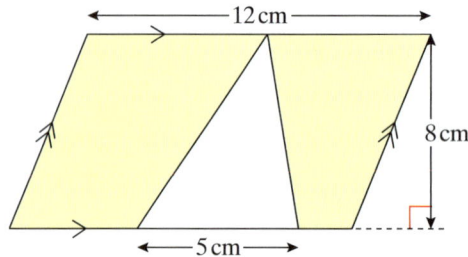

12. (i) ABCD is a parallelogram.

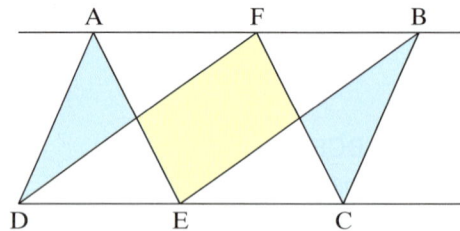

E is the midpoint of [DC] and F is the midpoint of [AB].
Prove that the area shaded in blue is equal to the area shaded in yellow.

(ii) In this parallelogram, E and F are **any** points on the sides [DC] and [AB] respectively.

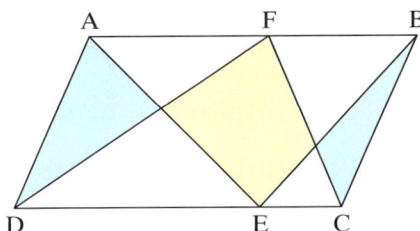

Join EF.

In this case, prove that the area shaded in blue is also equal to the area shaded in yellow.

13. ABCD is a rectangle. E and F are **any** points on the sides [AB] and [BC] respectively.

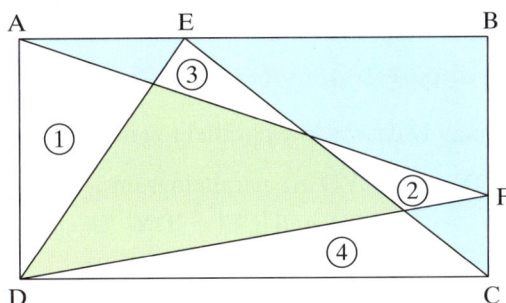

(i) Prove that the area of triangles ① + ② = area of triangles ③ + ④.
(ii) By numbering the remaining triangles, or otherwise, show that the region shaded in green is equal to the region shaded in blue.

Section 6.3 Ratio theorems

1. Transversals

In the given diagram, l, m and n are parallel lines.

The lines p and q are called **transversals**.

For the transversal p, $|AB| = |BC|$.

In this case we say that the parallel lines cut off **equal segments** on the transversal.

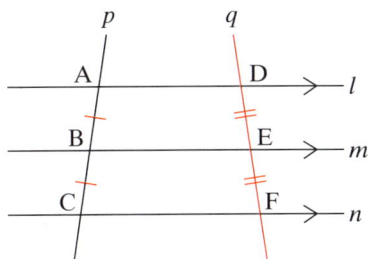

The line, q, is another transversal.
It can be shown that the line segments [DE] and [EF] are also equal in length.

The same property also holds for all other transversals.

Theorem 11
If three parallel lines cut off equal segments on some transversal line, then they will cut off equal segments on any other transversal.

Theorem 11 If three parallel lines make segments of equal length on a transversal, then they will also make segments of equal length on any other transversal.

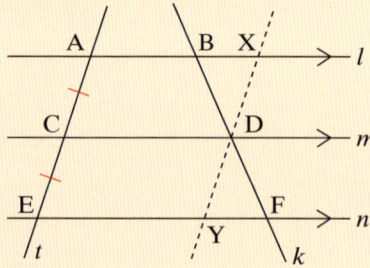

Given: Three parallel lines l, m and n intersecting the transversal t at the points A, C and E such that $|AC| = |CE|$.
Another transversal k intersects the lines at B, D and F.

To prove: $|BD| = |DF|$.

Construction: Through D draw a line parallel to t intersecting l at X and n at Y.

Proof: ACDX and CEYD are parallelograms.
  $\Rightarrow$ $|AC| = |XD|$ and $|CE| = |DY|$ …opposite sides
  But $|AC| = |CE|$.
  $\Rightarrow$ $|XD| = |DY|$
  In the triangles BDX and YDF,
      $|XD| = |DY|$
    $|\angle BDX| = |\angle YDF|$ …vertically opposite
    $|\angle DBX| = |\angle DFY|$ …alternate angles
  $\Rightarrow$ the triangles BDX and YDF are congruent
  $\Rightarrow$ $|BD| = |DF|$ …corresponding sides of congruent triangles

2. Line parallel to a side of a triangle

The diagram on the right shows the side [AB] of the triangle divided into three equal parts.

If lines are drawn through D and E parallel to BC, then the points X and Y will also divide the line [AC] into three equal parts.

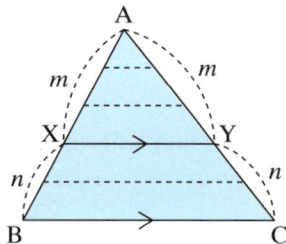

In the given triangle, X divides the side [AB] in the ratio $m : n$.

If [XY] is parallel to [BC], then Y will also divide [AC] in the ratio $m : n$, as shown.

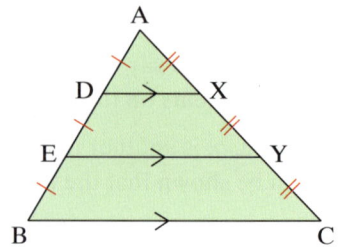

The diagram above illustrates a very important geometric result which states that:

Theorem 12
A line drawn parallel to one side of a triangle divides the other two sides in the same ratio.

In a triangle in which XY‖BC, the following ratios are always true:

(i) $\dfrac{|AX|}{|XB|} = \dfrac{|AY|}{|YC|}$ (ii) $\dfrac{|AB|}{|AX|} = \dfrac{|AC|}{|AY|}$ (iii) $\dfrac{|AB|}{|XB|} = \dfrac{|AC|}{|YC|}$

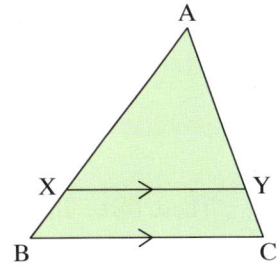

Mandatory Proof

Theorem 12	Let ABC be a triangle. If a line l is parallel to BC and cuts $[AB]$ in the ratio $s:t$, then it also cuts $[AC]$ also in the same ratio.

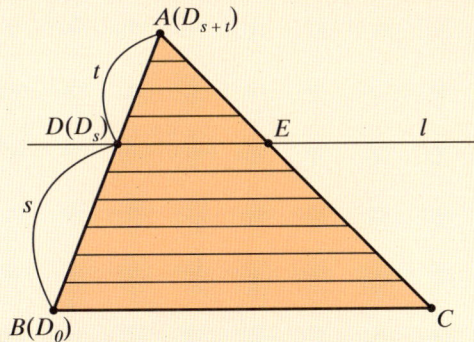

Given: The triangle ABC with l parallel to $[BC]$.
Let l cut $[AB]$ in D in the ratio $s:t$ $\therefore$ $|BD|:|DA| = s:t$

To Prove: $|CE|:|EA| = s:t$

Construction: Mark points $D_0\,(=B)$, D_1, D_2, ...$D_s\,(=D)$, D_{s+1}, ...$D_{s+t}\,(=A)$ equally spaced along $[AB]$.
i.e. the segments $[D_0D_1]$, $[D_1D_2]$, ...$[\,D_{s+t-1}\,D_{s+t}]$ all have equal length.
Draw lines D_1E_1, D_2E_2, ... parallel BC with E_1, E_2, E_3, ...on $[AC]$.

Proof: The line segments $[CE_1]$, $[E_1, E_2]$, $[E_2, E_3]$, ... $[E_{s+t+1}, D_{s+t}]$ all have the same length. ....(theorem 11)
and $E_s = E$ is the point where l cuts $[AC]$.
Hence E cuts $[AC]$ in the ratio $s:t$.
$\therefore$ $|CE|:|EA| = s:t$ Q.E.D.

Example 1

In the given figure, the lines l, m and n are parallel.

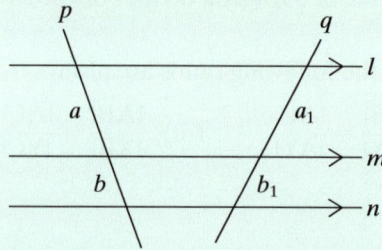

These three lines divide the transversal p in the ratio $a : b$.

The three lines divide the transversal q in the ratio $a_1 : b_1$.

Prove that $\dfrac{a}{a_1} = \dfrac{b}{b_1}$.

Draw another transversal (in red).

Let this transversal be divided in the ratio $x : y$.

In the blue triangle, the line m is parallel
to the base line n.

$$\Rightarrow \quad \frac{a}{b} = \frac{x}{y}$$

In the yellow triangle, the line m is parallel to the base l.

$$\Rightarrow \quad \frac{a_1}{b_1} = \frac{x}{y}$$

$$\Rightarrow \quad \frac{a}{b} = \frac{a_1}{b_1} = \frac{x}{y}$$

$$\Rightarrow \quad \frac{a}{a_1} = \frac{b}{b_1} \ldots$$

Given $\quad \dfrac{3}{4} = \dfrac{6}{8}$

$$\Rightarrow \quad \frac{3}{6} = \frac{4}{8}$$

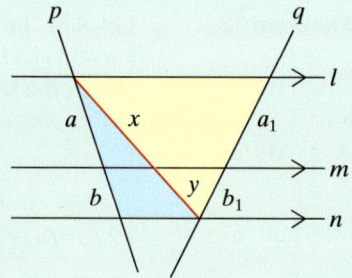

Example 2

In the given triangle, DE$\|$BC.
$|AD| = 8$, $|DB| = 4$ and $|AC| = 9$.
Find $|AE|$.

Let $\quad |AE| = x \quad \Rightarrow \quad |EC| = 9 - x$

$$\frac{|AD|}{|DB|} = \frac{|AE|}{|EC|}$$

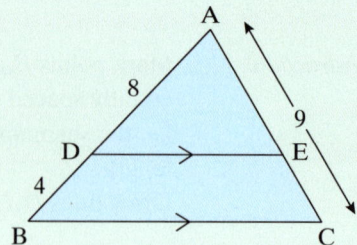

$$\Rightarrow \quad \frac{8}{4} = \frac{x}{9-x} \quad \Rightarrow \quad 4x = 8(9-x)$$
$$\Rightarrow \quad 4x = 72 - 8x$$
$$\Rightarrow \quad 12x = 72$$
$$\Rightarrow \quad x = 6$$
$$\Rightarrow \quad |AE| = 6$$

3. Similar triangles

The triangles ABC and DEF shown below have equal angles.

Notice that the triangles have the same shape but different sizes. These triangles are said to be **similar** or **equiangular** triangles.

The sides [AB] and [DE] are said to be **corresponding sides**, as they are both opposite the 60° angle.

Notice that $|DE| = 1\frac{1}{2}|AB|$ and $|DF| = 1\frac{1}{2}|AC|$.

Similarly $|EF|$ is $1\frac{1}{2}|BC|$.

This illustrates that $\dfrac{|AB|}{|DE|} = \dfrac{|AC|}{|DF|} = \dfrac{|BC|}{|EF|} = \dfrac{6}{9} = \dfrac{2}{3}$.

This important result for similar triangles is stated in the theorem below.

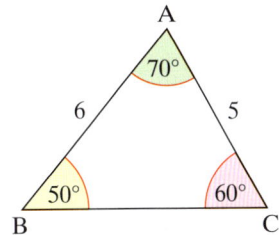

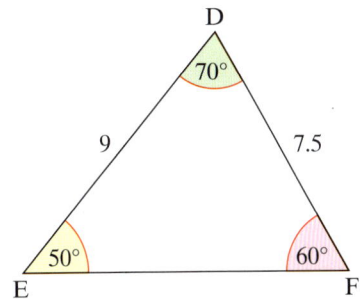

> **Theorem 13**
> If two triangles ABC and DEF are similar, then their sides are proportional, in order
> $$\frac{|AB|}{|DE|} = \frac{|BC|}{|EF|} = \frac{|AC|}{|DF|}$$

Note Two triangles will be similar if two angles in one triangle are equal to two angles in the second triangle. The remaining angles must be equal.

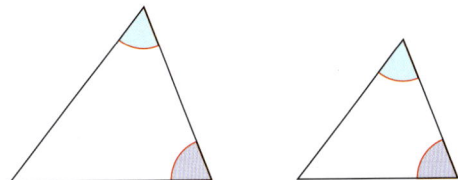

Theorem 13

If two triangles ABC and DEF are similar, then their sides are proportional in order:

$$\frac{|AB|}{|DE|} = \frac{|BC|}{|EF|} = \frac{|AC|}{|DF|}$$

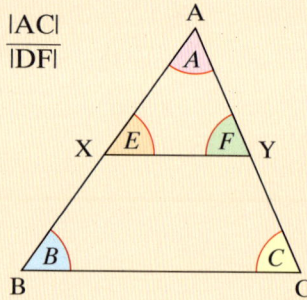

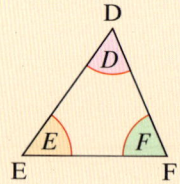

Given:

The triangles ABC and DEF, in which
$|\angle A| = |\angle D|, |\angle B| = |\angle E|$ and $|\angle C| = |\angle F|$.

To Prove:

$$\frac{|AB|}{|DE|} = \frac{|BC|}{|EF|} = \frac{|AC|}{|DF|}.$$

Construction:

Mark the point X on [AB] such that $|AX| = |DE|$.
Mark the point Y on [AC] such that $|AY| = |DF|$.
Join XY.

Proof:

The triangles AXY and DEF are congruent   ...(SAS)

∴ $|\angle AXY| = |\angle DEF|$ ...corresponding angles

∴ $|\angle AXY| = |\angle ABC|$

∴ $XY \| BC$

∴ $\dfrac{|AB|}{|AX|} = \dfrac{|AC|}{|AY|}$ ...a line parallel to one side divides the other side in the same ratio

∴ $\dfrac{|AB|}{|DE|} = \dfrac{|AC|}{|DF|}$

Similarly it can be proved that $\dfrac{|AB|}{|DE|} = \dfrac{|BC|}{|EF|}.$

∴ $\dfrac{|AB|}{|DE|} = \dfrac{|BC|}{|EF|} = \dfrac{|AC|}{|DF|}.$

Example 3

Find the length of the side marked x in the triangle below.

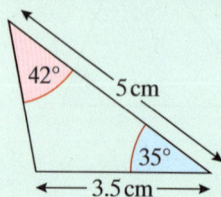

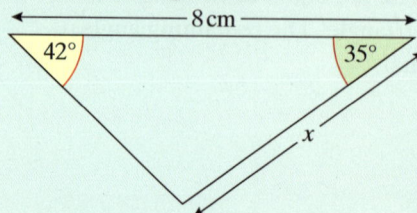

Corresponding sides are opposite equal angles.
The unmarked angles are equal.
The sides with lengths x and 3.5 cm are corresponding sides.

$$\frac{x}{3.5} = \frac{8}{5}$$
$$\Rightarrow \quad 5x = 8\,(3.5)$$
$$\Rightarrow \quad 5x = 28$$
$$\Rightarrow \quad x = 5.6\,\text{cm}$$

Exercise 6.3

1. In each of the following triangles, the arrows indicate that the lines are parallel.
   Find the length of the line segment marked x in each triangle:

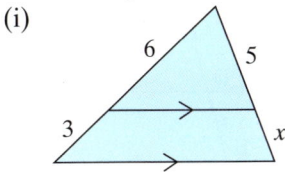

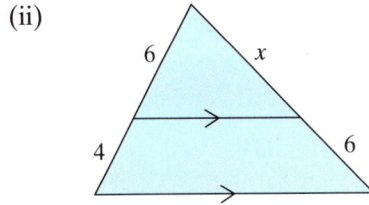

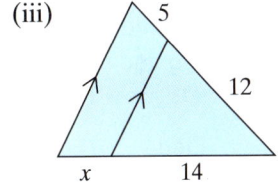

   (i)

   (ii)

   (iii)

2. In the following triangles, the arrows indicate that the lines are parallel.
   Find the length of the line segment marked with a letter in each triangle:

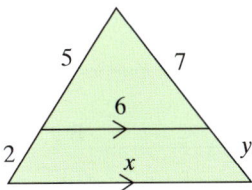

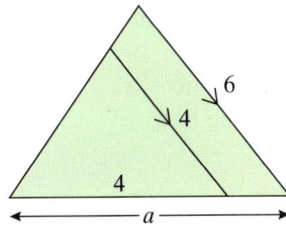

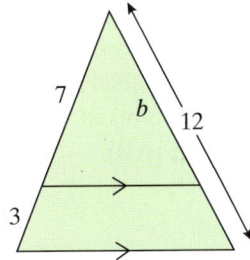

3. In the given triangle, XY∥ST.
   If $|XS| = 5$, $|YT| = 6$ and $|RS| = 12$,
   find $|RT|$.

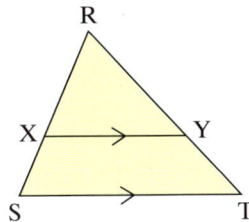

4. In the given triangle, XY∥BC.
   If $|AB| = 5$, $|BX| = 2$ and $|AC| = 8$,
   find $|AY|$.

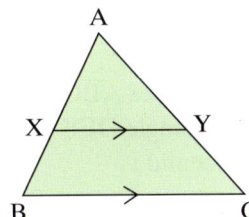

241

5. In the given triangle, PQ||BC.
Find |BC| and |BP|.

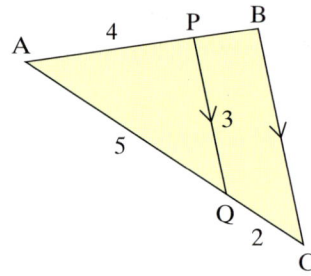

6. In the given triangle, XY||BC.
|AB| : |AX| = 3 : 2.
  (i) If |YC| = 10 cm, find |AY|.
  (ii) What is the ratio |XY| : |BC|?
  (iii) If |BC| = 30 cm, find |XY|.

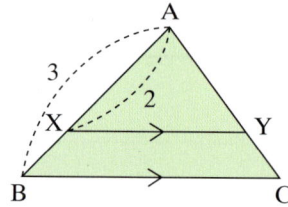

7. a, b and c are parallel lines.
p, q and r are three transversals intersecting a, b and c.
|DE| = |EF|, |GH| = 8 cm and |JK| = 7 cm.

Find (i) |HI| (ii) |GJ|.

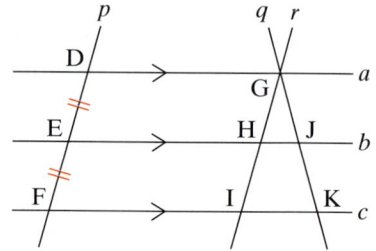

8. In the given figure, d, e and f are parallel lines.
p and q are two transversals.
The transversal p is divided in the ratio 4 : x.
Find, in terms of x, the length of the line
segment [AB].

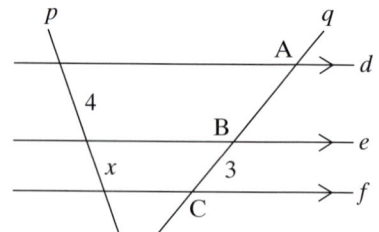

9.

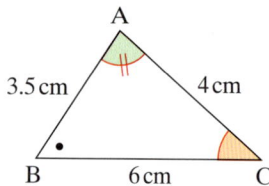

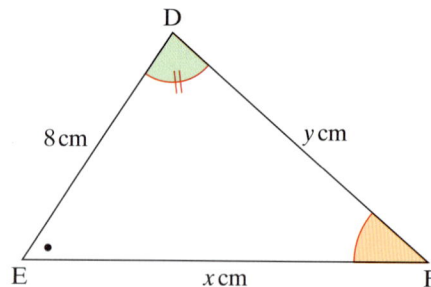

  (i) Explain why the triangles ABC and DEF are similar.
  (ii) Which side of the triangle DEF corresponds to the side [AC]?
  (iii) Find the values of x and y.

10. Find the value of x and the value of y in the given similar triangles.

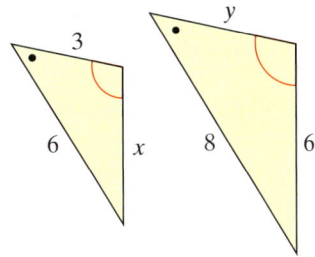

11. The triangles ABC and XYZ are similar.

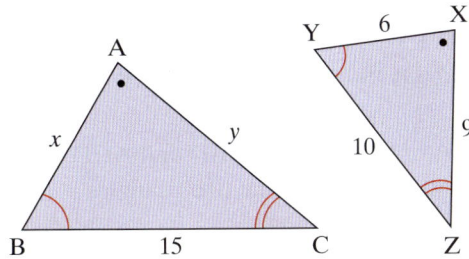

(i) Which side of the triangle XYZ corresponds to [AB]? Explain your answer.

(ii) Find the values of x and y.

12. Given below are two pairs of similar triangles.
The equal angles are marked.
Find the values of x and y for each pair.

(i)

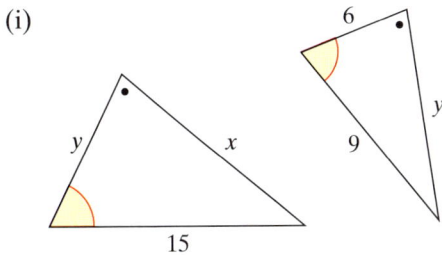

(ii)

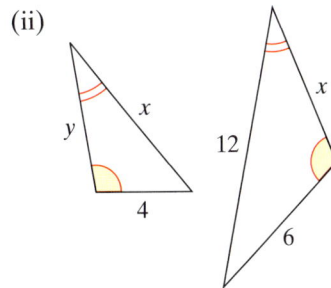

13. In the given figure, the diagonal [AC] bisects the angle BAD.
$|\angle ABC| = |\angle ACD|$.
Find   (i) $|CD|$
       (ii) $|AD|$.

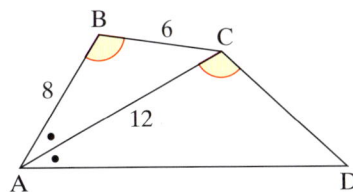

14. ABCD is a quadrilateral in which AB∥DC and |∠DAB| = |∠DBC|.

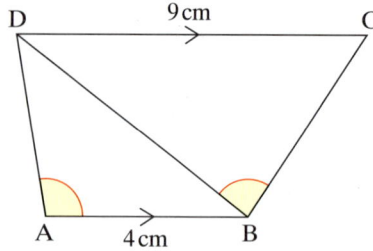

    (i) Prove that the triangles DAB and DBC are similar.

    (ii) If |AB| = 4 cm and |DC| = 9 cm, calculate |BD|.

15. Draw separate diagrams of the triangles ABD and ACD. Mark in equal angles and explain why the two triangles are similar.
Hence find |BD| and |AB|.

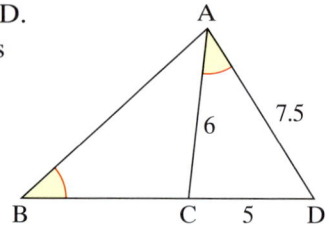

16. In the given figure, |∠BAD| = |∠CBD|.

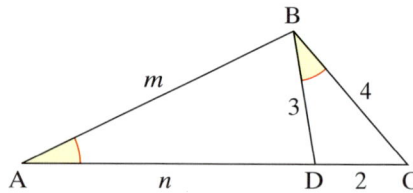

    (i) Name two similar triangles.   (ii) Hence find the values of *m* and *n*.

17. The triangles ABC and BED are similar but DE is not parallel to AC.
Work out the length of the side marked *x*.

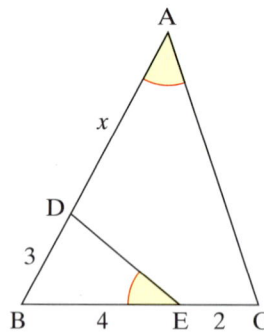

18. In the given figure, |∠WYZ| = |∠XWZ| = 90w°.

    (i) Which triangle is similar to the triangle WXY?

    (ii) Hence find the values of *v* and *w*.

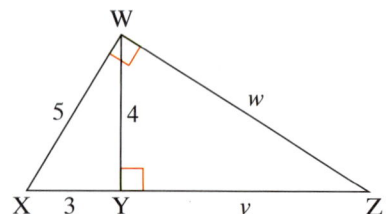

19. From the rectangle ABCD, a square is cut off to leave rectangle BCEF. Rectangle BCEF is similar to ABCD. Find x and hence state the ratio of the sides of rectangle ABCD.

Give x correct to 3 decimal places.

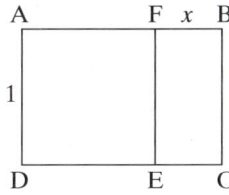

> ABCD is called the Golden Rectangle and is an important shape in architecture.

20. An A3 sheet of paper can be cut into two sheets of A4. The A3 and A4 sheets are mathematically similar.

Find the ratio: $\left(\dfrac{\text{long side of A3 sheet}}{\text{long side of A4 sheet}}\right)$ $\left[\text{that is, } \dfrac{x}{y}\right]$

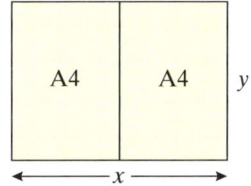

21. The diagram shows the side-view of a swimming pool being filled with water.

Calculate the length of x.

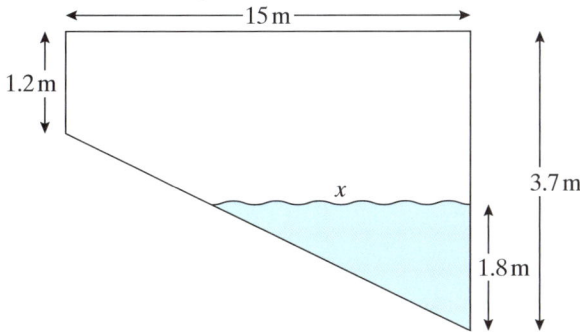

Section 6.4 Circle theorems

In this section we will deal with the geometry of the circle and look at some important mathematical results known as **circle theorems**.

Angles in circles

The diagram on the right shows the $\angle AOB$ at the centre and the $\angle ACB$ at the circumference of the circle, both standing on the arc AB.

An important circle theorem states that

> **Theorem 19**
> The angle subtended at the centre of a circle is twice the angle at the circumference.

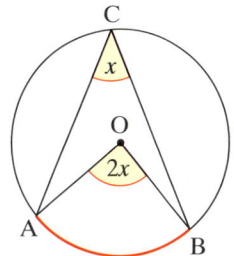

$|\angle AOB| = 2|\angle ACB|$

The theorem stated above gives rise to two important corollaries:

Corollary 2

Angles at the circumference on the same arc are equal in measure.

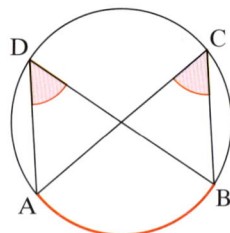

$|\angle ACB| = |\angle ADB|$

Corollary 3

Each angle in a semicircle is a right angle.

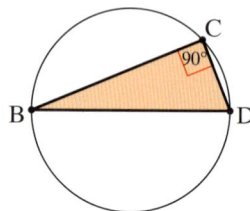

Corollary 4 (The *converse* of Corollary 3)

If the angle on a chord [BD] at some point on a circle is a right angle, then [BD] is a diameter.

Corollary 5

The sum of the opposite angles of a cyclic quadrilateral is 180°.

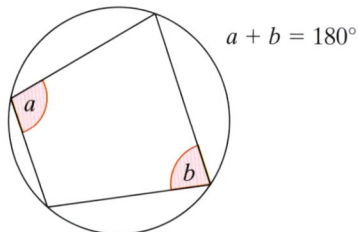

$a + b = 180°$

Example 1

In the given diagram, O is the centre of the circle, $|\angle AOB| = 110°$ and $|\angle OBC| = 30°$.

Find (i) $|\angle ACB|$ (ii) $|\angle OAC|$.

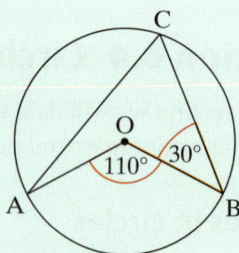

(i) $|\angle AOB| = 2|\angle ACB|$... angle at the centre is double angle at circumference

$\Rightarrow \quad 110° = 2|\angle ACB|$

$\Rightarrow \quad |\angle ACB| = \frac{1}{2}(110°) = 55°$

(ii) To find $|\angle OAC|$, join CO, as shown.

$|\angle OBC| = |\angle OCB| = 30°$... $|OB| = |OC| =$ radius

$|\angle ACB| = 55°$ ... from (i) above

$\Rightarrow \quad |\angle OCA| = 55° - 30°$, i.e., 25°

But $|\angle OAC| = |\angle OCA|$, since $|OA| = |OC| =$ radius.

$\Rightarrow \quad |\angle OAC| = 25°$.

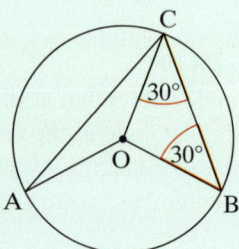

Tangents and chords

A tangent to a circle is a straight line that meets the circle at one point only.

In the given diagram, ℓ is a tangent to the circle.

T is called the **point of contact**.

[AB] and [CD] are **chords** of the circle.

In the given diagram, [OM] is perpendicular to the chord [AB].

$|AM| = |MB|$.

> **Theorem 21**
> The perpendicular from the centre of a circle to a chord bisects the chord.

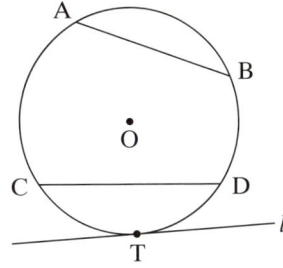

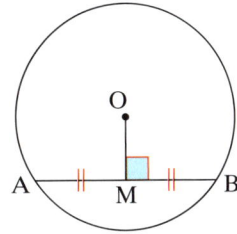

Example 2

Circle k has a diameter 20 cm in length.
$AB \perp CD$ and $|CD| = 16$ cm.
Find $|EB|$.

The diameter [AB] is perpendicular to the chord [CD].
$\Rightarrow \quad |CE| = |ED| = 8$ cm
$\quad\quad |OD| = 10$ cm $=$ radius

$\triangle ODE$ is right-angled.
$\Rightarrow \quad 10^2 = 8^2 + |OE|^2$
$\Rightarrow \quad 100 = 64 + |OE|^2$
$\Rightarrow \quad |OE|^2 = 36$
$\Rightarrow \quad |OE| = 6$ cm
$\Rightarrow \quad |EB| = (10 - 6)$ cm
$\Rightarrow \quad |EB| = 4$ cm

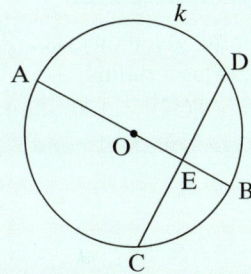

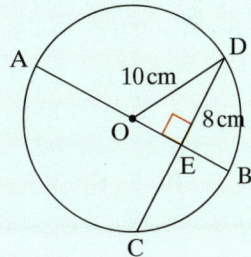

The diagram shows a tangent PT to the circle k with centre O.

T is the point of contact and [OT] is a radius.

$OT \perp TP$

This diagram illustrates that the angle between a tangent and a radius is 90°. This result is stated in the theorem below:

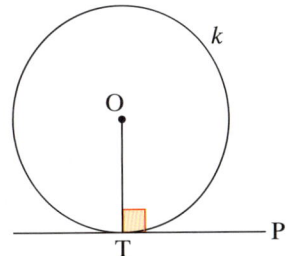

247

Theorem 20

1. A tangent is perpendicular to the radius that goes to the point of contact.
2. If a point T lies on a circle k and a line TP is perpendicular to the radius to T, then TP is a tangent to k.

Corollary 6

If two circles intersect at one point only, then the two centres and the point of contact are collinear.

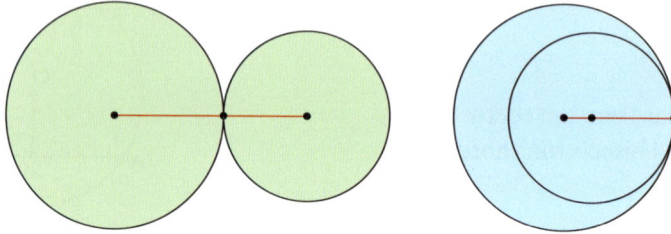

Example 3

In the given diagram, PT is a tangent to the circle and [OT] is a radius.
If $|\angle TOQ| = 120°$, find the measures of the angles marked x and y.

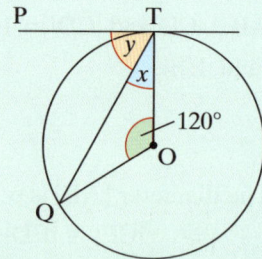

The triangle OTQ is isosceles as
$|OT| = |OQ| = $ radius

$\therefore \quad |\angle OTQ| = |\angle OQT| = x$

$\therefore \qquad 2x = 180° - 120°$

$\qquad\qquad = 60$

$\qquad\quad x = 30°$

Since $OT \perp PT \implies |\angle OTP| = 90°$

$\therefore \quad x + y = 90°$

$\qquad 30 + y = 90° \qquad \dots x = 30°$

$\qquad\qquad y = 90° - 30°$

$\qquad\qquad y = 60°$

Exercise 6.4

1. Find the measure of the angle marked with a letter in each of the following circles, where O is the centre.

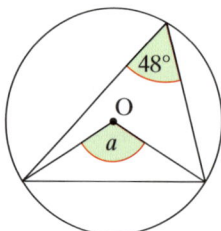

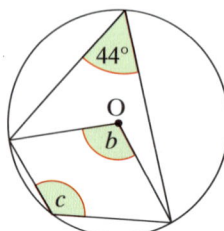

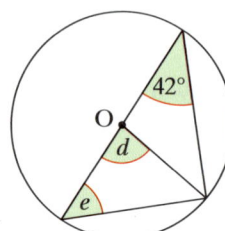

2. Find the measure of the angle marked with a letter in each of these circles:

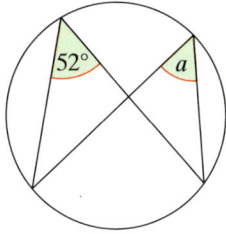

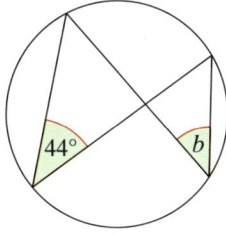

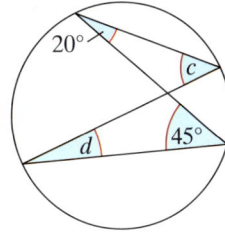

3. Find the measures of the angles marked *a*, *b* and *c* in
    the given diagram, where O is the centre of the circle.
    Explain your answer in each case.

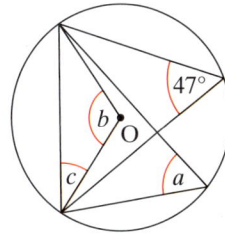

4. Find the measures of the angles marked *f*, *g* and *h* in
    the given circle.

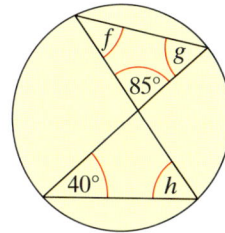

5. Find the measure of the angles marked with letters in the following circles, where O is
    the centre:

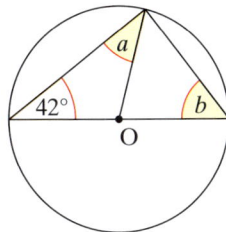

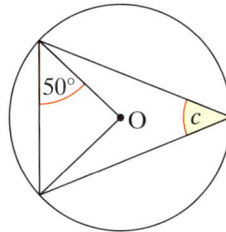

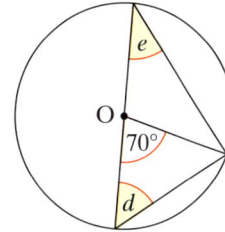

6. Find the measures of the angles marked with letters in the following circles, where
    equal line segments are indicated:

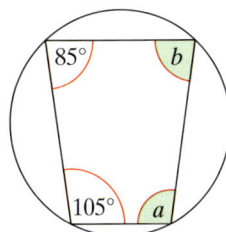

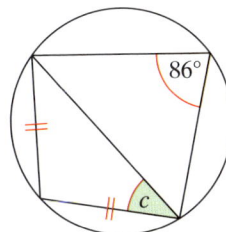

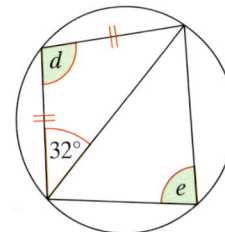

7. In the given diagram, O is the centre of the circle. Find the sizes of the three interior angles of the triangle ABC.
Give reasons for your answers.

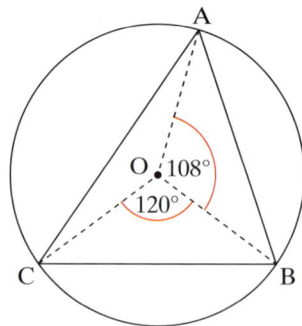

8. ST is a tangent to the given circle with O as centre. If $|\angle PST| = 40°$, find
    (i) $|\angle OST|$
    (ii) $|\angle OSP|$
  (iii) $|\angle OPS|$
  (iv) $|\angle SOP|$

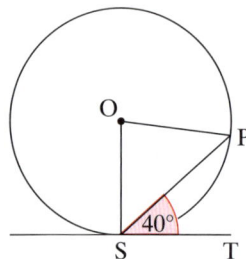

9. O is the centre of the given circles and t is a tangent in each case.
Work out the size of the angles marked with a letter.

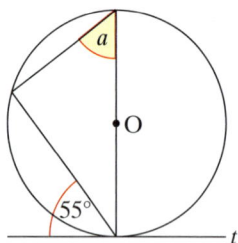

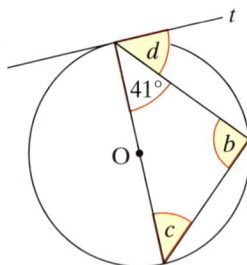

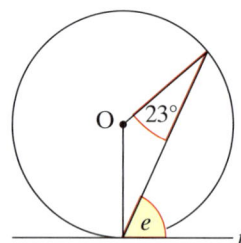

10. In the given figure, $|\angle BDC| = 62°$ and $|\angle DCA| = 44°$.
Find (i) $|\angle BAC|$
       (ii) $|\angle ABD|$.

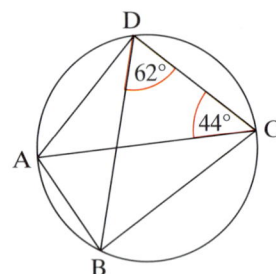

11. In the given diagram, O is the centre of the circle. PA and PB are tangents to the circle.
    (i) Prove that the triangles AOP and BOP are congruent.
    (ii) Hence show that $|PA| = |PB|$.
  (iii) Prove that $|\angle APB| + |\angle AOB| = 180°$.

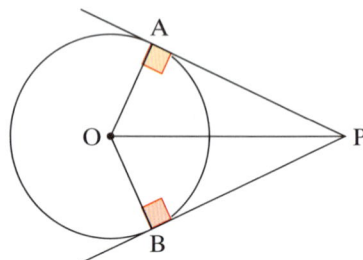

> The lengths of two tangents from a point to a circle are equal.

12. In the given diagram, PA and PT are tangents to the circle of centre O.
If $|\angle APT| = 40°$, find $|\angle ATO|$.

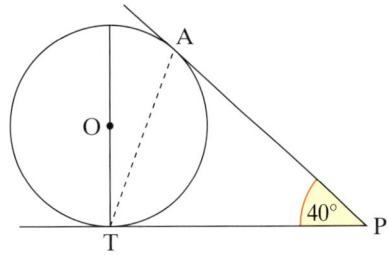

13. In the given circle, $|AB| = |BC|$ and $|\angle ADC| = 34°$.
Find   (i) $|\angle ABC|$
         (ii) $|\angle BAC|$.

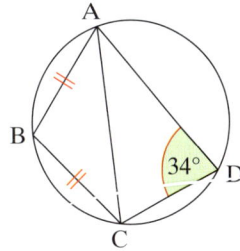

14. In the given diagram, O is the centre of the circle.
Prove that $x + y = 90°$.

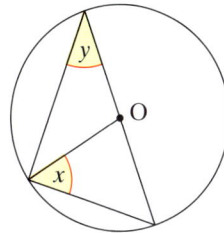

15. [RP], [PQ] and [QR] are tangents to the given circle.
X, Y and Z are the points of contact.
$|\angle PRQ| = 58°$ and $|\angle PQR| = 64°$.
  (i) Name three isosceles triangles.
  (ii) Find $|\angle PXY|$.
  (iii) Now find the measures of the interior angles
       of the triangle XYZ.

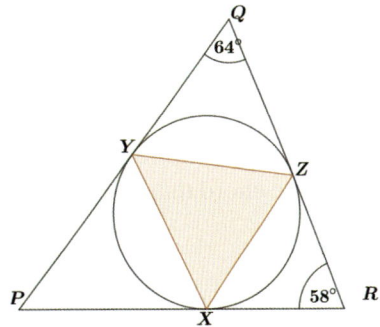

16. ABC is a triangle inscribed in a circle with centre O.
TA and TB are tangents to the circle.
If $|\angle ACB| = 53°$, find
  (i) $|\angle AOB|$
  (ii) $|\angle BTA|$
  (iii) $|\angle ABT|$.

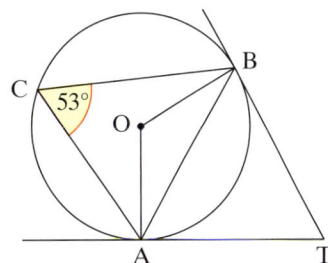

17. In the given figure, |AB| = |AD| and |∠DAB| = 84°.
   (i) Find |∠DBA|
   (ii) Find |∠BCA|.

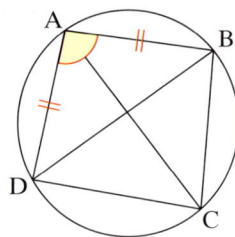

18. In the given circle, the chords [AC] and [BD] intersect at the point E.
Prove that the triangles ABE and ECD are similar.

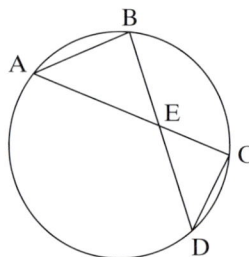

Revision Exercise 6 (Core)

1. The length of a rectangle is 3 m longer than its width. If the length of the perimeter is equal area of the rectangle find the length and width of the rectangle.

2. Find the value of the angle $a°$ in this diagram.
Give reasons for your answer.

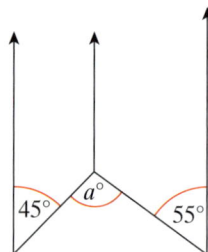

3. Two concentric circles with centre A have radii of 6 cm and 10 cm respectively. Find the length |BC| of the chord that is a tangent to the smaller circle.

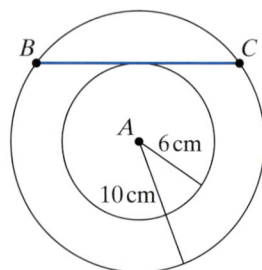

4. Find the value of the angle $b°$ in this diagram.
Give a reason for each deduction you make.

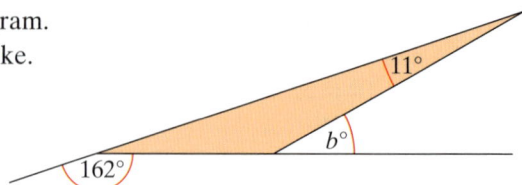

5. Prove that triangles BEF and DCF are similar.
(Give a reason for each deduction made).
Given that $|BF| = 6$ cm, $|EF| = 8$ cm, $|FD| = 2.5$ cm and
$|CD| = 3$ cm, find the lengths of the sides $[BE]$ and $[FC]$.

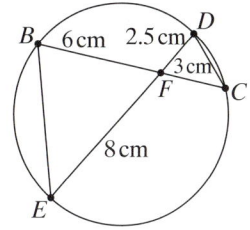

6. Find the area of this isosceles triangle.

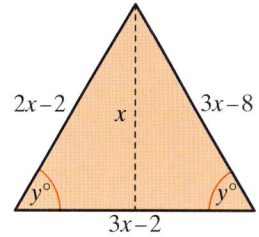

7. Given that $|\angle XZY| = 90°$ and $|XZ| = |AZ|$
find y in terms of x.

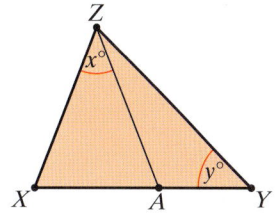

8. In the triangle ABC, $|\angle ADE| = |\angle ACB| = 90°$.
Find the value of x.

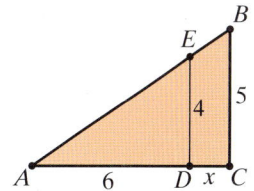

9. In the triangle ABC, $|\angle ABC| = 90°$.
$|AB| = 8$ cm, $|BC| = 6$ cm.
$[BD]$ is drawn perpendicular to $[AC]$
Find (i) $|BD|$ (ii) $|AD|$ (iii) $|DC|$

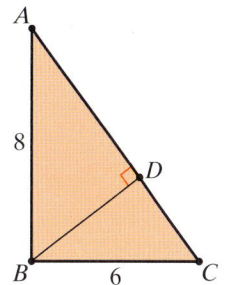

10. $\overleftrightarrow{CB}$ is a tangent to circle centre A at the point B.
If $|CD| = 2$ and $|CB| = 4$, find the length of
the radius $|AB|$.

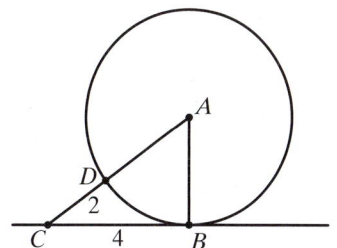

Revision Exercise 6 (Advanced)

1. *AED* and *ABC* are two right angled triangles.
Given that $|DE| = 1$ cm, $|AE| = 2$ cm, $|EB| = 3$ cm
find $|AC|$, leaving your answer in surd form.

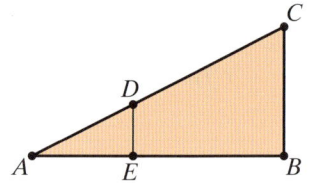

2. In the given diagram
$|AF| = |FE|$ and $|DF| = |FC|$
Prove each of the following:

(i) $|\angle ADF| = |\angle FCE|$

(ii) $|BD| = |BC|$

State your reasons for each deduction made.

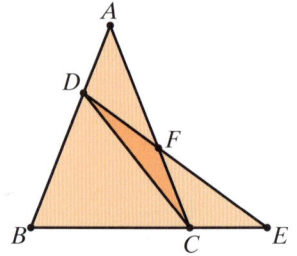

3. (i) A regular hexagon is drawn and divided
into 4 triangles. Using the triangles
calculate the size of the angle at each
point of the hexagon.

(ii) If a regular pentagon has 5 equal sides,
using the same procedure as above
find the size of angles in a pentagon.

(iii) Using the pattern formed from parts (i) and (ii) above write down a formula for an
n sided polygon and use it to find the measure of the internal angle of a decagon
(10 sides)

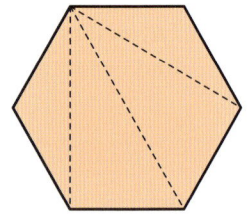

4. The given circle is inscribed in the triangle *ABC*.
Q, *R* and *S* are the points of contact.
$|\angle ARQ| = 70°$ and $|\angle RQS| = 54°$.
Find $|\angle ACB|$.

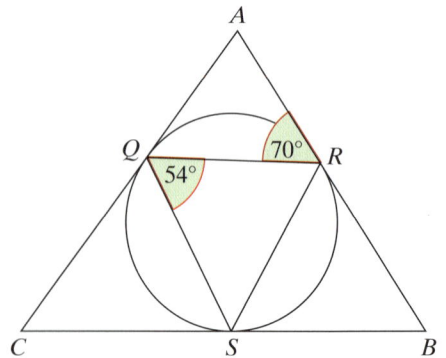

5. In the triangle *ABC*,
$|AB| = |AC|$,
$|\angle ADE| = |\angle AFE| = 90°$,
$|DE| : |EF| = 5 : 7$ and $|BC| = 48$
Find $|EC|$

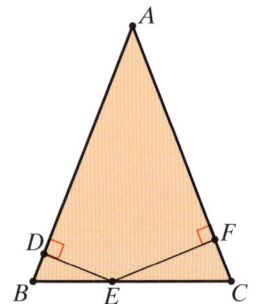

6. A chain fits tightly over two cogs of radii 19 cm and 12 cm as shown in the diagram. Given that the centres of the cogs are 41 cm apart, calculate the length of the straight section of chain, [AB].(The dotted line, parallel to [C_1C_2], may be useful.)

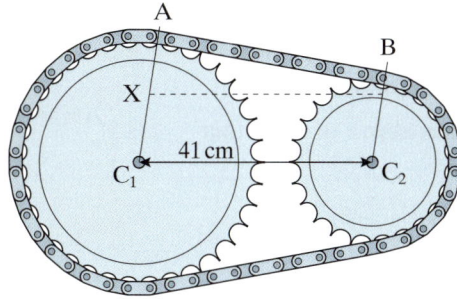

7. Given that T is a tangent to a circle centre O, explain why $\angle CAT = \angle ADC = \angle ABC = a°$. Hence find the measure of the angles marked x, y, d, c.

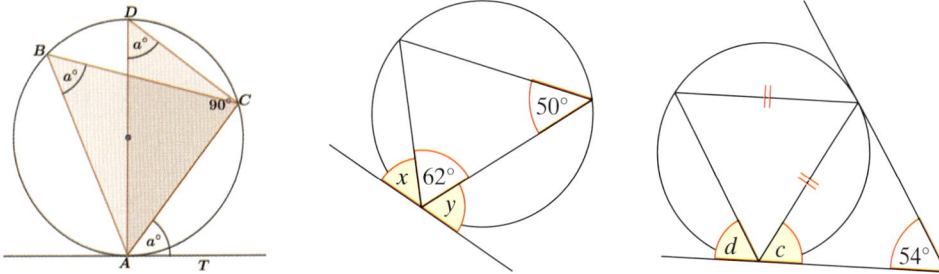

8. Sarah made this design of overlapping circles on cm squared paper. Show that the area of the blue-shaded region is 18 cm^2.

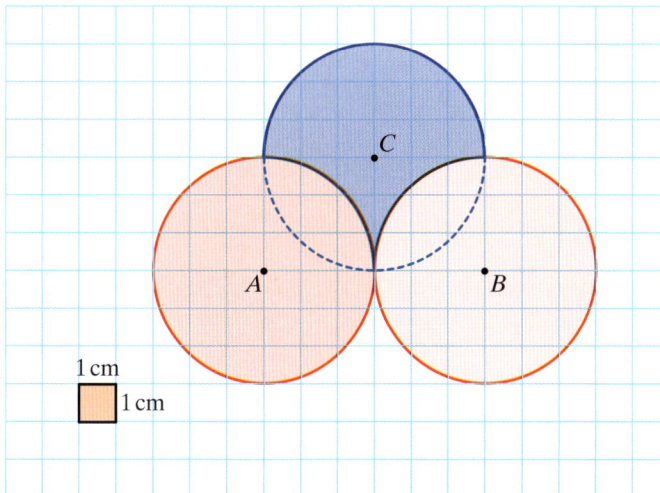

9. (i) Complete the following sentences
   1. "The external angle of a triangle is equal to ...."
   2. "In an isosceles triangle ...."

   (ii) [CD] is any chord of a circle centre A and [CD] is extended to E so that |DE| = radius r.

   E is joined to A and continued to N.

   Use the information above to show that

   $\angle DEB = \frac{1}{3}\angle CAN$

   (Hint: Join D to A and continue)

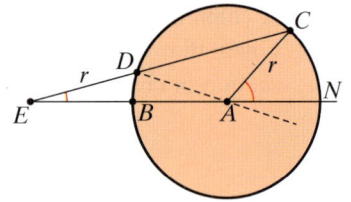

Archimedes (Book Of Lemmas)
Proposition 8

$\angle DEB = \frac{1}{3}\angle CAN$

Revision Exercise (Extended-Response Questions)

1. In the given circle with centre O, [PA] is a tangent and [PR] is a diameter of the circle.
   $|\angle APQ| = a°$.

   To prove that $|\angle APQ| = |\angle PTQ|$, copy and complete the following:

   $|\angle PQR| = 90°$, because …
   $\Rightarrow$ $|\angle PRQ| + |\angle RPQ| = 90°$, because …
   $\quad |\angle QPA| + |\angle RPQ| = 90°$, because …
   $\Rightarrow$ $|\angle PRQ| + |\angle RPQ| = |\angle QPA| + |\angle RPQ|$
   $\Rightarrow$ $|\angle PRQ| = |\angle QPA|$,

   But $|\angle PRQ| = |\angle PTQ|$, because …
   $\quad \Rightarrow$ $|\angle QPA| = |\angle PTQ|$, as required.

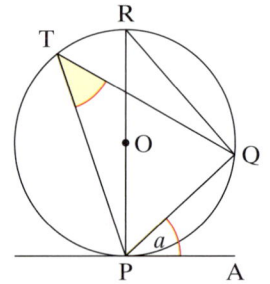

2. (i) Two spheres lie on a level surface and touch, as shown.
   The radius of the smaller sphere is 40 cm and the radius of the larger sphere is 70 cm.
   Find the distance |AB|, the length of the line between the points of contact of the spheres with the level surface.

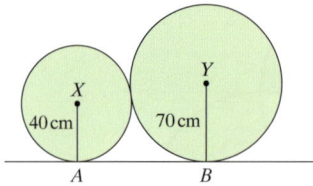

   (ii) A third sphere is placed beside the two spheres in part (i).

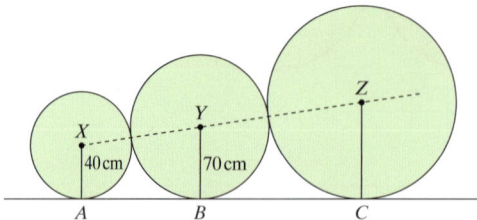

   In order to ensure that the three centres X, Y and Z are collinear, find |ZC|, the length of the radius of the third sphere, correct to the nearest cm.

256

3. (i) In the given diagram, $AB\|DC$.
Prove that the triangle AEB is isosceles.

(ii) If the diagram was redrawn so that E is the
centre of the circle and AB is still parallel to
DC, which of the following statements is not
always true?

    (a) $|AB| = |DC|$

    (b) The triangle ABE is equilateral

    (c) The triangles AEB and EDC are similar.

Give a reason for your answer.

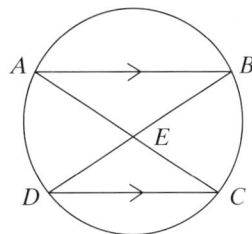

4. (i) A circular tunnel of radius 7 m has a road 9 m wide
as a base. Find the height h of the tunnel correct to
one place of decimals.

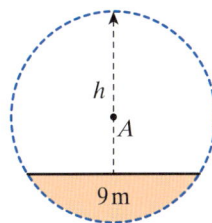

(ii) Two cylinders of radius 2 m are resting on
level ground. A cylinder of radius 1.5 m
rests on top of them as shown.
If the lines joining the centres of the circular
ends make an angle of 90° i.e. $\angle AEC = 90°$,
find:

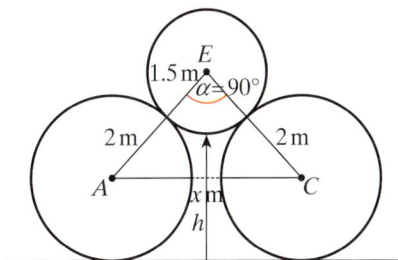

    (a) the distance between the bottom of the
smaller cylinder and the ground
i.e. find h.

(b) the distance between the larger cylinders i.e. find x.

Leave your answers in surd form.

5. (i) Prove that the sum of the angles of a quadrilateral add up to 360°.

(ii) Hence find the size of the angles marked with a letter in each of the following
diagrams.

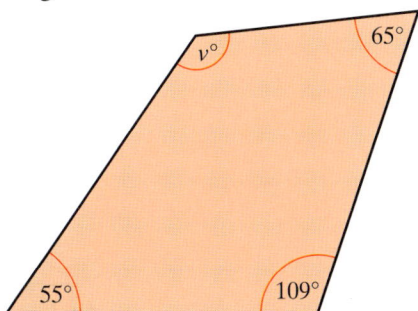

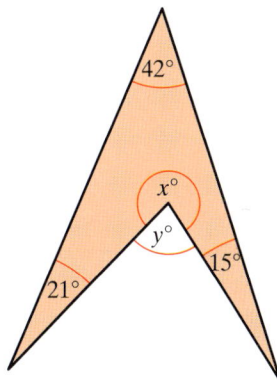

(iii) A cyclic quadrilateral $BCDE$ is one in which all vertices lie on the circumference of a circle.
Find the size of the angles $\angle BED$ and $\angle BCD$.

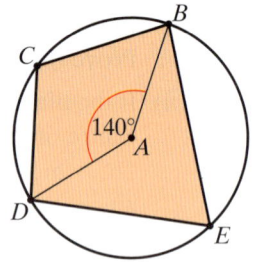

(iv) Sean has made a regular kite $ABCD$ with $|AB| = |AD|$ and $|BC| = |DC|$, if the $|\angle ABC| = 87°$ and $|\angle BCD| = 52°$ show that the kite does not form a cyclic quadrilateral.

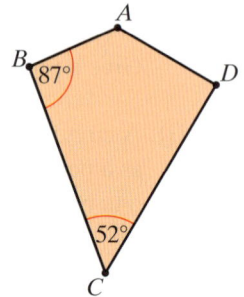

6. (i) Two tangents $[BC]$ and $[DC]$ are drawn to a circle centre A. Prove that the triangles ABC and ADC are congruent.

State your reasons for each deduction made

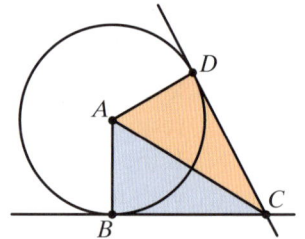

(ii) A circle, centre A, is inscribed in a quadrilateral $BCDE$ as shown. The sides of the quadrilateral are tangential to the circle.
If $|DF| = 9.6$ cm, $|EG| = 3.7$ and $|BC| = 12$ cm,
Find the length of the perimeter of $BCDE$.

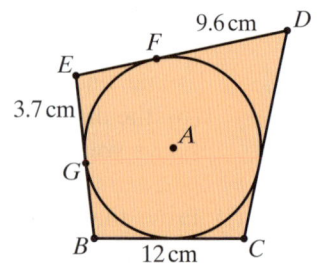

(iii) A square is inscribed in a circle which is inscribed in a square as shown. Find the ratio

$$\frac{(area\ of\ the\ larger\ square\ BCDE)}{(area\ of\ the\ smaller\ square\ FGHI)}$$

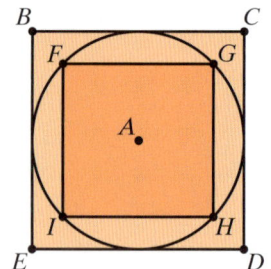

(iv) If a circle is inscribed in a square which is inscribed in a circle as shown, prove that

$$\frac{(area\ of\ the\ larger\ circle)}{(area\ of\ the\ smaller\ circle)} = 2$$

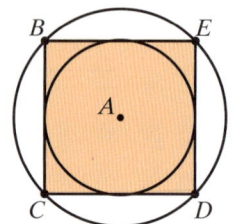

7. A thin circular sheet of aluminium of radius = 24 cm has a
   sector with an angle of 120° cut from it.
   The remaining sector is folded until the edges [CA] and [AB]
   match resulting in an aluminium funnel of radius r cm
   and height h cm.
     (i) Find the values of r and h
   Liquid is poured into the funnel.
    (ii) (a) What is the depth of the liquid when the radius of the
          surface of the liquid is half the radius of the funnel.
       (b) What fraction of the volume of the funnel is filled
          at this point.
   The funnel is filled with a viscous liquid and allowed to pour
   out through a hole in the bottom of the funnel at a rate of 20 cm³/min.
   (iii) At what depth should a sensor be placed so as to give a 10 min
        warning indicating that the funnel is nearly empty?

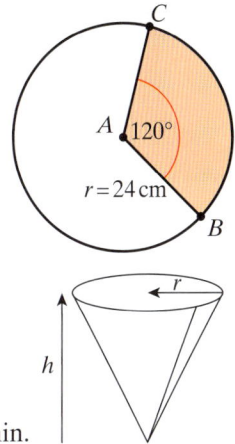

8. (i) A trapezium $ABCD$ is a quadrilateral with two
       parallel sides [BC] and [AD] as shown in diagram.
       If $|AD| = x$ and $|BC| = y$, show that the area
       of the trapezium can be written as
       Area of $ABCD = \frac{1}{2}(x + y)h$ where h is the
       perpendicular distance between the parallel sides
    (ii) A surveyor has a map of a trapezoidal field with
       side [AB] parallel to side[CD].
       $|AB| = 20$ cm and $|DC| = 30$ cm. He wants to
       mark the line of a fence [EF] on the map so that
       $|AE| = 3$ cm.
       Find the value of x so that the area of
       AEDF = area of CBEF.

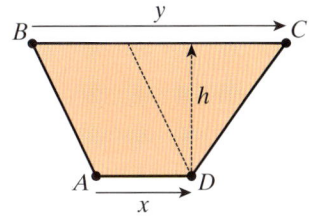

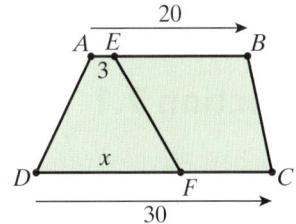

Differential Calculus

Key words

average rate of change   instantaneous rate of change   derived function

differentiation from first principles   product rule   quotient rule   chain rule

trigonometric function   inverse trigonometric function   exponential function

logarithmic function

Introduction to calculus

In this chapter, we begin the study of a very important branch of mathematics called *calculus*. Differential calculus is mainly concerned with measuring the rate of change of one quantity with respect to another. For example, the speed of a car is the rate at which the distance it travels changes with respect to time. However, we know that a car is unlikely to travel at a constant speed, even for a short time. If a car is accelerating, it is changing speed by the second. If 60 km/hr is registered on the speedometer, this tells us the **instantaneous** speed. Calculus is the mathematical tool that will enable us to find **instantaneous rates of change**.

Section 7.1 Average rate of change

We have already learned how to find the slope of a line if we are given two points on the line.

The slope, $m = \dfrac{y_2 - y_1}{x_2 - x_1}$.

We will now refer to this slope as the **rate of change** of y with respect to x.

The slope of a line will always be a fixed number as the slope is constant all along the line.

The curve on the right is the graph of a function $y = f(x)$.

How do we find the slope of a curve?

The slope of a curve at any point is defined as the slope of the tangent to the curve at that point.

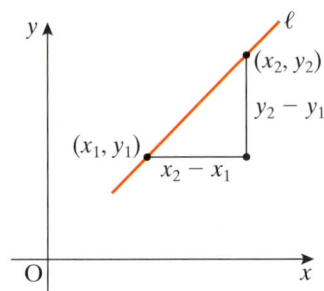

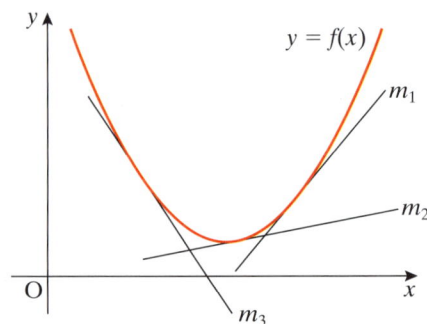

The diagram above also shows tangents drawn at three different points on the curve. The three tangents have different slopes – m_1, m_2 and m_3.

In the next section of this chapter, we will show how calculus can be used to find the slope of the tangent to a curve at any point on the curve.

Average rate of change

The curve on the right is the graph of
$f(x) = x^2$.
The points $(1, 1)$ $(2, 4)$ and $(3, 9)$ are shown on the curve.
Lines are drawn through $(1, 1)$ and $(3, 9)$ and also through $(1, 1)$ and $(2, 4)$.
These lines are marked l and m.

Slope of $l = \dfrac{y_2 - y_1}{x_2 - x_1} = \dfrac{9 - 1}{3 - 1} = \dfrac{8}{2} = 4$

Slope of $m = \dfrac{4 - 1}{2 - 1} = \dfrac{3}{1} = 3$

The slope of the line l joining $(1, 1)$ and $(3, 9)$ is generally referred to as the **average rate of change**.

The average rate of change of the line m = slope of m = 3.

In general, for any function $y = f(x)$, the average rate of change of y with respect to x over the interval $[a, b]$ is the slope of the line joining $(a, f(a))$ to $(b, f(b))$.

Average rate of change $= \dfrac{f(b) - f(a)}{b - a}$

> The interval $[a, b]$ represents $a \leqslant x \leqslant b$.

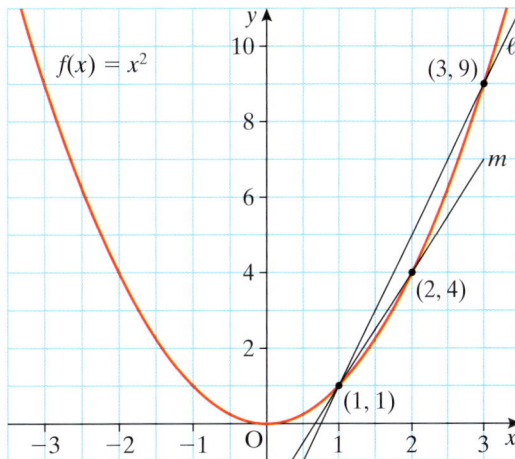

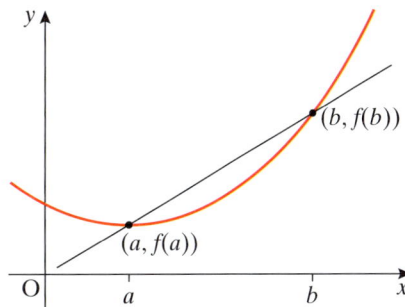

Example 1

Find the average rate of change of y with respect to x for the function $y = f(x)$ over the interval $[1, 4]$ as shown.

The average rate of change = slope$_{AB}$

$$= \frac{7 - 1}{4 - 1} = \frac{6}{3} = 2$$

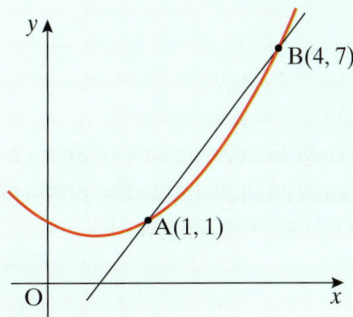

Example 2

The temperature T (°C) in a classroom on a particular day can be modelled by the equation

$$T = \frac{200}{t^2 + 2t + 20}, \text{ where } t \text{ is the time after 6.00 p.m..}$$

Find   (i)   the temperature in the room at 6.00 p.m.
       (ii) the temperature in the room at midnight
       (iii) the average rate of change of temperature from 6.00 p.m. to midnight.

  (i)   At 6.00 p.m., $t = 0$

  $$\Rightarrow T = \frac{200}{(0)^2 + 2(0) + 20} = 10°C$$

  (ii) At midnight, $t = 6$

  $$\Rightarrow T = \frac{200}{(6)^2 + 2(6) + 20} = 2.94°C$$

  (iii) The average rate of change $= \dfrac{10 - 2.94}{6 - 0} = 1.18°C/\text{hour}$

Exercise 7.1

1. The curve on the right is the graph of the function $f(x) = x^2 + x - 2$.
    The points A, B, C and D are shown.
    Find the average rate of change of y with respect to x of the line through

    (i)   A and B
    (ii) B and C
    (iii) C and D.

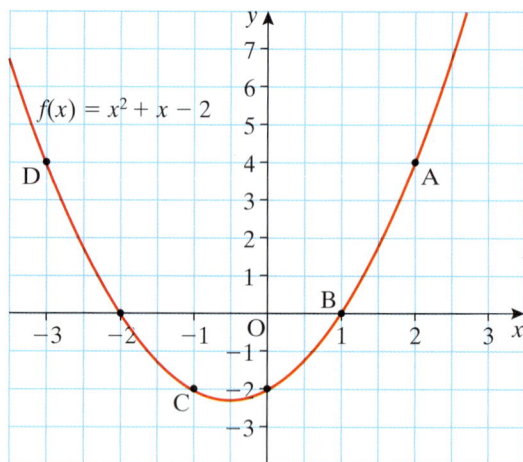

2. Find the average rate of change of the function depicted in the graph shown for the interval $[-2, 5]$.

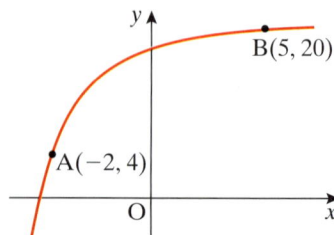

3. Find the average rate of change of y with respect to x from point A to point B for each of the following graphs.

(i)

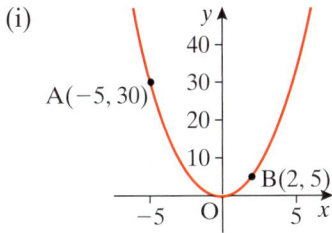

A(−5, 30)

B(2, 5)

(ii)

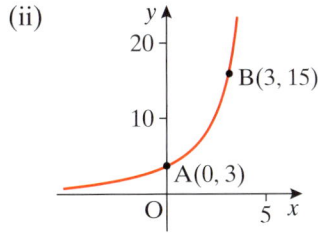

B(3, 15)

A(0, 3)

4. The depth, d cm, of water in a bath tub t minutes after the tap is turned on is modelled by the function $d(t) = \dfrac{-300}{(t + 6)} + 50, t \geqslant 0$.

Find the average rate of change of the depth of the water in the tub over the first 10 minutes after the tap is turned on.

5. The graph of a person's height h (cm) versus t (years) from some time after birth to age 20 is shown.

   (i) When is the growth rate greatest?
   (ii) Estimate the average rate of growth between the ages of 5 and 10 years.

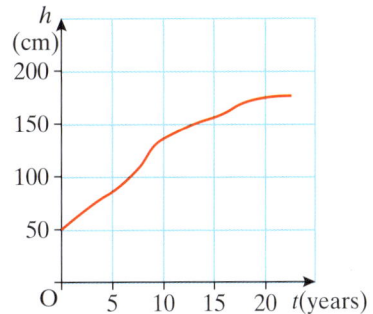

6. A cube has edge of length x cm.

   (i) Find an expression for the surface area, $S(x)$, of the cube.
   (ii) Find the average rate at which the surface area changes with respect to x as x increases from $x = 2$ cm to $x = 5$ cm.

7. The curve on the right is the graph of the function $y = x^2 - 2x$.
Q is the point $(3, 3)$.
P is any other point on the curve.

   (i) If P is the point $(4, 8)$, find the slope of PQ.
   (ii) If P is the point $(3.5, 5.25)$, find the slope of PQ.
   (iii) If P is the point $(3.1, 3.41)$, find the slope of PQ.
   (iv) What do the results in parts (i) to (iii) suggest for the slope of the tangent to the curve at Q?

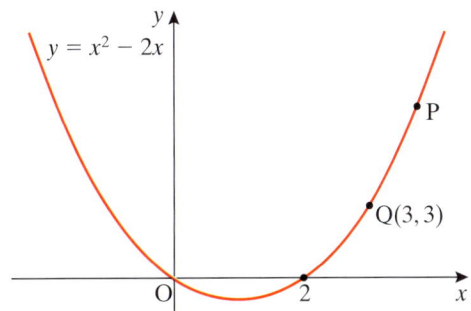

$y = x^2 - 2x$

P

Q(3, 3)

Section 7.2 Limits – Continuity

Introduction to limits

Consider this sequence of numbers: $\frac{1}{2}, \frac{1}{4}, \frac{1}{8}, \frac{1}{16}, \frac{1}{32}, \frac{1}{64}, \ldots$

If we add the first two numbers, we get $\frac{3}{4}$. If we add the first three, we get $\frac{7}{8}$.

If we add the first six numbers, we get $\frac{63}{64}$.

Notice that the more terms we add, the closer the result gets to 1 but it **never reaches** 1. In mathematics, we say that the **limit** of the sum of these numbers is 1.

We will now take the function $f(x) = x^2$ and consider its value as x **approaches** 3 from below and above 3

① $f(2) = 4$; $f(2.5) = 6.25$; $f(2.75) = 7.5625$; $f(2.9) = 8.41 \ldots$
② $f(4) = 16$; $f(3.5) = 12.25$; $f(3.25) = 10.5625$; $f(3.1) = 9.61 \ldots$

As x gets closer to 3, the value of x^2 gets closer to 9. 9 is said to be the limit of $f(x) = x^2$ as x **tends to** 3.

This is written as $\lim\limits_{x \to 3} (x^2) = 9$.

We generally use the abbreviation **lim** for limit.

In general, to find the limit of $f(x)$, we substitute a for x in the function.

For example, $\lim\limits_{x \to 2} \dfrac{3x + 2}{x + 4} = \dfrac{3(2) + 2}{2 + 4} = \dfrac{8}{6} = \dfrac{4}{3}$.

Now consider $\lim\limits_{x \to 3} \dfrac{x^2 - 9}{x - 3}$.

When we substitute 3 for x, we get $\dfrac{9 - 9}{3 - 3} = \dfrac{0}{0}$.

The result $\dfrac{0}{0}$ is known as an **indeterminate form** as its value cannot be determined.

> **Limit notation**
>
> $\lim\limits_{x \to a} f(x) = p$
> states that $f(x)$ approaches p as x gets close to a.

If after substitution the result is $\dfrac{0}{0}$, some other method must be found to obtain the limit.

The most common method used involves factorising the numerator and denominator and then dividing by the common factor.

Thus, $\lim\limits_{x \to 3} \dfrac{x^2 - 9}{x - 3} = \lim\limits_{x \to 3} \dfrac{(x + 3)\overset{1}{\cancel{(x - 3)}}}{\underset{1}{\cancel{(x - 3)}}} = \lim\limits_{x \to 3} (x + 3) = 6$.

Note: It is important to realise that if $f(x) = \dfrac{x^2 - 9}{x - 3}$, then $f(3)$ does not exist,
but the $\lim\limits_{x \to 3}(x)$ does exist.

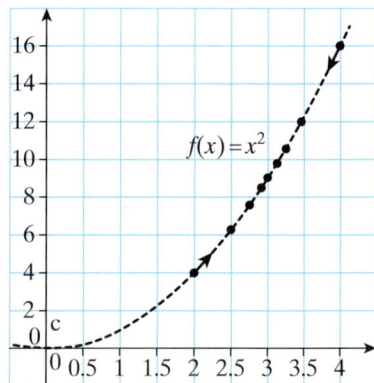

Example 1

Evaluate   (i) $\lim_{x \to 0} \dfrac{4x + 1}{2x + 3}$ (ii) $\lim_{x \to 2} \dfrac{x^2 + x - 6}{x - 2}$.

(i) $\lim_{x \to 0} \dfrac{4x + 1}{2x + 3} = \dfrac{0 + 1}{0 + 3} = \dfrac{1}{3}$

(ii) $\left[\lim_{x \to 2} \dfrac{x^2 + x - 6}{x - 2} = \dfrac{4 + 2 - 6}{2 - 2} = \dfrac{0}{0} \quad \text{... indeterminate} \right]$

We now factorise the numerator:

$$\therefore \quad \lim_{x \to 2} \dfrac{x^2 + x - 6}{x - 2} = \lim_{x \to 2} \dfrac{(x + 3)\overset{1}{(\cancel{x - 2})}}{\underset{1}{(\cancel{x - 2})}} = \lim_{x \to 2} (x + 3) = 5$$

Limit of a function as $x \to \infty$

In the example above, we investigated the limit of a function as the variable tended to a fixed number. Now we will examine the limit of a function as the variable tends to infinity. We use the symbol ∞ to denote infinity.

Now consider $\lim_{x \to \infty} \left(\dfrac{1}{x} \right)$.

When $x = 10, \dfrac{1}{x} = \dfrac{1}{10} = 0.1$. When $x = 1000, \dfrac{1}{x} = \dfrac{1}{1000} = 0.001$.

When $x = 1{,}000{,}000, \dfrac{1}{x} = \dfrac{1}{1{,}000{,}000} = 0.000001$.

These examples illustrate that as x increases,

the value of $\dfrac{1}{x}$ decreases and in fact tends to zero.

$$\lim_{x \to \infty} \dfrac{1}{x} = 0$$

If the numerator is any fixed number k, the $\lim_{x \to \infty} \dfrac{k}{x}$ is also zero.

Since $\lim_{x \to \infty} \dfrac{1}{x} = 0$, it follows that $\lim_{x \to \infty} \dfrac{1}{x^2} = 0$ and $\lim_{x \to \infty} \dfrac{k}{x^2} = 0$, where $k \in R$.

Example 2

Evaluate   (i) $\lim_{x \to \infty} \dfrac{4x + 1}{2x + 3}$ (ii) $\lim_{x \to \infty} \dfrac{3x^2 - 2x + 4}{5x^2 + 4x - 3}$

(In examples of this type, we divide the numerator and denominator by the

highest power of x in the expression and then use $\lim_{x \to \infty} \dfrac{1}{x} = 0$ or $\lim_{x \to \infty} \dfrac{k}{x} = 0$ to

evaluate the limit of the function.)

(i) $\lim\limits_{x \to \infty} \dfrac{4x + 1}{2x + 3} = \lim\limits_{x \to \infty} \dfrac{4 + \dfrac{1}{x}}{2 + \dfrac{3}{x}}$

$\qquad\qquad\qquad = \dfrac{4 + 0}{2 + 0} = 2 \quad \dots \left(\lim\limits_{x \to \infty} \dfrac{k}{x} = 0 \right)$

(ii) $\lim\limits_{x \to \infty} \dfrac{3x^2 - 2x + 4}{5x^2 + 4x - 3} = \lim\limits_{x \to \infty} \dfrac{3 - \dfrac{2}{x} + \dfrac{4}{x^2}}{5 + \dfrac{4}{x} - \dfrac{3}{x^2}}$ $\quad \dots$ divide each term by x^2

$\qquad\qquad\qquad\qquad = \dfrac{3 - 0 + 0}{5 + 0 - 0} = \dfrac{3}{5}$

Limits and slopes

In the next section on differential calculus, we will be required to find $\lim\limits_{h \to 0} \dfrac{f(x + h) - f(x)}{h}$
if we want to find the slope of the tangent to a curve at any point on the curve.

Example 3

Find $\lim\limits_{h \to 0} \dfrac{f(x + h) - f(x)}{h}$ given (i) $f(x) = 4x - 5$ (ii) $f(x) = x^2 + 1$.

(i) $f(x) = 4x - 5$
$f(x + h) = 4(x + h) - 5$
$f(x + h) - f(x) = 4(x + h) - 5 - (4x - 5)$
$\qquad\qquad\qquad = 4x + 4h - 5 - 4x + 5$
$\qquad\qquad\qquad = 4h$
$\dfrac{f(x + h) - f(x)}{h} = \dfrac{4h}{h} = 4$
$\lim\limits_{h \to 0} \dfrac{f(x + h) - f(x)}{h} = \lim\limits_{h \to 0} 4 = 4$

(ii) $f(x) = x^2 + 1$
$f(x + h) = (x + h)^2 + 1$
$f(x + h) - f(x) = (x + h)^2 + 1 - (x^2 + 1)$
$\qquad\qquad\qquad = x^2 + 2xh + h^2 + 1 - x^2 - 1$
$\qquad\qquad\qquad = 2xh + h^2$
$\dfrac{f(x + h) - f(x)}{h} = \dfrac{2xh + h^2}{h} = 2x + h$
$\lim\limits_{h \to 0} \dfrac{f(x + h) - f(x)}{h} = \lim\limits_{h \to 0} (2x + h) = 2x$

Continuity

A function $f(x)$ is said to be **continuous** when $x = a$ if the graph of $y = f(x)$ can be drawn through the point with coordinates $(a, f(a))$ without a break.
Otherwise, there is said to be a **discontinuity** at $x = a$.

Most of the functions that we encounter on our course are continuous functions.

The graph on the right is continuous as the graph can be traced with no jumps or breaks, that is, the pen does not have to leave the page.

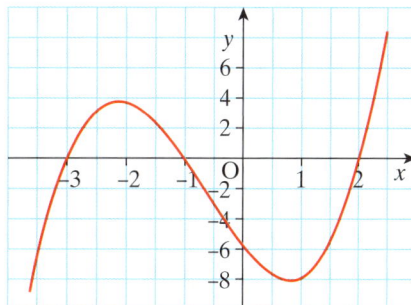

Consider the two graphs shown below:

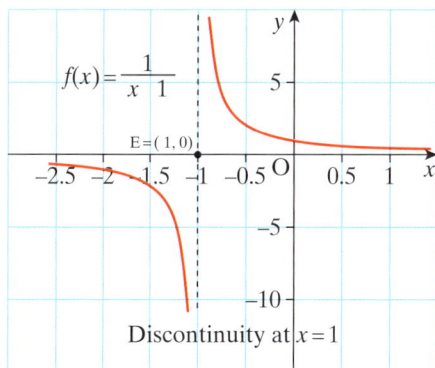

$f(x) = \dfrac{1}{x-1}$

$E = (1, 0)$

Discontinuity at $x = 1$

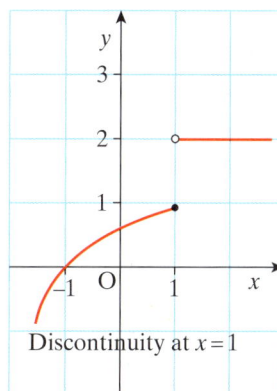

Discontinuity at $x = 1$

On the left above is the graph of the function $f(x) = \dfrac{1}{x + 1}$.

As x approaches -1 from below, the value of the function decreases rapidly.
As x approaches -1 from above, the value of the function increases rapidly.

$f(-1)$ cannot be found as $f(-1) = \dfrac{1}{-1 + 1} = \dfrac{1}{0}$, which is undefined.

We say that the graph is not continuous at $x = -1$.
Notice that the curve approaches but never touches the line $x = -1$.
We say that the line $x = -1$ is an **asymptote** to the curve.

Similarly, the graph on the right above shows a break at $x = 1$.
Again, we say that the curve is not continuous at $x = 1$.

Asymptote is a line that a curve approches as the curve and line go to infinity.

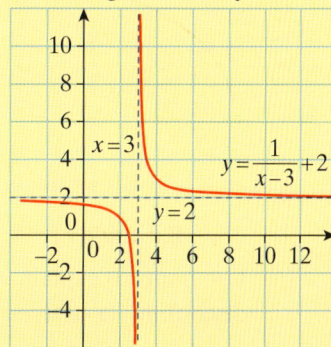

$x = 3$

$y = \dfrac{1}{x-3} + 2$

$y = 2$

Asymptotes: $x = 3$, $y = 2$

267

A more formal definition of continuity is given below:

A function f is continuous at $x = a$ if $\lim_{x \to a} f(x) = f(a)$.

Example 4

Show that $f(x) = \dfrac{3}{x-3}$ is not continuous at $x = 3$.

$f(x) = \dfrac{3}{x-3} \Rightarrow f(3) = \dfrac{3}{3-3} = \dfrac{3}{0}$, which is undefined.

Since $f(3)$ is undefined, a Real value for $f(x)$ does not exist at $x = 3$
Therefore, $f(x)$ is not continuous at $x = 3$.

Exercise 7.2

1. By examining the graphs below, write down the value(s) of x, if any, at which there is a discontinuity in the function:

(i)

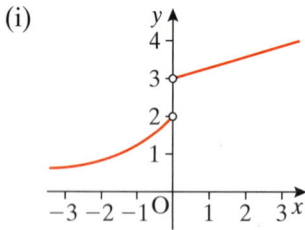

(ii)

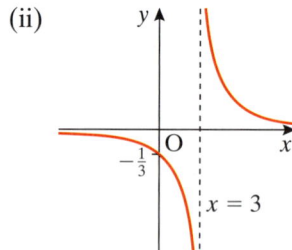

(iii)

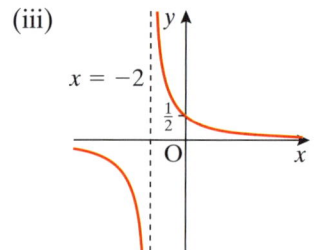

(iv)

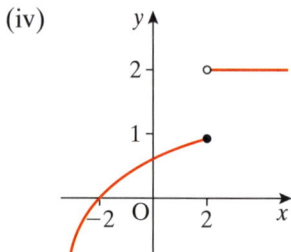

(v)

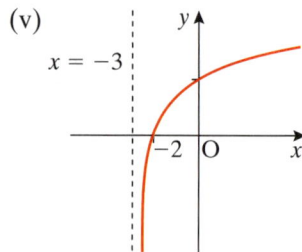

(vi)

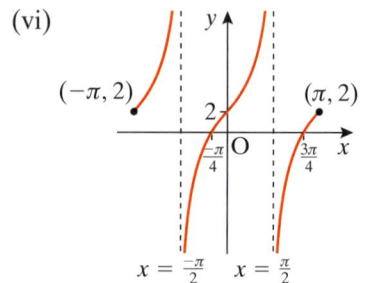

2. A sketch of the function $y = \dfrac{2}{x}$ is shown.

   (i) For what value of x is the function discontinuous?

   (ii) Use limits to explain why the function is discontinuous at this point.

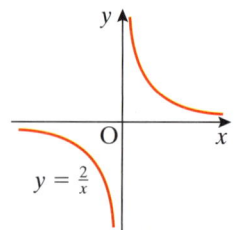

3. The graph of the function $y = \tan x$ is shown.

Use your knowledge of trigonometry to explain why the function is not continuous at $x = \dfrac{\pi}{2}$.

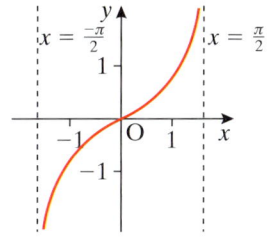

4. For what value(s) of x is each of these functions discontinuous?

(i) $f(x) = \dfrac{2}{x - 4}$

(ii) $f(x) = \dfrac{x}{(x + 5)(x - 5)}$

(iii) $f(x) = \dfrac{1}{x^2 - 3x - 4}$

5. Evaluate these limits:

(i) $\lim\limits_{x \to 2} \dfrac{x + 3}{x + 2}$

(ii) $\lim\limits_{x \to 0} (x^2 + 3x - 4)$

(iii) $\lim\limits_{x \to 3} \dfrac{x^2 - x - 3}{x + 1}$

6. Evaluate each of these limits:

(i) $\lim\limits_{x \to 0} \dfrac{x + 2}{x - 2}$

(ii) $\lim\limits_{x \to 0} \dfrac{6x - 3}{2 + x}$

(iii) $\lim\limits_{h \to 2} \dfrac{h^2 + 2h - 6}{h + 1}$

7. Evaluate each of these limits:

(i) $\lim\limits_{x \to 1} \dfrac{x^2 - 1}{x - 1}$

(ii) $\lim\limits_{x \to 2} \dfrac{x^2 - 4}{x - 2}$

(iii) $\lim\limits_{x \to 5} \dfrac{x^2 - 25}{x - 5}$

(iv) $\lim\limits_{x \to 1} \dfrac{x^2 - 3x + 2}{x - 1}$

(v) $\lim\limits_{x \to 1} \dfrac{x^2 + x - 2}{x - 1}$

(vi) $\lim\limits_{x \to -3} \dfrac{x + 3}{x^2 - x - 12}$

8. By completing the following table, show that $f(x) = \dfrac{x^2 - 9}{x - 3}$, has a limit as $x \to 3$ and write down its value.

x	2.5	2.9	2.999	2.9999	3.0000	3.0001	3.001	3.1	3.5
$f(x)$									

9. Write down the value of each of the following limits:

(i) $f(x) = \dfrac{1}{x}$ $\quad_{x \to \infty}$

(ii) $f(x) = \dfrac{4}{3x}$ $\quad_{x \to \infty}$

(iii) $f(x) = \dfrac{1}{x^2}$ $\quad_{x \to \infty}$

(iv) $f(x) = \dfrac{k}{x^3}$ $\quad_{x \to \infty}$

10. Evaluate each of the following limits:

(i) $\lim\limits_{x \to \infty} \dfrac{3x - 2}{2x + 3}$

(ii) $\lim\limits_{x \to \infty} \dfrac{4x - 3}{7x - 6}$

(iii) $\lim\limits_{x \to \infty} \dfrac{1 - 3x}{4x + 2}$

11. Evaluate each of these limits:

(i) $\lim\limits_{n \to \infty} \dfrac{n^2 + 4}{3n^2 - 4n}$

(ii) $\lim\limits_{n \to \infty} \dfrac{5n^2 - 3}{2n^2 - 6n + 5}$

(iii) $\lim\limits_{n \to \infty} \dfrac{2n^2 - 3n + 2}{6n^2 + 5n - 6}$

12. The slope of a function $y = f(x)$ is given by $\text{slope} = \lim_{h \to 0} \dfrac{f(x+h) - f(x)}{h}$.

Find the slope of each of these functions:

(i) $f(x) = 2x - 3$ (ii) $f(x) = x^2$ (iii) $f(x) = x^2 + 5$

13. Given that $x^3 - y^3 = (x - y)(x^2 + xy + y^2)$, evaluate $\lim_{x \to 3} \dfrac{x - 3}{x^3 - 27}$.

14. By completing the following table, find the $\lim_{n \to \infty} \left(1 + \dfrac{1}{n}\right)^n$.

n	1	2	5	10	100	1,000	10,000
$\left(1 + \dfrac{1}{n}\right)^n$							

The limit of this function should result in an approximate value for e.

Section 7.3 **Differentiating from first principles**

The graph of the function $y = x^2$ is shown.
We could find the slope of the tangent to the curve
at the point $(2, 4)$ by drawing an accurate curve and
tangent and then measure the slope by finding a
second point on the tangent. However, this method
will give only an estimate, so some other method must
be found.

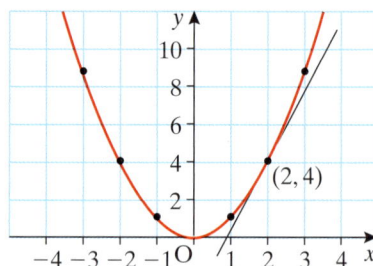

The method used to find the slope of a tangent
to a curve at any point is illustrated by the diagram
on the right. If we select points C and D on the
arc AB, we notice that the closer the point moves
towards A, the closer the approximation to the slope
of the tangent at A.

As the point gets very close to A, we say that

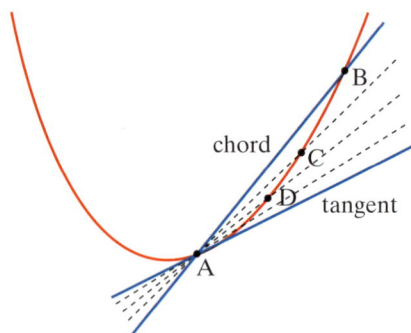

> the slope of the tangent = the limit of the
> slope of the chord as the point approaches A.

Differentiating from first principles

We will now consider the method of finding the slope of the tangent to the curve $y = f(x)$ at any point A $(x, f(x))$ on the curve.

Let B be another point on the curve such that the x-coordinate of B is $x + h$, where h represents a small increase.

Thus, the coordinates of B are

$$(x + h, f(x + h)).$$

From the diagram, the slope of

the chord $\text{AB} = \dfrac{f(x + h) - f(x)}{h}$

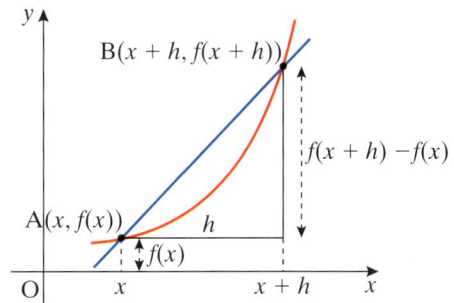

When h becomes very small, the slope of the tangent at A is the limit of the slope of the chord AB as $h \to 0$.

$\Rightarrow$ the slope of the tangent at A $= \lim\limits_{h \to 0} \dfrac{f(x + h) - f(x)}{h}$

$\lim\limits_{h \to 0} \dfrac{f(x + h) - f(x)}{h}$, if it exists, is called the **derived function**.

We use the notation $\dfrac{dy}{dx}$ (pronounced 'dee y dee x'), or $f'(x)$ (pronounced 'f dash of x')

to represent the derived function or simply the **derivative**.

The derived function

> In general, for the curve $y = f(x)$,
>
> $$\frac{dy}{dx} \left(\text{or } f'(x)\right) = \lim_{h \to 0} \frac{f(x + h) - f(x)}{h}$$
>
> represents the slope of the tangent to the curve at the point (x, y) on the curve.

The process of finding the derivative of a function $y = f(x)$ by finding $\lim\limits_{h \to 0} \dfrac{f(x + h) - f(x)}{h}$ is called **differentiating from first principles**.

In the next section of this chapter, we will see that there are basic rules that can be used to reduce the work involved in differentiating from first principles.

Note: When a function is given in the form $f(x) = \ldots$, the derivative is written as $f'(x) = \ldots$.

When the function is given in the form $y = \ldots$, the derivative is written in

the form $\dfrac{dy}{dx} = \ldots$.

For any function $y = f(x)$, $\dfrac{dy}{dx}$ may also be written as $\dfrac{d}{dx}(y)$.

This is pronounced 'the dee dee x of y'.

Example 1

Differentiate $f(x) = 3x + 8$ from first principles.

$$f(x) = 3x + 8$$
$$f(x + h) = 3(x + h) + 8$$
$$\overline{f(x + h) - f(x) = 3(x + h) + 8 - 3x - 8}$$
$$= 3x + 3h + 8 - 3x - 8$$
$$= 3h$$
$$\frac{f(x + h) - f(x)}{h} = \frac{3h}{h} = 3 \quad \text{... dividing both sides by } h$$
$$\lim_{h \to 0} \frac{f(x + h) - f(x)}{h} = \lim_{h \to 0} 3 = 3$$
$$\therefore \ f'(x) = 3$$

Note: Since the given function $f(x) = 3x + 8$ is linear, we expect the slope $\left(\dfrac{dy}{dx}\right)$ to be a constant.

Example 2

Differentiate $f(x) = x^2 - 6x$ from first principles.

$$f(x) = x^2 - 6x$$
$$f(x + h) = (x + h)^2 - 6(x + h)$$
$$= x^2 + 2hx + h^2 - 6x - 6h$$
$$\overline{f(x + h) - f(x) = x^2 + 2hx + h^2 - 6x - 6h - (x^2 - 6x)}$$
$$= x^2 + 2hx + h^2 - 6x - 6h - x^2 + 6x$$
$$= 2hx + h^2 - 6h$$
$$\frac{f(x + h) - f(x)}{h} = \frac{2hx + h^2 - 6h}{h} = 2x + h - 6$$
$$\lim_{h \to 0} \frac{f(x + h) - f(x)}{h} = \lim_{h \to 0} (2x + h - 6)$$
$$= 2x - 6$$
$$\therefore \ f'(x) = 2x - 6$$

Note: Since the graph of $f(x) = x^2 - 6x$ is a quadratic curve, the slope (rate of change) is not constant and varies as x varies, i.e. $(2x - 6)$ varies as x varies.

Example 3

Find, from first principles, the slope of the tangent to the curve with equation
$f(x) = x^2 + x + 5$ at the point where $x = 3$.

To get the slope of the tangent, we find $f'(x)$.

$$f(x) = x^2 + x + 5$$
$$f(x + h) = (x + h)^2 + (x + h) + 5$$
$$= x^2 + 2hx + h^2 + x + h + 5$$
$$f(x + h) - f(x) = x^2 + 2hx + h^2 + x + h + 5 - (x^2 + x + 5)$$
$$= x^2 + 2hx + h^2 + x + h + 5 - x^2 - x - 5$$
$$= 2hx + h^2 + h$$
$$\frac{f(x + h) - f(x)}{h} = 2x + h + 1$$
$$\lim_{h \to 0} \frac{f(x + h) - f(x)}{h} = \lim_{h \to 0} (2x + h + 1)$$
$$= 2x + 1$$
$$\therefore \quad f'(x) = 2x + 1$$

When $x = 3$, $f'(x) = 2(3) + 1 = 7$.

Hence, the slope of the tangent at the point where $x = 3$ is 7.

Exercise 7.3

1. Differentiate each of these from first principles:

   (i) $f(x) = 5x$
   (ii) $f(x) = 3x - 4$
   (iii) $f(x) = 6 - 4x$

2. Find the derivatives of each of the following from first principles:

   (i) $f(x) = x^2$
   (ii) $f(x) = 2x^2 + 9x$
   (iii) $f(x) = 3x^2 - 4x - 6$

3. $f(x) = x^2 - 2x + 5$

   (i) Find $f'(x)$ from first principles.
   (ii) Hence, find the slope of the tangent to the curve $y = f(x)$ at the point $(2, 5)$.
   (iii) Now find the equation of the tangent to the curve $y = f(x)$ at the point $(2, 5)$.

4. If $f(x) = kx^2$, show from first principles that $f'(x) = 2kx$ for all $x \in \mathbb{R}$.

5. Find the derivative of each of the following from first principles:

   (i) $f(x) = -x^2$
   (ii) $f(x) = 4x - x^2$
   (iii) $f(x) = 2 - x - 3x^2$

6. Use first principles to find the derivative of $f(x) = 2x^2 - 3x - 2$.
   Use your result to find

   (i) the slope of the tangent to the curve at the point $(3, 7)$

   (ii) the equation of the tangent to the curve at the point $(3, 7)$.

7. The area of a disc is given by the equation $A = \pi r^2$, where r is the radius of the disc.

   Use first principles to find $\dfrac{dA}{dr}$, the rate of change of A with respect to r.

8. If $f(x) = x^2 - 3x + 1$, find $f'(x)$ using first principles.
   Use your result to find the point on the curve $y = f(x)$ where the slope of
   the tangent is zero.

Section 7.4 Differentiation by rule

In the previous section, we found the derivative of a function from first principles.
This method becomes very tedious as the function becomes more complex.

We will now show how certain rules can be used to find the derivative of a function without
having to use the method of differentiation from first principles.

It can be shown from first principles that if

(i) $y = x^2$, then $\dfrac{dy}{dx} = 2x$

(ii) $y = 4x^2$, then $\dfrac{dy}{dx} = 8x$

(iii) $y = x^3$, then $\dfrac{dy}{dx} = 3x^2$

The pattern in these derivatives suggests a general result which is given below:

Differentiation by rule

1. If $y = x^n$, then $\dfrac{dy}{dx} = nx^{n-1}$ for all $n \in \mathbb{R}$.

2. If $y = ax^n$, then $\dfrac{dy}{dx} = nax^{n-1}$

In words, this rule may be expressed as follows:

To differentiate a term containing a power (index) of x, multiply the coefficient by the
power (index) and reduce the power (index) by 1.

Examples

(i) $y = 3x^2$

$\Rightarrow \dfrac{dy}{dx} = 6x$

(ii) $y = 7x^3$

$\Rightarrow \dfrac{dy}{dx} = 21x^2$

(iii) $f(x) = 5x$

$\Rightarrow f'(x) = 5x^0$

$= 5$

(iv) $f(x) = 6x^4$

$\Rightarrow f'(x) = 24x^3$

The derivative of a constant

Notice that if $y = 4$ (a constant), then this can be written as $y = 4x^0$. ... (any number to the power of zero is 1)

Thus, $y = 4x^0 \Rightarrow \dfrac{dy}{dx} = (0)4x^{-1} = 0$.

> The derivative of a constant is zero.

This shows that the derivative of a constant is zero.

The equation of the line l shown is $y = 4$.
The slope of l is zero.

Since $\dfrac{dy}{dx}$ represents the slope, the diagram illustrates

that the derivative of a constant is zero.

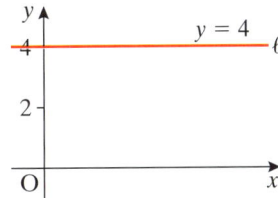

The derivative of a sum or difference of two functions

If a function $y = f(x)$ consists of more than one term, we differentiate each term in turn to find $f'(x)$.

> If $f(x) = u(x) + v(x)$, then $f'(x) = \dfrac{du}{dx} + \dfrac{dv}{dx}$.

Examples

(i) $y = 2x^2 + 5x$

$\Rightarrow \dfrac{dy}{dx} = 4x + 5$

(ii) $y = 6x^3 - 3x^2 + 4$

$\Rightarrow \dfrac{dy}{dx} = 18x^2 - 6x$

(iii) $y = 2 + 3x - 6x^2$

$\Rightarrow \dfrac{dy}{dx} = 3 - 12x$

To differentiate the function $y = \dfrac{1}{x^2}$, we rewrite the function as

$y = x^{-2}$ and so $\dfrac{dy}{dx} = -2x^{-2-1} = -2x^{-3} = -\dfrac{2}{x^3}$ ...-2 reduced by 1 gives -3

Example 1

Find the derivative of $f(x) = 6x^3 - 3x^2 + 4x$.
Hence, find $f'(2)$ and interpret the result.

$\begin{aligned}
f(x) &= 6x^3 - 3x^2 + 4x \\
f'(x) &= 3(6x^2) - 2(3x) + 4 \\
f'(x) &= 18x^2 - 6x + 4 \\
f'(2) &= 18(2)^2 - 6(2) + 4 = 64
\end{aligned}$

$f'(2) = 64$ states that the slope of the tangent to the curve at the point where $x = 2$ is 64.

Example 2

Find $\dfrac{dy}{dx}$ for each of the following:

(i) $y = 3x^2 + \dfrac{2}{x}$

(ii) $y = \sqrt{x} - \dfrac{4}{x^2}$

(i) $\qquad y = 3x^2 + \dfrac{2}{x}$

$\Rightarrow \quad y = 3x^2 + 2x^{-1}$

$\qquad \dfrac{dy}{dx} = 6x - 2x^{-2}$

$\qquad \dfrac{dy}{dx} = 6x - \dfrac{2}{x^2}$

(ii) $\qquad y = \sqrt{x} - \dfrac{4}{x^2}$

$\Rightarrow \quad y = x^{\frac{1}{2}} - 4x^{-2}$

$\qquad \dfrac{dy}{dx} = \dfrac{1}{2}x^{-\frac{1}{2}} + 8x^{-3}$

$\qquad \quad = \dfrac{1}{2x^{\frac{1}{2}}} + \dfrac{8}{x^3}$

$\qquad \dfrac{dy}{dx} = \dfrac{1}{2\sqrt{x}} + \dfrac{8}{x^3}$

Example 3

Find the slope of the tangent to the curve $y = 3x^2 + 4x - 5$ at the point $(1, 2)$. Hence, find the equation of the tangent at this point.

The slope of the tangent is $\dfrac{dy}{dx}$.

$\qquad y = 3x^2 + 4x - 5$

$\dfrac{dy}{dx} = 6x + 4$

$\qquad = 6(1) + 4 = 10 \quad \text{… at the point } (1, 2)$

We now use the formula $y - y_1 = m(x - x_1)$ to find the equation of the tangent at $(1, 2)$.

$\Rightarrow y - 2 = 10(x - 1) \quad \text{… slope = 10}$

$\Rightarrow y - 2 = 10x - 10$

$\Rightarrow 10x - y - 8 = 0$ is the equation of the tangent.

Example 4

Find the points on the curve $y = x^3 - 3x^2$ at which the slope of the tangent to the curve is 9.

$$y = x^3 - 3x^2$$
$$\Rightarrow \frac{dy}{dx} = 3x^2 - 6x$$
$$\Rightarrow 3x^2 - 6x = 9 \quad \text{... since the slope} = 9$$
$$\Rightarrow 3x^2 - 6x - 9 = 0$$
$$\Rightarrow x^2 - 2x - 3 = 0$$
$$\Rightarrow (x - 3)(x + 1) = 0$$
$$\Rightarrow x = 3 \text{ or } x = -1$$

When $x = 3$, $y = (3)^3 - 3(3)^2$ i.e. 0
$$\Rightarrow (3, 0) \text{ is one point.}$$
When $x = -1$, $y = (-1)^3 - 3(-1)^2$ i.e. -4
$$\Rightarrow (-1, -4) \text{ is the second point.}$$
Therefore the two points are $(3, 0)$ and $(-1, -4)$.

Exercise 7.4

1. Find $\dfrac{dy}{dx}$ for each of the following:

   (i) $y = 5x^5$
   (ii) $y = 5x^2 - 4x$
   (iii) $y = 6x^2 + 5x - 4$

   (iv) $y = x^3 - 8x + 2$
   (v) $y = x^2 + 2x + \dfrac{1}{x}$
   (vi) $y = 2x^3 + x^2 + \dfrac{1}{x^2}$

2. Find $f'(x)$ for each of the following:

   (i) $f(x) = 7x^2 - \dfrac{3}{x}$
   (ii) $f(x) = 3\sqrt{x}$
   (iii) $f(x) = 2\sqrt{x} + \dfrac{2}{x^2}$

   (iv) $f(x) = x^2 - 5\sqrt{x}$
   (v) $f(x) = \dfrac{3}{\sqrt{x}}$
   (vi) $f(x) = 3x^{-2} + \dfrac{1}{2\sqrt{x}}$

3. If $y = \dfrac{1}{3}x^3 + \dfrac{1}{2}x^2 - 6x$, find $\dfrac{dy}{dx}$.

4. Find $f'(x)$ for each of the following:

   (i) $f(x) = \sqrt[3]{x}$
   (ii) $f(x) = 3\sqrt{x} - \dfrac{1}{x^2}$
   (iii) $f(x) = \dfrac{4}{x} + \dfrac{3}{\sqrt{x}}$

   (iv) $f(x) = 6 - \dfrac{3}{x}$
   (v) $f(x) = 2\sqrt{x} + \sqrt[3]{x}$
   (vi) $f(x) = x^2 + 3 - \dfrac{4}{x^{-2}}$.

5. If $y = \sqrt{x}(1 + \sqrt{x})$, remove the brackets and then find $\dfrac{dy}{dx}$.
   Find also the value of $\dfrac{dy}{dx}$ when $x = 4$.

6. If $f(x) = x^3 + 2\sqrt{x}$, find $f'(x)$ and hence evaluate $f'(4)$.

7. If $f(x) = \dfrac{1}{\sqrt{x}}$, find $f'(4)$ and express your answer as a fraction.

8. Given that $y = x^{\frac{5}{2}}$, find $\dfrac{dy}{dx}$ and show that when $x = 2$, the value of $\dfrac{dy}{dx}$ can be written in the form $p\sqrt{2}$, where p is an integer to be found.

9. If $f(x) = x^2 + kx$ and $f'(-1)$ is 3, find the value of k.

10. If $y = \sqrt{x} + \dfrac{1}{\sqrt{x}}$, show that $\dfrac{dy}{dx}$ may be written in the form $\dfrac{x-1}{2x\sqrt{x}}$.

11. Find the slope of the tangent to the curve $y = x^2 - 2x - 3$ at the point $(2, 3)$.

12. Find the slope and hence the equation of the tangent to the curve $y = 2x^2 - 3x + 4$ at the point $(1, 3)$.

13. Find the slope and hence the equation of the tangent to the curve $y = 6 + x - x^2$ at the point $(2, 4)$.

14. Find the value of x at which the slope of the tangent to the curve $y = 8 + 2x - x^2$ is 6.

15. At what point on the curve $y = x^2 - x$ is the slope of the tangent equal to 1?

16. Find the point on the curve $y = 2x^2 - x - 4$ at which the slope of the tangent is 3.

17. Find the value of a if the slope of the tangent to the curve $y = x^2 + ax$ at the point where $x = -1$ is 3.

18. Show that the tangent to the curve $y = x^2 - 3x + 4$ at the point where $x = 1\frac{1}{2}$ is parallel to the x-axis.

19. Find the point on the curve $y = 2x^2 - 8x + 3$ where the tangent is parallel to the line $4x - y + 2 = 0$.

20. The tangent drawn to the curve $y = 2x^2 + 3x$ at the point $P(x, y)$ is parallel to the x-axis.
    Determine the coordinates of P.

21. The equation of a function is $y = a\sqrt{x} + b$, where a and b are constants.
    If $\dfrac{dy}{dx} = 3$ at the point $(4, 6)$, find the values of a and b.

22. The tangent drawn to the curve with equation $y = \dfrac{3}{x}$ at the point $(2, \frac{3}{2})$ meets the x-axis at A, and the y-axis at B.
    What is the area of the triangle AOB, where O is the origin?

Section 7.5 Product, Quotient and Chain Rules

1. The Product Rule

The function $y = (3x - 4)(x^2 + 2)$ can be differentiated by multiplying out the brackets and then differentiating the product.

Thus, $y = 3x^3 - 4x^2 + 6x - 8$

and $\dfrac{dy}{dx} = 9x^2 - 8x + 6.$

When the expansion of brackets becomes too tedious, a product can be differentiated in a much shorter way by using a method generally called the *Product Rule*.

Product Rule

> If $y = uv$, where u and v are both functions of x, then
> $$\frac{dy}{dx} = u\frac{dv}{dx} + v\frac{du}{dx}$$

Example 1

If $y = (6x^2 + 2x)(3x - 2)$, find $\dfrac{dx}{dy}$.

This is a product in which $\quad u = 6x^2 + 2x \quad$ *and* $\quad v = 3x - 2$

$$\Rightarrow \frac{du}{dx} = 12x + 2 \qquad\qquad \Rightarrow \frac{dv}{dx} = 3$$

$\dfrac{dy}{dx} = u\dfrac{dv}{dx} + v\dfrac{du}{dx}$

$\qquad = (6x^2 + 2x)(3) + (3x - 2)(12x + 2)$

$\qquad = 18x^2 + 6x + 36x^2 + 6x - 24x - 4$

$\therefore \dfrac{dy}{dx} = 54x^2 - 12x - 4$

Product Rule in words

> When a product consists of 2 factors, i.e. $y = $ (first)(second), then the product rule may be memorised as follows:
>
> "the first $\times$ by the derivative of the second + the second $\times$ by the derivative of the first".

2. The Quotient Rule

When differentiating a function of the form $y = \dfrac{u}{v}$, where u and v are both functions of x,

for example $y = \dfrac{2x - 3}{3x + 4}$, we use the *Quotient Rule* given below:

Example 2

If $f(x) = \dfrac{x^2 + 7}{3x - 1}$, find $f'(x)$.

$\dfrac{x^2 + 7}{3x - 1}$ is a quotient in which

$u = x^2 + 7$ and $v = 3x - 1$

$\Rightarrow \dfrac{du}{dx} = 2x$ $\Rightarrow \dfrac{dv}{dx} = 3$

$$f'(x) = \frac{dy}{dx} = \frac{v\dfrac{du}{dx} - u\dfrac{dv}{dx}}{v^2}$$

$$= \frac{(3x - 1)(2x) - (x^2 + 7)(3)}{(3x - 1)^2} = \frac{6x^2 - 2x - 3x^2 - 21}{(3x - 1)^2}$$

$$\Rightarrow f'(x) = \frac{3x^2 - 2x - 21}{(3x - 1)^2}$$

3. The Chain Rule

When we write $y = (3x - 4)^3$, we say that y is a function of x.

If we let $u = (3x - 4)$, then we have

$y = u^3$ and $u = 3x - 4$.

Now, y is a function of u and u is a function of x.

For this reason, the function $y = (3x - 4)^3$ is said to be a **composite function** or a **function of a function.**

Other examples of composite functions are:

(i) $y = (1 - 6x)^4$ (ii) $y = \sqrt{5x + 2}$ (iii) $y = \sqrt[3]{3x^2 + 6}$

The function $y = (3x - 4)^3$ could be differentiated by expanding the brackets and differentiating the result. However, it can also be differentiated in a more economical way by using a method called the *Chain Rule*.

To differentiate the function $y = (3x - 4)^3$, we let $u = 3x - 4$.
Then, $y = u^3$ and $u = 3x - 4$.

The Chain Rule states that $\dfrac{dy}{dx} = \dfrac{dy}{du} \cdot \dfrac{du}{dx}$.

$$\dfrac{dy}{dx} = \dfrac{dy}{du} \cdot \dfrac{du}{dx} \qquad\qquad y = u^3 \text{ and } u = 3x - 4$$

$$= 3u^2.3 \qquad\qquad \Rightarrow \dfrac{dy}{du} = 3u^2 \text{ and } \dfrac{du}{dx} = 3$$

$$= 9u^2 = 9(3x - 4)^3$$

The Chain Rule

> If y is a function of u, and u is a function of x,
> $$\dfrac{dy}{dx} = \dfrac{dy}{du} \cdot \dfrac{du}{dx}$$

Example 3

Find $\dfrac{dy}{dx}$ if (i) $y = (2x^2 - 1)^3$ (ii) $y = \sqrt{3x^2 - 2}$.

(i) $y = (2x^2 - 1)^3$

Let $u = 2x^2 - 1 \quad\Rightarrow\quad y = u^3$

$\Rightarrow \dfrac{du}{dx} = 4x \qquad$ and $\qquad \dfrac{dy}{du} = 3u^2$

$\dfrac{dy}{dx} = \dfrac{dy}{du} \cdot \dfrac{du}{dx}$

$\qquad = 3u^2.4x = 3(2x^2 - 1)^2.4x = 12x(2x^2 - 1)^2$

(ii) $y = \sqrt{3x^2 - 2} = (3x^2 - 2)^{\frac{1}{2}}$

Let $u = 3x^2 - 2 \quad\Rightarrow\quad y = \sqrt{u} = u^{\frac{1}{2}}$

$\Rightarrow \dfrac{du}{dx} = 6x \qquad\Rightarrow\qquad \dfrac{dy}{du} = \dfrac{1}{2}u^{-\frac{1}{2}} = \dfrac{1}{2u^{\frac{1}{2}}} = \dfrac{1}{2\sqrt{u}}$

$\dfrac{dy}{dx} = \dfrac{dy}{du} \cdot \dfrac{du}{dx}$

$\qquad = \dfrac{1}{2\sqrt{u}} \cdot 6x = \dfrac{1}{2\sqrt{3x^2 - 2}} \cdot 6x = \dfrac{3x}{\sqrt{3x^2 - 2}}$

In the examples above, u was substituted for the function of x inside the brackets.
In practice, we will omit this step and write down the derivative of a composite function
without the use of substitution.

Here are some examples:

(i) $y = (2x + 5)^3$

$\dfrac{dy}{dx} = 3(2x + 5)^2 \cdot \dfrac{d}{dx}(2x + 5)$

$\qquad = 3(2x + 5)^2(2)$

$\qquad = 6(2x + 5)^2$

(ii) $y = (x^2 - 3x)^4$

$\dfrac{dy}{dx} = 4(x^2 - 3x)^3 \dfrac{d}{dx}(x^2 - 3x)$

$\qquad = 4(x^2 - 3x)^3(2x - 3)$

$\qquad = 4(2x - 3)(x^2 - 3x)^3$

Example 4

Find $\dfrac{dy}{dx}$ if (i) $y = (x^2 - 3x)^4$ (ii) $y = \sqrt{x^2 - 6x}$.

(i) $y = (x^2 - 3x)^4$

$\dfrac{dy}{dx} = 4(x^2 - 3x)^3(2x - 3)$ ... $(2x - 3)$ is $\dfrac{d}{dx}(x^2 - 3x)$

$\qquad = 4(2x - 3)(x^2 - 3x)^3$

(ii) $y = \sqrt{x^2 - 6x} \;\Rightarrow\; y = (x^2 - 6x)^{\frac{1}{2}}$

$\dfrac{dy}{dx} = \dfrac{1}{2}(x^2 - 6x)^{-\frac{1}{2}}(2x - 6)$

$\qquad = \dfrac{2x - 6}{2(x^2 - 6x)^{\frac{1}{2}}} = \dfrac{2(x - 3)}{2\sqrt{x^2 - 6x}} = \dfrac{x - 3}{\sqrt{x^2 - 6x}}$

Example 5

If $y = \dfrac{x}{\sqrt{1 - x}}$, evaluate $\dfrac{dy}{dx}$ when $x = -3$.

Here we have a quotient in which $u = x$ and $v = \sqrt{1 - x}$

$\Rightarrow \dfrac{du}{dx} = 1$ and $\dfrac{dv}{dx} = \dfrac{1}{2}(1 - x)^{-\frac{1}{2}}(-1)$

$\qquad\qquad\qquad\qquad\qquad\qquad = \dfrac{-1}{2\sqrt{1 - x}}$

$$\frac{dy}{dx} = \frac{v\dfrac{du}{dx} - u\dfrac{dv}{dx}}{v^2}$$

$$= \frac{\sqrt{1-x}.1 - x\left(\dfrac{-1}{2\sqrt{1-x}}\right)}{1-x}$$

$$= \frac{\sqrt{1-x} + \dfrac{x}{2\sqrt{1-x}}}{1-x}$$

$$= \frac{2(1-x) + x}{2\sqrt{1-x}(1-x)} \quad \text{... multiply each term above and below by } 2\sqrt{1-x}$$

$$\frac{dy}{dx} = \frac{2-x}{2\sqrt{1-x}(1-x)}$$

When $x = -3$, $\dfrac{dy}{dx} = \dfrac{2-(-3)}{2\sqrt{1-(-3)}(1-(-3))} = \dfrac{5}{16}$

$$\therefore \frac{dy}{dx} = \frac{5}{16}$$

Exercise 7.5

1. Use the *Product Rule* to find the derivative of each of these:

   (i) $y = (3x + 4)(x - 2)$ (ii) $y = (3x - 4)(4x + 5)$ (iii) $y = (x^2 + 2)(x - 1)$

   (iv) $y = (2x - 1)(x^2 - 2)$ (v) $y = (1 - x)(2 - x^2)$ (vi) $y = (x^3 - 1)(2x + 1)$

2. Use the *Quotient Rule* to find $f'(x)$ of each of the following:

   (i) $f(x) = \dfrac{3x}{2x + 6}$ (ii) $f(x) = \dfrac{2x + 3}{x - 1}$ (iii) $f(x) = \dfrac{x^2}{2x + 3}$

   (iv) $f(x) = \dfrac{2x^2 - 1}{2x - 3}$ (v) $f(x) = \dfrac{2x^3}{1 - 2x}$ (vi) $f(x) = \dfrac{3x + 2}{x^2 - 3}$

3. Given that $y = \dfrac{x^2 + 1}{3x - 1}$, find the value of $\dfrac{dy}{dx}$ at $x = 0$.

4. Use the *Product Rule* to differentiate $y = \sqrt{x}(2x - 1)$ with respect to x and express your answer as a single fraction.

5. If $y = (\sqrt{x} + 4)(\sqrt{x} - 4)$, use the *Product Rule* to show that $\dfrac{dy}{dx} = 1$.

6. If $y = \dfrac{x}{1 - x^2}$, show that $\dfrac{dy}{dx} > 0$ for all $x \in \mathbb{R}$.

7. Differentiate each of the following using the *Chain Rule*:

(i) $y = (x + 4)^2$ (ii) $y = (2x - 1)^3$ (iii) $y = (3x + 5)^3$

(iv) $y = (x^2 - 1)^2$ (v) $y = (2x^2 + 3)^4$ (vi) $y = (1 - 3x)^5$

8. Find $f'(x)$ for each of the following:

(i) $f(x) = \sqrt{4x + 1}$ (ii) $f(x) = \sqrt{x^2 - 4}$ (iii) $f(x) = \sqrt{x^3 - 2x}$

9. Find $\dfrac{dy}{dx}$ for each of the following:

(i) $y = 2x(2x + 5)^3$ (ii) $y = (x^2 - 1)(3x + 2)^2$ (iii) $y = (x + 4)^2(x - 2)$

10. If $y = (x^2 - 3)^3$, find the value of $\dfrac{dy}{dx}$ when $x = 1$.

11. If $y = \dfrac{(2x - 1)^2}{3x + 4}$, find the value of $\dfrac{dy}{dx}$ at $x = 0$.

12. If $y = (2x^2 - 3)^7$, evaluate $\dfrac{dy}{dx}$ at $x = -1$.

13. If $f(x) = x\sqrt{x + 1}$, find $f'(x)$.

14. If $4x^2 + 2xy = 5$, express y in terms of x and hence find $\dfrac{dy}{dx}$.

15. If $y = \dfrac{x}{\sqrt{x + 1}}$, find $\dfrac{dy}{dx}$ and evaluate $\dfrac{dy}{dx}$ at $x = 1$.

16. If $y = \dfrac{3x + 1}{1 - 2x}$, express $\dfrac{dy}{dx}$ in the form $\dfrac{k}{(1 - 2x)^2}$, where k is a constant.

17. If $f(x) = \sqrt{3x^2 - 2}$, find the value of $f'(x)$ when $x = 1$.

18. Show that if $y = (x - 1)^{\frac{3}{2}} - 3(x - 1)^{\frac{1}{2}}$, then $\dfrac{dy}{dx} = \dfrac{3(x - 2)}{2\sqrt{x - 1}}$.

19. If $y = ax^3 + 2bx^2 + 3cx$ and $\dfrac{dy}{dx} = 6x^2 + 6x - 6$, find the values of the constants a, b and c.

20. If $f(x) = \sqrt{\dfrac{4x}{x + 3}}$, find the value of $f'(1)$.

21. Which of the following is the derivative of $(8 - 2x^2)^{\frac{2}{3}}$?

A: $-\frac{8}{3}x(8 - 2x^2)^{-\frac{1}{3}}$ B: $(8 - 4x)^{\frac{2}{3}}$ C: $\frac{2}{3}(8 - 4x)^{-\frac{1}{3}}$ D: $\frac{3}{5}(8 - 2x^2)^{\frac{5}{3}}$

22. Functions f and g are given by $f(x) = 3x + 1$ and $g(x) = x^2 - 2$.

(a) (i) Find $p(x)$ where $p(x) = f(g(x))$.

(ii) Find $q(x)$ where $q(x) = g(f(x))$.

(b) Solve $p'(x) = q'(x)$.

Section 7.6 Second derivatives

For any function $y = f(x)$, the first derivative is $\dfrac{dy}{dx}$ or $f'(x)$.

If we differentiate the resulting function, we get the **second derivative**.

The second derivative is denoted by $\dfrac{d^2y}{dx^2}$ or $f''(x)$.

$\dfrac{d^2y}{dx^2}$ is pronounced 'dee two y dee x squared'.

We learned earlier that for any function $y = f(x)$, $\dfrac{dy}{dx}$ represents the slope of the tangent to the curve at any point on the curve. When dealing with the graphs of functions in book 5, we will see that $\dfrac{d^2y}{dx^2}$ gives the rate at which the slope is changing over a given interval.

Example 1

Given that $y = x + \dfrac{1}{x}$, find $\dfrac{d^2y}{dx^2}$.

$$y = x + \frac{1}{x} \Rightarrow y = x + x^{-1}$$

$$\frac{dy}{dx} = 1 - x^{-2}$$

$$\Rightarrow \frac{d^2y}{dx^2} = 0 + 2x^{-3} = \frac{2}{x^3}$$

Example 2

If $y = \dfrac{3}{x} + 4x$, find $\dfrac{dy}{dx}$ and $\dfrac{d^2y}{dx^2}$; hence, show that $x^2\dfrac{d^2y}{dx^2} + x\dfrac{dy}{dx} - y = 0$.

$$y = \frac{3}{x} + 4x \Rightarrow y = 3x^{-1} + 4x$$

$$\Rightarrow \frac{dy}{dx} = -3x^{-2} + 4 = -\frac{3}{x^2} + 4$$

$$\Rightarrow \frac{d^2y}{dx^2} = 6x^{-3} = \frac{6}{x^3}$$

Now, $x^2 \dfrac{d^2y}{dx^2} + x \dfrac{dy}{dx} - y$

$$= x^2 \left(\dfrac{6}{x^3}\right) + x \left(-\dfrac{3}{x^2} + 4\right) - \left(\dfrac{3}{x} + 4x\right)$$

$$= \dfrac{6}{x} - \dfrac{3}{x} + 4x - \dfrac{3}{x} - 4x$$

$$= \dfrac{6}{x} - \dfrac{3}{x} - \dfrac{3}{x} = \dfrac{6 - 3 - 3}{x} = \dfrac{0}{x} = 0$$

$$\Rightarrow \quad x^2 \dfrac{d^2y}{dx^2} + x \dfrac{dy}{dx} - y = 0$$

Exercise 7.6

Find $\dfrac{d^2y}{dx^2}$ of the functions in numbers (1–9):

1. $y = x^3 + 2x^2$ **2.** $y = x^4 - 3x^2 + 6$ **3.** $y = \dfrac{1}{x}$

4. $y = \dfrac{1}{x^2} + 3x^2$ **5.** $y = 3x + \dfrac{1}{x} + 4$ **6.** $y = \sqrt{x}$

7. $y = \sqrt{2x + 3}$ **8.** $y = (3x - 2)^3$ **9.** $y = \dfrac{1}{x + 4}$

10. Given that $y = x^4 - x^3 + 4x - 1$, find $\dfrac{d^2y}{dx^2}$ and hence find the values of x for which $\dfrac{d^2y}{dx^2} = 0$.

11. If $y = 3x + \dfrac{4}{x}$, show that $x^2 \dfrac{d^2y}{dx^2} + x \dfrac{dy}{dx} - y = 0$.

12. Given that $f(x) = \dfrac{2}{x} + 4\sqrt{x}$, show that $f''(4) = -\dfrac{1}{16}$.

13. Given that $y = x^4$, show that $\dfrac{4x^4}{3} \left(\dfrac{d^2y}{dx^2}\right) - \left(\dfrac{dy}{dx}\right)^2 = 0$.

14. Given that $y = \dfrac{1}{\sqrt{x}}$, find $\dfrac{dy}{dx}$ and $\dfrac{d^2y}{dx^2}$.

Hence, show that $2x \left(\dfrac{d^2y}{dx^2}\right) + 3 \dfrac{dy}{dx} = 0$.

Section 7.7 The derivatives of trigonometric functions

The basic rules for differentiation apply to trigonometric functions also.
The derivatives of the three principal trigonometric functions are highlighted below:

Standard trigonometric derivatives

$$\frac{d}{dx}(\sin x) = \cos x \qquad \frac{d}{dx}(\cos x) = -\sin x \qquad \frac{d}{dx}(\tan x) = \sec^2 x$$

The following examples illustrate the use of the *Product Rule*, the *Quotient Rule* and the *Chain Rule* when differentiating trigonometric functions.

Example 1

Differentiate each of the following with respect to x:
  (i) $y = 3\sin x + 2\cos x$ (ii) $y = x^2 \sin x$

(i) $\dfrac{dy}{dx} = 3\cos x + 2(-\sin x) = 3\cos x - 2\sin x$

(ii) $y = x^2 \sin x$

  (Here we have a product where $u = x^2$ and $v = \sin x$.)

$$\frac{dy}{dx} = u\frac{dv}{dx} + v\frac{du}{dx}$$
$$= x^2(\cos x) + \sin x(2x)$$
$$\Rightarrow \frac{dy}{dx} = x^2 \cos x + 2x \sin x$$

Use of Chain Rule

The use of the Chain Rule is particularly important in the differentiation of trigonometric functions.

Chain Rule
$$\frac{dy}{dx} = \frac{dy}{du} \cdot \frac{du}{dx}$$

To differentiate $y = \sin 4x$, we let $u = 4x$.

$$y = \sin u \qquad \Rightarrow \frac{du}{dx} = 4$$
$$\Rightarrow \frac{dy}{dx} = \cos u$$

By the *Chain Rule*, $\dfrac{dy}{dx} = \dfrac{dy}{du} \cdot \dfrac{du}{dx}$
$$= \cos u \times 4 = 4\cos u = 4\cos 4x$$

In practice, we generally do not use the substitution method to apply the *Chain Rule*.

If $y = \sin 6x \Rightarrow \dfrac{dy}{dx} = \cos 6x . \dfrac{d}{dx}(6x) = \cos 6x.6 = 6\cos 6x$

Here are two more examples of the use of the *Chain Rule*:

(i) If $y = \sin x^2$

$$\frac{dy}{dx} = \cos x^2 . (2x)$$

$$= 2x \cos^2 x$$

(ii) If $y = \cos(3x^2 + x)$

$$\frac{dy}{dx} = -\sin(3x^2 + x).(6x + 1)$$

$$= -(6x + 1) \sin(3x^2 + x)$$

The derivative of $\sin^n x$ and $\cos^n x$

To differentiate $y = \sin^4 x$, we let $u = \sin x$.

$$\Rightarrow \quad y = u^4 \qquad \Rightarrow \frac{du}{dx} = \cos x$$

$$\Rightarrow \frac{dy}{du} = 4u^3$$

Now, $\dfrac{dy}{dx} = \dfrac{dy}{du} \cdot \dfrac{du}{dx} = 4u^3 . \cos x$

$$= 4 \sin^3 x . \cos x$$

$$\frac{dy}{dx} = 4 \sin^3 x . \cos x$$

Again, in practice we can write down the derivative of $\cos^3 x$, for example, without using a substitution.

If $y = \cos^3 x$

$$\frac{dy}{dx} = 3 \cos^2 x . \frac{d}{dx}(\cos x)$$

$$= 3 \cos^2 x . (-\sin x) = -3 \cos^2 x \sin x$$

Similarly, if $y = \tan(3x^2)$

$$\frac{dy}{dx} = \sec^2(3x^2).6x$$

$$= 6x \sec^2(3x^2)$$

Using the Chain Rule twice

Consider the function $y = \sin^3(5x + 2)$.

$$\Rightarrow y = [\sin(5x + 2)]^3$$

$$\boxed{\sin^3 x = (\sin x)^3}$$

Without using any substitution we can write down the derivative of $\sin^3(5x + 2)$ by

(i) finding the derivative of the power, i.e. $3 \sin^2(5x + 2)$

(ii) multiplying the result by the derivative of the trigonometric **function** $\sin(5x + 2)$, which is $\cos(5x + 2)$.

(iii) multiplying the two previous results by the derivative of the angle $(5x + 2)$, i.e. 5.

Thus, for $y = \sin^3(5x + 2)$

$$\frac{dy}{dx} = 3 \sin^2(5x + 2) \cos(5x + 2).5$$

$$= 15 \sin^2(5x + 2) \cos(5x + 2)$$

Similarly, if $y = \cos^4(3x - 1)$

$$\frac{dy}{dx} = 4 \cos^3(3x - 1)[-\sin(3x - 1).3]$$

$$= -12 \cos^3(3x - 1) \sin(3x - 1)$$

Example 2

Find the derivative of each of the following:

(i) $\cos(7x - 3)$ (ii) $\tan^2 3x$ (iii) $\sin^3(x^2 + 2)$

(i) Let $y = \cos(7x - 3)$

$$\frac{dy}{dx} = -\sin(7x - 3).7 = -7\sin(7x - 3)$$

(ii) Let $y = \tan^2 3x$

$$\frac{dy}{dx} = 2\tan 3x . \sec^2 3x . 3$$

$$= 6\tan 3x \sec^2 3x$$

(iii) Let $y = \sin^3(x^2 + 2)$

$$\frac{dy}{dx} = 3\sin^2(x^2 + 2).\cos(x^2 + 2).2x$$

$$= 6x\sin^2(x^2 + 2)\cos(x^2 + 2)$$

Example 3

If $f(x) = \dfrac{1 + \sin x}{\cos x}$, show that $f'(x) = \dfrac{1 + \sin x}{\cos^2 x}$ and hence evaluate $f'(\pi)$.

$\dfrac{1 + \sin x}{\cos x}$ is of the form $\dfrac{u}{v}$, so we use the *Quotient Rule* to find $f'(x)$.

$$f'(x) = \frac{v\dfrac{du}{dx} - u\dfrac{dv}{dx}}{v^2}$$

$$= \frac{\cos x(\cos x) - (1 + \sin x)(-\sin x)}{(\cos x)^2}$$

$$= \frac{\cos^2 x + \sin x + \sin^2 x}{\cos^2 x} = \frac{1 + \sin x}{\cos^2 x} \quad \dots (\sin^2 x + \cos^2 x = 1)$$

$$f'(\pi) = \frac{1 + \sin \pi}{\cos^2 \pi} = \frac{1 + 0}{(-1)^2} = \frac{1}{1} = 1$$

Exercise 7.7

1. Find $\dfrac{dy}{dx}$ for each of the following:

(i) $y = \sin 2x$ (ii) $y = \cos 6x$ (iii) $y = \tan 4x$

(iv) $y = \sin(2x + 3)$ (v) $y = \cos(3x - 1)$ (vi) $y = \tan(x^2)$

(vii) $y = \sin\frac{1}{2}x$ (viii) $y = \cos(x^2 - 1)$ (ix) $y = \sin 2x + \cos 4x$

2. Find $\dfrac{dy}{dx}$ for each of these:

    (i) $y = \sin^2 x$ (ii) $y = \cos^3 x$ (iii) $y = \tan^4 x$

    (iv) $y = \sin^3(4x)$ (v) $y = \cos^2(2x + 1)$ (vi) $y = \tan^3(4x + 3)$

3. Find $\dfrac{dy}{d\theta}$ for each of the following:

    (i) $y = 2\sin 3\theta + \cos 2\theta$ (ii) $y = \tan^2\theta + \tan 2\theta$

    (iii) $y = \cos 4\theta - \cos \dfrac{\theta}{4}$ (iv) $y = \tan^3\theta + 5$

4. Use the *Product Rule* to differentiate each of the following:

    (i) $y = x \sin 2x$ (ii) $y = x^2 \cos x$ (iii) $y = (x + 3)\sin x$

5. If $y = \sin x \cos x$, use the *Product Rule* to show that $\dfrac{dy}{dx} = \cos 2x$.

6. If $f(x) = \cos x \tan x$, show that $f'(x) = \cos x$.

7. Find the value of $\dfrac{dy}{dx}$ in each of the following at $x = \pi$:

    (i) $y = \sin 2x$ (ii) $y = x \cos x$ (iii) $y = \sin^2 x$.

8. Given that $\tan x = \dfrac{\sin x}{\cos x}$, use the *Quotient Rule* to show that $\dfrac{d}{dx}(\tan x) = \sec^2 x$.

9. Given that $f(x) = (\sin x + 1)^2$, find in surd form the value of $f'\left(\dfrac{\pi}{6}\right)$.

10. If $y = \sin x + 3 \cos x$, find $\dfrac{dy}{dx}$.

    Hence, show that $\cos x \dfrac{dy}{dx} + y \sin x = 1$.

11. Given that $y = \sin 2x - 2x$, find $\dfrac{dy}{dx}$.

    Give your answer in the form $k \sin^2 x$, where $k \in \mathbb{Z}$.

12. If $y = \cos(\frac{1}{4}\pi x)$, find the value of $\dfrac{dy}{dx}$ when $x = 4$.

13. Given that $f(x) = \cos^3(2x)$, find the value of $\dfrac{dy}{dx}$ when $x = \dfrac{\pi}{6}$.

14. It is given that $f(x) = \cos 2x$ and $g(x) = 2\sin^2 x$.

    Find (i) $f'(x)$ (ii) $g'(x)$ and show that $f'(x) + g'(x) = 0$.

15. Given that $y = \sin 3x$, show that $\dfrac{d^2y}{dx^2} = -9y$.

16. If $y = \tan x + \frac{1}{3}\tan^3 x$, show that $\dfrac{dy}{dx} = \sec^4 x$.

    (Hint: $\sec^2 x = 1 + \tan^2 x$).

17. If the slope of the curve $y = 3 \sin x + k \sin 3x$ is zero when $x = \frac{\pi}{3}$, find the value of k.

18. Find the values of a and b for which

$$\frac{d}{dx}\left(\frac{\sin x}{2 + \cos x}\right) = \frac{a + b \cos x}{(2 + \cos x)^2}.$$

Section 7.8 Differentiation of inverse trigonometric functions

Since $\sin \frac{\pi}{6} = \frac{1}{2}$, we use the notation $\frac{\pi}{6} = \sin^{-1}\frac{1}{2}$ to state that

"$\frac{\pi}{6}$ is an angle, the sine of which is $\frac{1}{2}$".

Thus, it is important to note that $\sin^{-1}\frac{1}{2}$ is an **angle**.

To differentiate the function $y = \sin^{-1}\frac{x}{a}$, we change the function to the form $\sin y = \frac{x}{a}$.

$\sin y = \frac{x}{a} \Rightarrow x = a \sin y$, where a is a constant.

We will now find $\frac{dx}{dy}$ and then write down the reciprocal of the answer to get $\frac{dy}{dx}$.

$x = a \sin y$

$\frac{dx}{dy} = a \cos y$

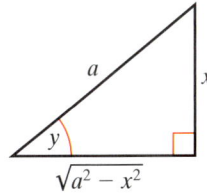

$\quad = a\left[\dfrac{\sqrt{a^2 - x^2}}{a}\right] = \sqrt{a^2 - x^2}$ ... see triangle

$\frac{dx}{dy} = \sqrt{a^2 - x^2} \Rightarrow \frac{dy}{dx} = \dfrac{1}{\sqrt{a^2 - x^2}}$

This shows that if $y = \sin^{-1}\frac{x}{a}$, then $\dfrac{dy}{dx} = \dfrac{1}{\sqrt{a^2 - x^2}}$

The standard derivatives for $f(x) = \sin^{-1}\frac{x}{a}$, $f(x) = \tan^{-1}\frac{x}{a}$ and $f(x) = \cos^{-1}\frac{x}{a}$ are given below.

Standard derivatives of inverse functions

$$f(x) = \sin^{-1}\left(\frac{x}{a}\right) \Rightarrow f'(x) = \frac{1}{\sqrt{a^2 - x^2}}$$

$$f(x) = \tan^{-1}\left(\frac{x}{a}\right) \Rightarrow f'(x) = \frac{a}{a^2 + x^2}$$

$$f(x) = \cos^{-1}\left(\frac{x}{a}\right) \Rightarrow f'(x) = -\frac{1}{\sqrt{a^2 - x^2}}$$

The next worked example shows how the function $y = \sin^{-1}\frac{5x}{3}$ can be differentiated using the standard derivative for $\sin^{-1}\frac{x}{a}$ and the *Chain Rule*.

Example 1

If $y = \sin^{-1}\dfrac{5x}{3}$, find $\dfrac{dy}{dx}$.

$$y = \sin^{-1}\frac{5x}{3} \qquad\qquad \text{Let} \quad u = \frac{5x}{3}$$

$$\Rightarrow \quad y = \sin^{-1}u \qquad\qquad \Rightarrow \quad \frac{du}{dx} = \frac{5}{3}$$

$$\frac{dy}{du} = \frac{1}{\sqrt{1-u^2}} \qquad \ldots a = 1$$

$$\frac{dy}{dx} = \frac{dy}{du}\cdot\frac{du}{dx}$$

$$= \frac{1}{\sqrt{1-u^2}}\cdot\frac{5}{3}$$

$$\frac{dy}{dx} = \frac{5}{3.\sqrt{1-\dfrac{25x^2}{9}}} = \frac{5}{3.\sqrt{\dfrac{9-25x^2}{9}}} = \frac{5}{3.\frac{1}{3}\sqrt{9-25x^2}} = \frac{5}{\sqrt{9-25x^2}}$$

Example 2

If $y = \tan^{-1}(2x + 1)$, find $\dfrac{dy}{dx}$.

$$y = \tan^{-1}(2x + 1) \qquad\qquad \text{Let} \quad u = 2x + 1$$

$$\Rightarrow \quad y = \tan^{-1}u \qquad\qquad \Rightarrow \quad \frac{du}{dx} = 2$$

$$\frac{dy}{du} = \frac{1}{1+u^2} \quad \ldots a = 1, \text{ since } 2x + 1 = \frac{2x+1}{1}$$

$$\frac{dy}{dx} = \frac{dy}{du}\cdot\frac{du}{dx}$$

$$= \frac{1}{1+u^2}\cdot 2 = \frac{2}{1+(2x+1)^2} = \frac{2}{1+4x^2+4x+1} = \frac{2}{2(2x^2+2x+1)}$$

$$= \frac{1}{2x^2+2x+1}$$

$$\frac{dy}{dx} = \frac{1}{2x^2+2x+1}$$

Exercise 7.8

1. Differentiate each of the following with respect to x:

    (i) $\sin^{-1}6x$ (ii) $\tan^{-1}3x$ (iii) $\sin^{-1}(2x+1)$ (iv) $\tan^{-1}(x^2)$

2. If $y = \sin^{-1}(3x - 1)$, show that $\dfrac{dy}{dx} = \dfrac{3}{\sqrt{6x - 9x^2}}$.

3. Find the value of the derivative of each of these:
   (i) $\sin^{-1} 2x$ at $x = 0$
   (ii) $\tan^{-1} 4x$ at $x = \frac{1}{4}$
   (iii) $\cos^{-1}(3x)$ at $x = 6$

4. Given $f(x)$, find $f'(x)$ for each of the following:
   (i) $f(x) = \sin^{-1} \dfrac{3}{x}$
   (ii) $f(x) = \tan^{-1} \dfrac{x}{4}$
   (iii) $\cos^{-1}\left(\dfrac{x}{2}\right)$

5. Use the *Product Rule* to differentiate each of these:
   (i) $y = x \sin^{-1} x$
   (ii) $2x \tan^{-1} x$

6. If $y = (\sin^{-1} x)^2$, show that $\dfrac{dy}{dx} = \dfrac{2 \sin^{-1} x}{\sqrt{1 - x^2}}$.

7. If $f(x) = \sin^{-1}(\cos x)$, show that $f'(x) = k, k \in Z$.

8. Given $f(x) = \tan^{-1}(\cos x)$, evaluate $f'\left(\dfrac{\pi}{6}\right)$.

9. If $y = \tan^{-1} \dfrac{1}{x}$, find the value of $\dfrac{dy}{dx}$ at $x = 1$.

10. If $y = \tan^{-1}(3x^2)$, find the value of $\dfrac{dy}{dx}$ at $x = \dfrac{1}{3}$.

11. If $y = \tan^{-1} x$, show that $\dfrac{d^2 y}{dx^2}(1 + x^2) + 2x \dfrac{dy}{dx} = 0$.

Section 7.9 Differentiation of exponential functions

The word **exponent** is often used instead of *index*.
A function such as $y = 2^x$, where the variable occurs in the index, is called
an **exponential function**.

The diagram on the right shows the graphs of these
three functions
   (i) $y = 2^x$ (ii) $y = e^x$ (iii) $y = 4^x$

The function illustrated by the red curve is $y = e^x$.
It is by far the most important exponential function.

It is generally referred to as **the** exponential function.
e is an irrational number whose value is 2.718,
correct to three decimal places.

This function will be studied more closely in chapter 12.

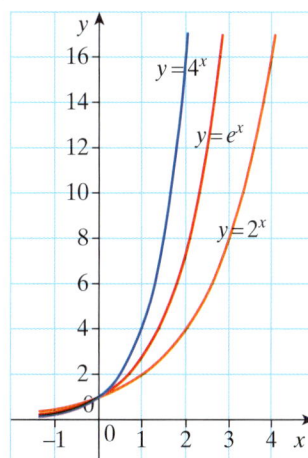

The importance of the function $y = e^x$ lies in the fact that the slope at any point on the curve is always the same as the y-value of the function.

For example, if $x = 2$, then $y = e^2 = 7.39...$
If an accurate diagram is drawn, it can be shown that the slope of the tangent at the point $x = 2$ is also 7.39. This leads us to a very important derivative, namely:

For $y = e^x$, $\dfrac{dy}{dx} = e^x$.

Notice that e^x is its own derivative and, in fact, is the only basic function which is its own derivative.

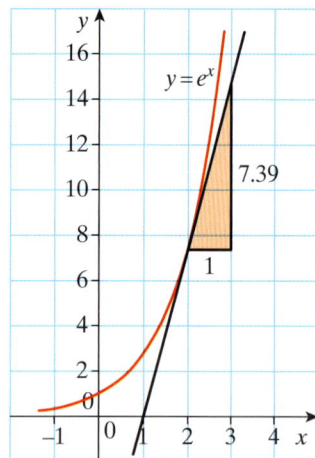

Standard derivative　　　　If $y = e^x$, then $\dfrac{dy}{dx} = e^x$.

Note: e^x is a continuously increasing function and can be used to model the growth of a cell, the spread of an infection, or the increase in size of a population.
e^{-x} is a decreasing function and can represent a rate of decay such as the rate at which a body loses heat or radioactive decay.

If $y = e^{ax}$, where a is a constant, it can be shown by using the *Chain Rule* that $\dfrac{dy}{dx} = ae^{ax}$.

If $y = e^{6x}$, then using the *Chain Rule*,

$$\frac{dy}{dx} = e^{6x}.\frac{d}{dx}(6x) = e^{6x}.6 = 6e^{6x}$$

Similarly, if $y = e^{x^2 + 4x}$, $\dfrac{dy}{dx} = e^{x^2 + 4x}(2x + 4)$

$$= (2x + 4)e^{x^2 + 4x}$$

Example 1

Find $\dfrac{dy}{dx}$ for each of the following:

(i) $y = 5e^{x^2}$　　　(ii) $y = e^{\cos x}$　　　(iii) $y = (e^x + 1)^4$

(i) $y = 5e^{x^2} \Rightarrow \dfrac{dy}{dx} = 5e^{x^2}.\dfrac{d}{dx}(x^2) = 5e^{x^2}.2x = 10xe^{x^2}$

(ii) $y = e^{\cos x} \Rightarrow \dfrac{dy}{dx} = e^{\cos x}.(-\sin x) = -\sin x(e^{\cos x})$

(iii) $y = (e^x + 1)^4 \Rightarrow \dfrac{dy}{dx} = 4(e^x + 1)^3.\dfrac{d}{dx}(e^x + 1)$

$$= 4(e^x + 1)^3.e^x = 4e^x(e^x + 1)^3$$

Example 2

If $y = e^{2x} \cos 2x$, find the value of $\dfrac{dy}{dx}$ at $x = \dfrac{\pi}{8}$.

$y = e^{2x} \cos 2x$

Here we use the *Product Rule*, $y = uv \Rightarrow \dfrac{dy}{dx} = u\dfrac{dv}{dx} + v\dfrac{du}{dx}$

$$\dfrac{dy}{dx} = e^{2x}(-2\sin 2x) + \cos 2x(2e^{2x}) \quad \dots u = e^{2x} \text{ and } v = \cos 2x$$

$$= -2\sin 2x.e^{2x} + 2\cos 2x.e^{2x}$$

$$\dfrac{dy}{dx} = 2e^{2x}(-\sin 2x + \cos 2x)$$

At $x = \dfrac{\pi}{8}$ $\dfrac{dy}{dx} = 2e^{\frac{\pi}{4}}\left(-\sin\dfrac{\pi}{4} + \cos\dfrac{\pi}{4}\right)$

$$= 2e^{\frac{\pi}{4}}\left(-\dfrac{1}{\sqrt{2}} + \dfrac{1}{\sqrt{2}}\right) = 2e^{\frac{\pi}{4}}(0) = 0$$

$$\therefore \dfrac{dy}{dx} = 0$$

Exercise 7.9

1. Find $\dfrac{dy}{dx}$ for each of the following:

   (i) $y = e^{4x}$ (ii) $y = e^{-3x}$ (iii) $y = e^{x^2}$

   (iv) $y = e^{2x+4}$ (v) $y = e^{x^2+3x}$ (vi) $y = e^{\sin x}$

2. Differentiate each of these:

   (i) $y = e^{\frac{x}{2}}$ (ii) $y = e^{\sin^2 x}$ (iii) $y = xe^{2x}$

3. Find $\dfrac{dy}{dx}$ for each of the following:

   (i) $y = e^{2x}\sin x$ (ii) $y = (e^x - 1)^2$ (iii) $y = \dfrac{e^{2x+1}}{e^x}$

4. Differentiate each of these:

   (i) $y = e^{2x}(1 + e^x)$ (ii) $t = \dfrac{e^{2x}}{x}$ (iii) $x^2 e^{\cos x}$

5. If $y = e^{3x}\sin(\pi x)$, find the value of $\dfrac{dy}{dx}$ when $x = 1$.

6. If $y = e^{2x}$, find $\dfrac{d^2y}{dx^2}$.

   Hence, show that $\dfrac{d^2y}{dx^2} - 3\dfrac{dy}{dx} + 2y = 0$.

7. Given that $y = e^x(\cos x - \sin x)$, show that $\dfrac{dy}{dx} = -2e^x \sin x$.

8. Given that $y = xe^x$, show that $\dfrac{d^2y}{dx^2} + y = 2\dfrac{dy}{dx}$.

9. If $f(x) = e^{2x} - ae^x$, show that $f'(x) = 0$ when $e^x = \dfrac{a}{2}$.

10. If $y = e^{mx}$, $m \in R$, find $\dfrac{d^2y}{dx^2}$.

   Hence, find m if $\dfrac{d^2y}{dx^2} - 3\dfrac{dy}{dx} - 4y = 0$.

11. Let $f(x) = \dfrac{e^x + e^{-x}}{2}$

   Show that $f''(x) = f(x)$, where $f''(x)$ is the second derivative of $f(x)$.

12. Find the equation of the tangent to the curve $y = 3e^x - \sin x + 5$ at the point where $x = 0$.

13. Line l_1 is the tangent to the curve $y = 2e^x - x$ at the point $(0,2)$.
    Line l_2 is the tangent to the curve $y = \sin 2x - x^2$ at the origin.

    Prove that the point of intersection of l_1 and l_2 is $(2, 4)$.

Section 7.10 Differentiating logarithmic functions

In the previous section we found the derivative of exponential functions. A log function is the inverse function of an exponential function and will be studied in detail in chapter 12.

The equation $8 = 2^3$ can be written as $\log_2 8 = 3$, where 2 is the **base** number.

Logarithms to the base e are called natural logarithms.

i.e. if $y = e^x$ then $x = \log_e y$ which is usually written $x = \ln y$

or if $x = e^y$ then $y = \ln x$.

For this reason, $y = \ln x$ is the inverse of the function $y = e^x$.

If $x = e^y$, then $y = \ln x$

To find the derivative of $y = \ln x$, we use the fact that if $y = \ln x$, then by definition $e^y = x$.

$$y = \ln x$$
$$\Rightarrow \quad x = e^y$$
$$\dfrac{dx}{dy} = e^y \quad \text{... differentiate with respect to } y$$
$$\Rightarrow \quad \dfrac{dy}{dx} = \dfrac{1}{e^y} \quad \text{... } \dfrac{dy}{dx} \text{ is the reciprocal of } \dfrac{dx}{dy}$$
$$\Rightarrow \quad \dfrac{dy}{dx} = \dfrac{1}{x}$$

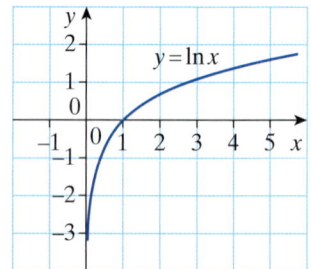

Standard derivative

If $y = \ln x$, then $\dfrac{dy}{dx} = \dfrac{1}{x}$.

When dealing with natural logarithms, the following results from chapter 12 are important:

(i) $\log_e 1 = 0$ ... (the log of 1 to any base is zero)

(ii) $\log_e e = 1$ ... ($\log_k k = 1$)

(iii) $\log_e e^x = x \log_e e = x$

$\ln e^x = x$, for all $x \in R$

The work involved in differentiating logarithmic functions can be simplified by using the laws of logarithms which are reproduced below:

Laws of Logarithms

(i) $\log_e(xy) = \log_e x + \log_e y$

(ii) $\log_e\left(\dfrac{x}{y}\right) = \log_e x - \log_e y$

(iii) $\log_e x^n = n \log_e x$

(iv) $\log_a x = \dfrac{\log_e x}{\log_e a}$

Note: If $y = \log_e(6x)$, we use logarithmic differentiation and the *Chain Rule* to find $\dfrac{dy}{dx}$.

$$y = \log_e(6x) \Rightarrow \dfrac{dy}{dx} = \dfrac{1}{6x} \cdot \dfrac{d}{dx}(6x) = \dfrac{1}{6x} \cdot \dfrac{6}{1} = \dfrac{1}{x}$$

In general,

If $y = \log_e(f(x))$, $\dfrac{dy}{dx} = \dfrac{1}{f(x)} \cdot f'(x)$

Example 1

Find $\dfrac{dy}{dx}$ if (i) $y = \log_e(4x^2 + 1)$ (ii) $y = \log_e(\sin^2 x)$.

(i) $y = \log_e(4x^2 + 1) \Rightarrow \dfrac{dy}{dx} = \dfrac{1}{4x^2 + 1} \cdot \dfrac{d}{dx}(4x^2 + 1)$

$$= \dfrac{1}{4x^2 + 1} \cdot 8x = \dfrac{8x}{4x^2 + 1}$$

(ii) $y = \log_e(\sin^2 x) \Rightarrow \dfrac{dy}{dx} = \dfrac{1}{\sin^2 x} \cdot \dfrac{d}{dx}(\sin^2 x)$

$$= \dfrac{1}{\sin^2 x} \cdot 2 \sin x \cos x = \dfrac{2 \cos x}{\sin x}$$

$$= 2 \cot x$$

Example 2

Given that $y = \log_e\left(\dfrac{1 + x}{1 - x}\right)$, show that $(1 - x^2)\dfrac{dy}{dx} = 2$.

$$y = \log_e\left(\dfrac{1 + x}{1 - x}\right)$$

$$\Rightarrow y = \log_e(1 + x) - \log_e(1 - x) \quad \ldots \left(\log_e\dfrac{a}{b} = \log_e a - \log_e b\right)$$

$$\dfrac{dy}{dx} = \dfrac{1}{1 + x} \cdot (1) - \dfrac{1}{1 - x} \cdot (-1)$$

$$= \dfrac{1}{1 + x} + \dfrac{1}{1 - x} = \dfrac{1 - x + 1 + x}{(1 + x)(1 - x)} = \dfrac{2}{1 - x^2}$$

$$\therefore (1 - x^2)\dfrac{dy}{dx} = (1 - x^2) \times \dfrac{2}{(1 - x^2)} = 2$$

Exercise 7.10

Find $\dfrac{dy}{dx}$ of the functions in numbers (1–9):

1. $y = \log_e 5x$
2. $y = \log_e(2x + 3)$
3. $y = \log_e(3x^2)$

4. $y = \log_e(\sin x)$
5. $y = \log_e(x^2 - 6x)$
6. $y = \log_e(\cos 3x)$

7. $y = x\log_e x$
8. $y = x^2 \ln(3x)$
9. $y = \dfrac{\ln x}{x}$

10. Use the rules of logarithms to simplify the following and then find $\dfrac{dy}{dx}$ of each function.

    (i) $y = \log_e(3x + 1)^3$
    (ii) $y = \log_e\left(\dfrac{2x + 1}{1 - 3x}\right)$
    (iii) $y = \log_e\sqrt{1 + x^2}$

    (iv) $y = \log_e\sqrt{\sin x}$
    (v) $y = \log_e(x^2 + 4)^2$
    (vi) $y = \log_e\sqrt{\dfrac{x}{1 + x}}$

11. If $y = \ln 3x^4$, find $\dfrac{d^2y}{dx^2}$.

12. If $y = [\log_e(x + 4)]^2$, show that $\dfrac{dx}{dy} = \dfrac{2\log_e(x + 4)}{x + 4}$.

13. If $y = x\log_e x$, find $\dfrac{d^2y}{dx^2}$.

14. Find the slope of the tangent to the curve $y = \log_e x - 2x + x^2$ at the point where $x = 2$.

15. If $y = (\ln x)^2$, find the value of $\dfrac{dy}{dx}$ at $x = e$.

16. Given that $y = \ln(1 + \sin t)$, find $\dfrac{dy}{dt}$.

    If $(1 + \sin t)\dfrac{d^2y}{dt^2} + k = 0$, find the value of $k \in N$.

17. If $y = \ln(e^x \cos x)$, show that $\dfrac{dy}{dx} = 1 - \tan x$.

Revision Exercise 7 (Core)

1. Find $\dfrac{dy}{dx}$ for each of the following:

    (i) $y = x^2 + \dfrac{1}{x}$ 　　　　(ii) $y = (2x + 3)^3$ 　　　　(iii) $y = \sqrt{1 + 3x}$

2. Differentiate $y = x^2 + 3x - 4$ from first principles.

3. Find $\dfrac{dy}{dx}$ for each of these:

    (i) $y = \frac{1}{3}(x + 2)^3$ 　　　　　　(ii) $y = \dfrac{2x}{x + 1}$

4. Find $f'(x)$ for each of these:

    (i) $f(x) = 2x^2 - \dfrac{3}{x^2}$ 　　(ii) $y = 4\sin 6x$ 　　(iii) $y = 3e^{x^2}$

5. Find the value of k for which $\dfrac{d}{dx}\left(\dfrac{2x + 3}{x - 4}\right) = \dfrac{k}{(x - 4)^2}$.

6. The point $P(x, y)$ lies on the curve with equation $y = 6x^2 - x^3$.

    (i) Find the value of x for which the gradient of the tangent at P is 12.

    (ii) Hence, find the equation of the tangent at P.

7. Find $\dfrac{dy}{dx}$ for each of these:

    (i) $y = 3x^2 - x + \dfrac{3}{x}$ 　　(ii) $y = \dfrac{3x^2}{x - 1}$ 　　(iii) $y = \cos^2 4x$

8. If $y = \dfrac{4x^2 + 6}{x}$, find $\dfrac{dy}{dx}$ without using the *Quotient Rule*.

9. $f(x) = a\sin 3x$, where a is a constant.

    If $f'(\pi) = 2$, find a.

10. The equation of a curve is $y = x\sin 2x$.

    Find the slope of the tangent to the curve at the point where $x = \dfrac{\pi}{3}$.

11. The gradient of the curve C is given by $\dfrac{dy}{dx} = (x + 1)(x - 2)$.

    The point $P(1, 2)$ lies on C.

    Find the equation of the tangent to C at P.

12. If $f(x) = \sqrt{x} + \dfrac{1}{x^2}$, evaluate $f'(4)$.

13. Given $y = 2x^2 - 1$, find

    (i) the average rate at which y changes over the interval $[1, 4]$

    (ii) the instantaneous rate of change of y with respect to x when $x = 4$.

14. Given that $y = \tan^{-1}(5x)$, find $\dfrac{dy}{dx}$.

15. The diagram shows a parabola with equation
$y = 2x^2 - 2x + 3$.
A tangent to the parabola has been drawn at P(1, 3).
Find the equation of this tangent.

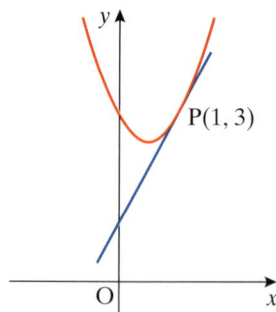

16. Given the function $f(x) = 2x^{-3} + \dfrac{k}{2}x^{-2} - x,\ x \neq 0,\ k \in R$.
If $f'(-2) = 0$, find the value of k.

Revision Exercise 7 (Advanced)

1. Find the rate of change of the function $y = \sin x - \cos x$ at the point where $x = \dfrac{\pi}{2}$.

2. Find the slope of the tangent to the curve $y = x^2 \sin x$ at the point where $x = \dfrac{\pi}{2}$.

3. Find the coordinates of the two points on the curve $y = x^2 + \ln x$ where the slope of the tangent to the curve is 3.

4. If $y = x - 1 + \dfrac{1}{x-1},\ x \neq 1$, find the values of x for which $\dfrac{dy}{dx} = 0$.

5. Differentiate each of these, expressing each answer in its simplest form:

(i) $y = \ln(3x^4)$ (ii) $y = \ln\left(\dfrac{3}{\sqrt{x}}\right)$

6. If $y = e^{nx}$, find $\dfrac{dy}{dx}$ and $\dfrac{d^2y}{dx^2}$.

Hence, find two values of n for which $\dfrac{d^2y}{dx^2} - 5\dfrac{dy}{dx} + 6y = 0$.

7. Find the coordinates of the two points on the curve $y = x^3 - 3x^2 - 5x + 10$ where the tangents to the curve are parallel to the line $y = 4x - 7$.

8. The slope of the curve $y = a\sqrt{x} - 5$ at the point $(4, b)$ is 2.
Find the values of a and b.

9. Water is being emptied from a tank and the volume remaining can be modelled by the equation $V = 80(30 - t)^3$.
The diagram on the next page shows part of the graph of the equation.

(i) Find the coordinates of A and B and explain the significance of the points with reference to the equation.

(ii) How much water remains in the tank after 10 minutes?

(iii) Find the average rate at which the water drains from the tank over the first 10 minutes.

(iv) Find the instantaneous rate at which the water is draining when $t = 10$ minutes.

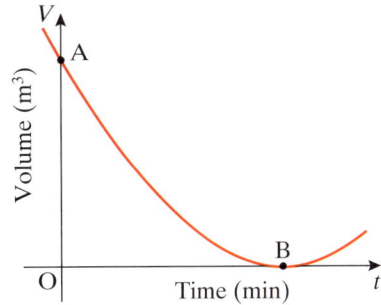

10. If $y = \dfrac{x}{\sqrt{1 - x^2}}$, find $\dfrac{dy}{dx}$ and express your answer in the form $\dfrac{1}{(1 - x^2)^k}$, where k is a rational number.

11. If $y = \tan^{-1}\left(\dfrac{1}{x}\right)$, find the value of $\dfrac{dy}{dx}$ at $x = 1$.

12. Find the equation of the tangent to the curve $y = x^3 e^x$ at the point where $x = 0$.

13. Given that $y = kx^2$ and $x\dfrac{dy}{dx} + \dfrac{1}{2}\left(\dfrac{dy}{dx}\right)^2 + y = 0$, find the value of the constant k, where $x \in R$ and $k \neq 0$.

14. x_1 is a first approximation to the root of the function $f(x) = x^3 + x^2 - 1$ and x_2 is a second approximation.

If the approximations are connected using the formula $x_2 = x_1 - \dfrac{f(x_1)}{f'(x_1)}$, find a value for x_2 if $x_1 = 1$.

15. If $y = \ln(1 + e^x)$, show that $\dfrac{d^2y}{dx^2} + \left(\dfrac{dy}{dx}\right)^2 = \dfrac{dy}{dx}$.

16. The diagram shows the curve $y = x^3 - x + 1$. The points A and B on the curve have x-coordinates -1 and $-1 + h$ respectively.

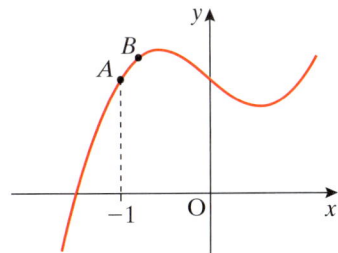

(i) Show that the y-coordinate of the point B is
$$1 + 2h - 3h^2 + h^3$$

(ii) Find the gradient of the chord AB in the form
$$p + qh + rh^2$$
where p, q and r are integers.

(iii) Explain how your answer to part (ii) can be used to find the gradient of the tangent to the curve at A. State the value of this gradient.

Revision Exercise 7 (Extended-response)

1. Consider the function $y = x(x - 2)$.

   (i) Write down the coordinates of the points at which the curve crosses the x-axis.

   (ii) Show that the slopes of the curve at these points differ only in sign and interpret the geometrical significance of this.

   (iii) Find the equations of the tangents to the curve at these points.

   (iv) Find the angle (θ) between the tangents.

   (v) Let $y = x(x - 2)(x - 5)$.

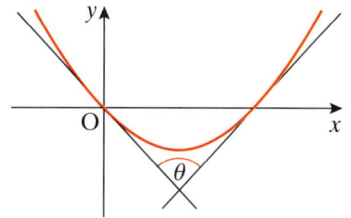

   If the slopes of the tangents to the curve at the points where the curve intersects the x-axis are p, q and r, prove that $\dfrac{1}{p} + \dfrac{1}{q} + \dfrac{1}{r} = 0$.

2. (i) Differentiate $y = 2 \ln (x\sqrt{x^2 + 1})$.

   Give your answer in the form $\dfrac{k(kx^2 + 1)}{x(x^2 + 1)}$, where k is to be found and $k \in N$.

   (ii) Find the equation of the tangent to the curve $y = 2 \ln (x\sqrt{x^2 + 1})$ at the point where $x = 1$.

3. The graph of the function $f(x) = \dfrac{x^2}{4} - x$ is shown on the right.
   The point B has coordinates $(3, -\frac{3}{4})$.

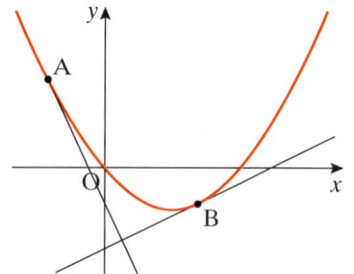

   (i) Find the equation of the tangent at B.

   (ii) The point A on the curve is such that the tangent at A is perpendicular to the tangent at B.
   Find the coordinates of A.

   (iii) If the tangents at A and B meet at the point C, find the coordinates of C.

   (iv) Show that the area of the triangle ABC is $\dfrac{125}{16}$.

4. P and Q are points on the curve $f(x) = x^3 - x$.

   (a) Find, in terms of h, the slope of the line through P(2, 6) and Q, where the x-coordinate of Q is $(2 + h)$.

   (b) Hence, find the slope of the line segment [PQ], where
       (i) $h = 0.5$ (ii) $h = 0.1$ (iii) $h = 0.01$ (iv) $h = 0.001$

   (c) To what value does the slope of PQ approach as $h \to 0$?

   (d) Hence, what is the slope of the curve at P?

   (e) If the coordinates of P are $(a, a^3 - a)$, and Q has x-coordinate $a + h$, find the slope of PQ in terms of a.

   (f) Hence, find the slope of the tangent to this curve at the point P$(a, a^3 - a)$.

5. (a) Let $f(x) = e^{-\frac{1}{2}x^2}$.

Show that the second derivative of $f(x)$ with respect to x is $f''(x) = (x^2 - 1)e^{-\frac{1}{2}x^2}$.

(b) At the point P in the first quadrant on the curve $f(x) = e^{-\frac{1}{2}x^2}$, $f''(x) = 0$.

Show that the tangent at P crosses the x-axis at $(2, 0)$.

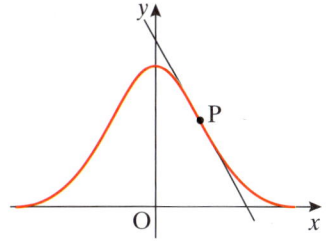

6. The diameter of a tree (D cm) t years after 1 January 1990 is given by $D = 50e^{kt}$.

(a) Prove that $\dfrac{dD}{dt} = cD$ for some constant c.

(b) If $k = 0.2$, find the rate of increase of D where $D = 100$.

Give your answer in cm/year, correct to the nearest cm.

7. (i) Find the slope of the curve $y = \ln\sqrt{1 + \sin 2x}$ at the point where $x = \dfrac{\pi}{2}$.

(ii) If $y = (x^2 - 1)^n, n \in R$, find $\dfrac{dy}{dx}$.

Hence, show that $(x^2 - 1)\dfrac{dy}{dx} - 2nxy = 0$.

(iii) If $f(x) = x^3 - 6x^2 + 12x + 5$, show that $f'(x)$ is always positive.

8. $f(x) = x(x - k)^2, k \in R$ defines a function.

(i) Find $f'(x)$ and express your answer in factorised form.

(ii) Find the coordinates of the points on the curve where the tangents are parallel to the x-axis.

(iii) Show that the equation of the line joining these points can be written as $y = -\dfrac{2k^2}{9}(x - k)$.

(iv) If the points found in (ii) above are A and B, show that AB intersects the curve at the midpoint of [AB].

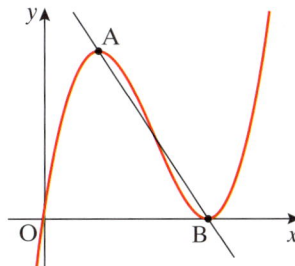

8 Trigonometry 2

Key words

identity   unit circle   sine rule   cosine rule   compound angle   surd form
double angle   half-angle formulae   product formulae $\sin^{-1} x$ (arc sine x)

Section 8.1 Trigonometric identities

We are already familiar with the three basic trigonometric ratios, namely sine, cosine and tangent.

Three related ratios are defined as:

$$\operatorname{cosec} A = \frac{1}{\sin A} \qquad \sec A = \frac{1}{\cos A} \qquad \cot A = \frac{1}{\tan A}$$

In the given triangle

$$\frac{\sin \theta}{\cos \theta} = \frac{y}{r} \div \frac{x}{r} = \frac{y}{r} \times \frac{r}{x} = \frac{y}{x} = \tan \theta$$

$$\Rightarrow \quad \tan \theta = \frac{\sin \theta}{\cos \theta}$$

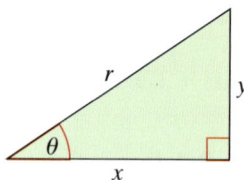

This relationship between trigonometric ratios is called an **identity** because it is true for **all values** of θ in a given domain.

The **mandatory proofs** of key standard trigonometric formulae are boxed separately and are flagged by a **Mandatory Proof** box. Other derivations are shown in the text and examples.

Mandatory Proof

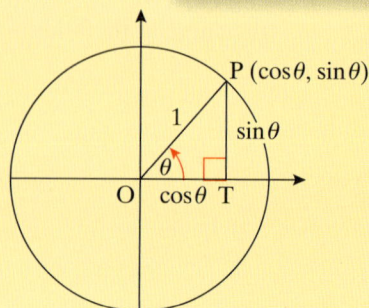

To prove that $\cos^2 \theta + \sin^2 \theta = 1$

We have already established that any point on the **unit circle** is defined by the coordinates $(\cos \theta, \sin \theta)$.

In the given diagram $|OP| = 1$

$$\Rightarrow \quad \sqrt{(\cos \theta - 0)^2 + (\sin \theta - 0)^2} = 1$$

$$\Rightarrow \quad \sqrt{\cos^2 \theta + \sin^2 \theta} = 1$$

$$\Rightarrow \quad \cos^2 \theta + \sin^2 \theta = 1 \ldots \text{(squaring both sides)}$$

If each term in the equation $\sin^2 \theta + \cos^2 \theta = 1$ is divided by $\cos^2 \theta$, we get,

$$\frac{\sin^2 \theta}{\cos^2 \theta} + \frac{\cos^2 \theta}{\cos^2 \theta} = \frac{1}{\cos^2 \theta}$$

$$\Rightarrow \quad \tan^2 \theta + 1 = \sec^2 \theta$$

$$\Rightarrow \quad \mathbf{1 + \tan^2 \theta = \sec^2 \theta}$$

The identities established above should be memorised as they are used very frequently to prove more complex identities. These identities are highlighted in the box below.

1. $\operatorname{cosec} \theta = \dfrac{1}{\sin \theta}$ **2.** $\sec \theta = \dfrac{1}{\cos \theta}$ **3.** $\tan \theta = \dfrac{\sin \theta}{\cos \theta}$

4. $\cot \theta = \dfrac{\cos \theta}{\sin \theta}$ **5.** $\sin^2 \theta + \cos^2 \theta = 1$ **6.** $1 + \tan^2 \theta = \sec^2 \theta$

It follows from **5** that $\mathbf{\sin^2 \theta = 1 - \cos^2 \theta}$ and $\mathbf{\cos^2 \theta = 1 - \sin^2 \theta.}$

The general method of proving an identity is to choose one side that allows development and show, by using known identities, that it can be simplified into the form of the other side.

This is illustrated in the following examples.

Example 1

Prove these identities:
  (i) $\sec A - \tan A \sin A = \cos A$ (ii) $\tan \theta \sqrt{1 - \sin^2 \theta} = \sin \theta.$

  (i) Here we change all ratios to sine and cosine ratios.

$$\sec A - \tan A \sin A = \frac{1}{\cos A} - \frac{\sin A}{\cos A} \cdot \sin A$$

$$= \frac{1}{\cos A} - \frac{\sin^2 A}{\cos A}$$

$$= \frac{1 - \sin^2 A}{\cos A} = \frac{\cos^2 A}{\cos A} = \cos A = \text{Right-hand side (RHS)}$$

  (ii) $\tan \theta \sqrt{1 - \sin^2 \theta} = \dfrac{\sin \theta}{\cos \theta} \cdot \sqrt{\cos^2 \theta} \ \dots \ 1 - \sin^2 \theta = \cos^2 \theta$

$$= \frac{\sin \theta}{\cos \theta} \cdot \frac{\cos \theta}{1} = \sin \theta = \text{RHS}$$

Example 2

Prove that $\dfrac{\tan \theta + \sin \theta}{\sec \theta + 1} = \sin \theta$.

$$\dfrac{\tan \theta + \sin \theta}{\sec \theta + 1} = \dfrac{\dfrac{\sin \theta}{\cos \theta} + \dfrac{\sin \theta}{1}}{\dfrac{1}{\cos \theta} + 1}$$

$$= \dfrac{\sin \theta + \sin \theta \cos \theta}{1 + \cos \theta} \quad \cdots \text{ (multiply each term above and below by } \cos \theta\text{)}$$

$$= \dfrac{\sin \theta (1 + \cos \theta)}{(1 + \cos \theta)} = \sin \theta = \text{RHS}$$

Identities involving the *Sine Rule* and *Cosine Rule*

The *Sine Rule* states that $\dfrac{a}{\sin A} = \dfrac{b}{\sin B}$

This can be also written as $\sin A = \dfrac{a \sin B}{b}$

The *Cosine Rule* states that $a^2 = b^2 + c^2 - 2bc \cos A$.

This can also be written as $\cos A = \dfrac{b^2 + c^2 - a^2}{2bc}$.

Identities involving the sides a, b and c of a triangle generally require the use of the *Sine* or *Cosine Rules* to prove them.

Example 3

Prove that in any triangle, $c \cos B - b \cos C = \dfrac{c^2 - b^2}{a}$

Using the Cosine Rule, we have

$$\cos B = \dfrac{c^2 + a^2 - b^2}{2ac} \text{ and } \cos C = \dfrac{a^2 + b^2 - c^2}{2ab}$$

Thus $c \cos B - b \cos C = \dfrac{c(c^2 + a^2 - b^2)}{2ac} - \dfrac{b(a^2 + b^2 - c^2)}{2ab}$

$$= \dfrac{c^2 + a^2 - b^2}{2a} - \dfrac{(a^2 + b^2 - c^2)}{2a}$$

$$= \dfrac{c^2 + a^2 - b^2 - a^2 - b^2 + c^2}{2a} = \dfrac{2c^2 - 2b^2}{2a}$$

$$= \dfrac{c^2 - b^2}{a} = \text{RHS}$$

Exercise 8.1

Prove the following identities:

1. $\cos A \tan A = \sin A$

2. $\sin \theta \sec \theta = \tan \theta$

3. $\sin \theta \tan \theta + \cos \theta = \sec \theta$

4. $\dfrac{\sin \theta}{\sqrt{1 - \sin^2 \theta}} = \tan \theta$

5. $\sec A - \sin A \tan A = \cos A$

6. $1 - \tan^2 \theta \cos^2 \theta = \cos^2 \theta$

7. $\dfrac{(1 + \cos \theta)(1 - \cos \theta)}{\cos^2 \theta} = \tan^2 \theta$

8. $\sec^2 A - \tan^2 A = 1$

9. $\dfrac{\sqrt{1 - \cos^2 \theta}}{\tan \theta} = \cos \theta$

10. $(1 + \tan^2 \theta) \cos^2 \theta = 1$

11. $(\cos \theta + \sin \theta)^2 + (\cos \theta - \sin \theta)^2 = 2.$

12. $(1 + \tan^2 A)(1 - \sin^2 A) = 1$

13. $(\sin \theta + \cos \theta)^2 - 2 \sin \theta \cos \theta = 1$

14. $\dfrac{1 - \cos^2 A}{\sin A \cos A} = \tan A$

15. $\dfrac{1}{1 - \sin A} + \dfrac{1}{1 + \sin A} = 2 \sec^2 A$

16. $(1 - \sin^2 A) \tan^2 A + \cos^2 A = 1$

17. $\operatorname{cosec}^2 \theta (\tan^2 \theta - \sin^2 \theta) = \tan^2 \theta$

18. $(1 - \sin A)(\sec A + \tan A) = \cos A$

Use the *Sine Rule* or *Cosine Rule* to prove the following identities:

19. $b \cos C + c \cos B = a$

20. $bc \cos A + ca \cos B = c^2$

21. $c = b \cos A + a \cos B$

22. $a \cos B - b \cos A = \dfrac{a^2 - b^2}{c}$

23. $ab \cos C - ac \cos B = b^2 - c^2$

24. $c \cos B - b \cos C = \dfrac{c^2 - b^2}{a}$

25. Use the *Sine Rule* to prove that $\dfrac{\sin A - \sin B}{\sin B} = \dfrac{a - b}{b}.$

26. Prove that $\dfrac{\cos A}{a} + \dfrac{\cos B}{b} + \dfrac{\cos C}{c} = \dfrac{a^2 + b^2 + c^2}{2abc}.$

Section 8.2 Compound angles

If A and B are two given angles, then $(A + B)$ and $(A - B)$ are called **compound angles**.

In this section we will establish formulae for $\cos(A \pm B)$, $\sin(A \pm B)$ and $\tan(A \pm B)$ by expressing them in terms of $\sin A$, $\cos A$ and $\tan A$.

We will first establish the formula for $\cos(A - B)$ and then use already established identities to prove the other formulae.

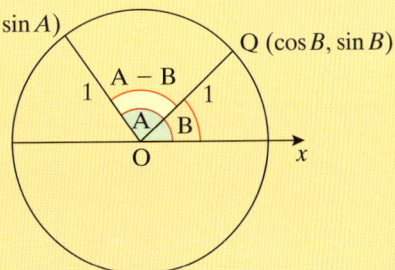

Mandatory Proof

To prove that $\cos(A - B) = \cos A \cos B - \sin A \sin B$

Let the radii [OP] and [OQ] make angles A and B with the positive x-axis.

$$|\angle POQ| = A - B$$

We now find $|PQ|$ using two different methods:

1. the standard formula for the distance between two points
2. the cosine rule.

1. Using the formula $\sqrt{(x_2 - x_1)^2 + (y_2 - y_1)^2}$, we have:

$$|PQ|^2 = (\cos A - \cos B)^2 + (\sin A - \sin B)^2$$
$$= \cos^2 A - 2\cos A \cos B + \cos^2 B + \sin^2 A - 2\sin A \sin B + \sin^2 B$$
$$\mathbf{= \cos^2 A + \sin^2 A - 2\cos A \cos B + \sin^2 B - 2\sin A \sin B}$$

But $\cos^2 A + \sin^2 A = 1$ and $\cos^2 B + \sin^2 B = 1$

$\Rightarrow \quad |PQ|^2 = 1 - 2\cos A \cos B + 1 - 2\sin A \sin B$
$$= 2 - 2(\cos A \cos B + \sin A \sin B) \ldots ①$$

2. Now using the cosine rule to find $|PQ|$, we have:

$$|PQ|^2 = |OP|^2 + |OQ|^2 - 2|OP|\,|OQ|\cos(A - B)$$
$$= 1 + 1 - 2(1)(1)\cos(A - B) \ldots |OP| = |OQ| = 1 = \text{radius}$$
$$= 2 - 2\cos(A - B) \ldots ②$$

Equating the two values for $|PQ|^2$, we have

$2 - 2(\cos A \cos B + \sin A \sin B) = 2 - 2\cos(A - B)$
$\Rightarrow \quad -(\cos A \cos B + \sin A \sin B) = -\cos(A - B)$
$\Rightarrow \quad \mathbf{\cos(A - B) = \cos A \cos B + \sin A \sin B} \ldots\ldots \textbf{(i)}$

Having established the formula for $\cos(A - B)$, we can derive the other formulae using the important identities shown on the right.

$\cos(-B) = \cos B$
$\sin(-B) = -\sin B$
$\sin(90° - A) = \cos A$
$\cos(90° - A) = \sin A$

Mandatory Proof

To prove that $\cos(A + B) = \cos A \cos B - \sin A \sin B$

To derive the formula for $\cos(A + B)$, we replace B with $(-B)$ in formula **(i)** on the previous page:

$\cos(A - B) = \cos A \cos B + \sin A \sin B$
$\Rightarrow \quad \cos[A - (-B)] = \cos A \cos(-B) + \sin A \sin(-B)$
$$= \cos A \cos B + \sin A (-\sin B)$$
$\Rightarrow \quad \mathbf{\cos(A + B) = \cos A \cos B - \sin A \sin B} \ldots\ldots \textbf{(ii)}$

Mandatory Proof

To prove that $\cos(2A) = \cos^2 A - \sin^2 A$

Replace B with A in $\cos(A + B)$
$\Rightarrow \quad \cos(A + A) = \cos A \cos A - \sin A \sin A$
$\Rightarrow \quad \mathbf{\cos(2A) = \cos^2 A - \sin^2 A}$

To prove that sin(A + B) = sin A cos B + cos A sin B

$\cos(A - B) = \cos A \cos B + \sin A \sin B$ ... from **(i)**

To derive the formula for $\sin(A + B)$, we replace A with $(90° - A)$.

$\Rightarrow \quad \cos[(90° - A) - B] = \cos(90° - A)\cos B + \sin(90° - A)\sin B$

$\qquad\qquad\qquad\qquad\quad = \sin A \cos B + \cos A \sin B$

$\Rightarrow \quad \cos[90° - (A + B)] = \sin A \cos B + \cos A \sin B$

$\Rightarrow \quad$ **sin(A + B) = sin A cos B + cos A sin B** ...... **(iii)**

Substituting $(-B)$ for B in formula **(iii)**, we get

$\qquad \sin(A - B) = \sin A \cos(-B) + \cos A \sin(-B)$ $\qquad$ $\boxed{\sin(-B) = -\sin B}$

$\Rightarrow \quad$ **sin(A − B) = sin A cos B − cos A sin B** ...... **(iv)**

Expressions for $\tan(A + B)$ and $\tan(A - B)$ can be derived from formulae **(i)** to **(iv)** established above:

To prove that tan(A + B) = $\dfrac{\tan A + \tan B}{1 - \tan A \tan B}$

$\tan(A + B) = \dfrac{\sin(A + B)}{\cos(A + B)} = \dfrac{\sin A \cos B + \cos A \sin B}{\cos A \cos B - \sin A \sin B}$

We now divide each term in the numerator and denominator by $\cos A \cos B$.

$\tan(A + B) = \dfrac{\dfrac{\sin A}{\cos A} + \dfrac{\sin B}{\cos B}}{1 - \dfrac{\sin A}{\cos A} \cdot \dfrac{\sin B}{\cos B}}$

$\Rightarrow \quad$ **tan(A + B) = $\dfrac{\tan A + \tan B}{1 - \tan A \tan B}$** ...... **(v)**

Substituting $(-B)$ for B in formula **(v)** we get:

$\qquad$ **tan(A − B) = $\dfrac{\tan A - \tan B}{1 + \tan A \tan B}$** ...... **(vi)** $\qquad$ $\boxed{\tan(-B) = -\tan B}$

Compound angle formulae

$\sin(A + B) = \sin A \cos B + \cos A \sin B$

$\sin(A - B) = \sin A \cos B - \cos A \sin B$

$\cos(A + B) = \cos A \cos B - \sin A \sin B$

$\cos(A - B) = \cos A \cos B + \sin A \sin B$

$\tan(A + B) = \dfrac{\tan A + \tan B}{1 - \tan A \tan B}; \tan(A - B) = \dfrac{\tan A - \tan B}{1 + \tan A \tan B}$

Note: The exact values of the sine, cosine and tangent of the angles 30°, 45° and 60° are given on page 13 of *Formulae and Tables*.

You may also use the triangles shown on the right to find the exact trigonometric ratios of 30°, 45° and 60°.

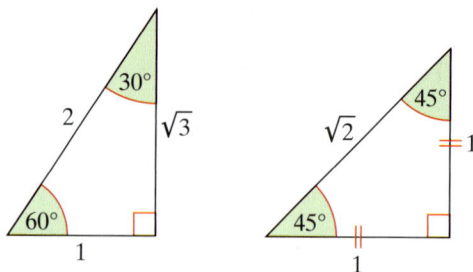

Example 1

Express in surd form   (i) $\sin 15°$ (ii) $\tan 105°$

(i) $\sin 15° = \sin(60° - 45°)$

$\qquad = \sin 60° \cos 45° - \cos 60° \sin 45°$

$\qquad = \dfrac{\sqrt{3}}{2} \cdot \dfrac{1}{\sqrt{2}} - \dfrac{1}{2} \cdot \dfrac{1}{\sqrt{2}}$

$\qquad = \dfrac{\sqrt{3}}{2\sqrt{2}} - \dfrac{1}{2\sqrt{2}}$

$\qquad = \dfrac{\sqrt{3} - 1}{2\sqrt{2}}$

| $\sin 60° = \dfrac{\sqrt{3}}{2}$
| $\cos 60° = \dfrac{1}{2}$
| $\sin 45° = \dfrac{1}{\sqrt{2}}$
| $\cos 45° = \dfrac{1}{\sqrt{2}}$

(ii) $\tan 105° = \tan(60° + 45°)$

$\qquad = \dfrac{\tan 60° + \tan 45°}{1 - \tan 60° \tan 45°}$

$\qquad = \dfrac{\sqrt{3} + 1}{1 - \sqrt{3}} = \dfrac{1 + \sqrt{3}}{1 - \sqrt{3}}$

$\qquad = \dfrac{1 + \sqrt{3}}{1 - \sqrt{3}} \cdot \dfrac{1 + \sqrt{3}}{1 + \sqrt{3}} = \dfrac{1 + 2\sqrt{3} + 3}{1 - 3} = \dfrac{4 + 2\sqrt{3}}{-2}$ ...

$\qquad = -2 - \sqrt{3}$

| $\tan 60° = \sqrt{3}$
| $\tan 45° = 1$

here we rationalised the denominator.

Example 2

If $\tan A = \dfrac{1}{4}$ and $\tan B = \dfrac{3}{5}$, find the value of $(A + B)$ without using a calculator.

$\tan(A + B) = \dfrac{\tan A + \tan B}{1 - \tan A \tan B}$

$\qquad = \dfrac{\dfrac{1}{4} + \dfrac{3}{5}}{1 - \dfrac{1}{4} \cdot \dfrac{3}{5}}$

$\qquad = \dfrac{5 + 12}{20 - 3}$ ... multiply each term above and below by 20

$\Rightarrow \quad \tan(A + B) = \dfrac{17}{17} = 1 \quad \Rightarrow \quad (A + B) = \tan^{-1} 1$

$\qquad\qquad\qquad\qquad\qquad\qquad = 45°$

Example 3

Prove that $\dfrac{\sin(A + B)}{\cos A \cos B} = \tan A + \tan B$.

$$\frac{\sin(A + B)}{\cos A \cos B} = \frac{\sin A \cos B + \cos A \sin B}{\cos A \cos B}$$

Divide each term in the numerator and denominator by $\cos A \cos B$.

$$\Rightarrow \quad \frac{\sin(A + B)}{\cos A \cos B} = \frac{\dfrac{\sin A \cos B}{\cos A \cos B} + \dfrac{\cos A \sin B}{\cos A \cos B}}{\dfrac{\cos A \cos B}{\cos A \cos B}}$$

$$= \frac{\dfrac{\sin A}{\cos A} + \dfrac{\sin B}{\cos B}}{1} = \tan A + \tan B$$

Exercise 8.2

1. Express, in surd form, the value of each of the following
   (i) $\cos 15°$
   (ii) $\sin 75°$
   (iii) $\cos 105°$

2. Express each of these in surd form:
   (i) $\tan 15°$
   (ii) $\sin 135°$
   (iii) $\tan 75°$

3. Use the triangles shown on the right to find the value of
   (i) $\cos(A + B)$
   (ii) $\tan(A - B)$.

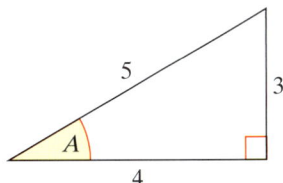

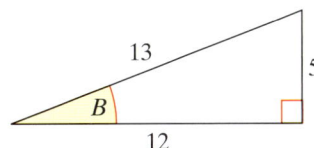

4. Express each of these as a function of a compound angle and evaluate:
   (i) $\sin 45° \cos 15° + \cos 45° \sin 15°$
   (ii) $\cos 40° \cos 50° - \sin 40° \sin 50°$
   (iii) $\cos 80° \cos 20° + \sin 80° \sin 20°$
   (iv) $\dfrac{\tan 25° + \tan 20°}{1 - \tan 25° \tan 20°}$.

5. Simplify each of the following:
   (i) $\dfrac{\tan 2A + \tan A}{1 - \tan 2A \tan A}$
   (ii) $\sin 2\theta \cos \theta + \cos 2\theta \sin \theta$

6. By using the formulae for compound angles, show that
   (i) $\sin(90° - A) = \cos A$
   (ii) $\cos(90° + A) = -\sin A$.

7. If $\tan(A - B) = 2$ and $\tan B = \frac{1}{4}$, find $\tan A$.

8. If $\tan A = \frac{1}{2}$ and $\tan B = \frac{1}{3}$, where A and $B < \dfrac{\pi}{2}$, find the value of the angle $(A + B)$.

9. If $\tan(A + B) = 1$ and $\tan A = \frac{1}{3}$, express $\tan B$ as a fraction.

10. If $\sin x = \frac{1}{2}$ and $0 \leqslant x \leqslant \dfrac{\pi}{2}$, find the value of $\sin\left(x + \dfrac{\pi}{4}\right)$ without using a calculator.

11. Express in surd form the value of tan 15°.
    Hence express the value of $\tan^2 15°$ in the form $p + q\sqrt{r}$, where p, q and r are integers.

12. Prove that $\tan\left(\dfrac{\pi}{4} + A\right) = \dfrac{\cos A + \sin A}{\cos A - \sin A}$.

13. Show that $\cos(A + B)\cos B + \sin(A + B)\sin B = \cos A$.

14. The diagram shows a triangle of height h m.
    The angles A and B are such that $A + B = 45°$.
    By using the expansion of $\tan(A + B)$, or otherwise,
    find the value of h.

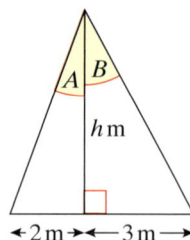

15. If $\sin A = \sin(A + 30°)$, show that $\tan A = 2 + \sqrt{3}$.

16. A triangle has sides 4, 5 and 6.
    The angles of the triangle are A, B and C, as shown.
    (i) Use the cosine rule to show that $\cos A + \cos C = \frac{7}{8}$
    (ii) Show that $\cos(A + C) = -\frac{9}{16}$.

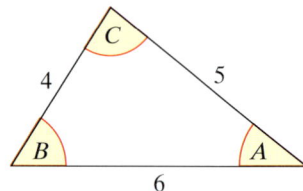

17. The diagram shows a right-angled triangle ABC
    in which $|AB| = h$ m and $|BC| = 6$ m.
    The point D lies on [BC] such that $|BD| = 1$ m
    and $|DC| = 5$ m.
    $$|\angle CAD| = 45° \text{ and } |\angle BAD| = \theta.$$
    By using the formula for $\tan(\theta + 45°)$, or otherwise,
    find the two possible values for h.

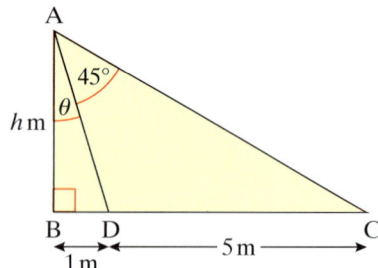

Section 8.3 Double-angle formulae

The compound angle formulae in the previous section deal with any two angles A and B.
If we replace B with A we get very useful formulae for $\sin 2A$, $\cos 2A$ and $\tan 2A$.

$$\sin(A + B) = \sin A \cos B + \cos A \sin B$$

Replacing B with A we get:

$$\sin 2A = \sin(A + A) = \sin A \cos A + \cos A \sin A = 2 \sin A \cos A$$

$$\cos 2A = \cos(A + A) = \cos A \cos A - \sin A \sin A = \cos^2 A - \sin^2 A$$

$$\tan 2A = \tan(A + A) = \frac{\tan A + \tan A}{1 - \tan A \tan A} = \frac{2 \tan A}{1 - \tan^2 A}$$

Using the identity $\sin^2 A + \cos^2 A = 1$, we get two further identities for $\cos 2A$:

$$\cos 2A = \cos^2 A - \sin^2 A \qquad\qquad\text{or}\qquad\qquad \cos 2A = \cos^2 A - \sin^2 A$$
$$= (1 - \sin^2 A) - \sin^2 A \qquad\qquad\qquad\qquad = \cos^2 A - (1 - \cos^2 A)$$
$$= 1 - 2\sin^2 A \qquad\qquad\qquad\qquad\qquad\quad = \cos^2 A - 1 + \cos^2 A$$
$$= 2\cos^2 A - 1$$

Double angle formulae

$$\cos 2A = \cos^2 A - \sin^2 A \qquad\qquad \sin 2A = 2\sin A \cos A$$
$$= 2\cos^2 A - 1$$
$$\tan 2A = \frac{2\tan A}{1 - \tan^2 A}$$
$$= 1 - 2\sin^2 A$$

By rearranging the formulae for $\cos 2A$, we can express $\cos^2 A$ and $\sin^2 A$ in terms of $\cos 2A$ as follows:

$$\cos 2A = 2\cos^2 A - 1 \qquad\qquad\text{or}\qquad\qquad \cos 2A = 1 - 2\sin^2 A$$
$$\Rightarrow\quad 2\cos^2 A = 1 + \cos 2A \qquad\qquad\qquad \Rightarrow\quad 2\sin^2 A = 1 - \cos 2A$$
$$\Rightarrow\quad \cos^2 A = \tfrac{1}{2}(1 + \cos 2A) \qquad\qquad\quad \Rightarrow\quad \sin^2 A = \tfrac{1}{2}(1 - \cos 2A)$$

$$\cos^2 A = \tfrac{1}{2}(1 + \cos 2A) \qquad\qquad \sin^2 A = \tfrac{1}{2}(1 - \cos 2A)$$

Example 1

Express $\sin 3A$ in terms of $\sin A$.

$$\sin 3A = \sin (2A + A)$$
$$= \sin 2A \cos A + \cos 2A \sin A$$
$$= 2\sin A \cos A \cos A + (1 - 2\sin^2 A)(\sin A)$$
$$= 2\sin A (\cos^2 A) + \sin A - 2\sin^3 A$$
$$= 2\sin A(1 - \sin^2 A) + \sin A - 2\sin^3 A$$
$$= 2\sin A - 2\sin^3 A + \sin A - 2\sin^3 A$$
$$\Rightarrow\quad \sin 3A = 3\sin A - 4\sin^3 A$$

Example 2

Given that θ is acute and that $\tan \theta = \tfrac{1}{2}$, evaluate
(i) $\sin 2\theta$ \qquad (ii) $\cos 2\theta$.

When $\tan \theta = \tfrac{1}{2}$, from the right-angled triangle shown we have:

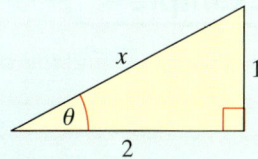

$$x^2 = 2^2 + 1^2 \quad\Rightarrow\quad x^2 = 5 \quad\Rightarrow\quad x = \sqrt{5}$$

$\Rightarrow \quad \sin \theta = \dfrac{1}{\sqrt{5}}$ and $\cos \theta = \dfrac{2}{\sqrt{5}}$

(i) $\sin 2\theta = 2 \sin \theta \cos \theta$

$\qquad = 2 \times \dfrac{1}{\sqrt{5}} \times \dfrac{2}{\sqrt{5}} = \dfrac{4}{5}$

(ii) $\cos 2\theta = \cos^2 \theta - \sin^2 \theta$

$\qquad = \left(\dfrac{2}{\sqrt{5}}\right)^2 - \left(\dfrac{1}{\sqrt{5}}\right)^2 = \dfrac{4}{5} - \dfrac{1}{5} = \dfrac{3}{5}$

The proofs of identities involving cos 2*A* often depend on selecting the appropriate formula for cos 2*A*. The choice is generally between $(2 \cos^2 A - 1)$ and $(1 - 2 \sin^2 A)$.

If we are given $1 + \cos 2A$, then to eliminate the 1 we select $(2 \cos^2 A - 1)$ for cos 2*A*. Thus $1 + \cos 2A$ becomes $1 + 2 \cos^2 A - 1 = 2 \cos^2 A$.

Example 3

Show that   (i) $\dfrac{\sin 2A}{1 + \cos 2A} = \tan A$ (ii) $\cos^4 \theta - \sin^4 \theta = \cos 2\theta$.

(i) $\dfrac{\sin 2A}{1 + \cos 2A} = \dfrac{2 \sin A \cos A}{1 + 2 \cos^2 A - 1}$

$\qquad\qquad = \dfrac{2 \sin A \cos A}{2 \cos^2 A} = \dfrac{\sin A}{\cos A} = \tan A$

(ii) $\cos^4 \theta - \sin^4 \theta = (\cos^2 \theta + \sin^2 \theta)(\cos^2 \theta - \sin^2 \theta)$ $x^4 - y^4 = (x^2 + y^2)(x^2 - y^2)$

$\qquad\qquad\qquad = (1)(\cos 2\theta)$

$\qquad\qquad\qquad = \cos 2\theta$

Expressing sin 2*A*, cos 2*A* and tan 2*A* in terms of tan *A*

When proving identities it is often useful to express sin 2*A*, cos 2*A* and tan 2*A* in terms of tan *A*.

We have already proved that $\tan 2A = \dfrac{2 \tan A}{1 - \tan^2 A}$.

On page 14 of *Formulae and Tables*, the following formulae are given:

(i) $\sin 2A = \dfrac{2 \tan A}{1 + \tan^2 A}$ (ii) $\cos 2A = \dfrac{1 - \tan^2 A}{1 + \tan^2 A}$

$$\sin 2A = \dfrac{2 \tan A}{1 + \tan^2 A} \qquad \cos 2A = \dfrac{1 - \tan^2 A}{1 + \tan^2 A} \qquad \tan 2A = \dfrac{2 \tan A}{1 - \tan^2 A}$$

Example 4

If $\cos 2\theta = \dfrac{7}{25}$, find the values of sin θ for $0° \leqslant \theta \leqslant 360°$.

$\qquad\qquad \cos 2\theta = 1 - 2 \sin^2 \theta$

$\Rightarrow \quad 1 - 2 \sin^2 \theta = \dfrac{7}{25} \quad \Rightarrow \quad 2 \sin^2 \theta = \dfrac{18}{25}$

$\qquad\qquad\qquad \Rightarrow \quad \sin^2 \theta = \dfrac{9}{25} \quad \Rightarrow \quad \sin \theta = \pm \dfrac{3}{5}$

Example 5

If $\sin 2A = \frac{3}{5}$, find the two values of $\tan A$ for $0° < A < 90°$.

Here we express $\sin 2A$ in terms of $\tan A$.

$$\sin 2A = \frac{2 \tan A}{1 + \tan^2 A}$$

$\Rightarrow \quad \frac{2 \tan A}{1 + \tan^2 A} = \frac{3}{5} \quad \Rightarrow \quad 3 + 3 \tan^2 A = 10 \tan A$

$\Rightarrow \quad 3 \tan^2 A - 10 \tan A + 3 = 0$

$\Rightarrow \quad (3 \tan A - 1)(\tan A - 3) = 0$

$\Rightarrow \quad 3 \tan A = 1 \quad$ or $\quad \tan A = 3$

$\Rightarrow \quad \tan A = \frac{1}{3} \quad$ or $\quad \tan A = 3$

Note: Since $\sin 2A = 2 \sin A \cos A$, it follows that

    (i) $\sin 4A = 2 \sin 2A \cos 2A$

    (ii) $\sin 6A = 2 \sin 3A \cos 3A$

    (iii) $\sin A = 2 \sin \frac{A}{2} \cos \frac{A}{2}$

Similarly, since $\cos 2A = 2 \cos^2 A - 1$

    (iv) $\cos 4A = 2 \cos^2 2A - 1$

    (v) $\cos A = 2 \cos^2 \frac{A}{2} - 1$

Exercise 8.3

1. If $\sin A = \frac{3}{5}$, where $0° < A < 90°$, find the value of

    (i) $\sin 2A$ (ii) $\cos 2A$ (iii) $\tan 2A$

2. If A is an acute angle and $\tan A = \frac{1}{2}$, find the value of

    (i) $\tan 2A$ (ii) $\sin 2A$.

3. From the given diagram, find the value of $\cos 2A$ without using a calculator.

4. If $\cos 2A = \frac{3}{8}$, $0° < A < 90°$, find the values of $\sin A$ and $\cos A$.

5. Given that $\sin 2A = 2 \sin A \cos A$ and $\cos 2A = \cos^2 A - \sin^2 A$, evaluate each of these without using a calculator:

    (i) $2 \sin 15° \cos 15°$ (ii) $2 \sin 75° \cos 75°$ (iii) $\cos^2 22\frac{1}{2}° - \sin^2 22\frac{1}{2}°$.

6. Simplify $\dfrac{2 \tan 22\frac{1}{2}°}{1 - \tan^2 22\frac{1}{2}°}$.

7. Prove that $\cos 3A = 4 \cos^3 A - 3 \cos A$.

8. Prove each of the following identities:

    (i) $(\sin A + \cos A)^2 = 1 + \sin 2A$
        (ii) $\dfrac{\cos 2A}{\cos A + \sin A} = \cos A - \sin A.$

9. Show that $1 - (\cos x - \sin x)^2 = \sin 2x.$

10. If $\tan A = \frac{1}{2}$, find $\tan 2A$ without using a calculator, given that A is an acute angle.

11. If $\cos A = \frac{3}{5}$, for $0 < A < 90°$, find the value of

    (i) $\sin 2A$
        (ii) $\cos 2A$

12. Prove that $\dfrac{1 - \cos 2A}{\sin 2A} = \tan A.$

13. Show that $\dfrac{2 \tan A}{1 + \tan^2 A} = \sin 2A.$

14. If $\tan 2\theta = \frac{4}{3}$, find the values of $\tan \theta$ for $0° \leqslant \theta \leqslant 180°.$

15. In the triangle XYZ, $|\angle XYZ| = 2\beta$ and $|\angle XZY| = \beta$.
    $|XY| = 3$ and $|XZ| = 5$.

    (i) Use this information to express $\sin 2\beta$ in the form

        $\dfrac{a}{b} \sin \beta$, where $a, b \in \mathbb{N}$.

    (ii) Hence express $\tan \beta$ in the form $\dfrac{\sqrt{c}}{d}$, where $c, d \in \mathbb{N}$.

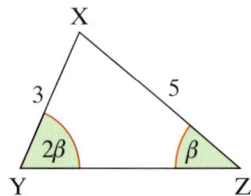

16. Two acute angles A and B are such that $\tan A = \frac{4}{3}$ and $\tan(A + B) = -1$.
    Without evaluating A or B,
    (i) show that $\tan B = 7$
    (ii) evaluate $\sin 2B$.

17. (i) Show that $\dfrac{\sin 2A}{1 + \cos 2A} = \tan A.$

    (ii) Hence, or otherwise, prove that $\tan 22\frac{1}{2}° = \sqrt{2} - 1.$

18. Given that $\cos 2A = 1 - 2\sin^2 A$ or $2\cos^2 A - 1$, express $\cos 4A$ in terms of
    (i) $\sin 2A$
        (ii) $\cos 2A$.

    Hence show that $\dfrac{1 - \cos 4A}{1 + \cos 4A} = \tan^2 2A.$

19. The lengths of the sides of a triangle are 21, 17 and 10.
    The smallest angle in the triangle is A.
    (i) Show that $\cos A = \frac{15}{17}.$
    (ii) Without evaluating A, find $\tan \frac{A}{2}.$

20. In the triangle PQR, $|\angle QRP| = 90°$ and $|RP| = h$.
    S is a point on [QR] such that $|\angle SPQ| = 2B$ and
    $|\angle RPS| = 45° - B, 0° < B < 45°.$
    (i) Show that $|SR| = h \tan (45° - B).$
    (ii) Hence, or otherwise, show that
        $|QS| = 2h \tan 2B.$

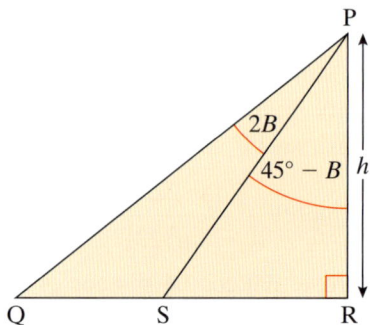

Section 8.4 Sum, difference and product formulae

Page 15 of *Formulae and Tables* contains important formulae for changing sums or differences into products. These formula are given, without proof, below.

Changing products to sums or differences

$$2 \sin A \cos B = \sin(A + B) + \sin(A - B)$$
$$2 \cos A \sin B = \sin(A + B) - \sin(A - B)$$
$$2 \cos A \cos B = \cos(A + B) + \cos(A - B)$$
$$-2 \sin A \sin B = \cos(A + B) - \cos(A - B)$$

Changing sums and differences to products

$$\sin A + \sin B = 2 \sin \frac{A + B}{2} \cos \frac{A - B}{2}$$
$$\sin A - \sin B = 2 \cos \frac{A + B}{2} \sin \frac{A - B}{2}$$
$$\cos A + \cos B = 2 \cos \frac{A + B}{2} \cos \frac{A - B}{2}$$
$$\cos A - \cos B = -2 \sin \frac{A + B}{2} \sin \frac{A - B}{2}$$

Note: When changing a sum or a difference to a product, it is advisable to have the larger angle first.

Thus $\sin 3x + \sin 5x$ should be changed to $\sin 5x + \sin 3x$.

Similarly, if we are given the product $2 \sin 2x \cos 3x$, we should change it to $2 \cos 3x \sin 2x$.

Example 1

Express as a sum or difference: (i) $2 \cos 3x \sin x$ (ii) $\cos \theta \cos 5\theta$

(i) $2 \cos 3x \sin x = \sin(3x + x) - \sin(3x - x)$
$$= \sin 4x - \sin 2x$$

(ii) $\cos \theta \cos 5\theta = \cos 5\theta \cos \theta$

Always put the bigger angle first.

$$= \tfrac{1}{2}[2 \cos 5\theta \cos \theta]$$
$$= \tfrac{1}{2}[\cos(5\theta + \theta) + \cos(5\theta - \theta)]$$
$$= \tfrac{1}{2}[\cos 6\theta + \cos 4\theta]$$

Example 2

Express as a product   (i) $\cos 5A + \cos 3A$ (ii) $\sin 3A - \sin A$

(i) $\cos 5A + \cos 3A = 2 \cos\left(\dfrac{5A + 3A}{2}\right) \cos\left(\dfrac{5A - 3A}{2}\right)$

$\qquad\qquad\qquad\qquad = 2 \cos 4A \cos A$

(ii) $\sin 3A - \sin A = 2 \cos\left(\dfrac{3A + A}{2}\right) \sin\left(\dfrac{3A - A}{2}\right)$

$\qquad\qquad\qquad\quad = 2 \cos 2A \sin A$

Example 3

Show that $\dfrac{\sin 3A - \sin 2A + \sin A}{\cos 3A + \cos A - \cos 2A} = \tan 2A.$

$\dfrac{\sin 3A - \sin 2A + \sin A}{\cos 3A + \cos A - \cos 2A} = \dfrac{(\sin 3A + \sin A) - \sin 2A}{(\cos 3A + \cos A) - \cos 2A}$

$\qquad\qquad\qquad\qquad\qquad = \dfrac{2 \sin 2A \cos A - \sin 2A}{2 \cos 2A \cos A - \cos 2A}$

$\qquad\qquad\qquad\qquad\qquad = \dfrac{\sin 2A(2 \cos A - 1)}{\cos 2A(2 \cos A - 1)} = \dfrac{\sin 2A}{\cos 2A} = \tan 2A$

Exercise 8.4

1. Express each of the following as a product:
    (i) $\sin 5x + \sin 3x$ (ii) $\sin 4x - \sin 2x$ (iii) $\cos 3x + \cos x$
    (iv) $\cos 7\theta - \cos 5\theta$ (v) $\cos 3\theta - \cos \theta$ (vi) $\sin 3\theta - \sin 7\theta$

2. Express as a product and simplify each of these:
    (i) $\cos 80° + \cos 40°$ (ii) $\sin 125° - \sin 55°$ (iii) $\cos 75° - \cos 15°$

3. Without using a calculator, show that each of the following is true:
    (i) $\sin 75° - \sin 15° = \dfrac{1}{\sqrt{2}}$ (ii) $\sin 10° + \sin 80° = \sqrt{2} \cos 35°.$

4. Express each of these as a product and give your answer in its simplest form:
    (i) $\cos(x + 45°) + \cos(x - 45°)$ (ii) $\cos(x + 60°) - \cos(x - 60°).$

5. Express each of the following as a sum or a difference:
    (i) $2 \sin 3A \cos 2A$ (ii) $2 \cos 4x \sin x$ (iii) $2 \cos 5A \cos 2A$
    (iv) $-2 \sin 6A \sin 2A$ (v) $\sin 2A \sin A$ (vi) $\sin x \cos 5x$

6. Express as a sum or difference and simplify:
    (i) $2 \sin 75° \cos 45°$ (ii) $10 \sin 67\frac{1}{2}° \sin 22\frac{1}{2}°.$

7. Show that

   (i) $2\cos(A + 45°)\sin(A - 45°) = \sin 2A - 1$

   (ii) $\dfrac{\cos 50° - \cos 70°}{\sin 70° - \sin 50°} = \sqrt{3}.$

8. Show that $\dfrac{\sin(\theta + 15°) + \sin(\theta - 15°)}{\cos(\theta + 15°) + \cos(\theta - 15°)} = \tan \theta.$

9. Show that $\dfrac{\sin 4A + \sin 2A}{2 \sin 3A} = \cos A.$

10. Show that $\dfrac{\sin 5A - \sin 3A}{\cos 5A + \cos 3A} = \tan A.$

11. Show that $2 \sin(135° + A) \sin(45° + A) = \cos 2A.$

12. Given that $\tan 3\theta = 2$, evaluate without using a calculator

$$\dfrac{\sin \theta + \sin 3\theta + \sin 5\theta}{\cos \theta + \cos 3\theta + \cos 5\theta}.$$

Section 8.5 Inverse trigonometric functions

In the given triangle $\sin x = \frac{3}{5}$.

We could also say that 'x is the angle whose sine is $\frac{3}{5}$.'

This is written as $\sin^{-1}\left(\frac{3}{5}\right) = x$.

$\sin^{-1}$ is pronounced 'arc sin'.

Again if (i) $\cos x = \dfrac{\sqrt{3}}{2}$ $\Rightarrow$ $x = \cos^{-1}\left(\dfrac{\sqrt{3}}{2}\right) = 30°$

(ii) $\tan x = 1$ $\Rightarrow$ $x = \tan^{-1}(1) = 45°.$

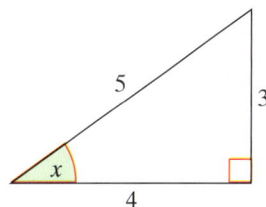

It should be clear from these two examples that $\cos^{-1}\left(\dfrac{\sqrt{3}}{2}\right)$ and $\tan^{-1}(1)$ are **angles** and that $\cos 30°$ and $\tan 45°$ are **ratios**.

Example 1

Write down the value of each of the following angles in the range $0°$ to $90°$.

(i) $\sin^{-1}\left(\dfrac{1}{2}\right)$ (ii) $\cos^{-1}\left(\dfrac{1}{\sqrt{2}}\right)$ (iii) $\tan^{-1}(\sqrt{3})$ (iv) $\cos^{-1}(0.8).$

(i) $\sin^{-1}\left(\dfrac{1}{2}\right) = 30°$

(ii) $\cos^{-1}\left(\dfrac{1}{\sqrt{2}}\right) = 45°$

(iii) $\tan^{-1}(\sqrt{3}) = 60°$

(iv) $\cos^{-1}(0.8) = 36.9°$ (by calculator)

Example 2

(i) Express $\cos(\sin^{-1} x)$ in terms of x.   (ii) Evaluate $\sin\left(2\tan^{-1}\frac{4}{3}\right)$.

(i) $\sin^{-1} x$ is the angle whose sine is x, as shown.

The third side is $\sqrt{1 - x^2}$.

$$\cos(\sin^{-1} x) = \frac{\sqrt{1 - x^2}}{1} = \sqrt{1 - x^2}$$

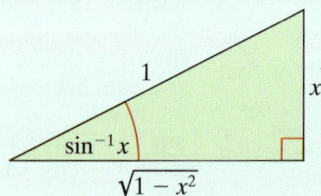

(ii) $2\tan^{-1}\left(\frac{4}{3}\right)$ is a double angle.

Let $\tan^{-1}\left(\frac{4}{3}\right) = A$.

A is shown in the given triangle.

$$\sin\left(2\tan^{-1}\frac{4}{3}\right) = \sin 2A$$
$$= 2\sin A \cos A$$
$$= 2\left(\frac{4}{5}\right)\left(\frac{3}{5}\right) = \frac{24}{25}$$

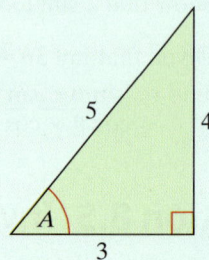

Exercise 8.5

1. Write down the value of each of these angles in the range $-90°$ to $180°$, without using a calculator:

(i) $\sin^{-1}\left(\frac{1}{\sqrt{2}}\right)$ (ii) $\cos^{-1}\left(\frac{1}{2}\right)$ (iii) $\tan^{-1}(1)$

(iv) $\cos^{-1}\left(\frac{\sqrt{3}}{2}\right)$ (v) $\sin^{-1}\left(-\frac{\sqrt{3}}{2}\right)$ (vi) $\tan^{-1}(-1)$

(vii) $\cos^{-1}\left(-\frac{1}{2}\right)$ (viii) $\tan^{-1}\left(-\frac{1}{\sqrt{3}}\right)$

2. In each of the following, draw a triangle to show that

(i) $\sin^{-1}\left(\frac{3}{5}\right) = \tan^{-1}\left(\frac{3}{4}\right)$ (ii) $\sin^{-1}\left(\frac{1}{2}\right) = \cos^{-1}\left(\frac{\sqrt{3}}{2}\right)$

(iii) $\sin^{-1}\left(\frac{5}{13}\right) = \tan^{-1}\left(\frac{5}{12}\right)$ (iv) $\tan^{-1}(x) = \sin^{-1}\left(\frac{x}{\sqrt{1 + x^2}}\right)$.

3. Simplify each of the following, expressing your answers in terms of x:

(i) $\sin(\sin^{-1} x)$ (ii) $\cos(\sin^{-1} x)$ (iii) $\sin(\tan^{-1} x)$.

4. Evaluate each of the following:

(i) $\sin\left(\cos^{-1}\frac{3}{5}\right)$ (ii) $\cos(\tan^{-1} 1)$ (iii) $\sin\left(\tan^{-1}\frac{8}{15}\right)$.

5. Evaluate

(i) $\sin\left(2 \cos^{-1} \frac{3}{5}\right)$ (ii) $\cos\left(2 \sin^{-1} \frac{5}{13}\right)$.

6. Use the formula for $\sin(A + B)$ to show that,

(i) $\sin\left[\sin^{-1}\left(\frac{5}{13}\right) + \sin^{-1}\left(\frac{4}{5}\right)\right] = \frac{63}{65}$.   (ii) $\sin\left[\sin^{-1}\frac{1}{\sqrt{5}} + \sin^{-1}\frac{1}{\sqrt{10}}\right] = \frac{1}{\sqrt{2}}$.

7. Evaluate $\tan\left(\sin^{-1}\frac{3}{5} + \sin^{-1}\frac{5}{13}\right)$.

8. Prove that $\sin\left(2 \tan^{-1}\frac{3}{4}\right) = \sin\left(\cos^{-1}\frac{7}{25}\right)$.

Revision Exercise 8 (Core)

1. Without using a calculator, find the value of $\sin 2x$ in the given diagram.

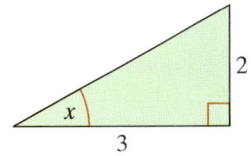

2. A and B are acute angles such that $\tan A = \frac{5}{12}$ and $\tan B = \frac{3}{4}$. Find $\cos(A - B)$ as a fraction.

3. Show that $(\cos A + \sin A)^2 = 1 + \sin 2A$.

4. If $\cos x = \frac{4}{5}$ and $0 \leqslant x \leqslant \frac{\pi}{2}$, find the value of $\tan 2x$.

5. Prove that $\sin^2 A + \cos^2 A = 1$.

6. A is an acute angle such that $\tan A = \frac{8}{15}$. Without evaluating A, find

(i) $\cos A$ (ii) $\sin 2A$.

7. (i) Express $\sin 75° \cos 15° - \cos 75° \sin 15°$ as a function of a compound angle and hence simplify.

(ii) Prove that $2 + 2 \cos 2x = 4 \cos^2 x$.

8. If $\tan 75° = a + b\sqrt{3}$, find the values of a and b, where $a, b \in \mathbb{Z}$.

9. (i) Show that $\tan \theta \sin \theta + \cos \theta = \sec \theta$.

(ii) If θ is an acute angle and $\cos \theta = \frac{5}{13}$, find the value of $\sin 2\theta$.

10. (i) Find the value of k for which $\sin 75° - \sin 15° = \frac{1}{\sqrt{k}}$, $k \in \mathbb{N}$.

(ii) If $A = \sin^{-1}\frac{1}{2}$, evaluate $\tan 2A$.

Revision Exercise 8 (Advanced)

1. (i) Using $\cos 2A = \cos^2 A - \sin^2 A$, or otherwise, prove that
$$\cos^2 A = \frac{1}{2}(1 + \cos 2A).$$

(ii) Write down the exact value of
$$\sin 40° \cos 20° + \cos 40° \sin 20°.$$

2. (i) If θ is an acute angle and $\sin \theta = \frac{4}{5}$, find the value of $\cos 2\theta$.

(ii) Show that $2 \cos^2 A - \cos 2A - 1 = 0$.

3. (i) Write $2 \sin 4\theta \cos 2\theta$ as a sum or difference of two trigonometric functions.

(ii) Show that $(\cos x + \sin x)^2 + (\cos x - \sin x)^2$ simplifies to a constant and write down its value.

4. (i) Prove that $\cos (45° + \theta) - (\cos 45° - \theta) = -\sqrt{2} \sin \theta$

(ii) Prove that $\dfrac{1}{\cos \theta} - \cos \theta = \tan \theta \sin \theta$

5. (i) By using a double angle formula, evaluate in surd form
$$\cos^2 15° - \sin^2 15.$$

(ii) Prove that $\dfrac{\sin 3\theta}{\sin \theta} - \dfrac{\cos 3\theta}{\cos \theta} = 2.$

6. (i) Show that $\tan 15° = 2 - \sqrt{3}$.

(ii) Prove that $\dfrac{\cos 5\theta - \cos 3\theta}{\sin 4\theta} = -2 \sin \theta.$

7. Prove that $\tan (A + B) = \dfrac{\tan A + \tan B}{1 - \tan A \tan B}.$

8. If $A + B = \dfrac{\pi}{4}$, write $\tan A$ in terms of $\tan B$.

Hence prove that $(1 + \tan A)(1 + \tan B) = 2$.

9. Find, in surd form, the value of $\sin 105° - \sin 15°$ without using a calculator.

10. QRST is a vertical wall of height h on level ground.
P is a point on the ground in front of the wall.
The angle of elevation of R from P is θ and the
angle of elevation of S from P is 2θ.
$|PQ| = 3|PT|$.
Find θ.

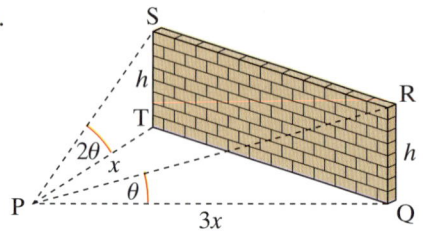

Revision Exercise 8 (Extended-Response Questions)

1. Given that $\cos(A + B) = \cos A \cos B - \sin A \sin B$, prove that
$$\cos 2x = 1 - 2 \sin^2 x.$$
Hence, by writing $\sin 3x$ as $\sin(2x + x)$, prove that
$$\sin 3x = 3 \sin x - 4 \sin^3 x.$$

2. Show that $(\cos A + \cos B)^2 + (\sin A + \sin B)^2 = 2 + 2 \cos (A - B).$

3. The diagram shows a rectangle ABCD inside a semicircle, centre O, and radius 5 cm, such that $|\angle BOA| = |\angle COD| = \theta$.

   (i) Show that the perimeter, p cm, of the rectangle is given by
   $$p = 20 \cos \theta + 10 \sin \theta.$$

   (ii) Find the value of k for which the area of the rectangle is $k \sin 2\theta \, \text{cm}^2$.

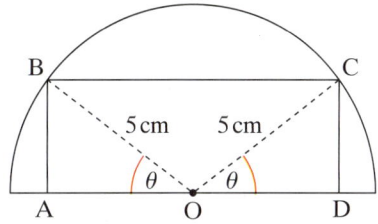

4. (i) Using the formula $\cos(A + B) = \cos A \cos B - \sin A \sin B$, derive a formula for $\cos(A - B)$.

   (ii) Hence prove that $\sin(A + B) = \sin A \cos B + \cos A \sin B$.

   (iii) Using page 13 of the formulae and tables booklet write down values for
   (a) $\cos (30°)$ (b) $\sin (30°)$

   (iv) Given that $\sin(A - 30°) = 3 \cos A$ for $0° < A < 360°$ show that $\tan A = \dfrac{7}{\sqrt{3}}$.

5. (i) Show that $\sqrt{2 \sin^2 \theta + 6 \cos^2 \theta - 2} = 2 \cos \theta$, for all θ.

   (ii) $x = 0°$ and $x = 60°$ are two solutions of the equation $a \sin^2 2x + \cos 2x - b = 0$, where $a, b \in \mathbb{N}$.
   Find the value of a and the value of b.

6. In the triangle ABC, $|AC| = 3$ cm, $|BC| = 2$ cm, $|\angle BAC| = \theta$ and $|\angle ABC| = 2\theta$.
   Calculate the value of θ correct to the nearest tenth of a degree.

   Hence find the size of the angle ACB and, without further calculation, explain why the length of [AB] is greater than 2 cm.

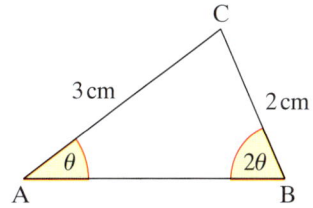

7. (i) Given that $\sin 2\theta = 1$ and that θ is acute, find the exact value of
   (a) $\sin \theta$ (b) $\tan \theta$

   (ii) Show that $\dfrac{\sin 4\theta \, (1 - \cos 2\theta)}{\cos 2\theta(1 - \cos 4\theta)} = \tan \theta$.

8. In the given diagram
   $|AC| = |CB| = |DC| = |EC| = x$,
   $|\angle ACB| = 4\theta$ and $|\angle DCE| = 2\theta$.

   (i) If area of $\triangle ACB$ = area of $\triangle DCE$, show that $\theta = 30°$.

   (ii) Using $\theta = 30°$, find the value of x, given that $|AB|^2 + |DE|^2 = 24$.
   Give your answer in surd form.

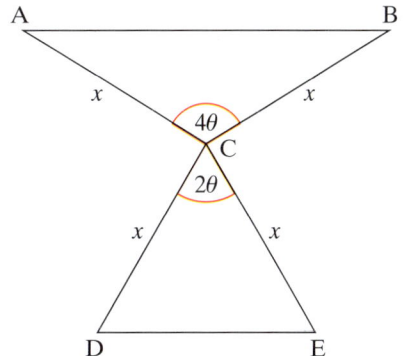

9. In the given diagram, C is the centre of a circle of radius 2 cm.
    ADBC is a sector of the circle, with angle 2θ radians.
    Find (i) the area of the sector ADBC in terms of θ.
         (ii) the area of the triangle ABC in terms of $\sin 2\theta$.

    If the area of $\triangle$ABC is three-quarters the area of the sector
    ADBC, show that
    $$2 \sin 2\theta = 3\theta.$$
    If the area of $\triangle$ABC is $\sqrt{3}$ cm^2, find θ in radians.

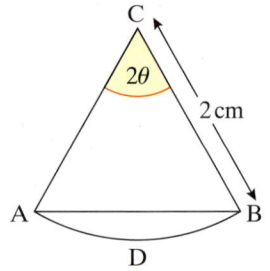

10. [AB] is the diameter of a semicircle of centre O and radius
     length r.
     [AC] is a chord such that $|\angle CAB| = \alpha$, where α is in radians.

     (i) Find $|AC|$ in terms of r and α.
     (ii) [AC] bisects the area of the semicircular region.

        Show that $2\alpha + \sin 2\alpha = \dfrac{\pi}{2}$.

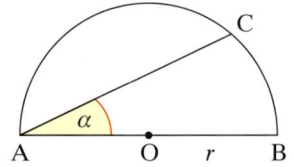

Sequences –Series – Patterns

chapter 9

Key words

number sequence   arithmetic sequence   series   sigma (Σ)

geometric sequence   exponential sequence   geometric series   recurring decimal

finite difference   composite function   quadratic function

Section 9.1 Sequences

A **number sequence** is a set of numbers written down in a definite order.
In most cases all the terms of the sequence are connected by a rule.

Examine the following sequences and state in words the rule that connects one term to
the next. Hence find the next two terms of each sequence.

(i) 1, 3, 5, 7, ...

(ii) 2, 5, 8, 11, ...

(iii) $\frac{1}{3}, \frac{1}{6}, \frac{1}{12}, \frac{1}{24}, \ldots$

(iv) 1, 2, 4, 8, ...

(v) $1^3, 2^3, 3^3, 4^3, \ldots$

(vi) $\frac{1}{2}, \frac{2}{3}, \frac{3}{4}, \frac{4}{5}, \ldots$

(vii) 1, 4, 9, 16, ...

(viii) 1, 2, 6, 24, 120, ...

(ix) $1, \frac{2}{3}, \frac{3}{9}, \frac{4}{27}, \ldots$

(x) 4, 2, 0, -2, ...

(xi) 1, -1, 1, -1, ...

(xii) $1, -\frac{1}{2}, \frac{1}{4}, -\frac{1}{8}, \ldots$

The most basic number sequence is the set of natural numbers, N = {1, 2, 3, 4, ... n}; all other
sequences can be compared to it.

Consider the natural numbers   1,   2,   3,   4,   5, ... n

and compare them with the sequence $\rightarrow$ 1,   3,   5,   7,   9, ... $2n - 1$

$T_1, T_2, T_3, T_4, T_5, \ldots\ldots T_n$

The first term is T_1 ; the second term is T_2.

T_n is called the nth term and it gives us the rule needed to find any term of the sequence.

$T_n = 2n - 1$

Let $n = 1$, $T_1 = 2(1) - 1 = 1$

Let $n = 2$, $T_2 = 2(2) - 1 = 3$

Let $n = 3$, $T_3 = 2(3) - 1 = 5$

Let $n = 4$, $T_4 = 2(4) - 1 = 7$ etc.

Hence the rule $T_n = 2n - 1$ produces
the sequence 1, 3, 5, 7, ...

Sequences are often derived from patterns created by different processes. In biology the
arrangement of leaves on a stem can be described by the 'Fibonacci sequence' 0, 1, 1, 2, 3, 5, 8, 13, ...

Sequences are used in computational software. In physics they occur in the study of waves; sequence patterns control robot movements and are used extensively in digital technology.

Consider the following patterns and describe how to add two more elements to each pattern.

(i) 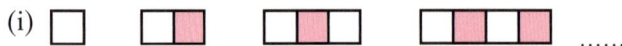 ......

(ii) 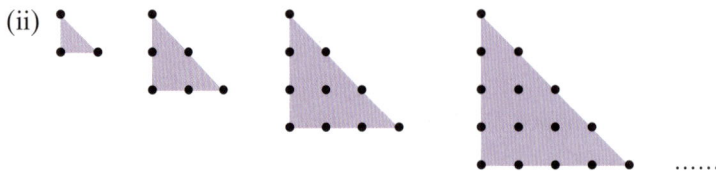 ......

(iii) 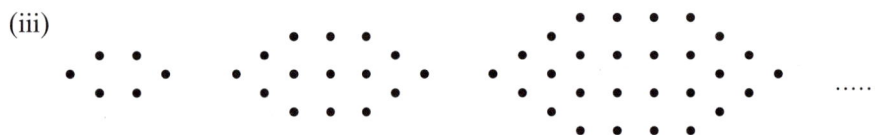 ......

Example 1

Write down the first four terms of each of the following sequences:

(i) $T_n = n^2 + n$ (ii) $T_n = 2^n - 3n$

(i) $T_n = n^2 + n$

Let $n = 1$, $T_1 = 1^2 + 1 = 2$
$n = 2$, $T_2 = 2^2 + 2 = 6$
$n = 3$, $T_3 = 3^2 + 3 = 12$
$n = 4$, $T_4 = 4^2 + 4 = 20$

The sequence is $2, 6, 12, 20$.

(ii) $T_n = 2^n - 3n$

Let $n = 1$, $T_1 = 2^1 - 3(1) = -1$
$n = 2$, $T_2 = 2^2 - 3(2) = -2$
$n = 3$, $T_3 = 2^3 - 3(3) = -1$
$n = 4$, $T_4 = 2^4 - 3(4) = 4$

The sequence is $-1, -2, -1, 4$.

Example 2

The following rectangular patterns are made from two sets of coloured tiles.

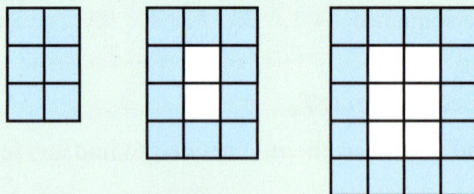

(i) Draw the next two patterns of tiles.
(ii) Write a number sequence for the blue tiles used in each of these patterns.
(iii) Write a number sequence for the total number of tiles used in each of these patterns.
(iv) Write a number sequence for the white tiles used in each of these patterns.
(v) Write out the next 3 terms in each sequence found in (ii), (iii), (iv).

(i)

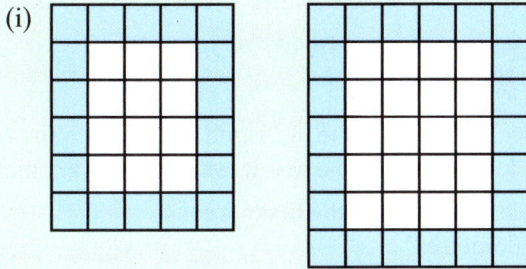

(ii) 6, 10, 14, 18, 22 is the sequence for the blue tiles

(iii) 6, 12, 20, 30, 42 is the sequence for the total number of tiles

(iv) 0, 2, 6, 12, 20 is the sequence for the white tiles.

(v) (ii) We notice that 6, 10, 14, 18, 22, ... each term increases by 4.

⇒ the next three terms are $\quad$ 22 + 4 = 26 $\quad$⎤
$\qquad\qquad\qquad\qquad\qquad$ 26 + 4 = 30 $\quad$⎬ 26, 30, 34
$\qquad\qquad\qquad\qquad\qquad$ 30 + 4 = 34 $\quad$⎦

(iii) 6, 12, 20, 30, 42, ... each term increases according to the pattern 6, 8, 10, 12 ..., i.e. the gap between terms is increasing by 2.

⇒ the next three terms are $\quad$ 42 + 14 = 56 $\quad$⎤
$\qquad\qquad\qquad\qquad\qquad$ 56 + 16 = 72 $\quad$⎬ 56, 72, 90
$\qquad\qquad\qquad\qquad\qquad$ 72 + 18 = 90 $\quad$⎦

(iv) The white tile sequence is 0, 2, 6, 12, 20, ... and has a rectangular property $(0 \times 1), (1 \times 2), (2 \times 3), (3 \times 4), (4 \times 5), ...$

⇒ the next three terms are $\quad (5 \times 6), (6 \times 7), (7 \times 8)$
$\qquad\qquad\qquad\qquad\qquad\quad$ = 30 $\qquad$ 42 $\qquad$ 56

[Note: This sequence could also be found by subtracting sequence (ii) from sequence (iii)]

Exercise 9.1

1. Write down the next three terms of each of the following sequences:

(i) 6, 12, 18, 24, ...

(ii) 7, 12, 17, 22, ...

(iii) 4.7, 5.9, 7.1, 8.3, ...

(iv) 2, −1, −4, −7, ...

(v) 2, 3, 6, 11, 18, 27, ...

(vi) 78, 70, 62, 54, ...

(vii) 10, 5, 0, −5, −10, ...

(viii) −64, −55, −46, −37, ...

(ix) 2, 6, 18, ...

(x) 2, 6, 12, 20, ...

(xi) $\frac{3}{4}, \frac{1}{4}, -\frac{1}{4}$

(xii) 1, 2, 4, 7, 11, ...

(xiii) 0, 3, 8, 15, 24, ...

(xiv) 3, −6, 12, −24, ...

(xv) $\frac{1}{2}, \frac{1}{6}, \frac{1}{12}, \frac{1}{20}, ...$

2. Find the first four terms of the following sequences, given the nth term (T_n) in each case.

(i) $T_n = 4n - 2$

(ii) $T_n = (n + 1)^2$

(iii) $T_n = n^2 - 2n$

(iv) $T_n = (n + 3)(n + 1)$

(v) $T_n = n^3 - 1$

(vi) $T_n = \dfrac{n}{n + 2}$

(vii) $T_n = 2^n$

(viii) $T_n = (-3)^n$

(ix) $T_n = n.2^n$

3. A spider is climbing up a wall. It crawled 5 cm in the first minute. Every minute after the first, it crawled 4 cm further than the previous minute.

   (i) Write a sequence to show how far the spider crawled every minute.
   (ii) How far did the spider crawl in the fifth minute?

4. Joan was training for a marathon race. Each week she increased the distance she ran in the previous week by 1, 2, 3, 4, 5, … kilometres. In the first week, she ran 1 kilometre.

   (i) Write down how far she ran each week during the first 6 weeks.
   (ii) In which week did she run 29 kilometres?

5. If $T_n = 4n - 3$, find T_1, T_5, T_{10}.

6. If $T_n = (-2)^{n+1}$, find T_1, T_6, T_{11}.

7. By inspection, draw the next three patterns of each of the following sequences. Write a number sequence for each set of patterns.

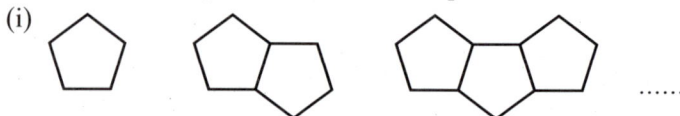

   (i)

   (ii)

   (iii)

8. Match each nth term (T_n) with one of the sequences given:

   (i) $T_n = 4n - 2$ A: 2, 4, 8, 16, …
   (ii) $T_n = 2n^2$ B: 2, 8, 18, 32, …
   (iii) $T_n = n(n + 1)$ C: 2, 6, 10, 14, …
   (iv) $T_n = 2^n$ D: 2, 6, 12, 20, …

9. Given the set of natural numbers, N = 1, 2, 3, 4, 5, … n. By inspection, find the nth term (T_n) of each of the following sequences:

   (i) 5, 6, 7, 8, 9, …   (vi) −1, 1, −1, 1, −1, …
   (ii) 2, 4, 6, 8, 10, …   (vii) 1, 5, 9, 13, 17, …
   (iii) 2, 5, 8, 11, 14, …   (viii) 1, $\frac{1}{2}$, $\frac{1}{3}$, $\frac{1}{4}$, $\frac{1}{5}$, …
   (iv) 1, 4, 9, 16, 25, …   (ix) $\frac{2}{3}$, $\frac{3}{4}$, $\frac{4}{5}$, $\frac{5}{6}$, $\frac{6}{7}$, …
   (v) 2, 5, 10, 17, 26, …   (x) (2×3), (3×4), (4×5), (5×6), …

10. The first eight terms of the Fibonacci sequence are given below. Describe in words how the sequence is formed and hence write out the next four terms of the sequence.

    0, 1, 1, 2, 3, 5, 8, 13, 21, … .

11. Shown opposite are the first 5 rows of 'Pascal's triangle'.

Copy these 5 rows and, by finding the pattern, continue 'Pascal's triangle' up to row 8.

By examining the triangle, find the nth term, T_n, for

Row 1			1		
Row 2		1		1	
Row 3		1	2	1	
Row 4	1	3	3	1	
Row 5	1	4	6	4	1

  (i) the sequence formed by the second numbers in each row

  (ii) the sequence of numbers produced by the third numbers in each row

 (iii) the sequence given by the sum of the numbers in each row

 (iv) the sequence created by adding the second and third numbers in each row.

Section 9.2 Arithmetic sequences

A sequence in which each term changes by the same fixed amount is called an **arithmetic sequence**.

For example,

$$\overset{+4\quad+4\quad+4}{3,\quad 7,\quad 11,\quad 15, \ldots} \text{ each term increases by 4.}$$

$$\overset{-2\quad-2\quad-2}{3,\quad 1,\quad -1, -3, \ldots} \text{ each term decreases by 2.}$$

If we let the first term be $a\ (= T_1)$, and the difference between consecutive terms be d (called the common difference), then every arithmetic sequence can be represented by

$$\overset{+d\qquad\quad +d\qquad\quad +d}{T_1,\qquad T_2,\qquad T_3,\qquad T_4 \qquad \ldots \qquad T_n}$$
$$a,\qquad a+d\quad a+2d,\quad a+3d,\quad \ldots\quad a+(n-1)d$$

For the sequence: $3, 7, 11, 15, \ldots$

$$\left.\begin{array}{l} a = 3 \\ d = 7 - 3 = 4 \end{array}\right\} \qquad \begin{array}{l} T_n = a + (n-1)d \\ \quad = 3 + (n-1)4 \\ \quad = 3 + 4n - 4 \\ T_n = 4n - 1. \end{array}$$

> In every arithmetic sequence,
> $$T_1 = a$$
> $$T_2 - T_1 = d$$
> $$T_n - T_{n-1} = d$$
> $$T_n = a + (n-1)d$$

Example 1

Find the nth term (T_n) of the arithmetic sequence:

$$-2,\quad 3,\quad 8,\quad 13, \ldots$$

and hence find (i) T_{20} (ii) T_{21} (iii) $T_{21} - T_{20}$.

$$\left.\begin{array}{l} a = -2 \\ d = 3 - (-2) = 5 \\ (\text{also, } d = 8 - 3 = 5) \end{array}\right\} \qquad \begin{array}{l} T_n = a + (n-1)d \\ T_n = -2 + (n-1)5 \\ \quad = -2 + 5n - 5 \\ T_n = 5n - 7 \end{array}$$

$$\therefore\ \ T_{20} = 5(20) - 7 \quad \text{and} \quad T_{21} = 5(21) - 7$$
$$\qquad\quad = 93 \qquad\qquad\qquad\qquad = 98$$
$$\Rightarrow\ \ T_{21} - T_{20} = 98 - 93 = 5\ (=d).$$

The sequence $3, 1, -1, -3, \ldots$ has an infinite number of terms.

The sequence $3, 1, -1, -3, \ldots -35$ has a finite number of terms.

If we are given $T_n = -35$, we can find the number of terms (n) in the sequence if we know the formula for T_n.

Example 2

Find the number of terms in the sequence
$$1, \quad -3, \quad -7, \quad -11, \quad \ldots \ldots \quad -251.$$

In this sequence, $\left.\begin{array}{l} a = 1 \\ d = -3 - 1 = -4 \\ T_n = -251 \end{array}\right\}$

$T_n = a + (n - 1)d$

$-251 = 1 + (n - 1)(-4)$

$-251 = 1 - 4n + 4$

$4n = 256$

$n = \frac{256}{4} = 64$

There are 64 terms in this sequence.

Example 3

In an arithmetic sequence, $T_4 = 6$ and $3T_2 = T_{10}$, find the values of a and d and hence write out the first 6 terms of the sequence.

$T_n = a + (n - 1)d$

$T_4 = a + (4 - 1)d = a + 3d$

$T_2 = a + (2 - 1)d = a + d$

$T_{10} = a + (10 - 1)d = a + 9d$

$\begin{array}{ll} \qquad\quad T_4 = 6 \qquad \text{and} & \qquad 3T_2 = T_{10} \\ \Rightarrow \quad a + 3d = 6 & \qquad 3(a + d) = a + 9d \\ & \qquad 3a + 3d = a + 9d \\ & \qquad 2a - 6d = 0 \\ & \Rightarrow \quad a - 3d = 0 \end{array}$

Using simultaneous equations,

$\begin{array}{l} a - 3d = 0 \\ \underline{a + 3d = 6} \\ 2a \qquad = 6 \text{ ... adding both lines} \\ \qquad a = 3 \end{array}$

Also, $\quad a - 3d = 0$

$3 - 3d = 0$

$-3d = -3$

$d = \left(\dfrac{-3}{-3}\right) = 1$

The sequence is $3, 4, 5, 6, 7, 8, \ldots$

❯ Given an arithmetic sequence $T_1, T_2, T_3, T_4, T_5, \ldots\ldots T_n,$

$T_3 - T_2 = T_4 - T_3 = T_5 - T_4 =$ the common difference (d).

In general terms:

$T_{n+1} - T_n = d$ (the common difference).

A corollary to this is as follows:

To prove that a sequence is arithmetic, we must show that $T_{n+1} - T_n$ is a constant.

❯ Also, if $T_{n+1} - T_n > 0$, then the sequence is increasing

if $T_{n+1} - T_n < 0$, then the sequence is decreasing.

Note, to find T_{n+1}, substitute $(n + 1)$ for n in T_n.

If $T_n = 3n + 1$,

$T_{n+1} = 3(n + 1) + 1 = 3n + 4.$

Example 4

If $p + 2, 2p + 3$ and $5p - 2$ are three consecutive terms of an arithmetic sequence, find the value of $p, p \in R$.

Because we have three consecutive terms of an arithmetic sequence,

$$\Rightarrow \quad (2p + 3) - (p + 2) = (5p - 2) - (2p + 3)$$
$$2p + 3 - p - 2 = 5p - 2 - 2p - 3$$
$$p + 1 = 3p - 5$$
$$-2p = -6$$
$$p = \left(\frac{-6}{-2}\right) = 3.$$

Note: The three terms of the sequence are $5, 9, 13$.

Example 5

Given (i) $T_n = \dfrac{n + 1}{2}$

(ii) $T_n = \dfrac{2}{n + 1}$, determine whether

(a) the sequence is arithmetic or not

(b) the sequence is increasing or decreasing.

(i)
$$T_n = \frac{n+1}{2}$$

$$T_{n+1} = \frac{(n+1)+1}{2}$$

$$= \frac{n+2}{2}$$

$$T_{n+1} - T_n = \frac{n+2}{2} - \frac{n+1}{2}$$

$$= \frac{\cancel{n}+2-\cancel{n}-1}{2}$$

$$T_{n+1} - T_n = \frac{1}{2}$$

∴ $T_{n+1} - T_n$ is a constant

∴ T_n is an arithmetic sequence

Also, since $T_{n+1} - T_n = \frac{1}{2}$,

i.e. > 0,

⇒ T_n is an increasing sequence.

(ii)
$$T_n = \frac{2}{n+1}$$

$$T_{n+1} = \frac{2}{(n+1)+1} = \frac{2}{n+2}$$

$$T_{n+1} - T_n = \frac{2}{n+2} - \frac{2}{n+1}$$

$$= \frac{2(n+1) - 2(n+2)}{(n+2)(n+1)}$$

$$= \frac{2\cancel{n} + 2 - 2\cancel{n} - 4}{(n+2)(n+1)}$$

$$T_{n+1} - T_n = \frac{-2}{(n+2)(n+1)}$$

≠ constant … since the value depends on n.

∴ T_n is not arithmetic

Also,

$$T_{n+1} - T_n = \frac{-2}{(n+2)(n+1)} < 0.$$

Since $n \in N$ and is always positive,
∴ T_n is a decreasing sequence.

Exercise 9.2

1. Find T_n, the nth term of the following arithmetic sequences.
   Hence find T_{22} for each sequence.

   (i) 8, 13, 18, 23, ...   (ii) 16, 36, 56, 76, ...   (iii) 10, 7, 4, 1, ...

2. The nth term of an arithmetic sequence is given by $T_n = 5n - 2$.
   Write down the first four terms.

3. Find the number of terms in each of the following arithmetic sequences:

   (i) $-5, -1, 3, 7, \ldots\ldots 75$ (ii) $2, 5, 8, 11, \ldots\ldots 59$ (iii) $-\frac{3}{2}, -1, -\frac{1}{2}, 0, \ldots\ldots 14.$

4. In an arithmetic sequence, $T_1 = 4$ and $T_7 = 22$. Using simultaneous equations, find

   (i) the values of a and d (ii) the first five terms of the sequence   (iii) T_{20}.

5. Niamh made wall hangings using the following designs:

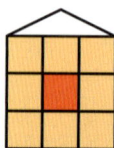      

Design 1   Design 2   Design 3

    (i) How many red and orange tiles will she need for design 8?

    (ii) Will any of her designs need 38 tiles? Explain your answer.

6. In an arithmetic sequence, $T_{13} = 27$ and $T_7 = 3T_2$. Find expressions in terms of n for T_{13}, T_7 and T_2 and hence find the values of a and d.
Write down the first six terms of the sequence.

7. (i) If $2k + 2, 5k - 3$ and $6k$ are three consecutive terms of an arithmetic sequence, find the value of $k, k \in Z$.

    (ii) Given that $4p, -3 - p$ and $5p + 16$ are three consecutive terms of an arithmetic sequence, find the value of $p, p \in Z$.

8.

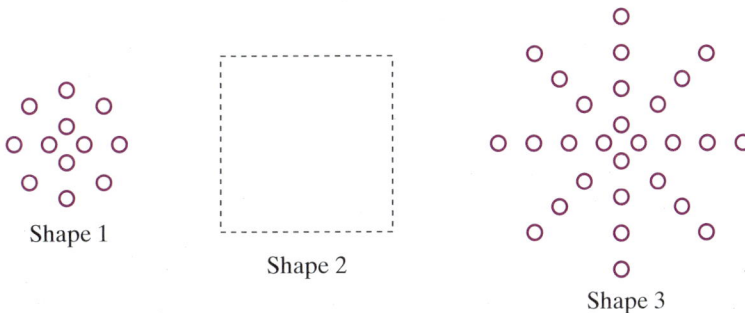

Shape 1

Shape 2

Shape 3

Three shapes were drawn on a wall.
The second shape was removed accidentally. Given that the shapes were drawn in arithmetic sequence, draw shape 2.

    (i) Write a number sequence for the number of circles used in each shape and hence find T_n for the sequence.

    (ii) How many circles are needed for shape 15?

    (iii) Which shape requires 164 circles?

9. The nth term of a sequence is given by $T_n = 4n - 2$.
Verify that the sequence is arithmetic.

10. If $T_n = n(n + 2)$ for a given sequence, verify that the sequence is not arithmetic.

11. Continue the following pattern by adding two more shapes.

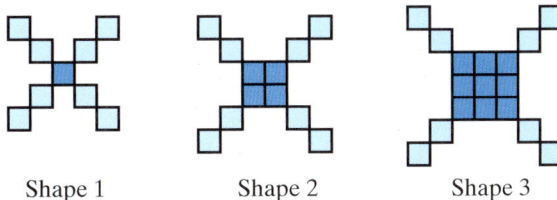

Shape 1   Shape 2   Shape 3

    (i) How many light-coloured tiles will be needed for shape 7?

    (ii) How many dark-coloured tiles will be needed for shape 7?

    (iii) By inspection, write down an expression for T_n, the number of tiles needed for the nth shape.

    (iv) Prove that the sequence generated is not arithmetic.

12. Sandrine made the following hexagon patterns with matchsticks.

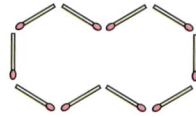 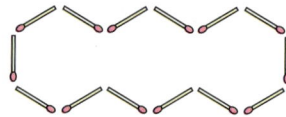

1 hexagon   2 "hexagons"   3 "hexagons"

She hoped to continue this pattern and find an expression for T_n.
Copy and complete the following table.

Number of "hexagons"	1	2	3	4	...	...	10	...	( )	...	...	...	30
Perimeter		6	10	( )	( )	...	...	( )	...	82	...	...	...	( )

(i) Having finished a number of "hexagons", Sandrine counted 87 matchsticks left over. Has she enough to complete other designs with no matchsticks left over? Explain your answer.

(ii) Prove that the sequence formed by the number of sticks in the shapes generates an arithmetic sequence.

(iii) Sandrine then decided to change her design to create a stacked hexagon pattern, removing the matchsticks in the centre.

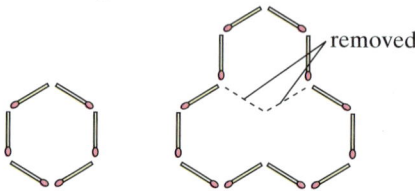

removed

How many completed levels could she make with 122 matchsticks, and how many matchsticks would be left over?

13. After knee surgery, your trainer changes your jogging programme slowly. He suggests jogging for 12 minutes each day for the first week. Each week thereafter, he suggests that you increase that time by 6 minutes a day.
In which week will you be jogging 60 minutes a day?

Section 9.3 Arithmetic series ————————————————

When the terms of a sequence are added, a **series** is formed.

$T_1, T_2, T_3, T_4, \ldots T_n$ is a sequence ;   e.g. $3, 6, 9, 12, \ldots$

$T_1 + T_2 + T_3 + T_4, \ldots + T_n$ is a series ;   e.g. $3 + 6 + 9 + 12 + \ldots$

We use S_n to represent the sum of n terms of a series,

i.e. $S_n = T_1 + T_2 + T_3 + T_4 + \ldots T_n$

To find an expression for S_n, we note that in an arithmetic sequence,

$T_n = a + (n - 1)d$ (where $a = T_1$, the first term, and d = the common difference)

$\Rightarrow$ $T_{n-1} = a + [(n - 1) - 1]d$
$= a + (n - 2)d$
$T_3 = a + 2d$
$T_2 = a + d$
$T_1 = a$

Hence,	$S_n =$	T_1	T_2	T_3	$... T_{n-1}$	T_n
$\Rightarrow$	$S_n =$	a	$+ a + d$	$+ a + 2d$	$.... + a + (n-2)d$	$+ a + (n-1)d$
Also,	$S_n =$	$a + (n-1)d$	$+ a + (n-2)d$	$a + (n-3)d$	$... + a + d$	$+ a$ (reversing the order)
$\Rightarrow$	$2S_n =$	$2a + (n-1)d$	$+ 2a + (n-1)d$	$2a + (n-1)d$	$.... + 2a + (n-1)d$	$+ 2a + (n-1)d$

$\Rightarrow$ $2S_n = n[2a + (n-1)]d$ ... since there are n identical terms in the sum.

$\Rightarrow$ $S_n = \frac{n}{2}[2a + (n-1)]d$ ... where a is the first term, d is the common difference, n is the number of terms.

Example 1

Find the sum of the series $4 + 11 + 18 + 25 + ... + 144$.

Examining the series, we find: $a = 4$
$$d = 11 - 4 = 7$$

To find n, the number of terms up to the term 144, we use

$T_n = a + (n-1)d$
$144 = 4 + (n-1)7 = 4 + 7n - 7$
$144 = 7n - 3$
$7n = 147$
$n = \left(\frac{147}{7}\right) = 21$ ... i.e. there are 21 terms in this sequence.

$\therefore \quad S_n = \frac{n}{2}\{2a + (n-1)d\}$

$S_{21} = \frac{21}{2}\{2(4) + (21-1)7\}$

$S_{21} = 1554.$

Example 2

To celebrate the birth of his niece, an uncle offers to open a savings account with a deposit of €50. He also offers to every year add €10 more than he did the previous year until his niece is 21 years of age.
(i) Find an expression for S_n, the sum of money on deposit after n years.
(ii) Find S_{21}, the total saved after 21 years.

$a = $€$50$
$d = $€$10$

$S_n = \frac{n}{2}\{2a + (n-1)d\}$

$= \frac{n}{2}\{2(50) + (n-1)10\}$

$= \frac{n}{2}\{100 + 10n - 10)\}$

$\Rightarrow \quad S_n = \frac{n}{2}\{10n + 90\}$

$S_{21} = \frac{21}{2}\{10(21) + 90\} = $€$3150$

We note that
$$S_1 = T_1$$
$$S_2 = T_1 + T_2$$
$$S_3 = T_1 + T_2 + T_3 \text{ etc.}$$
$$\therefore \quad S_3 - S_2 = \qquad T_3$$

Generally,
$$S_n - S_{n-1} = T_n$$

Given S_n to find T_n :
$$S_n - S_{n-1} = T_n$$

Example 3

Given $S_n = n^2 - 4n$, find an expression for T_n and hence determine if the sequence is arithmetic.

$$S_n = n^2 - 4n$$

$$S_{n-1} = (n-1)^2 - 4(n-1) \quad \text{... replace } n \text{ with } n-1$$
$$= n^2 - 2n + 1 - 4n + 4$$
$$\Rightarrow \quad S_{n-1} = n^2 - 6n + 5$$

$$T_n = S_n - S_{n-1} = n^2 - 4n - (n^2 - 6n + 5)$$
$$= n^2 - 4n - n^2 + 6n - 5.$$
$$T_n = 2n - 5$$

If a sequence is arithmetic, $T_n - T_{n-1}$ must be a constant.
$$\Rightarrow \quad T_n - T_{n-1} = 2n - 5 - [2(n-1) - 5]$$
$$= 2n - 5 - (2n - 7)$$
$$= 2n - 5 - 2n + 7$$
$$= 2 \text{ , i.e. a constant.}$$

Therefore the sequence is arithmetic.

Example 4

A lighting company is making a sequence of light panels with the number of bulbs per panel in arithmetic sequence.

For the first 10 panels, 165 bulbs were used.

If the third panel is as shown in the diagram, find a, the first term of the sequence, and d, the common difference.

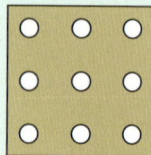

3rd panel (9 bulbs)

Hence draw a diagram of the first four panels.

$T_n = a + (n - 1)d$ Also, $S_n = \frac{n}{2}\{2a + (n - 1)d\}$

$T_3 = a + (3 - 1)d$

$T_3 = a + 2d = 9$ ..... we know that $S_n = 165$ when $n = 10$

$$\Rightarrow \quad S_{10} = \frac{10}{2}\{2a + (10 - 1)d\}$$

$$S_{10} = 10a + 45d = 165.$$

$$a + 2d = 9$$
$$\Rightarrow \quad 10a + 20d = 90$$
$$\text{and} \quad 10a + 45d = 165$$
$$\overline{ -25d = -75} \text{ ... subtracting}$$

$$\Rightarrow \quad d = \left(\frac{-75}{-25}\right) = 3$$

If $d = 3$, then $a + 2(3) = 9$

$$\Rightarrow \quad a \quad = 3$$

The sequence of bulbs in the panels is 3, 6, 9, 12.

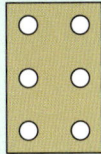

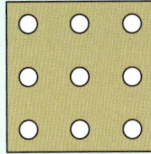

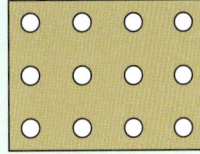

Sigma (Σ) notation

An efficient way of representing a series is to use the sigma notation.

$$S_n = T_1 + T_2 + T_3 + T_4 + ... T_n$$

$$= \sum_{r=1}^{n} T_r \text{ which reads as the sum of all the values of } T_r \text{ as } r \text{ changes from 1 to } n.$$

$$\sum_{r=1}^{6} (2r + 1) = 3 + 5 + 7 + 9 + 11 + 13 \ (n = 6 \text{ terms})$$

$$\sum_{r=2}^{5} \frac{r^2}{3} = \frac{4}{3} + \frac{9}{3} + \frac{16}{3} + \frac{25}{3} \ (n = 4 \text{ terms})$$

$$\sum_{r=0}^{4} r(r + 1) = 0(0 + 1) + 1(1 + 1) + 2(2 + 1) + 3(3 + 1) + 4(4 + 1)$$
$$= \quad 0 \quad + \quad 2 \quad + \quad 6 \quad + \quad 12 \quad + \quad 20 \quad (n = 5 \text{ terms})$$

$\sum$ = the sum of

$\sum_{r=1}^{4} T_r$ is the sum of $T_1 + T_2 + T_3 + T_4$

Example 5

(i) Use the sigma notation ($\sum$) to represent $2 + 6 + 10 + 14 + \ldots$ for 45 terms.

(ii) For what value of n is $\displaystyle\sum_{r=1}^{n} (3r - 5) = 90$?

(iii) Find the value of $\displaystyle\sum_{r=1}^{8} (4r - 1)$.

(i) $2 + 6 + 10 + \ldots \quad \begin{aligned} a &= 2 \\ d &= 4 \end{aligned} \quad \begin{aligned} T_n &= a + (n-1)d \\ &= 2 + (n-1)4 \end{aligned}$

$\qquad\qquad\qquad\qquad\qquad T_n = 4n - 2$

$\qquad\qquad\qquad\qquad \Rightarrow \quad T_r = 4r - 2.$

$\therefore \quad 2 + 6 + 10 + \ldots \text{ for 45 terms} = \displaystyle\sum_{r=1}^{r=45} (4r - 2)$

(ii) $\displaystyle\sum_{r=1}^{n} (3r - 5) = [3(1) - 5] + [3(2) - 5] + [3(3) - 5)] + \ldots 3n - 5$

$\qquad\qquad\qquad = \quad -2 \quad + \quad 1 \quad + \quad 4 \quad + \ldots 3n - 5.$

$\Rightarrow \quad \begin{aligned} a &= -2 \\ d &= 1 - (-2) = 3 \\ S_n &= 90 \end{aligned} \quad \begin{aligned} S_n &= \frac{n}{2}\{2a + (n-1)d\} \\ 90 &= \frac{n}{2}\{2(-2) + (n-1)(3)\} \\ 180 &= n(-4 + 3n - 3) \\ 180 &= n(3n - 7) \end{aligned}$

$\qquad\qquad\qquad\qquad \Rightarrow \quad 3n^2 - 7n - 180 = 0$

$\qquad\qquad\qquad\qquad (3n + 20)(n - 9) = 0$

$\Rightarrow \quad n - 9 = 0 \quad \text{or} \quad 3n + 20 = 0$

$\therefore \qquad n = 9 \quad \text{or} \quad n = \frac{-20}{3}$

$\therefore \qquad n = 9 \quad \text{since} \quad n \in N$

(iii) $\displaystyle\sum_{r=1}^{8} (4r - 1) = 3 + 7 + 11 + \ldots (n = 8 \text{ terms})$

$\qquad \begin{aligned} a &= 3 \\ d &= 7 - 3 = 4 \end{aligned} \quad \therefore \quad \begin{aligned} S_n &= \frac{n}{2}\{2a + (n-1)d\} \\ S_8 &= \frac{8}{2}\{2(3) + (8-1)4\} \\ &= 4(34) = 136 \end{aligned}$

$\therefore \quad \displaystyle\sum_{r=1}^{8} (4r - 1) = 136$

Exercise 9.3

1. Find S_n and S_{20} of each of the following arithmetic series:
   (i) $1 + 5 + 9 + 13 + \dots$
   (ii) $50 + 48 + 46 + 44 + \dots$
   (iii) $1 + 1.1 + 1.2 + 1.3 + \dots$
   (iv) $-7 - 3 + 1 + 5 + \dots$

2. Find the sum of each of the following:
   (i) $6 + 10 + 14 + 18 + \dots + 50$
   (ii) $1 + 2 + 3 + 4 + \dots + 100$
   (iii) $80 + 74 + 68 + 62 + \dots -34$

3. How many terms of the series $5 + 8 + 11 + 14 + \dots$ must be added to make a total of 98?

4. Given $T_n = 5 - 3n$, write down the first term a, and the common difference d.
   Hence find S_{10}.

5. Anna saves money each week to buy a printer which costs €190. Her plan is to start with €10 and to put aside €2 more each week (i.e. €12, €14, etc.) until she has enough money to buy the printer.
   At this rate, how many weeks will it take Anna to save for the printer?

6. Evaluate (i) $\displaystyle\sum_{r=1}^{6}(3r + 1)$ (ii) $\displaystyle\sum_{r=0}^{5}(4r - 1)$ (iii) $\displaystyle\sum_{r=1}^{100} r$

7. Write each of the following series in sigma notation.
   (i) $4 + 8 + 12 + 16 + \dots + 124$
   (ii) $-10 - 9\frac{1}{2} - 8 - 7\frac{1}{2} + \dots + 4$
   (iii) $10 + 10.1 + 10.2 + 10.3 + \dots + 50$

8. In an arithmetic series, $T_4 = 15$ and $S_5 = 55$.
   Find the first five terms of the series.

9. The third term of an arithmetic sequence is 18 and the seventh term is 30.
   Find the sum of the first 33 terms.

10. In an Art class, a student experiments with a design for a dreamcatcher using rings and threads. The first three designs are shown below.
    He wishes to continue his pattern of designs. How many rings will he need for
    (i) design 10
    (ii) design 20?
    How many rings in total will he need to make all 20 designs?

Design 1

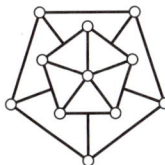

Design 2

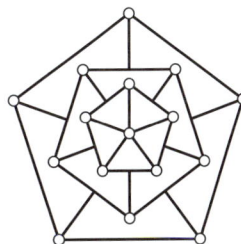

Design 3

11. The first term of an arithmetic sequence is -12 and the last term is 40. If the sum of the series is 196, find the number of terms in the sequence and the common difference.

12. Show that the sum of the natural numbers from 1 to n is $\frac{n}{2}(n+1)$ and use the formula to find the sum of $1 + 2 + 3 + 4 + \ldots 99$.

13. The twenty-first term of an arithmetic sequence is $5\frac{1}{2}$ and the sum of the first twenty-one terms is $94\frac{1}{2}$.

Find the first term and the common difference.

Hence find S_{30}, the sum of the first thirty terms.

14. In an arithmetic sequence, $T_{21} = 37$ and $S_{20} = 320$. Find the sum of the first ten terms.

15. Show that $S_n = \dfrac{n(a+l)}{2}$ is the sum to n terms of an arithmetic sequence where l is the last term.

16. Explain why S_∞ (the sum to infinity) for an arithmetic sequence cannot be found.

Section 9.4 Geometric sequences

A **geometric sequence** is formed when each term of the sequence is obtained by multiplying the previous term by a fixed amount.

For example, $\overset{\times 3 \quad \times 3 \quad \times 3}{2, \quad 6, \quad 18, \quad 54, \ldots}$ each term increasing by a factor of 3.

$\overset{\times\frac{1}{2} \quad \times\frac{1}{2} \quad \times\frac{1}{2}}{4, \quad 2, \quad 1, \quad \frac{1}{2}, \ldots}$ each term decreasing by a factor of $\frac{1}{2}$.

For any geometric sequence, the first term is denoted by a and the ratio between consecutive terms is r (called the common ratio); then every geometric sequence can be represented by

$$\overset{+r \qquad +r \qquad +r \qquad +r}{T_1, \qquad T_2, \qquad T_3, \qquad T_4, \qquad T_5, \qquad \ldots \qquad T_n}$$

$$a, \qquad ar, \qquad ar^2, \qquad ar^3, \qquad ar^4, \qquad \ldots \qquad ar^{n-1}$$

Consider the sequence:

$$2, \qquad 6, \qquad 18, \qquad 54, \qquad \ldots \quad a.r^{n-1}$$
$$= \quad 2, \quad 2 \times 3, \quad 2 \times 3^2, \quad 2 \times 3^3, \quad \ldots \quad 2 \times 3^{n-1}$$

$a = 2$

$r = \frac{6}{2} = 3$

$T_n = ar^{n-1}$

$T_n = 2.3^{n-1}$

Example 1

Find T_n and T_{10} of the geometric sequence $1, \frac{1}{4}, \frac{1}{16}, \frac{1}{64}, \ldots$

$\left.\begin{array}{l} a = 1 \\[2mm] r = \dfrac{\frac{1}{4}}{1} = \dfrac{1}{4} \end{array}\right\}$

$\begin{aligned} T_n &= a.r^{n-1} \\ &= 1.\left(\tfrac{1}{4}\right)^{n-1} \\ &= \dfrac{1}{4^{n-1}} \end{aligned}$

$T_n = 4^{-n+1} = 4^{1-n}$

$T_{10} = 4^{1-10} = 4^{-9} = \dfrac{1}{262\,144}$

In every geometric sequence:

$T_1 = a$

$\dfrac{T_2}{T_1} = r$

$T_n = ar^{n-1}$

$\dfrac{T_{n+1}}{T_n} = r$

Example 2

In a geometric sequence, $T_3 = 32$ and $T_6 = 4$.

Find a and r and hence write down the first six terms of the sequence.

$T_n = a.r^{n-1}$
$T_3 = a.r^{3-1} = ar^2 = 32$
$T_6 = a.r^{6-1} = ar^5 = 4$

Dividing these terms:

$\dfrac{\cancel{a}r^5}{\cancel{a}r^2} = \dfrac{4}{32}$

$r^3 = \dfrac{1}{8}$

$r = \sqrt[3]{\dfrac{1}{8}} = \dfrac{1}{2}$

If $\quad r = \tfrac{1}{2}$,

then $\quad ar^2 = 32$

$\Rightarrow \quad a.\left(\tfrac{1}{4}\right) = 32$

$a = 128.$

The sequence is $128, 64, 32, 16, 8, 4$.

Note:

> Given three consecutive terms of a geometric sequence, T_1, T_2, T_3, we note that

$\dfrac{T_2}{T_1} = \dfrac{T_3}{T_2} = $ (common ratio, r).

> We also note that $\dfrac{a}{r}, a, ar$ are three consecutive terms of a geometric sequence, with first term $\dfrac{a}{r}$ and common ratio r.

Multiplying these terms gives $\dfrac{a}{\cancel{r}} \times a \times a\cancel{r} = a^3$, i.e. the cube of the middle term.

For example: $2, 6, 18$ are in geometric sequence,

$\Rightarrow \quad 2 \times 6 \times 18 = 216 = 6^3$

Also, $\quad 1, \frac{1}{4}, \frac{1}{16}$ are in geometric sequence,

$\Rightarrow \quad 1 \times \frac{1}{4} \times \frac{1}{16} = \frac{1}{64} = \left(\frac{1}{4}\right)^3$

Example 3

$3, x, x + 6, \ldots$ are the first three terms of a geometric sequence of positive terms.
Find
   (i) the value of x (ii) the tenth term of the sequence.

(i) For a geometric sequence, $\dfrac{T_2}{T_1} = \dfrac{T_3}{T_2}$, i.e., $\dfrac{x}{3} = \dfrac{x + 6}{x}$

$$\therefore \quad x^2 = 3x + 18$$
$$\therefore \quad x^2 - 3x - 18 = 0$$
$$\therefore \quad (x - 6)(x + 3) = 0$$
$$\Rightarrow \quad x = 6 \text{ or } x = -3.$$

$x = 6$ since the terms are positive $\Rightarrow$ sequence is $3, 6, 12, \ldots$

(ii) $T_n = a.r^{n-1}$

$$T_{10} = a.r^{10-1} = a.r^9 = 3.2^9 = 1536$$

Example 4

The product of the first three terms of a geometric sequence is 216 and their
sum is 21. Given that the common ratio r is less than 1, find the first three terms
of the sequence.

Let $\dfrac{a}{r}, a, ar$ be the first three terms.

$$\Rightarrow \quad \frac{a}{r} \times a \times ar = a^3 = 216$$
$$\Rightarrow \quad a = \sqrt[3]{216} = 6$$

Also, $\dfrac{a}{r} + a + ar = 21$

$$\frac{6}{r} + 6 + 6r = 21$$
$$\frac{6}{r} + 6r - 15 = 0$$
$$6 + 6r^2 - 15r = 0$$
$$\therefore \quad 6r^2 - 15r + 6 = 0$$
$$(2r - 1)(r - 2) = 0$$
$$\Rightarrow \quad r = \tfrac{1}{2} \text{ or } r = 2.$$

Since $r < 1 \Rightarrow r = \tfrac{1}{2}$.

Therefore the first three terms are $\dfrac{a}{r}, a, ar = \dfrac{6}{\left(\frac{1}{2}\right)}, 6, 6\left(\tfrac{1}{2}\right) = 12, 6, 3.$

Example 5

Find the number of terms in the geometric sequence $81, 27, 9, \ldots \frac{1}{27}$.

$$a = 81$$
$$r = \frac{27}{81} = \frac{1}{3}$$

Let $T_n = \frac{1}{27}$

$$T_n = a.r^{n-1}$$
$$= 81.\left(\frac{1}{3}\right)^{n-1} = \frac{1}{27}$$

$$\Rightarrow \quad \frac{1}{3^{n-1}} = \frac{1}{27 \times 81}$$
$$\Rightarrow \quad 3^{n-1} = 27 \times 81$$
$$\Rightarrow \quad 3^{n-1} = 3^3 \times 3^4 = 3^7$$

$$\therefore \quad n - 1 = 7$$
$$n = 8 \quad \Rightarrow \quad \text{there are eight terms in the sequence.}$$

Note: When solving an equation such as $4^{n-1} = 4096$, we can use two different methods.

Method A: Express 4096 as a power of 4 using a calculator and trial and error.

$$\therefore \quad 4^{n-1} = 4096 = 4^6$$
$$n - 1 = 6$$
$$n = 7$$

Method B: Using logs (see chapter 12)

$$4^{n-1} = 4096$$
$$\Rightarrow \quad n - 1 = \log_4 4096$$

Definition of logs:
If $\quad a^x = y$
then $\log_a y = x$

$$\Rightarrow \quad n - 1 = 6 \text{ (using the } \boxed{\log_\blacksquare \square} \text{ key on the calculator).}$$
$$\therefore \quad n = 7$$

Exponential sequences

Exponential functions of the form $y = Aa^x$, where A is the initial value and a the multiplier or common ratio, produce geometric sequences.

Consider a ball dropping from a height of 10 m.

If the ball bounces back to $\frac{2}{3}$ of its original height on each bounce, the height of the ball is given by the following pattern:

After 1 bounce: $\quad 10 \times \frac{2}{3} = 10\left(\frac{2}{3}\right)^1$

After 2 bounces: $\quad 10 \times \frac{2}{3} \times \frac{2}{3} = 10\left(\frac{2}{3}\right)^2$

After 3 bounces: $\quad 10 \times \frac{2}{3} \times \frac{2}{3} \times \frac{2}{3} = 10\left(\frac{2}{3}\right)^3$

After n bounces: $\quad 10 \times \left(\frac{2}{3}\right)^n$

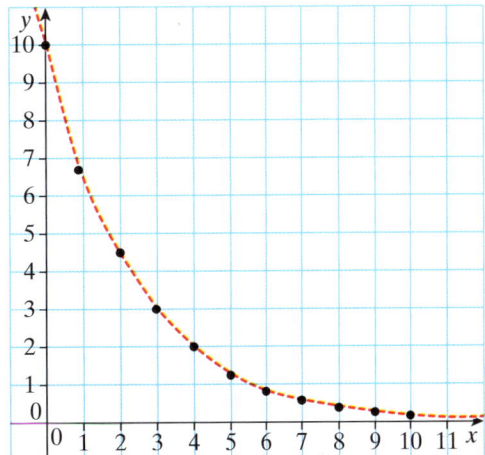

Example 6

A ball is dropped from a height of 27 m and loses $\frac{2}{3}$ of its height on each bounce.

(i) Find the height of the ball on each of its first four bounces.
(ii) Hence write down the height of the ball after the 10th bounce.
(iii) After which bounce will the ball be at most 2.5 m above the ground?

(i) After the 1st bounce, the ball is $27 \times \frac{1}{3} = 9$ m above the ground.

After the 2nd bounce, the ball is $27 \times \frac{1}{3} \times \frac{1}{3} = 3$ m.

After the 3rd bounce, the ball is $27 \times \frac{1}{3} \times \frac{1}{3} \times \frac{1}{3} = 1$ m.

After the 4th bounce, the ball is $27 \times \frac{1}{3} \times \frac{1}{3} \times \frac{1}{3} \times \frac{1}{3} = \frac{1}{3}$ m.

(ii) After the 10th bounce, the ball is $27 \times \left(\frac{1}{3}\right)^n = 27 \times \left(\frac{1}{3}\right)^{10} = 0.00046$ m.

(iii) To find n, the number of bounces needed to produce a height of 2.5 m,

let $\quad 27 \times \left(\frac{1}{3}\right)^n = 2.5$

$$\left(\frac{1}{3}\right)^n = 0.093$$

$$\ln\left(\frac{1}{3}\right)^n = \ln(0.093)$$

$$n\ln\left(\frac{1}{3}\right) = \ln(0.093) \quad \Rightarrow n = \left(\frac{\ln(0.093)}{\ln\left(\frac{1}{3}\right)}\right) = 2.16 \text{ bounces.}$$

Since the number of bounces of a ball has to be a discrete (whole) number, after two bounces the ball *will* be above 2.5 m.

Therefore it will require three bounces of the ball to guarantee the ball is below 2.5 m.

Exercise 9.4

1. Determine which of the following sequences are geometric.

Find the common ratios of these sequences and write down the next two terms of each sequence.

(i) 3, 9, 27, 81, ...

(ii) 1, $\frac{1}{3}$, $\frac{1}{9}$, $\frac{1}{27}$, ...

(iii) -1, 2, -4, 8, ...

(iv) 1, -1, 1, -1, ...

(v) 1, $1\frac{1}{2}$, $1\frac{1}{4}$, $1\frac{1}{8}$, ...

(vi) a, a^2, a^3, a^4, ...

(vii) 1, 1.1, 1.21, 1.331, ...

(viii) $\frac{1}{2}$, $\frac{1}{6}$, $\frac{1}{12}$, $\frac{1}{36}$, ...

(ix) 2, 4, -8, -16, ...

(x) $\frac{3}{4}$, $\frac{9}{2}$, 27, 162, ...

2. Each of the following sequences is geometric.
Find a and r and hence find the indicated term.

(i) 5, 10, ... (T_{11})

(ii) 10, 25, ... (T_7)

(iii) 1.1, 1.21, ... (T_8)

(iv) 24, -12, 6, ... (T_{10})

3. Given $T_2 = 12$ and $T_5 = 324$, find a and r and hence write down the first five terms of the sequence.

4. Find the value of r given that the third term is 6 and the eighth term is 1458.

5. Write down the first five terms of the geometric sequence that has a second term 4 and a fifth term $-\frac{1}{16}$.

6. A:

......etc.

B:

......etc.

C:

......etc.

D:

......etc.

By inspection, decide which of the above patterns generate a geometric sequence. Draw the next pattern of those that are geometric.

7. The three numbers $n - 2, n$ and $n + 3$ are the first three terms of a geometric sequence. Find the value of n and hence write down the first four terms of the sequence.

8. The third term of a geometric sequence is -63 and the fourth term is 189. Find
(i) the values of a and r
(ii) an expression for T_n.

9. The first term of a geometric sequence is 16 and the fifth term is 9.
What is the value of the seventh term?

10. The product of the first three terms of a geometric sequence is 27 and their sum is 13. Find the first four terms of the sequence.

11. The nth term, T_n, of a geometric sequence is $T_n = 3 \times 2^{n-1}$.
Write down the first five terms of the sequence in their simplest form.

12. Given $T_n = 8\left(\frac{3}{4}\right)^n$, write out the first four terms of the sequence.

13. Write out the first four terms of the sequence defined by $T_n = (-1)^{n+1} \times \frac{5}{2^{n-4}}$.

14. If each of the following are the first three terms of a geometric sequence, find one or two possible values of x and hence write down possible sequence(s) for each.

    (i) $x - 3, x$ and $3x + 4$ (ii) $x + 1, x + 4$ and $3x + 2$

    (iii) $x - 2, x$ and $x + 3$ (iv) $x - 6, 2x$ and x^2.

15. Show that the sequence whose nth term is $T_n = 2 \times 3^n$ is a geometric sequence.

> To show that a sequence is geometric, we must show
> that $\dfrac{T_{n+1}}{T_n} = $ a constant (r).

16. Investigate if the sequence $T_n = 3 \times n^2$ is geometric.

17. Find the number of terms in each of the following geometric sequences:

    (i) $5, 15, 45, \ldots\ldots 3645$ (ii) $48, 6, \tfrac{3}{4}, \ldots\ldots \dfrac{3}{2048}$

18. A rubber orb is dropped from a height of 27 m on to a concrete floor. Each time it hits the concrete, it bounces back to $\frac{2}{3}$ of the original height. Find

    (i) the height of each of the first four bounces

    (ii) a formula for the height of the nth bounce

    (iii) the height of the 12th bounce using the formula found in (ii).

19. The value of a sum of money on deposit at 3% per annum compound interest is given by $A = $ €4000 $(1.03)^t$ where t is the number of years of the investment. Find

    (i) the amount of money on deposit

    (ii) the value of the investment at the end of each of the first four years

    (iii) the value of the investment at the end of the 10th year

    (iv) the number of years, correct to the nearest year, needed for the investment to double in value.

20. The value, A, of an investment is given by $A = P(1 + i)^t$ where P is the sum on deposit, t the number of years and i the rate of interest, expressed as a decimal.

    Given that over a 10 year period €2500 on deposit amounted to €3047, calculate the rate of interest (correct to 1 place of decimals).

Section 9.5 Limits of sequences

As the number of terms in the sequence becomes very large, in some cases the terms of the sequence converge to a fixed value which we call the *limit* of the sequence.

If such a limit exists, the sequence is said to be convergent.

A sequence which does converge is said to be divergent.

The sequence 0.3, 0.33, 0.333, 0.3333,... converges to 1/3.

Consider the sequence $T_n = \dfrac{n+2}{n^2}$, $n \in N$ as n increases the value of $\dfrac{n+2}{n^2}$ tends to zero.

We write this as $n \to \infty$, $T_n \to 0$.

i.e. n^{th} term of the sequence $3, 1, \frac{5}{9}, \frac{6}{16}, \frac{7}{25}, \ldots$ "**tends to**" zero.

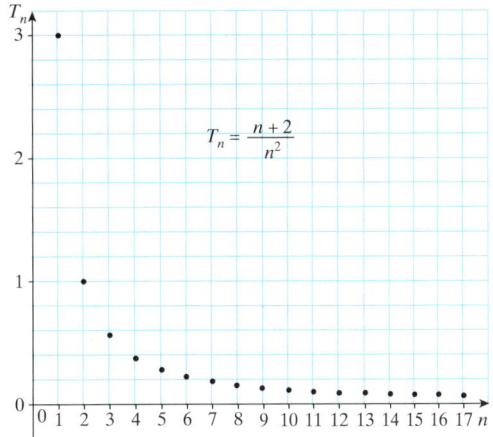

$$T_n = \frac{n+2}{n^2}$$

Note: Although the nth term (T_n) never becomes zero, by taking n large enough we can make the difference between T_n and zero so small, it is negligible.

In chapter 7 we have already stated that

$\lim\limits_{n \to \infty} \frac{1}{n} = 0$ and therefore $\lim\limits_{n \to \infty} \frac{k}{n} = 0$

Also $\lim\limits_{n \to \infty} \frac{k}{n^p} = 0$ where $p > 0$ the following rules, as $n \to \infty$, should also be noted.

> **Limit notation**
>
> $$\lim_{n \to \infty} T_n = L$$
>
> States that as n gets close to ∞, T_n approaches the value L.

$$\lim_{n \to \infty} C = C$$

$$\lim_{n \to \infty} (T_n + R_n) = \lim_{n \to \infty} (T_n) + \lim_{n \to \infty} (R_n)$$

$$\lim_{n \to \infty} (T_n \times R_n) = \lim_{n \to \infty} (T_n) \times \lim_{n \to \infty} (R_n)$$

$$\lim_{n \to \infty} \left(\frac{T_n}{R_n} \right) = \frac{\lim\limits_{n \to \infty} T_n}{\lim\limits_{n \to \infty} R_n}$$

1. The limit of a constant C is C

2. The limit of a sum is the sum of the limits.

3. The limit of a product is the product of the limits

4. The limit of a quotient is the quotient of the limits

In practice (as in Ch 7) to evaluate the limit of a fraction, divide both numerator and denominator by the highest power of n in the expression, and then use the appropriate rule above. Remember: $\lim\limits_{n \to \infty} \frac{k}{n^p} = 0$.

Example 1

Evaluate (i) $\lim\limits_{n \to \infty}\left(\dfrac{3n^2}{n^2 + 5}\right)$ (ii) $\lim\limits_{n \to \infty}\left(\dfrac{n^3 - 4n}{n^2 - 2}\right)$ (iii) $\lim\limits_{n \to \infty}\left(\dfrac{n^2 + 4n}{n^4 - 2n^3}\right)$

(i) $\lim\limits_{n \to \infty}\left(\dfrac{3n^2}{n^2 + 5}\right) = \lim\limits_{n \to \infty}\left(\dfrac{3}{1 + \frac{5}{n^2}}\right)$ (dividing above and below by n^2)

$$= \dfrac{3}{1 + 0} = 3 \qquad \left(\lim\limits_{n \to \infty}\dfrac{5}{n^2} = 0\right)$$

(ii) $\lim\limits_{n \to \infty}\left(\dfrac{n^3 - 4n}{n^2 - 2}\right) = \lim\limits_{n \to \infty}\left(\dfrac{1 - \frac{4}{n^3}}{\frac{1}{n} - \frac{2}{n^3}}\right)$ (dividing above and below by n^3)

$$= \dfrac{1 - 0}{0 - 0} = \dfrac{1}{0} = \infty \text{ i.e. there is no limit}$$

(iii) $\lim\limits_{n \to \infty}\left(\dfrac{n^2 + 4n}{n^4 - 2n^3}\right) = \lim\limits_{n \to \infty}\left(\dfrac{\frac{1}{n} + \frac{4}{n^2}}{1 - \frac{2}{n}}\right)$ (dividing above and below by n^4)

$$= \dfrac{0 - 0}{1 - 0} = \dfrac{0}{1} = 0$$

Exercise 9.5

1. Find the limit of each of the following sequences as $n \to \infty$:

(i) $\dfrac{n + 2}{3n - 4}$ (ii) $\dfrac{5n - 4}{n - 4}$ (iii) $\dfrac{n^2 + 2}{n^2 - 4}$

2. Evaluate each of the following:

(i) $\lim\limits_{n \to \infty}\dfrac{n^3 + 2n}{2n^3 - 4n^2 + 3n}$ (ii) $\lim\limits_{n \to \infty}\dfrac{8}{n(n - 6)}$ (iii) $\lim\limits_{n \to \infty}\dfrac{(n + 3)(n - 1)}{n^2 - 9}$

3. Determine the limit (if it exists) of the following sequences:

(i) $T_n = \dfrac{n^3 + 2n^2 - 3n}{n^2}$ (ii) $T_n = \dfrac{4n^2 + 2}{n^2}$ (iii) $T_n = \dfrac{6n^2 + 5n}{n^3}$

4. Evaluate each of the following limits:

(i) $\lim\limits_{n \to \infty}\left(4 + \dfrac{5n - 4}{n - 4}\right)$ (ii) $\lim\limits_{n \to \infty}\left(\dfrac{1}{2} - \dfrac{n^2 - 2n}{3n^2}\right)$ (iii) $\lim\limits_{n \to \infty}(3n)\left(\dfrac{n + 4}{n - 1}\right)$

5. Find the limit as $n \to \infty$ of each of the following:

(i) $T_n = \dfrac{5n + 2}{3n^2 + 2}$ (ii) $T_n = \dfrac{n - 2n^3}{n^2 + 2n}$ (iii) $T_n = \dfrac{7n^3}{n^2 + 3n - 4}$

6. Find the limit as $n \to \infty$ of $T_n = \dfrac{an^p + cn^q}{bn^p + dn^s}$ where $p > q > s$.

Section 9.6 Geometric series

When the terms of a geometric sequence are added, a geometric series is created.

For example, $2 + 6 + 18 + 54 + \ldots$ is a geometric series.

To find the sum of a series, $a_1 + a_2 + a_3 + a_4 + \ldots$ we consider a sequence of partial sums where $S_1 = a_1$, $S_2 = a_1 + a_2$, $S_3 = a_1 + a_2 + a_3$ and $S_n = a_1 + a_2 + a_3 + \ldots a_n$.

To find a formula for S_n, we use the following procedure:

$$S_n = a + ar + ar^2 + \ldots\ldots ar^{n-3} + ar^{n-2} + ar^{n-1}$$

$$\Rightarrow \quad r.S_n = \quad\quad ar + ar^2 + \ldots\ldots ar^{n-3} + ar^{n-2} + ar^{n-1} + ar^n \quad \text{... multiplying each term by } r$$

Subtracting: $\quad S_n - rS_n = \quad\quad a - ar^n$

$$\therefore \quad S_n(1 - r) = a(1 - r^n)$$

$$\therefore \quad S_n = \frac{a(1 - r^n)}{1 - r}$$

The sum to n terms of a geometric sequence,

$$S_n = \frac{a(1 - r^n)}{1 - r}, \quad \text{where } a \text{ is the first term and } r \text{ is the common ratio.}$$

Example 1

Find T_5 and S_5 of each of the following:

(i) $1 + 3 + 9 + \ldots$
                              (ii) $1 + \frac{1}{4} + \frac{1}{16} + \ldots$

(i) $\left.\begin{array}{l} a = 1 \\ r = \frac{3}{1} = 3 \end{array}\right\}$
    $T_n = ar^{n-1}$

$\qquad\qquad\qquad\quad T_n = 1.3^{n-1}$

$\qquad\qquad\qquad\qquad = 3^{n-1}$

$\qquad\qquad\quad \therefore\ T_5 = 3^{5-1}$

$\qquad\qquad\qquad\qquad = 3^4$

$\qquad\qquad\qquad\qquad = 81$

$S_n = \dfrac{a(1 - r^n)}{1 - r}$

$\quad = \dfrac{1(1 - 3^n)}{1 - 3}$

$\quad = \dfrac{1 - 3^n}{-2}$

$S_n = \dfrac{3^n - 1}{2}$

$\therefore\ S_5 = \dfrac{3^5 - 1}{2} = 121$

(ii) $\left.\begin{array}{l} a = 1 \\ r = \frac{\frac{1}{4}}{1} = \frac{1}{4} \end{array}\right\}$
  $T_n = ar^{n-1}$

$\qquad\qquad\qquad\quad = 1.\left(\frac{1}{4}\right)^{n-1}$

$\qquad\qquad\qquad T_n = \dfrac{1}{4^{n-1}}$

$\qquad\qquad \therefore\ T_5 = \dfrac{1}{4^{5-1}}$

$\qquad\qquad\quad T_5 = \dfrac{1}{4^4}$

$\qquad\qquad\qquad\quad = \dfrac{1}{256}$

$S_n = \dfrac{a(1 - r^n)}{1 - r}$

$\quad = \dfrac{1\left(1 - \left(\frac{1}{4}\right)^n\right)}{1 - \frac{1}{4}}$

$\quad = \dfrac{1 - \frac{1}{4^n}}{\frac{3}{4}}$

$S_n = \dfrac{4}{3}\left(1 - \dfrac{1}{4^n}\right)$

$\therefore\ S_5 = \dfrac{4}{3}\left(1 - \dfrac{1}{4^5}\right) = \dfrac{341}{256}$

Example 2

In a geometric series, $T_3 = 32$ and $T_6 = 4$; find a and r and hence find S_8, the sum of the first eight terms.

$$T_n = ar^{n-1}$$
$$T_3 = ar^{3-1} = ar^2 = 32$$
$$T_6 = ar^{6-1} = ar^5 = 4$$

Dividing these equations, we get $\dfrac{\cancel{a}r^2}{\cancel{a}r^5} = \dfrac{32}{4}$

$$\frac{1}{r^3} = 8$$
$$r^3 = \frac{1}{8}$$
$$r = \sqrt[3]{\frac{1}{8}} = \frac{1}{2}$$

If $r = \frac{1}{2}$, then $a\left(\frac{1}{2}\right)^2 = 32$

$$a\left(\frac{1}{4}\right) = 32$$
$$a = 128.$$

$$\therefore \ S_n = \frac{a(1 - r^n)}{1 - r}$$
$$= \frac{128\left(1 - \left(\frac{1}{2}\right)^n\right)}{1 - \frac{1}{2}}$$
$$S_n = 256\left(1 - \frac{1}{2^n}\right)$$
$$S_8 = 256\left(1 - \frac{1}{2^8}\right)$$
$$= 255$$

It is very important to understand the effect the value of r has on the sum of a geometric series. Consider three geometric sequences – A, B and C – where A has a common ratio of $r = 2$, B has a common ratio of $r = 1$, and C has a common ratio of $r = \frac{1}{2}$.

Starting with a first term value of 1, we get:

Sequence	r	T_1	T_2	T_3	T_4	T_5	T_6	.....	T_{100}
A	2	1	2	4	8	16	32		6.3×10^{29}
B	1	1	1	1	1	1	1		1
C	$\frac{1}{2}$	1	$\frac{1}{2}$	$\frac{1}{4}$	$\frac{1}{8}$	$\frac{1}{16}$	$\frac{1}{32}$		1.6×10^{-30}

Series	r	S_1	S_2	S_3	S_4	S_5	S_6	.....	S_{100}
A	2	1	3	7	15	31	63		1.3×10^{30}
B	1	1	2	3	4	5	6		100
C	$\frac{1}{2}$	1	1.5	1.75	1.875	1.9375	1.96875		2

If $|r| > 1$, the values of T_n and S_n, as n gets bigger, increase very rapidly.

If $|r| = 1$, then the sequence behaves like an arithmetic sequence with a constant amount added each term.

If $|r| < 1$, then the value of S_n is said to have a "limiting value".

In series C above, the sum S_n approaches the value 2.

By taking a sufficiently large value of n, we can make S_n as near to 2 as we wish, that is, we can make $2 - S_n$ as small as we wish.

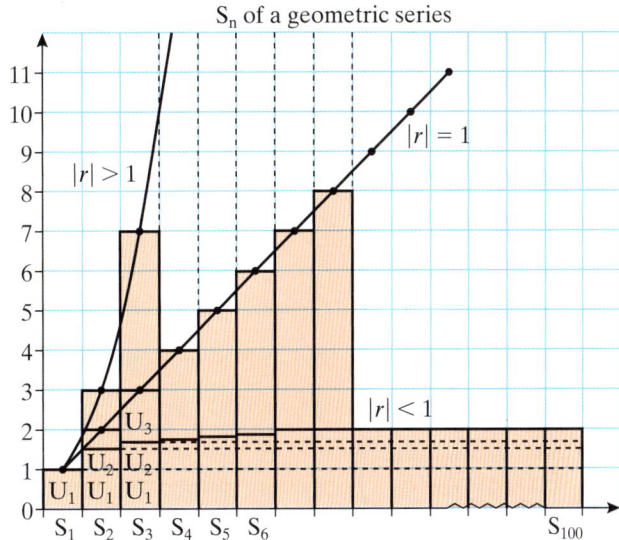

S_n of a geometric series

We say that S_n approaches
a limiting value of 2 as n approaches infinity.

This is written as: $S_n \to 2$ as $n \to \infty$ or $\lim_{n \to \infty} S_n = 2$.

In words, we say that "the limit of the partial sum S_n, as n tends to infinity, is 2."

Now consider the formula for the sum to n terms of a geometric series if $|r| < 1$.

$$S_n = \frac{a(1 - r^n)}{1 - r}$$

When $|r| < 1$, r^n will approximate to zero for large values of n, i.e. $r^n \to 0$ as $n \to \infty$.

Thus, $S_n = \dfrac{a(1 - r^n)}{1 - r}$ becomes $S_n = \dfrac{a(1 - 0)}{1 - r}$

$$\therefore \quad S_n = \frac{a}{1 - r} \quad \text{as} \quad n \to \infty.$$

or $\lim_{n \to \infty} S_n = \dfrac{a}{1 - r}$

> For a geometric series with $|r| < 1$,
> $$\lim_{n \to \infty} S_n = \frac{a}{1 - r}.$$

Example 3

Find the sum to infinity of the geometric series $16 + 12 + 9 + \ldots$

$\left. \begin{array}{l} a = 16 \\ r = \frac{12}{16} = \frac{3}{4} \end{array} \right\} \Rightarrow \lim_{n \to \infty} S_n = \dfrac{a}{1 - r}$

$$= \frac{16}{1 - \frac{3}{4}} = 64$$

Recurring decimals

Recurring decimals can be expressed as a sum to infinity of a geometric sequence, where the common ratio $r < 1$.

For example, $0.\dot{3} = 0.3333\ldots\ldots = \dfrac{3}{10} + \dfrac{3}{10^2} + \dfrac{3}{10^3} + \dfrac{3}{10^4} + \ldots\ldots$

$\times\frac{1}{10} \quad \times\frac{1}{10} \quad \times\frac{1}{10}$

where $a = 0.3$ and $r = \dfrac{1}{10}$.

Similarly,

$0.2\dot{3}\dot{5} = 0.2353535\ldots\ldots = 0.2 + [0.035 + 0.00035 + \ldots\ldots]$

$= 0.2 + \dfrac{35}{1000} + \dfrac{35}{100000} + \ldots\ldots$

$= 0.2 + \text{an infinite geometric series}$

where $a = \dfrac{35}{1000}$ and $r = \dfrac{1}{100}$.

Example 4

Write the recurring decimal $0.\dot{2}\dot{3}$ as a fraction in the form $\dfrac{a}{b}$, $a, b, \in N$.

$0.\dot{2}\dot{3} = 0.232323\ldots\ldots = 0.23 + 0.0023 + 0.000023 + \ldots\ldots$

$= \dfrac{23}{100} + \dfrac{23}{10000} + \dfrac{23}{1000000} + \ldots\ldots$

$\Rightarrow \quad a = \dfrac{23}{100}$ and $r = \dfrac{23}{10000} \div \dfrac{23}{100} = \dfrac{1}{100}$

$\Rightarrow \quad \lim\limits_{n \to \infty} S_n = \dfrac{a}{1 - r} = \dfrac{\frac{23}{100}}{1 - \frac{1}{100}} = \dfrac{23}{100} \times \dfrac{100}{99} = \dfrac{23}{99}$

$\left[\text{Note:} \quad \lim\limits_{n \to \infty} S_n \text{ is often written as } S_\infty . \text{ Thus, } S_\infty = \dfrac{23}{99}\right]$

Note: If we let $x = 0.232323\ldots$,

then $100x = 23.232323\ldots$

$\Rightarrow \quad 99x = 23$ ... subtracting both lines

$\therefore \quad x = \dfrac{23}{99}$

Exercise 9.6

1. Find the sum of the first 10 terms of the series $2 + 6 + 18 + 54 + \ldots\ldots$

2. Find the number of terms, n, in the following series:
   $1024 + 512 + 256 + \ldots\ldots 32$. Hence find the sum of the series.

3. Find S_8 of the series $1 + 2 + 4 + 8 + \ldots\ldots$

4. Find S_{10} of the series $32 + 16 + 8 + \ldots\ldots$

5. Find S_6 of the series $4 - 12 + 36 - 108 + \ldots\ldots$

6. Find the number of terms in the series $729 - 243 + 81 - \ldots\ldots - \dfrac{1}{3}$.
   Hence find the sum of the series.

7. Write out the first three terms of the series $\displaystyle\sum_{r=1}^{6} 4^r$ and hence find the sum of the series.

8. Evaluate $\displaystyle\sum_{r=1}^{8} 2 \times 3^r$.

9. Find the sum of $\displaystyle\sum_{r=1}^{10} 6 \times \left(\frac{1}{2}\right)^r$ correct to three places of decimals.

10. Write each of the following recurring decimals as an infinite geometric series.
    Hence express each as a decimal in the form $\frac{a}{b}$, $a, b \in N$.

    (i) $0.\dot{7}$ (ii) $0.\dot{3}\dot{5}$ (iii) $0.2\dot{3}$ (iv) $0.\dot{3}7\dot{0}$ (v) $0.1\dot{6}\dot{2}$ (vi) $0.3\dot{2}\dot{1}$

11. Find S_n, the sum to n terms, of $1 + \frac{1}{2} + \left(\frac{1}{2}\right)^2 + \left(\frac{1}{2}\right)^3 + \dots + \left(\frac{1}{2}\right)^{n-1}$ and hence find S_∞, the sum to infinity of the series.
    Find the least value of n such that $S_\infty - S_n < 0.001$.

Section 9.7 Other sequences

In some cases terms of a sequence might be defined as a function of preceding terms:

(i) $T_{n+1} = 2T_n + 2$ where $T_1 = 2$

(ii) $T_{n+2} = T_{n+1} - T_n$ where $T_1 = 3$ and $T_2 = 1$

In each case a relationship between terms is given and a starting value T_1 (or T_1 and T_2)

These are referred to as **recurrence relations**.

Example 1

Write out the first five terms of the sequence defined by

$$T_{n+2} = T_{n+1} + T_n, \text{ where } T_1 = 1 \text{ and } T_2 = 2$$

Let $n = 1$, $\Rightarrow T_{1+2} = T_{1+1} + T_1$ $\therefore$ $T_3 = T_2 + T_1 = 2 + 1 = 3$

Let $n = 2$, $\Rightarrow T_{2+2} = T_{2+1} + T_2$ $\therefore$ $T_4 = T_3 + T_2 = 3 + 2 = 5$

Let $n = 3$, $\Rightarrow T_{3+2} = T_{3+1} + T_3$ $\therefore$ $T_5 = T_4 + T_3 = 5 + 3 = 8$

The first five terms are $1, 2, 3, 5, 8$.

Example 2

Write out the first four terms of the sequence defined by

$$T_{n+1} = 2T_n + 1, \text{ given that } T_1 = 1$$

Let $n = 1$, $\Rightarrow T_{1+1} = 2T_1 + 1$ $\therefore$ $T_2 = 2T_1 + 1 = 2(1) + 1 = 3$

Let $n = 2$, $\Rightarrow T_{2+1} = 2T_2 + 1$ $\therefore$ $T_3 = 2T_2 + 1 = 2(3) + 1 = 7$

Let $n = 3$, $\Rightarrow T_{3+1} = 2T_3 + 1$ $\therefore$ $T_4 = 2T_3 + 1 = 2(7) + 1 = 15$

The first five terms are $1, 3, 7, 15$.

1. Write down the first five terms of the sequence defined by

    $T_1 = 2, T_n = 4T_{n-1}$

2. Write down the first five terms of the sequences defined by the following recurrence relations:

    (i) $G_1 = 2, G_n = 2 + 3G_{n-1}$
    (ii) $G_1 = 1, G_2 = 3, G_n = 2G_{n-1} + G_{n-2}$
    (iii) $G_1 = 0, G_2 = 1, G_n = 3G_{n-1} - G_{n-2}$

3. Write down the first five terms of the sequence formed from the recurrence relation defined by

    $$S_0 = 6, \quad S_n = 2 + S_{n-1}$$

    And hence show that it can also be represented by the linear equation $S_n = 2n + 6$.

4. Any term of the Fibonacci sequence is obtained by finding the sum of the two previous terms.

    Write out a recurrence relation for the Fibonacci sequence and use the relation to write down the first eight terms of the sequence. (Given that the first two terms are 0, 1).

5. Find the fourth term of each of the following sequences:

    (i) $T_1 = 1, T_2 = 3$ given that $T_n = 3T_{n-1} - T_{n-2}$ for $n > 2$
    (ii) $T_1 = 5$ and $T_{n+1} = T_n - 2$

6. Find the first five terms of the sequence formed from the recurrence relation
    $G_1 = 2$ and $G_{n+1} = (G_n - 2)^2$

7. The pattern of triangles given below can be described in two ways using recurrence relations:

    (i) For the number of triangles, $T_{n+1} = T_n + 2, T_1 = 1$
    (ii) For the number of sides $S_{n+1} = S_n + 4, S_1 = 3$

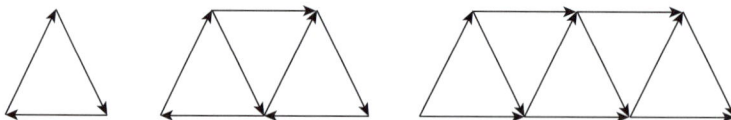

   If the pattern is continued, use these relations to answer the following:
   (a) (i) Find T_4, T_5, T_6 the number of triangles in the next three patterns.
       (ii) Find S_4, S_5, S_6 the number of sides in the next three patterns.
   (b) Show that each of sequences formed for T_n and S_n is arithmetic.
   (c) If the number of sides S_n can be written as $S_n = an + b$, find the values of a and b.
   (d) Find the number of sides in the 20th pattern, S_{20}

Section 9.8 Number patterns – Revisited

Linear, Quadratic and Cubic patterns

In our study of algebra, we discovered that we can identify patterns in certain number sequences by calculating differences.

The sequence $-4, 0, 4, 8, 12, \ldots$ has a first difference of $+4$ creating a formula for $T_n = 4n + a$, where $n = 1, 2, 3, \ldots$ etc.

Sequence		-4	0	4	8	12
1st difference			$+4$	$+4$	$+4$	$+4$

Therefore, if $n = 1$, then $T_1 = 4(1) + a = -4$

$$\Rightarrow \quad a = -8$$

$\therefore$ A constant first difference gives rise to an arithmetic (**linear**) pattern, $T_n = 4n - 8$.

As the following table indicates, the sequence $7, 17, 31, 49, 71, \ldots$ does not have a constant first difference.

Sequence		7	17	31	49	71
1st difference			10	14	18	22
2nd difference				4	4	4

A constant second difference indicates a **quadratic** (n^2) pattern, $\boldsymbol{an^2 + bn + c}$.

Consider $T_n = an^2 + bn + c$ for all values of $n \geq 1$.
The following table evaluates the first and second differences in terms of a, b and c.

T_1	T_2	T_3	T_4	T_5	
$a + b + c$	$4a + 2b + c$	$9a + 3b + c$	$16a + 4b + c$	$25a + 5b + c$	
	$3a + b + c$	$5a + b + c$	$7a + b + c$	$9a + b + c$	1st difference
	$2a$		$2a$	$2a$	2nd difference

From this table we can see that the second difference of a quadratic pattern of numbers is always $2a$, twice the coefficient of n^2.

$\therefore$ if the second difference is $+4 \Rightarrow 2a = 4$

$$a = 2$$

$\therefore \quad T_n = 2n^2 + bn + c$ for $n = 1, 2, 3$, etc.

To find b and c, we use simultaneous equations as follows.

$\quad T_n = 2n^2 + bn + c$ for $n = 1, 2, 3$, etc.

Let $n = 1$, $T_1 = 2(1)^2 + b(1) + c = 7$

$$\Rightarrow \quad b + c = 5$$

Let $n = 2$, $T_2 = 2(2)^2 + b(2) + c = 17$

$$\Rightarrow \quad 2b + c = 9$$
$$\underline{\quad\quad b + c = 5}$$
$$\therefore \quad b = 4$$

If $b = 4$, then $4 + c = 5$,

$$\Rightarrow \quad c = 1$$

$\therefore \quad T_n = 2n^2 + 4n + 1$ for $n = 1, 2, 3$, etc.

The method of finite differences can be used to study patterns of numbers with higher powers.

If the third difference is constant we have a **cubic pattern**, $T_n = an^3 + bn^2 + cn + d$ etc.

	Pattern	To find a
1st difference constant	$T_n = an + b$	a = 1st difference
2nd difference constant	$T_n = an^2 + bn + c$	$2a$ = 2nd difference
3rd difference constant	$T_n = an^3 + bn^2 + cn + d$	$6a$ = 3rd difference

Example 1

Express the nth term of the number pattern $-1, 13, 51, 125, 247, \ldots$ as a cubic polynomial.

Since the 3rd difference is constant, the number pattern has a cubic part and $6a$ = third difference.

$$\Rightarrow \quad a = \tfrac{1}{6} \times 12 = 2$$

Sequence	-1		13		51		125		247
1st difference		14		38		74		122	
2nd difference			24		36		48		
3rd difference				12		12			

$\therefore \quad T_n = 2n^3 + bn^2 + cn + d$ for $n \geqslant 1$

$T_1 = 2 + b + c + d = -1$

$\quad \Rightarrow \quad b + c + d = -3$

$T_2 = 2(2)^3 + b(2)^2 + c(2) + d = 13$

$\quad\quad \Rightarrow \quad 4b + 2c + d = -3$

$T_3 = 2(3)^3 + b(3)^2 + c(3) + d = 51$

$\quad\quad \Rightarrow \quad 9b + 3c + d = -3$

Solving the equations:

1. $b + c + d = -3$

2. $4b + 2c + d = -3$

3. $9b + 3c + d = -3$

we get $b = 0, c = 0, d = -3$

$\therefore \quad T_n = 2n^3 - 3$ for $n \geqslant 1$.

Example 2

A mosaic arrangement is constructed on a floor as shown.
Find the number of tiles needed for the 30th pattern.

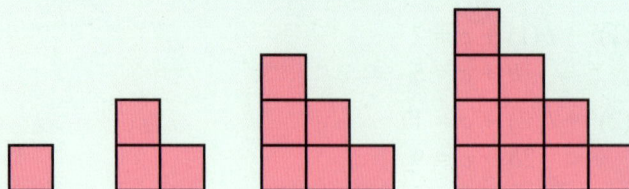

The number of tiles required forms the pattern 1, 3, 6, 10, ...

Checking differences, we find a constant 2nd difference.
Therefore, a quadratic pattern –
$T_n = an^2 + bn + c$ – exists.

Sequence	1		3		6		10
1st difference		2		3		4	
2nd difference			1		1		

And $2a = 1 \Rightarrow a = \frac{1}{2}$

$\therefore \quad T_n = \frac{1}{2}n^2 + bn + c$

$T_1 = \frac{1}{2}(1)^2 + b(1) + c = 1$

$\Rightarrow \quad b + c = \frac{1}{2}$

$T_2 = \frac{1}{2}(2)^2 + b(2) + c = 3$

$\Rightarrow \quad 2b + c = 1$

Solving these equations, we find
$b = \frac{1}{2}, c = 0$

$\therefore \quad T_n = \frac{1}{2}n^2 + \frac{1}{2}n$, for $n \geqslant 1$

$\therefore \quad T_{30} = \frac{1}{2}(30)^2 + \frac{1}{2}(30) = 465.$

In summary, when a process is examined and a number pattern identified, we can create a formula for successive elements under such headings as (i) Arithmetic (Linear) (ii) Quadratic (iii) Cubic (iv) Geometric (Exponential) by identifying the link between elements of the pattern.

Exercise 9.8

1. Using the method of differences, find the nth term, T_n, for each of the following number patterns:

    (i) 5, 9, 13, 17, 21, ...　　(ii) 1, 4, 7, 10, 13, ...　　(iii) 11, 16, 21, 26, 31, ...

2. Find a formula for T_n, the nth term, of the following number patterns:

    (i) 2, 1, 0, −1, −2, ...　　(ii) 0, −2, −4, −6, −8, ...　　(iii) −6, −4, −2, 0, 2, ...

3. If each square in this pattern measures 5 mm × 5 mm, find

    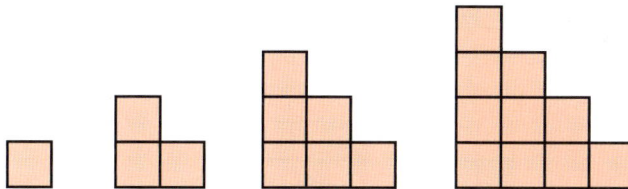

    (i) the area　　　　(ii) the perimeter　of the 28th pattern.

4. If each triangle has an area of 1 cm², convert this triangular pattern into a number pattern. Hence find,

    (i) the area of the 30th part of the design

    (ii) which part would have an area of 441 cm²

    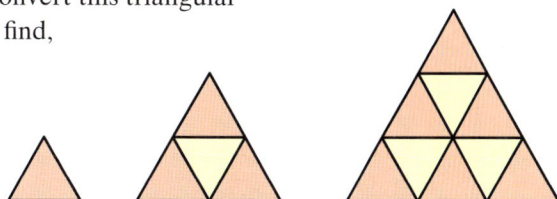

5. If this pattern of triangles continues, find

    (i) the area of the 100th triangle   (ii) which triangle has an area of $240\,cm^2$.

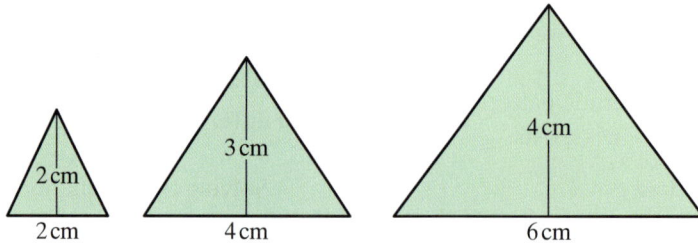

6. Each of the following number patterns can be written in the form $an^3 + bn^2 + cn + d$. Find the values of $a, b, c,$ and d in each case:

    (i) 6, 27, 74, 159, 294

    (ii) 3, −1, −1, 9, 35

   (iii) −1, 2, 17, 50, 107

7. Form a rule for determining the number of bright tiles in each of the following patterns. Determine the number of bright and dark tiles needed for the 24th pattern of each.

    (a)

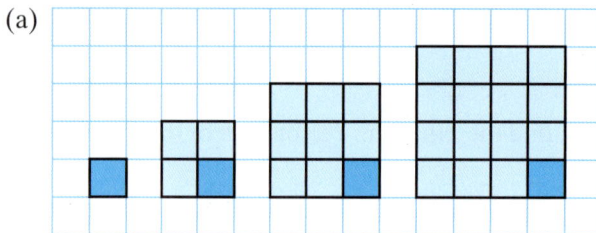

    (b)

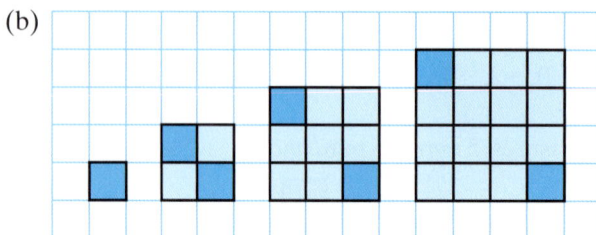

    (c)

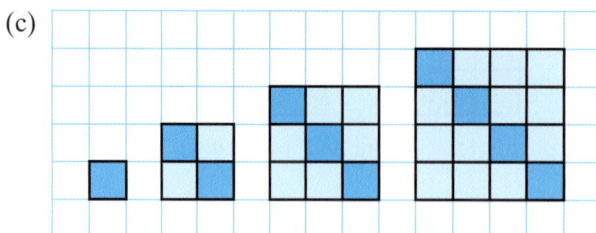

8. Write a formula for the nth term of each of the following number sequences.

    (i) 7, 16, 31, 52, 79, ...   (ii) 1, 0, −3, −8, −15, ...

  (iii) −1, 14, 53, 128, 251, ...   (iv) −2, 2, 6, 10, 14, ...

    (v) 4, 31, 98, 223, 424, ...

Revision Exercise 9 (Core)

1. Find the first four terms of these sequences given the nth term in each case:

   (i) $T_n = 3n + 4$
   (ii) $T_n = 6n - 1$
   (iii) $T_n = 2^{n-1}$
   (iv) $T_n = (n + 3)(n + 4)$
   (v) $T_n = n^3 + 1$

2. The third term of an arithmetic sequence is 71 and the seventh term is 55.
   Find the first term and the common difference.

3. In a geometric series, the first term is 12 and the sum to infinity is 36.
   Find the common ratio.

4. Find the common ratio in each of the following geometric progressions and hence write an expression for T_n, the nth term.

   (i) $-2, 4, -8, \ldots$
   (ii) $1, \frac{1}{2}, \frac{1}{4}, \ldots$
   (iii) $2, -6, 18, \ldots$

5. Using matchsticks, a series of cubes are made and joined as cuboids, as shown in the diagram.

   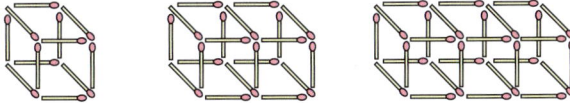

   (i) Determine the number of matchsticks needed for the nth cuboid.
   (ii) Determine the maximum number of cubes in the cuboid if there are 2006 matchsticks left for the construction.

6. The second term of a geometric sequence is 21.
   The third term is -63.
   Find   (i) the common ratio   (ii) the first term.

7. €2000 is invested in a savings scheme which offers 2.5% compound interest.
   Explain how the expression $A = €2000(1.025)^5$ represents the value of the investment after 5 years.

8. Find the sum of the first 200 natural numbers.

9. The fifth term of an arithmetic sequence is twice the second term.
   The two terms also differ by 9.
   Find the sum of the first 10 terms of the sequence.

10. Evaluate $\displaystyle\sum_{r=3}^{16} (2r + 1)$.

Revision Exercise 9 (Advanced)

1. A set of mirrors is arranged, as shown in the diagram. A lamp of 2000 lumens shines its light so that it reflects continuously from consecutive mirrors.
   (**Note:** A lumen is a measure of brightness)

   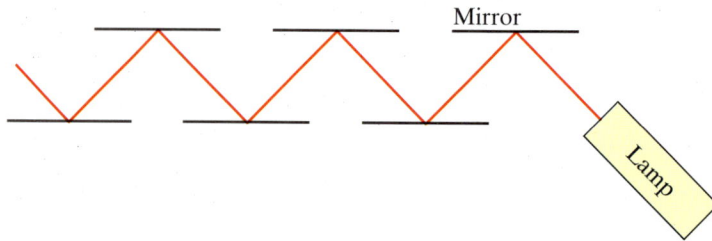

   Each mirror reflects $\frac{3}{5}$ of the light that hits it.
   (i) Find the intensity of the light reflecting from the 10th mirror.
   (ii) Write an equation representing the intensity of the light reflecting from the nth mirror.
   (iii) After how many reflections (mirrors) will the intensity be reduced to $\frac{1}{10}$ of its original value?

2. The value of a sum of money, €P, on deposit for t years is given by $A = P(1 + i)^t$, where i is the interest rate over the saving period.

   (i) Show that the time taken for the initial investment to double in value for any investment depends only on the interest rate i and not on the sum invested. Hence find an expression, in terms of i, the interest rate, for the time taken for an investment to double in value.
   (ii) Hence calculate the time taken for a sum of money to double in value if invested at an interest rate of
   (a) 2%   (b) 5%   (c) 10%.

3. A ball is dropped from a height of 10 m and bounces back up to 6m and then to 3.6 m and so on, as shown in the diagram. Copy the graph and add in the next five heights of the ball from the ground.

   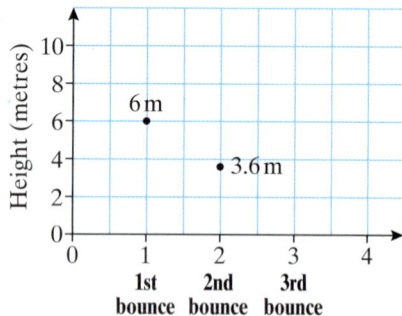

   (i) Write down a series of numbers representing the total distance travelled by the ball.
   (ii) Describe what type of series is generated.
   (iii) Find the total distance travelled by the ball.
   (iv) How is the size of the ball accounted for in this problem?

4. (i) Write an equation for the *nth* term of the sequence 3, 6, 12, 24, 48 ...

    (ii) Use logs to find the first term of this sequence to exceed one million.

5. A rich auntie is pleased to see you take up the game of chess. To encourage you, she says that she will put 1 cent on the first square of the board and tells you that she will double the amount for each week that you continue to learn the game.
    How much money, in euros, will your aunt owe you by the end of

    (i) week 32

    (ii) week 64 ?

6. An arithmetic sequence has three consecutive terms with a sum of 33 and a product of 935. Find these terms.

7. The value of a car depreciates by 13% per year. If the car is bought new for €30 000,

    (i)   find a formula linking the value €V of the car with its age a

    (ii) find the value of the car after five years

    (iii) find the year in which the car is worth less than €6000.

8. A sequence of numbers is given by the formula $T_n = 3\left(\frac{2}{3}\right)^n - 1$, where n is a positive integer.

    (i)   Find T_1, T_2, T_3 of this sequence.

    (ii) Show that $T_{n+1} = 2\left(\frac{2}{3}\right)^n - 1$.

    (iii) If $3T_{n+1} - 2T_n = k$, find k if $k \in Z$.

    (iv) Show that $\sum\limits_{n=1}^{15} \left[3\left(\frac{2}{3}\right)^n - 1\right] = -9.014$ correct to 4 significant figures.

9. Given that S_n is the sum to n terms of a series,

    (i)   show that $T_n = S_n - S_{n-1}$, where T_n is the *nth* term of the series

    (ii) if $S_n = 3n^2 + n$, find an expression for T_n

    (iii) obtain an expression, in terms of n, for $\sum\limits_{r=1}^{n}(T_r)^2$, given that $\Sigma n = \frac{n}{2}(n+1)$ and $\Sigma n^2 = \frac{n}{6}(n+1)(2n+1)$.

10. Express $\log_4 x$ in terms of $\log_2 x$ in its simplest form.
    Hence show that $\log_2 x$, $\log_4 x$ and $\log_{16} x$ are three consecutive terms of a geometric series and state the value of the common ratio.
    If the sum to infinity of the geometric series is $k \log_2 x$, find the value of k.
    (See Chapter 7 for the rules for logs.)

Revision Exercise 9 (Extended-Response Questions)

1. A cubic sequence can be represented by the nth term $T_n = an^3 + bn^2 + cn + d$, where $a, b, c \in R$ and $a \neq 0$.

   (i) Complete the following Table 1 in terms of a, b, and c.

T_1	T_2	T_3	T_4	T_5
$a + b + c + d$				
				1st difference
			2nd difference	
		3rd difference		

Table 1

   (ii) Based on this table, copy and complete the following statement:
      The third difference for all cubic sequences is always ....

  (iii) Compete the following two statements about quadratic sequences:
      (a) The second difference for all quadratic sequences is always ....
      (b) The first difference, $T_2 - T_1$, for all quadratic sequences is always ....

  (iv) Complete Table 2 for the sequence 5, 12, 25, 44, ...

T_1	T_2	T_3	T_4
5	12	25	44
			1st difference
		2nd difference	

Table 2

   (v) Use your expressions for first and second differences in (iii) to find a, b and c.
  (vi) Hence evaluate T_{20}.

2. A ball is dropped from an initial height of 40 m onto a concrete floor. On the tenth bounce, it rises 1 m up from the floor.

   (i) Write an expression for the height of the ball after n bounces.
  (ii) What percentage of the height from which it fell does the ball bounce back up each time?
  (iii) Find the heights of the ball after each of its first 5 bounces and hence complete the table:

Bounce	1st	2nd	3rd	4th	5th
Height					

  (iv) Draw a graph representing the height of the ball after each bounce.
   (v) Estimate from your sketch the number of bounces needed before the bounce does not exceed 2 m.
  (vi) Using the expression in part (i), calculate the minimum number of bounces needed for the ball to stay under 2 m.
 (vii) According to the expression in part (i) and the graph in part (iv), the ball could go on bouncing forever. Explain why this does not actually happen.

3. Ronan is in his Leaving Certificate year.

At the end of fifth-year, his parents gave him €20 a week pocket money.

To encourage him to work harder in sixth-year, they proposed two types of "pocket money schemes" for Ronan.

> Scheme 1: €20 in week one. €22 in week two … and so on, increasing by €2 each week.
>
> Scheme 2: €20 in week one. €21 in week two … and so on, increasing by a constant factor of $\frac{21}{20}$ each week.

  (i) Find separately the total amount in euro he would receive in week n for Scheme 1 and Scheme 2, leaving each answer in its simplest form.

 (ii) Assuming that a school year consists of 36 "five-day" weeks, which scheme do you think Ronan should choose? Justify your answer.

(iii) Ronan is interested in saving for a new games console which costs €400.
If he spends just €1.50 per school day and saves the rest of his pocket money, which is the earliest week he will be able to buy the games console?
Assume that he has chosen Scheme 1 above for his pocket money.

4. A liquid is kept in a barrel. At the start of the year 2010, 160 litres of liquid is poured into the barrel. If 15% of the volume of the liquid is lost by evaporation during the year,

  (i) evaluate the amount of liquid in the barrel at the end of the year

 (ii) show that the amount of liquid in the barrel at the end of 2020 is approximately 31.5 litres.

At the start of each year, starting in 2010, a new barrel is filled with 160 litres of liquid. This process is continued for twenty years until 2030.

(iii) Calculate the total amount of liquid in the barrels after evaporation at the end of the year 2030.

5. A company bought a new graphics machine for €15 000 at the start of 2005.
Each year the value of the machine decreases by 20% of its value at the start of the year.

  (i) Show that the value of the machine at the start of 2007 was €9,600.

 (ii) When the value of the machine falls below €500, the company plans to replace it. Find the year in which the machine will need to be replaced.

(iii) To plan for the replacement, the company pays €1000 at the start of each year into a savings account. The interest rate on the account is 5% per annum. If the first payment is made when the machine was first bought, and the last payment made at the start of the year in which the machine is to be replaced, using your answer to part (ii), find the value of the account when the machine is replaced.

(iv) If the amount saved is to fully cover the total cost of a new machine, calculate the upper limit on the average annual inflation rate over the period of the investment.

Statistics 1

Key words

discrete data   continuous data   categorical data   primary data
secondary data   univariate   bivariate   surveys   questionnaires
control group   population   sample   stratified   systematic   quota
cluster   convenience   mode   mean   median   outlier
interquartile range   standard deviation   percentile   stem and leaf diagram
histogram   positive skew   negative skew   explanatory variable
response variable   random sample

Introduction to statistics

The aim of statistics is to help us make sense of large amounts of information or data.
In pursuit of this aim, statistics divides the study of data into three parts:

  (i) Collecting data

 (ii) Describing and presenting data

(iii) Drawing conclusions from data.

In this chapter, we will discuss the variety of ways that information or data can be collected.
These include questionnaires, experiments and observations. Once data has been gathered,
we must then concern ourselves with the **description** of data so that ordinary people can
understand it. We can do this by representing the data graphically. You will meet a variety of
graphical methods in this chapter, as shown below. These are known as **descriptive statistics**.

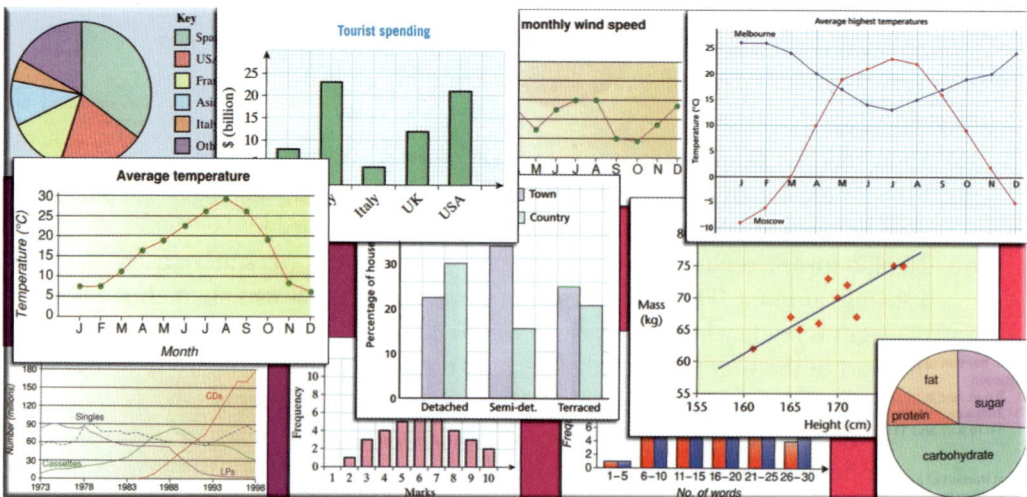

Another way of making a large amount of data easily understood is by **summarising** the data. Data may be summarised by simply finding an average or some other number that could be representative of the data as a whole. These numbers are known as **summary statistics**.

One of the most widely-used and important statistical processes is concerned with gathering information from a small group of people (or items) and using this data to draw conclusions about a much larger group of people. A good example of this is provided by the opinion poll. A poll is taken of a few thousand people. From the information that these people provide, remarkably accurate conclusions can be drawn that refer to the whole population, which is many times greater in number. Collecting information from a small group to draw conclusions about a large group is know as **inferential statistics**.

Section 10.1 Types of data

When we observe, count or measure something, we end up with a collection of numbers. These numbers are called **data**. Data is the plural of **datum** which means a piece of information.

1. Numerical data

Data which can be counted or measured is called **numerical** data because the answer is a number. Numerical data can be either **discrete** or **continuous**.

Discrete data

Data which can take only certain individual values is called **discrete data**. Here are some examples of **discrete data**:

> The number of goals scored by football teams on a Saturday
> The number of desks in the classrooms of the school
> The marks achieved in a test

Continuous data

Continuous data is measured on some scale and can take any value on that scale. Here are some examples of **continuous data**:

> The heights of students in your class
> The speed of cars passing a certain point on a road
> The time taken to complete a 100-metre sprint

Example 1

For each of these types of data, write down whether it is discrete or continuous.
  (i)   the number of coins in your pocket
 (ii)   the number of tickets sold for a concert
(iii)   the time taken to complete a puzzle
 (iv)   the weights of students in your class
  (v)   dress sizes

  (i) discrete   (ii) discrete   (iii) continuous
 (iv) continuous   (v)   discrete

2. Categorical data

The answer to the question, 'What colour is your car?' will not be a numerical value.
Rather, it will fit into a group or category such as blue, red, black, white, ...
Data which fits into a group or category is called **categorical data**.

Here are some examples of categorical data:

> gender (male, female)

> country of birth (Ireland, France, Spain, Nigeria ...)

> favourite sport (soccer, hurling, tennis, basketball ...)

The three examples of data above are generally referred to as **nominal categorical data**.

Categorical data in which the categories have an obvious order such as first division, second
division, third division, etc, is called **ordinal data**.

Other examples of ordinal data are:

> type of house (1-bedroomed, 2-bedroomed, 3-bedroomed)

> attendance at football matches (never, sometimes, very often)

> opinion scales (strongly disagree, disagree, neutral, agree, strongly agree).

The data you collect can be divided into two broad categories, namely, **primary data** and
secondary data.

3. Primary data

Data that is collected by an organisation or an individual who is going to use it is called
primary data.

Primary data is generally obtained

> by using a questionnaire

> by carrying out an expeirment

> by investigations

> by making observations and recording the results.

4. Secondary data

Data which is already available, or has been collected by
somebody else for a different purpose, is called secondary data.

Secondary data is obtained

> from the internet, e.g., the National Census

> from published statistics and databases

> from tables and charts in newspapers and magazines.

5. Univariate data

When one item of information is collected, for example, from each member of a group of
people, the data collected is called univariate data.

Examples of univariate data include:

> colour of eyes
> distance from school
> height in centimetres.

6. Bivariate data

Data that contains **two items** of information, such as the height and weight of a person, is generally called **paired data** or **bivariate data**.

Examples of bivariate data are:

> hours of study per week and marks scored in an examination
> the age of a car and the price of that car
> the engine sizes of cars and the number of kilometres travelled on a litre of petrol.

Colour of hair and gender is an example of **bivariate categorical data**.

The number of rooms in a house and the number of children in the house is an example of **bivariate discrete data**.

Example 2

For each of these sets of data, write down whether it is numerical or categorical:
  (i)   the sizes of shoes sold in a shop
  (ii) the colours of socks sold in a shop
  (iii) the subjects offered to Leaving Certificate students
  (iv) the marks given by judges in a debating competition
  (v)   the crops grown on a village farm
  (vi) the area of your classroom.

| (i) numerical | (ii) categorical | (iii) categorical |
| (iv) numerical | (v) categorical | (vi) numerical |

Exercise 10.1

1. State whether each of the following is categorical or numerical data:
    (i)   The number of bicycles sold by a shop in a particular week
    (ii) The colours of cars sold by a garage last month
    (iii) The number of horses in the six races at a meeting
    (iv) The favourite sports of all the students in a school.

2. State if each of the following data is discrete or continuous:
    (i)   The number of rooms in each of the houses on a road
    (ii) The number of CDs that have been sold
    (iii) The weights of the eggs in a carton
    (iv) Shoe sizes

(v) The time taken to complete a crossword puzzle

(vi) The score obtained when a dice is thrown

(vii) The number of spanners in a toolbox

(viii) The marks given by judges in a competition

3. Imelda bought a new dress.
   She wrote down (i) the colour of the dress
   (ii) the number of buttons on the dress
   (iii) the length of the dress.
   For each of these data types, write down whether it is numerical or categorical.
   Which of the three is discrete data?

4. Sonia recorded how long it took her to run a cross-country race and the race-number on her bib.
   Say if each of these variables is discrete or continuous.

5. State if each of the following is paired data:
   (i) The colours of shirts on a stand
   (ii) The ages and the heights of a group of students
   (iii) The number of brothers and their ages that each pupil in a class has
   (iv) The ages of all the people living on my street

6. *The amount of flour and the number of eggs needed to make a cake.*
   (i) Explain why this is paired data.
   (ii) Which part of the data is discrete?
   (iii) Which part of the data is continuous?

7. A doctor records information about her patients.
   The variables that she uses are described below:
   (i) the colour of the patient's eyes
   (ii) the patient's waist-size and height
   (iii) the patient's shoe size
   (iv) the patient's blood group.
   State if each variable is (a) categorical (b) numerical.
   Which of the four data types is discrete?
   Describe in full the data type given in part (ii).

8. State whether each of the following statements is true or false.
   Give a reason for your answer in each case.
   (i) The number of pockets on a jacket is discrete data.
   (ii) The types of trees in a forest is categorical data.
   (iii) The countries in which people like to holiday is numerical data.
   (iv) The number of bedrooms in each house on my street is categorical data.
   (v) The age of a tree and the circumference of the tree is bivariate data.
   (vi) The birth month of the students in your class is categorical data.

(vii) The number of matches played and the number of goals scored is bivariate and discrete data.

(viii) The weights of horses in a race and the times taken by the horses to complete the race is bivariate and continuous data.

9. Cars are often categorised as small, economy, family, executive and luxury.
   This is an example of **ordinal data**.
   Give three more examples of ordinal data.

10. Write down whether each of the following is an example of primary data or secondary data:
    (i) Alan counted the number of red vans passing the school gate.
    (ii) Helen examined records at a maternity hospital to find out how many babies were born each day in December.
    (iii) Robbie threw a dice 100 times and recorded the results to investigate if the dice was fair.
    (iv) Niamh used the internet to check the number of gold medals won by each competing country at the Beijing Olympics.

11. Roy and Damien want to predict next season's football league champions.
    Roy looks at the results for the last 5 years.
    Damien looks at the results for the 5 years before that.
    (i) What type of data are they using?
    (ii) Whose data is likely to be the more reliable and why?

12. Give one example of bivariate data which will be
    (i) discrete
    (ii) continuous.

Section 10.2 Collecting data

Data is collected for a variety of reasons and from a variety of sources.

Companies do market research to find out what customers like or dislike about their products and to see whether or not they would like new products. The government carries out a **census** of every person in the country every five years. Local government, education authorities and other organisations use the information obtained for further planning.

Data can be collected through direct observation such as a naturalist observing animal behaviour. In an observational study, the observer wishes to record data without interfering with the process being observed.

Apart from observational studies, data may also be collected by
> carrying out a survey
> doing an experiment
> conducting interviews or completing questionnaires
> using a data logger which records data or readings over a period of time, using a sensor.

1. Surveys

Surveys are particularly useful for collecting data that is likely to be personal.

The main survey methods are:
> postal surveys in which people are asked questions
> personal interviews in which people are asked questions; this type of survey is very widely-used in market research
> telephone surveys; here the interview is conducted by phone
> **observation**, which involves monitoring behaviour or information.

Survey method	Advantages	Disadvantages
Observation	> Systematic and mechanical	> Results are prone to chance
Personal interview and telephone survey	> Many questions can be asked > High response rate	> Expensive > Interviewer may influence responses
Postal survey	> Relatively cheap > Large amounts of data can be collected	> Limited in the type of data that can be collected > Poor response rate

2. Questionnaires

One of the most commonly-used methods of conducting a survey is by means of a questionnaire.

A **questionnaire** is a set of questions designed to obtain data from individuals.

People who answer questionnaires are called **respondents**.

There are two ways in which the questions can be asked.
> An interviewer asks the questions and fills in the questionnaire.
> People are given a questionnaire and asked to fill in the responses themselves.

When you are writing questions for a questionnaire,
> be clear on what you want to find out and what data you need
> ask short, concise questions
> start with simple questions to encourage the person who is giving the responses
> provide response boxes where possible: Yes ☐ No ☐
> avoid leading questions such as
>> 'Don't you agree that there is too much sport on television?'
> or 'Do you think that professional footballers are overpaid?'
> avoid personal questions such as,
>> 'Do you live in an affluent area?'
> or 'Are you well educated?'
> or 'Are you overweight?'

A choice of responses can be very useful in replying to the question, 'What age are you?'

Here is an example: Tick your age in one of the boxes below:

☐ ☐ ☐ ☐
Under 18 years   18–30   31–50   Over 50

Notice that there are no gaps in the ages and that only one response applies to each person.

When you are collecting data, you need to make sure that your survey or experiment is **fair** and avoids **bias**. If bias exists, the data collected might be unrepresentative.

The boxes given below contain questions that should be avoided because they either are too **vague**, too **personal**, or may **influence** the answer.

How often do you play tennis?

Sometimes ☐   Occasionally ☐   Often ☐

The three words *sometimes*, *occasionally* and *often* mean different things to different people.

Normal people enjoy swimming.
Do you enjoy swimming?

Yes ☐   No ☐

This is a leading question and may cause the result to be biased.
The first sentence should not be there.

Have you ever stolen goods from a supermarket?

Yes ☐   No ☐

Few people are likely to answer this question honestly if they have already stolen.

Whenever you undertake a survey or experiment, it is advisable to do a pilot survey. A pilot survey is one that is carried out on a very small scale to make sure the design and methods of the survey are likely to produce the information required. It should identify any problems with the wording of the questions and likely responses.

3. Designed experiments

In statistics, the word 'experiment' generally refers to a situation where the experimentor carries out some activity and records the results by counting or measuring or simply observing.

Thus an experiment may consist of
> tossing three coins and recording the number of times two heads show
> measuring the circumference of oak trees in a wood
> throwing a dice several times to determine if it is biased
> recording the side-effects of a new drug
> investigating whether people are better at remembering words, numbers or pictures.

4. Control group

If we wish to investigate whether a new drug has any effect on those who take it, we select a group of patients, chosen at random, to form a sample. The sample is then divided randomly into two groups. Both groups think that they are taking the new drug, but only the first group actually take it.

The second group are given an inactive substance (or placebo) but they think they have taken the drug. This second group is called a **control group**. If more patients get better in the first group, then the drug has an effect.

Explanatory and response variables

In a statistical experiment, one of the variables will be controlled while its effect on the other variable is observed.

The controlled variable is called the **explanatory variable**.
The effect being observed is called the **response variable**.

> ### Example 1
>
> A research team is investigating whether the adding of fish oil to the daily diet of school students increases their IQ. A school of 500 students is selected. Two groups, each of 50 students, are selected at random.
> Group A is given a daily ration of fish oil.
> Group B is given the same food as Group A, but no fish oil.
> (i) Which group is the control group?
> (ii) What is the explanatory variable in this experiment?
> (iii) What is the response variable?
>
> (i) Group B is the control group.
> (ii) The explanatory variable is the fish oil; that is, the variable whose effect on the response variable we wish to study.
> (iii) The response variable is the IQ of the student; that is, the variable whose changes we wish to study.

Exercise 10.2

1. Jack wants to find out what students think about the library service at his college. Part of the questionnaire he has written is shown.

   > **Q1.** What is your full name? ....
   >
   > **Q2.** How many times a week do you go to the library?
   > ☐ Often   ☐ Sometimes   ☐ Never

   (i) Why should Q1 not be asked?
   (ii) What is wrong with the choices offered in Q2?

2. Carol wants to find out what people think of the HSE. Part of the questionnaire she has written is shown.

   > **Q1.** What is your date of birth? ....
   >
   > **Q2.** Don't you agree that waiting times for operations are too long?
   > Yes ☐   No ☐
   >
   > **Q3.** How many times did you visit your doctor last year?
   > ☐ less than 5   ☐ 5–10   ☐ 10 or more

(i) Why should Q1 not be asked?

(ii) Give a reason why Q2 is unsuitable.

(iii) (a) Explain why the responses to Q3 are unsuitable in their present form.

(b) Rewrite a more suitable question to be included in the questionnaire.

3. Give a reason why questions A and B below should be re-worded before being included in a questionnaire.

Rewrite each one showing exactly how you would present it in a questionnaire.

Question A: Do you live in a working-class or middle-class area?

Question B: The new supermarket seems to be a great success. Do you agree?

4. Decide if the given question is suitable for use in a questionnaire. If it is not, give a reason why and rewrite the question to improve it.

How much pocket money do you get?

a little ☐   some ☐   a lot ☐

5. A market research company is conducting a survey to find out whether, last year, most people had a holiday in Ireland, elsewhere in Europe or in the rest of the world.

It also wants to know if they stayed in self-catering accommodation, hotels or went camping.

Design **two** questions that could be used in a questionnaire to efficiently find out all this information.

6. Which of the following questions do you think are biased?

Write down their letters and explain what makes them biased.

A: Did you go to a cinema in the last month?

B: It is important to eat fruit. Do you eat fruit?

C: How many hours of television do you watch each week?

D: In view of the huge number of road accidents outside this school, do you think the speed limit should be reduced?

7. Megan has to carry out a survey into the part-time jobs of all the 16-year-olds in her school.

She has to find out:

➤ what proportion of these 16-year-olds have part-time jobs

➤ whether more girls than boys have part-time jobs.

Design **two** questions which she could include in her questionnaire.

8. Richie is convinced that people with longer legs run faster in sprint races. He conducts an experiment to test his theory.

What are the explanatory and response variables he should measure?

9. The HSE has the following data on operations carried out in a large Dublin hospital.

Number of operating theatres	3	4	5	6	7
Number of operations per day	15	21	24	28	37

(i) What is the explanatory variable?

(ii) What is the response variable?

10. A medical research company wishes to investigate whether a new drug is effective in controlling blood-pressure.

They select 80 people who suffer from high blood-pressure and divide them randomly into two groups of 40.

Group A is given the drug. Group B is not given the drug, but they believe that they are taking it.

At the end of the study, the blood pressures of both groups are taken to see if the drug is effective.

   (i)   Which group is the control group?

  (ii)   What is the explanatory variable in the experiment?

 (iii)   What is the response variable?

 (iv)   Which of these would best describe the research?

       (a)   a designed experiment

       (b)   an observational study.

Section 10.3 Populations and sampling

In a statistical enquiry, you often need information about a particular group. This group is known as the population and it could be small, large or even infinite.

Examples of populations include
  (i)   all second-level pupils in Ireland
 (ii)   paid-up members of golf clubs
(iii)   people entitled to vote in a general election.

If information is obtained from all members of a population, the survey is called a census.

Sample survey

When a population is large, taking a census can be very time-consuming and difficult to do with accuracy. So when a census is ruled out as being impractical, information is normally taken from a small part of the population. The chosen members of the population are called a **sample** and an investigation using a sample is called a **sample survey**. Data from a sample can be obtained relatively cheaply and quickly. If the data is representative of the population, a sample survey can give an accurate indication of the population characteristic that is being studied.

The **size** of a sample is important. If the sample is too small, the results may not be very reliable.
If the sample is too large, the data may take a long time to collect and analyse.
However, large samples are more likely to give reliable information than small ones.

Bias in sampling

The sample you select for your study is very important. If the sample is not properly selected, the results may be **biased**. If **bias** exists, the results will be distorted and so may not be representative of the population as a whole.

Bias in a sample may arise from any of the following:

> **Choosing a sample which is not representative**
  Example   Cara is doing a survey on people's attitude towards gambling. If she stands outside a casino and questions people as they enter or leave, the results will be biased as these people are already involved in gambling.

> **Not identifying the correct population**
  Example   The school principal wants to find out about students' attitudes to school uniforms. She questions ten Leaving Certificate students only. This may lead to biased results as the opinions of the younger students (from 1st year to 5th year) are not included.

> **Failure to respond to a survey**
  Many people do not fill in responses to questionnaires sent through the post. Those who do respond may not be representative of the population being surveyed.

> **Dishonest answers to questions**

Sampling methods

The purpose of sampling is to gain information about the whole population by selecting a sample from that population. If you want the sample to be representative of the population, you must give every member of the population an equal chance of being included in the sample. This is known as **random sampling**. Before a random sample is selected, a **sampling frame** must be used to identify the population. A sampling frame consists of all the items in the population to ensure that every item has a chance of being selected in the sample.

Some of the most commonly-used sampling methods are given below.

1. Simple random sampling

A sample of size n is called a **simple random sample** if every possible sample of size n has an equal chance of being selected. In practice, this means that each member of the population has an equal chance of being selected.

There are many ways of doing this.

Methods for choosing a **simple random sample** could involve giving each member of the population a number and then selecting the numbers for the sample in one of these ways:

> putting the numbers into a hat and then selecting however many you need for the sample
> using a random number table
> using a random number generator on your calculator or computer

Any of these methods are suitable only if the population is relatively small and the sampling frame is clearly identified.

2. Stratified sampling

Most populations contain identifiable strata. For example male / female or Retired / working / in education etc.

<40 yrs	40–60 yrs	>60 yrs
45%	40%	15%

Assume this table reflected the age distribution of a particular county. If samples are being used to determine preferences in music or film or technological innovation in this county and if the sample (randomly selected) contain proportions (of age) which do not reflect their proportion in the population then there will obviously be an inbuilt bias and a misleading view of the population. **Stratified sampling** is used when the population can be split into separate groups or strata that are quite different from each other. The number selected from each group is proportional to the size of the group. Separate random samples are then taken from each group.

Example 1

A survey to estimate the number of vegetarians in a mixed college with 660 boys and 540 girls is carried out.
A sample of 40 students is required.
How many boys and girls should be included?

The total number of students is $660 + 540 = 1200$.

Boys: $\dfrac{660}{1200} \times \dfrac{40}{1} = 22$ boys

Girls: $\dfrac{540}{1200} \times \dfrac{40}{1} = 18$ girls

So 22 boys and 18 girls should be chosen.

---

3. Systematic sampling

A sample which is obtained by choosing items at regular intervals from an unordered list is called a **systematic sample**. For example, if you wish to choose 20 students from 200 students, you could take every tenth student from the register. Select a random number between 1 and 10, e.g., 4. Thus you could select the 4th, 14th, 24th, 34th … until you get 20 students

4. Quota sampling

Quota sampling is widely used in market research and in opinion polls. First the population is divided into groups in terms of age, general education levels, social class, etc. The interviewer is then told how many people (the quota) to interview in each of these groups, but the interviewer makes the choice of who exactly is asked. A disadvantage of quota sampling is that the actual people or items chosen are left to the discretion of the interviewer which could lead to bias. An advantage of quota sampling is that no sampling frame is required.

5. Cluster sampling

If the population is geographically widely spread, simple random sampling would be very difficult and very expensive. In this case the population is divided into clusters (regions). The smaller the cluster the better.

A possible procedure is then:
   (i)   Select a cluster (region) at random
   (ii) Select every member of the cluster or a random sample of members in each Cluster.
   Opinion polls generally use cluster sampling.

6. Convenience sampling

Convenience sampling involves selecting a group of people because it is easy for us to contact them and they are willing to answer our questions. For example, a sample of 40 students in a school could be selected by simply taking the first 40 names on the school register. Convenience sampling is very quick and easy to organise but it can lead to high levels of bias and so is very likely to be unrepresentative.

Example 2

Simon wanted to investigate whether people in Ireland measured their height in metric or imperial units. He went to his local supermarket and asked the first twenty people he met how tall they were.
  (i)   For this survey, state the sampling frame, the sampling method used and why it might be biased.
  (ii) Outline a better method of choosing a sample.

  (i)   The sampling frame could be the whole population of Ireland.
        The sampling method used is convenience sampling.
        It may be biased as everyone chosen most likely lives in the same area and so may not provide a cross-section of social class and age-groups. Also, the sample is too small.
  (ii) A better method would be to use stratified sampling. In this way, you could ensure that men and women across all age-groups, different ethnic groups and different social classes were represented in the sample.

Exercise 10.3

1. Explain briefly the difference between a **census** and a **sample**.
   Give two reasons why a sample may be preferred to a census.

2. There are 100 students in Transition Year.
   Generate random numbers on your calculator to select a sample of 10 students from Transition Year.
   Describe briefly what is meant by a simple random sample.

3. For each of the following methods, say whether it would give a random sample or whether it is likely to be biased:
   (i)   Interview all the people in a local supermarket.
   (ii) Take every tenth person from a list.
   (iii) Put all the names in a hat and pick without looking.
   (iv) Test the first article produced each hour by a machine.
   (v)   Number all the items and then select by using random number tables.

4. Describe briefly what is meant by convenience sampling.

   Jack is doing a statistical project. He decides to take a sample of 20 people.
   The sample he chooses is the first 20 names on a register.
   (i) What sort of sample is he choosing?
   (ii) Give two major problems with this method of taking a sample.

5. What type of sampling is being used in each of the following surveys?
   (i) Kate is doing a survey to find out how often people go to the cinema and how they travel to get there. She stands outside her local cinema and questions 20 people as they go in.
   (ii) Enda wants to know people's voting intentions as they enter the polling station on election day. He questions every 5th person as they enter the polling station.
   (iii) There are 60 girls and 40 boys in 5th year.
   The school principal wants to interview a sample of 20 students from 5th year. She randomly selects 12 girls and 8 boys.

6. After plans for a bypass to a large town were announced, the local newspaper received twelve letters on the subject. Eleven were opposed to it.
   The newspaper claimed

   OVER 90% ARE AGAINST NEW BYPASS

   (i) Give two reasons why the newspaper could be criticised for making this claim.
   (ii) The local council is to carry out a survey to find the true nature of local opinion.
   Give two factors that should be taken into account when selecting the sample.

7. Gillian wanted to find out how much people in Ireland were prepared to spend on holidays abroad. She asked people in the street where she lived.
   (i) What sampling method was Gillian using?
   (ii) Explain why the sample may be biased.
   (iii) Describe a better method of choosing the sample.

8. There are 1000 students in Nigel and Sonia's school.
   Nigel is carrying out a survey of the types of food eaten at lunchtime.
   (i) Explain how Nigel could take a random sample of students to carry out this survey.

   This table shows the gender and the number of students in each year group.

Year group	Number of boys	Number of girls	Total
1	100	100	200
2	90	80	170
3	120	110	230
4	80	120	200
5	100	100	200

Sonia is carrying out a survey about how much homework students are given.
She decides to take a stratified sample of 100 students from the whole school.
   (ii) Calculate how many in the stratified sample should be
      (a) students from year group 3
      (b) boys from year group 4.

9. A research company was asked to do a survey on people's attitudes to the HSE. They divided the population into ten groups of roughly equal size, based on gender, age and annual income. They then asked fifty interviewers to question twenty people from each group and record their responses.
   (i) What sampling method did the research company use?
   (ii) Give one advantage and one disadvantage of this method.

10. Explain briefly
    (i) Why it is often desirable to take a sample rather than a census
    (ii) What you understand by the term 'sampling frame'.

11. In a school, there are 460 pupils in Junior Cycle and 420 pupils in Senior Cycle.
    (i) How many pupils from each cycle of the school should be included in a stratified random sample of size 100?
    (ii) Explain briefly in what circumstances a stratified random sample might be taken rather than a simple random sample.

12. Julia and her friends are investigating the part-time jobs of the Senior Cycle students in their school. There are eight Senior Cycle classes.
    (i) Julia chooses one class at random and questions every pupil in this class.
        What sampling method is she using?
    (ii) Brian goes into the school hall at morning break and chooses ten girls and ten boys.
        What sampling method is he using?
    (iii) Leah has a list of all the pupils in Senior Cycle, arranged in alphabetical order. For her sample, she chooses the third pupil on the list and then every tenth pupil after that.
        What sampling method is she using?

Section 10.4 Measures of location

When we are presented with a huge mass of numbers (data), we need just one or two numbers that would convey most of the essential information. These numbers are generally referred to as **summary statistics**.

There are two main types of summary statistic, namely, **measures of location** and **measures of spread**. Measures of location answer the question 'What value is typical of the values in the data?' Measures of spread answer the questions 'How much do the values vary?' or 'How spread out are the values?'

In this section, we will deal with measures of location or averages.
There are three different types of average in statistics.
These are the **mode**, the **mean** and the **median**.

1. The Mode

The **mode** is the most common value in a set of data. The mode is very useful when one value appears much more often than any other. It is easy to find and can be used for non-numerical data such as the colours of cars sold by a car dealership.

The following numbers represent the ages of students on a school bus.

    10, 11, 12, 12, 12, 13, 13, 14, 14, 15, 15, 15, 15, 16, 16, 16, 17, 17

The number in this list with the greatest frequency is 15.

∴   the mode = 15 years.

2. The Mean

To find the mean of a set of numbers,

1.   Find the sum of all the numbers.
2.   Divide this sum by the number of numbers.

The mean is the most frequently-used 'average'.

$$\text{The mean is} = \frac{\text{sum of the numbers}}{\text{number of numbers}}$$

It is important because it considers every piece of data. However, it can be affected by extreme values.

The mean of the numbers   12, 14, 10, 17, 21 and 22 is:

$$\text{Mean} = \frac{12 + 14 + 10 + 17 + 21 + 22}{6} = \frac{96}{6} = 16$$

The mean of a frequency distribution

The table below shows the marks (from 1 to 10) scored by the twenty pupils in a class.

Marks	1	2	3	4	5	6	7	8	9	10
No. of pupils	1	1	1	3	5	3	2	2	1	1

The average or mean mark of this distribution is found by dividing the total number of marks by the total number of pupils.

To find the total number of marks, we multiply each mark (or *variable*) by the number of pupils (*frequency*) who received that mark.

∴   the mean $= \dfrac{1(1) + 2(1) + 3(1) + 4(3) + 5(5) + 6(3) + 7(2) + 8(2) + 9(1) + 10(1)}{1 + 1 + 1 + 3 + 5 + 3 + 2 + 2 + 1 + 1}$

$$= \frac{110}{20} = 5.5 \text{ marks}$$

If x stands for the variable and f stands for the frequency, then

$$\text{mean} = \frac{\Sigma fx}{\Sigma f}$$

$$\text{Mean} = \frac{\Sigma fx}{\Sigma f}$$

where Σfx is the sum of all the variables multiplied by the corresponding frequencies and Σf is the sum of the frequencies.

Grouped frequency distributions

The grouped frequency distribution table below shows the marks (out of 25) achieved by fifty students in a test.

Marks achieved	1–5	6–10	11–15	16–20	21–25
No. of students	11	12	15	9	3

While it is not possible to find the exact mean of a grouped frequency distribution, we can find an estimate of the mean by taking the **mid-interval value** of each class. The mid-interval value in the (1–5) class is found by adding 1 and 5 and dividing by 2,

i.e., $\dfrac{1+5}{2} = 3$

Similarly, the mid-interval value of the (6–10) class is $\dfrac{6+10}{2} = 8$.

The table given on the previous page is reproduced, with the mid-interval values written in smaller size over each class interval.

	3	8	13	18	23
Marks achieved	1–5	6–10	11–15	16–20	21–25
No. of students	11	12	15	9	3

Mean $= \dfrac{\Sigma fx}{\Sigma f} = \dfrac{11(3) + 12(8) + 15(13) + 9(18) + 3(23)}{11 + 12 + 15 + 9 + 3} = \dfrac{555}{50} = 11.1$

3. The Median

To find the median of a list of numbers, put the numbers in order of size, starting with the smallest. The **median** is the middle number.

If there are 11 numbers in the list, the middle value is $\frac{1}{2}(11 + 1)$, i.e., the 6th value.

If there are 10 numbers in the list, the middle number is $\frac{1}{2}(10 + 1)$, i.e., the $5\frac{1}{2}$th value.

This value is half the sum of the 5th and 6th values.

> If there are n numbers in a list, the middle value is $\frac{1}{2}(n + 1)$.
>
> If $\frac{1}{2}(n + 1) = 4$, then the 4th value is the median.

Example 1

Find the median of these numbers: 5, 8, 12, 4, 9, 3, 7, 2.

Writing the numbers in order of size, we get:

$$2, \ 3, \ 4, \ \boxed{5, \ 7,} \ 8, \ 9, \ 12$$

The median is $\frac{1}{2}(5 + 7) = \dfrac{5 + 7}{2} = \dfrac{12}{2} = 6$

> Write the numbers in order of size to find the median.

∴ the median = 6

The mode and median of a frequency distribution

The frequency table below shows the number of letters in the answers to a crossword.

No. of letters in word	3	4	5	6	7
Frequency	3	4	9	5	2

The **mode** is the number of letters (in the word) that occurs most frequently.
Thus the mode is 5 as it occurs more often than any other number.

The **median** is the middle number in the distribution.

The total frequency is $3 + 4 + 9 + 5 + 2$, i.e., 23.

The middle value of the 23 values is $\frac{1}{2}(23 + 1)$, i.e., the 12th value.

We take the frequency row and find the column that contains the 12th number.
The sum of the first two frequencies is $3 + 4 = 7$.
The sum of the first three frequencies is $3 + 4 + 9 = 16$.
Thus the 12th value occurs in the third column, where the number of letters in the word is 5.
$\therefore$ the median = 5

When dealing with grouped frequency distributions, we use the same procedure to find the **class interval** in which the median lies.

Deciding which average to use

The three averages, the **mean**, the **mode** and the **median**, are all useful but one may be more appropriate than the others in different situations.

The **mode** is useful when you want to know, for example, which shoe size is the most common.

The **mean** is useful for finding a 'typical' value when most of the data is closely grouped. The mean may not give a typical value if the data is very spread out or if it includes a few values that are very different from the rest. These values are known as **outliers**.

Take, for example, a small company where the chief executive earns €12 100 a month and the other eleven employees each earn €2500 a month.

Here the mean monthly salary is €3300 which is not typical of the monthly salaries.

In situations like this, the **median** or middle value may be more typical.

The table below, which compares the advantages and disadvantages of each type of average, should help you make the correct decision.

Average	Advantages	Disadvantages
Mode	› Easy to find › Not influenced by extreme values	› May not exist › Not very useful for further analysis
Median	› Unaffected by extremes › Easy to calculate if data is ordered	› Not always a given data value › Not very useful for further analysis
Mean	› Uses all the data › Easy to calculate › Very useful for further analysis	› Distorted by extreme results › Mean is not always a given data value

Example 2

There are 10 apartments in a block.
On a particular day, the number of letters delivered to each of the apartments is

$$2, \ 0, \ 5, \ 3, \ 4, \ 0, \ 1, \ 0, \ 3, \ 15$$

Calculate the mean, mode and median number of letters.
Which of these averages is the most suitable to represent this data?
Give a reason for your answer.

$$\text{Mean} = \frac{2 + 0 + 5 + 3 + 4 + 0 + 1 + 0 + 3 + 15}{10} = \frac{33}{10} = 3.3$$

Mode $= 0$

Median: 0, 0, 0, 1, $\boxed{2, \ 3,}$ 3, 4, 5, 15

$$\text{Median} = \frac{2 + 3}{2} = \frac{5}{2} = 2\tfrac{1}{2}$$

Here the mean has been distorted by the large number of letters delivered to one apartment. It is, therefore, not a good measure of the 'typical' number of letters delivered.
Neither is the mode a good measure of the 'typical' number of letters, since seven out of ten apartments do receive some letters.
The median is the best measure of the 'typical' number of letters delivered since half of the apartments receive more than the median and half receive less than the median.

Outliers

An outlier is a very high or very low value that is not typical of the other values in a data set. If the data set is small, an outlier can have a significant effect on the mean.

Exercise 10.4

1. Rewrite each of the following arrays of numbers in order of size and then write down
   (i)   the mode   (ii)   the median.
      (a) 8, 11, 2, 5, 8, 7, 8, 2, 5   (b) 3, 3, 7, 8, 7, 9, 8, 5, 7, 11, 12

2. The speeds, in kilometres per hour, of 11 cars travelling on a road are shown:
      41, 42, 31, 36, 42, 43, 42, 34, 41, 37, 45
   (i)   Find the median speed.   (ii)   Find the mean speed.

3. A rugby team played 10 games.
   Here are the numbers of points the team scored:
      12, 22, 14, 11, 7, 18, 22, 14, 36, 14
   (i)   Write down the mode.
   (ii)   What is the median number of points scored?
   (iii)   Find the mean number of points scored.

4. The mean of four numbers is 19. Three of them are 21, 25 and 16. Find the fourth number.

5. Kate's marks in four tests were: 8, 4, 5, 3.
What marks did she get in her fifth and sixth tests if her modal mark was 4 and her mean mark was 5 after the six tests?

6. Find (i) the mean (ii) the median of these numbers:

    9, 11, 11, 15, 17, 18, 100

   Which of these two averages would you choose to best describe these numbers?

7. The mean of five numbers is 39.
Two of the numbers are 103 and 35 and each of the other three numbers is equal to x.
Find   (i) the total of the five numbers
       (ii) the value of x.

8. There are 12 children in Phil's group. Their mean mark in a Maths test is 76%. In Paul's group, there are only 8 children.
Their mean mark is 84%. Find the overall mean mark for the 20 children.

9. A teacher sets a test.
He wants to choose a minimum mark for a distinction so that 50% of his students score higher than this mark.
Should he use the modal mark, the median mark or the mean mark?
Give a reason for your answer.

10. A class took a test.
The mean mark of the 20 boys in the class was 17.4.
The mean mark of the 10 girls in the class was 13.8.
  (i) Calculate the mean mark for the whole class.

   Five pupils in another class took a different test.
   Their marks, written in order, were 12, 18, 20, 25 and x.
   The mean of these 5 marks was 2 greater than the median of the 5 marks.
  (ii) Calculate the value of x.

11. A test consisted of ten questions, 1 mark per question, and 0 for an incorrect solution.
The following table shows how a class of students scored in the test:

Marks	3	4	5	6	7	8	9
No. of students	3	2	6	10	0	3	1

  (i) How many students were in the class?
  (ii) Write down the mode of the data.
  (iii) Calculate the mean mark per student.
  (iv) How many students scored better than the mean mark?
  (v) Find the median mark.

12. Paula has 6 people in her family. She wonders how many people are in her friends' families. She asks each of her friends and records the information in a table.

Number in family	2	3	4	5	6	7	8
Frequency	2	4	6	5	2	0	1

   (i)   Write down the modal number of people in these families.
   (ii) Find the median number of persons per family.
   (iii) Calculate the mean of the distribution.

13. The ages of some people watching a film are given in this frequency table:

Age (in years)	10–20	20–30	30–40	40–50
No. of people	4	15	11	10

   (i)   Use the mid-interval value of each class to estimate the mean of the distribution, giving your answer correct to the nearest year.
   (ii) In which interval does the median lie?

14. Joe collects six pieces of data x_1, x_2, x_3, x_4, x_5 and x_6. He works out that Σx is 256.2.
   (i)   Calculate the mean for these data.

He collects another piece of data. It is 52.
   (ii) Write down the effect this piece of data will have on the mean.

15. The frequency distribution table below shows the ratings of a disco by a random sample of 40 students.
A capital A means they enjoyed it very much.
A capital E means that they did not enjoy it at all.

Rating	A	B	C	D	E
Number of students	6	13	10	7	4

   (i)   Work out (a) the mode, (b) the median for this distribution.
   (ii) Explain why you cannot write down the mean of this distribution.

16. The rainfall in a certain seaside holiday resort was measured, in millimetres, every week for ten weeks. The hours of sunshine were also recorded. The data is shown in the table.

Rainfall (mm)	0	1	2	3	3	26	3	2	3	0
Sunshine (hours)	70	15	10	15	18	0	15	21	21	80

   (i)   Calculate the mean rainfall per week.
   (ii) Calculate the mean number of hours of sunshine per week.
   (iii) Write down the modal amount of rainfall and the modal amount of sunshine per week.
   (iv) Work out the median rainfall and the median amount of sunshine per week.

The council plans to produce a brochure and in it they wish to promote the resort as having lots of sunshine and little rain.

(v) Write down, with reasons, which of the mean, mode or median they should quote in their brochure as the average rainfall and hours of sunshine.

17. An ordinary dice was thrown 50 times and the resulting scores were summarised in a frequency table.
    The mean score was calculated to be 3.42.
    It was later found that the frequencies 12 and 9 of two consecutive scores had been swapped.
    What is the correct value of the mean?

Section 10.5 Measures of variability

When dealing with **averages** in the previous section, we were looking for a data value that was typical or representative of all the data values.

In this section, we will discuss the measure of the spread of the data about the mean to help us describe the data more fully.

The three most common ways of measuring the spread or **variability** of data are the **range**, the **interquartile range** and **standard deviation**.

1. The range

The **range** of a set of data is the highest value of the set minus the lowest value.

It shows the **spread** of the data.

It is very useful when comparing two sets of data.

> The range of a set of data is the largest value minus the smallest value.

The range is a crude measure of spread because it uses only the largest and smallest value of the data.

The range of the numbers 14, 18, 11, 27, 21, 19, 33, 24 is

$$\text{Range} = 33 - 11 = 22$$

2. Quartiles and Interquartile range

When data is arranged in order of size, we have already learned that the median is the value halfway into the data. So we can say that the median divides the data into two halves.
The data can also be divided into four quarters.

When the data is arranged in ascending order of size:

> the **lower quartile** is the value one quarter of the way into the data
> the **upper quartile** is the value three quarters of the way into the data
> the upper quartile minus the lower quartile is called the **interquartile range**.

The lower quartile is written Q_1; the median is Q_2; the upper quartile is Q_3.

Consider the following data which is arranged in order of size. It contains 15 numbers.

| The lower quartile is the value one quarter of the way along. Written as Q_1 | The median is the value halfway along. Written as Q_2 | The upper quartile is the value three quarters of the way along. Written as Q_3 |

0	2	4	5	7	8	10	12	12	12	13	14	14	15	16

Q_1 is the 4th value $\qquad$ Q_2 is the 8th value $\qquad$ Q_3 is the 12th value

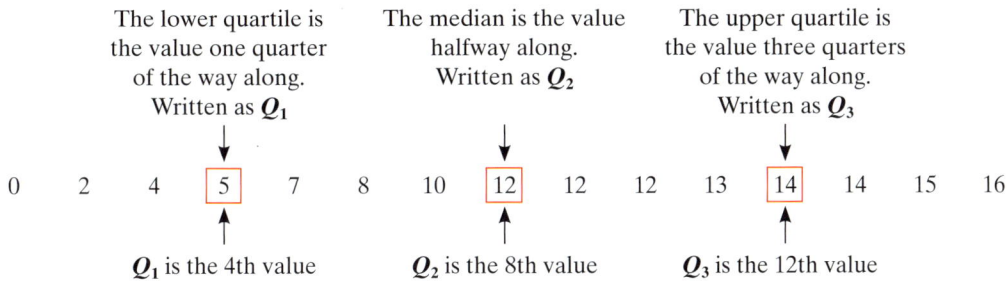

The lower quartile $Q_1 = 5$.
The median $Q_2 = 12$.
The upper quartile $Q_3 = 14$.
The interquartile range $= Q_3 - Q_1 = 14 - 5 = 9$.

> The interquartile range is
> upper quartile − lower quartile
> $= Q_3 - Q_1$

When n data values are written in order:

❯ the lower quartile, Q_1, is the $\frac{1}{4}(n + 1)$th value

❯ the median, Q_2, is the $\frac{1}{2}(n + 1)$th value

❯ the upper quartile, Q_3, is the $\frac{3}{4}(n + 1)$th value.

If you get a non-integer value for $\frac{1}{4}(n + 1)$ or $\frac{3}{4}(n + 1)$, e.g., $3\frac{3}{4}$, find the mean of the 3rd and 4th pieces of data.

If you get a non-integer for $\frac{1}{2}(n + 1)$, take the mean of the two data values on either side.
For example if $\frac{1}{2}(n + 1) = 3\frac{1}{2}$, find the mean of the 3rd and 4th data values.

Example 1

These are the test marks of 11 students:

$$52,\ 78,\ 61,\ 49,\ 79,\ 47,\ 54,\ 58,\ 72,\ 62,\ 73$$

Find　　(i) the median　　　(ii) the lower quartile
　　　(iii) the upper quartile　　(iv) the interquartile range.

We first rewrite the numbers in order, starting with the smallest:

$$47,\ 49,\ 52,\ 54,\ 58,\ 61,\ 62,\ 72,\ 73,\ 78,\ 79$$

(i) The median is the middle value of the list.
Since there are 11 values, the middle value is
$\frac{1}{2}(11 + 1)$ i.e. the 6th value.
The 6th value is $61 \Rightarrow$ the median $= 61$.

(ii) The lower quartile is the value that is $\frac{1}{4}$ way through the distribution.
This value is found by getting $\frac{1}{4}(11 + 1) =$ the 3rd value.
The 3rd value is $52 \Rightarrow$ the lower quartile $(Q_1) = 52$.

(iii) The upper quartile is the value that is $\frac{3}{4}$ way through the distribution.
This value is found by getting $\frac{3}{4}(11 + 1) =$ the 9th value.
This ninth value is $73 \Rightarrow$ the upper quartile $(Q_3) = 73$.

(iv) The interquartile range $= Q_3 - Q_1$
$$= 73 - 52 = 21$$

3. Standard deviation

One of the most important and frequently-used measures of spread is called **standard deviation**. It shows how much variation there is from the average (mean). It may be thought of as the average difference of the scores from the mean, that is, how far they are away from the mean. A low standard deviation indicates that the data points tend to be very close to the mean; a high standard deviation indicates that the data is spread out over a large range of values.

The Greek letter σ is used to denote standard deviation.

Take, for example, all adult men in Ireland. The average height is about 177 cm with a standard deviation of about 8 cm.

For this large population, about 68% of the men have a height within 8 cm of the mean.

> If the mean is $\bar{x}$ and σ is the standard deviation of a large sample, then 68% will lie between $\bar{x} + \sigma$ and $\bar{x} - \sigma$

Procedure for finding the standard deviation

The steps used to find the standard deviation of a set of numbers are as follows:

1. Calculate the mean of the numbers. This is written $\bar{x}$.

2. Find the deviation (or difference) of each variable, x, from the mean. This is denoted by $(x - \bar{x})$.

3. Square each of these deviations, i.e., find $(x - \bar{x})^2$.

4. Find the sum (Σ) of these values, i.e., find $\Sigma(x - \bar{x})^2$.

5. Divide this result by n, the number of numbers.

   This gives $\dfrac{\Sigma(x - \bar{x})^2}{n}$.

6. Finally, get the square root of the result in **5**.

   There is no need to use this formula if you can remember the steps listed above.
   Alternatively, you may use a calculator.

> **Standard deviation**
>
> $$\sigma = \sqrt{\frac{\Sigma(x - \bar{x})^2}{n}}$$

Example 2

Find the standard deviation of the numbers 6, 9, 10, 12, 13.

The mean $= \dfrac{6 + 9 + 10 + 12 + 13}{5} = \dfrac{50}{5} = 10$.

$$\sigma = \sqrt{\frac{(6 - 10)^2 + (9 - 10)^2 + (10 - 10)^2 + (12 - 10)^2 + (13 - 10)^2}{5}}$$

$$= \sqrt{\frac{(-4)^2 + (-1)^2 + (0)^2 + (2)^2 + (3)^2}{5}}$$

$$= \sqrt{\frac{16 + 1 + 0 + 4 + 9}{5}} = \sqrt{\frac{30}{5}} = \sqrt{6} = 2.45$$

$\therefore$ the standard deviation is 2.45

Finding the Standard Deviation of a Frequency Distribution

When finding the standard deviation from a frequency distribution, the deviation of each variable from the mean is squared and then multiplied by the frequency (f) of that variable. The result is then divided by the sum of the frequencies.

Finally, we get the square root of the result.

This procedure can be represented by the formula

$$\sqrt{\frac{\Sigma f(x - \bar{x})^2}{\Sigma f}}$$

where $\Sigma f(x - \bar{x})^2$ is the sum of the $f(x - \bar{x})^2$ column and Σf is the sum of the frequencies.

The worked example below will show you how to lay out your work when finding the standard deviation of a frequency distribution.

Example 3

Find the standard deviation of the following frequency distribution:

Variable (x)	1	2	3	4	5	6
Frequency (f)	9	9	6	4	7	3

First find the mean of the distribution.

$$\text{The mean} = \frac{(9 \times 1) + (9 \times 2) + (6 \times 3) + (4 \times 4) + (7 \times 5) + (3 \times 6)}{9 + 9 + 6 + 4 + 7 + 3}$$

$$\Rightarrow \quad \bar{x} = \frac{114}{38} = 3$$

Now set out a table like this.

x	f	$x - \bar{x}$	$(x - \bar{x})^2$	$f(x - \bar{x})^2$
1	9	−2	4	36
2	9	−1	1	9
3	6	0	0	0
4	4	1	1	4
5	7	2	4	28
6	3	3	9	27
	↓			↓
	$\Sigma f = 38$			$\Sigma f(x - \bar{x})^2 = 104$

$$\sigma = \sqrt{\frac{\Sigma f(x - \bar{x})^2}{\Sigma f}} = \sqrt{\frac{104}{38}} = 1.65$$

Note: To calculate the standard deviation of a grouped frequency distribution, take the mid-interval values of the variables and proceed as in Example 3 above.

Use of calculator to find standard deviation

The tedious work involved in calculating the standard deviation of a large set of data can be substantially reduced by using a scientific calculator.

In the following examples, we will use the **Casio fx-83ES** calculator to illustrate the keys and steps involved in finding standard deviation.

Example 4

Find (a) the mean (b) the standard deviation of the following set of numbers:
(i) 5, 3, 1, 8, 2
(ii) 10, 6, 2, 16, 4

(i) Key in [MODE] and select [2] for statistics mode.

Then select [1] for 1 − VAR.

Now input the numbers [5] [=]
                        [3] [=]
                        [1] [=]
                        [8] [=]
                        [2] [=]

CASIO		fx-83ES
	X	FREQ
1	5	1
2	3	1
3	1	1
4	8	1
5	2	1

To get your answers, key in [AC] to clear, and [SHIFT] [1] to go to menu.

Now select [5] to get statistics on variables.

Then select [2] for $\bar{x}$ (the mean), then [=]

The mean $\bar{x}$ is 3.8.

To proceed to get the standard deviation, key in [AC] to clear.

Now key in [SHIFT] [1] to go to menu and select [5] to get statistics on variables.

Now key in [3] for $x\,\sigma\,n$ (standard deviation) [=]

The result is 2.4819... = 2.5
∴ standard deviation = 2.5

(ii) 10, 6, 2, 16, 4.
Here is the sequence of keys to find the mean and standard deviation.
[MODE] [2] [1]

[10] [=] [6] [=] [2] [=] [16] [=] [4] [=]

[AC] [SHIFT] [1] [5] [2] [=]   7.6 = mean

[AC] [SHIFT] [1] [5] [3] [=]   4.963869... = 5.0 = standard deviation

4. Percentiles

Percentiles divide data into 100 equal parts.

Percentiles give a measure of your position relative to others in a data set. If you are told that you are on the 70th percentile in a competitive test, this means that 70% of the competitors had scores lower than yours (or 30% higher than yours). It is important not to confuse percentiles with percentages. For example, you could achieve a score of 70% in a state examination but you could be at the 80th percentile.

Percentiles are denoted by P_1, P_2, P_3, P_{40} ...

How to find P_k of a data set

When asked to find the 40th percentile, P_{40}, we are required to find the value of the number that is 40% of the way into the data set.

Thus to find P_k of a data set:

1. Order the numbers in the data set from smallest to largest.

2. Now find $k\%$ of the total number of data points in the set.
   i.e. find $\dfrac{k}{100} \times n$, where n is the number of numbers in the set.

3. (i) If the answer in 2 is a whole number, for example 5, then the kth percentile is the mean of the 5th and 6th numbers in the data set.
   (ii) If the answer in 2 is not a whole number, for example $6\frac{1}{4}$, round up to 7. The 7th number in the data set will be the kth percentile.

Example 5

Here are the marks of 24 students in a science test:

| 48 | 54 | 76 | 34 | 82 | 67 | 76 | 92 | 54 | 72 | 86 | 47 |
| 80 | 73 | 64 | 57 | 68 | 36 | 82 | 74 | 71 | 62 | 46 | 52 |

(i) Find P_{60}
(ii) Find P_{75}
(iii) If Sinead scored 74 in the test, find on what percentile is her score.

First we order the data, starting with the smallest:

| 34 | 36 | 46 | 47 | 48 | 52 | 54 | 54 | 57 | 62 | 64 | 67 |
| 68 | 71 | 72 | 73 | 74 | 76 | 76 | 80 | 82 | 82 | 86 | 92 |

(i) $P_{60} = \frac{60}{100} \times \frac{24}{1} = 14.4$

Since 14.4 is not a whole number, we go to the next whole number, i.e. 15.

P_{60} = the 15th number in the set.

This number is 72. Thus $P_{60} = 72$.

(ii) $P_{75} = \frac{75}{100} \times \frac{24}{1} = 18$

As this is a whole number, we find the mean of the 18th and 19th numbers in the data set.

These numbers are 76 and 76.

$$\therefore \quad P_{75} = \frac{76 + 76}{2} = 76$$

(iii) If Sinead scored 74, this means that 16 students scored lower than she did. We now find the percentile that corresponds to 16.

Percentile $= \frac{16}{24} \times \frac{100}{1} = 66.66$

Therefore Sinead is in the 67th percentile.

Example 6

Leah lives near the local bus stop. One day she recorded the number of people waiting in the queue for each bus. The table below shows her data.

Number of people	3	4	5	6	7	8	9	10	11
Frequency	4	6	3	8	0	7	5	9	8

(i) Find P_{40} (ii) Find P_{82}

(i) To find P_{40}, we find $\frac{40}{100}$ of the total frequency.

The total frequency is 50.

$$P_{40} = \frac{40}{100} \times \frac{50}{1} = 20 \Rightarrow P_{40} = \frac{\text{20th value} + \text{21st value}}{2}$$

The 20th and 21st values lie in the fourth column, i.e., 6 people.

$$\therefore \quad P_{40} = 6 \text{ people}$$

(ii) $P_{82} = \frac{82}{100} \times \frac{50}{1} = 41 \Rightarrow P_{82} = \frac{\text{41st value} + \text{42nd value}}{2}$

The 41st and 42nd values lie in the eight column, i.e., 10 people.

$$\therefore \quad P_{82} = 10 \text{ people}$$

Exercise 10.5

1. Find the range for each of the following sets of data:
   (i) 6, 3, 8, 2, 9, 5, 10   (ii) 21, 16, 72, 40, 67, 65, 55, 34, 17, 48, 32, 19, 44, 61, 73

2. Nine students submitted their assignments which were marked out of 40.
   The marks obtained were:

   37, 34, 34, 29, 27, 27, 10, 4, 34

   (i) Write down the range of marks.   (ii) Write down the median mark.
   (iii) Find (a) the lower quartile   (b) the upper quartile   (c) the interquartile range.

3. Here are the times, in minutes, for a bus journey:

   15, 7, 9, 12, 9, 19, 6, 11, 9, 16, 8

   (i) Find the range of these times.   (ii) Find the lower quartile.
   (iii) Find the upper quartile.   (iv) Write down the interquartile range.

4. A group of boys and girls took a French test. These are the marks which the boys got:

   13, 14, 14, 15, 14, 14, 15, 17, 16, 14, 16, 12

   (i) Find the range of the boys' marks.
   (ii) Calculate the mean mark of the boys.

   The mean mark for the girls in the class was 13.2 and the girls' marks had a range of 7.
   (iii) Make two statements about the differences between the boys' and girls' marks in
         the French test.

5. Conor played nine rounds of crazy golf. Here are his scores:

   51, 53, 50, 41, 59, 64, 66, 65, 50

   Find   (i)   the range   (ii) the lower quartile
            (iii) the upper quartile   (iv) the interquartile range.

6. The blood glucose of 30 adults is recorded.
   The results, in mmol/litre, are given below:

   3.1 3.6 3.7 2.2 2.3 4.0 4.4 4.0 5.1 4.0 4.5 3.7 3.8 3.8 2.3

   4.6 4.8 3.8 3.9 2.5 3.8 2.7 3.9 3.9 5.5 2.2 4.7 3.2 3.7 4.0

   (i) Find Q_1 and Q_3 and hence find the interquartile range.
   (ii) If an outlier can be identified as being $1\frac{1}{2}$ times the interquartile range above the
        upper quartile or $1\frac{1}{2}$ times the interquartile range below the lower quartile, find any
        outliers in the distribution.

7. Calculate the standard deviation of each of the following arrays of numbers, giving your
   answer correct to one decimal place:
   (i) 1, 3, 7, 9, 10   (ii) 8, 12, 15, 9   (iii) 1, 3, 4, 6, 10, 12
   Use your calculator to verify your answer in each case.

8. Find the standard deviation of the numbers: 2, 3, 4, 5, 6.

   Now find the standard deviation of these numbers: 12, 13, 14, 15, 16.

   (i)   What is the relationship between the two sets of numbers?
   (ii) What is the relationship between their standard deviations?
   (iii) What conclusion can you draw from the results?

9. Use your calculator, or otherwise, to show that the standard deviation of the numbers

   3   4   6   2   8   8   5   is 2.17.

10. There are two routes for a worker to get to his office.
Both the routes involve hold-ups due to traffic lights.
He records the time it takes over a series of six journeys for each route.
The results are shown in the table.

Route 1	15	15	11	17	14	12
Route 2	11	14	17	15	16	11

(i) Work out the mean time taken for each route.

(ii) Calculate the standard deviation of each of the two routes.

(iii) Using your answers to (i) and (ii), suggest which route you would recommend. State your reason clearly.

11. Verify that 2 is the mean of this distribution.
Hence calculate the standard deviation, correct to 1 decimal place.

Variable	0	2	3	4
Frequency	4	3	2	3

12. Show that the mean of the given frequency distribution is 3 and hence find the standard deviation, correct to 2 decimal places.

Variable	1	2	3	4
Frequency	1	4	9	6

13. Use the mid-interval values to show that the mean of the grouped frequency distribution below is 5.
Hence find the standard deviation of the distribution.

Class	1–3	3–5	5–7	7–9
Frequency	4	3	9	2

14. Use the mid-interval values to find the mean and standard deviation of the given grouped frequency distribution:

Variable	0–4	4–8	8–12	12–16	16–20
Frequency	2	3	9	7	3

15. The number of letters delivered to a business premises on each day of the 5-day working week were as follows:

18, 26, 22, 34, 25

(i) Calculate the mean number of letters delivered.

(ii) Calculate the standard deviation, correct to one decimal place.

(iii) If $\bar{x}$ is the mean and σ is the standard deviation, find the values of $\bar{x} + \sigma$ and $\bar{x} - \sigma$.

(iv) On how many days is the number of letters delivered within one standard deviation of the mean?

16. The mean of the numbers 1, 9, a and $3a - 2$ is $\bar{x}$ and the standard deviation is σ.
    (i) Express $\bar{x}$ in terms of a.
    (ii) If $\sigma = \sqrt{20}$, find the value of a, if $a \in Z$.

17. Jack is wondering if he is taller or smaller than other boys in his age-group.
After investigating, he discovered that he is at the 80th percentile.
What percentage of boys in his age-group are
    (i) smaller than Jack   (ii) taller than Jack?

18. (i) The scores in a test ranged from 1 to 100.
       If Elaine's score was 85, does this mean that her score is in the 85th percentile?
       Explain your answer.
    (ii) In a national examination, Tanya's mark was at the 40th percentile.
       If 800 people took the examination, how many people did better than Tanya?

19. Here are the marks, out of 100, of 20 students in a maths test:

        38 43 44 44 52 55 58 63 65 66

        68 69 71 72 72 77 79 79 84 85

    (i) What score indicates the 25th percentile?
    (ii) What score indicates the 75th percentile?
    (iii) Find the difference between the 40th and 75th percentile.
    (iv) How many students have scores greater than or equal to the 80th percentile?
    (v) Eoin received 65 marks in the test. At what percentile is Eoin's mark?

20. Here are the prices (in €) of gents' T-shirts in a sports shop:

        21 22 22 22 23 25 26 26 26 27 28 29

        29 32 32 32 33 37 40 40 42 42 46 48

        52 55 55 57 59 60 60 65 70 70 75 80

    (i) Calculate P_{70}, the 70th percentile.   (ii) Calculate P_{40}, the 40th percentile.
    (iii) How many of the T-shirts are lower in price than the 40th percentile.
    (iv) Find P_{80} and then find the number of T-shirts that are more expensive than the
       price at the 80th percentile.
    (v) If the price of a T-shirt is €40, find what percentile this price represents.

21. The numbers $a, b, 8, 5, 7$ have a mean of 6 and a standard deviation of $\sqrt{2}$.
Express a in terms of b and hence find the values of a and b for $a > b$.

Section 10.6 Stem and leaf diagrams (stemplots)

A **stem and leaf diagram** is a very useful way of presenting data. It is useful because it shows all the original data and also gives you the overall picture or shape of the distribution.

It is similar to a horizontal bar chart, with the numbers themselves forming the bars.

Stem and leaf diagrams are suitable only for small amounts of data.

Often the stem shows the tens digit of the values and the leaves show the units digit.
If you put them together, you get the original value.

For example 4|2 represents 42.

A typical stem and leaf diagram is shown below.

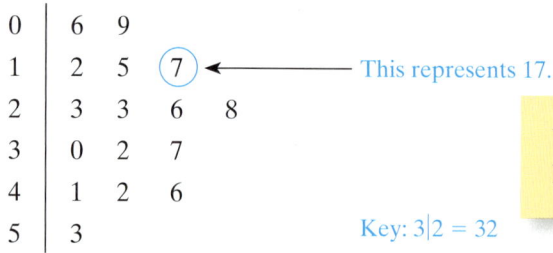

```
0 | 6  9
1 | 2  5  (7) ←──────────── This represents 17.
2 | 3  3  6  8
3 | 0  2  7
4 | 1  2  6
5 | 3                    Key: 3|2 = 32
```

You must always add a key to show how the stem and leaf combine.

The data represented above is:

6, 9, 12, 15, 17, 23, 23, 26, 28, 30, 32, 37, 41, 42, 46, 53

Example 1

Here are the marks gained by a class of students in a science test.

58　65　40　59　68　63　81　76　63　57　44　47　53　70　80
68　81　61　57　49　70　54　75　69　65　59　52　63　63　74

(i) Construct a stem and leaf diagram to represent this data.
(ii) What is the mode of the data?
(iii) What is the median?
(iv) What is the range of the data?

(i) First draw the stem of the diagram.
The smallest value in the list is 40 and the largest value is 81.
The stem of the diagram will be the tens digits from 4 to 8.
Now work through the data values and put the second digit on the appropriate row.

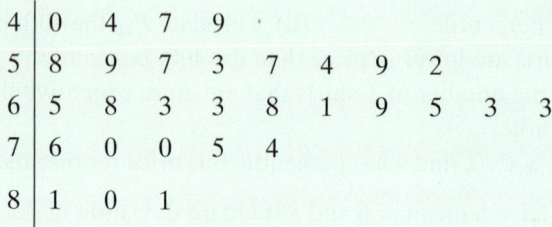

```
4 | 0  4  7  9
5 | 8  9  7  3  7  4  9  2
6 | 5  8  3  3  8  1  9  5  3  3
7 | 6  0  0  5  4
8 | 1  0  1
```

For the first value, 58, the 8 will go on the 5 row.

The numbers on the right of the diagram are the leaves.

Finally, rewrite the diagram with all the leaves in order, with the smallest nearest to the stem.
Remember to include a key.

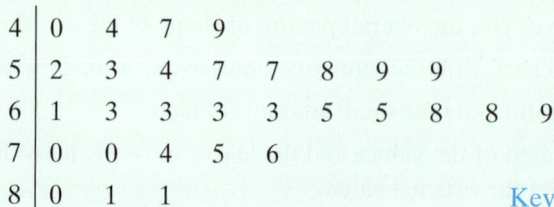

```
4 | 0  4  7  9
5 | 2  3  4  7  7  8  9  9
6 | 1  3  3  3  3  5  5  8  8  9
7 | 0  0  4  5  6
8 | 0  1  1                  Key: 6|3 = 63
```

(ii) The mode is 63 as this is the value that occurs most often.

(iii) As there are 30 values, the median will be the mean of the 15th and 16th values.

Count the values in the stem and leaf diagram to find the 15th and 16th values.

Since these are both 63, the median is 63.

> If there are 30 values, the middle value is $\frac{1}{2}(30+1)$, i.e., $15\frac{1}{2}$.
> This will be half the sum of the 15th and 16th values.

(iv) The range is the highest value minus the lowest value.

$$= 81 - 40 = 41$$

Different values for the stems

In a stem and leaf diagram, each leaf consists of one digit only.
The stem may have more than one digit.

Here are the times, in seconds, for the contestants in a 60-metre race.

6.6   4.9   5.7   7.6   8.2   6.3   6.5   7.4   5.1   5.3   6.2   7.8

This time we will use the units as the stems.

Step 1   Draw the first diagram.
The units are the stems.
The tenths are the leaves.

4	9			
5	7	1	3	
6	6	3	5	2
7	6	4	8	
8	2			

Key: 6|3 = 6.3 seconds

Step 2   Put the leaves in numerical order.

4	9			
5	1	3	7	
6	2	3	5	6
7	4	6	8	
8	2			

Back-to-back stem and leaf diagrams

Two stem and leaf diagrams can be drawn using the same stem.

These are known as **back-to-back stem and leaf diagrams**.

The leaves of one set of data are put to the right of the stem.

The leaves of the other set of data are put on the left.

A back-to-back stem and leaf diagram is very useful to compare two sets of data.

Jack and Ciara compared the length of time they spent each evening on their homework.

Their times are shown in this back-to-back stem and leaf diagram.

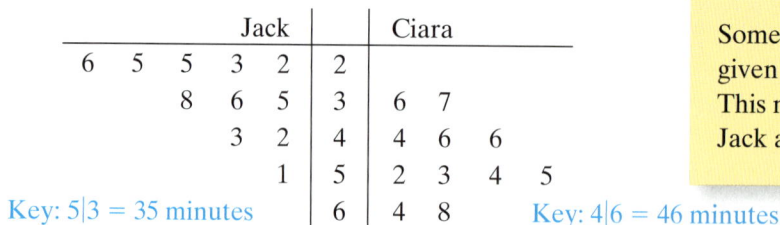

Jack		Ciara
6 5 5 3 2	2	
8 6 5	3	6 7
3 2	4	4 6 6
1	5	2 3 4 5
	6	4 8

Key: 5|3 = 35 minutes   Key: 4|6 = 46 minutes

> Sometimes the key is given as 5|3|6.
> This means 35 for Jack and 36 for Ciara.

We read Jack's times from the stem to the left.

Thus Jack's times are:

22, 23, 25, 25, 26, 35, 36, …

Ciara's times are:

36, 37, 44, 46,46, 52, …

The following example shows how a back-to-back stem and leaf diagram can be used to compare two sets of data.

Example 2

Robert and Jane compared the lengths of time they spent each evening watching television.

Their times are shown in the following back-to-back stem and leaf diagram.

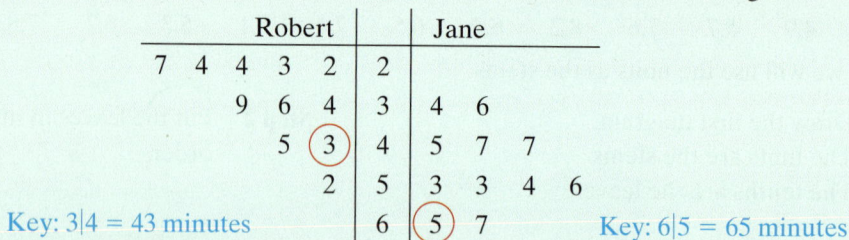

Robert		Jane
7 4 4 3 2	2	
9 6 4	3	4 6
5 (3)	4	5 7 7
2	5	3 3 4 6
	6	(5) 7

Key: 3|4 = 43 minutes   Key: 6|5 = 65 minutes

(i)   What does the diagram show about the lengths of time Robert and Jane spent watching television?
(ii) What was Jane's median time spent watching television?
(iii) What was Robert's median time?
(iv) Do these median times support your conclusion in (i) above?

(i)   By looking at the diagram, we can see that most of Robert's times are between 22 and 39 minutes.
      Most of Jane's times are between 45 and 67 minutes.
      This shows that Jane spends more time watching television than Robert does.
(ii) For Jane, the value that is halfway through the distribution is 53.
      Thus her median time spent watching television is 53 minutes.
(iii) Robert's median time is 34 minutes.
(iv) Because Jane's median time is greater than Robert's, it supports the view, expressed in (i) above, that she spends more time than Robert watching television.

Finding the interquartile range from a stem and leaf diagram

In Section 10.5 of this chapter, we found that the lower quartile is the value in the data that is one quarter way through the distribution. The upper quartile is the value that is three quarters way through the distribution. The difference between the upper quartile and the lower quartile is the **interquartile range**.

We will now show how to find the two quartiles and the interquartile range of a distribution presented as a stem and leaf diagram.

Example 3

The stem and leaf diagram below shows the marks, out of 50, obtained in a maths test.

Marks obtained

```
1 | 2  8
2 | 1  4  7  7  8
3 | 1  4  5  7
4 | 1  2  8
5 | 0            Key: 2|1 = 21
```

Find (i)   the median mark   (ii)   the lower quartile
      (iii) the upper quartile   (iv)   the interquartile range.

(i)   The median mark is the mark that is halfway through the distribution.
      There are 15 data values.

      The halfway value is $\frac{1}{2}(15 + 1)$ i.e. the 8th value.

      Starting at the lowest value, the 8th value is 31.
      ∴   the median = 31

(ii) The lower quartile is the value that is one quarter way through the distribution.

      This value is $\frac{1}{4}(15 + 1)$ i.e. the 4th value

      This value is 24.
      ∴   the lower quartile = 24

(iii) The upper quartile is the value that is three quarters of the way through the distribution.

      This value is $\frac{3}{4}(15 + 1)$ i.e. the 12th value.

      This value is 41.
      ∴   the upper quartile = 41

(iv) The interquartile range = upper quartile minus lower quartile
                             = 41 − 24
                             = 17

Exercise 10.6

1. The stem and leaf diagram below shows the ages, in years, of 25 people who wished to enter a 10 km walking competition.

```
1 | 4  4  6  9
2 | 1  3  7  7  7  8
3 | 3  6  6  7  9
4 | 0  2  3  3  8  8
5 | 1  3  4  7
```
Key: 1|6 means 16 years old

   (i)   How many people were less than 20 years old?
   (ii) Write down the modal age.
   (iii) How many people were between 35 and 45 years old?
   (iv) What was the median age?

2. Twenty four pupils were asked how many CDs they had in their collection. The results are shown below:

23	2	18	14	7	4	25	21	32	26	31	6
17	6	18	19	31	21	12	1	0	8	14	15

   (i)   Draw a stem and leaf diagram to represent this information.
   (ii) How many pupils had more than twenty CDs?
   (iii) What is the median number of CDs per pupil?

3. The times, in seconds, taken to answer 24 telephone calls are shown.

3.2	5.6	2.4	3.5	4.3	3.6	2.8	5.8	3.3	2.6	3.5	2.8
5.6	3.5	4.2	1.5	2.7	2.5	3.7	3.1	2.9	4.2	2.4	3.0

Copy and complete the stem and leaf diagram on the right to represent this information.

```
1 |
2 |
3 | 2
4 |
5 |
```
Key: 3|2 means 3.2 seconds

   (i)   How many of the calls took longer than 4 seconds to answer?
   (ii) What is the difference, in seconds, between the shortest and the longest times to answer the calls?
   (iii) What is the median length of time taken to answer the calls?
   (iv) What is the modal length of time?

4. The stem and leaf diagram below shows the marks achieved by 19 students in a test.

```
stem | leaf
  2  | 2
  3  | 4  6
  4  | 2  7  9
  5  | 3  4  5  8  9
  6  | 0  2  6  7
  7  | 2  6
  8  | 1  4
```
Key: 4|2 = 42 marks

   (i)   Write down the range of the marks.   (ii) Find the value of the lower quartile.
   (iii) What is the upper quartile?   (iv) What is the interquartile range?

5. The number of laptops sold by a store was recorded each month for a period of 26 months. The results are shown in the stem and leaf diagram below.

stem	leaf
1	8
2	3 6 7 9 9
3	2 6 6 6 7 8 8
4	4 5 5 5 7 7 7 7 9
5	2 7 7 9

Key: 1|8 means 18 laptops

  (i)   Find the median.
  (ii) Find the lower quartile.
  (iii) Find the upper quartile.
  (iv) Work out the interquartile range.
  (v)   Write down the modal number of laptops sold.

6. The results for examinations in Science and French for a class of students are shown in the back-to-back stem and leaf diagram below:

```
          Science      |   | French
              7   5   | 2 |
              8   0   | 3 | 6
              5   5   | 4 | 0  5  7  8
    9  5  4  3  2     | 5 | 1  5  8
          9  7  5     | 6 | 2  4  4  5  7
              3   1   | 7 | 2  4  5  6
              6   3   | 8 | 3  5
                  1   | 9 |
```

Key: 1|7 = 71 marks

Key: 3|6 = 36 marks

  (i)   How many students took the examinations?
  (ii) What is the range of marks in   (a) Science   (b) French?
  (iii) What is the median mark in Science?
  (iv) What is the interquartile range of the French marks?

7. The back-to-back stem and leaf diagram below shows the rested pulse rates of a group of college students. They are split into those who smoked and those who didn't.

```
         Smoke      |   | Do not smoke
               5    | 5 | 0  8  9
        9   8   5   | 6 | 0  4  4  5  6  6  6  8  8
  6  6  5  0  0     | 7 | 0  1  1  8  9
  8  8  6  3  0     | 8 | 0  1  6  8  8
            2   0   | 9 |
```

Key: 5|6 = 65 bpm

Key: 5|8 = 58 bpm

  (i)   Find the median and range of the pulse rates of the group who smoked.
  (ii) Find the median and range of the pulse rates of the group who did not smoke.
  (iii) If a lower pulse rate indicates a higher level of fitness, which of the two groups is the fitter? Explain your answer.

8. The table below gives the examination marks in French and English for a class of 20 pupils.

French	75	69	58	58	46	44	32	50	53	78
	81	61	61	45	31	44	53	66	47	57
English	52	58	68	77	38	85	43	44	56	65
	65	79	44	71	84	72	63	69	72	79

   (i)   Construct a back-to-back stem and leaf diagram to represent these results.
   (ii)   What is the median mark in French?
   (iii)   What is the median mark in English?
   (iv)   In which subject did the pupils perform better? Explain your answer.

9. The lengths of time (in minutes) that twenty people had to wait to buy tickets at two cinema complexes were recorded.
The back-to-back stem and leaf diagram below shows the results.

Cinema

Movie Matrix 1		Movie Matrix 2
6 5 3 2 2	0	2 4 5 6
8 7 6 5 3 1	1	0 2 4 ☐ 6 7 8 8 9
8 6 4 3 3 2 1	2	1 2 4 5 5
2 0	3	3 3

Key: 1|2 = 21 mins   Key: 2|4 = 24 mins

   (i)   What is the range of waiting times at Movie Matrix 2?
   (ii)   What is the median waiting time at Movie Matrix 1?
   (iii)   One time is missing from Movie Matrix 2.
          Give a possible value for this missing time.
   (iv)   A patron is selected at random from Movie matrix 1.
          What is the probability that this person waited longer than 10 minutes for tickets?
   (v)   At which cinema would you have the shorter wait?
          Justify your answer.

10. Ten men and ten women were asked how much television they watched the previous weekend. Their times, in minutes, were as follows:

Men	40	41	42	52	52	52	64	65	65	71
Women	40	41	51	62	63	75	87	88	93	95

Copy and complete the back-to-back stem and leaf diagram opposite.

Men		Women
	4	0
	5	
4	6	
	7	
	8	
	9	

Key: 4|6 = 64 mins   Key: 4|0 = 40 mins

   (i)   What is the modal time for men?
   (ii)   What is the median time for
          (a) men   (b) women?
   (iii)   What is the range of times for
          (a) men   (b) women?
   (iv)   Use the results in (ii) and (iii) to show that women spend more time watching television than men do.

Section 10.7 Histograms

One of the most common ways of representing a frequency distribution is by means of a **histogram**.

Histograms are very similar to bar charts but there are some important differences:

> there are no gaps between the bars in a histogram
> histograms are used to show **continuous data**
> the data is always **grouped**; the groups are called classes
> the **area** of each bar or rectangle represents the frequency.

Histograms may have equal or unequal class intervals.

For our course, we will confine our study to histograms with **equal class intervals**.

When the class intervals are equal, drawing a histogram is very similar to drawing a bar chart.

Example 1

The frequency table below shows the times taken by 32 students to solve a problem.

Time (in secs)	0–10	10–20	20–30	30–40	40–50	50–60
No. of students	1	2	8	12	6	3

(i)   Draw a histogram to represent this data.
(ii)   Write down the modal class.
(iii)   In which interval does the median lie?

We first draw two axes at right angles to each other.

We plot the variables (time in this case) on the horizontal axis and plot the frequencies (number of students) on the vertical axis.

(i)   The histogram is shown below.

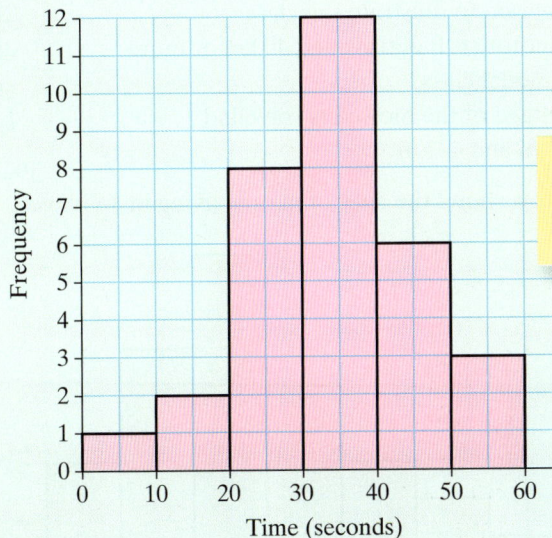

It is important to label each axis.

(ii) The modal class is the class with the highest frequency.
This is the (30–40) second class.

∴ the modal class is (30–40) seconds.

(iii) The median is the value halfway through the distribution.

There are 32 students altogether; so the middle students are the 16th and 17th students.

The sum of the numbers of students in the first three intervals is

1 + 2 + 8 i.e. 11

The 16th and 17th students will lie in the next interval, i.e., (30–40) seconds.

Thus the median lies in the (30–40) second interval.

Note:

If a table of results does not contain equal class-intervals proceed as follows:

Time (secs)	0–20	20–30	30–40	40–50	50–60
No. of pupils	6	8	10	6	4

Time	0–10	10–20	20–30	30–40	40–50	50–60
No. of pupils	3	3	8	10	6	4

Two equal intervals are made by halving the frequency of the original interval.

Exercise 10.7

1. At the end of their journeys, 30 motorists were asked how many kilometres they had travelled. Their responses are shown in the table opposite.
   (i) Draw a histogram to illustrate this data.
   (ii) How many motorists had travelled 40 km or more?
   (iii) What is the modal class?
   (iv) What percentage of the motorists travelled between 20 km and 40 km?

Distance (in km)	Frequency
0–20	6
20–40	12
40–60	7
60–80	4
80–100	1

[0–20 means ⩾0 and <20]

2. The histogram below shows the ages of people living in a village.

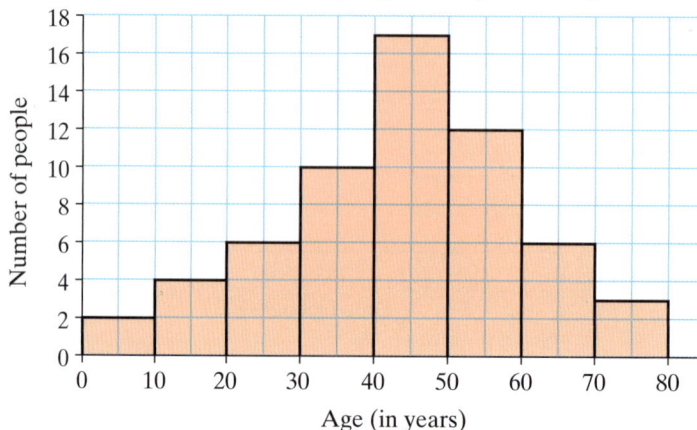

If there were 4 people in the (10–20) year age-group, answer the following questions:
   (i)   How many people were aged between 30 years and 40 years?
   (ii) Which is the modal class?
   (iii) How many people were aged under 30 years?
   (iv) How many people lived in the village?
   (v)   Which interval contains 20% of the people surveyed?
   (vi) In which interval does the median age lie?

3. The frequency table below gives the waiting times of a group of patients at a doctor's surgery.

Waiting time (in mins)	0–4	4–8	8–12	12–16	16–20
No. of patients	2	6	10	12	8

   (i)   Draw a histogram to illustrate this data.
   (ii) How many patients were included in the survey?
   (iii) Which is the modal class?
   (iv) In which interval does the median lie?
   (v)   What is the greatest number of patients who could have waited longer than 10 minutes?
   (vi) What is the least number of patients who could have waited longer than 14 minutes?

4. The histogram below shows the times taken, in seconds, for a group of pupils to solve a puzzle.

   (i)   How many pupils took 15 seconds or longer to solve the puzzle?
   (ii) How many pupils took part?
   (iii) Which is the modal class?
   (iv) In which interval does the median lie?
   (v)   What is the greatest number of pupils who could have solved the puzzle in less than 8 seconds?
   (vi) What is the least number of pupils who could have solved the puzzle in less than 12 seconds?

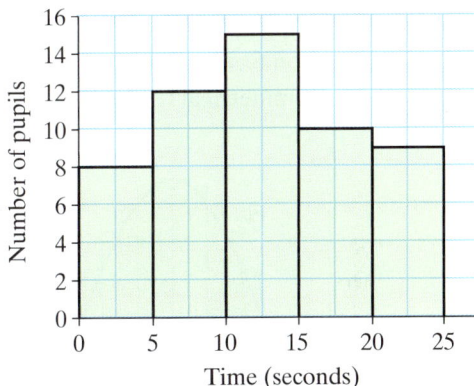

5. The grouped frequency table opposite shows the minutes spent in a shopping complex by a number of people:

Minutes	Number of people
5–15	8
15–25	14
25–35	28
35–45	20

   (i)   Draw a histogram to illustrate the data.
   (ii) Write down the modal class.
   (iii) In which interval does the median lie?
   (iv) Which interval contains exactly 20% of the people?
   (v)   What is the greatest number of people who could have spent more than 30 minutes in the shopping complex?
   (vi) Use the mid-interval values to calculate the mean time spent in the shopping complex, correct to the nearest minute.

Section 10.8 The shape of a distribution

In the previous section, we encountered histograms of various shapes.

The diagrams below show four histograms, all with different shapes.

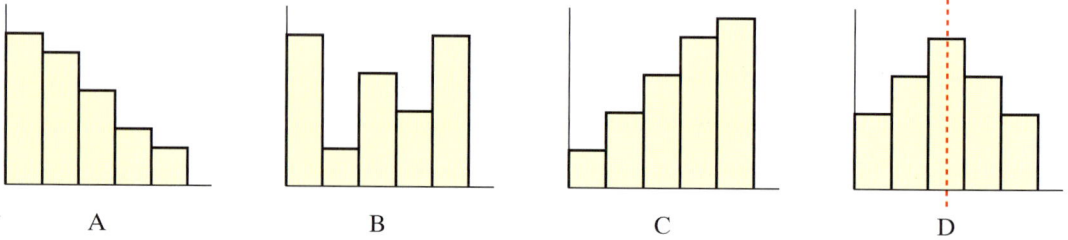

A   B   C   D

Only histogram D appears balanced or symmetrical as it has an axis of symmetry.
The other three histograms are less balanced or **skewed** in some way.

Histograms are very useful when you want to see where the data lies and so get a clear picture of the shape of the distribution. For example, in histogram A above, we can see that most of the data is concentrated at the lower values. In histogram C, the data is concentrated at the higher values.

There are some shapes that occur frequently in distributions and you should be able to recognize and name them. The most common and frequently occurring shapes follow.

1. Symmetrical distributions

> This distribution has an axis of symmetry down the middle.
> It is called a symmetrical (or bell-shaped) distribution.

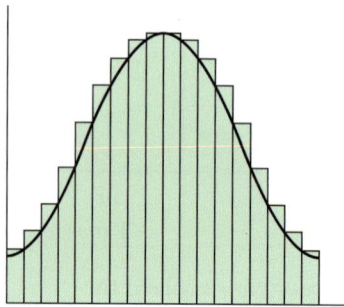

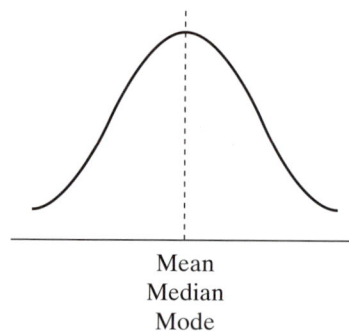

Mean
Median
Mode

Mean = Median = Mode

> One of the most important symmetrical distributions in statistics is the **normal distribution**.

> Real-life examples of a symmetrical (or normal) distribution are
>   (i)   the heights of a random sample of people
>   (ii) the intelligence quotients (IQ) of a population.

2. Positive skew

› When a distribution has most of the data at the lower values, we say it has a **positive skew**. The following histogram shows a positive skew as most of the data, represented by the higher bars, is mainly to the left.

Notice that there is a long tail to the right of the distribution.

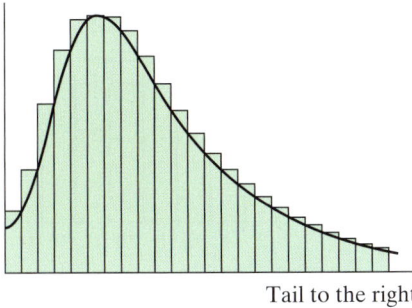

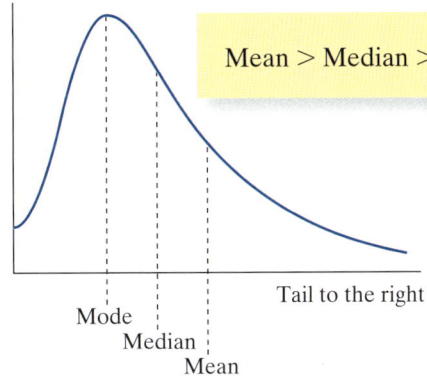

Tail to the right

Mean > Median > Mode

Mode
Median
Mean

Tail to the right

› Real-life examples of a distribution with a positive skew are
  (i)   the number of children in a family
  (ii) the age at which people first learn to ride a bicycle
  (iii) the age at which people marry.

3. Negative skew

› When a distribution has most of the data at the higher values, we say that the distribution has a **negative skew**.

When a distribution has a negative skew, the tail will be to the left.

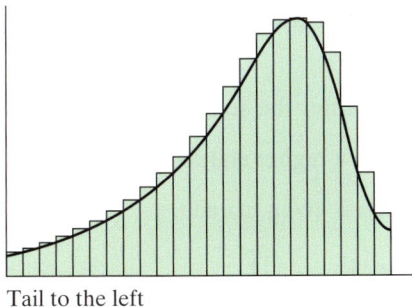

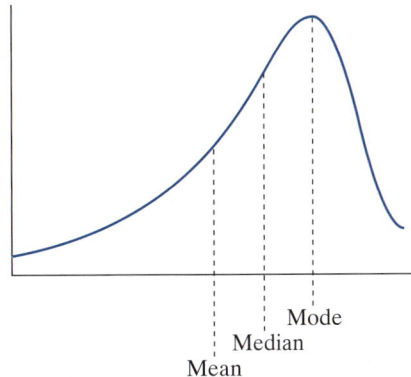

Tail to the left

Mode
Median
Mean

In a distribution with a **positive** skew, the tail is to the **right**; with a **negative** skew, the tail is to the **left**.

Mean < Median < Mode

› Real-life examples of a distribution with a negative skew are
  (i) the ages at which people have to get their first pair of reading glasses
  (ii) the heights of players playing in a professional basketball league.

4. Uniform distributions

In a uniform distribution, the data is evenly spread throughout.

It does not have a modal class.

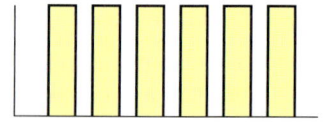

5. Bimodal distributions

This distribution has two modes.

It is called a **bimodal distribution**.

The modes are 6 and 16.

A distribution that has three or more modes is said to be **multimodal**.

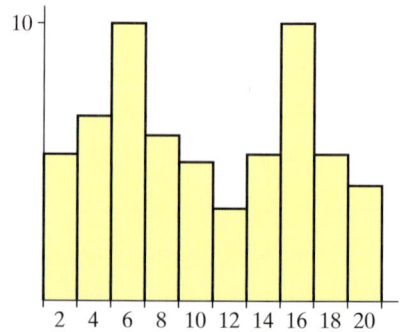

6. Distributions and standard deviation

Consider the two distributions, (A) and (B), shown below:

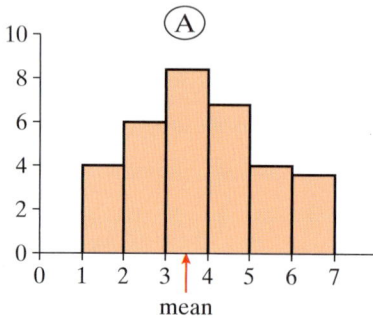

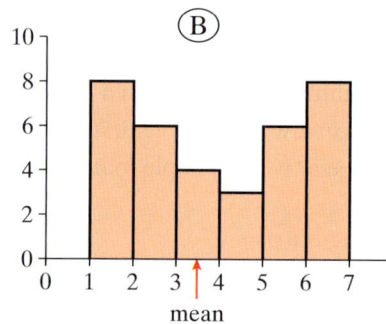

In distribution (A), most of the data lies between 2 and 5.

In distribution (B), the data is more spread out and further from the mean than the data in distribution (A).

The more spread out the data is in a distribution, the greater the standard deviation will be.

In the distributions above, we can conclude that (B) has a higher standard deviation than (A).

In the two distributions (C) and (D) below, the mean μ is given in each.

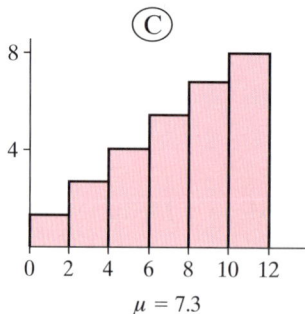

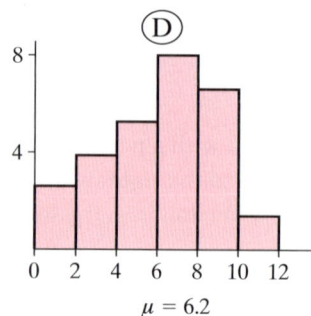

From the diagrams, we can see that more of the data is further from the mean in (C) than in (D).

Thus distribution (C) has the greater standard deviation.

1. Describe the distribution shown.
   (i) What is this distribution commonly known as?
   (ii) Give one real-life example of this distribution.

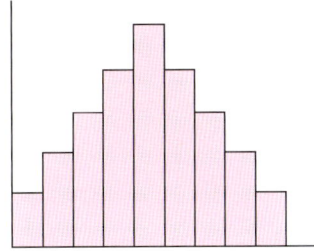

2. Is this distribution positively or negatively skewed?
   You will notice that most of the values are
   at the lower end of the distribution.
   Give one real-life situation that is an example
   of this type of distribution.

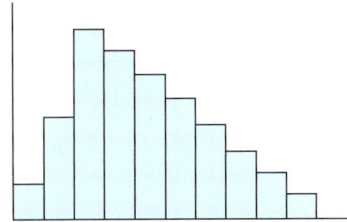

3. Here are three distributions:

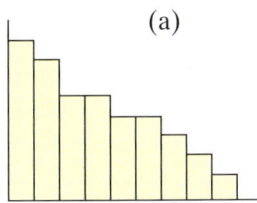

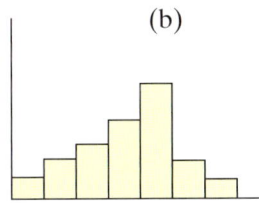

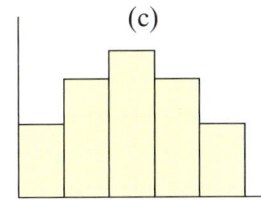

   (i) Which of these distributions is symmetrical?
   (ii) Which distribution is positively skewed?
   (iii) Which distribution is negatively skewed?
   (iv) Which distribution is the most likely to represent this data?
        'The weights of international rugby players'.
   (v) Which distribution best represents this data?
        'The intelligence quotients (IQ) of a large number of second-level students.'

4. Describe the distribution illustrated below.

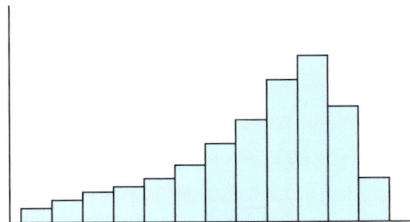

   For the mode, mean and median of this distribution,
   (i) state which of the three is the smallest
   (ii) state which of the three is the largest.

5. Consider the two distributions (A) and (B) shown below.

Explain why the standard deviation of the data in (B) is greater than the standard deviation of the data in (A).

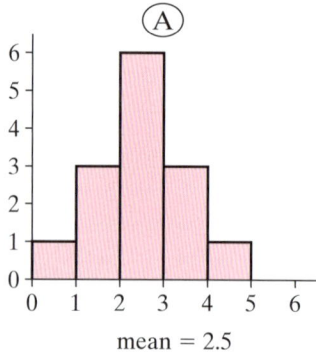

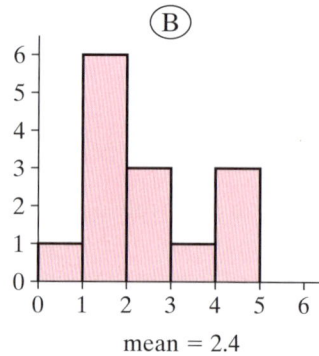

mean = 2.5

mean = 2.4

For each of the following pairs of distributions, state whether (A) or (B) has the larger standard deviation.

If they are the same, state so.

6. (i)

mean = 2.6

mean = 3.5

(ii)

mean = 3

mean = 3

7. (i)

mean = 2.5

mean = 2.5

(ii)

mean = 0.75

mean = 4.75

8. (i)

mean = 3.2

mean = 3.5

(ii)

mean = 3

mean = 2.9

9. (i)

$\mu = 2.2$ $\mu = 2.5$

(ii)

$\mu = 1.9$ $\mu = 2.5$

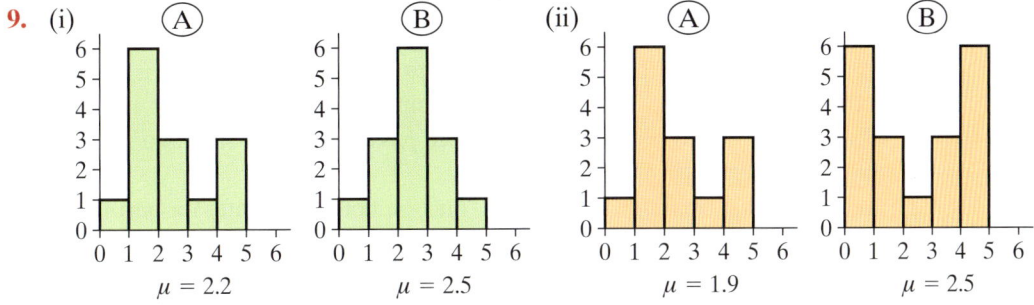

10. The shapes of the histograms of four different sets of data are shown below.

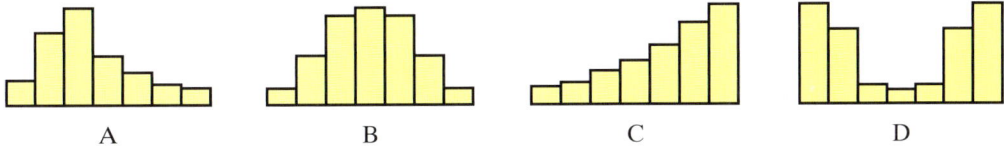

A   B   C   D

(i) Complete the table below, indicating whether the statement is correct (✓) or incorrect (✗) with respect to each data set.

	A	B	C	D
The data is skewed to the left.				
The data is skewed to the right.				
The mean is equal to the median.				
The mean is greater than the median.				
There is a single mode.				

(ii) Assume that the four histograms are drawn on the same scale.
State which of them has the largest standard deviation, and justify your answer.

Revision Exercise 10 (Core)

1. State whether each of the following is primary data or secondary data:
   (i) Counting the number of hatchback cars passing the school gate.
   (ii) Looking at records to see how many people passed through Shannon Airport each day in June one year.
   (iii) Phoning local supermarkets and stores to find the hourly pay rates for part-time work.
   (iv) Going online to see how many medals each country won at the Vancouver Winter Olympics.
   (v) Examining tourist brochures to find the average midday temperatures of selected cities for the month of June.

2. Here are the times, in minutes, for a bus journey:

   15, 7, 9, 12, 9, 19, 6, 11, 9, 16, 8

   (i) Find the range of these times.
   (ii) Find the lower quartile.
   (iii) Find the upper quartile.
   (iv) Write down the interquartile range.

3. The mean of the numbers $3, 6, 7, x$ and 14 is 8.
   Find x and the standard deviation of the set of numbers.

4. (i) What is the main difference between obtaining information by census and by sampling?
   (ii) A student discovered that his mark in a recent test was at the 72nd percentile. If 90 students took the test, how many students received a higher mark than he did?

5. The following stem and leaf diagram shows the amounts of money spent on a Friday night by a group of college students.

			Males			Females					
				8	0	6					
		7	6	5	1	0	5	5	5	8	8
9	9	9	8	6	2	5	5	8	8	9	
	8	8	5	5	3	5	5				
			8	5	4	0					

   Key: 5|4 = €45   Key: 3|5 = €35

   (i) How many students were in the group?
   (ii) Write down the largest amount of money spent by the males.
   (iii) What is the median amount of money spent by the females?
   (iv) What is the median amount of money spent by the males?
   (v) Comment on whether males or females spent the most money.

6. (i) Without doing any calculations, state which of the following arrays of numbers has the greater standard deviation:
   (a) 2, 7, 10, 11, 12, 14, 15
   (b) 1, 5, 9, 10, 15, 18, 21
   Give a reason for your answer.

(ii) The data below gives the number of books read in the last month by a class of 20 students.

Number of books, x	0	1	2	3	4
Number of students, f	2	5	6	5	2

Find the mean and standard deviation of the number of books.

7. The principal of an 800-pupil school wishes to carry out a survey to determine how the pupils feel about the introduction of e-books instead of hard-copy textbooks. There are roughly the same number of pupils in each of the five year-groups. The principal decides to take a random sample of 100 students, with equal numbers from each year-group.
   (i) The principal is using two sampling methods in this survey.
       Name these two methods.
   (ii) How many students should she select from the first-year group?
   (iii) Describe one method of selecting a random sample of 10 students from 100 students.

8. A pollster working for RTE wants to know how many people are watching a new series which is being shown. She questions 200 people as they are leaving a supermarket between 10:00 and 12:00 one Thursday.
   (i) Do you think that this sample might be biased? Explain your answer.
   (ii) Suggest a more suitable way of selecting a sample.

9. Explain what is meant by **stratified sampling** and **cluster sampling**.
   Your explanation should include
   (i) a clear indication of the difference between the two methods
   (ii) one reason why each method might be chosen instead of simple random sampling.

10. Alexandrine enjoys listening to popular music.
    On one CD she noted that the lengths of the tracks varied greatly.
    These are the times, in minutes, of the tracks.

    4.6 3.8 4.0 3.1 4.2 3.2 3.5 4.7
    4.7 3.3 4.7 4.1 3.6 3.4 4.6 5.9

    (i) Construct a stem and leaf diagram to show these times.
    (ii) Write down the mode of the distribution.
    (iii) Find the median and interquartile range.

Revision Exercise 10 (Advanced)

1. The table below lists some statistics for the performances of Nicola and David in their mathematics tests over a term.

Student	Mean	Standard deviation	Range
Nicola	70	3.8	11
David	64	2.5	11

Which student, Nicola or David, had the more consistent test results?
Give a reason for your answer.

2. Here are the marks, out of 100, of 24 students in a national test:

46	73	68	65	37	48	74	68	76	55	42	38
57	63	68	71	46	54	82	78	66	46	64	59

(i) Find P_{40}, the 40th percentile.
(ii) Gillian scored 71 marks in the test.
     At what percentile was her mark?

3. The size, mean, and standard deviation of four different data sets are given in the table below.

	A	B	C	D
size (N)	1000	100	100	10
mean (μ)	10	100	1000	100
standard deviation (σ)	20	30	20	10

Complete the sentences below by inserting the relevant letter in each space:
(i) The biggest data set is _____ and the smallest is _____.
(ii) In general, the data in set _____ is the biggest and the data in set _____ is the smallest.
(iii) The data in set _____ is more spread out than the data in the other sets.
(iv) Set _____ must contain some negative numbers.
(v) If the four sets are combined, the median is most likely to be a value in set _____.

4. Using the mid-interval values, find the standard deviation of the given grouped frequency distribution. Give your answer correct to 1 decimal place.

Class interval	1–3	3–5	5–7	7–9
Frequency	4	3	0	2

5. The histogram below represents a certain distribution.

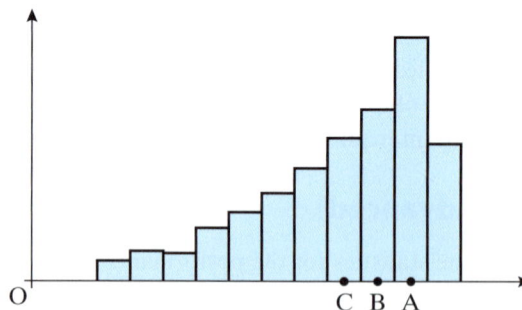

(i) Is the distribution positively or negatively skewed?
    Explain your answer.
(ii) The mean, mode and median of the distribution are represented by the points A, B and C.
    State what each point represents.
(iii) Give a real-life example of a distribution that is likely to have this shape.

6. A meat-canning factory supplies a supermarket with cans of meat in three sizes: large, medium and small.

   The regular consignment is of 300 large cans, 500 medium cans and 400 small cans.

   If the supermarket applies the method of *stratified random sampling* to select a sample of 60 cans to test the quality of the goods, how many of each size should be selected?

7. The number of road accidents recorded per day at a busy junction were recorded over a 400-day period as follows:

Accidents per day	0	1	2	3	4	5	6
Number of days	26	90	57	19	5	3	200

   (i) Calculate the mean number of accidents per day.
   (ii) Calculate the standard deviation of the number of accidents per day.

   An earlier study at the same road junction produced the results shown below.

Daily road accidents	
Mean	3.2
Standard deviation	1.15

   (iii) Compare the results of the two studies.

8. State which is the explanatory variable and which is the response variable in each of the following.
   (i) The wheat yield per hectare and the quantity of fertilizer applied.
   (ii) The number of suitable habitats and the number of species.
   (iii) The length of time it takes for a container of hot water to cool and the amount of water in the container.
   (iv) The petrol consumption of a car and the size of its engine.

9. Name the sampling method employed in each of the following surveys:
   A: Taking every 20th name from a school list arranged in alphabetical order.
   B: Surveying the first 50 people you meet in the street.
   C: Putting all the names into a box and picking out 20 names without looking.
   D: Selecting a random sample of boys and girls from each year-group in proportion to their numbers.
   E: Selecting 40 interviewers and asking each interviewer to question fifty people in any way they wish.

10. The runs scored by a cricketer in 11 innings during a season were as follows:

    47 63 0 28 40 51 *a* 77 0 13 35

    The exact value of *a* was unknown but it was greater than 100.

    (i) Calculate the median and interquartile range of these 11 values.
    (ii) Give a reason why, for these 11 values,
       (a) the mode is **not** an appropriate measure of average
       (b) the range is **not** an appropriate measure of spread.

Revision Exercise 10 (Extended-Response Questions)

1. For each of the football seasons 2008/09 and 2009/10 of a major European league, a count is made of the number of goals scored in each of the 380 matches. The results are shown in the table on the right:

   (i) For the number of goals scored in a match during the 2008/09 season,
   - (a) determine the median and the interquartile range
   - (b) calculate the mean and standard deviation, correct to 2 decimal places.

   (ii) Two statistics students, Jole and Katie, independently analyse the data on the number of goals scored in a match during the 2009/10 season.
   - › Jole determines correctly that the median is 2 and that the interquartile range is also 2.
   - › Katie calculates correctly, to two decimal places, that the mean is 2.48 and that the standard deviation is 1.59.

   Use your answers from part (i), together with Jole's and Katie's results, to compare briefly the two seasons with regard to the average and the spread of the number of goals scored in a match.

Number of goals scored in a match	Number of matches	
	2008/09	2009/10
0	30	32
1	79	82
2	99	95
3	68	78
4	60	48
5	24	30
6	11	9
7	6	6
8	2	0
9	1	0
Total	**380**	**380**

2. Sophie and Jack do a survey every day for three weeks. Sophie counts the number of pedal cycles using Market Street. Jack counts the number of pedal cycles using Strand Road. The data they collected is summarised in the back-to-back stem and leaf diagram.

Sophie	Stem	Jack
9 9 7 5	0	6 6
7 6 5 3 3 2 2 2 1 1	1	1 1 5
5 3 3 2 2	2	1 2 2 2 3 7 7 8 9
2 1	3	2 3 4 7 7 8
	4	2

Key: 1|3 = 31   Key: 2|1 = 21

   (i) Write down the modal number of pedal cycles using Strand Road.
   The quartiles for these data are summarised in the table opposite.

   (ii) Find the values for X, Y and Z.

	Sophie	Jack
Lower quartile	X	21
Median	13	Y
Upper quartile	Z	33

   (iii) Write down the road you think has the most pedal cycles travelling along it overall. Give a reason for your answer.

3. The diagrams show the age distribution of road-user casualties.

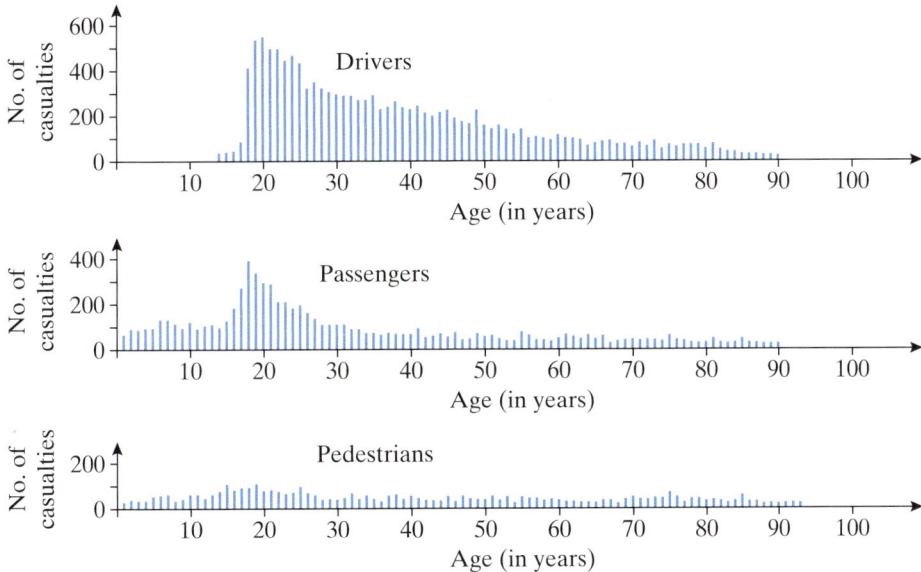

   (i) Comment on the shape of the distributions of driver and passenger casualties mentioning skewness and clustering.
   (ii) At what age are you most likely to be injured in a road accident if your are
        (a) the driver   (b) a passenger?
   (iii) Comment on the shape of the distribution of pedestrian casualties.
   (iv) If you were running a road safety campaign to help lower the number of casualties on our roads, whom would you target and why?

4. Some research was carried out into the participation of girls and boys in sport. The researchers selected a simple random sample of fifty male and fifty female teenagers enrolled in GAA clubs in the greater Cork area. They asked the teenagers the question: *How many sports do you play?*

   The data collected was as follows:

Boys	Girls
0, 4, 5, 1, 4, 1, 3, 3, 3, 1,	3, 3, 3, 1, 1, 3, 3, 1, 3, 3,
1, 2, 2, 2, 5, 3, 3, 4, 1, 2,	2, 2, 4, 4, 4, 5, 5, 2, 2, 3,
2, 2, 2, 3, 3, 3, 4, 5, 1, 1,	3, 3, 4, 1, 6, 2, 3, 3, 3, 4,
1, 1, 1, 2, 2, 2, 2, 2, 3, 3,	4, 5, 3, 4, 3, 3, 3, 4, 4, 3,
3, 3, 3, 3, 3, 3, 3, 3, 3, 3	1, 1, 3, 2, 1, 3, 1, 3, 1, 3

   (i) Display the data in a way that gives a picture of each distribution.
   (ii) State **one difference** and **one similarity** between the distributions of the two samples.
   (iii) Do you think that there is evidence that there are differences between the two populations?
   (iv) The researchers are planning to repeat this research on a larger scale.
        List **two** improvements they could make to the design of the research to reduce the possibility of bias in the samples. Explain why each improvement you suggest will reduce the likelihood of bias.

417

5. 224 athletes completed a triathlon which consisted of a 750 metre swim, followed by a 20 kilometre cycle, followed by a 5 kilometre run.

Some of the summary statistics are given in the table below:
Three of the entries in the table have been removed and replaced with question marks (?).

	Swim	Cycle	Run
Mean	18.329	41.927	?
Median	17.900	41.306	?
Mode			
Standard Deviation	?	4.553	3.409
Sample Variance	10.017	20.729	11.622
Skewness	1.094	0.717	0.463
Range	19.226	27.282	20.870
Minimum	11.350	31.566	16.466
Maximum	30.576	58.847	37.336
Count	224	224	224

Histograms of the times for the three events were produced.
Here are the three histograms without their titles.

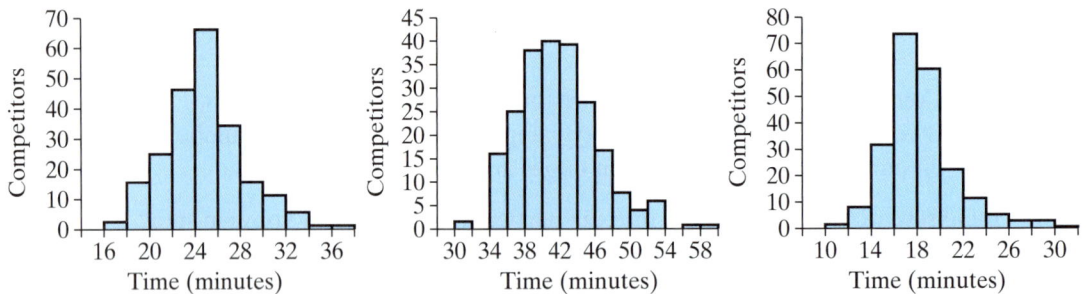

(i) Use the summary statistics in the table to decide which histogram corresponds to each event.

(ii) The mean and median time for the run are approximately equal. Estimate this value from the corresponding histogram.

(iii) Estimate, from the relevant histogram, the standard deviation of the times for the swim.

(iv) When calculating the summary statistics, the software failed to find a *mode* for the data sets. Why do you think this is?

6. Some students are using a database of earthquakes to investigate the times between the occurrences of serious earthquakes around the world. They extract information about all of the earthquakes in the 20th century that caused at least 1000 deaths. There are 115 of these.

The students wonder whether there are patterns in the timing of these earthquakes, so they look at the number of days between each successive pair of earthquakes.

They make the following table, showing the number of earthquakes for which the time interval from the previous earthquake is as shown.

Time in days from previous earthquake	0–100	100–200	200–300	300–400	400–500	500–600	600–700	700–800	800–1000	1000–1300
Number of earthquakes	31	24	12	14	8	7	5	6	5	3

[Source: National geophysical data center, significant earthquake database: www.ngdc.noaa.gov]

(i) Create a suitable graphical representation of the distribution.

(ii) Describe the distribution. Your description should refer to the shape of the distribution and should include an estimate of the median.

(iii) The mean time between these earthquakes is 309 days and the standard deviation is 277 days. Suppose that such an earthquake has just occurred and that we want to find the probability that the time to the next one will be between 100 and 200 days. Explain why it would **not** be correct to use standard normal distribution tables (z-tables) to do this.

(iv) Based on the information presented in this question so far, what is the best estimate for the probability described in part (iii) above? Explain your reasoning.

(v) As stated at the beginning, the students chose to analyse earthquake timings by looking at the time intervals between the occurrences of a particular type of earthquake. Suggest a different way that they could have looked at the data in the database in order to try to find patterns in the timing of earthquakes.

Coordinate Geometry: The Circle

Key words

centre   radius   tangent   chord   **perpendicular   parallel   intersection**
common chord   point of contact   internally   externally   common tangent

Section 11.1 The equation of a circle with centre (0, 0)

Definition

A circle is a set of points equidistant from a given point called the **centre**.

[OP] is always equal in length to the radius.

The circle on the right has centre $(0, 0)$ and radius r.

Let $P(x, y)$ be any point on the circle.

In the given right-angled triangle we have,

$$x^2 + y^2 = r^2.$$

This is the **equation** of the circle with centre $(0, 0)$ and radius r.

To find the equation of a circle, we require
  (i) the centre of the circle   (ii) the length of the radius.

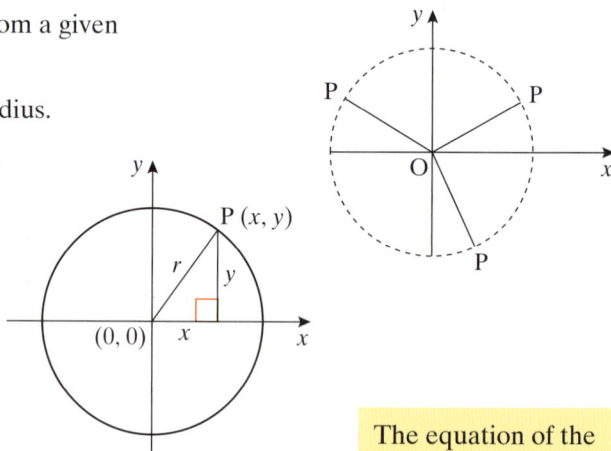

> The equation of the circle with centre $(0, 0)$ and radius r is
> $$x^2 + y^2 = r^2.$$

Example 1

A circle has its centre at $(0, 0)$ and passes through the point $(3, -1)$.
   (i) Find the length of the radius of the circle.
   (ii) Find the equation of the circle.

   (i) The length of the radius is the distance from $(0, 0)$ to $(3, -1)$.
      This distance is $\sqrt{(x_2 - x_1)^2 + (y_2 - y_1)^2}$
      $$= \sqrt{(3 - 0)^2 + (-1 - 0)^2} = \sqrt{9 + 1} = \sqrt{10}$$

(ii) Equation of circle: $x^2 + y^2 = r^2$

$$\Rightarrow \quad x^2 + y^2 = (\sqrt{10})^2$$
$$\Rightarrow \quad x^2 + y^2 = 10 \text{ is the required equation.}$$

If we are given the centre and the equation of a tangent
to the circle, then the radius is found by getting the
length of the perpendicular from the centre of
the circle to the tangent.

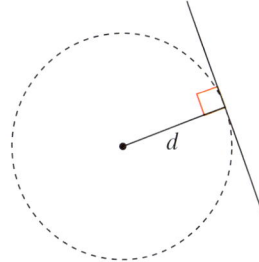

$d = $ length of radius

Example 2

The line $2x + 3y - 13 = 0$ is a tangent to a circle with centre $(0, 0)$.
Find the equation of this circle.

The radius of the circle is the perpendicular
distance from $(0, 0)$ to $2x + 3y - 13 = 0$.

Using the formula $\dfrac{|ax_1 + by_1 + c|}{\sqrt{a^2 + b^2}}$,

the radius $= \dfrac{|2(0) + 3(0) - 13|}{\sqrt{4 + 9}}$

$$= \frac{13}{\sqrt{13}} = \frac{13\sqrt{13}}{13} = \sqrt{13}$$

The equation of the circle is $x^2 + y^2 = r^2$ $r = \sqrt{13}$
i.e. $x^2 + y^2 = 13$

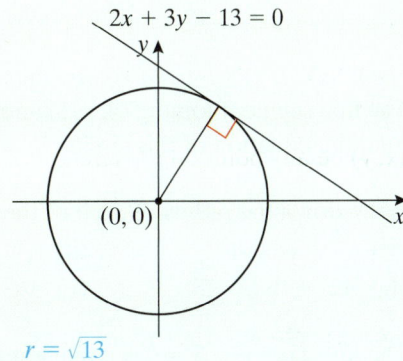

Finding the radius of a circle from its equation

The circle whose equation is $x^2 + y^2 = r^2$ has centre $(0, 0)$ and radius $= r$.

$\Rightarrow$ the circle $x^2 + y^2 = 8$ has centre $(0, 0)$ and radius $\sqrt{8}$.

If the equation of the circle is $4x^2 + 4y^2 = 9$, then divide each term by 4 so that the equation
is in the form $x^2 + y^2 = r^2$.

$$4x^2 + 4y^2 = 9 \quad \Rightarrow \quad x^2 + y^2 = \frac{9}{4}$$
$$\Rightarrow \qquad r^2 = \frac{9}{4}$$
$$\Rightarrow \qquad r = \frac{3}{2}$$

Exercise 11.1

1. Write down the equation of the circle with centre $(0, 0)$ and radius
   (i) 2   (ii) 5   (iii) $\sqrt{2}$ (iv) $3\sqrt{2}$ (v) $\frac{3}{4}$ (vi) $2\frac{1}{2}$

2. A circle with centre $(0, 0)$ contains the point $(3, 4)$.
   Find the equation of the circle.

3. Find the equation of the circle with centre $(0, 0)$ and which passes through the point $(-4, 1)$.

4. The points $(4, 3)$ and $(-4, -3)$ are the end points of the diameter of a circle.
   Find   (i)   the coordinates of the centre of the circle
            (ii)   the length of the radius
            (iii)   the equation of the circle.

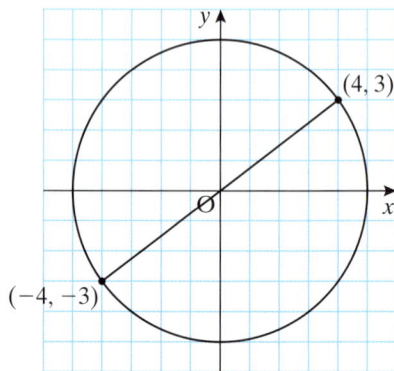

5. The line segment joining $(4, -1)$ and $(-4, 1)$ is the diameter of a circle. Find the equation of this circle.

6. Write down the radius of each of these circles:
   (i) $x^2 + y^2 = 9$ (ii) $x^2 + y^2 = 1$ (iii) $x^2 + y^2 = 27$
   (iv) $4x^2 + 4y^2 = 25$ (v) $9x^2 + 9y^2 = 4$ (vi) $16x^2 + 16y^2 = 49$.

7. The line $2x + y - 5 = 0$ is a tangent to the circle with centre $(0, 0)$.

   (i) Find the length of the radius of the circle.
   (ii) Write down the equation of the circle.

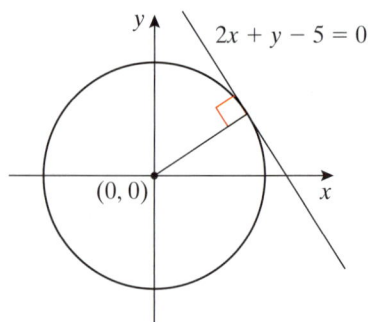

8. Find the equation of the circle of centre $(0, 0)$ if the line $4x - 3y - 25 = 0$ is a tangent to it.

9. The line $3x - y + 10 = 0$ is a tangent to a circle with centre $(0, 0)$.
   Find the equation of the circle.

10. Find the equation of the circle s with centre $(0, 0)$ and radius $2\sqrt{5}$.

t is the line $x - 2y + 10 = 0$.

By finding the distance from the centre of s to the line t, determine whether t is a tangent to s.

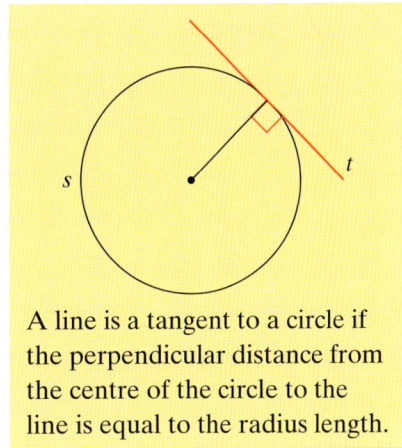

A line is a tangent to a circle if the perpendicular distance from the centre of the circle to the line is equal to the radius length.

Section 11.2 Equations of a circle with centres not at (0, 0)

1. The equation of a circle with centre (h, k) and radius r

The diagram on the right shows a circle with centre $C(h, k)$ and radius r.

Let $P(x, y)$ be any point on the circle.

The distance from C to P is equal to the radius.

From the diagram,

$$|CP|^2 = (x - h)^2 + (y - k)^2$$

But $|CP| = r$

$$\Rightarrow \quad (x - h)^2 + (y - k)^2 = r^2$$

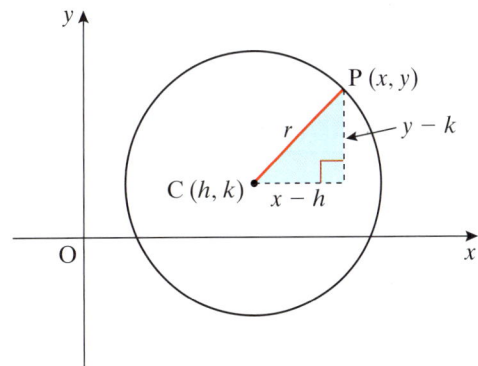

The equation of the circle with centre (h, k) and radius r is

$$(x - h)^2 + (y - k)^2 = r^2$$

Example 1

Find the equation of the circle with centre $(3, -1)$ and radius 4.

The equation is $(x - h)^2 + (y - k)^2 = r^2$
$$(x - 3)^2 + (y + 1)^2 = 4^2$$
$$\Rightarrow \quad x^2 - 6x + 9 + y^2 + 2y + 1 = 16$$
$$\Rightarrow \quad x^2 + y^2 - 6x + 2y - 6 = 0 \text{ is the equation}$$

Example 2

Find the centre and radius of the circle

$$(x - 3)^2 + (y + 4)^2 = 36$$

$$(x - 3)^2 + (y + 4)^2 = 36$$

centre = $(3, -4)$ radius = $\sqrt{36} = 6$

2. The general equation of a circle

Consider the equation $(x - 3)^2 + (y + 4)^2 = 36$
in Example 2 above

$$(x - 3)^2 + (y + 4)^2 = 36$$
$$\Rightarrow \quad x^2 - 6x + 9 + y^2 + 8y + 16 = 36$$
$$\Rightarrow \quad x^2 + y^2 - 6x + 8y - 11 = 0$$

If the equation of a circle is in the form
$$x^2 + y^2 + 2gx + 2fy + c = 0$$
(i) the centre = $(-g, -f)$
(ii) the radius = $\sqrt{g^2 + f^2 - c}$,
provided $g^2 + f^2 - c > 0$

The centre is $(3, -4)$ where 3 is $-\left(\frac{1}{2} \text{ coefficient of } x\right)$

and -4 is $-\left(\frac{1}{2} \text{ coefficient of } y\right)$

The radius is $\sqrt{(3)^2 + (-4)^2 - (-11)}$

$$= \sqrt{9 + 16 + 11} = \sqrt{36} = 6$$

Example 3

Find the centre and the radius of the circle $x^2 + y^2 - 2x + 4y - 8 = 0$.

Centre = $\left(-\frac{1}{2} \text{ coefficient of } x, -\frac{1}{2} \text{ coefficient of } y\right)$

$= (1, -2)$

Radius = $\sqrt{g^2 + f^2 - c}$

$= \sqrt{(1)^2 + (-2)^2 - (-8)}$

$= \sqrt{1 + 4 + 8} = \sqrt{13}$

$\therefore$ the centre = $(1, -2)$ and radius = $\sqrt{13}$

Note: 1. The equation of a circle can be written in two ways
(i) $(x - h)^2 + (y - k)^2 = r^2$ ... centre = (h, k) and radius = r
(ii) $x^2 + y^2 + 2gx + 2fy + c = 0$ ... centre = $(-g, -f)$ and radius = $\sqrt{g^2 + f^2 - c}$

2. When finding the centre and radius of a circle whose equation is in the form
$x^2 + y^2 + 2gx + 2fy + c = 0$, ensure that the coefficients of x^2 and y^2 are both one.

3. The equation of circle has these characteristics:
(i) The equation is of the second degree in x and y.
(ii) The coefficients of x^2 and y^2 are equal.
(iii) There is no term in xy.

Points and circles

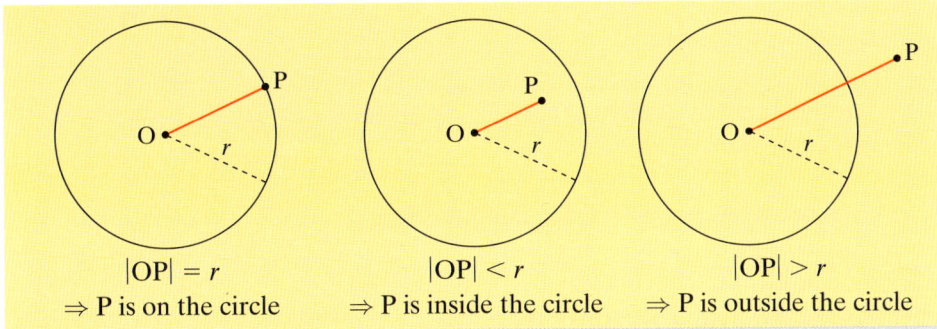

$|OP| = r$
$\Rightarrow$ P is on the circle

$|OP| < r$
$\Rightarrow$ P is inside the circle

$|OP| > r$
$\Rightarrow$ P is outside the circle

Note: If the coordinates of a point satisfy the equation of a circle, then that point is on the circle.

Example 4

Investigate if the point P(4, 1) is inside the circle $x^2 + y^2 - 6x + 4y + 4 = 0$.

Centre of circle = $(3, -2)$

Radius of circle = $\sqrt{(3)^2 + (-2)^2 - 4} = \sqrt{9 + 4 - 4} = \sqrt{9} = 3$

Distance from $(3, -2)$ to P(4, 1) is
$$\sqrt{(4 - 3)^2 + (1 + 2)^2} = \sqrt{1 + 9} = \sqrt{10}$$

Since this distance, i.e. $\sqrt{10}$, is greater than the radius 3,

$\Rightarrow$ P(4, 1) is outside the circle

Exercise 11.2

1. Find the equation of each of the following circles in the form $(x - h)^2 + (y - k)^2 = r^2$.

   (i) centre (3, 1); radius = 2

   (ii) centre (1, −4); radius = $\sqrt{8}$

   (iii) centre (4, 0); radius = $2\sqrt{3}$

   (iv) centre (0, −5); radius = $3\sqrt{2}$

2. The given circle has centre (2, 2). If the circle contains the point (5, 1), find its equation.

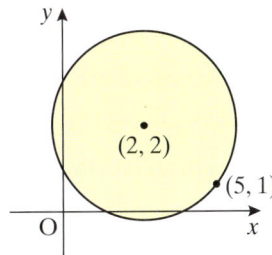

3. The line segment joining (3, 5) and (−1, 1) is the diameter of a circle.

   (i) Find the coordinates of the centre of the circle.

   (ii) Write down the equation of the circle.

4. Write down the centre and radius of each of the following circles:

   (i) $(x - 3)^2 + (y - 2)^2 = 16$

   (ii) $(x + 2)^2 + (y - 6)^2 = 8$

   (iii) $(x - 3)^2 + y^2 = 5$

   (iv) $x^2 + (y + 2)^2 = 10$

5. Find the equation of the circle of centre $(-2, 5)$ and whose radius is equal to the diameter of the circle $(x - 3)^2 + (y + 4)^2 = 18$.

6. The given circle touches both the x-axis and y-axis. If the radius of the circle is 3, write down the coordinates of C, the centre. Hence write down the equation of the circle.

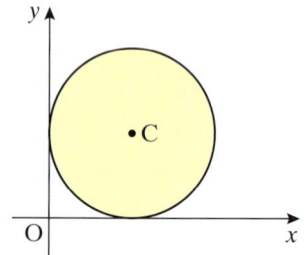

7. Find the centre and radius of each of the following circles:

   (i) $x^2 + y^2 - 4x + 8y - 5 = 0$

   (ii) $x^2 + y^2 - 2x - 6y - 15 = 0$

   (iii) $x^2 + y^2 - 8x - 8 = 0$

   (iv) $x^2 + y^2 + 5x - 6y = 5$

   (v) $2x^2 + 2y^2 - 4x + 3y = 0$

   (vi) $4x^2 + 4y^2 - 28y + 33 = 0$

8. Show that the point $(5, -5)$ is on the circle $x^2 + y^2 - 4x + 2y - 20 = 0$.

9. Show that the point $(3, 6)$ is outside the circle $x^2 + y^2 + 2x - 4y - 20 = 0$.

10. Investigate if the point $(3, 1)$ is inside or outside the circle $x^2 + y^2 - 2x + 4y - 15 = 0$.

11. Is the point $(1, 1)$ inside, on, or outside the circle $x^2 + y^2 - 6x + 4y + 4 = 0$?

12. The length of the radius of the circle $x^2 + y^2 - 8x + 10y + k = 0$ is 7. Find the value of k.

13. The point $(-4, 3)$ is the centre of a circle k. The y-axis is a tangent to k.

   (i) Draw a sketch of the circle k.

   (ii) Write down the radius of the circle.

   (iii) Write down the equation of the circle.

14. The diagram shows four circles of equal radius length. The circles are touching as shown. The equation of k_1 is $x^2 + y^2 = 4$.

   (i) Write down the radius of k_1.

   (ii) Write down the coordinates of the centre of k_3.

   (iii) Write down the equation of k_3.

   (iv) Is $x^2 + (y + 4)^2 = 4$ the equation of k_2 or k_4? Explain your answer.

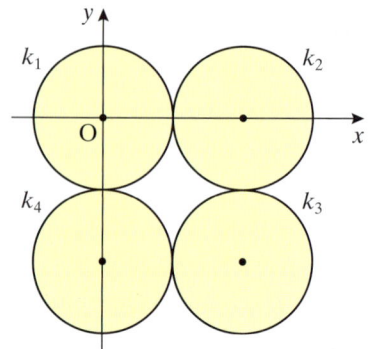

15. The centre of a circle k is in the second quadrant and the length of the radius is 4.
The x-axis and y-axis are both tangents to k.
Draw a sketch of this circle and hence write down its equation.

16. The line $4x - 3y - 40 = 0$ touches the circle
$(x - 2)^2 + (y - 6)^2 = 100$ at $P(10, 0)$.

    (i) Write down the coordinates of C,
        the centre of the circle.

    (ii) Show that CP is perpendicular to
         the given line.

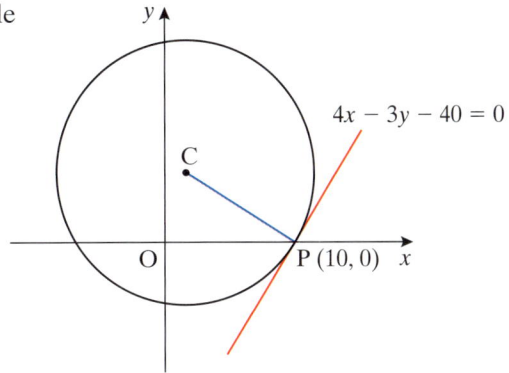

17. On a street plan, two roads are represented by
straight lines with equations $y = -x + 4$
and $y = x$.
The intersection of these lines marks the
centre of a roundabout whose diameter
is 2 units on the plan.
Find the equation of the circle representing
the roundabout.

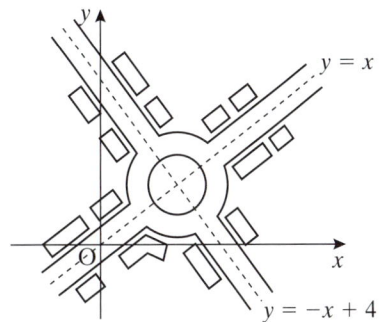

18. The small circle, centre C, has equation
$$(x + 2)^2 + (y + 1)^2 = 25$$
The large circles, centres A and B, touch the
small circle and AB is parallel to the x-axis.
Find (i) the centre and radius of each of the
           three circles

       (ii) the equation of the circle with centre A.

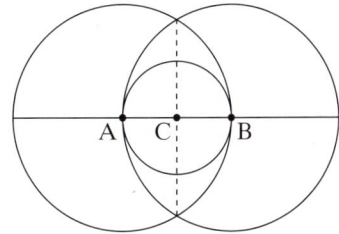

Section 11.3 Finding the equation of a circle

To find the equation of a circle we generally require,
(i) the centre and (ii) the radius of the circle.

In the more difficult questions these two pieces of information are not given directly. We have
to rely, therefore, on our knowledge of the geometry of the circle to find the centre and the
radius.

Three geometrical properties of the circle are particularly important.

1. **The perpendicular from the centre of a circle to a chord bisects the chord**

   In the given figure, $CM \perp AB$

   $$|AM| = |MB|$$

   The corollary to this theorem is property 2, given below.

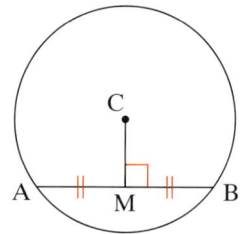

2. **The perpendicular bisector of a chord contains the centre**

   In the given diagram, l is the perpendicular bisector of the chord $[AB]$ and m is the perpendicular bisector of the chord $[BC]$.

   Each of these bisectors contains the centre, O.

   The point of intersection of these two perpendicular bisectors is the centre of the circle.

   Note: This property is very useful when we require the equation of a circle containing three given points.

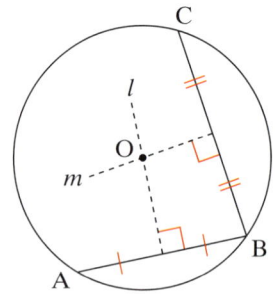

3. **The perpendicular to a tangent at the point of contact passes through the centre of the circle**

   In the given diagram the tangent, t, touches the circle at the point P.

   The perpendicular to t through P contains the centre O.

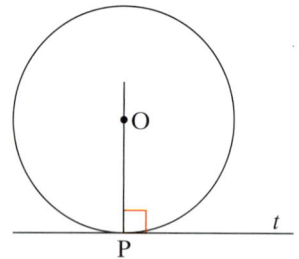

1. Equation of circle containing three given points

> ### Example 1
>
> Find the equation of the circle which contains the points $A(2, 1)$, $B(0, 5)$ and $C(-1, 2)$.
>
> The given diagram shows the circle containing the three given points.
>
> l is the perpendicular bisector of $[CA]$
>
> m is the perpendicular bisector of $[BC]$.
>
> We now find the equations of l and m.

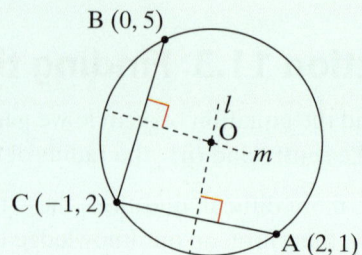

Equation of *l*:

Slope of AC $= \dfrac{1-2}{2+1} = -\dfrac{1}{3}$

$\Rightarrow$ slope of $l = 3$

Midpoint of $[AC] = \left(\dfrac{2-1}{2}, \dfrac{1+2}{2}\right)$

$= \left(\dfrac{1}{2}, \dfrac{3}{2}\right)$

Equation of *l*: point $= \left(\dfrac{1}{2}, \dfrac{3}{2}\right)$

slope $= 3$

$y - \dfrac{3}{2} = 3\left(x - \dfrac{1}{2}\right)$

$\Rightarrow \quad y - \dfrac{3}{2} = 3x - \dfrac{3}{2}$

$\Rightarrow \quad 2y - 3 = 6x - 3$

$\Rightarrow \quad 6x - 2y = 0$

$\Rightarrow \quad 3x - y = 0 \;...\text{①}$

Equation of *m*:

Slope of BC $= \dfrac{5-2}{0+1} = \dfrac{3}{1} = 3$

$\Rightarrow$ slope of $m = -\dfrac{1}{3}$

Midpoint of $[BC] = \left(\dfrac{0-1}{2}, \dfrac{5+2}{2}\right)$

$= \left(-\dfrac{1}{2}, \dfrac{7}{2}\right)$

Equation of *m*: point $= \left(-\dfrac{1}{2}, \dfrac{7}{2}\right)$

slope $= -\dfrac{1}{3}$

$\Rightarrow \qquad y - \dfrac{7}{2} = -\dfrac{1}{3}\left(x + \dfrac{1}{2}\right)$

$\Rightarrow \qquad y - \dfrac{7}{2} = -\dfrac{x}{3} - \dfrac{1}{6}$

$\Rightarrow \qquad 6y - 21 = -2x - 1$

$\Rightarrow \quad 2x + 6y - 20 = 0$

$\Rightarrow \quad x + 3y - 10 = 0 \;...\text{②}$

Solving the equations for *l* and *m* we get:

①: $\quad 3x - y = 0 \quad \Rightarrow \quad 3x - y = 0$

②: $\quad x + 3y = 10 \quad \Rightarrow \quad \underline{3x + 9y = 30}$

$\qquad\qquad\qquad\qquad\qquad -10y = -30 \quad \Rightarrow \quad y = 3$

$y = 3 \quad \Rightarrow \quad x = 1$

$\therefore$ the centre of the circle is O(1, 3).

Radius of the circle is $|OA|$.

$\quad |OA| = \sqrt{(1-2)^2 + (3-1)^2} = \sqrt{1+4} = \sqrt{5}$

Equation of circle with centre (1, 3) and radius $\sqrt{5}$ is

$\quad (x-1)^2 + (y-3)^2 = (\sqrt{5})^2$

$\Rightarrow \quad (x-1)^2 + (y-3)^2 = 5$ is the required equation

Alternative method

The equation of a circle containing three points can also be found by using the general equation of the circle, $x^2 + y^2 + 2gx + 2fy + c = 0$. By substituting the three sets of values for x and y we will then have 3 simultaneous equations.

This is illustrated in the following example.

429

Example 2

Find the equation of the circle which contains the points $(0, 0)$, $(3, 1)$ and $(3, 9)$.

Let the equation of the circle be $x^2 + y^2 + 2gx + 2fy + c = 0$.

$(0, 0) \in$ the circle $\Rightarrow$ $0 + 0 + 0 + 0 + c = 0$ $\Rightarrow$ $c = 0$ ... ①
$(3, 1) \in$ the circle $\Rightarrow$ $9 + 1 + 6g + 2f + c = 0$
$\Rightarrow$ $6g + 2f = -10$ ... ② ... $(c = 0)$
$(3, 9) \in$ the circle $\Rightarrow$ $9 + 81 + 6g + 18f + c = 0$
$\Rightarrow$ $6g + 18f = -90$ ... ③ ... $(c = 0)$

We now solve equations ② and ③.

②: $6g + 2f = -10$
③: $\underline{6g + 18f = -90}$
        $-16f = 80$
$\Rightarrow$ $16f = -80$ $\Rightarrow$ $f = -5$
②: $6g + 2(-5) = -10$
        $6g = 0$ $\Rightarrow$ $g = 0$
$\therefore$ $g = 0, f = -5$ and $c = 0$

We now substitute these values in the equation

$x^2 + y^2 + 2gx + 2fy + c = 0$ $\Rightarrow$ $x^2 + y^2 - 10y = 0$ is the required
equation

Note: If one of the three points on a circle is $(0, 0)$, the method of finding the equation shown in Example 2 may be easier than the method shown in Example 1.

2. Equation of circle when given the equation of a tangent, the point of contact and one other point

Example 3

Find the equation of the circle which touches the line $3x - 4y - 3 = 0$ at the point A$(5, 3)$ and which passes through the point B$(-2, 4)$.

A rough sketch of the circle is shown on the right.

The centre O lies on the perpendicular bisector of [AB].

The centre also lies on the line through A$(5, 3)$, perpendicular to the tangent $3x - 4y - 3 = 0$.

The centre, O, is the point of intersection of these two lines.

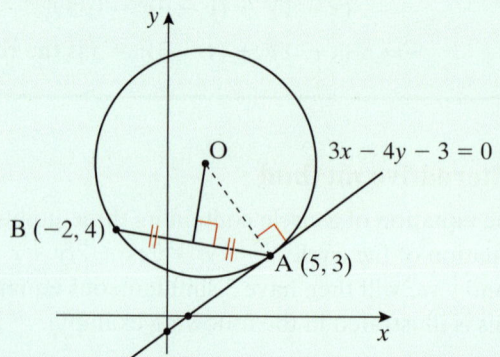

(i) Equation of the perpendicular bisector of [AB]:

Slope of AB $= \dfrac{3-4}{5+2} = -\dfrac{1}{7}$

$\Rightarrow$ Slope of perpendicular to AB $= 7$

Midpoint of [AB] $= \left(\dfrac{-2+5}{2}, \dfrac{4+3}{2}\right) = \left(\dfrac{3}{2}, \dfrac{7}{2}\right)$

Equation of perpendicular bisector of [AB]:

$\quad$ point $= \left(\dfrac{3}{2}, \dfrac{7}{2}\right)$; $\quad$ slope $= 7$

$\quad y - \dfrac{7}{2} = 7\left(x - \dfrac{3}{2}\right)$

$\Rightarrow \quad y - \dfrac{7}{2} = 7x - \dfrac{21}{2}$

$\Rightarrow \quad 2y - 7 = 14x - 21 \quad \Rightarrow \quad 14x - 2y - 14 = 0$

$\qquad\qquad\qquad\qquad\qquad \Rightarrow \qquad 7x - y - 7 = 0 \dots \text{①}$

(ii) Equation of line through A perpendicular to $3x - 4y - 3 = 0$:

Slope of $3x - 4y - 3 = 0$ is $\dfrac{3}{4}$ $\Rightarrow$ slope of perpendicular line $= -\dfrac{4}{3}$.

Equation of line: $\quad y - 3 = -\dfrac{4}{3}(x - 5)$

$\Rightarrow \qquad\qquad 3y - 9 = -4x + 20$

$\Rightarrow \quad 4x + 3y - 29 = 0 \dots \text{②}$

Solving equations ① and ② we get:

① $\times$ 3: $\quad 21x - 3y = 21$

② $\quad$: $\quad \underline{4x + 3y = 29}$

$\qquad\qquad 25x \qquad = 50 \quad \Rightarrow \quad x = 2 \text{ and } y = 7$

$\Rightarrow \quad (2, 7)$ is the centre of the circle

The radius of the circle is the distance from $(2, 7)$ to $(-2, 4)$.

$\therefore \quad$ the radius $= \sqrt{(-2-2)^2 + (4-7)^2}$

$\qquad\qquad\qquad = \sqrt{16 + 9} = \sqrt{25} = 5$

The equation of the circle with centre $(2, 7)$ and radius $= 5$ is

$\qquad (x - 2)^2 + (y - 7)^2 = 25$

3. Equation of circle through two given points with its centre on a given line

The given diagram shows a circle k containing two points A and B and a line l which contains the centre of k.

The centre of the circle is found by getting the point of intersection of l and the perpendicular bisector of [AB].

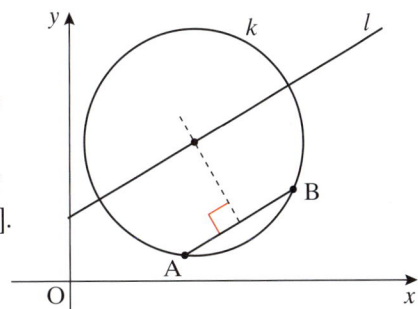

Example 4

Find the equation of the circle whose centre is on the line l: $3x - y - 7 = 0$ and which passes through the points A(1, 1) and B(2, −1).

m is the perpendicular bisector of [AB]. The centre of the circle is the point of intersection of m and the line $3x - y - 7 = 0$.

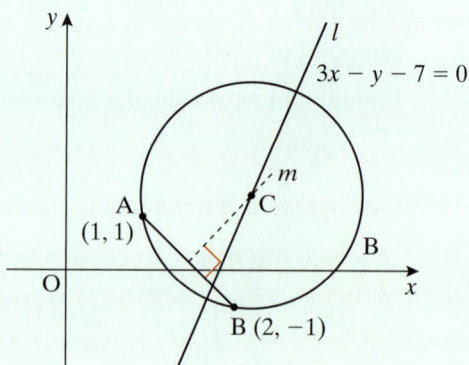

Midpoint of $[AB] = \left(\frac{3}{2}, 0\right)$

Slope of $AB = \frac{-1-1}{2-1}$

$\qquad = -2$

Slope of $m = \frac{1}{2}$

Equation of m: point $= \left(\frac{3}{2}, 0\right)$ and slope $= \frac{1}{2}$

$$y - y_1 = m(x - x_1)$$
$$y - 0 = \frac{1}{2}\left(x - \frac{3}{2}\right)$$
$$\Rightarrow \qquad y = \frac{x}{2} - \frac{3}{4}$$
$$\Rightarrow \qquad 4y = 2x - 3 \Rightarrow 2x - 4y - 3 = 0 \text{... equation of } m$$

We now find the point of intersection of ℓ and m.

l: $\quad 3x - y = 7 \quad (\times 2)$: $\quad 6x - 2y = 14$

m: $\quad 2x - 4y = 3 \quad (\times 3)$: $\quad \underline{6x - 12y = 9}$

$\qquad\qquad\qquad\qquad\qquad 10y = 5 \Rightarrow y = \frac{1}{2}$

l: $\quad 3x - \frac{1}{2} = 7$

$\Rightarrow \quad 3x = 7\frac{1}{2} \Rightarrow 3x = \frac{15}{2} \Rightarrow x = \frac{5}{2}$

$\therefore$ centre of circle, $C = \left(\frac{5}{2}, \frac{1}{2}\right)$

The radius length is the distance from $\left(\frac{5}{2}, \frac{1}{2}\right)$ to (1, 1).

$$\Rightarrow \text{ radius} = \sqrt{\left(\frac{5}{2} - 1\right)^2 + \left(\frac{1}{2} - 1\right)^2}$$
$$= \sqrt{\frac{9}{4} + \frac{1}{4}} = \sqrt{\frac{10}{4}}$$

The equation of the circle is $(x - h)^2 + (y - k)^2 = r^2$

$$\Rightarrow \left(x - \frac{5}{2}\right)^2 + \left(y - \frac{1}{2}\right)^2 = \frac{10}{4}$$
$$\Rightarrow \left(x - \frac{5}{2}\right)^2 + \left(y - \frac{1}{2}\right)^2 = \frac{5}{2}$$

Note   **1.**   The question in Example 4 may also be done by using the general equation
$x^2 + y^2 + 2gx + 2fy + c = 0$.

By substituting the points $(1, 1)$ and $(2, -1)$ we get two equations in g, f and c.

Since the line $3x - y - 7 = 0$ contains the centre $(-g, -f)$, we get the equation
$-3g + f - 7 = 0$.

We then solve the three equations to get the values of g, f and c.

2.   A line is a tangent to a circle if it touches the circle at one point only.

Also, the perpendicular distance from the centre of a circle to a tangent is equal to the radius of the circle.

3.   Showing that a line is a tangent to a circle

A line is a tangent to a circle if the perpendicular distance from the centre of the circle to the line is equal to the radius.

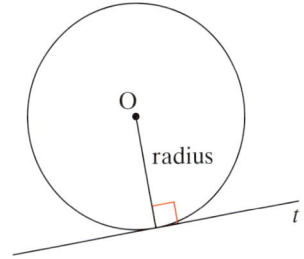

Example 5

Show that the line $x + 6y - 9 = 0$ is a tangent to the circle
$x^2 + y^2 - 4x + 10y - 8 = 0$.

The centre of the circle $= (2, -5)$ and radius $= \sqrt{(2)^2 + (-5)^2 + 8} = \sqrt{37}$.

The perpendicular distance from $(2, -5)$ to the line $x + 6y - 9 = 0$ is

$$\frac{|2(1) + 6(-5) - 9|}{\sqrt{1^2 + 6^2}} = \frac{|2 - 30 - 9|}{\sqrt{37}} = \frac{|-37|}{\sqrt{37}} = \frac{37\sqrt{37}}{37} = \sqrt{37}$$

Since this perpendicular distance is equal to the radius,

$\Rightarrow$ the line is a tangent to the circle

Exercise 11.3

1.   Find the centre and radius of the circle $x^2 + y^2 = 10$.
By finding the perpendicular distance from the centre of the circle to the line
$l: 3x + y + 10 = 0$, show that l is a tangent to the circle.

2.   Write down the centre and the radius of the circle $(x - 3)^2 + (y + 4)^2 = 50$.
Hence show that the line $x - y + 3 = 0$ is a tangent to the circle.

3.   Investigate if the line $3x - 4y - 12 = 0$ is a tangent to the circle $(x + 2)^2 + (y - 1)^2 = 16$.

4.   The line $2x - 3y - 5 = 0$ is a tangent to a circle k.
If $(-1, 2)$ is the centre of k, find its equation.

5.   Find the equation of the circle with centre $(2, 1)$ and which touches the line $x - y + 5 = 0$.

6. The equation of a circle is $x^2 + y^2 - 2x - 2y + 1 = 0$.

    (i) Write down the coordinates of the centre of the circle.

    (ii) Find the radius of the circle.

    (iii) Draw a sketch of the circle.

    (iv) Explain why the circle touches both axes.

7. Write down the equation of the circle with centre $(2, 2)$ and which touches both axes.

8. Find the equation of the circle whose centre is $(2, 3)$ and which touches the y-axis.

9. The equation of a circle s is $x^2 + y^2 - 4x + 6y - 12 = 0$.

    (i) Find the coordinates of the centre and length of the radius of s.

    (ii) Find the values of k if the line $3x + 4y - k = 0$ is a tangent to s.

10. The points $A(1, 2)$, $B(0, -2)$ and $C(4, -3)$ are shown in the given diagram.

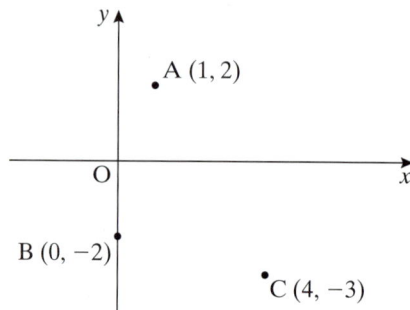

    (i) Find the equation of the perpendicular bisector of $[AB]$.

    (ii) Find the equation of the perpendicular bisector of $[BC]$.

    (iii) Find the point of intersection of these two bisectors.

    (iv) Find the length of the radius of the circle through the three points.

    (v) Write down the equation of the circle.

11. Using the general equation $x^2 + y^2 + 2gx + 2fy + c = 0$, find the equation of the circle which passes through the points $(0, 0)$, $(2, 0)$ and $(3, -1)$.

12. Find the equation of the circle which passes through the points $(0, 0)$, $(-2, 4)$ and $(-1, 7)$.

13. A circle passes through the points $(3, 5)$ and $(-1, 3)$.
Its centre is on the line $x + 2y - 6 = 0$.
Using the equation $x^2 + y^2 + 2gx + 2fy + c = 0$ to represent the circle, write down three equations in g, f and c to represent the given information.
Hence write down the equation of the circle.

14. The centre of the circle $x^2 + y^2 + 2gx + 2fy + c = 0$ is $(-g, -f)$.
If the centre of the circle is on the x-axis, find the value of f.
Now find the equation of the circle which has its centre on the x-axis and which passes through the points $(4, 5)$ and $(-2, 3)$.

15. The circle $x^2 + y^2 - 4x - 6y + k = 0$ touches the x-axis at the point T.

    (i) Write down the length of the radius of the circle.

    (ii) Hence find the value of k and the coordinates of T.

16. A circle k has its centre in the first quadrant and touches both the x-axis and y-axis.

    (i) If the centre of the circle is $(-g, -f)$, what can you say about the values of g and f?

    (ii) If the distance from the centre of the circle to the origin is $3\sqrt{2}$, find the equation of the circle k.

17. The line $3x + 2y - 12 = 0$ is a tangent to the circle k at B$(4, 0)$.
The circle also contains the point A$(3, -5)$.

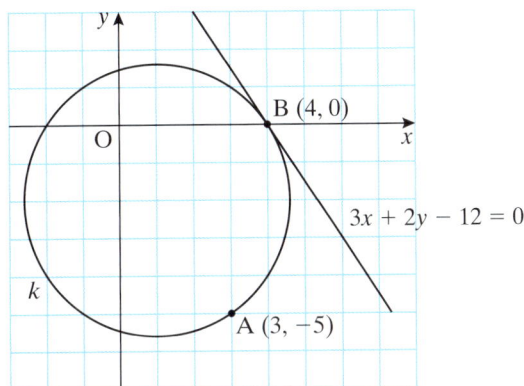

    (i) Explain why the perpendicular to the line $3x + 2y - 12 = 0$ at the point B contains the centre of the circle.

    (ii) Find the equation of this perpendicular.

    (iii) Find the equation of the perpendicular bisector of [AB].

    (iv) Hence find the centre and radius length of the circle.

    (v) Write down the equation of the circle.

18. A circle passes through the points $(7, 2)$ and $(7, 10)$. The line $x = -1$ is a tangent to the circle. Find the equation of the circle.

> Hint: Let the centre of the circle be $(-g, -f)$

19. A circle of radius length $\sqrt{20}$ contains the point $(-1, 3)$.
Its centre lies on the line $x + y = 0$.
Find the equations of the two circles that satisfy these conditions.

20. In a computer game a tractor is drawn. The front wheel's rim has equation

$$(x - 5)^2 + (y - 3)^2 = 4.$$

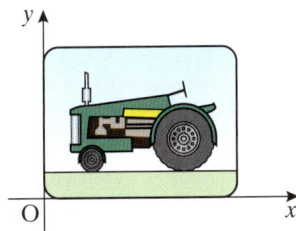

    (i) The ground is a line parallel to the x-axis. Write down the equation of this line.

    (ii) The rear wheel's radius is 3 times the size of the front one's. If the points of contact of the wheels with the ground are 10 units apart, find the equation of the rear wheel's rim.

    (iii) The tractor moves 2 units to the left. Find the new equation of the rim of the rear wheel.

Section 11.4 Tangents to a circle

A line is a tangent to a circle if it intersects the circle at one and only one point.

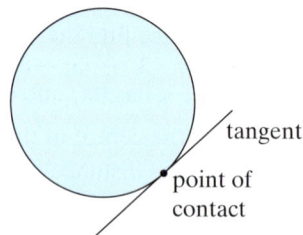

tangent

point of contact

1. Finding the equation of the tangent to a circle at the point P on the circle

In the given diagram, t is a tangent to the circle at the point P and C is the centre of the circle. CP is perpendicular to t.

To find the equation of t:
  (i) Find the slope of CP.
 (ii) Write down the slope of t.
(iii) Find the equation of t using
     $y - y_1 = m(x - x_1)$.

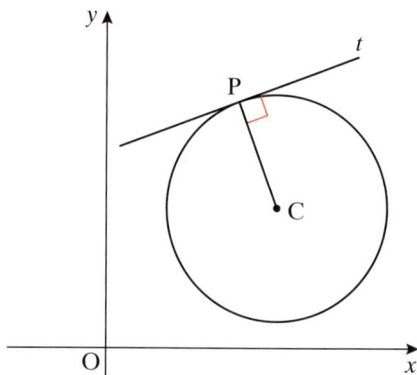

Example 1

Find the equation of the tangent to the circle $x^2 + y^2 - 4x + 2y - 20 = 0$ at the point $(5, -5)$ on the circle.

The centre of the circle is C(2, −1).

$$\text{Slope of CP} = \frac{-1 + 5}{2 - 5} = \frac{4}{-3} = -\frac{4}{3}$$

$$\Rightarrow \quad \text{slope of } t = \frac{3}{4}$$

Equation of t: $y + 5 = \frac{3}{4}(x - 5)$

$$\Rightarrow \quad 4y + 20 = 3x - 15$$

$$\Rightarrow \quad 3x - 4y - 35 = 0 \text{ is the equation of the tangent}$$

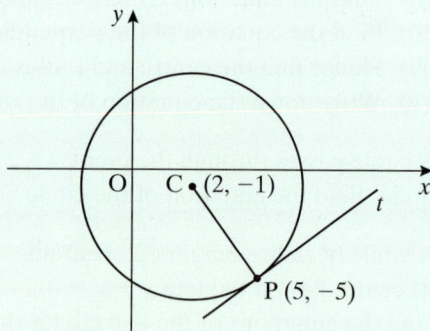

2. Tangents to a circle parallel or perpendicular to a given line

Parallel and perpendicular lines.

1. Any line parallel to $ax + by + c = 0$
    has equation $ax + by + k = 0$
2. Any line perpendicular to $ax + by + c = 0$
    has equation $bx - ay + k = 0$

Example 2

Find the equations of the two lines parallel to the line $3x + 4y - 6 = 0$ and which are tangents to the circle $x^2 + y^2 = 25$.

A sketch of the line and circle are shown.

The two tangents parallel to $3x + 4y - 6 = 0$ are shown in red.

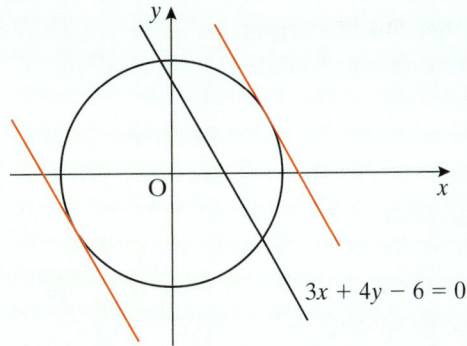

$3x + 4y - 6 = 0$

The equation of any line parallel to $3x + 4y - 6 = 0$ is $3x + 4y + k = 0$.

The radius of the circle is $\sqrt{25} = 5$.

The perpendicular distance from the centre of the circle, $(0, 0)$, to $3x + 4y + k = 0$ is equal to 5.

$$\Rightarrow \frac{|3(0) + 4(0) + k|}{\sqrt{3^2 + 4^2}} = 5$$

$$\Rightarrow \frac{|k|}{5} = 5$$

$$\Rightarrow \frac{k}{5} = 5 \quad \text{or} \quad \frac{k}{5} = -5$$

$$\Rightarrow k = 25 \quad \text{or} \quad k = -25$$

> If $|x| = 5$
> $\Rightarrow x = 5 \quad \text{or} \quad x = -5$

The equations of the two tangents are

$$3x + 4y + 25 = 0 \quad \text{or} \quad 3x + 4y - 25 = 0.$$

3. Tangents to a circle from a point P not on the circle

The diagram below illustrates that two tangents can be drawn to a circle from a point outside the circle, i.e. PA and PB are tangents to the circle k.

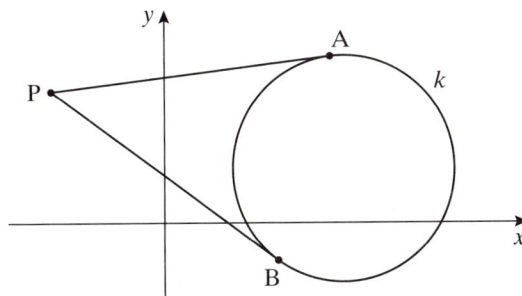

If we are asked to find the equations of the two tangents from the point $(2, 3)$, for example, to a given circle, we first find in terms of the slope, m, the equation of any line through $(2, 3)$.

This equation is $y - 3 = m(x - 2)$

i.e. $mx - y + 3 - 2m = 0$.

We then find the perpendicular distance from the centre of the circle to this line and equate it to the radius to find the two values of m.

Remember

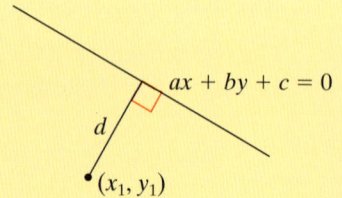

Example 3

Find the equations of the tangents to the circle $x^2 + y^2 = 5$ from the point $(5, 0)$.

The equation of any line through $(5, 0)$ is

$$y - y_1 = m(x - x_1)$$
$$\Rightarrow \quad y - 0 = m(x - 5)$$
$$\Rightarrow \quad y = m(x - 5)$$
$$\Rightarrow \quad mx - y - 5m = 0$$

Centre of circle $= (0, 0)$

Radius of circle $= \sqrt{5}$

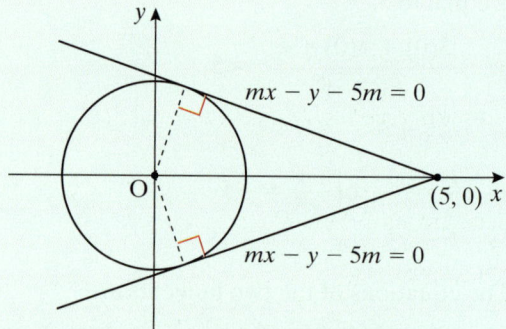

If the line $mx - y - 5m = 0$ is a tangent to the circle, then the perpendicular distance from the centre of the circle, i.e. $(0, 0)$, to the line is equal in length to the radius.

$$\Rightarrow \quad \frac{|0.m + 0(-1) - 5m|}{\sqrt{m^2 + (-1)^2}} = \sqrt{5}$$

$$= \frac{|-5m|}{\sqrt{m^2 + 1}} = \sqrt{5}$$

$$\Rightarrow \quad \frac{25m^2}{m^2 + 1} = 5$$

$$\Rightarrow \quad 25m^2 = 5(m^2 + 1)$$

$$\Rightarrow \quad 20m^2 = 5$$

$$\Rightarrow \quad m^2 = \tfrac{1}{4} \quad \Rightarrow \quad m = \pm\tfrac{1}{2}$$

The equations of the tangents are

$m = \tfrac{1}{2}$: $\quad y - 0 = \tfrac{1}{2}(x - 5)$

$\quad \Rightarrow \quad 2y = x - 5$

$\quad \Rightarrow \quad x - 2y - 5 = 0$

$m = -\tfrac{1}{2}$: $\quad y - 0 = -\tfrac{1}{2}(x - 5)$

$\quad \quad 2y = -x + 5$

$\quad \Rightarrow \quad x + 2y - 5 = 0$

The equations of the two tangents are

$\quad x - 2y - 5 = 0 \quad$ and $\quad x + 2y - 5 = 0$.

4. Length of a tangent to a circle from a given point

When dealing with problems involving tangents, it is important to remember that the line joining the centre of the circle to the point of tangency is perpendicular to the tangent.

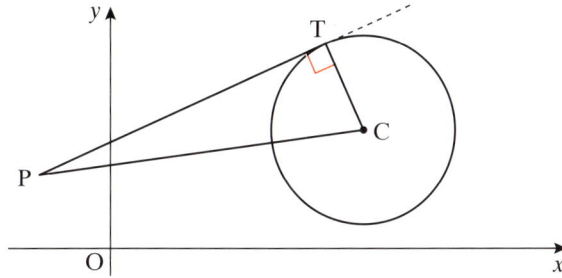

We will use this information to find the length of a tangent to a circle from a given point.

This is illustrated in the following example.

> To find the length of the tangent [PT],
> $$|CP|^2 = |PT|^2 + |CT|^2$$
> $$\Rightarrow \quad |PT|^2 = |CP|^2 - |CT|^2$$

Example 4

Find the length of the tangent from the point $(-5, 8)$ to the circle $x^2 + y^2 - 4x - 6y + 3 = 0$.

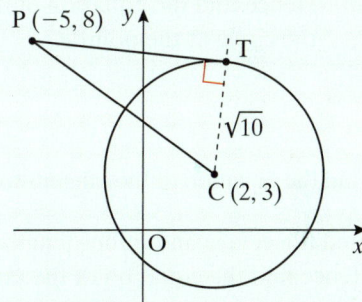

The centre of the circle is $(2, 3)$.

The radius $= \sqrt{g^2 + f^2 - c}$

$\qquad\qquad = \sqrt{4 + 9 - 3} = \sqrt{10}$

$\Rightarrow \quad |CT| = \sqrt{10}$

$|CP| = \sqrt{(2 + 5)^2 + (3 - 8)^2}$

$\qquad = \sqrt{49 + 25} = \sqrt{74}$

Since $\triangle CTP$ is right-angled $\quad \Rightarrow \quad |PT|^2 = |CP|^2 - |CT|^2$

$\qquad\qquad\qquad\qquad\qquad\qquad\qquad = 74 - 10 = 64$

$\qquad\qquad\qquad \Rightarrow \quad |PT| = \sqrt{64} = 8$

$\therefore$ the length of the tangent is 8

Exercise 11.4

1. Find the equation of the tangent, t, to the given circle $x^2 + y^2 = 8$ at the point $P(2, 2)$.

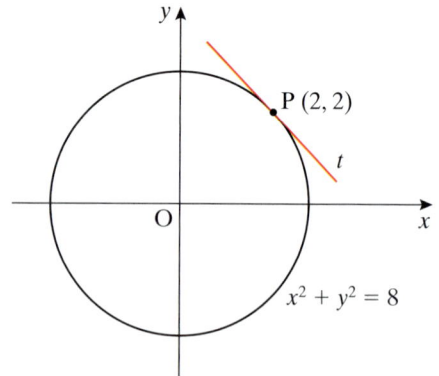

2. Find the equation of the tangent to the circle $x^2 + y^2 = 10$ at the point $(-3, 1)$.

3. Find the equation of the tangent to the circle $x^2 + y^2 = 17$ at the point $(4, -1)$.

4. The equation of the given circle is
$$(x - 1)^2 + (y + 2)^2 = 20$$

   (i) Verify that the point $P(3, 2)$ is on the circle.
   (ii) Write down the coordinates of C, the centre of the circle.
   (iii) Hence find the equation of the tangent to the circle at the point P.

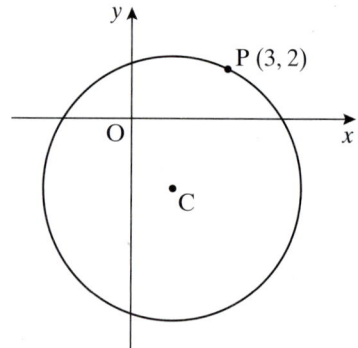

5. Find the equation of the tangent to the circle $(x + 4)^2 + (y - 3)^2 = 17$ at the point $(0, 2)$.

6. Find the centre and radius length of the circle $x^2 + y^2 - 4x + 10y - 8 = 0$.
   Hence find the equation of the tangent to the circle at the point $(3, 1)$.

7. Find the perpendicular distance from $(0, 0)$ to the line $3x - 4y - 25 = 0$.
   Hence show that the line $3x - 4y - 25 = 0$ is a tangent to the circle $x^2 + y^2 = 25$.

8. Find the centre and radius length of the circle $x^2 + y^2 - 6x - 4y + 8 = 0$.
   Hence show that $x + 2y - 12 = 0$ is a tangent to the circle.
   Explain your conclusion.

9. Write down the centre and radius length of the circle $x^2 + y^2 - 6x - 2y - 15 = 0$.
   If the line $3x + 4y + c = 0$ is a tangent to this circle, find the two values of c.

10. For what values of k is the line $2x - ky - 3 = 0$ a tangent to the circle $x^2 + y^2 + 4x - 4y - 5 = 0$?

11. Show that the tangent to the circle $x^2 + y^2 = 13$ at the point $(-2, 3)$ is also a tangent to the circle $x^2 + y^2 - 10x + 2y - 26 = 0$.

12. Find the equation of the circle, c, whose centre is $(2, -1)$ and which touches the line $3x + y = 0$.

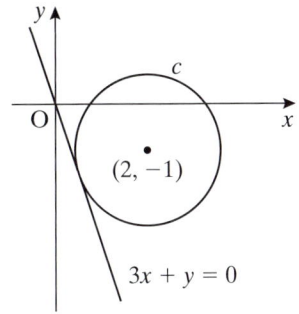

13. Write down the equation of the line which contains the origin and whose slope is m. Hence find the equations of the tangents from the origin to the circle $x^2 + y^2 - 4x - 2y + 4 = 0$.

14. Find the equation of the line through the point $(3, 5)$ with slope m. Hence find the equations of the two tangents from the point $(3, 5)$ to the circle $x^2 + y^2 + 2x - 4y - 4 = 0$.

15. Write down the equation of any line parallel to $3x + 4y - 6 = 0$. Hence find the equations of the tangents to the circle $x^2 + y^2 - 2x - 2y - 7 = 0$ and which are parallel to the line $3x + 4y - 6 = 0$.

16. A circle has centre $(3, 5)$ and touches the line $y = 2x + 4$.
   (i) Find the length of the radius of the circle.
   (ii) Find the equation of the circle.
   (iii) Find the equation of the tangent to the circle at the point $(1, 4)$.

17. The equation of a circle with radius length 7 is $x^2 + y^2 - 10kx + 6y + 60 = 0$, where $k > 0$.
   (i) Find the centre of the circle in terms of k.
   (ii) Find the value of k.
   (iii) The line $3x + 4y + d = 0$ is a tangent to the circle, where $d \in Z$.
       Show that one value for d is 17.
       Find the other value for d.

18. The diagram shows the circle $x^2 + y^2 + 4x - 2y - 4 = 0$.
   (i) Write down the radius length of the circle.
   (ii) If PT is a tangent to the circle, explain why PT is perpendicular to the radius [CT].
   (iii) Hence find the length of the tangent [PT] to the circle.

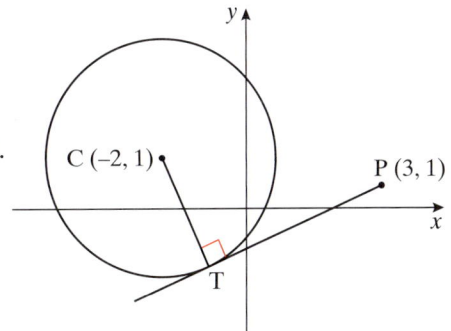

19. Find the centre and radius length of the circle $x^2 + y^2 - 14x - 2y + 34 = 0$. Hence find the length of the tangent from the point $(2, 5)$ to the circle.

20. Find the length of the tangent from the origin to the circle $x^2 + y^2 - 8x - 4y + 10 = 0$.

21. Find the length of the tangent from the point $(7, 8)$ to the circle $(x - 2)^2 + (y - 5)^2 = 16$.

22. If the length of the tangent from the point $(1, 1)$ to the circle $x^2 + y^2 - 4x - 6y + c = 0$ is 2 units, find the value of c.

Section 11.5 Lines and circles: Common chord

1. Points of intersection of a line and a circle

We use simultaneous equations to find the point(s) of intersection of a line and a circle.

If there are two solutions, then the line intersects the circle at two points.

If there is only one point of intersection, the line is a tangent to the circle, as shown below.

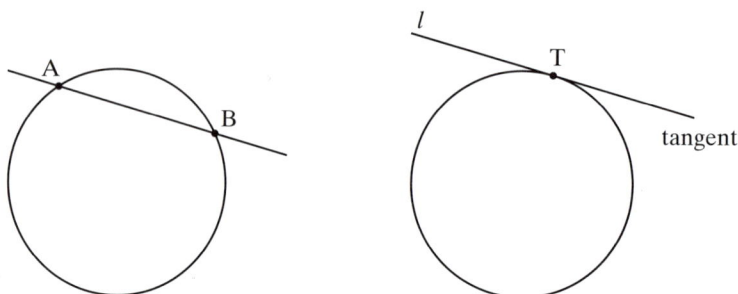

Example 1

Find the points of intersection of the line $x + 2y - 1 = 0$ and the circle $x^2 + y^2 + 2x + 8y - 8 = 0$.

We start with the equation of the line and express x in terms of y or y in terms of x. (Avoid fractions, if possible.)

$$x + 2y - 1 = 0 \Rightarrow x = -2y + 1$$

We now substitute $(-2y + 1)$ for x in the equation of the circle.

$$(-2y + 1)^2 + y^2 + 2(-2y + 1) + 8y - 8 = 0$$
$$\Rightarrow \quad 4y^2 - 4y + 1 + y^2 - 4y + 2 + 8y - 8 = 0$$
$$\Rightarrow \qquad\qquad\qquad 5y^2 - 5 = 0 \Rightarrow y^2 - 1 = 0$$
$$\Rightarrow \qquad\qquad\qquad\qquad (y - 1)(y + 1) = 0$$
$$\Rightarrow \qquad\qquad\qquad\qquad y = 1 \quad \text{or} \quad y = -1$$

For each value for y, we find the corresponding x-value.

$$y = 1 \Rightarrow x = -1; \quad y = -1 \Rightarrow x = 3$$

The points of intersection are $(-1, 1)$ and $(3, -1)$.

Example 2

Find the point(s) of intersection of the line $2x - y + 8 = 0$ and the circle $x^2 + y^2 + 4x + 2y = 0$ and hence show that the line is a tangent to the circle.

Line: $2x - y + 8 = 0 \Rightarrow y = 2x + 8$

Circle: $\quad x^2 + (2x + 8)^2 + 4x + 2(2x + 8) = 0$

$\Rightarrow \quad x^2 + 4x^2 + 32x + 64 + 4x + 4x + 16 = 0$

$\Rightarrow \qquad\qquad\qquad 5x^2 + 40x + 80 = 0$

$\Rightarrow \qquad\qquad\qquad\quad x^2 + 8x + 16 = 0$

$\Rightarrow \qquad\qquad\qquad (x + 4)(x + 4) = 0$

$\Rightarrow \qquad\qquad\qquad\qquad\quad x = -4 \dots$ one value only

The corresponding y value is: $2(-4) - y + 8 = 0 \Rightarrow y = 0$

The point of intersection is $(-4, 0)$.

Since there is only one point of intersection, the line is a tangent to the circle.

2. Where a circle intersects the axes

A circle intersects the x-axis at the points where $y = 0$.

A circle intersects the y-axis at the points where $x = 0$.

Example 3

Find the length of the intercept the circle $x^2 + y^2 - 10x + 8y + 16 = 0$ makes on the x-axis.

The circle intersects the x-axis at the points where $y = 0$.

$\quad y = 0 \Rightarrow x^2 - 10x + 16 = 0$

$\qquad\quad \Rightarrow (x - 8)(x - 2) = 0$

$\qquad\quad \Rightarrow x = 8 \quad\text{or}\quad x = 2$

The circle intersects the x-axis at $(2, 0)$ and $(8, 0)$.

$\therefore$ the intercept on the x-axis is 6.

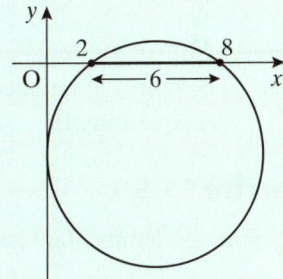

3. The common chord or common tangent of two circles

Take the circles s_1: $x^2 + y^2 - 4x - 2y - 4 = 0$

$\qquad$ and s_2: $x^2 + y^2 - 6x + 4y - 3 = 0$

$s_1 - s_2$: $\qquad\qquad 2x - 6y - 1 = 0$

This is the equation of the line which passes through the points of intersection of the two circles.

(i) If the two circles intersect, then the line is the **common chord** of the two circles.
(ii) If the circles touch internally or externally, then the line is the **common tangent**.

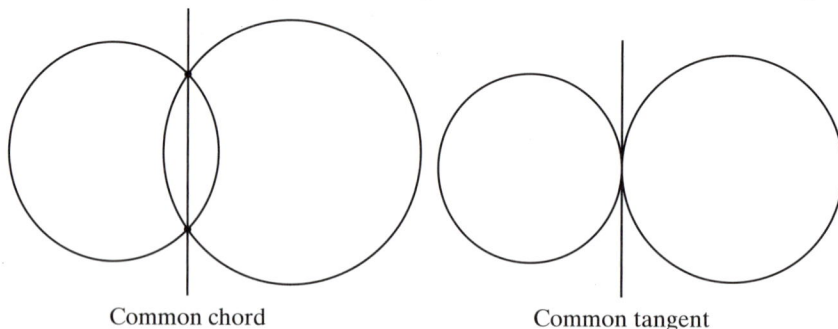

Common chord   Common tangent

The points of intersection of two circles may be found by following these steps:
(i) find the equation of the common chord
(ii) find the points of intersection of the chord and any one of the circles.

Example 4

Find the equation of the common chord of the two circles
$x^2 + y^2 - 6x + 2y + 4 = 0$ and $x^2 + y^2 + 2x - 4y - 6 = 0$.

The equation of the common chord is

$$x^2 + y^2 - 6x + 2y + 4 - (x^2 + y^2 + 2x - 4y - 6) = 0$$
$$\Rightarrow \quad x^2 + y^2 - 6x + 2y + 4 - x^2 - y^2 - 2x + 4y + 6 = 0$$
$$\Rightarrow \quad -8x + 6y + 10 = 0$$
$$\Rightarrow \quad 4x - 3y - 5 = 0 \text{ is the required equation}$$

The common chord of two circles $s_1 = 0$ and $s_2 = 0$ is

$$s_1 - s_2 = 0.$$

Note: The points of intersection of the two circles in Example 4 above are found by solving the equations $4x - 3y - 5 = 0$ and $x^2 + y^2 - 6x + 2y + 4 = 0$.

Exercise 11.5

1. Find the points of intersection of the line $3x - y + 5 = 0$ and the circle $x^2 + y^2 = 5$.

2. Show that the line $x - 3y - 10 = 0$ is a tangent to the circle $x^2 + y^2 = 10$ and find the coordinates of the point of contact.

3. Find the point of intersection of the line $2x - y - 5 = 0$ and the circle $x^2 + y^2 = 5$.

4. Find the points of intersection of the given line and circle in each of the following:
   (i) $x + y = 6$ and $x^2 + y^2 + 2x - 4y - 20 = 0$
   (ii) $2x + y - 2 = 0$ and $x^2 + y^2 - 10x - 4y - 11 = 0$
   (iii) $3x - y - 5 = 0$ and $x^2 + y^2 - 2x + 4y - 5 = 0$.

5. Show that the line $x - 2y + 12 = 0$ is a tangent to the circle $x^2 + y^2 - x - 31 = 0$ by finding the point of contact.

6. The line $x - 2y - 1 = 0$ intersects the circle $x^2 + y^2 + 2x - 8y - 8 = 0$ at the points L and M.
   (i) Find the coordinates of L and M.
   (ii) Find the midpoint of [LM].
   (iii) Find the equation of the circle with [LM] as diameter.

7. Find the coordinates of the points where the circle $x^2 + y^2 - 4x - 6y - 12 = 0$ intersects the x-axis.
   Hence write down the length of the intercept the circle makes on the x-axis.

8. Find the coordinates of the points of intersection of the circle $x^2 + y^2 - 4x + 6y - 7 = 0$ and the y-axis.
   Hence write down the length of the chord that the circle makes on the y-axis.

9. The circle $x^2 + y^2 - 4x + 11y - 12 = 0$ meets the positive x-axis and positive y-axis at A$(a, 0)$ and B$(0, b)$ respectively.
   Find the value of a and b.

10. k is the circle $x^2 + y^2 - 4x - 8y - 5 = 0$.
    Find the length of the intercept the circle cuts off the x-axis.

11. Find the equation of the common chord of the circles $x^2 + y^2 - 3x + 5y - 4 = 0$ and $x^2 + y^2 - x + 4y - 7 = 0$.
    Hence find the coordinates of the points of intersection of the two circles.

12. Find the equation of the common tangent to the circles $x^2 + y^2 + 14x - 10y - 26 = 0$ and $x^2 + y^2 - 4x + 14y + 28 = 0$.
    Use this tangent to find the point of intersection of the two circles.

13. Find the points of intersection of the circles $x^2 + y^2 + 4x - 2y - 5 = 0$ and $x^2 + y^2 + 14x - 12y + 65 = 0$.

14. Stars revolve around the Pole Star once each night.
    A particular star traces out the circle,
    $x^2 + y^2 + 2x - 8y + 4 = 0$, in a chosen set of
    coordinate axes.
    The horizon has equation $y = 1$.
    (i) State the coordinates of the Pole Star.
    (ii) Calculate the coordinates of the points of rising and setting of the moving star.

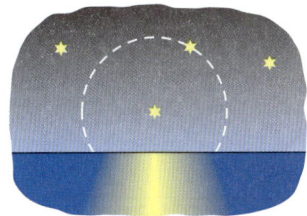

Section 11.6 Touching circles – Chords and circles

1. Circles touching externally or internally

Two circles touch if they meet at one point only.

If two circles touch **externally**, then the distance between their centres is equal to the sum of their radii. In the given diagram d is the distance between the two centres.
Since the circles touch externally,

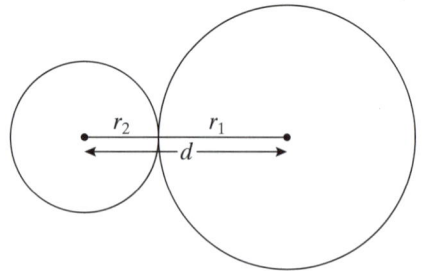

$$d = r_1 + r_2$$

If two circles touch **internally**, then the distance between their centres is equal to the difference of their radii.
In the given diagram,

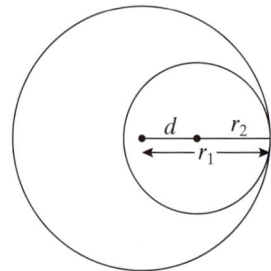

$$d = r_1 - r_2$$

Example 1

Show that the circles s_1: $x^2 + y^2 - 6x - 4y + 11 = 0$
and s_2: $x^2 + y^2 + 4x + 6y - 19 = 0$ touch externally.

s_1: $x^2 + y^2 - 6x - 4y + 11 = 0$ $\Rightarrow$ centre $= (3, 2)$ and
$$\text{radius} = \sqrt{3^2 + 2^2 - 11} = \sqrt{2}$$

s_2: $x^2 + y^2 + 4x + 6y - 19 = 0$ $\Rightarrow$ centre $= (-2, -3)$ and
$$\text{radius} = \sqrt{(-2)^2 + (-3)^2 + 19} = \sqrt{32} = 4\sqrt{2}$$

Distance between the centres $= \sqrt{(3 + 2)^2 + (2 + 3)^2} = \sqrt{50}$
$$= 5\sqrt{2}$$

Sum of the two radii $= \sqrt{2} + 4\sqrt{2} = 5\sqrt{2}$

Since the distance between the centres = the sum of the radii $= 5\sqrt{2}$, the circles touch externally.

2. Chords and circles

We have already encountered the very useful geometrical property of the circle which states that:

The perpendicular from the centre of a circle to a chord bisects the chord.

In the given diagram, d is the length of the perpendicular from the centre, O, to the chord.

We use the Theorem of Pythagoras to find d, r or p as required.

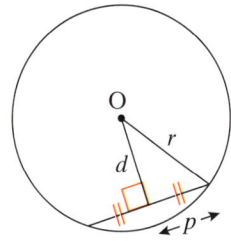

Example 2

A circle k has centre $C(4, 2)$ and makes a chord 6 units in length on the y-axis. Find the equation of k.

If the centre is $(4, 2)$, then the length of the perpendicular [BC] is 4 units.

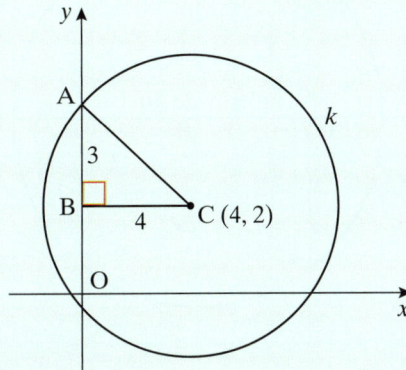

$|AB| = \frac{1}{2}$ length of chord on y-axis

$\Rightarrow \quad |AB| = 3$

$|AC|^2 = 3^2 + 4^2$

$\Rightarrow \quad |AC|^2 = 25 \quad \Rightarrow \quad |AC| = 5 \quad \Rightarrow \quad$ radius $= 5$

$\therefore$ the circle has centre $(4, 2)$ and radius 5

Equation of circle: $(x - 4)^2 + (y - 2)^2 = 25$

Exercise 11.6

1. Find the centre and the radius of each of these circles:
   $s_1: x^2 + y^2 - 2x - 15 = 0$ and $s_2: x^2 + y^2 - 14x - 16y + 77 = 0$.
   Hence show that the circles touch externally.

2. Show that the circles $x^2 + y^2 + 4x - 6y + 12 = 0$ and $x^2 + y^2 - 12x + 6y - 76 = 0$ touch internally.

3. Find the centre and radius of each of the circles,
   $x^2 + y^2 - 4x - 2y - 20 = 0$ and $x^2 + y^2 - 16x - 18y + 120 = 0$.
   Deduce that the two circles touch externally.

4. Determine whether the circles $x^2 + y^2 - 16y + 32 = 0$ and $x^2 + y^2 - 18x + 2y + 32 = 0$ touch internally or externally.

5. $x^2 + y^2 - 4x - 6y + 5 = 0$ and $x^2 + y^2 - 6x - 8y + 23 = 0$ are two circles.
   (i) Prove that the circles touch internally.
   (ii) Find the equation of the common tangent.
   (iii) Hence find the coordinates of the point of contact of the two circles.

6. The given diagram shows a circle with centre $(3, 0)$ making an intercept 8 units in length on the y-axis.

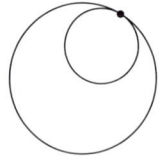

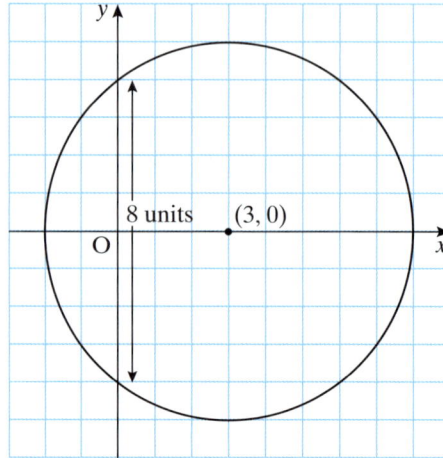

   (i) Use the *Theorem of Pythagoras* to find the length of the radius.
   (ii) Hence write the equation of the circle in the form
   $$(x - a)^2 + (y - b)^2 = c^2.$$

7. A circle has centre $(2, 3)$ and radius 4 units in length.
   (i) Draw a sketch of this circle.
   (ii) Show that the distance between the points where the circle intersects the y-axis is $4\sqrt{3}$.
   (iii) Find the length of the intercept the circle cuts off the x-axis.

8. A circle of radius length 5 units has its centre in the first quadrant.
   It touches the x-axis and makes an intercept of length 6 units on the y-axis, as shown.
   (i) Find the coordinates of the centre, C.
   (ii) Find the equation of the circle.

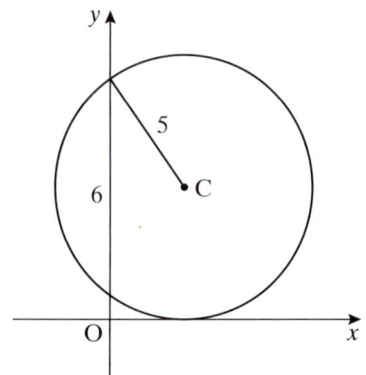

9. A circle with centre in the first quadrant touches the y-axis at the point $(0, 2)$.
   If the circle makes a chord of length 3 units on the x-axis, find its equation.

10. A circle k has centre $(-1, -4)$.
    The midpoint of a chord of length $2\sqrt{5}$ is $(2, 0)$.
    (i) Find the length of the radius of k.
    (ii) Write down the equation of k.

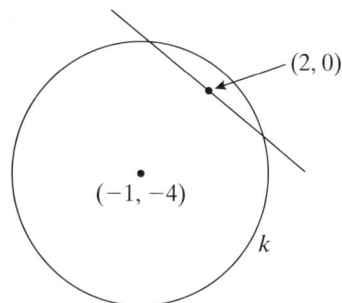

11. A circle passes through the points $(0, 0)$ and $(0, 8)$.
    The centre of the circle is in the first quadrant and the length of the radius is 5 units.
    (i) Find the coordinates of the centre of the circle.
    (ii) Find the equation of the circle.

12. $x^2 + y^2 - 6x + 4y - 12 = 0$ is the equation of a circle.
    Write down the coordinates of its centre and the length of its radius.
    $x^2 + y^2 + 12x - 20y + k = 0$ is another circle, where $k \in R$.
    If the two circles touch externally, find the value of k.

Section 11.7 Circles touching the x-axis or y-axis

If a circle touches the x-axis or y-axis, then the radius of the circle is equal to one of coordinates of its centre.

1. Circle touching the x-axis

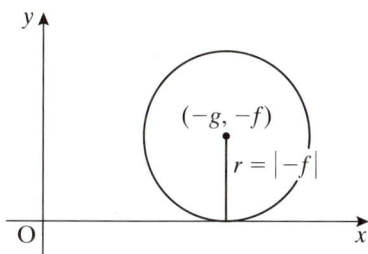

Radius $= |-f|$
$$\Rightarrow \quad \sqrt{g^2 + f^2 - c} = |-f|$$
$$\Rightarrow \quad g^2 + f^2 - c = f^2$$
$$\Rightarrow \quad g^2 - c = 0$$
$$\Rightarrow \quad g^2 = c$$

2. Circle touching the y-axis

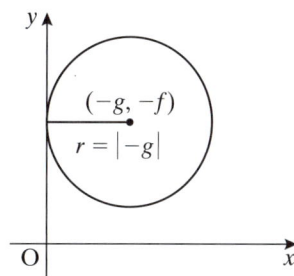

Radius $= |-g|$
$$\Rightarrow \quad \sqrt{g^2 + f^2 - c} = |-g|$$
$$\Rightarrow \quad g^2 + f^2 - c = g^2$$
$$\Rightarrow \quad f^2 - c = 0$$
$$\Rightarrow \quad f^2 = c$$

Example 1

Find the equations of the two circles which contain the points $(3, -2)$ and $(2, -1)$ and which touch the x-axis.

Let the equation of the circle be

$$x^2 + y^2 + 2gx + 2fy + c = 0.$$

$(2, -1) \in$ the circle

$$\Rightarrow \quad 4 + 1 + 2g(2) + 2f(-1) + c = 0$$

$$\Rightarrow \qquad\qquad 4g - 2f + c = -5 \dots ①$$

$(3, -2) \in$ the circle

$$\Rightarrow \quad 9 + 4 + 2g(3) + 2f(-2) + c = 0$$

$$\Rightarrow \qquad\qquad 6g - 4f + c = -13 \dots ②$$

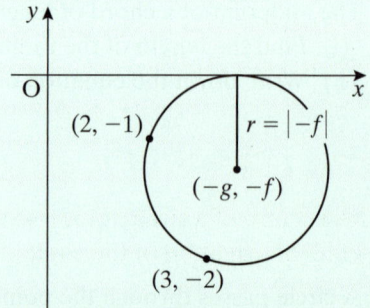

If the circle touches the x-axis, the radius $= |-f|$

$$\Rightarrow \quad \sqrt{g^2 + f^2 - c} = |-f|$$

$$\Rightarrow \quad g^2 + f^2 - c = f^2$$

$$\Rightarrow \qquad\qquad g^2 = c \dots ③$$

We now use equations ① and ② to eliminate f.

①: $4g - 2f + c = -5$	① $\times$ 2: $8g - 4f + 2c = -10$
②: $6g - 4f + c = -13$	②: $\underline{6g - 4f + c = -13}$
	$2g + c = 3$
	$\Rightarrow \quad c = -2g + 3$

We now substitute $(-2g + 3)$ for c in equation ③

③: $g^2 = c$

$$\Rightarrow \qquad\qquad g^2 = -2g + 3$$

$$\Rightarrow \qquad g^2 + 2g - 3 = 0$$

$$\Rightarrow \quad (g - 1)(g + 3) = 0$$

$$\Rightarrow \quad g = 1 \quad \text{or} \quad g = -3$$

$g = 1 \quad \Rightarrow \quad c = -2(1) + 3 \quad \Rightarrow \quad c = 1$

$g = -3 \quad \Rightarrow \quad c = -2(-3) + 3 \quad \Rightarrow \quad c = 9$

Substituting these values for g and c in equation ① we get:

$$4g - 2f + c = -5 \dots ①$$

$g = 1$ and $c = 1$: $\qquad\qquad 4(1) - 2f + 1 = -5$

$$\Rightarrow \quad -2f = -10 \quad \Rightarrow \quad f = 5$$

$g = -3$ and $c = 9 \quad \Rightarrow \qquad 4(-3) - 2f + 9 = -5$

$$\Rightarrow \qquad\qquad -12 - 2f + 9 = -5$$

$$\Rightarrow \qquad\qquad\qquad -2f = -2 \quad \Rightarrow \quad f = 1$$

The two sets of values for g, f and c are

Circle 1: $g = 1, f = 5$ and $c = 1$ **Circle 2:** $g = -3, f = 1$ and $c = 9$

Circle 1: $x^2 + y^2 + 2x + 10y + 1 = 0$
Circle 2: $x^2 + y^2 - 6x + 2y + 9 = 0$

Exercise 11.7

1. The centre of a circle is $(3, -4)$ and the x-axis is a tangent to the circle.
    Find the equation of the circle.

2. The y-axis is a tangent to a circle, k.
    If the centre of k is $(-3, 2)$, find its equation.

3. The coordinates of the centre of a circle are $(5, y)$, $y > 0$.
    The x-axis and y-axis are both tangents to this circle.
    (i) Write down the value of y.
    (ii) Write down the equation of the circle.
    (iii) Write down the equation of the tangent to the circle that is parallel to the y-axis.

4. The x-axis and the line $y = 8$ are both tangents to a circle k.
    The centre of the circle lies on the line $2x - 3y = 0$.
    (i) Draw a rough sketch of the circle.
    (ii) Write down the length of the radius.
    (iii) Find the coordinates of the centre of the circle.
    (iv) Write down the equation of the circle.

5. The y-axis and the line $x = 8$ are tangents to a circle.
    The centre of the circle lies on the line $2x - y - 3 = 0$.
    (i) Write down the length of the radius of the circle.
    (ii) Find the coordinates of the centre of the circle.
    (iii) Find the equation of the circle.

6. The x-axis is a tangent to the circle $x^2 + y^2 + 2gx + 2fy + c = 0$.
    Show that $g^2 = c$.
    The x-axis is a tangent to a circle k at the point $(4, 0)$.
    If the circle contains the point $(1, 3)$, find its equation.

7. The y-axis is a tangent to the circle $x^2 + y^2 + 2gx + 2fy + c = 0$.
    Prove that $f^2 = c$.
    A circle touches the y-axis at the point $(0, -3)$ and it contains the point $(4, 1)$.
    Find the equation of this circle.

8. The x-axis and the line $y = 10$ are tangents to a circle.
    If the circle also contains the point $(1, 5)$, find the equations of the two circles that
    satisfy these conditions.

Revision Exercise 11 (Core)

1. A circle has centre $(-1, 5)$ and passes through the point $(1, 2)$.
   (i) Find the the length of the radius of the circle.
   (ii) Write down the equation of the circle.

2. Find the coordinates of the centre and radius length of the circle $x^2 + y^2 - 2x - 4y - 9 = 0$. Hence write down the equation of the circle with the origin as centre and which has the same radius length as the given circle.

3. Find the equation of the circle with centre $(2, 3)$ and which touches the x-axis.

4. Show that the line $3x - 4y + 25 = 0$ is a tangent to the circle $x^2 + y^2 = 25$.

5. $A(-1, -3)$ and $B(3, 1)$ are the end-points of a diameter of a circle. Write down the equation of the circle.

6. The circle $(x - 5)^2 + y^2 = 36$ meets the x-axis at P and Q. Find the coordinates of P and Q.

7. Write down the centre and radius of the circle
   $$x^2 + y^2 - 2x + 4y + 4 = 0$$
   Draw a sketch of this circle.
   If the line $x = k$ is a tangent to the circle, find the two values of k.

8. The circles k_1 and k_2 touch externally.
   Circle k_1 has centre $(8, 5)$ and radius 6.
   Circle k_2 has centre $(2, -3)$.
   Calculate the radius of k_2.

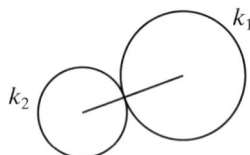

9. Show that $(0, 0)$ lies inside the circle $(x - 5)^2 + (y + 2)^2 = 30$.

10. David took a photograph of the Big Wheel at the Fairground. Using the axes shown, he estimated A to be $(1, 6)$ and B$(11, 10)$.
    Find the equation of the circular part of the Big Wheel through A and B.

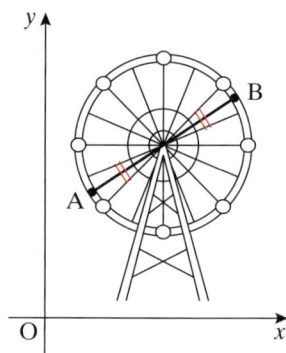

11. Two satellites orbit the earth. The equation of the orbit of the first satellite is $x^2 + y^2 = 2250000$. The second satellite orbits 200km away (from the centre of the earth) than the first. How much further does the second satellite travel to the nearest km.

Revision Exercise 11 (Advanced)

1. Write down the centre and radius of the circle
$$x^2 + y^2 - 6x - 2y - 3 = 0.$$
Hence find the equation of the tangent to this circle at the point $(5, 4)$.

2. Circle k has centre $(5, -1)$.
The line l: $3x - 4y + 11 = 0$ is a tangent to k.
   (i) Show that the radius of k is 6.
   (ii) The line $x + py + 1 = 0$ is also a tangent to k.
   Find two possible values of p.

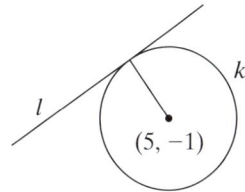

3. Find the two values of k for which $8x + 3y + k = 0$ is a tangent to the circle
$x^2 + y^2 + 4x - 3y - 12 = 0$.

4. The point A$(5, 2)$ is on the circle k: $x^2 + y^2 + px - 2y + 5 = 0$.
   (i) Find the value of p.
   (ii) The line $x - y - 1 = 0$ intersects the circle k.
   Find the coordinates of the points of intersection.

5. c_1: $x^2 + y^2 + 2x - 2y - 23 = 0$ and
c_2: $x^2 + y^2 - 14x - 2y + 41 = 0$ are two circles.
   (i) Prove that c_1 and c_2 touch externally.
   (ii) k is a third circle.
   Both c_1 and c_2 touch k internally.
   Find the equation of k.

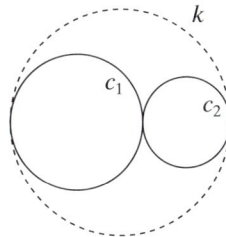

6. A circle with centre C has equation $x^2 + y^2 - 10y + 20 = 0$.
   (i) Write down the coordinates of C.
   (ii) Find the radius of the circle, leaving your answer in surd form.
   A line has equation $y = 2x$.
   (iii) Show that the line $y = 2x$ is a tangent to the given circle and find the coordinates of the point of contact.

7. Find the centre and the radius of each of the circles $x^2 + y^2 = 4$ and
$x^2 + y^2 - 8x - 6y + 16 = 0$ and show that they touch externally.
Write down the equation of the common tangent to these circles.

8. Points $(2, 5)$ and $(-2, 1)$ lie on the circle $x^2 + y^2 + 2gx + 2fy + 7 = 0$.
   (i) Make two equations in g and f.
   (ii) Solve this pair of equations to find the values of g and f.
   (iii) Hence find the equation of the circle, and give its centre and radius.

9. A circle passes through the origin and the point $(4, 2)$.
If its centre is on the line $x + y = 1$, find its equation.

10. A circle with centre C has equation $(x + 3)^2 + (y - 2)^2 = 25$.
Write down   (i)   the coordinates of C
                      (ii)   the radius of the circle.
Verify that N$(0, -2)$ lies on the circle.
The point P has coordinates $(2, 6)$.
Find the length of the tangent drawn from P to the circle.

11. The centre of a circle lies on the line $x - 2y - 1 = 0$.
The x-axis and the line $y = 6$ are tangents to the circle.
Find the equation of this circle.

12. 6 identical metal barrels are stacked as shown.
The equation of the end of the barrel
centre C is $(x - 4)^2 + (y - 5)^2 = 1$
  (i) Find the equation of the end of
       the barrel centre H.
 (ii) Find the area trapped between
       the 6 barrels correct to 3 places of decimals.

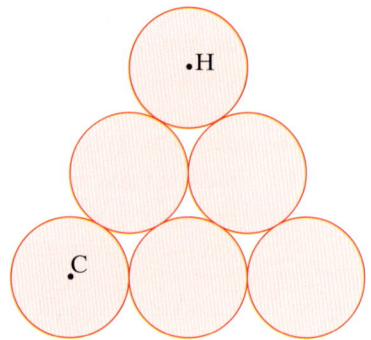

Revision Exercise 11 (Extended-Response Questions)

1.   (i)   Find the length of the intercept which the circle $x^2 + y^2 - 8x - 7y + 12 = 0$
            cuts off the y-axis.
  (ii)   Find also the length of the tangent to the circle from the point $(9, 2)$
 (iii)   Find the equation of the image of this circle under the translation
            $(0, 0) \rightarrow (4, -3.5)$

2.   (i)   Write down the equation of any line parallel to the line $3x - 4y + 1 = 0$.
  (ii)   Write down the centre and radius of the circle $x^2 + y^2 - 8x + 2y - 8 = 0$
 (iii)   Find the equations of two tangents to this circle which are parallel to
            $3x - 4y + 1 = 0$.

3. A, B, C and D are the vertices of a square.
The coordinates of A and B are $(2, 7)$
and $(8, 7)$ respectively.
  (i) Write down the coordinates of C and D.
 (ii) Write down the coordinates of the
       centre of the circle that passes through
       A, B, C and D.
(iii) Find the equation of the largest circle
       that can be drawn inside the square
       ABCD.

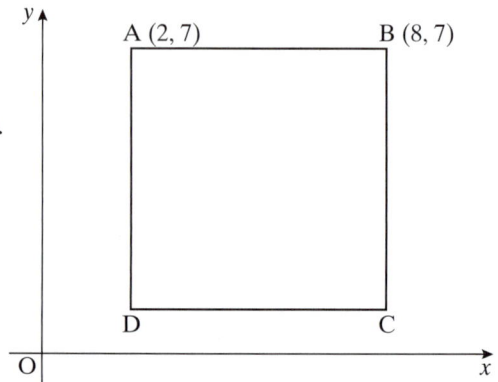

4. The x and y-axes are tangents to the circle $x^2 + y^2 + 2gx + 2fy + c = 0$
   (i) Prove that $g^2 = f^2 = c$
   (ii) Find the equations of the two circles that pass through the points $(-3, 6)$ and $(-6, 3)$ and which have the y-axis as a tangent.
   (iii) Show that the x-axis is also a tangent to these circles.
   (iv) One of these circles is an enlargement of the other with the origin $(0, 0)$ as the centre of enlargement. Find the scale factor k of the enlargement.
   (v) Show that the circumference of the larger circle = $k \times$ circumference of the smaller circle.

5. A metal plate is used to strengthen the struts of a push-chair. The holes have radius 4 units and their centres form an isosceles triangle with sides 20, 20 and 24 units long.
If the equation of the edge of the top hole is $(x - 20)^2 + (y - 18)^2 = 16$, find the equations of the edges of the other two holes.

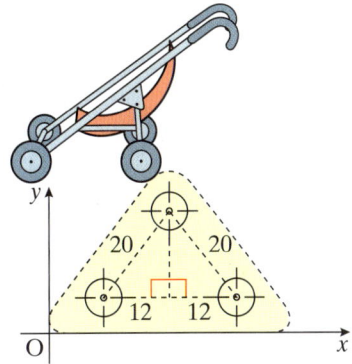

6. The line $3x - y - 6 = 0$ is a tangent to a circle at the point $(3, 3)$.
The circle also contains the point $(4, 1)$.
   (i) Sketch the line $3x - y - 6 = 0$ and the points $(3, 3)$ and $(4, 1)$.
   (ii) Draw a rough sketch of the circle.
   (iii) Find the equation of the circle.
   (iv) Find the equation of the image of circle by reflection in the line $3x - y - 6 = 0$.

> A perpendicular to a tangent at the point of contact contains the centre of the circle.

7. A circle has its centre in the first quadrant.
The x-axis is a tangent to the circle at the point $(3, 0)$.
The circle cuts the y-axis at points C and F where $|CF| = 8$
   (i) Find the equation of the circle.
A tangent is drawn to the circle at the point C.
   (ii) Find the equation of the tangent and the coordinates of the point D.
A perpendicular tangent touches the circle at the point J.

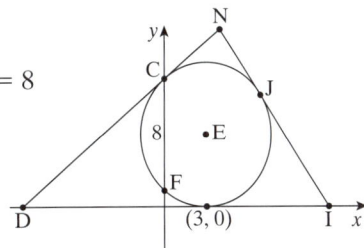

   (iii) Find the equation of the perpendicular tangent and the coordinates of the point I.
   (iv) Hence find the length of the perimeter of the triangle.

8. A circle has equation $x^2 + y^2 - 2ax - 2by + b^2 = 0$.
   (i) Find the centre and radius of the circle.
   (ii) Prove that the circle touches the y-axis.
   (iii) Find the equations of the two circles that pass through the points $(1, 2)$ and $(2, 3)$ and which touch the y-axis.
   (iv) Find the distance between their centres.

12 Algebra 3

Key words

inequality   quadratic inequality   rational inequality   modulus

modular equations   modular inequalities   direct proof   proof by contradiction

absolute value   abstract inequalities   indices   base number

exponential growth   exponential decay   logarithm   proof by induction

Section 12.1 Revision

The inequality symbols $>, \geqslant, <, \leqslant$ are needed when solving problems in which a range of possible values satisfy the given conditions.

$>$	greater than
$\geqslant$	greater than or equal to
$<$	less than
$\leqslant$	less than or equal to

e.g. If $3x - 4 > 5$,

$\qquad 3x > 9$,

and $x > 3$, which means that **all values of x**
greater than 3 satisfy $3x - 4 > 5$.

An expression such as $3x - 4 > 5$ is called an **inequality**.

Basic rules of inequalities

Adding or subtracting a constant, a	$x > y$	$x \pm a > y \pm a$
Multiplying or dividing by a **positive** number, $a > 0$	$x > y$	$ax > ay$ $\dfrac{x}{a} > \dfrac{y}{a}$

When multiplying or dividing by a negative number, the inequality symbol is **reversed**.

E.g. $5 > 2$; if both sides are multiplied by (-1), we get $5 \times (-1) < 2 \times (-1)$, i.e. $-5 < -2$.

Multiplying or dividing by a **negative** number, $a < 0$	$x > y$	$ax < ay$ $\dfrac{x}{a} < \dfrac{y}{a}$

Also,

Combining inequalities	$x > y$ $y > z$	$x > z$
	$x > y > 0$ $a > b > 0$	$ax > by$

Graphical construction

If a graph of the function is given or is easily constructed, this provides an extra technique in helping to understand and solve inequalities.

If $f(x) = (x + 3)(x - 1)(x - 4) \geqslant 0$,

then the points $x = -3$, $x = 1$ and $x = 4$ are the critical points in determining the solution set.

The set of values of x for which

$$f(x) = (x + 3)(x - 1)(x - 4) \geqslant 5$$

can also be estimated.

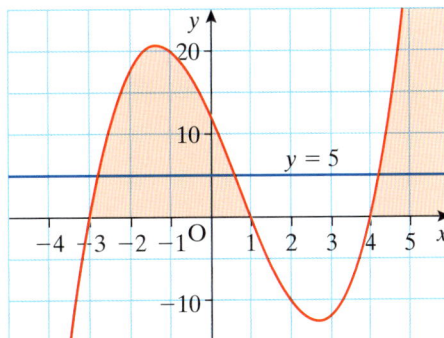

Note:

(i) When solving inequalities, the solution is often restricted to specific number systems, i.e. $\in N, \in Z, \in R$, and the resulting range of numbers plotted on the number line. e.g. $5x - 1 > 14, x \in N$.

(ii) An inequality creates an ordered pair (a, b); If $a > b$, then if the order is reversed (b, a), the inequality is also reversed, i.e. $b < a$.

Example 1

Solve the inequality $3x + 7 \geqslant x + 2, x \in Z$, and plot the solution on a number line.

$3x + 7 \geqslant x + 2$

$2x + 7 \geqslant 2$ ... subtracting x from both sides

$\quad 2x \geqslant -5$ ... subtracting 7 from both sides

$\quad\quad x \geqslant \dfrac{-5}{2}, x \in Z.$

(All integer values greater than or equal to $-2\frac{1}{2}$ will satisfy the original inequality.)

Example 2

Solve the inequality $\frac{1}{6}(x - 1) \geqslant \frac{1}{3}(x - 4), x \in R$.

Graph your solution on a number line.

$\frac{1}{6}(x - 1) \geqslant \frac{1}{3}(x - 4)$

$\Rightarrow x - 1 \geqslant 2x - 8$ ... multiplying both sides by 6

$\qquad \Rightarrow -x \geqslant -7$ ... adding 1 and subtracting $2x$ from both sides

$\qquad\quad \Rightarrow x \leqslant 7$ ... multiplying both sides by (-1) and reversing the inequality sign.

(**Note:** A closed circle on 7 indicates that 7 is included in the range.)

Example 3

Solve the inequality $-9 < 3 - 4x \leqslant 1, x \in R$.

Graph your solution on the number line.

$\qquad -9 < 3 - 4x \leqslant 1$

$\Rightarrow -12 < -4x \leqslant -2$ ... subtracting 3 from each part of the inequality

$\qquad \Rightarrow 3 > x \geqslant \frac{1}{2}$ ... dividing each part of the inequality by -4 and reversing

$\qquad\qquad$ the inequality symbol

$\qquad \Rightarrow \frac{1}{2} \leqslant x < 3$ ... reversing the order

(**Note:** An open circle on 3 indicates that it is not to be included.)

Example 4

(i) Find the solution set A, $\{x \mid 7 \leqslant 10 - 3x, x \in R\}$.

(ii) Find the solution set B, $\{x \mid 2 > \frac{4}{3} - 2x, x \in R\}$.

(iii) Find the set $A \cap B$ and graph the solution on the number line.

A: $7 \leqslant 10 - 3x$ $\qquad\qquad$ B: $2 > \frac{4}{3} - 2x$

$\qquad 3x \leqslant 3$ $\qquad\qquad\qquad\quad 2x > \frac{4}{3} - 2$

$\qquad\quad x \leqslant 1$ $\qquad\qquad\qquad\quad 2x > \frac{-2}{3}$

$\qquad\qquad\qquad\qquad\qquad\qquad\quad x > \frac{-1}{3}$

$\therefore$ $A \cap B$ is the set of values $\frac{-1}{3} < x \leqslant 1$.

Exercise 12.1

1. Graph on a number line the set of values of $x \in N$ for which
   (i) $3x - 5 > x + 3$ (ii) $6x - 5 \leqslant 2x - 1$ (iii) $1 - 3x > 10$.

2. Solve each of the following inequalities and plot the solution set on a number line.
   (i) $\frac{x}{2} + 2 < 7, x \in N$ (ii) $\frac{1}{6}(x - 1) \geqslant \frac{1}{3}(x - 4), x \in Z$
   (iii) $\frac{4 - x}{2} > \frac{2 - x}{3}, x \in R$

3. Plot the solution of each of the following inequalities on a number line, $x \in R$.
   (i) $12x - 3(x - 3) < 45$ (ii) $x(x - 4) \geqslant x^2 + 2$ (iii) $x - 2(5 + 2x) < 11$

4. Plot on a number line the set of values of $x \in R$ for which
   (i) $-2 \leqslant x + 1 \leqslant 3$ (ii) $13 > 1 - 3x \geqslant 7$ (iii) $3 \geqslant 4x + 1 > -1$.

5. Solve each of the following inequalities, $x \in R$.
   (i) $3 > \frac{3}{5}(x - 2) > 0$ (ii) $-4 \leqslant \frac{2}{5}(1 - 3x) \leqslant 1$ (iii) $3 \leqslant 2 - \frac{x}{7} < 4$

6. Find the set of values for which $3(x - 2) > x - 4$ and $4x + 12 > 2x + 17, x \in R$, and plot your answers on a number line.

7. (i) Find the solution set A of $2x - 5 < x - 1, x \in R$.
   (ii) Find the solution set B of $7(x + 1) > 23 - x, x \in R$.
   (iii) Plot the solution set $A \cap B$ on a number line.

8. (i) Find the solution set C of $2x - 3 > 2, x \in R$.
   (ii) Find the solution set D of $3(x + 2) < 12 + x, x \in R$.
   (iii) Plot the solution set $C \cap D$ on a number line.

9. (i) Find the solution set E of $15 - x < 2(11 - x), x \in Z$.
   (ii) Find the solution set F of $5(3x - 1) > 12x + 19, x \in Z$.
   (iii) Find the set of values $E \cap F$.

10. (i) Find the set of values G for which $3x + 8 \leqslant 20, x \in N$.
    (ii) Find the set of values H for which $2(3x - 7) \geqslant x + 6, x \in N$.
    (iii) Find the set of values $G \cap H$.

11. A 38 m rope is used to form a rectangular area on a sports day. If the width of the rectangle has to be at least 2 m long, and the length has to be exactly 1 m longer than its width, find the maximum dimensions of the rectangle.

12. If $a < n < b$, and $100 < 2^n < 200$, find the values of a and b, where $a, b \in R$ and n where $n \in N$.

13. Give one example to show that if $a > b > 0$ and $n > 0 \Rightarrow a^n > b^n$.
Now give an example to show that if $a > b > 0$ and $n < 0 \Rightarrow a^n < b^n$.

Write an equivalent set of conclusions for these:
(i) If $a < b < 0$ and $n \ (odd) > 0$ .....
(ii) If $a < b < 0$ and $n \ (even) > 0$ .....
(iii) If $a < b < 0$ and $n \ (odd) < 0$ .....
(iv) If $a < b < 0$ and $n \ (even) < 0$ .....

14. Find x if $x \in Z$ and $Z = \{5 - 3x < -10\} \cap \{4x + 6 < 32\}$.

Section 12.2 Quadratic and rational inequalities _____

1. Quadratic inequalities

$ax^2 + bx + c \geqslant 0$ is an example of a quadratic inequality.

To solve a quadratic inequality of the form $ax^2 + bx + c \geqslant 0$ (or $\leqslant 0$), proceed as follows:

1. Solve $ax^2 + bx + c = 0$ to find the (real) roots of the quadratic equation.

2. Draw a rough sketch of the graph using these roots.

(i) If $a > 0$, the graph is $\cup$-shaped.
(ii) If $a < 0$, the graph is $\cap$-shaped.

3. Use the graph to find the set of values of x that satisfies the inequality.

Example 1

Solve the inequality $x^2 - 2x - 8 \leqslant 0$.

Step 1. Solve $x^2 - 2x - 8 = 0$.
$$\Rightarrow x^2 - 2x - 8 = (x + 2)(x - 4) = 0$$
$$\Rightarrow x = -2 \text{ or } x = 4$$

Step 2. Since $a = +1$, i.e. > 0, $\therefore$ a $\cup$-shaped graph.

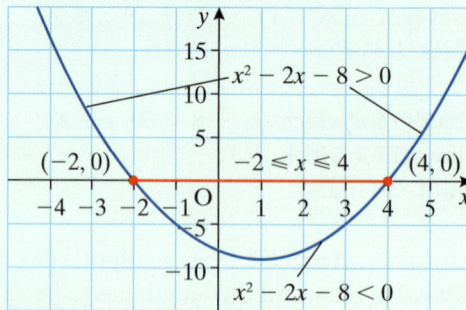

Step 3. The solution of the inequality is the set of values of x that produces the points of the graph that are on or below the x-axis, i.e. $x^2 - 2x - 8 \leqslant 0$. The solution is $-2 \leqslant x \leqslant 4$.

Questions involving values for which the roots of an equation are real, i.e. $b^2 - 4ac \geq 0$, result in quadratic inequalities as shown in the following example.

Example 2

Find the range of values of k for which the equation $x^2 + (k - 4)x + (k - 1) = 0$ has real roots.

Condition for real roots: $b^2 - 4ac \geq 0$.

$a = 1, b = (k - 4), c = (k - 1)$

$\Rightarrow b^2 - 4ac = (k - 4)^2 - 4(1)(k - 1)$

$\qquad = k^2 - 8k + 16 - 4k + 4$

$\qquad = k^2 - 12k + 20$

$b^2 - 4ac \geq 0 \Rightarrow k^2 - 12k + 20 \geq 0$.

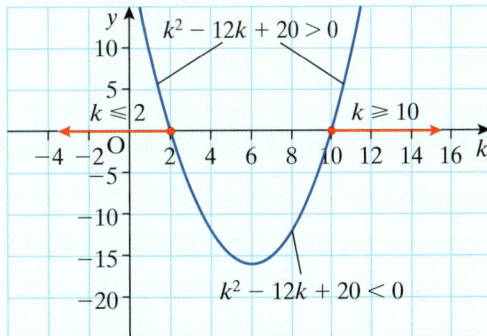

(i) Solving $k^2 - 12k + 20 = 0$;

$\qquad \Rightarrow (k - 2)(k - 10) = 0$

$\qquad \Rightarrow k = 2$ and $k = 10$ are the roots.

(ii) Sketch the graph; $a = +1$, i.e. > 0,

$\qquad \therefore$ a $\cup$-shaped graph.

The solution of the inequality is the set of values of k that produces points on a graph that are on or above the k-axis, i.e. $k^2 - 12k + 20 \geq 0$.

The solution is $k \leq 2$ and $k \geq 10$.

2. Rational inequalities

$f(x) = \dfrac{3x - 2}{x + 1}$ is a *rational function* as the denominator and numerator are both polynomials in x.

$\dfrac{3x - 2}{x + 1} \geq 2$ is a *rational inequality*.

Since we do not know if $(x + 1)$ is positive or negative, we cannot simply multiply both sides by $(x + 1)$ when solving for x as the inequality symbol would have to be reversed if $(x + 1)$ was negative.

However, if we multiply both sides by $(x + 1)^2$, we can retain the same inequality sign since $(x + 1)^2$ is always positive.

$\qquad \Rightarrow \dfrac{3x - 2}{x + 1} \times (x + 1)^2 \geq 2 \times (x + 1)^2$

$\qquad \Rightarrow (3x - 2)(x + 1) \geq 2(x^2 + 2x + 1)$

$\qquad \Rightarrow 3x^2 + x - 2 \geq 2x^2 + 4x + 2$

$\qquad \Rightarrow x^2 - 3x - 4 \geq 0$, creating a quadratic inequality (with the same solution set) from the rational inequality.

461

Example 3

Find the range of values of x for which $\dfrac{2x+1}{x+2} < \dfrac{1}{2}$.

Since $\dfrac{2x+1}{x+2} < \dfrac{1}{2}$,

multiply both sides by $(x+2)^2$.

$[(x+2)^2$ is always positive for all values of x.]

$\Rightarrow \dfrac{2x+1}{x+2} \times (x+2)^2 < \dfrac{1}{2} \times (x+2)^2$

$\Rightarrow (2x+1)(x+2) < \dfrac{1}{2}(x^2+4x+4)$

$\Rightarrow 2x^2 + 5x + 2 < \dfrac{1}{2}(x^2+4x+4)$

$\Rightarrow 4x^2 + 10x + 4 < x^2 + 4x + 4$

$\Rightarrow 3x^2 + 6x < 0$

$\Rightarrow x^2 + 2x < 0.$

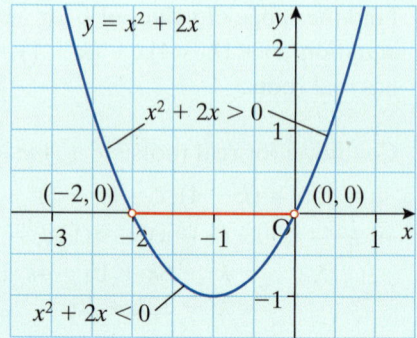

$\left[\textbf{Note:}\ \dfrac{2x+1}{x+2} < \dfrac{1}{2}\ \text{has the same solution set as}\ x^2 + 2x < 0.\right]$

(i) Solving the equation $x^2 + 2x = 0$;   (ii) Sketch the graph; $a = +1$, i.e. >0,

$\Rightarrow (x)(x+2) = 0$ $\therefore$ a $\cup$-shaped graph.

$\Rightarrow x = 0$ and $x = -2$ are the roots.

$\Rightarrow$ The solution of the inequality is the set values of x that produces points on the graph that are below the x-axis (i.e. $x^2 + 2x < 0$).

The solution is $-2 < x < 0$.

Exercise 12.2

In each of the following questions, $x \in R$ unless otherwise stated.

1. Solve each of the following quadratic inequalities:
    (i) $x^2 - x - 6 \geqslant 0$ (ii) $x^2 + 3x - 10 \leqslant 0$ (iii) $2x^2 - 5x + 2 < 0$.

2. Solve each of the following inequalities for x:
    (i) $6 - x - x^2 \geqslant 0$ (ii) $12 - 5x - 2x^2 > 0$ (iii) $-2x^2 - 7x \geqslant 0$.

3. Find the set of values of x for which
    (i) $6x^2 - x > 15$ (ii) $16 - x^2 \leqslant 0$ (iii) $2(x^2 - 6) \geqslant 5x$.

4. Find the set of values of x for which $(4 - x)(1 - x) < x + 11$.

5. If $x^2 - 6x + 2 \leqslant 0$, show that $3 - \sqrt{7} \leqslant x \leqslant 3 + \sqrt{7}$.

6. Find the range of values of k for which $x^2 + (k + 1)x + 1 = 0$ has real roots.

7. Find the range of values of k for which the equation $kx^2 + 4x + 3 + k = 0$ has real roots.

8. Find the range of values of p for which the quadratic equation $px^2 + (p + 3)x + p = 0$ has real roots.
   If $x = -2$ is a root of the equation, find the value of p.

9. Solve each of the following rational inequalities for x.

   (i) $\dfrac{x + 3}{x + 2} < 2, x \neq -2$ (ii) $\dfrac{x + 5}{x - 3} > 1, x \neq 3$ (iii) $\dfrac{2x - 1}{x + 3} > 3, x \neq -3$

10. Find the range of values of x for which

   (i) $\dfrac{3x + 4}{x - 5} > 2, x \neq 5$ (ii) $\dfrac{1 - 2x}{4x + 2} > 2, x \neq \dfrac{-1}{2}$ (iii) $\dfrac{3 + 4x}{5x - 1} > 3, x \neq \dfrac{1}{5}$

11. Find the set of values of x for which each of the following inequalities is true.

   (i) $\dfrac{x}{2x - 3} \leqslant 1, x \neq \dfrac{3}{2}$ (ii) $\dfrac{2x - 4}{x - 1} < 1, x \neq 1$ (iii) $\dfrac{x - 5}{x - 1} \leqslant 3, x \neq 1$

12. Solve these inequalities:

   (i) $\dfrac{2x - 7}{x + 3} < 1, x \neq -3$ (ii) $\dfrac{2x - 3}{x - 5} < \dfrac{3}{2}, x \neq 5$ (iii) $\dfrac{x + 2}{x - 1} \leqslant 3, x \neq 1$

13. Examine the graphs of $y = 2x^2 + 4x$ and $y = x^2 - x - 6$ and estimate the range of values of x for which

   $$2x^2 + 4x > x^2 - x - 6.$$

   By simplifying the quadratic inequality, find the range of values of x for which $2x^2 + 4x > x^2 - x - 6, x \in R$.

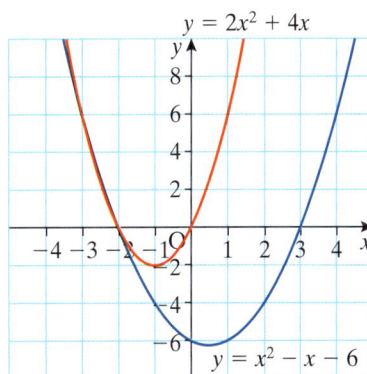

$y = 2x^2 + 4x$

$y = x^2 - x - 6$

ICT: Study the functions in **Q13.** using graphics software. Enlarge the scale on the x-axis and focus particularly on the domain $-3 < x < -2$.

14. Show that $x^2 + x + 1 > 0$ for all values of x.

15. The path of a ball is given by the expression $f(t) = -11 + 13t - 2t^2$, where t represents time.
    Find the range of values of t that satisfies each of the following inequalities.
    (i) $f(t) \leqslant 4$
    (ii) $f(t) \geqslant 7$, and hence deduce the set of values of t that satisfies
    (iii) $4 < f(t) < 7$.

16. Examine the graphs of the following quadratic functions.

Find, as accurately as the graph allows, the range of values of x that satisfies each of the following inequalities.

    (i) $f(x) > 0$
    (ii) $g(x) \leqslant 8$
    (iii) $f(x) \leqslant g(x)$
    (iv) $g(x) > 0$

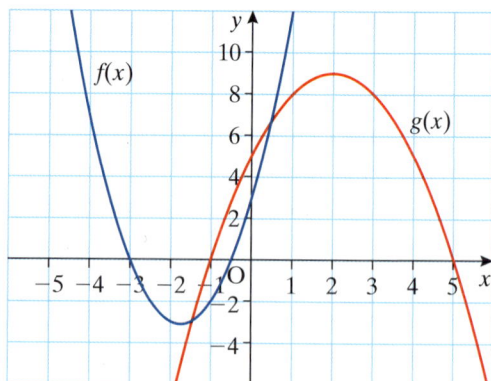

17. The width of a rectangle is to be 3 m shorter than its length. If the ratio of the length to the width is to be less than 5, find the range of possible dimensions for

    (i) the length of the rectangle
    (ii) the width of the rectangle.

18. The graphs of $x^2 - 2px + p + 6$ are shown for $p = 1.5, 2, 2.5$.

Find the range of values of p for which the graphs are always positive, for all real values of x.

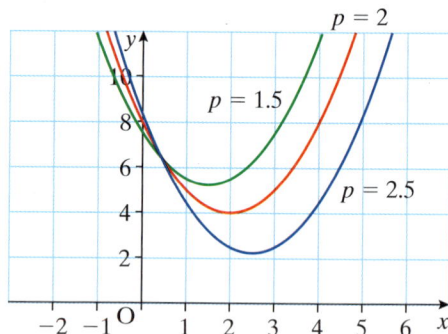

19. Find the range of values of x for which

    (i) the perimeter of this rectangle is less than 50 m
    (ii) the area of this rectangle is greater than 12 m²
    (iii) the perimeter of this rectangle is less than 50 m and the area is greater than 12 m².

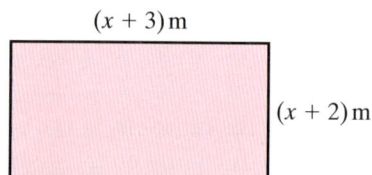

$(x + 3)\,\text{m}$

$(x + 2)\,\text{m}$

20. Find the range of values of $x, x \in Z$, so that the perimeter of this triangle is between 8 m and 12 m long.

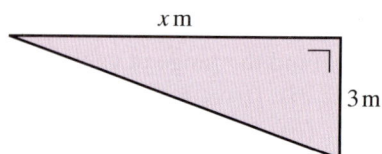

$x\,\text{m}$

$3\,\text{m}$

Section 12.3 Modulus

1. Modular equations

The modulus of a number is a measure of its size or magnitude and is written as $|x|$.

> If $|x| = a$, then $x = +a$ or $-a$ and $|x|^2 = a^2$.

$|3| = 3, |-4| = 4, |15.5| = 15.5, |-6.2| = 6.2 \ldots$ in other words, for all $x \in R$, $|x|$ is the positive value of the number.

Conversely, if $|x| = 6$, then $x = +6$ or -6.
And therefore, $|x|^2 = 36$.

Geometrically, the modulus function multiplies any negative part of the graph by (-1).

Compare the following graphs:

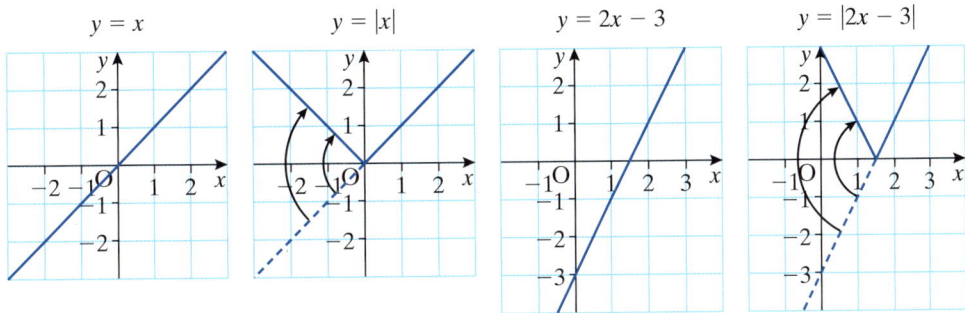

$y = x$ $y = |x|$ $y = 2x - 3$ $y = |2x - 3|$

The graph of $f(x) = |x|$ is found from the graph of $f(x) = x$ by reflecting, in the x-axis, that part of the graph for which $f(x) < 0$.

Example 1

Sketch the graph of $f(x) = |3x + 5|$ and hence solve the equation $|3x + 5| = 2$
(i) graphically and (ii) algebraically.

(i) Graphically:

Given $f(x) = 3x + 5$.

At $x = 0$, $f(x) = 5 \Rightarrow (0, 5)$ is the $f(x)$ intercept.

At $f(x) = 0; 0 = 3x + 5 \Rightarrow x = \dfrac{-5}{3} \Rightarrow \left(\dfrac{-5}{3}, 0\right)$ is the x-axis intercept.

$f(x) = 3x + 5$ is the line passing through $(0, 5)$ and $\left(\dfrac{-5}{3}, 0\right)$.

Reflecting the negative region of the graph in the x-axis creates the graph of $f(x) = |3x + 5|$.

The x-coordinates of the intersection points of $f(x) = |3x + 5|$ and $f(x) = 2$ give the solution to the equation $|3x + 5| = 2$.

The x-coordinates are $x = -1$ and $x \cong -2.3$.

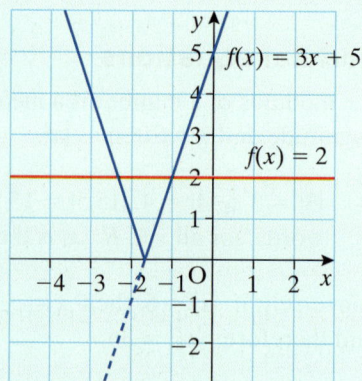

(ii) Algebraically:

Method 1

Since $|3x + 5| = 2$,

$\Rightarrow 3x + 5 = +2 \qquad \therefore x = -1$

$or \ 3x + 5 = -2 \qquad \therefore x = \dfrac{-7}{3}$

The solution is $x = \dfrac{-7}{3}$ or $x = -1$

Method 2

$|3x + 5| = 2$

$\Rightarrow (3x + 5)^2 = (2)^2$

$\Rightarrow 9x^2 + 30x + 25 = 4$

$\Rightarrow 9x^2 + 30x + 21 = 0$

$\Rightarrow 3x^2 + 10x + 7 = 0$

$\Rightarrow (3x + 7)(x + 1) = 0$

$\Rightarrow$ The solution is $\left(-\frac{7}{3}, -1\right)$

Note 1: The method of "squaring both sides" of a modular equation can be useful when the modulus sign appears on both sides of the equation, e.g. $|3x + 5| = |x - 2|$.

Note 2: Getting the modulus of an expression is sometimes referred to as getting the **absolute value** of the expression.

2. Modular inequalities

If $|x| < 1$, then the value of x must lie between $+1$ and -1, i.e. $-1 < x < +1$.

If $|x| > 1$, then the value of x must lie outside this range, i.e. $x > 1$ or $x < -1$.

Example 2

Sketch the graph of $f(x) = |2x - 5|$ and hence solve the inequality $|2x - 5| < 3$.

$f(x) = 2x - 5$ is drawn first by using two points on the line, e.g. $(2.5, 0)$ and $(4, 3)$.

$f(x) = |2x - 5|$ is then drawn by reflecting the negative portion of the graph in the x-axis as before.

Drawing the line $f(x) = 3$ on the same axes, the red segment represents where $|2x - 5| < 3$.

The x-values that create that portion of the graph are $1 < x < 4$.

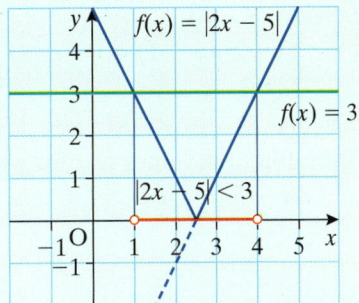

Note :   If $|2x - 5| = 3$, then $2x - 5 = 3$ or $2x - 5 = -3$.

If $|2x - 5| < 3$, then $-3 < 2x - 5 < 3$.

$$\therefore \quad 2 < 2x < 8 \quad \text{... adding 5 to each part of the inequality}$$

$$1 < x < 4 \quad \text{... dividing each part of the inequality by 2}$$

This produces the same solution set as above.

Example 3

Draw a graph of $f(x) = |x + 3|$ and $f(x) = |3x - 7|$.
Solve the inequality $|x + 3| < |3x - 7|$ algebraically and indicate graphically the solution set.

$$|x + 3| < |3x - 7|$$
$$\Rightarrow (x + 3)^2 < (3x - 7)^2$$
$$\Rightarrow x^2 + 6x + 9 < 9x^2 - 42x + 49$$
$$\Rightarrow -8x^2 + 48x - 40 < 0$$
$$\Rightarrow x^2 - 6x + 5 > 0.$$

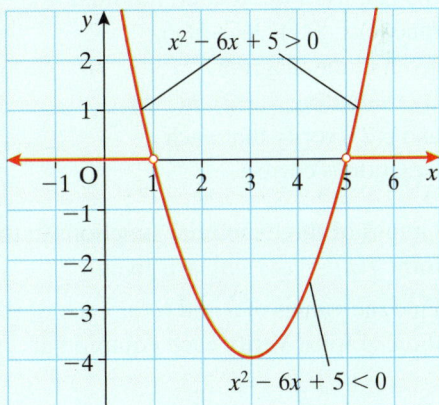

Solving $x^2 - 6x + 5 = 0$,
$$(x - 5)(x - 1) = 0$$
$$\Rightarrow x = 5 \text{ or } x = 1$$

Therefore, the values of x for which
$x^2 - 6x + 5 > 0$ are $x < 1$ and $x > 5$.

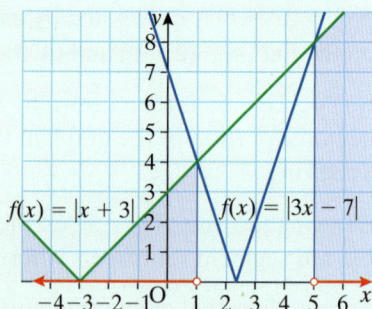

$f(x) = |x + 3|$ $f(x) = |3x - 7|$

Exercise 12.3

1. Solve each of the following inequalities for $x \in R$.

   (i) $|x + 3| = 1$ (ii) $|x - 2| = 4$ (iii) $|2x - 1| = 5$

   (iv) $|3x - 2| = x$ (v) $2|x - 3| = 2$ (vi) $|x - 5| = |x + 1|$

2. Copy and complete the following table and hence sketch a graph of $f(x) = |3x - 2|$.

x	-3	-2	-1	0	1	2	3
$f(x) = |3x - 2|$							

   Use your graph to solve the equation $|3x - 2| = 5$.

3. Write an equation for each of
   the graphs of the related modular
   functions, $f(x), g(x), h(x)$,
   given in the diagram.
   By evaluating $f(-2), h(-5)$
   and $g(2)$, verify that each
   equation is correct.

   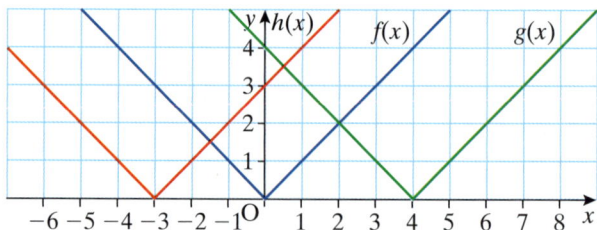

4. Graphs of three modular functions in the
   form $f(x) = |ax + b|$ are given.

   Find the values of a and b for each of the
   three graphs. Verify each equation at $x = -2$.

   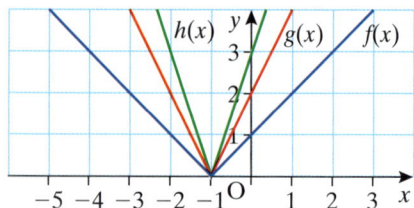

5. On the same set of axes, sketch the graphs of the functions

   $$f : x \rightarrow |x - 2| \text{ and } g : x \rightarrow |x - 6|.$$

   Hence solve the equation $|x - 2| = |x - 6|$.

   Verify your answer algebraically.

6. Solve each of the following inequalities for $x \in R$.

    (i) $|x - 6| < 2$ (ii) $|x + 2| \leqslant 4$ (iii) $|2x - 1| \geqslant 5$

    (iv) $|2x - 1| \geqslant 11$ (v) $|3x + 5| < 4$ (vi) $|x - 4| < 3$

7. Solve the following inequalities, $x \in R$.

    (i) $|2x - 1| \geqslant 7$ (ii) $|3x + 4| \leqslant |x + 2|$ (iii) $2|x - 1| \leqslant |x + 3|$

8. On the same set of axes, sketch the graphs of the functions

$$f(x) = |x| - 4 \text{ and } g(x) = \tfrac{1}{2}x.$$

    Hence solve the inequality $|x| - 4 \leqslant \tfrac{1}{2}x$.

9. Sketch the graph of the function $f(x) = |\tfrac{1}{4}x + 3|$ and hence find the solution to the inequality $|\tfrac{1}{4}x + 3| \geqslant 3$.

10. Solve the inequality $|1 + 2x| < |x + 2|$ for $x \in R$.

11. For what real values of $x \in R$ is $\left| \dfrac{1}{1 + 2x} \right| = 1, x \neq -\dfrac{1}{2}$?

    Hence solve the inequality $\left| \dfrac{1}{1 + 2x} \right| < 1$.

12. Use the graphs of the functions $f(x) = |x + 1|$, $g(x) = |3x - 6|$ and $h(x) = 3$ to estimate the range of values of x that satisfies each of the following inequalities.

    (i) $f(x) < h(x)$
    (ii) $h(x) < f(x)$
    (iii) $g(x) < f(x)$
    (iv) $g(x) < h(x) < f(x)$
    (v) $g(x) < f(x) < h(x)$
    (vi) $f(x) > h(x) > g(x)$
    (vii) $f(x) > g(x) > h(x)$

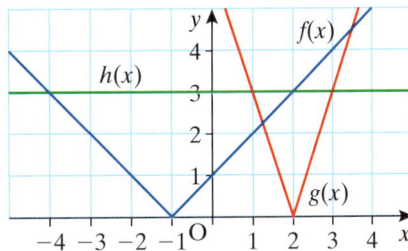

13. Solve each of the following for $x \in R$.

    (i) $\dfrac{x}{2x - 1} < -2$ (ii) $|x - 3| = 2|x - 1|$ (iii) $|x - 1| - |2x + 1| > 0$

Section 12.4 Mathematical proof

In mathematics, we use deductive reasoning to prove that a statement is *always* true.

The statement, when proved true, then becomes a theorem. e.g. Pythagoras' theorem.

The different methods of proof include direct proofs, proofs by contradiction and proofs by induction (see Section 12.12).

1. Direct proof

Direct proof uses axioms, definitions and other proven theorems to verify the new statement.

Example 1

Prove that the sum of two even integers x and y is always even.

Proof:

Since x is even, we can write it as $x = 2a$, where $a \in Z$.

Also since y is even, $y = 2b$, where $b \in Z$.

Therefore, $x + y = 2a + 2b = 2(a + b)$.

Since $x + y$ has a factor of $2 \Rightarrow x + y$ must be even.

$\therefore$ The sum of two even integers is always even.

2. Proof by contradiction

In a proof by contradiction, we show that if we claim some statement to be true, then a logical contradiction occurs which proves that the original statement must be false.

Example 2

Prove that $\sqrt{2}$ is irrational.

Proof: Assume $\sqrt{2}$ is a rational number.

$\therefore$ $\sqrt{2}$ can be written as $\frac{a}{b} : a, b \in Z$ and $b \neq 0$, and a and b have no common factor.

$\therefore$ $2 = \frac{a^2}{b^2}$ ... squaring both sides

$\therefore$ $a^2 = 2b^2$

$\therefore$ a^2 is even since it is equal to $2 \times (b^2)$ .... any integer multiplied by 2 is even

$\therefore$ a is even

$\therefore$ a can be written as $a = 2c$ ... since a is divisible by 2

$\therefore$ $a^2 = 4c^2 = 2b^2$

$\therefore$ $2c^2 = b^2$

$\therefore$ b is also even

$\therefore$ a and b have a common factor of 2 which contradicts our assumption.

$\therefore$ $\sqrt{2}$ is not a rational number.

$\therefore$ $\sqrt{2}$ is an irrational number, i.e. it cannot be written as $\frac{a}{b}$ with no common factors.

Exercise 12.4

1. Prove by contradiction that there are no positive integer solutions to $x^2 - y^2 = 1$. (Hint: Assume that x and y are both positive integers and use the difference of two squares.)

2. Prove by contradiction that if a is a rational number and b an irrational number, then $a + b$ is an irrational number.

3. Prove by contradiction that there are no positive integer solutions to $x^2 - y^2 = 10$. (Hint: Assume that x and y are both positive integers and use the difference of two squares.)

4. Prove that if a divides b, and b divides c, then a divides c.

5. Prove that if a divides b, and a divides c, then a divides $(b + c)$.

6. If a and b are real numbers, prove that $a^2 + b^2 \geqslant 2ab$. (Abstract inequality proof.)

7. Prove that the sum of two rational numbers is a rational number.

8. Prove that the sum of two odd numbers is always even.

Section 12.5 Proofs of abstract inequalities

If $a > 0$ and $b > 0$, then $\dfrac{a}{b} + \dfrac{b}{a} \geqslant 2$ is an example of an **abstract inequality** (see Example 2).

To prove that an inequality statement is true, we will use two important facts:

  (i) (Any real number)$^2 \geqslant 0$
  (ii) $-$(Any real number)$^2 \leqslant 0$.

If both sides of an inequality are squared, the inequality sign is retained only if both sides of the inequality are positive.

For example, $4 > 3 \Rightarrow 4^2 > 3^2$, i.e. $16 > 9$.

> If a and b are real numbers, then
> $$a^2 \geqslant 0 \text{ and } b^2 \geqslant 0$$
> $$(a + b)^2 \geqslant 0$$
> $$(a - b)^2 \geqslant 0$$
> $$-(a + b)^2 \leqslant 0$$
> $$-(a - b)^2 \leqslant 0$$

However, if one or both sides are negative, then this does not hold.

E.g. $2 > -3 \nRightarrow 2^2 > (-3)^2$,
           i.e. $4 \ngtr 9$.

To prove an abstract inequality;

1. Write down the statement you are asked to prove.
2. Use the rules of inequalities to adapt the inequality until …
3. you arrive at an inequality that is obviously true.

Example 1

Prove that $a^2 + b^2 \geqslant 2ab$ for all $a, b \in R$.

If: $a^2 + b^2 \geqslant 2ab$,

then $a^2 - 2ab + b^2 \geqslant 0$ ... subtracting $2ab$ from both sides.

$\therefore \quad (a - b)^2 \geqslant 0$ ... factorising the left-hand side.

which is always true. $\quad \therefore \quad a^2 + b^2 \geqslant 2ab$.

Example 2

If $a > 0$ and $b > 0$, prove that $\dfrac{a}{b} + \dfrac{b}{a} \geqslant 2$.

If: $\dfrac{a}{b} + \dfrac{b}{a} \geqslant 2$,

then $a^2 + b^2 \geqslant 2ab$ ... multiply each term by the common denominator ab.

$\therefore \quad a^2 - 2ab + b^2 \geqslant 0$

$\therefore \quad (a - b)^2 \geqslant 0$ ... which is always true.

$\therefore \quad \dfrac{a}{b} + \dfrac{b}{a} \geqslant 2$.

Example 3

Show that $x^2 + 4x + 6 > 0$ (i.e. is positive) for all $x \in R$.

If: $x^2 + 4x + 6 > 0$,

then $x^2 + 4x + \mathbf{4} - \mathbf{4} + 6 > 0$ ... adding and subtracting $\left(\dfrac{4}{2}\right)^2$ to complete the square.

$\Rightarrow (x + 2)^2 - 4 + 6 > 0$ ... completing the square.

$\Rightarrow (x + 2)^2 + 2 > 0$ ... which is true for all values of x, since $(x + 2)^2 > 0$ for all values of x.

$\therefore \quad x^2 + 4x + 6 > 0$ for all $x \in R$.

Example 4

Show for all real numbers $a, b > 0$ that $(a + b)\left(\dfrac{1}{a} + \dfrac{1}{b}\right) \geqslant 4$.

If: $(a + b)\left(\dfrac{1}{a} + \dfrac{1}{b}\right) \geqslant 4$,

then $(a + b)\left(\dfrac{a + b}{ab}\right) \geqslant 4$ ... using the common denominator ab to add the fractions.

$\therefore \dfrac{(a + b)^2}{ab} \geqslant 4$ ... simplifying.

$\therefore (a + b)^2 \geqslant 4ab$ ... multiplying both sides by ab.

$\therefore a^2 + 2ab + b^2 \geqslant 4ab$ ... expanding the left-hand side.

$\therefore a^2 - 2ab + b^2 \geqslant 0$ ... subtracting $4ab$ from both sides.

$\therefore (a - b)^2 \geqslant 0$ ... which is true for all $a, b \in R$.

$\therefore (a + b)\left(\dfrac{1}{a} + \dfrac{1}{b}\right) \geqslant 4$.

Exercise 12.5

1. Prove that (i) $a^2 + 2ab + b^2 \geqslant 0$ (ii) $a^2 + 2ab + 2b^2 \geqslant 0$ for all $a, b \in R$.

2. Prove that $(a + b)^2 \geqslant 4ab$ for all $a, b \in R$.

3. Prove that $-(a^2 + 2ab + b^2) \leqslant 0$ for all $a, b \in R$.

4. If $a > 0$ and $b > 0$, show that

   (i) $a + \dfrac{1}{a} \geqslant 2$ (ii) $\dfrac{1}{a} + \dfrac{1}{b} \geqslant \dfrac{2}{a + b}$.

5. Prove that $a^2 - 6a + 9 + b^2 \geqslant 0$ for all real values of a and b.

6. Prove that for all real values of x,

   (i) $x^2 + 6x + 9 \geqslant 0$ (ii) $x^2 - 10x + 25 \geqslant 0$ (iii) $x^2 + 4x + 6 > 0$
   (iv) $x^2 - 6x + 10 > 0$ (v) $4x^2 + 12x + 11 > 0$ (vi) $4x^2 - 4x + 2 > 0$.

7. Show that (i) $-x^2 + 10x - 25 \leqslant 0$ (ii) $-x^2 - 4x - 7 \leqslant 0$ for all $x \in R$.

8. Prove that for all real numbers p and q,

   (i) $p^2 + 4q^2 \geqslant 4pq$ (ii) $(p + q)^2 \leqslant 2(p^2 + q^2)$.

9. Factorise $a^3 + b^3$.
   Hence prove that $a^3 + b^3 > a^2b + ab^2$ for all real $a > 0$ and $b > 0$.

10. Given that $a^2 + b^2 \geqslant 2ab$, deduce an expression for (i) $a^2 + c^2$ and (ii) $b^2 + c^2$.
Use these results to prove that
$$a^2 + b^2 + c^2 \geqslant ab + bc + ca \text{ for all real values of } a, b \text{ and } c.$$

11. If $p > 0$ and $q > 0$ and $p \neq q$, prove that $\dfrac{p + q}{2} > \sqrt{pq}$.

12. Show that $(ax + by)^2 \leqslant (a^2 + b^2)(x^2 + y^2)$ for all $a, b, x, y \in R$.

13. Prove that $a^4 + b^4 \geqslant 2a^2b^2$ for all $a, b \in R$.

14. If a and b are positive numbers, show that
$$(a + 2b)\left(\frac{1}{a} + \frac{1}{2b}\right) \geqslant 4.$$

15. Show that for all real a, $\dfrac{a}{(a + 1)^2} < \dfrac{1}{4}, a \neq -1$.

16. (i) Express $a^4 - b^4$ as the product of (a) two factors (b) three factors.
(ii) Factorise $a^5 - a^4b - ab^4 + b^5$.
(iii) Use the results from (i) and (ii) to show that $a^5 + b^5 > a^4b + ab^4$, where a and b are positive unequal real numbers.

17. If $a^2 + b^2 = 1$ and $c^2 + d^2 = 1$, show that $ab + cd \leqslant 1$.
(Hint: Use the result that $a^2 + b^2 \geqslant 2ab$.)

18. Prove that $\sqrt{ab} > \dfrac{2ab}{a + b}$ if a and b are positive and unequal.

19. Prove that $a + \dfrac{9}{a + 2} \geqslant 4$, where $a + 2 > 0$.

20. If a, b, c, d are positive numbers and $\dfrac{a}{b} > \dfrac{c}{d}$, prove that $\dfrac{a + c}{b + d} > \dfrac{c}{d}$.

21. Explain why $(a^3 - b^3)(a - b)$ is always positive for $a > b$.
Hence prove that $a^4 + b^4 \geqslant a^3b + ab^3$ for all $a, b \in R$ and $a > b$.

Section 12.6 Indices

When a number is multiplied by itself many times, we use the index form to represent the product.

$4 \times 4 \times 4 \times 4 \times 4 = 4^5$, i.e. 4 to the power of 5.

In this case, 5 is the **index** (plural indices) and 4 is the **base number**.

Revision of the rules of indices.

	Example	Rule
1.	$6^3 \times 6^4 = 6^7$	$a^p a^q = a^{p+q}$
2.	$\dfrac{4^5}{4^2} = 4^3$, also $\dfrac{4^5}{4^7} = 4^{-2}$	$\dfrac{a^p}{a^q} = a^{p-q}$
3.	$(2^4)^3 = 2^{12}$	$(a^p)^q = a^{pq}$
4.	$3^0 = 5^0 = 9^0 = (-3)^0 = \left(\frac{1}{4}\right)^0 = 1$	$a^0 = 1$
5.	$3^{-1} = \frac{1}{3}$, $3^{-4} = \dfrac{1}{3^4}$	$a^{-p} = \dfrac{1}{a^p}$
6.	$7^{\frac{1}{2}} = \sqrt[2]{7}$, $5^{\frac{1}{3}} = \sqrt[3]{5}$	$a^{\frac{1}{q}} = \sqrt[q]{a}$
7.	$8^{\frac{2}{3}} = \left(8^{\frac{1}{3}}\right)^2$ or $(8^2)^{\frac{1}{3}}$	$a^{\frac{p}{q}} = \sqrt[q]{a^p} = (\sqrt[q]{a})^p$
8.	$(2 \times 5)^2 = 2^2 \times 5^2$	$(ab)^p = a^p a^p$
	$\left(\dfrac{5}{6}\right)^4 = \dfrac{5^4}{6^4}$	$\left(\dfrac{a}{b}\right)^p = \dfrac{a^p}{b^p}$

Each of these rules can be verified by expanding the powers and simplifying, e.g.

$(2^4)^3 = 2^4 \times 2^4 \times 2^4 = 2^{12} = 4096$

Note: $\sqrt{x} = \sqrt[2]{x} = x^{\frac{1}{2}} = $ the square root of x.

$\sqrt[3]{x} = x^{\frac{1}{3}} = $ the cube root of x.

$\sqrt[4]{x} = x^{\frac{1}{4}} = $ the fourth root of x ... etc.

Note: $25^{\frac{3}{2}} = \left(25^{\frac{1}{2}}\right)^3 = (5)^3 = 125$ (most often, it is easier to get the root first and then raise to the power.)

Example 1

Evaluate each of the following.

(i) $27^{\frac{1}{3}}$ (ii) $36^{\frac{3}{2}}$ (iii) $64^{-\frac{2}{3}}$ (iv) $\left(\frac{27}{125}\right)^{-\frac{2}{3}}$

(i) $27^{\frac{1}{3}} = \sqrt[3]{27} = 3$ ... (i.e. 3 multiplied by itself three times equals 27)

(ii) $36^{\frac{3}{2}} = \left(36^{\frac{1}{2}}\right)^3 = (\sqrt{36})^3 = 6^3 = 216$

(iii) $64^{-\frac{2}{3}} = \dfrac{1}{64^{\frac{2}{3}}} = \dfrac{1}{\left(64^{\frac{1}{3}}\right)^2} = \dfrac{1}{(4)^2} = \dfrac{1}{16}$

(iv) $\left(\frac{27}{125}\right)^{-\frac{2}{3}} = \left(\frac{125}{27}\right)^{\frac{2}{3}} = \left[\left(\frac{125}{27}\right)^{\frac{1}{3}}\right]^2 = \left(\frac{5}{3}\right)^2 = \frac{25}{9}$

Numerical expressions containing complex fractions with indices can be simplified and evaluated with a calculator.

Since the procedure on each calculator may be slightly different, it is important to gain practice on your calculator, particularly when dealing with fractional powers.

However, it is most important to understand the rules of indices and to be able to apply them to general problems containing unknowns.

Example 2

Simplify each of the following. (i) $\left(\dfrac{x^2 y^{-3}}{x^{-4} y^5}\right)^{\frac{1}{2}}$ (ii) $\dfrac{\sqrt{a^3}}{\sqrt[4]{a} \times \sqrt[3]{a^2}}$

(i) $\left(\dfrac{x^2 y^{-3}}{x^{-4} y^5}\right)^{\frac{1}{2}} = (x^6 y^{-8})^{\frac{1}{2}} = (x^6)^{\frac{1}{2}}(y^{-8})^{\frac{1}{2}} = x^3 y^{-4} = \dfrac{x^3}{y^4}$

(ii) $\dfrac{\sqrt{a^3}}{\sqrt[4]{a} \times \sqrt[3]{a^2}} = \dfrac{a^{\frac{3}{2}}}{a^{\frac{1}{4}} \times a^{\frac{2}{3}}} = \dfrac{a^{\frac{3}{2}}}{a^{\frac{3+8}{12}}} = \dfrac{a^{\frac{3}{2}}}{a^{\frac{11}{12}}} = a^{\frac{3}{2} - \frac{11}{12}} = a^{\frac{7}{12}}$

Example 3

Show that $\dfrac{5^{n+1} - 4.5^n}{5^{n-2} + 5^n} = \dfrac{25}{26}$.

$\dfrac{5^{n+1} - 4.5^n}{5^{n-2} + 5^n} = \dfrac{5^n . 5^1 - 4.5^n}{5^n . 5^{-2} + 5^n} = \dfrac{5.5^n - 4.5^n}{\dfrac{5^n}{25} + 5^n} = \dfrac{5^n}{\dfrac{5^n + 25.5^n}{25}} = \dfrac{5^n}{\dfrac{26.5^n}{25}} = \dfrac{25}{26}$

Exercise 12.6

1. Simplify each of the following:

   (i) $a^2 \times a^3$ (ii) $x.x.x^2$ (iii) $2x^3 \times 3x^3$ (iv) $\dfrac{x^5}{x^2}$ (v) $\dfrac{x^4}{x^5}$

   (vi) a^0 (vii) $\sqrt[3]{27}$ (viii) $(a^3)^2$ (ix) $\dfrac{(x^3)^2}{x^3}$ (x) $(3ab)^2$

2. Express each of the following as a rational number:

   (i) $\sqrt[3]{64}$ (ii) 3^{-2} (iii) $\dfrac{1}{2^{-3}}$ (iv) $\dfrac{2^{-2}}{3^{-2}}$ (v) $\dfrac{1}{4^{-\frac{1}{2}}}$

3. Express as rational numbers,

   (i) $8^{\frac{2}{3}}$ (ii) $16^{\frac{3}{4}}$ (iii) $27^{\frac{2}{3}}$ (iv) $81^{\frac{3}{4}}$ (v) $125^{\frac{2}{3}}$.

4. Simplify each of these:

   (i) $\left(\dfrac{2}{3}\right)^{-2}$ (ii) $\left(\dfrac{4}{9}\right)^{-\frac{1}{2}}$ (iii) $\left(\dfrac{9}{25}\right)^{-\frac{3}{2}}$ (iv) $\left(\dfrac{27}{125}\right)^{-\frac{2}{3}}$ (v) $\left(3\dfrac{3}{8}\right)^{\frac{1}{3}}$

5. Express $\dfrac{4^2 \times 16^{\frac{1}{2}}}{64^{\frac{2}{3}} \times 4^3}$ in the form $4^n, n \in Z$.

6. Find the value of the rational number p for which $\dfrac{3^{\frac{1}{4}} \times 3 \times 3^{\frac{1}{6}}}{\sqrt{3}} = 3^p$.

7. Simplify each of the following, writing your answers with positive indices.

   (i) $\dfrac{(xy^2)^3 \times (x^2y)^{-2}}{xy}$ (ii) $\left(\dfrac{p^2q}{p^{-1}q^3}\right)^4$ (iii) $a^{\frac{1}{4}} \times a^{-\frac{5}{4}}$

   (iv) $\left(\dfrac{y^{-2}}{y^{-3}}\right)^{\frac{2}{3}}$ (v) $\dfrac{(a\sqrt{b})^{-3}}{\sqrt{a^3b}}$ (vi) $\dfrac{\sqrt[4]{x^7}}{\sqrt{x^3}}$

8. Simplify each of these

   (i) $\dfrac{x^{\frac{1}{2}} + x^{-\frac{1}{2}}}{x^{\frac{1}{2}}}$ (ii) $\left(x + x^{\frac{1}{2}}\right)\left(x - x^{\frac{1}{2}}\right)$ (iii) $\dfrac{\sqrt{x} + \sqrt{x^3}}{\sqrt{x}}$

9. By multiplying the numerator and denominator by $(x-1)^{\frac{1}{2}}$, simplify

   $$\dfrac{(x-1)^{\frac{1}{2}} + (x-1)^{-\frac{1}{2}}}{(x-1)^{\frac{1}{2}}}.$$

10. The expression $\sqrt{3^{2n+1}} \times \sqrt[3]{3^{-3n}}$ can be written in the form 3^k; find k.

11. The keys on a piano are tuned so that each key (white and black) produces a note that has a frequency of $2^{\left(\frac{1}{12}\right)}$ times that of the previous note. If the A key (2 keys below middle C) is tuned to a frequency of $220\,\text{Hz}$, find, correct to the nearest whole number, the frequency (in Hz) of middle C.

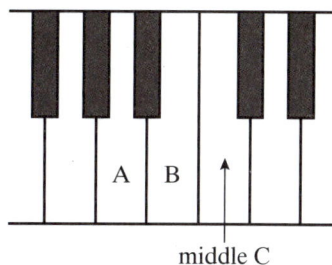

A   B

middle C

12. The surface area of a sphere is given by

   $A = 4\pi r^2$ and its volume V by $\frac{4}{3}\pi r^3$, where r is the radius of the sphere.

   Show that if we have two spheres of radii r_1 and r_2 respectively, then the ratio of the surface areas can be written as $\dfrac{A_1}{A_2} = \left(\dfrac{V_1}{V_2}\right)^{\frac{2}{3}}$.

If two such spheres have volumes 162 cm³ and 384 cm³ respectively, find the ratio of their

areas, expressing your answer in the form $\frac{a}{b}$, where $a, b \in N$.

13. Given $f(n) = 3^n$, find expressions for (i) $f(n + 3)$ (ii) $f(n + 1)$.
    Hence find the value of k such that $f(n + 3) - f(n + 1) = k f(n)$, where $k \in N$.

14. Given $f(n) = 3^{n-1}$, find the value of k such that $f(n + 3) + f(n) = k f(n)$, where $k \in N$.

Section 12.7 Exponential equations

$y = 3^x$ is an example of an exponential function.
$3^x = 27$ is an example of an **exponential equation**.

As in the last section, 3 is the **base number** and x is the **index** (power) or **exponent.**

When solving exponential equations, it is important to identify the base number (usually a prime number) that is common to all the individual terms of the equation.

E.g. $3^x = 27$; 3 is the base number for both sides. ... ($3^x = 3^3$)

$\quad\ \ 25^x = 125$; 5 is the base number. ... ($5^x = 5^3$)

Example 1

Solve these equations. (i) $\frac{1}{8^x} = 16^{\frac{1}{3}}$ (ii) $27^{x-3} = 3 \times 9^{x-2}$

(i) $\frac{1}{8^x} = 16^{\frac{1}{3}}$ (the base number is 2)

$\frac{1}{(2^3)^x} = (2^4)^{\frac{1}{3}}$

$2^{-3x} = 2^{\frac{4}{3}} \implies -3x = \frac{4}{3}$

$\implies x = -\frac{4}{9}$

(ii) $27^{x-3} = 3 \times 9^{x-2}$
(the base number is 3)

$(3^3)^{x-3} = 3 \times (3^2)^{x-2}$

$\implies 3^{3x-9} = 3^1 \times 3^{2x-4}$

$\implies 3^{3x-9} = 3^{2x-3}$

$\implies 3x - 9 = 2x - 3$

$\implies x = 6$

By using a suitable **change of variable,** an exponential equation can be transformed into a quadratic equation and then solved.

Note: If $2^x = y$,

$\implies 3 \cdot 2^x = 3y$

$\implies 2^{2x} = (2^x)^2 = y^2$

$\implies 2^{x+2} = 2^x \cdot 2^2 = 4y$

Example 2

If $y = 3^x$, express 3^{2x} in terms of y.

Hence solve the equation $3^{2x} - 4.3^x + 3 = 0$.

(i) $3^{2x} = (3^x)^2 = y^2$

(ii) Given $3^{2x} - 4.3^x + 3 = 0$.

$\Rightarrow y^2 - 4y + 3 = 0$ ... using the substitution $3^x = y$ and $3^{2x} = y^2$

$\Rightarrow (y - 1)(y - 3) = 0$

$\Rightarrow y = 1$ or $y = 3$ ... are the solutions of the new quadratic equation

$\Rightarrow 3^x = 1$ or $3^x = 3$ ... re-substituting to find values of x

$\Rightarrow 3^x = 3^0$ or $3^x = 3^1$ ... using the base number 3

$\therefore \quad x = 0$ or $x = 1$ are the solutions.

Exercise 12.7

1. Find the value of x in each of these equations:

   (i) $2^x = 32$ (ii) $16^x = 64$ (iii) $25^x = 125$ (iv) $3^x = \frac{1}{27}$

2. Solve each of these index (exponential) equations.

   (i) $9^x = \frac{1}{27}$ (ii) $4^x = \frac{1}{32}$ (iii) $4^{x-1} = 2^{x+1}$ (iv) $\frac{1}{9^x} = 27$

3. Find the value of x in each of these equations:

   (i) $2^x = \frac{\sqrt{2}}{2}$ (ii) $25^x = \frac{125}{\sqrt{5}}$ (iii) $\frac{1}{8^x} = \sqrt{2}$ (iv) $7^x = \frac{1}{\sqrt[3]{7}}$

4. Write $\sqrt{32}$ as a power of 2 and hence solve the equation $16^{x-1} = 2\sqrt{32}$.

5. If $27^x = 9$ and $2^{x-y} = 64$, find the values of x and y.

6. Express (i) 2^{x+2} and (ii) $2^x + 2^x$ in the form $k2^x$, where $k \in N$.
   Hence solve for c in the equation $2^x + 2^x = 2^{x+2}(c - 2)$.

7. By letting $3^x = y$, solve the equation $3^{2x} - 12(3^x) + 27 = 0$.

8. Solve the equation $2^{2x} - 3(2^x) - 4 = 0$ and verify your answer by substitution.

9. Solve each of these equations: (i) $2^{2x} - 9(2^x) + 8 = 0$ (ii) $3^{2x} - 10(3^x) + 9 = 0$

10. If $y = 2^x$, write (i) 2^{2x} (ii) 2^{2x+1} and (iii) 2^{x+3} in terms of y.
    Hence solve the equation $2^{2x+1} - 2^{x+3} - 2^x + 4 = 0$.

11. By using the substitution $y = 3^x$, find the two values of x such that $3.3^x + 3^{-x} = 4$ and verify each solution by substitution into the original exponential equation.

12. Solve the equation $2(4^x) + 4^{-x} = 3$.

13. Solve the equation $3^x - 28 + 27(3^{-x}) = 0$.

14. By letting $2^x = y$, solve the equation $2^{x+1} + 2(2^{-x}) - 5 = 0$.

15. Solve the exponential equation $3^x + 81(3^{-x}) - 30 = 0$.

Section 12.8 **Exponential functions** _____

Exponential functions such as $f(x) = a^x$ are used in modelling many physical occurrences. These include:

(i) the growth of a biological cell

(ii) changes in population, e.g. algae growth on stagnant water

(iii) compounded interest and depreciation

(iv) radioactive decay

(v) the rate at which a body loses heat (Newton's law of cooling).

> **ICT:** Functions of the form $y = a^x$, a = constant, can be studied graphically. Remember, when using a keyboard, to use the "^" button to raise a power (exponent), i.e. $y = 2 \wedge x$.
> Proper use of brackets is essential, i.e. $y = 2 \wedge (2x) = 2^{2x}$.

All of the graphs associated with exponential functions have a characteristic shape and are easily identified. From this diagram we can see that graphs of the form $f(x) = a^x$, where $a > 0$ and $a \neq 1$, have the following properties;

1. At $x = 0$, $f(0) = a^0 = 1$.

$\Rightarrow (0, 1)$ is a point on all graphs.

2. At $x = 1$, $f(1) = a^1 = a$.

$\Rightarrow (1, a)$ is a point on all graphs.

3. At $x = -1$, $f(-1) = a^{-1} = \dfrac{1}{a}$.

$\Rightarrow \left(-1, \dfrac{1}{a}\right)$ is a point on all graphs.

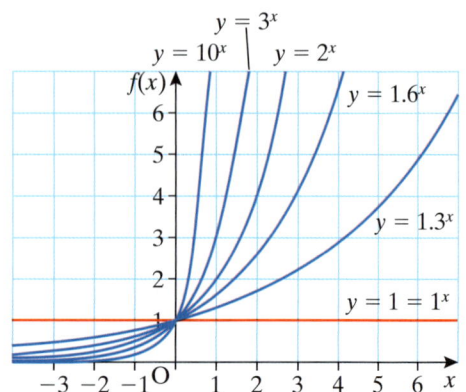

4. They are defined for all real values of x.

5. The x-axis is a horizontal asymptote to all the curves $\Rightarrow f(x) = a^x$ is always positive.

6. If $a > 1$, all of the curves increase as x increases. As a increases, the curves rise more steeply.

7. If $0 < a < 1$, then the curve $f(x) = a^x$ reflects in the y-axis, producing a set of curves that decrease rapidly as x increases.

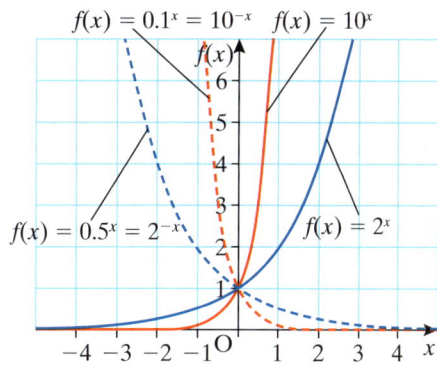

$f(x) = 0.1^x = 10^{-x}$ $f(x) = 10^x$

$f(x) = 0.5^x = 2^{-x}$ $f(x) = 2^x$

Note: If $a = \left(\frac{1}{2}\right) = 2^{-1}$

$\Rightarrow f(x) = \left(\frac{1}{2}\right)^x = (2^{-1})^x = 2^{-x}$

Note: The general formula for an increasing exponential function is $f(x) = Aa^x$, where A is the value at the start, i.e. when $x = 0$.

Exponential functions $f(x) = A.a^x$

Increasing exponential functions $a > 1$.

Decreasing exponential functions $0 < a < 1$.

$(0, A)$ is the y-axis intercept.

Decreasing functions can be written in the form

$$f(x) = A.a^{-x}$$

Example 1

A bacterial colony doubles every hour. If 10 bacteria cells were present at the start of an experiment, (i) complete the following table   (ii) draw a graph of the number of bacteria present up to 5 hours.

Time in hours	0	1	2	3	4	5
Number of bacteria						

(iii) By how many would the population increase in the 6th hour?

(iv) What percentage increase in the population occurred in the 6th hour by comparison to the first hour?

(v) Write an expression for the size of the population (N) after t hours.

(i)

Time in hours	0	1	2	3	4	5
Number of bacteria	10	20	40	80	160	320

(ii)

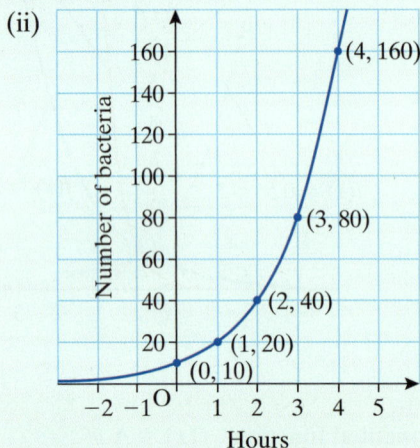

(iii) At $t = 5$ hours, there are 320 bacteria.

At $t = 6$ hours, there are 640 bacteria.

$\Rightarrow$ an increase of 320 bacteria.

(iv) Percentage increase

$$= \left(\frac{320}{10}\right) \times \frac{100}{1}\ \%$$

$$= 3200\%$$

(v) After t hours, $N = A.a^t$.

At $t = 0, N = 10 = A.a^0$.

$\Rightarrow 10 = A$.

At $t = 1, N = 10.a^1 = 20$.

$\Rightarrow a = 2$.

$\therefore\ \ N = 10.2^t$.

Example 2

The graphs of two exponential functions, $y = Aa^x$, are given in this diagram. Find the values of A and a for each graph.

(i) $f(x) = Aa^x$

$f(0) = 1, \therefore Aa^0 = 1 \Rightarrow A = 1$.

$f(1) = 2, \therefore a^1 = 2 \Rightarrow a = 2$

$[\therefore f(x)$ is an increasing function$]$

$\therefore f(x) = 2^x$

(ii) $h(x) = Aa^x$

$f(0) = 4, \therefore Aa^0 = 4 \Rightarrow A = 4$.

$f(1) = 2, \therefore 4a^1 = 2 \Rightarrow a = \frac{2}{4} = \frac{1}{2}$.

$[\therefore f(x)$ is a decreasing function$]$

$h(x) = 4\left(\frac{1}{2}\right)^x = 4.2^{-x}$

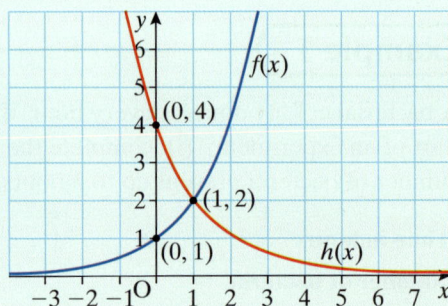

The magnitude (or size) M of an earthquake is measured on a scale called the Richter scale.

During earthquakes, the amplitude (A) of the earth's movement is a measure of the intensity (I) of the quake i.e. $I \sim A$ and is given by the exponential formula $I = k10^M$, where k is a constant.

The energy released by the earthquake of magnitude M is $E = 10^{1.5M + 4.4}$ joules

An earthquake of magnitude 2 on the Richter scale releases 25,118,864 Joules of energy.

An earthquake of magnitude 6 on the Richter scale releases 25,118,864,315,096 Joules of energy.

Example 3

Given that the intensity of an earthquake is represented by the formula $I = k10^M$, and the energy released during a quake by the formula $E \cong 10^{1.5M + 4.8}$, where I is the Intensity and M is the magnitude on the Richter scale, compare
(i) the intensity (ii) the energy of an earthquake of magnitude 6.1 on the Richter scale with a quake of magnitude 4.7.

(i) $M_1 = 6.1 \Rightarrow I_1 = k10^{6.1}$
   $M_2 = 4.7 \Rightarrow I_2 = k10^{4.7}$

$\Rightarrow \dfrac{I_1}{I_2} = \dfrac{k10^{6.1}}{k10^{4.7}} = 10^{1.4} \cong 25$

$\Rightarrow I_1 \cong 25I_2$

(ii) $E_1 \cong 10^{1.5M + 4.8} = 10^{1.5 \times 6.1 + 4.8} = 10^{13.95}$
    $E_2 \cong 10^{1.5M + 4.8} = 10^{1.5 \times 4.7 + 4.8} = 10^{11.85}$

$\Rightarrow \dfrac{E_1}{E_2} = \dfrac{10^{13.95}}{10^{11.85}} = 10^{2.1} \cong 126$

$E_1 \cong 126E_2$

Exercise 12.8

1. Match each of the following exponential functions with one of the graphs.

   (i) $y = 2^x$
   (ii) $y = (0.1)^x$
   (iii) $y = 10^x$
   (iv) $y = (0.5)2^x$

A

B

C

D

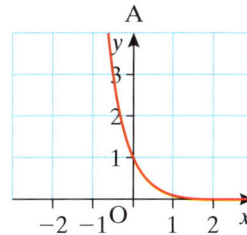

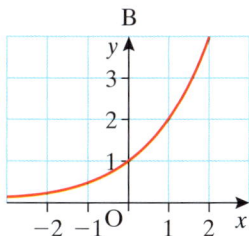

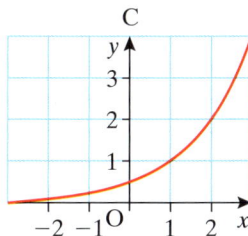

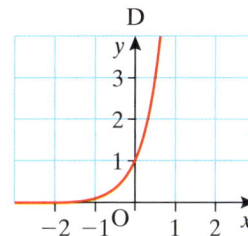

2. An entomologist monitoring a grasshopper plague notices that the area affected by the grasshoppers is given by $A(n) = 1000 \times 2^{0.2n}$ hectares, where n is the number of weeks that have elapsed after the initial observation. Find

   (i) the area originally affected
   (ii) the affected area after (a) 10 weeks (b) 12 weeks.
   (iii) Draw a graph of $A(n)$ against n for $0 \leqslant n \leqslant 10$.
   (iv) From the graph or otherwise, calculate the "doubling time" for the colony.

3. State whether each of the following graphs is increasing or decreasing.
    (i) $y = \left(\frac{1}{4}\right)^x$
    (ii) $y = (0.8)^x$
    (iii) $y = 4 \times 2^x$
    (iv) $y = 3 \times 4^{-x}$

4. What is the y-intercept of each of the following curves?
    (i) $y = (0.6)2^x$
    (ii) $y = 3.2^{-x}$
    (iii) $y = 8.2^x$
    (iv) $y = 6.4^{-x}$

5. For each of the following, use one set of axes to sketch the graphs ($-2 \leqslant x \leqslant 4$).
    (i) $y = 2^x$ and $y = 3^x$
    (ii) $y = 2^{-x}$ and $y = 3^{-x}$
    (iii) $y = 3.2^x$ and $y = 2.3^{-x}$
    (iv) For what values of x is $2^x > 3^x$?
    (v) For what values of x is $2^x < 3^x$?
    (vi) For what value(s) of x is $2^x = 3^x$?
    (vii) For what values of x is $\left(\frac{1}{2}\right)^x > \left(\frac{1}{3}\right)^x$?

6. The number of days, D, that yoghurt stays fresh, if stored at the temperature $T°C$, is
    $$D = 18(0.72)^T.$$
    (i) Is this an example of exponential growth or decay? Explain your answer.
    (ii) For how many days will the yoghurt stay fresh if stored at
        (a) 5°C   (b) 2°C   (c) 0°C ?
    (iii) Estimate the temperature required to keep the yoghurt fresh for at least 5 days.

7. Carbon-14, the radioactive element of carbon, decays according to the formula
    $P = 100(0.99988)^n$, where P is the percentage of the original mass of Carbon-14 that
    remains after n years.
    (a) Find the percentage of Carbon-14 that remains after (i) 200 years   (ii) 500 years.
    (b) Estimate (using trial and error) how long it will take the Carbon-14 sample to
        decay to half its original mass. Give your answer correct to the nearest 10 years.
    (c) A bone containing 79% of its original Carbon-14 was discovered in a bog in
        County Offaly. Estimate its age.

8. A science researcher monitoring a mosquito plague notices that the area affected by the
    mosquitoes is given by $A(n) = 1000 \times 2^{0.2n}$ hectares, where n is the number of weeks
    after the initial observation.
    (i) Find the original area affected.
    (ii) Find the area affected after (a) 5 weeks (b) 10 weeks (c) 12 weeks.
    (iii) Using the answers to (i) and (ii), draw a graph of A(n) against n.

9. The pulse rate, P(t), of a runner, t-minutes after he finishes training, is given by
    $$P(t) = 90 \times 3^{-0.25t} + 50.$$
    (i) Sketch the graph of P(t) using the values of $t = 0, 2, 4, 6, 8, 10$ min.
    (ii) Find the pulse rate immediately after finishing training.
    (iii) How long did it take for his pulse rate to drop to
        (a) 70 beats per minute   (b) 55 beats per minute?
    (iv) What is the runner's normal pulse rate? Explain your answer.

10. The energy released by an earthquake is given by $E \cong 10^{1.5M+4.8}$ where A is the amplitude and M is the magnitude on the Richter scale.
How many times greater is the energy released by an earthquake of magnitude 7 compared to an earthquake of magnitude 5?

11. In an experiment involving a population of flies, the model $P(t) = 40b^t$ was established for the population $P(t)$ after t days from the beginning of the experiment, $t \geqslant 0$.
    (i) How many flies were there initially?
    (ii) After 1 day, there were 48 flies. Find the value of b and interpret it.
    (iii) Sketch a graph of $P(t)$ versus t for $0 \leqslant t \leqslant 5$.

Section 12.9 Logarithmic function

The **logarithm** is a function that focuses on the index (or exponent) of a number.
If $y = 2^5$, then $y = 32$ is easily calculated.
However, if $200 = 2^x$, it is not as easy to find the index x that gives the number 200.
To find x, we use logarithms (**logs** for short).

Consider the result $32 = 2^5$; using log notation, **$\log_2 32 = 5$.**
This is read as "the log of 32 to the base 2 is 5",
i.e., **5 is the index (power)** to which the base number 2 must be raised to get 32.

Similarly, $10^2 = 100$ can be rewritten using logs as $\log_{10} 100 = 2$
(the log of 100 in the base 10 is 2),
i.e., **2 is the index (power)** to which the base number 10 must be raised to get 100.

Thus, the equations $2^3 = 8$ and $\log_2 8 = 3$ are **identical and interchangeable**.

Index form	Log form
$32 = 2^5$	$\log_2 32 = 5$
$100 = 10^2$	$\log_{10} 100 = 2$
$200 = 2^x$	$\log_2 200 = x$

The **logarithm** of a number is the **power** to which the base number must be raised to get that number.

$a^x = y$ is equivalent to $\log_a y = x$

From this definition of a log, it is clear that
(i) $\log_5 25 = 2$ (ii) $\log_3 27 = 3$ (iii) $\log_2 16 = 4$ (iv) $\log_3 81 = 4$,
i.e. to what power must 5 be raised, to get 25 ...? Answer $= 2 ...$ etc.

If the log or base is not a whole number, proceed as follows.

> ### Example 1
>
> Without using a calculator, evaluate   (i) $\log_9 27$ (ii) $\log_{\frac{1}{3}} 9$ (iii) $\log_{\sqrt{2}} 8$.
>
> (i) Let $\log_9 27 = x$.
>
> $\Rightarrow 9^x = 27$
>
> $\Rightarrow (3^2)^x = 3^3$
>
> $\Rightarrow 2x = 3$
>
> $\Rightarrow x = \frac{3}{2}$
>
> (ii) Let $\log_{\frac{1}{3}} 9 = x$.
>
> $\Rightarrow \left(\frac{1}{3}\right)^x = 9$
>
> $\Rightarrow (3^{-1})^x = 3^2$
>
> $\Rightarrow -x = 2$
>
> $\Rightarrow x = -2$
>
> (iii) Let $\log_{\sqrt{2}} 8 = x$.
>
> $\Rightarrow (\sqrt{2})^x = 8$
>
> $\Rightarrow (2^{\frac{1}{2}})^x = 2^3$
>
> $\Rightarrow \frac{x}{2} = 3$
>
> $\Rightarrow x = 6$

1. The laws of logarithms

When the rules of indices are expressed in logarithm form, we produce the very important laws of logarithms.

These laws enable us to solve many complex equations.

Using your calculator, verify each of the following.

1. $\log_{10} 4 + \log_{10} 3 = \log_{10} 12 = 1.0792$

2. $\log_{10} 8 - \log_{10} 6 = \log_{10}\left(\frac{8}{6}\right) = 0.1249$

3. $\log_{10} 8^3 = 3\log_{10} 8 = 2.7093$

4. $\log_{10} 10 = 1$

5. $\log_{10} 1 = 0$

The Laws of Logarithms

1. $\log_a xy = \log_a x + \log_a y$

2. $\log_a\left(\dfrac{x}{y}\right) = \log_a x - \log_a y$

3. $\log_a x^n = n\log_a x$

4. $\log_a a = 1$

5. $\log_a 1 = 0$

6. $\log_a x = \dfrac{\log_b x}{\log_b a}$

The rules of logs apply to any base, however, the two most widely-used bases in logs are the base 10 and the base e (2.718).

Base ten logs, e.g. **$\log_{10} 1000$,** are used for calculation purposes and are referred to as **common logs**.

Base e ($= 2.718$), e.g. **$\log_e 1000$**, is used when dealing with naturally-occurring events, e.g. earthquakes, growth of colonies etc., and hence are called **natural logs** and are written **$\log_e x = \ln x$**.

Example 2

Without using a calculator, simplify the following number:

$$2\log_{10}3 + \log_{10}16 - 2\log_{10}\left(\frac{6}{5}\right)$$

$$2\log_{10}3 + \log_{10}16 - 2\log_{10}\left(\frac{6}{5}\right) = \log_{10}3^2 + \log_{10}16 - \log_{10}\left(\frac{6}{5}\right)^2$$

$$= \log_{10}(3^2 \times 16) - \log_{10}\left(\frac{36}{25}\right)$$

$$= \log_{10}\frac{9 \times 16}{\left(\frac{36}{25}\right)}$$

$$= \log_{10}100 = 2$$

Example 3

Without using a calculator, simplify the following number:

$$\log_2 128 + \log_3 45 - \log_3 5$$

$$\log_2 128 + \log_3 45 - \log_3 5 = \log_2 128 + \log_3\left(\frac{45}{5}\right) = \log_2 128 + \log_3 9$$

(Since the bases are different, these logs cannot be added!)

Let $\log_2 128 = x \Rightarrow 128 = 2^x$ also, let $\log_3 9 = y \Rightarrow 9 = 3^y$

$\qquad\qquad\qquad\qquad 2^7 = 2^x \qquad\qquad\qquad\qquad\qquad\quad 3^2 = 3^y$

$\qquad\qquad\qquad\qquad\quad 7 = x \qquad\qquad\qquad\qquad\qquad\qquad 2 = y$

$$\therefore \quad \log_2 128 + \log_3 9 = 7 + 2 = 9$$

Example 4

Evaluate the following number correct to two significant figures:

$$\log_8 11 - \log_6 4$$

Using the log key on the calculator

Press [log■□], 8, →, 11, →, −, [log■□], 6, →, 4, →, =

> → is the forward key on the cursor button.

$= 0.379438$

$= 0.38$ correct to two significant figures.

Note: For all bases,

(i) if $\log_e(e)^k = x$ also (ii) if $a^{(\log_a n)} = x$

$\Rightarrow k\log_e(e) = x$ $\Rightarrow \log_a a^{(\log_a n)} = \log_a x$ ... taking the log of both sides.

but $\log_e(e) = 1$ $\therefore \log_a n . \log_a a = \log_a x$

$\Rightarrow k = x$ $\therefore \log_a n . 1 = \log_a x$

> The log of a number to its own base is 1.

$\Rightarrow n = x$

> If e is a positive integer, $e \geqslant 2, k > 0$ (i) $\log_e(e)^k = k$ and (ii) $e^{(\log_e k)} = k$

2. Solving logarithmic equations

- When solving log equations, always check that each term has the same base. If this is not the case, *the change of base rule* must first be used to change to a common base.
- If no base is given, the equation holds true for all bases.
- If $\log_a b = \log_a c$, then $b = c$.
- If $\log_a b = k$, then $b = a^k$.
- Check all solutions to make sure they do not produce logs of negative numbers as these are not defined. (See page 492.)

Example 5

Solve the equation $2\log_3 x - \log_3(18 - x) = 1$.

$2\log_3 x - \log_3(18 - x) = 1$

$\Rightarrow \log_3 x^2 - \log_3(18 - x) = 1$

$\Rightarrow \log_3\left(\dfrac{x^2}{18 - x}\right) = 1$

$\Rightarrow \left(\dfrac{x^2}{18 - x}\right) = 3^1 = 3$

$\Rightarrow x^2 = 54 - 3x$

$\Rightarrow x^2 + 3x - 54 = 0$

$\Rightarrow (x - 6)(x + 9) = 0$

$\Rightarrow x = 6$ or $x = -9$.

If $x = -9$, the equation becomes

$2\log_3(-9) - \log_3(18 + 9) = 1$.

Since the $\log_3(-9)$ is undefined, $x = -9$ is rejected as an answer.

$\Rightarrow x = 6$.

Example 6

Solve the equation $\log_3 x + 3\log_x 3 = 4$.

This equation contains logs with different bases.
Therefore, we need to change base 3 to base x (or vice versa).

$$\log_3 x = \frac{\log_x x}{\log_x 3} = \frac{1}{\log_x 3} \quad \text{because } \log_x x = 1$$

$$\therefore \quad \log_3 x + 3\log_x 3 = 4 \quad \Rightarrow \quad \frac{1}{\log_x 3} + 3\log_x 3 = 4$$

Using the substitution $\log_x 3 = y$,

$$\frac{1}{y} + 3y = 4 \qquad\qquad \therefore \quad \log_x 3 = 1 \Rightarrow 3 = x^1$$
$$\qquad\qquad\qquad\qquad\qquad \Rightarrow 3 = x$$
$$\Rightarrow 1 + 3y^2 = 4y$$
$$3y^2 - 4y + 1 = 0 \qquad\qquad \text{or } \log_x 3 = \tfrac{1}{3} \Rightarrow 3 = x^{\frac{1}{3}}$$
$$(3y - 1)(y - 1) = 0 \qquad\qquad\qquad \Rightarrow 3^3 = x$$
$$\therefore \quad y = 1 \text{ or } y = \tfrac{1}{3} \qquad\qquad\qquad \Rightarrow 27 = x$$

$\therefore \quad x = 3$ or 27 (both solutions give positive logs and thus are acceptable).

Note: This result can be verified by repeating the procedure using the base 3 instead of the base x: $\log_x 3 = \dfrac{\log_3 3}{\log_3 x} = \dfrac{1}{\log_3 x}$.

Exercise 12.9

Without using a calculator answer questions 1–6.

1. Write down the value of each of these:
   (i) $\log_2 4$ (ii) $\log_3 81$ (iii) $\log_{10} 1000$ (iv) $\log_2 64$

2. Find the value of each of the following:
   (i) $\log_8 16$ (ii) $\log_9 27$ (iii) $\log_{16} 32$ (iv) $\log_{\frac{1}{2}} 8$ (v) $\log_{\frac{1}{3}} 81$

3. Change each of the following to index form and solve for x.
   (i) $\log_{\frac{1}{3}} 27 = x$ (ii) $\log_{\sqrt{2}} 4 = x$ (iii) $\log_8 x = 2$ (iv) $\log_{64} x = \tfrac{1}{2}$

4. Solve each of the following equations:
   (i) $\log_2 x = -1$ (ii) $\log_3 \sqrt{27} = x$ (iii) $\log_x 2 = 2$ (iv) $\log_2(0.5) = x$

5. Simplify each of the following, expressing your answers without logs.
   (i) $\log_4 2 + \log_4 32$ (ii) $\log_6 9 + \log_6 8 - \log_6 2$ (iii) $\log_6 4 + 2\log_6 3$

6. Write each of the following in the form $\log_a x$ and then simplify:
   (i) $\log_3 2 + 2\log_3 3 - \log_3 18$ (ii) $\log_8 72 - \log_8\left(\dfrac{9}{8}\right)$

7. If the $\log_3 5 = a$, find in terms of a,

     (i) $\log_3 15$ (ii) $\log_3\left(\dfrac{5}{3}\right)$ (iii) $\log_3\left(8\tfrac{1}{3}\right)$ (iv) $\log_3\left(\dfrac{25}{27}\right)$ (v) $\log_3 75$.

8. Use common logarithms (i.e. logarithms to the base 10) to find, correct to three significant figures, the value of x in each of the following:

     (i) $200 = 2^x$ (ii) $5^x = 500$ (iii) $3^{x+1} = 25$ (iv) $5^{2x+3} = 51$

9. Let $y = 2^{x-1} + 3$.

     (i) Express x in terms of y using common logarithms.

     (ii) Hence find, correct to 4 decimal places, the value of x for which $y = 8$.

10. If $\log_{10} x = 1 + a$ and $\log_{10} y = 1 - a$, show that $xy = 100$.

11. If $p = \log_a\left(\dfrac{21}{4}\right)$, $q = \log_a\left(\dfrac{7}{3}\right)$ and $r = \log_a\left(\dfrac{7}{2}\right)$, show that $p + q = 2r$.

12. If $\log_a x = 4$ and $\log_a y = 5$, find the exact values of:

     (i) $\log_a x^2 y$ (ii) $\log_a axy$ (iii) $\log_a \dfrac{\sqrt{x}}{y}$

13. Use the change of base law to show that $\log_{25} x = \tfrac{1}{2}\log_5 x$.

14. Using a calculator, evaluate each of the following logs correct to three significant figures:

     (i) $\log_{10} 4$ (ii) $\log_{10} 27$ (iii) $\log_{10} 356$ (iv) $\log_{10} 5600$
     (v) $\log_{10} 29\,000$ (vi) $\log_{10} 350\,000$ (vii) $\log_{10} 3\,870\,000$.

15. If the $\log_{10} x = 3.123$, and using the results of Q14, find the max and min values of x without using your calculator.

16. Find, correct to three significant figures, the value of each of the following:

     (i) $\log_3 15 - \log_2 5$ (ii) $\log_5 6 - \log_2 18$ (iii) $\log_2 42 - \log_3 215$

17. Evaluate   (i) $\log_{27} 81$ (ii) $\log_{32} 8$.

18. Show that $\log_b a = \dfrac{1}{\log_a b}$.

19. If $x > 0$ and $x \neq 1$, show that $\dfrac{1}{\log_2 x} + \dfrac{1}{\log_3 x} + \dfrac{1}{\log_5 x} = \dfrac{1}{\log_{30} x}$.

20. If $\log_r p = \log_r 2 + 3\log_r q$, use the laws of logarithms to express p in terms of q.

21. If $\log_3 a + \log_9 a = \tfrac{3}{4}$, $a > 0$, find the exact value of a.

22. Find the value of $3\ln 41.5 - \ln 250$, correct to three significant figures.

Solve the following log equations:

23. $\log_2(x - 2) + \log_2 x = 3$

24. $\log_{10}(x^2 + 6) - \log_{10}(x^2 - 1) = 1$

25. $\log 2x - \log(x - 7) = \log 3$

26. $\log(2x + 3) + \log(x - 2) = 2\log x$

27. $\log_{10}(17 - 3x) + \log_{10} x = 1$

28. $\log_{10}(x^2 - 4x - 11) = 0.$

29. Given that $2\log_2 x = y$ and $\log_2(2x) = y + 4$, find the value of x.

30. If $\log_6 x + \log_6 y = 1$, $x, y > 0$, show that $x = \dfrac{6}{y}$.

Hence solve the simultaneous equations $\log_6 x + \log_6 y = 1$
$$5x + y = 17.$$

31. Use the change of base rule to solve each of the following equations:

(i) $4\log_x 2 - \log_2 x - 3 = 0$ (ii) $2\log_4 x + 1 = \log_x 4.$

Section 12.10 The graph of $y = \log_a(x)$

Using computer software, the graphs of $\log_{10}(x)$, $\log_e(x)$ [i.e. $\ln(x)$] and $\log_2(x)$ are drawn in the domain $0 \leq x \leq 10$.

Comparing the graphs, we conclude that $y = \log_a(x)$ has the following properties:

1. $\log_{(\text{any base})} 1 = 0.$
2. $\log_2 2 = \log_e e = \log_{10} 10 = 1.$
3. All graphs of log functions are increasing.
4. $y = \log_a(x)$ is defined for $x > 0$ **only**.
5. $y = \log_a(0)$ is not defined.
6. The y-axis is a vertical asymptote to all curves.

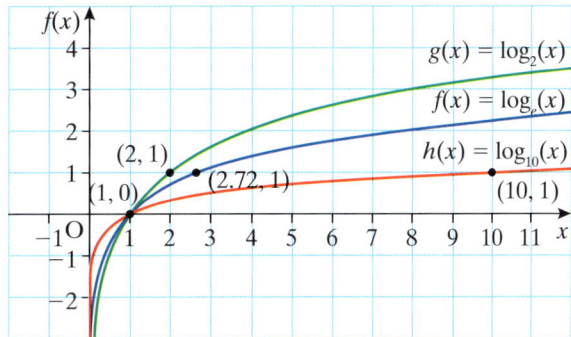

Comparing $\log_a(x)$ with $y = a^x$

If we let $a = 2$; comparing $y = 2^x$ and $y = \log_2(x)$, we have

x	$y = 2^x$	x	$y = \log_2 x$
0	$y = 2^0 = 1$	1	$y = \log_2 1 = 0$
1	$y = 2^1 = 2$	2	$y = \log_2 2 = 1$
2	$y = 2^2 = 4$	4	$y = \log_2 4 = 2$
3	$y = 2^3 = 8$	8	$y = \log_2 8 = 3$
4	$y = 2^4 = 16$	16	$y = \log_2 16 = 4$

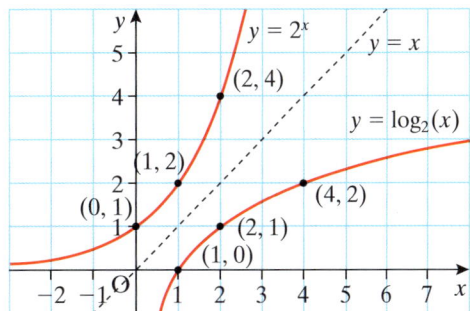

The points $(0, 1), (1, 2), (2, 4), (3, 8), (4, 16), \ldots$ are on the curve $y = 2^x$.

The points $(1, 0), (2, 1), (4, 2), (8, 3), (16, 4), \ldots$ are on the curve $y = \log_2(x)$.

$\therefore$ $y = \log_2(x)$ is the inverse function of $y = 2^x$.

Also, $y = \log_{10}x$ is the inverse function of $y = 10^x$.

The graphs of $y = 2^x$ and $y = \log_2(x)$ reflect in the line $x = y$.

Exercise 12.10

1. Using your knowledge of indices, explain properties 1, 2 and 5 on the previous page.

2. Using a graphics calculator or computer software, plot $y = 10^x$ and $y = \log_{10}x$ on the same axes and find the axis of symmetry.
   From your graph, estimate correct to one place of decimals, the value of $y = 10^{1.5}$ by enlarging the scale on the y-axis.

3. Consider the function $y = \log_3 x$.

   (i) Complete the following table.

x		$\frac{1}{9}$		1	3	
$y = \log_3 x$			-1			2

   (ii) Using the values in this table, sketch the graph of $y = \log_3 x$.
   (iii) Estimate the value of $\log_3 2.5$ from your graph.

4. On the same axes, sketch the graphs of

   (i) $y = 5^x, 0 \leqslant x \leqslant 2$ (ii) $y = \log_5 x, 0 < x \leqslant 25$
   (iii) What is the relationship between the two graphs?

5. On the same axes, sketch the graphs of

   (i) $y = \log_2 x$ at $x = 1, 2, 4, 6, 8$.
   (ii) $y = \log_2 2x$ at $x = 1, 2, 4, 6, 8$.
       Use the log rule: $\log_2 xy = \log_2 x + \log_2 y$, to explain the transformation that has occurred in the new graph.
   (iii) $y = \log_2(x - 2)$ at $x = 3, 4, 6, 8, 10$.
        By comparing this graph with the graph of $y = \log_2 x$, describe the transformation that has occurred.

6. On the same axes, sketch the graphs of $y = \log_{10}x$, $y = \log_{10}\frac{x}{2}$ and $y = \log_{10}(x + 2)$.

7. Given $y = 3^{x+2} - 5$,
   (i) express x in terms of y using common logarithms.
   (ii) If $y = 30$, find correct to 3 places of decimals, the value of x.

8. Copy this graph of the function $y = \log_{10}x$ into your copybook (or using a computer) and use it to draw rough sketches of the following functions:
   (i) $y = \log_{10}x + 2$ (ii) $y = \log_{10}(x + 2)$
   (iii) $y = \log_{10}x - 2$ (iv) $y = 2\log_{10}x$
   (v) $y = -\log_{10}x$

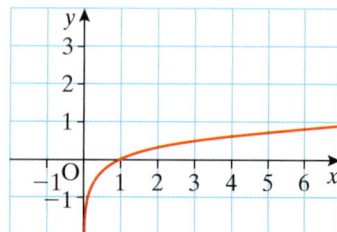

9. Copy this graph of the function $y = \log_{10} x$ into your copybook and use it to draw rough sketches of the following functions:

(i) $y = \log_{10}(2x)$
(ii) $y = \log_{10}\left(\dfrac{x}{2}\right)$

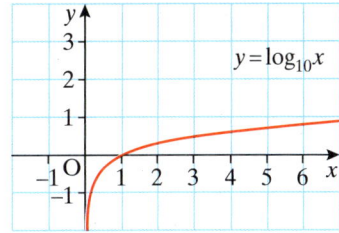

10. Copy this graph of the function $y = 2^x$ into your copybook and use it to draw rough sketches of the following functions:

(i) $y = 2^x + 1$
(ii) $y = 1 - 2^x$
(iii) $y = 2^{x+1}$
(iv) $y = \left(\dfrac{1}{2}\right) \cdot 2^x$

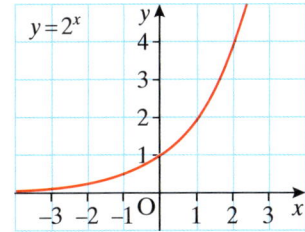

Section 12.11 Problem-solving with exponential and log functions

As stated already, exponential and log functions are used to model a wide variety of problems.

The loudness of sounds, the acidity of a solution and the intensity of earthquakes on the Richter scale are some examples, among many, of their application.

Example 1

The acidity of a substance is determined by the ion concentration formula $pH = -\log[H^+]$, where a pH of 7 is defined as neutral, <7 acidic, >7 alkaline. Determine the acidity of each of the following substances.

(a) Apple juice with a $[H^+]$ ion concentration of 0.0003.
(b) Ammonia with a $[H^+]$ ion concentration of 1.3×10^{-9}.

(a) $[H^+] = 0.0003 \implies pH = -\log[H^+]$
$$= -\log[0.0003]$$
$$= 3.52 \quad \therefore \quad \text{the apple juice is acidic}$$

(b) $[H^+] = 1.3 \times 10^{-9} \implies pH = -\log[H^+]$
$$= -\log[1.3 \times 10^{-9}]$$
$$= 8.87 \quad \therefore \quad \text{the ammonia solution is alkaline}$$

Example 2

The loudness of a sound of intensity I is given by the formula $dB = 10 \log\left(\dfrac{I}{I_o}\right)$,

where dB is measured in decibels and I_o is the threshold intensity of hearing $(I_o = 1 \times 10^{-12}\, \text{Wm}^{-2})$.

(a) Find the loudness (in decibels) of a sound at the threshold of hearing.

(b) Given that prolonged exposure to sounds over 85 decibels can cause hearing damage, and that a gunshot from a .22 rifle has an intensity of $I = 2.5 \times 10^{13}\, I_o$, should you wear ear protection when firing this gun?

(a) Threshold of hearing $= 1 \times 10^{-12}\, \text{Wm}^{-2}$

$$dB = 10 \log\left(\frac{I}{I_o}\right) = 10 \log\left(\frac{1 \times 10^{-12}}{1 \times 10^{-12}}\right) = 10 \log 1 = 0\, dB, \text{ i.e. no loudness.}$$

(b) $I = 2.5 \times 10^{13}\, I_o$

$$dB = 10 \log\left(\frac{I}{I_o}\right) = 10 \log\frac{2.5 \times 10^{13}\, I_o}{I_o} = 10 \log 2.5 \times 10^{13} = 134\, dB.$$

Yes, since the loudness is well above 85 dB, you should wear ear protection.

Compound interest (increasing value)

The final value, €A, of a sum of money, €P, invested at a rate of i (expressed in decimal form) compound interest for t years, is given by the formula $A = P(1 + i)^t$. It is often required that we calculate the time, t (the index), for a particular investment to mature. This can be done by using logs as follows;

If $\qquad A = P(1 + i)^t$,

$\Rightarrow \qquad \dfrac{A}{P} = (1 + i)^t$ ... dividing both sides by P

$\Rightarrow \quad \ln\left(\dfrac{A}{P}\right) = \ln(1 + i)^t$ ... taking the natural log of both sides

$\Rightarrow \quad \ln\left(\dfrac{A}{P}\right) = t.\ln(1 + i)$ ... $\ln B^n = n.\ln B$

$\Rightarrow \quad \dfrac{\ln\left(\dfrac{A}{P}\right)}{\ln(1 + i)} = t.$

Example 3

How long would it take €5000 to increase in value to €6000, if invested in a credit union at a yearly compound interest rate of 2%?

Since $A = P(1 + i)^t$, where €P is invested for t years at $i\%$,

$A =$ €6000 $\qquad P =$ €5000 $\qquad i = 2\% = 0.02 \qquad \therefore \quad 1 + i = 1.02$

$\Rightarrow$ €6000 = €5000 $(1.02)^t$

$\dfrac{6000}{5000} = (1.02)^t$

$1.2 = (1.02)^t$

$\ln 1.2 = \ln(1.02)^t$ ... taking the natural log of both sides

$\ln 1.2 = t.\ln 1.02$

$\dfrac{\ln 1.2}{\ln 1.02} = t$

Method 2

$1.2 = (1.02)^t$

$\Rightarrow \quad \log_{(1.02)} 1.2 = t$

$\Rightarrow \quad t = 9.2069 = 9.21$ years.

9.21 years $= t \cong 9$ years and 77 days

Depreciation (reducing value)

If a quantity reduces by a fixed amount over a given term (e.g. per annum), the same equation can be adapted to track the reducing value over time.

The present population P then becomes $P = P_0(1 - i)^t$ where P_0 was the initial population.

For example, if the population of red squirrels is reducing at a rate of 5% per year, then $P = P_0(1 - 0.05)^t = P_0(0.95)^t$ is the number of red squirrels after "t" years.

Example 4

The population of red squirrels in a given region was estimated to be 5000 at the start of 2003. Assuming a rate of decrease of 5% per year, estimate the size of the population in 2013.

Since $P = P_0(1 - i)^t$ and $i = 5\% = 0.05$,

and given that $P_0 = 5000$ and $t = 10$ years,

$\therefore \quad P = 5000(1 - 0.05)^{10} = 5000(0.95)^{10} = 2994$ squirrels

Doubling time

The **doubling time** is the time required for a quantity to double in size or value.

If a quantity is growing exponentially, then the number (or value) present at time t can be expressed by $y = A.e^{bt}$, where A is the amount or value at the start (i.e. $t = 0$) and b is a growth constant, specific to a particular organism.

If this quantity doubles in size, then there are 2A present.

∴ $2A = Ae^{bT}$, where T is the time taken to produce $2A$, i.e. the doubling time.

∴ $2 = e^{bT}$

∴ $\ln 2 = \ln e^{bT} = bT \ln e = bT$

$\Rightarrow \dfrac{\ln 2}{b} = T$, the doubling time.

> $\ln x^n = n.\ln x$
>
> and $\ln e = 1$

Example 5

A certain type of bacteria is growing exponentially, where $y = Ae^{bt}$ is the number of bacteria present after t (hours) and b is the growth constant. Under certain conditions, the bacteria doubles in population every 6.5 hours. If at the start of the experiment under these conditions there are 100 bacteria present, find (i) the growth constant b (ii) how many bacteria will be present after 2 days.

Since $y = Ae^{bt}$, then $200 = 100e^{6.5b}$ ... since 100 doubles to 200 in 6.5 hours

$\quad\quad\quad ∴ \quad 2 = e^{6.5b}$

$\quad\quad\quad ∴ \quad \ln 2 = \ln e^{6.5b} = 6.5b \ln e = 6.5b.$

(i) The growth constant $b = \dfrac{\ln 2}{6.5} = 0.1066$ per hour.

(ii) Two days = 48 hours

The number present after 48 hours $= 100\, e^{0.1066 \times 48}$

$\quad\quad\quad\quad\quad\quad\quad\quad\quad\quad\quad\quad = 16\,680$ bacteria.

Exercise 12.11

1. Anne invests €5000 in a fixed-term account paying 0.6% per month compound interest. Find
   (i) the money in Anne's account after
      (a) 1 month   (b) 2 months   (c) 3 months
   (ii) a formula for the amount Anne has saved after t-months
   (iii) the minimum time for which Anne needs to invest her money if she wants to double her money.

2. A biologist puts 100 bacteria into a controlled environment at the start of an experiment.
   Six hours later, she returns and counts 450 bacteria in the colony.
   Assuming exponential growth of the form $y = Ae^{bt}$ where b is the growth constant, find a value for b, correct to two decimal places.

3. Milk for a baby, which was heated up to 45°C, is left to cool. The temperature $T°C$ of the milk, after t minutes left cooling, is given by the rule $T = 15 + 30 \times 10^{-0.02t}$.

(i) Verify that the initial temperature was 45°C.

(ii) If the milk is to be given to a baby when it has cooled to 35°C, find how long it has to be left to cool to reach this temperature.

(iii) Use this rule to find the room temperature, explaining your answer.

4. The loudness L (measured in dB) of a sound is given by the formula $L = 10 \log_{10}\left(\dfrac{I}{I_o}\right)$, where I_o is the threshold of hearing $(1 \times 10^{-12}\,\text{Wm}^{-2})$ and I the intensity of the sound.

(i) If thunder can have a range of loudness between $100-110\,\text{dB}$, what is the corresponding range of intensities in Wm^{-2}?

(ii) The threshold of pain is generally assumed to be $10\,\text{Wm}^{-2}$. Find in dB the loudness of a sound that starts to cause pain.

> Watts per m² = Wm⁻²

Watts per m^2 = Wm^{-2}

5. The amplitude of an earthquake is given by $A = 10^M$, where M is the magnitude (size) of the quake on the Richter scale. The energy released by the earthquake is $E \cong 10^{1.5M + 4.8}$ joules. Using the rules of logs, find a and b such that $E = 10^a A^b$, $a, b \in Q$.

6. The consumer price index (CPI) measures the cost of goods and services on a yearly basis. Assuming that a commodity was valued at €100 in 2000, and that the CPI has been rising exponentially at 4.5% since that year, find

(i) the value of that commodity in €, t years after 2000

(ii) the predicted cost of that commodity in 2010.

(iii) Using the same predicted rate of increase, what was the value of that commodity in 1995?

7. During the early stages of development, the weight W kg of a certain mammal, t months after birth, is given by the formula $W = 0.6 \times 1.15^t$.

(i) What was the weight of the mammal at birth?

(ii) State the growth constant per month as a percentage.

(iii) How long does it take this mammal to double its weight?

8. The decay of Polonium-210, a radioactive substance, is given by the formula $M = M_0 e^{-kt}$, where M_0 is the mass at the start,
$\qquad$ M is the mass after t days,
$\qquad$ k is a decay constant specific to Polonium.

If $M = 10\,\text{g}$ when $t = 0$, and $M = 5\,\text{g}$ when $t = 140$ days, find

(i) the value of M_0 and k

(ii) the mass of Polonium after 70 days

(iii) after how many days there will be 2 g of Polonium left.

Section 12.12 Proofs by induction

Many theorems in mathematics are proven true using the method of mathematical induction.

To prove a statement true by induction, we follow clearly-defined steps.

(i) The statement is proven true for some fixed value, usually $n = 1$ or $n = 2$.

(ii) The statement is then assumed true for $n = k$.

(iii) Based on this assumption, we must show that the statement is true for $n = k + 1$.

(iv) In conclusion, a "rolling proof" is formed:

    a. Since it was true for $n = 1$,

    b. it is now true for $n = 1 + 1 = 2$.

    c. Since it is true for $n = 2$, it is true for $n = 2 + 1 = 3$, etc.

    d. It is therefore true for all values of n.

Example 1

Prove that **for all values of n**, $1 + 2 + 3 + 4 + \ldots n = \dfrac{n}{2}(n + 1)$.

Proof:

(i) Prove the statement true for $n = 1$.

$$\Rightarrow 1 = \tfrac{1}{2}(1 + 1) = \tfrac{1}{2}(2) = 1, \text{ which is true.}$$

(ii) Assume true for $n = k$.

$$\Rightarrow 1 + 2 + 3 + 4 + \ldots k = \frac{k}{2}(k + 1).$$

(iii) Based on this assumption, we must show that the statement is true for $n = k + 1$.

$$1 + 2 + 3 + 4 + \ldots k + (k + 1) = \frac{k}{2}(k + 1) + (k + 1) \quad \ldots \text{adding } (k + 1) \text{ to both sides.}$$

$$= (k + 1)\left(\frac{k}{2} + 1\right) \quad \ldots \text{factorising } (k + 1) \text{ from RHS.}$$

$$= (k + 1)\left(\frac{k + 2}{2}\right) \quad \ldots \text{getting a common denominator.}$$

$$= \left(\frac{k + 1}{2}\right)(k + 2) \quad \ldots \text{re-arranging the denominator.}$$

$$= \left(\frac{k + 1}{2}\right)[(k + 1) + 1]$$

$\therefore$ It is true for $n = k + 1$.

(iv) But since it is true for $n = 1$, it now must be true for $n = 1 + 1 = 2$. And if it is true for $n = 2$, it is true for $n = 2 + 1 = 3$, … etc.

(v) Therefore, it is true for all values of n.

Note 1: Although we could prove this statement true for many discrete values of n, the important feature of this method of proof is that it proves the statement true **for all values of n**.

Note 2: Mathematical induction is not a means of discovering a result, but when we have a result that seems to be true, this method provides us with a rigorous proof.

Note 3: Proof by induction can be applied to several different categories of results including;

    (i) Results involving **series of numbers**   e.g. $1 + 2 + 3 + 4 + \ldots n = \frac{n}{2}(n + 1)$.

    (ii) Results involving **factors of expressions**   e.g. $10^n - 7^n$ is divisible by 3.

    (iii) Results involving **inequalities**   e.g. $3^n > 3n + 1$, for $n \geqslant 2$.

Example 2

Prove that for all values of $n \in N$, $3 + 3^2 + 3^3 + 3^4 + 3^5 + \ldots 3^n = \frac{3}{2}(3^n - 1)$.

Proof:

(i) Prove the statement true for $n = 1$.

$$3^1 = \tfrac{3}{2}(3^1 - 1) = \tfrac{3}{2}(2) = 3 \;\; \ldots \text{which is true.}$$

(ii) Assume true for $n = k$.

$$3 + 3^2 + 3^3 + 3^4 + 3^5 + \ldots 3^k = \tfrac{3}{2}(3^k - 1).$$

(iii) Based on this assumption, we must now show that the statement is true for $n = k + 1$.

$$3 + 3^2 + 3^3 + 3^4 + 3^5 + \ldots 3^k + \mathbf{3^{k+1}} = \tfrac{3}{2}(3^k - 1) + \mathbf{3^{k+1}}. \;\; \ldots \text{adding } 3^{k+1}$$
$$\text{to both sides.}$$

$$= \tfrac{3}{2}(3^k - 1) + 3^k.3^1$$

$$= 3\left(\frac{(3^k - 1)}{2} + 3^k \right) \;\; \ldots \text{factorising 3.}$$

$$= 3\left(\frac{3^k - 1 + 2.3^k}{2} \right) \;\; \ldots \text{common}$$
$$\text{denominator.}$$

$$= \tfrac{3}{2}(3.3^k - 1) \;\; \ldots \text{rearranging.}$$

$$= \tfrac{3}{2}(3^{k+1} - 1)$$

    $\therefore$ It is true for $n = k + 1$.

(iv) But since it is true for $n = 1$, it now must be true for $n = 1 + 1 = 2$. And if it is true for $n = 2$, it is true for $n = 2 + 1 = 3$, ... etc.

(v) Therefore, it is true for all values of n.

Example 3

Prove by induction that $\frac{1}{1.2} + \frac{1}{2.3} + \frac{1}{3.4} + \ldots \frac{1}{n(n+1)} = \frac{n}{n+1}, n \in N.$

Proof:

(i) Prove the statement true for $n = 1$.

$$\frac{1}{1(1+1)} = \frac{1}{1+1} = \frac{1}{2} \ldots \text{which is true.}$$

(ii) Assume true for $n = k$.

$$\frac{1}{1.2} + \frac{1}{2.3} + \frac{1}{3.4} + \ldots \frac{1}{k(k+1)} = \frac{k}{k+1}, k \in N.$$

(iii) Based on this assumption, we must now show that the statement is true for $n = k + 1$.

$$\frac{1}{1.2} + \frac{1}{2.3} + \frac{1}{3.4} + \ldots \frac{1}{k(k+1)} + \frac{1}{(k+1)(k+2)} = \frac{k}{k+1} + \frac{1}{(k+1)(k+2)}$$

$$= \frac{k(k+2) + 1}{(k+1)(k+2)}$$

$$= \frac{k^2 + 2k + 1}{(k+1)(k+2)}$$

$$= \frac{\cancel{(k+1)}(k+1)}{\cancel{(k+1)}(k+2)} = \frac{(k+1)}{(k+1)+1}$$

∴ It is true for $n = k + 1$.

(iv) But since it is true for $n = 1$, it now must be true for $n = 1 + 1 = 2$. And if it is true for $n = 2$, it is true for $n = 2 + 1 = 3, \ldots$ etc.

(v) Therefore, it is true for all values of n.

Exercise 12.12(A)

In each of the following questions, prove the results by mathematical induction for all positive integer values of n.

1. $2 + 4 + 6 + 8 + \ldots 2n = \sum\limits_{n=1}^{n} 2n = n(n+1).$

2. $1 + 4 + 7 + 10 + \ldots (3n - 2) = \frac{n}{2}(3n - 1).$

3. $1(2) + 2(3) + 3(4) + 4(5) + \ldots n(n+1) = \sum\limits_{n=1}^{n} n(n+1) = \frac{n}{3}(n+1)(n+2).$

4. $\frac{1}{2(3)} + \frac{1}{3(4)} + \frac{1}{4(5)} + \frac{1}{5(6)} + \ldots \frac{1}{(n+1)(n+2)} = \frac{n}{2(n+2)}.$

5. $\frac{1}{4(5)} + \frac{1}{5(6)} + \frac{1}{6(7)} + \frac{1}{7(8)} + \ldots \frac{1}{(n+3)(n+4)} = \sum\limits_{n=1}^{n} \frac{1}{(n+3)(n+4)} = \frac{n}{4(n+4)}.$

6. $1^3 + 2^3 + 3^3 + 4^3 + \ldots n^3 = \sum_{n=1}^{n} n^3 = \dfrac{n^2}{4}(n+1)^2.$

7. $\sum_{n=1}^{n} n(n+2) = \dfrac{n(n+1)(2n+7)}{6}.$

8. $x + x^2 + x^3 + x^4 + \ldots x^n = \dfrac{x(x^n-1)}{x-1}, x \neq 1.$

Divisibility proofs

> ### Example 4
>
> Prove that for all $n \in N$, 3 is a factor of $4^n - 1$.
>
> **Proof:**
>
>   (i) Prove the statement true for $n = 1$.
>
>   3 is a factor of $4^1 - 1 = 3$ ... true.
>
> (ii) Assume true for $n = k$.
>
> $\Rightarrow$ 3 is a factor of $4^k - 1, k \in N$.
>
> (iii) Based on this assumption, we must now show that the statement is true for $n = k + 1$.
>
>   Is 3 a factor of $4^{k+1} - 1$?
>
> $$= 4^k.4^1 - 1$$
> $$= 4^k.(3+1) - 1$$
> $$= 3.4^k + 1.4^k - 1$$
> $$= 3.4^k + (4^k - 1).$$
>
>   Since 3.4^k is divisible by 3 and $(4^k - 1)$ is assumed divisible by 3,
>
> $\therefore$ $3.4^k + (4^k - 1)$ is divisible by 3.
>
> $\therefore$ It is true for $n = k + 1$.
>
> (iv) But since it is true for $n = 1$, it now must be true for $n = 1 + 1 = 2$.
>
>   And if it is true for $n = 2$, it is true for $n = 2 + 1 = 3$, ... etc.
>
> (v) Therefore, it is true for all values of n.

Example 5

Prove by induction that $8^n - 7n + 6$ is divisible by 7 for all $n \in N$.

Proof:

(i) Prove the statement true for $n = 1$.

$\quad$ 7 is a factor of $8^1 - 7.1 + 6 = 7$ ... which is true.

(ii) Assume true for $n = k$.

$\quad \Rightarrow$ 7 is a factor of $8^k - 7k + 6, k \in N$.

(iii) Based on this assumption, we must now show that the statement is true for $n = k + 1$.

$\quad$ Is 7 a factor of $8^{k+1} - 7(k + 1) + 6$?

$$= 8^k.8^1 - 7k - 7 + 6$$
$$= 8^k.(7 + 1) - 7k - 7 + 6$$
$$= 7.8^k + 1.8^k - 7k - 7 + 6$$
$$= 7.8^k + (8^k - 7k + 6) - 7$$

Since 7.8^k is divisible by 7, $(8^k - 7k + 6)$ is assumed divisible by 7 and -7 is divisible by 7,

$\quad \therefore \quad 8^{k+1} - 7(k + 1) + 6$ is divisible by 7.

$\quad \therefore \quad$ It is true for $n = k + 1$.

(iv) But since it is true for $n = 1$, it now must be true for $n = 1 + 1 = 2$.

And if it is true for $n = 2$, it is true for $n = 2 + 1 = 3$, ... etc.

(v) Therefore, it is true for all values of n.

Example 6

Show that $n(n + 1)(n + 2)$ is divisible by 3 for $n \in N$.

Proof:

(i) Prove the statement true for $n = 1$.

$\quad$ 3 is a factor of $n(n + 1)(n + 2) = 1(1 + 1)(1 + 2)$
$$= 6. \text{ ... which is true.}$$

(ii) Assume true for $n = k$.

$\quad \Rightarrow$ 3 is a factor of $k(k + 1)(k + 2), k \in N$.

(iii) Based on this assumption, we must now show that the statement is true for $n = k + 1$.

Is 3 a factor of $(k + 1)(k + 1 + 1)(k + 1 + 2)$?

$$= (k + 1)(k + 2)[k + 3]$$
$$= (k + 1)(k + 2)k + (k + 1)(k + 2)3$$
$$= k(k + 1)(k + 2) + 3(k + 1)(k + 2)$$

Since 3 is assumed a factor of $k(k + 1)(k + 2)$, and 3 is a factor of $3(k + 1)(k + 2)$,

$\therefore$ $(k + 1)(k + 2)(k + 3)$ is divisible by 3.

$\therefore$ It is true for $n = k + 1$.

(iv) But since it is true for $n = 1$, it now must be true for $n = 1 + 1 = 2$. And if it is true for $n = 2$, it is true for $n = 2 + 1 = 3, \ldots$ etc.

(v) Therefore, it is true for all values of n.

Exercise 12.12(B)

Prove by induction that

1. $6^n - 1$ is divisible by 5 for $n \in N$.

2. $5^n - 1$ is divisible by 4 for $n \in N$.

3. $9^n - 5^n$ is divisible by 4 for $n \in N$.

4. $3^{2n} - 1$ is divisible by 8 for $n \in N$.

5. $7^n - 2^n$ is divisible by 5 for $n \in N$.

6. $7^{2n+1} + 1$ is divisible by 8 for $n \in N$.

7. $2^{3n-1} + 3$ is divisible by 7 for $n \in N$.

8. $5^n - 4n + 3$ is divisible by 4 for $n \in N$.

9. $7^n + 4^n + 1$ is divisible by 6 for $n \in N$.

10. $n(n + 1)(2n + 1)$ is divisible by 3 for $n \in N$.

11. $n^3 - n$ is divisible by 3 for $n \in N$.

12. $13^n - 6^{n-2}$ is divisible by 7 for $n \geqslant 2$, $n \in N$.

Inequality proofs

When dealing with inequalities we noted two important deductions, namely

   (i) If $a > b$, then $a - b > 0$

   (ii) (any real number $)^2 > 0$.

Example 7

Prove by induction that $2^n > n^2$ for $n \geq 5, n \in N$.

Proof:

  (i) Prove the statement true for $n = 5$.
$$2^5 > 5^2$$
$$32 > 25 \ \text{... which is true.}$$

  (ii) Assume true for $n = k, k \geq 5$.
$$\Rightarrow 2^k > k^2, k \in N \text{ and } k \geq 5.$$

  (iii) Based on this assumption, we must now show that the statement is true for $n = k + 1$.

        Is $\ 2^{k+1} > (k + 1)^2$?

        Since $\ 2^k > k^2$ (assumed)

        $\therefore \ \ 2^k . 2 > 2k^2$

        $\therefore \ \ 2^{k+1} > 2k^2$

  $\therefore$ we need to prove that $2k^2 > (k + 1)^2$.
$$2k^2 > k^2 + 2k + 1$$
$$k^2 - 2k - 1 > 0$$
$$k^2 - 2k + 1 - 1 - 1 > 0 \ \text{... completing the square by adding and}$$
$$k^2 - 2k + 1 - 2 > 0 \ \ \ \text{subtracting half the coefficient of } k \text{ squared.}$$
$$(k - 1)^2 - 2 > 0 \ \text{which is true for } k \geq 5.$$

      $\therefore \ \ 2^{k+1} > 2k^2 > (k + 1)^2$

      $\therefore$ It is true for $n = k + 1$.

  (iv) But since it is true for $n = 5$, it now must be true for $n = 5 + 1 = 6$. And if it is true for $n = 6$, it is true for $n = 6 + 1 = 7, \ldots$ etc.

  (v) Therefore, it is true for all values of $n \geq 5, n \in N$.

Example 8

Prove by induction that $n! > 2^n, n \geq 4, n \in N$.

Proof:

  (i) Prove the statement true for $n = 4$.
$$4! > 2^4$$
$$24 > 16 \ \text{... which is true.}$$

(ii) Assume true for $n = k, k \geqslant 4$.

$\Rightarrow k! > 2^k, k \in N$ and $k \geqslant 4$.

(iii) Based on this assumption, we must now show that the statement is true for $n = k + 1$.

Is $(k + 1)! > 2^{k+1}$?

Is $(k + 1)k! > 2^k . 2$? ... $(k + 1)k! = (k + 1)!$

Since $k! > 2^k$ (assumed),

$\therefore \quad (k + 1)k! > (k + 1)2^k$

$\therefore \quad$ we need to prove that $(k + 1)2^k > 2^k . 2$

$(k + 1)2^k > 2.2^k$ which is obviously true if $k > 1$.

$\therefore \quad (k + 1)! > 2^{k+1}$

$\therefore \quad$ It is true for $n = k + 1$.

(iv) But since it is true for $n = 4$, it now must be true for $n = 4 + 1 = 5$.

And if it is true for $n = 5$, it is true for $n = 5 + 1 = 6, \dots$ etc.

(v) Therefore, it is true for all values of $n \geqslant 4, n \in N$.

Example 9

Prove that $(1 + x)^n \geqslant 1 + nx$ for $n \geqslant 1, n \in N, x \in R$.

Proof:

(i) Prove the statement true for $n = 1$.

$\Rightarrow (1 + x)^1 \geqslant 1 + 1.x$ ... which is true.

(ii) Assume true for $n = k, k \geqslant 1$.

$(1 + x)^k \geqslant 1 + kx, k \in N$ and $k \geqslant 1$.

(iii) Based on this assumption, we must now show that the statement is true for $n = k + 1$.

Is $(1 + x)^{k+1} \geqslant 1 + (k + 1)x$?

Is $(1 + x)^k(1 + x) \geqslant 1 + kx + x$?

Since $(1 + x)^k \geqslant 1 + kx$ ... (assumed).

$\therefore \quad (1 + x)^k(1 + x) \geqslant (1 + kx)(1 + x)$

$\therefore \quad$ we need to prove that $(1 + kx)(1 + x) \geqslant 1 + kx + x$

$1 + x + kx + kx^2 \geqslant 1 + kx + x$.

$\Rightarrow kx^2 \geqslant 0$ which is true for $k \geqslant 1$ and $x \in R$.

$\therefore \quad$ It is true for $n = k + 1$.

(iv) But since it is true for $n = 1$, it now must be true for $n = 1 + 1 = 2$.

And if it is true for $n = 2$, it is true for $n = 2 + 1 = 3, \dots$ etc.

(v) Therefore, it is true for all values of $n \geqslant 1, n \in N$.

Exercise 12.12(C)

Prove by induction each of the following statements:

1. $2^n > 2n + 1$ for $n \geqslant 3, n \in N$.

2. $3^n > n^2$ for $n \geqslant 2, n \in N$.

3. $3^n > 2n + 2$ for $n \geqslant 2, n \in N$.

4. $n! > 2^{n-1}$ for $n \geqslant 3, n \in N$.

5. $(n + 1)! > 2^n$ for $n \geqslant 2, n \in N$.

6. $(1 + 2x)^n \geqslant 1 + 2nx$ for $x > 0, n \in N$.

7. $(1 + ax)^n \geqslant 1 + anx$ for $a > 0, x > 0, n \in N$.

Revision Exercise 12 (Core)

1. Find the values of x that satisfy the following inequality:

$$-1 \leqslant \frac{2x + 4}{3} \leqslant 2 , x \in R.$$

2. (a) Using the log and 10^x keys on your calculator, evaluate each of the following:
    (i) $10^{3.5}$ (ii) $\log_{10} 4.5$ (iii) 10^{3t}, where $t = 0.04$ (iv) $\log 5n$, where $n = 100$.
   (b) Using the ln and e^x keys on the calculator, evaluate
    (i) $e^{3.4}$ (ii) $ln\, 589$ (iii) $e^{-0.02t - 4}$, where $t = 40$ (iv) $\ln\left(\dfrac{10}{k}\right)$, where $k = 3.7$.

3. An exponential function is defined by $f(x) = 3 \times 4^x$. Find
   (i) the value of a if $(a, 6)$ lies on $f(x)$
   (ii) the value of b if $\left(\dfrac{-1}{2}, b\right)$ lies on $f(x)$.

4. Solve the equation $|x - 8| = 3$.

5. Solve each of the following:
   (i) $5^{2n} \times 25^{2n-1} = 625$ (ii) $27^{n-2} = 9^{3n+2}$

6. A graph of the exponential curve $y = a2^x + b$
   is shown in the diagram.

   (i) Write down two equations in terms of a and b.
   (ii) Solve the simultaneous equations to find the
       values of a and b.

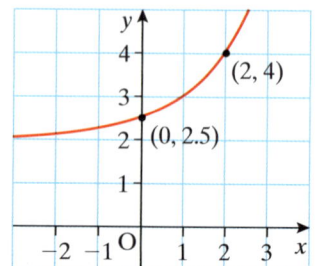

7. The graphs of the log functions
    (i) $\ln(x)$
    (ii) $\ln(x + 1)$
    (iii) $\ln(x) + 1$
    are shown in this diagram. Identify each curve,
    giving a reason for your answers.

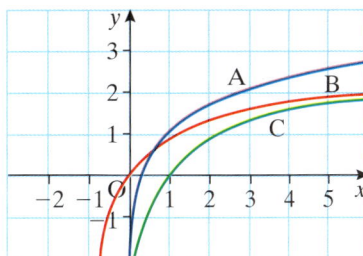

8. Solve the equation $\ln(x - 1) + \ln(x + 2) = \ln(6x - 8)$.

9. $y = Ae^{bt}$. Given that $y = 6$ when $t = 1$, and $y = 8$ when $t = 2$, find the values
    of A and b.

10. Find the values of a and b if the graph of $y = a\log_2(x - b)$ passes through the
    points $(5, 2)$ and $(7, 4)$.

11. Solve $32^{x-1} = 28$ for x, correct to two places of decimals.

12. Prove by induction that
$$3 + 6 + 9 + 12 + \ldots . 3n = \frac{3n}{2}(n + 1), \text{ for all positive integer values.}$$

13. Prove by induction that
    $8^n + 6$ is divisible by 7 for $n \in N$.

14. Prove by induction that
    $n^2 > 4n + 3$ for $n \geqslant 5, n \in N$.

Revision Exercise 12 (Advanced)

1. Find the range of values of x that satisfies
    (i) $3x + 4 < x^2 - 6$ (ii) $x^2 - 6 < 9 - 2x$.
    Hence find the range of values of x that satisfies $3x + 4 < x^2 - 6 < 9 - 2x$

2. The mass M of a radioactive material remaining after t years is given by the formula
    $M = 30 \times 2^{-0.001t}$ grams. Find
    (i) the original mass
    (ii) how long it would take for the material to decay to 10 grams
    (iii) how long it would take to decay to the "safe level" of 1% of its original mass.

3. The exponential curve $I = I_0 \times 10^{0.1S}$ measures the loudness of sounds compared to
    the threshold intensity of hearing I_0, where S is the perceived loudness (in decibels).
    (i) How many times louder than the threshold intensity is a sound of 30 decibels?
    (ii) How many times louder is a sound of 28 dB than a sound of 15 dB, give your
        answer correct to the nearest integer?

4. By choosing a suitable base, solve the following equation for x.
$$\log_5 x - 1 = 6 \log_x 5$$

5. Solve $0.7^x \geqslant 0.3$ for x, giving your answer correct to 3 significant figures.

6. Using the same axes, draw a sketch of each of the following in the domain $-3 \leqslant x \leqslant 3$.
    (i) $f(x) = |x|$
    (ii) $g(x) = |x| + 2$
    (iii) $h(x) = |x + 2|$.
    (iv) Find the values of x that satisfy $f(x) \cap h(x)$.
    (v) For what values of x is $g(x) > h(x)$?

7. Sketch the graph of $y = \ln(x - 3)$.
    Express x in terms of y and hence sketch the image of $y = \ln(x - 3)$ in the line $y = x$.

8. Sketch the graph of the function $f(x) = |\frac{1}{4}x + 3|$ and hence find the solution to the inequality $|\frac{1}{4}x + 3| \geqslant 3$.

9. Simplify $\dfrac{x^{\frac{3}{2}} - x^{\frac{-1}{2}}}{x^{\frac{1}{2}} - x^{\frac{-1}{2}}}$.

10. Prove by induction that
$$\frac{1}{(1 + r)^n} \leqslant \frac{1}{1 + nr} \text{ for } r > 0 \text{ and } n \in N.$$

11. Prove that $\dfrac{4x}{(x + 1)^2} \leqslant 1$ for all $x \in R, x \neq -1$.

12. Given that k is real, find the set of values of k for which the roots of the quadratic equation $(1 + 2k)x^2 - 10x + (k - 2) = 0$
    (i) are real
    (ii) have a sum which is greater than 5.

13. Prove by induction that
$$1 + 2.2 + 3.2^2 + 4.2^3 + \ldots . n.2^{n-1} = (n - 1)2^n + 1.$$

14. If for all integers n, $u_n = (n - 20)2^n$, write an expression for u_{n+1}, u_{n+2}. Hence verify that $u_{n+2} - 4u_{n+1} + 4u_n = 0$.

15. Solve the following simultaneous equations for $x, y \geq 0$.

$$2 \log y = \log 2 + \log x \quad \text{and} \quad 2^y = 4^x$$

16. The population of a city grows according to the law $P = 40\,000\,(1.03)^n$, where n is the time in years and P is the population size.

    (i) What type of function is this?

    (ii) Estimate the size of the population in 12 years time.

    (iii) What was the initial population of the city before the city started growing?

    (iv) Determine when the population will have doubled (to the nearest half-year).

17. The population of a town was 8000 at the beginning of the year 2000 and 15 000 at the end of the year 2007. Assuming that the growth was exponential,

    (i) write an expression for the growth of the population, defining each of the terms used

    (ii) find the population at the end of the year 2009.

    (iii) In what year will the population be double that of the year 2007?

Revision Exercise 12 (Extended-Response Questions)

1. The manufacturer of a facial cream *SPOTLESS* claims that the population of bacteria which create spots will be halved within five days of using their cream.
During a trial in his laboratory, Professor Snape finds that the number of bacteria N in the population is given by the formula $N = 5000e^{-0.15t}$, where t is time, measured in days.

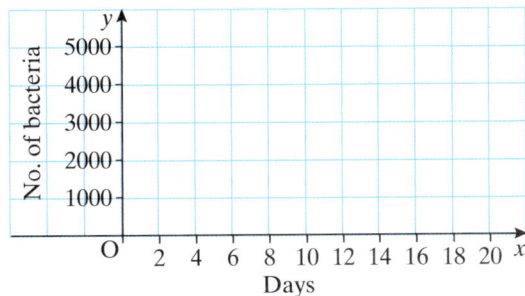

    (i) Using this formula, test the claim that the bacteria population will halve in five days.

    (ii) According to Professor Snape's equation, what will the level of bacteria be after 10 days?

    (iii) How many bacteria are present at the beginning of the trial?

    (iv) After how many days will the population reduce to 100?

    (v) Copy this grid and sketch a graph of the number of bacteria in the population over a 20-day trial.

2.

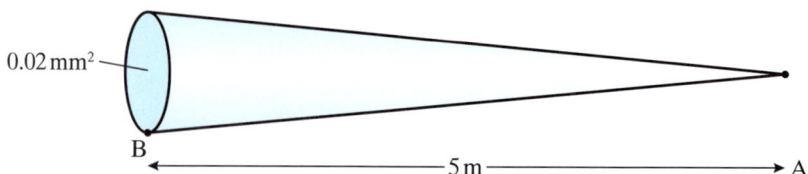

The diagram shows a conical glass fibre.

The circular cross-sectional area at the end B is $0.02\,\text{mm}^2$.

The cross-sectional area reduces along the length from B to A by a factor of $(0.92)^{\left(\frac{1}{10}\right)}$ per metre length of the fibre.

The total length of the fibre is 5.0 m.

   (i) Write down a rule for the cross-sectional area of the fibre at a distance x m from B.

  (ii) What is the cross-sectional area of the fibre at a point one-third of its length from B?

 (iii) The strength of the fibre increases from B to A.

At a distance x m from B, the strength of the fibre is given by the formula

$$S = (0.92)^{10-3x}.$$

If the weight that the fibre will support at each point before breaking is given by Weight = Strength × Cross-sectional area, write down an expression, in terms of x, for the weight the fibre will support at a distance x m from B.

  (iv) A piece of glass fibre is needed to carry weights of up to $0.02 \times (0.92)^{2.5}$ units. How much of the 5 m could be used for this purpose?

3. A trans-european train developed a fault in the lighting systems in two carriages A and B. Before the fault, the light intensity in carriage A was **I** units and in carriage B was $0.66\mathbf{I}$ units.

At each station at which the train stopped, the light intensity in carriage A decreased by 17% and in carriage B by 11%.

   (i) Write down exponential expressions for the expected light intensity in each carriage after n station-stops.

  (ii) At some time after the initial fault, the light intensity in both carriages was the same. At how many stations did the train stop before this occurred?

4. There are approximately ten times as many red squirrels as grey squirrels in a particular region.

If the population of red squirrels is reducing at a rate of 5% per year, and the grey squirrel population is increasing at a rate of 11% per year,

   (i) write an expression for the size of the population of grey squirrels after t years

  (ii) write an expression for the size of the population of red squirrels after t years.

 (iii) After how many years, correct to 1 place of decimals, will the populations of both species be equal (assuming the present increase/decrease rates continue)?

 (iv) Find how many years it will take (again, assuming the present increase/decrease rates continue) before the proportions of the squirrel populations will be reversed.

  (v) Using the same axes, draw exponential graphs indicating your answers to (i), (ii), (iii), (iv) above. [Take $t = 0, 5, 10, 15, \ldots$, years.]

5. The number of bacteria in a colony is given by the formula $n = A(1 - e^{-bt})$, where n is the size of the population after t hours.

A and b are positive constants.

   (i) Is this a graph of growth or decay? Explain your answer.

  (ii) If $t = 2$ when $n = 10\,000$, and $t = 4$ when $n = 15\,000$, show that
$$2e^{-4b} - 3e^{-2b} + 1 = 0.$$

 (iii) Using the substitution $a = e^{-2b}$, show that
$$2a^2 - 3a + 1 = 0.$$

 (iv) Solve this equation for a.

  (v) Find the exact value of b.

 (vi) Find the exact value of A.

 (vii) Sketch the graph of n against t.

(viii) After how many hours is the population of the bacteria $18\,000$?

Answers

Chapter 1: Algebra 1

Exercise 1.1

1. (i) 3   (ii) -9 (iii) 5
2. (i) 2   (ii) 3   (iii) 4
3. (i) $\frac{3}{2}$ is not an integer
   (ii) $-4x^{-1}$, -1 is not a positive power
4. (i) $8x^2 - 4x - 2$ (ii) $4x^3 + 2x^2 - 6x$
   (iii) $7x^2 - 5x$ (iv) $9x^2 - 9x - 19$
5. (i) $22x^3 - 19x^2$ (ii) $9x^4 - 26x^3$
   (iii) $7x^4 - 5x^3 + 5x^2$ (iv) $15x^3 - 31x^2 + 3x$
6. (i) $2x^2 + 13x + 20$ (ii) $2x^2 - x - 6$
   (iii) $3x^2 + 7x - 6$ (iv) $12x^2 - 11x + 2$
   (v) $6x^2 + 13x - 5$ (vi) $8x^2 - 22x - 6$
   (vii) $x^2 - 4$ (viii) $4x^2 - 25$
   (ix) $a^2x^2 - b^2y^2$
7. (i) $x^2 + 4x + 4$ (ii) $x^2 - 6x + 9$
   (iii) $x^2 + 10x + 25$ (iv) $a^2 + 2ab + b^2$
   (v) $x^2 - 2xy + y^2$ (vi) $a^2 + 4ab + 4b^2$
   (vii) $9x^2 - 6xy + y^2$ (viii) $x^2 - 10xy + 25y^2$
   (ix) $4x^2 + 12xy + 9y^2$
8. (i) $x^2 + x + \frac{1}{4}$ (ii) $8x^2 - 4x + \frac{1}{2}$
   (iii) $-x^2 + 2x - 1$
9. (i) No   (ii) No   (iii) Yes.
   Parts (i) and (ii) cannot be expressed in the form $(ax + b)^2$
10. $p = 4$ **11.** $t = 20$ **12.** $s = 16$
13. (i) $x^3 + 4x^2 + 10x + 12$
    (ii) $2x^3 - 5x^2 - 13x + 4$
    (iii) $2x^3 - 3x^2 - 5x + 6$
    (iv) $6x^3 - 16x^2 + 14x - 4$
14. Proof
15. Proof
16. 14
17. $2x^3 - x^2 - 25x - 12$
18. $2x^4 - 10x^3 + 9x^2 + 5x - 2$
19. -47
20. (i) $x + 2$ (ii) $x + 2$
    (iii) $x^2 - 2x$ (iv) $3x - 2y$
21. (i) $2x + 3y - 1$ (ii) $2x^2 - 3x + 4$
22. (i) $4a$ (ii) $4ab$ (iii) $2yz$ (iv) $\frac{y}{x}$
23. (i) $x + 3$ (ii) $2x + 4$ (iii) $2x + 3$
24. (i) $x^2 - 7x + 12$ (ii) $x^2 - 1$
    (iii) $x^2 - 1$ (iv) $4x^2 + 5x - 6$
    (v) $x^2 - 5x + 3$ (vi) $2x^2 + 3x + 6$
25. (i) $x - 2$ (ii) $x - 3$
    (iii) $3x - 1$ (iv) $x + 2$
26. (i) $x^2 + 2x + 4$ (ii) $4x^2 + 6xy + 9y^2$

Exercise 1.2

1. (i) $x^2 + 4x$ (ii) $4x + 8$
2. (i) $2x + 2$ (ii) $10x + 2$
3. (a) $2x^3 + 5x^2 + 3x$
   (b) $8x^2 + 15x + 6$
   (c) (i) $390 \, \text{cm}^3$ (ii) $281 \, \text{cm}^2$
4. (a) -4 (b) -8 (c) -14
   (d) $54a^3 - 9a^2 - 15a - 4$
5. (a) 6   (b) 46   (c) 7.75
   (d) $\frac{a^2}{16} - \frac{3a}{4} + 6$
6. (a) $2x^2 + xy - 3y^2$ (b) $6x + 4y$
7. (a) $2x^3 - 10x^2$ (b) $18x^2 - 50x$
8. (i) Number of diagonals in a 4-sided polygon (2)
   (ii) Number of diagonals in a 5-sided polygon (2), (5), (9) A triangle has no diagonal
9. $a^2 - 3a - 8$
10. (i) $4t^2 + 6t + 6$ (2)   (ii) $t^4 - 3t^2 + 6$ (4)
    (iii) $t^2 - 7t + 16$ (2)
11. (i) $1372\pi \, \text{cm}^3$ (ii) $\frac{1}{3}\pi r^3$ (iii) $\frac{4}{3}\pi h^3$
12. $4x^2 - 84x^2 + 432x$, $a = 0$, $b = 9$
13. $\frac{40}{\pi^2}$ m
14. 3 m
15. (i) 10   (ii) 15   (iii) 45; 17

Exercise 1.3

1. $5x(x - 2)$
2. $6b(a - 2c)$
3. $3x(x - 2y)$
4. $2x^2(y - 3z)$
5. $2a(a^2 - 2a + 4)$

6. $5xy(y - 4x)$

7. $2ab(a - 2b + 6c)$

8. $3xy(x - 3y + 5z)$

9. $2\pi r(2r + 3h)$

10. $(3a - 4)(2b - c)$

11. $(x - 9)(x + 3)$

12. $(c - 2d)(2c + 1)$

13. $(2x + y)(4a - 3b)$

14. $(y - 3b)(7y + 2a)$

15. $(2x - 3y)(3y - 4z)$

16. $(2x - 3y)(3x - 2a)$

17. $(x - y)(x + y)(3a - 4b)$

18. $(a - b)(a + b)$

19. $(x - 2y)(x + 2y)$

20. $(3x - y)(3x + y)$

21. $(4x - 5y)(4x + 5y)$

22. $(6x - 5)(6x + 5)$

23. $(1 - 6x)(1 + 6x)$

24. $(7a - 2b)(7a + 2b)$

25. $(xy - 1)(xy + 1)$

26. $(2ab - 4c)(2ab + 4c)$

27. $3(x - 3y)(x + 3y)$

28. $5(3 - x)(3 + x)$

29. $5(3a - 2)(3a + 2)$

30. $(2x + y - 2)(2x + y + 2)$

31. $(3a - 2b - 3)(3a - 2b + 3)$

32. $(a - b)(a + b)(a^2 + b^2)$

33. $(x + 2)(x + 7)$

34. $(2x + 1)(x + 3)$

35. $(2x + 7)(x + 2)$

36. $(x - 2)(x - 7)$

37. $(x - 4)(x - 7)$

38. $(2x - 1)(x - 3)$

39. $(3x - 5)(x - 4)$

40. $(7x - 4)(x - 2)$

41. $(2x + 3)(x - 5)$

42. $(3x - 4)(x + 5)$

43. $(4x - 5)(3x + 1)$

44. $(3x + 5)(2x - 3)$

45. $(3x - 2)(x + 5)$

46. $(3x - 1)(2x - 3)$

47. $(9x - 4)(4x + 1)$

48. $(5x + 2)(3x - 4)$

49. $(3y - 5)(2y + 7)$

50. $(4x - y)(3x + 5y)$

51. (i) $(x + 2\sqrt{3})(x + \sqrt{3})$
    (ii) $(x + 3\sqrt{5})(x - \sqrt{5})$
    (iii) $(2x + \sqrt{2})(x - 3\sqrt{2})$

52. (i) $(a + b)(a^2 - ab + b^2)$
    (ii) $(a - b)(a^2 + ab + b^2)$
    (iii) $(2x + y)(4x^2 - 2xy + y^2)$

53. (i) $(3x - y)(9x^2 + 3xy + y^2)$
    (ii) $(x - 4)(x^2 + 4x + 16)$
    (iii) $(2x - 3y)(4x^2 + 6xy + 9y^2)$

54. (i) $(2 + 3k)(4 - 6k + 9k^2)$
    (ii) $(4 - 5a)(16 + 20a + 25a^2)$
    (iii) $(3a + 4b)(9a^2 - 12ab + 16b^2)$

55. (i) $(a - 2bc)(a^2 + 2abc + 4b^2c^2)$
    (ii) $5(x + 2y)(x^2 - 2xy + 4y^2)$
    (iii) $(x + y - z)((x + y)^2 + z(x + y) + z^2)$

Exercise 1.4

1. (i) $\dfrac{4}{y^2}$ (ii) $\dfrac{a}{2b}$ (iii) x

   (iv) $\dfrac{7 + 2y}{7}$ (v) $\dfrac{x}{3 + 2a}$

2. (a) $\dfrac{26x}{15}$ (b) $\dfrac{x}{10}$

   (c) $\dfrac{10x + 9}{12}$ (d) $\dfrac{13x + 1}{20}$

   (e) $\dfrac{-(x + 6)}{6}$ (f) $\dfrac{3x + 5}{12}$

   (g) $\dfrac{17x + 11}{20}$ (h) 0

   (i) $\dfrac{11x + 4}{20}$ (j) $\dfrac{8}{15x}$

   (k) $\dfrac{1}{8x}$ (l) $\dfrac{2x + 3}{x(x + 3)}$

   (m) $\dfrac{5x + 14}{(x + 2)(x + 4)}$ (n) $\dfrac{7x - 8}{(x - 2)(2x - 1)}$

   (o) $\dfrac{17 - x}{(3x - 1)(x + 3)}$ (p) $\dfrac{13x + 13}{(2x - 7)(5x + 2)}$

   (q) $\dfrac{13 - 3x}{4(3x - 5)}$ (r) $\dfrac{-x - 7}{(2x - 1)(x - 2)}$

   (s) $\dfrac{x^2 + y^2}{x^2 - y^2}$ (t) $\dfrac{4x + 9y - 2}{3xy}$

   (u) $\dfrac{x - 7}{x(x - 1)}$

3. (i) $\dfrac{z - 2}{z - 5}$ (ii) $\dfrac{y + 2}{y - 5}$

   (iii) $\dfrac{t + 4}{t - 2}$ (iv) $\dfrac{2}{(x + 2)(x - 2)}$

   (v) $\dfrac{a - 8}{(a + 3)(a - 3)}$ (vi) $\dfrac{2x + 1}{(x + 2)(x - 2)}$

4. (i) $\dfrac{-4}{(2x + 1)}$ (ii) $\dfrac{-1}{2x + 1}$

5. (i) $\dfrac{-x - 4}{(x + 3)(x - 3)(x + 2)}$

   (ii) $\dfrac{x + 5}{(x + 1)(x - 1)(x + 2)}$

   (iii) $\dfrac{5}{(3x + 4)(3x - 4)(2x + 1)}$

   (iv) $\dfrac{1}{xy}$

6. (i) 5   (ii) 4   (iii) $x - 1$

7. (i) $\dfrac{1 + x}{1 - x}$ (ii) $\dfrac{1 + 2x}{x}$ (iii) xy

8. (i) $\dfrac{8y - 3}{4}$ (ii) $\dfrac{2x - 1}{2x}$

    (iii) $\dfrac{3x^2 + 1}{2x}$ (iv) $\dfrac{4y + 1}{2}$

9. (i) $\dfrac{6z - 2}{6z - 3}$ (ii) 2

    (iii) $\dfrac{6z^2 - 3}{6z^2 - 2}$ (iv) $\dfrac{x^2 + x - 1}{x^2 - 1}$

10. (i) $\dfrac{x - 2}{x}$ (ii) $\dfrac{1}{x^2}$ (iii) $x + 2$

11. (i) $\dfrac{2b}{a - b}$ (ii) $\dfrac{x^2}{x^2 - 3}$ (iii) $\dfrac{3y - 1}{3y + 1}$

12. Proof (constant = 3)

Exercise 1.5

1. (i) 35   (ii) 15   (iii) 15   (iv) 1365   (v) 10
2. (i) 1   (ii) 10   (iii) 1   (iv) 1   (v) 18
3. $k = 9$
4. $k = 4$
5. $a^4 + 8a^3b + 24a^2b^2 + 32ab^3 + 16b^4$
6. 1 6 15 20 15 6 1
7. $10 \times 8 = 80$
8. (i) $a^4 - 8a^3b + 24a^2b^2 - 32ab^3 + 16b^4$
    (ii) $8x^3 - 12x^2y + 6xy^2 - y^3$
    (iii) $p^4 + 12p^3q + 54p^2q^2 + 108pq^3 + 81q^4$
    (iv) $1 + 10y + 40y^2 + 80y^3 + 80y^4 + 32y^5$
9. (i) $64 + 576p + 2160p^2 + 4320p^3 +$
     $4860p^4 + 2916p^5 + 729p^6$
    (ii) $1 - 7b + 21b^2 - 35b^3 + 35b^4 - 21b^5 + 7b^6 - b^7$
    (iii) $p^5 - 20p^4q + 160p^3q^2 - 640p^2q^3 +$
     $1280pq^4 - 1024q^5$
10. 1 7 21 35 35 21 7 1
11. $70x^4y^4$
12. $-84x^6y^3$
13. $8064x^5y^5$
14. 7 terms, 160
15. (i) $256x^8 - 1024x^7y + 1792x^6y^2 -$
     $1792x^5y^3 + 1120x^4y^4 - 448x^3y^5 +$
     $112x^2y^6 - 16xy^7 + y^8$
    (ii) $a^9 + 18a^8b + 144a^7b^2 + 672a^6b^3 +$
     $2016a^5b^4 + 4032a^4b^5 + 5376a^3b^6 +$
     $4608a^2b^7 + 2304ab^8 + 512b^9$
16. $\dbinom{10}{2}(5x)^8 = 17578125x^8$
17. -283.5

Exercise 1.6

1. $a = 6, b = -1, c = -12$
2. $p = 13, q = -10$
3. $a = 3, b = 7$
4. $a = 2, b = -10$
5. $p = 2, q = \dfrac{5}{4}, r = \dfrac{23}{8}$
6. $a = 3, b = 9$
7. $m = 9, n = 2$
8. (i) $a, b, c, d = 1, 10, 31, 30$
    (ii) $p, q, r = 5, 33, 52$
9. $p = 2, q = -5$
10. $a = 7.5, b = 37.75, c = 4.5$
11. $p = -12, q = 48$
12. $a = -3, b = 1$
13. $b = 4, c = 3$
14. $a = \dfrac{-2c}{5}$
15. $pq = 8$
16. Proof
17. $A = -\dfrac{1}{2}, B = \dfrac{1}{2}$
18. $C = -\dfrac{1}{5}, D = \dfrac{1}{5}$
19. $A = \dfrac{1}{3}, B = -\dfrac{1}{3}$
20. $a = -27, b = 54$
21. $p = -12, q = 16$
22. $c = 3, d = -4; (x - 2)(x + 2)(x + 3)$
23. 5
24. $a = 9 - p^2, b = 9p, p = 8, 1$
25. Proof
26. Proof
27. Proof
28. $2x - 1$
29. $A = 2, B = -1, C = -1$

Exercise 1.7

1. (i) $x = \dfrac{4 + 2y}{3}$ (ii) $x = \dfrac{4c + b}{2}$

    (iii) $x = \dfrac{y + 8}{10}$ (iv) $x = \dfrac{2y + 15}{5}$

    (v) $x = 9y + 6$ (vi) $x = \dfrac{yz}{y - z}$

2. (i) $x = \dfrac{y + 1}{6}$ (ii) $x = \dfrac{y - 3z}{2}$

    (iii) $x = \dfrac{a}{b + c}$

3. (a) $r = \sqrt{\dfrac{V}{\pi h}}$ (b) $r = \dfrac{A}{2\pi h}$ (c) Proof

4. (a) πr^2 (b) $4r^2$

    (c) $r^2(4 - \pi)$ (d) $\dfrac{r^2}{4}(16 - \pi)$

5. (i) $u = \dfrac{c(f^1 - f)}{f^1}$ (ii) $c = \dfrac{f^1 u}{f^1 - f}$

6. (i) $l = \dfrac{T^2 g}{4\pi^2}$ (ii) $l = 2.3\,\text{m}$

7. (i) $a = \dfrac{b(x + y)}{x - y}$ (ii) $a = \dfrac{b}{2}$

8. (i) $v = \dfrac{3u - 4y}{3}$ (ii) $v = \dfrac{2s - ut}{t}$

9. (i) $i = 100\sqrt[3]{\dfrac{A}{P}} - 100$ (ii) 2.0%

10. (i) $c = \dfrac{a - b}{ad^2}$ (ii) $c = \dfrac{b - 1}{b - 2}$

11. (i) $h = \sqrt{225 - r^2}$ (ii) $h = 10\sqrt{2}$
    (iii) $h = 13\,\text{cm}$

12. (i) $L = 300 - 2W$
    (ii) $A = W(300 - 2W)$
    (iii) $W = 50, L = 200$ or $W = 100, L = 100$

Exercise 1.8

1. (a) Linear   (b) Linear
    (c) Quadratic   (d) Quadratic
    (e) Quadratic   (f) Quadratic
    (g) Quadratic   (h) Linear
    (i) Quadratic   (j) Quadratic

2. (a) $4x^2 - 1$ (b) $4 - x^2$

3. (i) $5x + 2$ (ii) $4x - 6$ (iii) $3 - x$
    (iv) $-2 - 5x$ (v) $\dfrac{x}{2} + 3$ (vi) $-1 + \dfrac{x}{5}$

4. $2x + 5$

5. $2x + 5$

6. (a) $3x; 45$ (b) $4x; 60$ (c) $2x + 1$; 31

7. $70 + 35x; 125 + 24x$; 5 months

8. $f(t) = 2t^2 + t + 4$; in the 16th hour

Exercise 1.9

1. (i) x^2 is not of degree 1
    (ii) $(x - 1)^{-1}$ is not of degree 1
    (iii) $y^2 = 3x + 4 \Rightarrow y = \sqrt{3x + 4}$;
    not of degree 1

2. (i) 7   (ii) 3   (iii) -3

3. (i) 2   (ii) 2   (iii) -1 (iv) 2.5

4. (i) 2   (ii) 11   (iii) 7

5. (i) 2   (ii) 12   (iii) 3

6. (i) 3   (ii) 9   (iii) -5 (iv) 1.5

7. (i) 2.5   (ii) -2

Exercise 1.10

1. (i) $(4, 2)$ (ii) $(2, 5)$ (iii) $(3, 1)$

2. (i) $(3, -2)$ (ii) $(2, 5)$ (iii) $\left(3, 2\tfrac{1}{2}\right)$

3. $(10, 5)$

4. $(10, 7)$

5. (i) $(x, y, z) = (2, 3, 1)$
    (ii) $(x, y, z) = (2, -3, 1)$
    (iii) $(x, y, z) = (5, 0, 1)$

6. (i) $(a, b, c) = (1, 4, 2)$
    (ii) $(x, y, z) = (2, 3, -1)$
    (iii) $(x, y, z) = (3, 1, -2)$

7. $(x, y, z) = (-1, 2.5, -0.5)$

8. $(a, b, c) = (1, -1, 2)$

9. $(a, b, c) = (2, 5, -6)$

10. 32 000

11. 17 years, 15 years

12. $y = \tfrac{1}{2}x + 4$

13. $N_1 = 88, N_2 = 22$

14. $a = 1, b = -1$

15. $c = \tfrac{4}{5}, d = -\tfrac{4}{5}$

16. 25 litres

17. $x = 15, y = 11$

18. $a = 0.5, u = -1.5$

19. $(4, 26), (8, 13)$

20. $(a, b, c) = (3, -2, 1)$

21. (i) $(x, y, z) = (3, 4, 1)$
    (ii) $(x, y, z) = (6, 4, -3)$

22. $(a, b, c) = (-2, -2, 1)$

23. 4(small), 6(medium), 5(large)

24. A€3000, B€6000, C€1500

25. $W = 2, B = 4, G = 6$

Revision Exercise 1 (Core)

1. (i) $\dfrac{1}{3m^6 n^7}$ (ii) $\dfrac{3x + 1}{5 + 4x}$ (iii) $\dfrac{1}{2x - 8}$

2. (i) $(x, y) = (-2, 2)$
    (ii) $(x, y) = \left(\dfrac{6}{5}, \dfrac{17}{5}\right), (3, -2)$

3. $x^2 + 2x - 1$

4. $3x^3 + 6x^2 + 3x + 33$

5. (i) $(0, 3, -3)$ (ii) $\tfrac{1}{2}, 2$

6. $k = 25$

7. (i) $32x^5 + 240x^4 + 720x^3 + 1080x^2 + 810x + 243$
    (ii) $x^6 - 12x^5 + 60x^4 - 160x^3 + 240x^2 - 192x + 64$

8. $(x - 3)(x^2 + 3x + 9)$

9. $(p, q, r) = (2, 3, -13)$

10. $(x, y, z) = (2, -1, 4)$

11. $6b^2 + 2$

12. (i) $3n^2$ (ii) $5n^2$ (iii) $\dfrac{n^2}{2}$

13. $n^2 + 3n + 2$; 10 302

14. $l = 21\,\text{cm}, w = 15\,\text{cm}$

15. (i) $r = \dfrac{2uv}{u + v}$ (ii) $m = \dfrac{v}{u}$

Revision Exercise 1 (Advanced)

1. $\dfrac{n(n + 1)}{2}$; 1225

2. $0.5\,\text{m}^3$

3. (i) $x + y = 8.4, 0.6x + 0.4y = 0.5(x + y)$
    (ii) $4.2\,\text{kg}$

4. Proof

5. $-\dfrac{1}{2}$

6. (i) $7.5\,l$ (ii) $2.5\,l$

7. A:1 500, B:4 500, C:17 000

8. (i) $a = 0.3; b = 0.28$ (ii) $3.57\,\text{m/sec}$

9. (i) $-\dfrac{224}{27}\,x^5$ (ii) $192456x^5$

10. $-336798x^6$

11. 83 026 944

Revision Exercise 1 (Extended Response Questions)

1. (a) (i) 436   (ii) 112   (iii) 0.7956
    (b) €58 358

2. (ii) $x + 1.5y = 26$
    (iii) 14 standard, 8 deluxe

3. (i) $h = \dfrac{40}{x^2}$ (ii) Proof

(iii)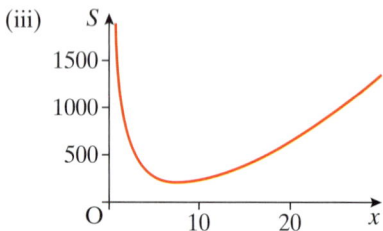

(iv) $x = 4, h = 2.5\,\text{cm}$ or $x = 2.9, h = 4.76\,\text{cm}$

4. (i) $C(x) = 3500 + 10.5x$
    (ii) $I(x) = 11.5x$
    (iii)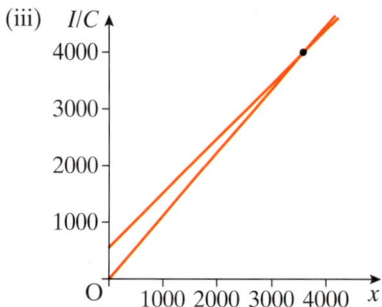

(iv) 3500

(v) Profit

(vi) 5500 games

5. (a) €110.40
    (b) 12 blue, 84 white

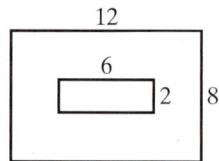

6. (i) $C = 40x + 30\,000$
    (ii) €45
    (iii) 5000
    (iv) $R = 80x$
    (v) R/C

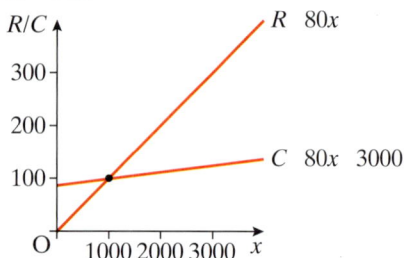

(vi) 751
(vii) $P = 40x - 30\,000$

Chapter 2: Algebra 2

Exercise 2.1

1. (a) (i) $-5, 4$ (ii) $3, 4$ (iii) $-1, 5$
    (b) (i) $-3, 5$ (ii) $-5, \dfrac{3}{2}$ (iii) $-\dfrac{2}{3}, 5$
    (c) (i) $-\dfrac{2}{5}, 3$ (ii) $-\dfrac{5}{3}, \dfrac{4}{3}$ (iii) $-\dfrac{5}{4}, \dfrac{3}{2}$
    (d) (i) ± 3 (ii) $0, \dfrac{10}{3}$ (iii) $0, \dfrac{8}{5}$
    (e) (i) $-5, \dfrac{3}{2}$ (ii) $-\dfrac{5}{3}, 2$ (iii) $-2, 1$
    (f) (i) $-5, \pm 4$ (ii) $3, \pm 1$
    (g) (i) $-\dfrac{4}{3}, \pm 2$ (ii) $-4, -3, 5$

2. (a) (i) $-0.7, 2.7$ (ii) $-3.6, 0.6$ (iii) $0.6, 2.4$
    (b) (i) $0.6, 5.4$ (ii) $0.1, 2.5$ (iii) $-2.9, 0.9$

3. (a) (i) $\dfrac{-2 \pm \sqrt{19}}{3}$ (ii) $\dfrac{6 \pm \sqrt{46}}{2}$
    (iii) $\dfrac{3 \pm 2\sqrt{2}}{2}$
    (b) (i) $-2 \pm 2\sqrt{3}$ (ii) $\dfrac{-2 \pm \sqrt{14}}{5}$
    (iii) $\dfrac{1 \pm \sqrt{5}}{2}$

4. (a) (i) $2, 3$ (ii) $\dfrac{2}{3}, 2$ (iii) $-2, 3$

(b) (i) $\dfrac{9 \pm \sqrt{57}}{6}$ (ii) $0, 7$

    (iii) $\dfrac{3}{2}$

5. (a) (i) $\pm\sqrt{2}, \pm\sqrt{5}$ (ii) $\dfrac{-5 \pm \sqrt{17}}{2}$

    (iii) $\pm\sqrt{1 \pm \sqrt{3}}$ (iv) $\dfrac{11 \pm \sqrt{41}}{4}$

  (b) (i) $-\dfrac{3}{2}, 4$ (ii) $1, 2$

  (c) $1, 2, 4$

  (d) $-1, -\dfrac{1}{2}, \dfrac{5}{2}, 5$

6. $-\dfrac{\sqrt{3}}{2}, \sqrt{3}$

7. (a) $-4.2, 1.2$ (b) $-2.3, 1.3$
  (c) $-9.5, -0.5$ (d) $-1.6 \leqslant x \leqslant 0.6$
  (e) $-1.6, 0.6$ (f) $-3, 1$
  (g) $-3.6, 0.6$ (h) $-4.2 \leqslant x \leqslant -0.8$

8. Graph does not intercept the x-axis

9. (a) 21 units   (b) 25 units

10. (a) $-0.5, 2$ (b) -0.8
  (c) $-0.5, 2.4$

11. (i) 1   (ii) 4
    Only one solution is real in each case

12. (i) $-\sqrt{7}, 2\sqrt{7}$ (ii) $-3\sqrt{5}, -\dfrac{\sqrt{5}}{2}$

Exercise 2.2

1. (i) Curve f (ii) Curve h (iii) Curve g
  (iv) 1. Curve f has roots = 1.5 and 4.5
       2. Curve h has roots = 3
       3. Curve g has no real roots

2. $A = \left(\dfrac{-b - b\sqrt{b^2 - 4ac}}{2a}, 0 \right)$

  $B = \left(\dfrac{-b + b\sqrt{b^2 - 4ac}}{2a}, 0 \right)$

3. (i) $-39 < 0$ $\therefore$ No real roots
  (ii) $17 > 0$ $\therefore$ Roots are real and different
  (iii) $16 > 0$ $\therefore$ Roots are real and different
  (iv) $-8 < 0$ $\therefore$ No real roots
  (v) 0 $\therefore$ Roots are real and equal
  (vi) 0 $\therefore$ Roots are real and equal

4. $k < -12$ or $k > 12$

5. (i) $k = 25$ (ii) $k = \pm 12$
  (iii) $k = 0, 3$

6. $k = -\dfrac{1}{3}, 1$

10. $k = -\dfrac{1}{12}$

12. $a = \dfrac{b^2}{4}; -\dfrac{2}{b}$

Exercise 2.3

1. $x = -3, y = 9$ or $x = 1, y = 1$
2. $x = -2, y = -1$ or $x = 1, y = 2$
3. $x = -1, y = 4$ or $x = \dfrac{1}{2}, y = 1$
4. $x = 1, y = 0$ or $x = 4, y = -3$
5. $x = 3, y = 4$ or $x = 4, y = 3$
6. $x = 2, y = 3$
7. $x = 2, y = 2$ or $x = 5, y = 11$
8. $x = 3, y = 1$
9. $x = 2, y = 0$ or $x = 0, y = 1$
10. $x = -2, y = -2$ or $x = 1, y = 4$
11. $x = 1, y = 1$ or $x = \dfrac{7}{2}, y = -4$
12. $x = 0, y = 3$ or $x = -2, y = 1$
13. $t = 2, s = 3$ or $t = -\dfrac{4}{3}, s = -\dfrac{11}{3}$
14. $t = -7, s = -5$ or $t = 1, s = -1$
15. $t = 2, s = 1$ or $t = 11, s = 7$

Exercise 2.4

1. $-6, -5$ or $5, 6$
2. $-6, -4$ or $4, 6$
3. (i) $2x + 2y = 62; xy = 198$
  (ii) Length = 22 m, width = 9 m
4. Sides are 3, 4, 5 and perimeter = 12 units
5. $t = 2.68$ or $t = 9.32$
6. $x = -3$ or $x = 5$
7. 0.25 seconds or 1.25 seconds
8. 12 cm
9. $-1, 1$ or $7, 9$
10. 9 cm
11. Length = 10 m, width = 6 m
12. $-1, 0, 1$ or $7, 8, 9$
13. Width = 2 m
14. Length = 24 m, width = 10 m
15. 9.35 m
16. $t = 3, s = 5$
  Negative values are not valid
17. $(-2.2, 2.4); (6.2, -0.4)$
  $k > 10$

Exercise 2.5

1. (a) (i) -9 (ii) 4
  (b) (i) 2 (ii) -5
  (c) (i) 7 (ii) 2
  (d) (i) 9 (ii) -3
  (e) (i) $\dfrac{7}{2}$ (ii) $\dfrac{1}{2}$
  (f) (i) $-\dfrac{1}{7}$ (ii) $-\dfrac{1}{7}$
  (g) (i) $-\dfrac{10}{3}$ (ii) $-\dfrac{2}{3}$

(h) (i) -2 (ii) $\frac{1}{5}$

(i) (i) -2 (ii) -3

(j) (i) $\frac{3}{4}$ (ii) $\frac{5}{4}$

2. (a) $x^2 + 3x - 1 = 0$

(b) $x^2 - 6x - 4 = 0$

(c) $x^2 - 7x - 5 = 0$

(d) $3x^2 + 2x - 7 = 0$

(e) $2x^2 + 5x - 4 = 0$

(f) $2x^2 + 3x - 10 = 0$

(g) $12x^2 + 3x - 4 = 0$

(h) $6x^2 + 10x + 3 = 0$

3. (i) $x^2 - 10x + 24 = 0$

(ii) $x^2 + x - 6 = 0$

(iii) $x^2 + 6x + 5 = 0$

(iv) $x^2 - (4 + \sqrt{5})x + 4\sqrt{5} = 0$

(v) $x^2 - 4ax + 3a^2 = 0$

(vi) $25x^2 - 25x + 6 = 0$

(vii) $b^2x^2 - 5bx + 6 = 0$

(viii) $10x^2 - 31x + 15 = 0$

Exercise 2.6

1. (i) 196   (ii) 9   (iii) $\frac{25}{4}$

2. (i) $(x - 4)^2 - 19$ (ii) $(x - 1)^2 - 6$

(iii) $(x - 1)^2$

3. (i) $(x + 2)^2 - 10$ (ii) $(x + \frac{9}{2})^2 - \frac{65}{4}$

(iii) $(x - \frac{7}{2})^2 - \frac{61}{4}$

4. (i) $(-1, -7)$ (ii) $(1, -4)$

(iii) $(-\frac{1}{2}, 2)$

5. $k > 9$

6. $2(x - 3)^2 - 11$

8. (i) $(-1, -5), (2, -1), (4, 1)$

(ii) (a) $y = (x + 1)^2 - 5$

(b) $y = x^2 + 2x - 4$

(a) $y = (x - 2)^2 - 1$

(b) $y = x^2 - 4x + 3$

(a) $y = (x - 4)^2 + 1$

(b) $y = x^2 - 8x + 17$

9. (i) 3   (ii) -2 (iii) $\frac{1}{3}$

10. Maximum point $= (3, 9)$

Greatest height $= 9$ units

11. (i) $C; y = (x - 3)^2 - 1$

(ii) $B; y = (x - 3)^2$

(iii) $A; y = (x - 3)^2 + 1$

12. Curve C: $y = 16 - (x - 2)^2 \Rightarrow p = 16, a = 1,$
$q = 2$

Curve D: $y = 4 - (x - 2)^2 \Rightarrow p = 4, a = 1,$
$q = 2$

13. $f(x) = -\frac{1}{2}x^2 + 1\frac{1}{2}x + 9$ or
$f(x) = 9 - \frac{1}{2}(x - 1\frac{1}{2})^2$

14. $f(x) = x^2 + 2x + 4$ or $f(x) = (x + 1)^2 + 3$

15. (i) $f(x) = 4 - (0.1)(x - 6)^2$

(ii) $(6 - 2\sqrt{10}, 0)$ and $(6 + 2\sqrt{10}, 0)$

(iii) $4\sqrt{10}$

17. $40\,^\circ\text{C}$, 4 hrs

Exercise 2.7

1. (i) $2\sqrt{2}$ (ii) $3\sqrt{3}$ (iii) $3\sqrt{5}$

(iv) $10\sqrt{2}$ (v) $9\sqrt{2}$

2. (i) $5\sqrt{2}$ (ii) $5\sqrt{2}$ (iii) $7\sqrt{2}$

(iv) $5\sqrt{3}$ (v) $9\sqrt{2}$ (vi) $7\sqrt{5}$

3. (i) $\frac{\sqrt{3}}{3}$ (ii) $\frac{\sqrt{2}}{2}$ (iii) $\frac{\sqrt{2}}{5}$

(iv) $2\sqrt{2}$ (v) $\frac{\sqrt{2}}{2}$

4. (i) $4\sqrt{6}$ (ii) 30   (iii) $6 + 2\sqrt{3}$

(iv) 22   (v) 2   (vi) $a^2 - 4b$

5. (i) $\sqrt{5} - 1$ (ii) $\dfrac{12(3 + \sqrt{2})}{7}$

(iii) $-9 + 4\sqrt{5}$ (iv) $\dfrac{\sqrt{2}}{2}$

6. (i) 2   (ii) 4

7. (i) 7   (ii) $-12 - 2\sqrt{5}$

8. (i) $4\sqrt{2}$ (ii) $\sqrt{6}$

(iii) $\dfrac{13}{2}$ (iv) $\dfrac{19 + 8\sqrt{3}}{13}$

10. $5(2 - \sqrt{3})$

11. $\sqrt{2}$

13. $\dfrac{-9 - 5\sqrt{3}}{6}$

Exercise 2.8

1. $\sqrt{2(x^2 + 4)}\,\text{m}$

2. (a) $\sqrt{14}\,\text{km}$

(b) (i) $2(4 - \sqrt{14})\,\text{km}$

(ii) 12 seconds

3. $(8 + 2\sqrt{6})\,\text{km}$

4. (i) $2\sqrt{a}$ (ii) $\dfrac{2}{\sqrt{a}}; 2$

5. (i) $x = 4$ (ii) $x = 5$

(iii) $x = 9$ (iv) $x = 2, 3$

(v) $x = 2$ (vi) $x = -2, 8$

6. (i) $x = 4$ (ii) $x = \frac{2}{9}, 2$

(iii) $x = 9$ (iv) $x = 2, 6$

7. $a = 1, b = 2; x = \dfrac{-31}{16}$

8. 5

9. $a + \dfrac{1}{a} + 1$

10. $a = 2, b = 5$

11. (i) $\sqrt{2x^2 + 8}$

(ii) $\sqrt{3x^2 + 8}\,; x = 4\,\text{m}$

Exercise 2.9

5. True

7. True

8. $k = 8$

9. $p = 11$

10. $(x - 1)(x + 2)$

11. $(x - 2)(x - 3)$

12. (i) $(x - 1)(x - 4)(x + 1)$

(ii) $(x - 1)(x - 3)(x - 4)$

(iii) $(x - 2)(x + 3)(x + 5)$

(iv) $(x - 1)(x + 1)(3x - 4)$

(v) $(x + 1)(x - 3)(2x + 1)$

(vi) $(x - 2)^2(2x + 5)$

13. $(x + 2)(x + 5)(2x - 1)$

14. $a = 2; (x - 1)(x + 1)$

15. $(x - 2)(x - 3)(x + 4); x = 2, 3, -4$

16. $-4, -2$

17. (i) $-1, 1, 4$ (ii) $-1, -4, 3$

(iii) $-1, 1, \dfrac{4}{3}$ (iv) $-1, -2, 3$

18. $a = 7, b = 2; (2x - 1); -1, -3, \dfrac{1}{2}$

19. $k = -8; (x - 2)(x + 6)$

20. $a = 3, b = -30; (2x + 5)$

21. $a = -5, b = 19; -1, 3, -\dfrac{2}{5}$

22. (i) $\left(\dfrac{b + c}{a}\right)^{\frac{1}{3}}$ (ii) $\left(\dfrac{c}{a}\right)^{\frac{1}{3}} - b$

Exercise 2.10

1. (i) $f(x) = x^3 - 3x^2 - x + 3$

(ii) $f(x) = x^3 + x^2 - 10x + 8$

2. (i) $f(x) = x^3 + x^2 - 6x$

$g(x) = 3x^3 + 3x^2 - 18x$

(ii) $f(x) = -x^3 + 6x^2 - 11x + 6$

$g(x) = -2x^3 + 12x^2 - 22x + 12$

3. $a = 6, b = 3, c = -15, d = 6$

4. $a = 0, b = -7, c = -6$

5. (i) $f(x) = x^3 + 2$

(ii) $g(x) = x^3$

(iii) $h(x) = 2x^3$

$A = (2^{\frac{1}{3}}, 4)$

6. $f(2) = 16, f(5) = -5$

7. $f(0) = 6$

$f\left(\dfrac{1}{2}\right) = 3\dfrac{3}{8}$

$f(2) = -4$

8. (i) $f(x) = -1(x + 1)(x - 1)(x - 2)^2$

(ii) $a = -1, b = 4, c = -3, d = -4, e = 4$

9. (i) $a = -2$

(ii) $f(x) = (x + 2)^2(x - 1)^2$

$g(x) = -\dfrac{1}{2}(x + 2)^2(x - 1)^2$

10. (i) $x^3 - 6x^2 + 3x + 10 = 0$

(ii) $x^3 + 4x^2 + 3x = 0$

(iii) $4x^3 - 5x^2 - 23x + 6 = 0$

(iv) $2x^3 - 13x^2 + 22x - 8 = 0$

11. (i) $f(x) = 2x^3 - 17x^2 + 27x + 18$

(ii) $f(x) = -4x^3 - 8x^2 + 37x + 20$

12. $a = -\dfrac{1}{3}, b = -18$

13. (i) $-1, 0, 2$

(ii) $-1\dfrac{1}{4}, 0, 2\dfrac{1}{4}$

(iii) $-1.3, 0, 2.3$

14. (i) $V = x(x - 1)(x + 1)$

(ii) $x = 3\,\text{cm}$

15. $V = \dfrac{\pi}{4}h^3 = ah^3$

$a = 0.79$

$V = 1051.49\,\text{cm}^3$

$d = 6.5\,\text{cm}$

16. $x = 4.8$ (from graph); $x = 4.84$ (algebra);

$x = 3.6$

Revision Exercise 2 (Core)

1. $x = 1, 5; t = -2, -1, 3, 6$

2. $x = 1 \pm \sqrt{13}$

3. $p > 1$

5. $a = -21, b = 8$

6. (i) One of $2, -3, 5$

(ii) $(x - 2)(x + 3)(x - 5)$

(iii) Roots are $2, -3, 5$

7. (i) Real roots

(ii) Imaginary roots

(iii) Imaginary roots

8. $y^2 - 12y + 27 = 0; x = 1, 2$

Revision Exercise 2 (Advanced)

1. $2(x - 1)^2 - 7$

(i) $1 \pm \sqrt{\dfrac{7}{2}}$

(ii) $(1, -7)$

2. $11 - 4\sqrt{6}$

3. $\dfrac{\sqrt{35}+5}{25}$

4. 7

5. (i) t has a value slightly less than 1

(ii) $t = 0.90$ (iii) 0.49%

6. $p = \dfrac{1}{2} \pm \dfrac{\sqrt{1-4n\sigma^2}}{2}$

7.

	$k < 0$	$0 < k < \frac{1}{4}$	$k > \frac{1}{4}$
k	Negative	Positive	Positive
$4k$	Negative	Positive	Positive
$4k - 1$	Negative	Negative	Positive
$k(4k - 1)$	Positive	Negative	Positive

$0 < k < \frac{1}{4}$

9. $B(-\sqrt{2}, 1 - 5\sqrt{2})$ $A(\sqrt{2}, 1 + 5\sqrt{2})$

10. $k = -3$

11. -6

12. $(2, -7), \left(-\dfrac{13}{5}, \dfrac{34}{5}\right)$

13. Length $= 18$ m, width $= 6$ m

14. $y \leqslant -4$ or $y \geqslant 0$

15. $y = -2x^2 - x + 5$

16. (iii) $f(0) = -6, f(1) = 0, f(2) = 0, f(3) = 0,$
$f(3) = 0, f(4) = 6$

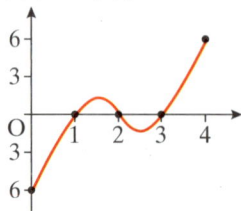

17. (i) $2, 5$

(ii) $f(x) = p(x - 2)(x - 5)^2$

(iii) $a = 2, b = -24, c = 90, d = -100$

(iv) $f(x) = -2x^3 + 24x^2 - 90x + 100$

(v) $f(x) = -2x^3 - 24x^2 - 90x - 100$

Revision Exercise 2 (Extended Response Questions)

1. (i) $a = 0.0002$

(ii) 10 hours

(iii) Because a is so small, the effect of at^3 is not noticed until it is near 10

2. (i) $6x^2 + 7xy + 2y^2$

(ii) $k = 7$

(iii) $x = \dfrac{1}{2}$ m

$3.5y + 2y^2 = 1$

$\Rightarrow y = \dfrac{1}{4}$ m

3. (a) $V = x(96 - 4x)(48 - 2x) = 8x(24 - x)^2$

(b) (i) $0 < x < 24$

(ii) Maximum volume occurs at A
No volume exists at B and C

(iii) Maximum $= 16\,382$ cm³; $x = 8$ cm

(iv) $15\,680$ cm³   (v) $14\,440$ cm³

(vi) 9720 cm³

(c) $a = 4, b = 24, c = 48$

4. (ii) Roots $= 0, 40$

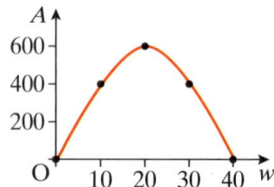

(iii) $A = 600 - (w - 20)^2$
Maximum area $= 600$ m²

(iv) $w = 20$ m

(v) width $= 20$ m, length $= 15$ m

5. (a) (i) 1 second or 3 seconds

(ii) 4.5 seconds

(b) 4.45 seconds

(c) $h = 6 - (t - 2)^2; (p, q) = (2, 6)$

6.

No. of price hikes	Price per rental	Number of rentals	Total income (I)
	€12	36	€432
1 price hike	€12.5	34	€425
2 price hikes	€13	32	€416
3 price hikes	€13.5	30	€405
x price hikes	$12 + 0.5x$	$36 - 2x$	$(12 + 0.5x) \times (36 - 2x)$

(i) $I = (12 + 0.5x)(36 - 2x) = 432 - 6x - x^2$

(ii) $441 - (x + 3)^2$

(iii) €441

(iv) Reduce rental price

7. (a) $A = xy + \dfrac{\pi}{2}x^2$

(b) (i) $y = 100 - \pi x$

(ii) $A = 100x - \dfrac{\pi}{2}x^2$

(iii) $0 < x < \dfrac{100}{\pi}$

(c) $51.2, 12.4$

(d) (i) $\frac{x^2}{50}\left(100 - \frac{\pi}{2}x\right)$

    (ii) $247.6\,\text{m}^2$

    (iii) $18.8\,\text{m}$

8. (a) $B\left(\dfrac{3-\sqrt{33}}{2}, 3-\sqrt{33}\right)$,

      $A\left(\dfrac{3+\sqrt{33}}{2}, 3+\sqrt{33}\right)$

  (b) $d = 6 + 3x - x^2$

  (c)

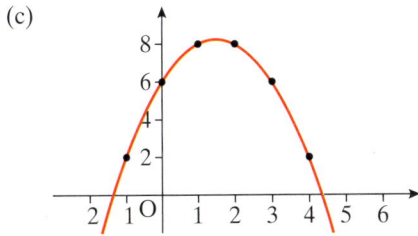

  (d) $y = 8\frac{1}{4} - (x - 1\frac{1}{2})^2$

  (e) $(1\frac{1}{2}, 8\frac{1}{4})$

  (f) $0 \le d \le 8\frac{1}{4}$

9. (iii)

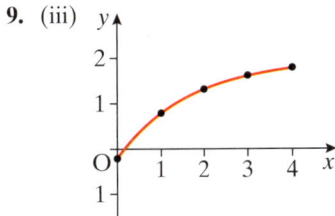

  (iv) $(\frac{1}{4}, \frac{1}{4})$

  (v) (a) $k < 0$ (b) $k = 0$ (c) $k > 0$

Chapter 3: Trigonometry 1

Exercise 3.1

1. (i) $\frac{\pi}{6}$ (ii) $\frac{\pi}{4}$ (iii) $\frac{5\pi}{6}$ (iv) $\frac{3\pi}{4}$

  (v) $\frac{\pi}{5}$ (vi) $\frac{4\pi}{3}$ (vii) $\frac{13\pi}{6}$

2. (i) $180°$ (ii) $90°$ (iii) $30°$

  (iv) $150°$ (v) $80°$ (vi) $330°$ (vii) $75°$

3. (i) $8\,\text{cm}$ (ii) $16\,\text{cm}$ (iii) $10\,\text{cm}$ (iv) $5\,\text{cm}$

4. (i) 1 radian   (ii) 2 radians

  (iii) $\frac{1}{2}$ radian   (iv) $1\frac{1}{2}$ radians

  (v) $1\frac{1}{4}$ radians

5. $7\frac{1}{2}\,\text{cm}$

6. $15\,\text{cm}^2$

7. $1\frac{1}{4}$ radians

8. $\frac{\pi}{6}$

9. $\frac{3}{2}$ radians

10. $\frac{15\pi}{2}\,\text{cm}^2$

11. (i) $\frac{5}{2}$ radians   (ii) $143°$

12. $(4 - \pi)\,\text{cm}^2$

13. $64\,\text{cm}^2$

14. (ii) $2\pi\,\text{cm}$ (iii) $(12\pi - 18\sqrt{3})\,\text{cm}^2$

15. (i) $\theta = \dfrac{40 - 2r}{r}\left(\text{or } \theta = \dfrac{200}{r^2}\right)$

  (ii) $r = 10$ (iii) $\theta = 2$ radians

Exercise 3.2

1. (i) 0.7431 (ii) 0.2756 (iii) 0.5407

  (iv) 0.7266 (v) 0.5914

2. (i) $48°$ (ii) $69°$ (iii) $55°$

  (iv) $78°$ (v) $42°$ (vi) $12°$

3. (i) $42°$ (ii) $53°$ (iii) $41°$

  (iv) $24°$

6. $42 + 12\sqrt{3}$

7. (i) 13.9 (ii) $44°$

8. (i) $\sqrt{2}$ (ii) $\sqrt{6}$; $1 + \sqrt{3}$

Exercise 3.3

1. (i) 0.7660 (ii) -0.7660 (iii) 0.6428

  (iv) -0.6428 (v) -0.8192 (vi) 0.5736

2. (i) 0.6691 (ii) -0.8480

  (iii) -0.9004 (iv) -0.9336

3. (i) $\sin 50°$ (ii) $-\cos 65°$

  (iii) $-\tan 20°$ (iv) $-\cos 40°$

  (v) $-\sin 70°$ (vi) $-\tan 60°$

4. (i) $\dfrac{\sqrt{3}}{2}$ (ii) $-\dfrac{1}{\sqrt{2}}$ (iii) $-\dfrac{\sqrt{3}}{2}$

  (iv) $-\dfrac{1}{2}$ (v) $\dfrac{\sqrt{3}}{2}$ (vi) 1

  (vii) $-\dfrac{\sqrt{3}}{2}$ (viii) $-\dfrac{\sqrt{3}}{2}$

5. (i) 3rd (ii) 1st (iii) 2nd (iv) 1st

6. (i) $124°$ (ii) $68°$ (iii) $240°$

  (iv) $345°$ (v) $75°$

7. $13°$ and $167°$

8. (i) $147°$ and $213°$ (ii) $224°$ and $316°$

  (iii) $43°$ and $223°$

9. $30°$ and $150°$

10. 1 and -1

11. $\dfrac{\sqrt{3}}{2}$ and $-\dfrac{\sqrt{3}}{2}$

12. $\dfrac{1}{2}$ and $-\dfrac{1}{2}$

13. 233°

14. $-\dfrac{3}{4}$

15. $-\dfrac{\sqrt{3}}{2}$

16. $-\dfrac{1}{\sqrt{5}}$

17. (i) $\dfrac{\sqrt{3}}{2}$ (ii) $-\dfrac{1}{\sqrt{2}}$ (iii) $\sqrt{3}$

Exercise 3.4

1. (i) 6.4 m   (ii) 18.7 m   (iii) 6.7 m

2. (i) 44°   (ii) 35°   (iii) 41°

3. (i) 68°16′   (ii) 9.7
    (iii) 36 sq. units

4. (i) 28.3 cm²   (ii) 9.5 cm²   (iii) 29.5 cm²

5. (i) 35°   (ii) 90°   (iii) 42°

6. (i) 23 cm   (ii) 182 cm²

7. (i) 2 m

8. $x = 4$ cm

9. 72.5° and 107.5°

10. (i) 7.3 cm   (ii) 2.0 cm

11. 36.8 m

12. 103 km

13. 406 m, 622 m

14. 13.7 km

Exercise 3.5

1. (i) 7.2 cm   (ii) 8.6 cm   (iii) 9.4 cm

2. (i) 106°   (ii) 44°   (iii) 108°

4. 15.2 sq. units

5. (i) 4.0   (ii) 120°

6. 146.5 m

7. (i) 46°   (ii) 10.9 cm

8. (i) $\dfrac{1}{8}$ (ii) $a = 3, b = 8$

10. 18.3 cm

11. (i) $x = 4$ (ii) $\dfrac{15\sqrt{3}}{4}$

12. (i) 21.5 cm   (ii) 582 cm

13. 70°

14. 97.2°

15. (i) 127.7°   (ii) 161 cm²

16. 19°

17. 54.4 km

18. (i) 88.79 km, 17.32.

Exercise 3.6

1. (i) 11.87 cm   (ii) 19.7°

2. (i) 25.7 m   (ii) 38.7°   (iii) 29.8 m
    (iv) 21.9°

3. (i) $|\text{PY}| = 180$ m; $|\text{QY}| = 297$ m
    (ii) 331 m

4. (i) 18.4°   (ii) 31.9 cm   (iii) 15.8°

5. (i) 7 m   (ii) 13 m

6. (i) 3.3 m   (ii) 17.6 m²

7. 29 m

8. (i) 14.8 m   (ii) 19.7°   (iii) 28.5°

9. $x = 8$

10. 11.9 m

11. 6.1 m

12. (i) 28.6 m²   (ii) 29.2 m²

13. (i) 160 m   (ii) 340 m   (iii) 525 m
    (iv) 200 m

14. (i) 169.7 cm   (ii) 177 cm   (iii) 43°

Exercise 3.7

1.

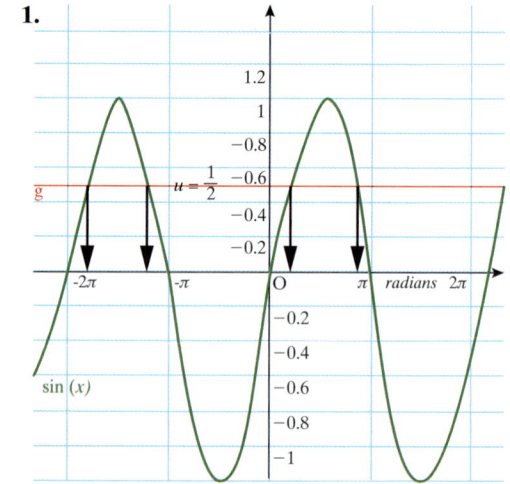

4 Angles

2.

x	0	45	90	135	180	225	270	315	360	405	450	495	540
sin x	0	0.7	1	0.7	0	−0.7	−1	−0.7	0	0.7	1	0.7	0

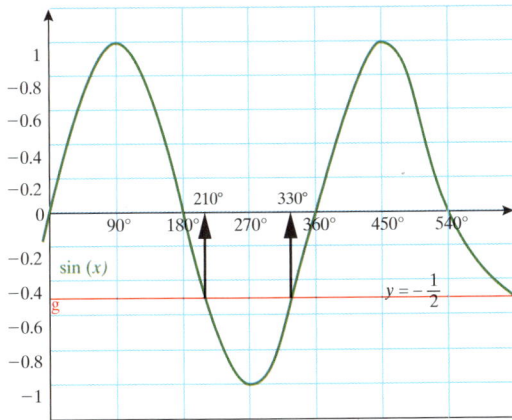

3.

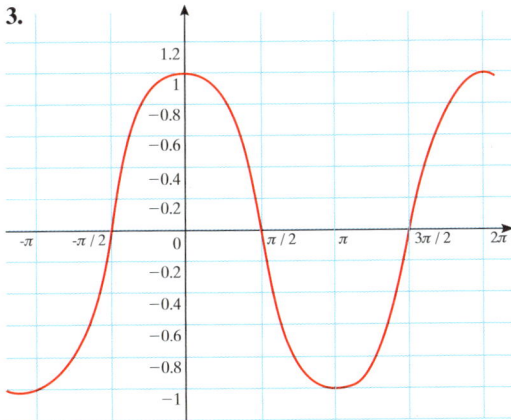

, (0,1) or $(2\pi ,1)$

5.

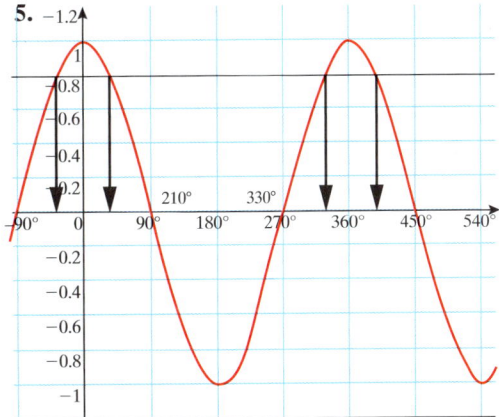

, $-26°, 26°, 332°, 386°. 0.84$

4.   (i) $y = \tan x, 0 \leqslant x \geqslant \dfrac{3\pi}{2}$

   (ii) $y = \cos x, -\pi \leqslant x \leqslant \pi$

6. (iv) $\frac{|GH|}{1} = 0.58$,

(v)

x	0	10	20	30	40	50	60	70	80	85
$tan\ x$	0	0.18	0.36	0.58	0.84	1.2	1.7	2.7	5.7	11.4

(vi)

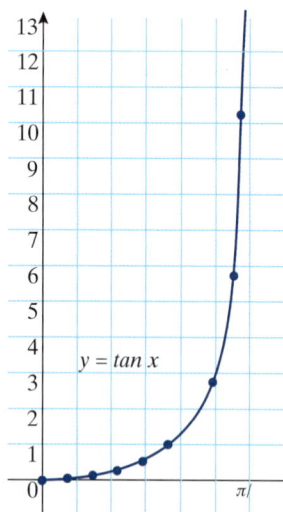

$y = tan\ x$

(vii) 2.2, (viii) 2.5%

7. (i) $\frac{\pi}{4}, \frac{5\pi}{4}$ (ii) $0, \pi, 2\pi$ (iii) $\frac{\pi}{4} \leqslant x \leqslant \frac{5\pi}{4}$

(iv) $0 < x > \frac{\pi}{2}, \pi < x < \frac{3\pi}{2}$

Exercise 3.8

1. (i) $3, 2\pi$ (ii) $2, 2\pi$ (iii) $4, \frac{\pi}{2}$, (iv) $\frac{1}{4}, \pi$

2. (i) π (ii) $2\frac{\pi}{3}$ (iii) 8π (iv) $\frac{\pi}{3}$

3. (i) $[-2, 2]$ (ii) $[-5, 5]$ (iii) $[-8, 8]$

(iv) $[-6, 6]$

4. (i) $a = 3, b = 2$ (ii) $a = 4, b = \frac{1}{2}$

5. $a = 3, b = 2$

6. (i) $\pi, [-1, 1], \cos 2x$ (ii) $4\pi, [-2, 2], 2\sin\frac{x}{2}$

(iii) $\frac{\pi}{2}, [-0.5, 0.5], \frac{1}{2}\sin 4x$

(iv) $\pi, [-4, 4], 4\cos 2x$

7. (i) $f(x) = 3\cos 2x, g(x) = 2\cos 3x$

(ii) $A = \frac{\pi}{6}, B = \frac{\pi}{2}, C = 5\frac{\pi}{6}, D = 7\frac{\pi}{4}$

8. (i) $y = 4, [2, 6], 2\pi$ (ii) $y = -1, [-3, 1], 2\frac{\pi}{3}$

(iii) $-2, [-3, -1], \frac{\pi}{2}$, (iv) $2, [-3, 7], 8\pi$

9. (i) $y = 2$, period $= \pi, y = 2 + 2\cos 2x$

(ii) $y = -1$, period $= 4\pi, y = -1 - 3\cos\frac{x}{2}$

(iii) $y = 2$, period $= 2\pi, y = 2 + \sin x$

(iv) $y = -2$, period $= 2\frac{x}{3}, y = -2 - 3\sin 3x$

10.

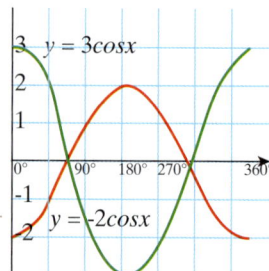

11.

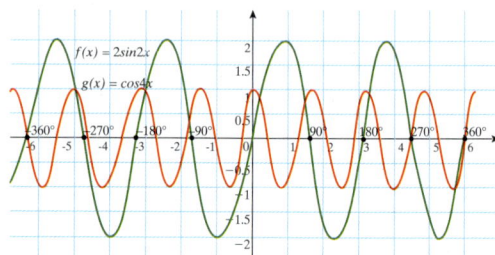

12. $y = \cos 2x, y = \sin\frac{x}{2}, 5\pi$

13. (i) $a = 25\ 000, b = 15\ 000, c = 30°$

or $\frac{\pi}{6}$ radians (ii) 6 times (iii) 4 months

14. (i) 2m, 6m

(ii)

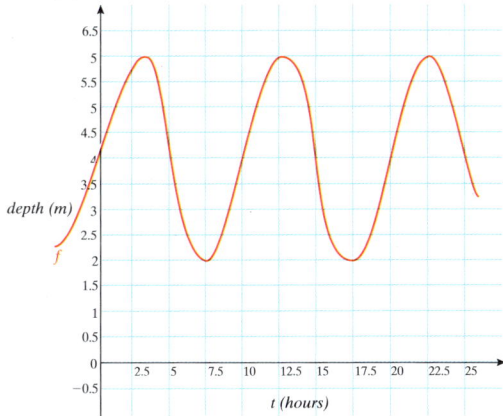

depth (m) vs *t (hours)*

(iii) 5.18m

(iv) between 00.50 and 04.10 or
10.50 and 14.10 or 20.50 and 24.10

Exercise 3.9

1. 30° and 150°

2. 30° and 330°

3. $\dfrac{\pi}{4}$ and $\dfrac{5\pi}{4}$

4. $\dfrac{\pi}{12} + n\pi$ or $\dfrac{5\pi}{12} + n\pi$

5. $10° + n(120°)$ or $110° + n(120°)$

6. $\dfrac{4\pi}{9} + \dfrac{2n\pi}{3}$ or $\dfrac{5\pi}{9} + \dfrac{2n\pi}{3}$

7. $\dfrac{\pi}{12} + \dfrac{n\pi}{2}$ or $\dfrac{5\pi}{12} + \dfrac{n\pi}{2}$

8. (i) $\dfrac{5\pi}{12} + n\pi$ or $\dfrac{7\pi}{12} + n\pi$

(ii) $n = 0, \dfrac{5\pi}{12}, \dfrac{7\pi}{12}$

$n = 1, \dfrac{17\pi}{12}, \dfrac{19\pi}{12}$

$n = 2, \dfrac{29\pi}{12}, \dfrac{31\pi}{12}$

$n = 3, \dfrac{41\pi}{12}, \dfrac{43\pi}{12}$

9. $x = 75°, 105°, 195°, 225°, 315°, 345°$

10. 75°, 105°, 255°, 285°

11. (i) $\dfrac{\pi}{12} + \dfrac{2n\pi}{3}$ or $\dfrac{7\pi}{12} + \dfrac{2n\pi}{3}$

(ii) $n = 0, \dfrac{\pi}{12}, \dfrac{7\pi}{12}$

$n = 1, \dfrac{3\pi}{4}$

12. $\dfrac{\pi}{24} + \dfrac{n\pi}{2}$ or $\dfrac{11\pi}{24} + \dfrac{n\pi}{2}$

13. $\theta = 40°, 80°, 160°, 200°, 280°, 320°$

14. $\theta = 17°, 43°, 137°, 167°, 257°, 283°$

Revision Exercise 3 (Core)

1. $23.1\,\text{cm}^2$

2. 150° and 330°

3. (i) $\dfrac{6}{5}$ radians (ii) 24 cm

4. $16\dfrac{4}{5}\,\text{cm}^2$

5. (i) Period $= 180°$; Range $= [-2, 2]$

(ii) $a = 2, b = 2$

6. 2 sq. units

7. $-\dfrac{3}{4}$

8. 30° or 150°

9. 49° or 131°

10. $\dfrac{1}{2}$

11.

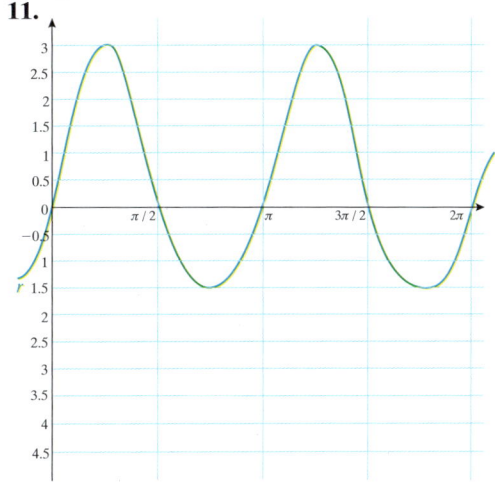

Revision Exercise 3 (Advanced)

1. (i) 115° (ii) $43.5\,\text{cm}^2$

2. (i) $n\pi + \dfrac{5\pi}{12}$ or $n\pi + \dfrac{7\pi}{12}$

(ii) $1\dfrac{1}{2}$ radians

3. (i) 57° (ii) 39 cm

4. 36 km/h

5. (i) $a = 5$ (ii) $\dfrac{25\sqrt{3}}{2}$

6. 2.9 m

7. (i) $[-4, 4]$ (ii) π (iii) -4

(iv) $g(x) = 4\cos x$; $f(x) = 2\sin 2x$

(v) $P = \left(\dfrac{5\pi}{4}, 2\right)$

8. 3.13 m

9. (a) (i) 9.4 m (ii) 42°

(b) No; eye moves 32.4°

10. (i) (a) 10.4 cm (b) $\dfrac{5}{4}$ radians

11. 12m

525

12. $\left(\frac{32\pi}{3} - 8\sqrt{3}\right)$cm²

13. (i) $a = (0, 4)$, $b = (0, -4)$, $c = (\frac{\pi}{6}, 0)$,

$d = (\pi/2, 0)$, $e = (\frac{5\pi}{6}, 0)$, $f = (\frac{4\pi}{3}, 0)$

(ii) 20.5 m

14. (i) $\theta = n\pi + \frac{\pi}{12}$ or $n\pi + \frac{11\pi}{12}$

(ii) $\theta = \frac{\pi}{12}, \frac{11\pi}{12}, \frac{13\pi}{12}, \frac{23\pi}{12}$

15. 38°

Revision Exercise 3 (Extended Response Questions)

1. (i) 6.5 m   (ii) 21.0 m   (iii) 63.4°

(iv) 23.3 m   (v) 16.2°

2. (i) $k - \frac{8}{\tan\theta}$ (ii)   49°

3. (i) $4 - 2\sqrt{2}$

(ii) $8 - 8\pi + 4\pi\sqrt{2}$

(iii) $8\sqrt{3} - 4\pi$

4. Proof

5. (i) $\frac{h}{\tan 25°}$ (ii) $\frac{h}{\tan 33°}$ (iii) 22.7 m

6. (i) $p = 5$, $q = 3$

(ii)

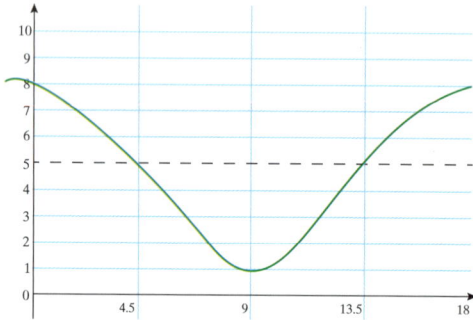

(iii) 3 hrs after low tide

7. (i) (a) 9 m (b) 3 m

(ii) (a) 0.524 s (b) 1.571 s

(iii) (a) 3 m (b) [3m, 9m]

(iv) $\frac{2\pi}{3}$ radians

(v)

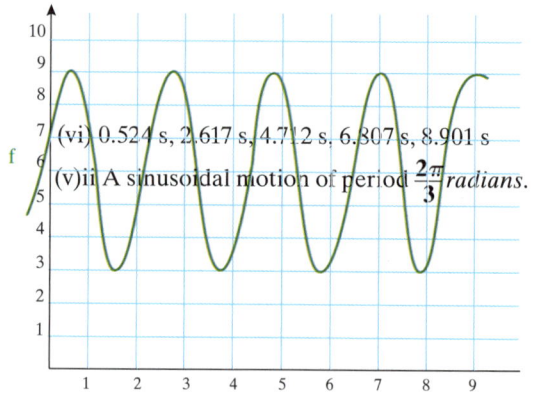

(vi) 0.524 s, 2.617 s, 4.712 s, 6.807 s, 8.901 s

(vii) A sinusoidal motion of period $\frac{2\pi}{3}$ radians.

8. (i) 23.5°, 23°

(ii) 27

(iii)

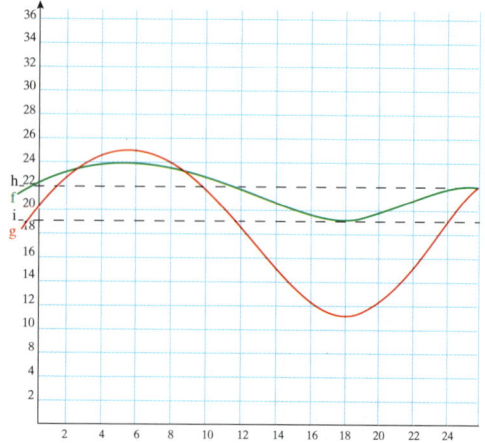

(iv) 10.28, 17.32

Chapter 4: Coordinate Geometry: The Line

Exercise 4.1

1. (i) $\sqrt{41}$ (ii) $2\sqrt{5}$
   (iii) $-\frac{1}{6}$ (iv) $(4, 0)$
2. $(-1, -1)$
3. (i) $\frac{3}{4}$ (ii) $-\frac{4}{3}$
6. $k = 5$
7. $p = -5$
8. (i) $\frac{1}{2}, -2, -\frac{1}{3}$
9. (i) a and c (ii) b and d
10. Slope of $a = \frac{2}{3}$; slope of $b = \frac{3}{2}$; slope of $c = 2$
11. Line is falling from left to right; $m = -\frac{1}{2}$
12. $a = -5$ or 9
13. $k = 3, 11$
14. (i) $\frac{1}{2}$ (ii) $-2, k = 6$
    (iii) $4\sqrt{5}$ (iv) 10 sq. units
15. (i) $q = 4$ or $\frac{32}{3}$

Exercise 4.2

1. (i) $\frac{5}{2}$ (ii) $\frac{27}{2}$ (iii) $\frac{5}{2}$ (iv) 5
2. $B' = (-7, -2)$, $C' = (1, -2)$; 8 sq. units
3. (i) $\frac{9}{2}$ (ii) $\frac{33}{2}$
4. 14 sq. units
5. $k = 7, -21$
6. $k = 5, -\frac{23}{5}$
7. $k = 1, 8$
8. Area $= 0$; points collinear
9. $k = 8$ or 16
10. $b = 6$; 5 sq. units
11. $k = 1$
12. (i) 15 sq. units (ii) $2\sqrt{10}$ (iii) $\frac{3\sqrt{10}}{2}$

Exercise 4.3

1. (i) $3x - y - 13 = 0$ (ii) $2x + y + 12 = 0$
2. $2x - 3y + 9 = 0$
3. (i) $\frac{1}{3}$ (ii) $x - 3y - 15 = 0$
4. (i) 6 (ii) $x + 6y - 4 = 0$
5. $k = 2$
6. $t = \frac{8}{3}$
7. $k = 2$
8. $(6, 0)$ and $(0, -2)$
9. $a = -5$
10. (i) $C = (-3, 0)$ (ii) $3x + 2y + 9 = 0$

11. $-\frac{2}{5}$; $2x + 5y - 11 = 0$
12. (i) neither (ii) perpendicular
    (iii) perpendicular (iv) parallel
    (v) parallel (vi) perpendicular
13. $(5, -2)$
14. $(2, 3)$; $2x - 3y + 5 = 0$
15. $3x - y - 7 = 0$
16. (ii) $k = 3$
17. $x - 5y + 11 = 0$
18. $\left(\frac{k}{3}, 0\right)$; $\left(0, \frac{k}{4}\right)$; $k = 24$
19. $2x - 3y + c = 0$; $2x - 3y - 2 = 0$
20. $4x + y = k$; $4x + y - 12 = 0$
21. (a) It does not. (b) 1.58 km

Exercise 4.4

1. $\left(\frac{17}{5}, -\frac{12}{5}\right)$
2. $(1, -4)$
3. $\left(\frac{24}{7}, \frac{24}{7}\right)$
4. $\left(\frac{13}{5}, -\frac{6}{5}\right)$
5. $\left(\frac{17}{4}, 6\right)$
6. $\left(\frac{14}{3}, \frac{17}{3}\right)$
7. $x = 8, y = 3$
8. $x = 6, y = 4$
9. $x = 21, y = -14$
10. $1 : 2$

Exercise 4.5

1. (i) $(1, 2)$ (ii) $(4, 1)$
2. $(2, 1)$
3. $(3, -2)$
4. $\left(\frac{4}{3}, \frac{5}{3}\right)$
5. $(2, 0)$
7. $k = -5$

Exercise 4.6

1. 1
5. $c = 10$ or $c = -40$
6. $\frac{3\sqrt{10}}{4}$
7. Yes
8. $a = -\frac{1}{3}, 3$
9. $a = -3$
12. No
13. $4x + 3y + c = 0$; $4x + 3y + 11 = 0$;
    $4x + 3y - 9 = 0$

14. $4x + 3y + k = 0$; $4x + 3y + 13 = 0$;
$4x + 3y - 27 = 0$

15. $mx - y + 4m + 2 = 0$; $y - 2 = 0$;
$4x + 3y + 10 = 0$

16. $y - 5 = 0$; $15x + 8y - 85 = 0$

17. (i) 2
(ii) Area = 5 sq. units

18. (a) red: $3x + 2y - 2 = 0$, blue: $3x + 2y + 2 = 0$
(b) $\dfrac{4}{\sqrt{13}}$

19. No they live on opposite sides of the town.

20. (a) $8x - 10y + 3 = 0$
(b) $\dfrac{1}{\sqrt{41}}\, km$

Exercise 4.7

1. (i) 1   (ii) $\dfrac{7}{4}$ (iii) 8
2. 45°
3. 135°
4. 82°
5. 135°
6. 30°
7. $-\dfrac{1}{5}$ or 5
8. $5x + y = 0$; $x - 5y = 0$
9. $3x - y + 4 = 0$; $x + 3y - 2 = 0$
10. $x + 5y - 14 = 0$; $5x + y - 22 = 0$
11. $2x + 3y - 6 = 0$
12. (i) Slope $= -t$ (ii) $t = -\dfrac{1}{3}$ or 3

Exercise 4.8

1. (a) (i) 95°F (ii) 58°F (iii) 10°C (iv) 38°C
(b) $5x - 9y - 160 = 0$
(c) 203°F
2. (i) €320   (ii) 45 m²   (iii) €440
3. (i) €400, €800, €1200
(ii) $I = 400T$
(iii) $8\dfrac{3}{4}$ years
(iv) $A = 400T + 5000$
4. (ii) $5P + 4N = 700$ (iii) €69.60
(iv) 85
5. (ii) **A**: $P = 5 + 2D$; **B**: $P = 2.2D$
(iii) 25 km   (iv) Firm **B**
6. (ii) €40 and 28 articles

Revision Exercise 4 (Core)

1. $2x + 3y - 10 = 0$
2. 4 square units
3. $a = -8$

4. $a = 9$
5. (i) $\dfrac{3}{2}$ (ii) $\left(\dfrac{4}{3}, 0\right)$ and $(0, -2)$
(iii) $\dfrac{4}{3}$ sq. units
6. $\dfrac{2}{5}$; $2x - 5y + 3 = 0$
7. (i) $k = -\dfrac{1}{2}$ (ii) $(-4, 11)$
8. (a) Yes   (b) Yes
(c) Yes   (d) No
9. $2x - y - 8 = 0$
10. $k = 9$

Revision Exercise 4 (Advanced)

1. (i) 3   (ii) $k = -32$
2. (i) $(-1, 1)$ (ii) (a) $(3, 0)$ and $\left(0, \dfrac{6}{k}\right)$
(b) $k = 3$
3. (i) $2x + y = 9$ (ii) (a) $x - 2y = 1 - 2k$
(b) $k = \dfrac{1}{2}$
4. $(3, 3)$
5. $(4\dfrac{1}{2}, 1)$
6. (i) $y - 6 = m(x + 4)$
(ii) $\left(\dfrac{-6 - 4m}{m}, 0\right)$, $(0, 6 + 4m)$
(iii) $m = \dfrac{3}{4}$ or $m = 3$
7. (i) $k = -3\dfrac{1}{2}$ (ii) $3x - 4y - 23 = 0$
8. $4x - 3y + 20 = 0$; $4x - 3y - 20 = 0$
9. $3x - y - 2 = 0$ and $x + 3y - 14 = 0$
10. (ii) $4x + 3y + c = 0$
(iii) $4x + 3y + 5 = 0$; $4x + 3y - 15 = 0$

Revision Exercise 4 (Extended Response Questions)

1. (i) $2x + y = 5$ (ii) 5 m   (iii) 559 cm
2. (i) $mx - y + (5 - 2m) = 0$
(ii) $\left(\dfrac{-5 + 2m}{m}, 0\right)$, $(0, 5 - 2m)$
(iii) $m = -\dfrac{1}{2}$ or $m = -\dfrac{25}{2}$
3. (i) $\dfrac{4 - k}{2}$ (ii) $k = -2, 3$
(iii) 15 sq. units
4. (i) $Q = (8, 0)$, $R = (0, -12)$ (ii) $c = \pm 12\sqrt{2}$
5. (i) $(1, -1)$ (ii) $\sqrt{65}$ (iii) 65π
6. (i) $x - 4y + 10 = 0$
(ii) $A = (4, 1)$; $C = (-2, 2)$
7. (i) $k = 2$ (ii) $T = (2, 12)$
8. (ii) $4I - 3S + 77 = 0$ (iii) €41 million
(iv) $10\dfrac{3}{4}\%$

10. (i) $m = \dfrac{-t}{t+2}$ (ii) $t = -\dfrac{3}{2}$ or $t = 1$

11. (i) $y = \dfrac{5}{3}x - 4$ (ii) $\left(\dfrac{66}{7}, \dfrac{82}{7} \right)$ (iii) $\dfrac{5}{3}$

    (iv) $c = 15$ (v) $\dfrac{629}{14}u^2$

Chapter 5: Probability 1

Exercise 5.1

1. 60   **2.** 42

3. 1872   **4.** 240

5. 720   **6.** 5040; 1440

7. 120;   (i) 24   (ii) 6

8. 5040;   (i) 1440   (ii) 1440

9. (i) 480   (ii) 240   (iii) 240

10. (i) 720   (ii) 1440

11. 5040; 720

12. (i) 720   (ii) 144

13. 840   **14.** 360

15. 336   **16.** 1440

17. (i) 504   (ii) 648

18. 24;   (i) 6   (ii) 6   (iii) 12

19. 4536;   (i) 1008   (ii) 504

20. 72; 24

21. 100;   (i) 60   (ii) 20

22. (i) 300   (ii) 60

23. 36   **24.** 60 480

25. 5040;   (i) 1440   (ii) 3600

26. (i) 720   (ii) 336   (iii) 48

Exercise 5.2

1. (i) 15   (ii) 35   (iii) 45

    (iv) 66   (v) 153

3. 56

4. 364; 286

5. 126;   (i) 70   (ii) 35

6. 126; 70

7. 22 100; 286

8. (i) 56   (ii) 126   (iii) 35

9. 40

10. (i) 26 400   (ii) 22 275

11. 20;   (i) 12   (ii) 16

12. 28; 6

13. (i) 15   (ii) 18

14. 360

15. (i) 70   (ii) 15   (iii) 15

16. 10; 3

17. (i) 15   (ii) 6

18. (i) 35   (ii) 70   (iii) 120

19. 560

20. 288

21. (i) $n = 5$ (ii) $n = 10$ (iii) $n = 7$

Exercise 5.3

1. (i) Impossible   (ii) V. likely

    (iii) V. unlikely   (iv) V. unlikely

    (v) Evens   (vi) Certain

    (vii) Unlikely

2. (i) 6   (ii) 4   (iii) 0   (iv) 2

3. (i) 6   (ii) 8   (iii) 2

4. (i) $\dfrac{1}{6}$ (ii) $\dfrac{1}{3}$ (iii) $\dfrac{1}{2}$ (iv) $\dfrac{1}{2}$

    (v) $\dfrac{1}{3}$ (vi) $\dfrac{1}{2}$

5. (i) $\dfrac{1}{13}$ (ii) $\dfrac{1}{4}$ (iii) $\dfrac{3}{13}$ (iv) $\dfrac{1}{26}$

    (v) $\dfrac{5}{13}$

6. (i) $\dfrac{9}{17}$ (ii) $\dfrac{8}{17}$ (iii) $\dfrac{5}{17}$ (iv) $\dfrac{4}{17}$

7. (i) $\dfrac{1}{8}$ (ii) $\dfrac{1}{4}$ (iii) $\dfrac{3}{8}$ (iv) $\dfrac{1}{2}$

8. (i) $\dfrac{1}{2}$ (ii) $\dfrac{1}{6}$ (iii) $\dfrac{2}{3}$ (iv) $\dfrac{1}{2}$

9. (i) $\dfrac{1}{12}$ (ii) $\dfrac{1}{4}$ (iii) $\dfrac{1}{6}$ (iv) $\dfrac{1}{3}$

10. (i) $\dfrac{1}{36}$ (ii) $\dfrac{1}{12}$ (iii) $\dfrac{1}{9}$

11. $\dfrac{2}{5}$

12. (i) $\dfrac{3}{5}$ (ii) 3   (iii) 3

13. (i) $\dfrac{1}{12}$ (ii) $\dfrac{1}{6}$ (iii) $\dfrac{1}{2}$; 9 most often; $\dfrac{1}{4}$

14. (i) $\dfrac{2}{9}$ (ii) $\dfrac{1}{9}$

15. (i) $\dfrac{1}{8}$ (ii) $\dfrac{1}{8}$ (iii) $\dfrac{3}{8}$

16. (i) $\dfrac{1}{2}$ (ii) $\dfrac{8}{25}$ (iii) $\dfrac{8}{25}, \dfrac{16}{25}$

17. (i) $\dfrac{1}{6}$ (ii) $\dfrac{7}{12}$

18. (i) 286   (ii) 22 100   (iii) $\dfrac{11}{850}$

19. (i)

	M	W	Tot
Coffee	10	20	30
~~Coffee~~	15	5	20
Total	25	25	50

    (ii)

	M	W	Tot
Coffee	0.2	0.4	0.6
~~Coffee~~	0.3	0.1	0.4
Total	0.5	0.5	1

    (iii) (a) 0.3   (b) 0.4

20. $\frac{2}{13}$

21. (i) $\frac{1}{6}$ (ii) $\frac{171}{1296}$

22. (i) (a) 330 (b) $(100+15)=115$ (ii) $\frac{2}{11}$

Exercise 5.4

1. (i) 150 (ii) 150 (iii) 300

2. (i) $\frac{1}{2}$ (ii) (a) 200 (b) 150

3. (i) $\frac{17}{50}$

  (ii) No; as 34 is well below the expected value of 50

4. (i) (a) $\frac{1}{5}$ (b) $\frac{2}{15}$

  (ii) (a) $\frac{1}{6}$ (b) $\frac{1}{6}$ (iii) No

5. (i) $\frac{77}{150}$

  (ii) No; far more red than one would expect

6. No; after 300 spins the results should be close to the expected value

7. (i) $x=0.1$ (ii) 0.6 (iii) 200

8. $\frac{7}{10}$

9. $\frac{33}{200}$; largest no. of trials

10. (i) Bill's (ii) Biased

  (iii) $\frac{63}{290}$ (v) 322

11. (i) $\frac{1}{3}$ (ii) 1, 2, 2, 3, 3, 4

12. (i) (17.5)17 (ii) 14

13. (i) 0.196 (ii) 0.084 (iii) 0.0168

Exercise 5.5

1. (i) $\frac{1}{2}$ (ii) $\frac{1}{4}$ (iii) $\frac{3}{4}$

2. (i) $\frac{1}{4}$ (ii) $\frac{3}{26}$ (iii) $\frac{19}{52}$

3. (i) $\frac{1}{3}$

  (ii) $\frac{1}{5}$; As 15 and 30 are multiples of both 3 and 5; $\frac{7}{15}$

4. (i) $\frac{1}{2}$ (ii) $\frac{1}{3}$ (iii) $\frac{2}{3}$

5. (i) $\frac{1}{4}$ (ii) $\frac{1}{13}$ (iii) $\frac{4}{13}$

  (iv) $\frac{1}{2}$ (v) $\frac{1}{13}$ (vi) $\frac{7}{13}$

6. (i) $\frac{1}{6}$ (ii) $\frac{5}{36}$ (iii) $\frac{5}{18}$

7. (i) $\frac{1}{2}$ (ii) $\frac{3}{4}$ (iii) $\frac{2}{7}$

  (iv) $\frac{11}{14}$ (v) $\frac{3}{4}$ (vi) 0

8. (i) $\frac{4}{25}$ (ii) $\frac{1}{2}$ (iii) $\frac{53}{100}$

9. (i) $\frac{1}{4}$ (ii) $\frac{1}{4}$ (iii) $\frac{7}{16}$

  (iv) $\frac{3}{4}$ (v) $\frac{1}{4}$ (vi) $\frac{7}{8}$

  (vii) $\frac{5}{8}$

10. 5

11. (i) $\frac{2}{5}$ (ii) $\frac{7}{10}$ (iii) $\frac{7}{10}$

12. (i) $\frac{1}{25}$ (ii) $\frac{13}{100}$ (iii) $\frac{16}{25}$

13. (i) (a) N (b) N (c) N (d) Y (e) Y

  (ii) $\frac{1}{2}$

  (iii) No; not mutually exclusive events

14. (i) $\frac{2}{5}$ (ii) $\frac{11}{20}$ (iii) $\frac{17}{20}$

15. (i) 0.6 (ii) 0.5 (iii) 0.9
  (iv) 0.2

16. (i) 12 (ii) $\frac{3}{5}$ (iii) $\frac{1}{10}$

  (iv) $\frac{21}{25}$ (v) $\frac{37}{50}$

17. (i) 40 (ii) $\frac{3}{40}$ (iii) $\frac{3}{11}$

  (iv) $\frac{5}{24}$ (v) $\frac{2}{3}$

18. (ii) 52% (iii) 26%

19. $\frac{1}{2}$ **20.** $\frac{1}{5}$

21. 0.5 **22.** 1

23. (i) $\frac{13}{15}$ (ii) No

24. $\frac{22}{35}$

25. (a)

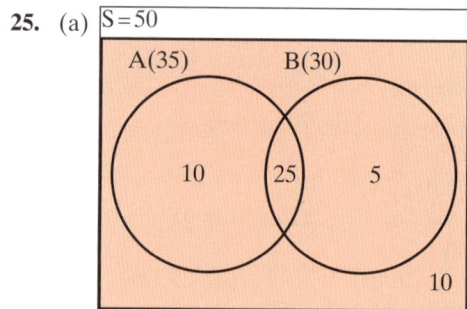

  (b) The students who did not go to the cinema or watch movies at home

(c) $P(S) = 1$

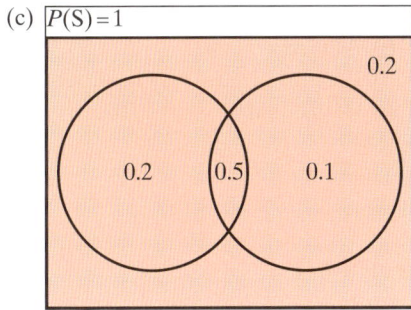

(d) 0.2

(e) (i) 0.7   (ii) 0.6

Exercise 5.6

1. (i) $\frac{4}{25}$ (ii) $\frac{1}{25}$ (iii) $\frac{4}{25}$ (iv) $\frac{2}{25}$

2. (i) $\frac{1}{36}$ (ii) $\frac{1}{12}$ (iii) $\frac{1}{6}$

3. (i) $\frac{1}{12}$ (ii) $\frac{1}{4}$

4. (i) $\frac{1}{4}$ (ii) $\frac{1}{169}$ (iii) $\frac{1}{104}$

5. (i) $\frac{4}{25}$ (ii) $\frac{6}{25}$ (iii) $\frac{6}{25}$ (iv) $\frac{9}{25}$

    (v) $\frac{13}{25}$

6. $\frac{1}{2}$

7. (i) $\frac{1}{4}$ (ii) $\frac{1}{16}$ (iii) $\frac{3}{169}$

    (iv) $\frac{1}{676}$ (v) $\frac{1}{2704}$

8. $\frac{1}{72}$

9. (i) 0.04   (ii) 0.32

10. (i) 0.504   (ii) 0.006   (iii) 0.994

11. (i) $\frac{1}{3}$ (ii) $\frac{1}{6}$ (iii) $\frac{1}{2}$

12. (i) 0.336   (ii) 0.788

13. (i) $\frac{125}{216}$ (ii) $\frac{91}{216}$ (iii) $\frac{25}{72}; \frac{1}{36}$

14. (i) $\frac{1}{49}$ (ii) $\frac{1}{7}$ (iii) $\frac{6}{7}$ (iv) $\frac{13}{49}$

15. (i) $\frac{216}{343}$ (ii) $\frac{108}{343}$ (iii) $\frac{127}{343}$

Exercise 5.7

1. (i) $\frac{1}{2}$ (ii) $\frac{1}{13}$ (iii) $\frac{1}{3}$

2. (i) $\frac{7}{9}$ (ii) $\frac{4}{5}$ (iii) $\frac{19}{25}$

3. (i) $\frac{1}{6}$ (ii) $\frac{2}{3}$

4. (i) $\frac{3}{8}$ (ii) $\frac{7}{11}$ (iii) $\frac{5}{9}$

5. (i) $\frac{5}{8}$ (ii) $\frac{5}{14}$ (iii) $\frac{3}{28}$ (iv) $\frac{13}{28}$

6. (i) $\frac{2}{11}$ (ii) $\frac{3}{11}$ (iii) $\frac{3}{11}$ (iv) $\frac{5}{11}$

    (v) $\frac{5}{11}$

7. (i) $\frac{1}{20}$ (ii) $\frac{1}{10}$ (iii) $\frac{2}{5}$

8. $\frac{1}{14}$

9. (i) $\frac{20}{33}$ (ii) $\frac{4}{13}$ (iii) $\frac{1}{13}$ (iv) $\frac{3}{8}$

10. (i) 0.48   (ii) 0.52

11. $\frac{3}{5}$

12. (i) 0.6   (ii) 0.2   (iii) 0.9   (iv) 0.4

    (v) $0.3\dot{3}$

13. (i) $\frac{2}{5}$ (ii) $\frac{2}{15}$ (iii) $\frac{4}{5}$ (iv) $\frac{1}{4}$; No

14. (i) 0.35   (ii) 0.4   (iii) 0.5

15. (i) 0.3   (ii) 0.7   (iii) 0.7   (iv) 0.3

    (v) 0.4   (vi) $0.3\dot{3}$

16. (ii) 0.2   (iii) 0.2   (iv) No

17. (i) 0.5   (ii) 0.35   (iii) 0.375   (iv) 0.4

18. (i) 0.7   (ii) $0.6\dot{6}$ (iii) 0.8   (iv) 0.1

19. (i) $\frac{1}{20}$ (ii) $\frac{3}{20}$

20. (i) 0.42   (ii) 0.1

    (iii) 0.476 (or $\frac{10}{21}$)   (iv) $0.16\dot{6}$ (or $\frac{1}{6}$)

    (v) 0.48   (vi) 0.2

Revision Exercise 5 (Core)

1. 60;   (i) 12   (ii) 36

2. (i) 330   (ii) 150

3. (i) $\frac{1}{36}$ (ii) $\frac{1}{6}$ (iii) $\frac{1}{6}$

4. (i) 0.15   (ii) '1'   (iii) 50

5. (i) 720   (ii) 240

6. (i) (a)   (ii) $\frac{11}{15}$

7. (i) $\frac{1}{3}$ (ii) $\frac{1}{9}$ (iii) $\frac{4}{27}$

8. $\frac{12}{143}$

9. (i) 0.3   (ii) $\frac{1}{2}$ (iii) $\frac{19}{20}$

10. (i) $\frac{11}{25}$ (ii) $\frac{7}{13}$ (iii) $\frac{1}{30}$

Revision Exercise 5 (Advanced)

1. (i) $\frac{1}{6}$ (ii) $\frac{5}{36}$ (iii) $\frac{11}{36}$

2. (i) 70   (ii) 35   (iii) 40

3. (i) 5040   (ii) 120   (iii) 1440

4. (i) $\frac{2}{9}$ (ii) $\frac{1}{18}$ (iii) $\frac{4}{9}$

5. (ii) (a) 7315   (b) 1330   (c) $\frac{2}{11}$

6. (i) $\frac{4}{15}$ (ii) $\frac{8}{15}$ (iii) $\frac{2}{5}$

7. (i) 0.4   (ii) 0.5   (iii) 0.9

    (iv) $\frac{3}{7}$

8. (i) $\frac{4}{7}$ (ii) $\frac{26}{35}$ (iii) $\frac{8}{13}$

    (iv) $\frac{16}{35}$ (v) $\frac{6}{7}$; Not mutually exclusive

9. (i) $\dfrac{x(x-1)}{(x+6)(x+5)}$

    (ii) 14   (iii) $\frac{15}{91}$

10. $\frac{7}{10}$

Revision Exercise 5 (Extended Response Questions)

1. (i) $\frac{1}{6}$ (ii) $\frac{20}{21}$ (iii) $\frac{25}{42}$

2. (i) 0.8%   (ii) 7.2%   (iii) 9.2%

3. (i) Equally likely outcomes

    (ii) $\dfrac{P(A \cap B)}{P(B)}$

    (iii) (a) $\frac{1}{15}$ (b) $\frac{4}{5}$ (c) $\frac{1}{5}$

4. (i) $\frac{4}{5}$ (ii) $\frac{2}{25}$; $\frac{32}{625}$

5. (ii) $\frac{1}{5}$ (iii) 36

6. (i) 0.030   (ii) 0.146   (iii) 0

7. (i) $\frac{1}{3}$ (ii) $\frac{1}{3}$

    (iii) (a) {3, 4, 5} or {5, 4, 3} or {2, 6, 4} or ...

      (b) 10

    (iv) (a) 3   (b) $\frac{1}{216}$

8. (i) $x = 0.2$, $y = 0.2$, $z = 0.05$

    (ii) $\frac{3}{8}$ (iii) $\frac{2}{7}$ (iv) 0.25

    (v) 0.95

9. (i) $\frac{11}{36}$ (ii) $\frac{5}{36}$ (iii) $\frac{1}{18}$

    (iv) $\frac{7}{18}$ (v) $\frac{2}{5}$

10. (ii) 0.512   (iii) 0.064   (iv) 0.479

11. (i) 60   (ii) $\frac{1}{12}$ (iii) $\frac{23}{144}$

    (iv) (a) €60   (b) Lose €12   (c) $\frac{3}{18}$ (d) €3

Chapter 6: Geometry 1

Exercise 6.1

1. $a = 46°$, $b = 134°$, $c = 80°$, $d = 100°$, $e = 65°$

2. $a = 111°$, $b = 74°$, $c = 112°$, $d = 65°$, $e = 40°$,

    $f = 52\frac{1}{2}°$, $g = 60°$, $h = 30°$

3. $a = 62°$, $b = 110°$, $c = 55°$, $d = 34°$

4. (i) $x = 55°$, $y = 45°$ (ii) $x = 116°$, $y = 52°$

    (iii) $x = 80°$, $y = 30°$

5. (i) $\sqrt{76}$ $(= 2\sqrt{19})$ (ii) $4\sqrt{2}$ (iii) $2\sqrt{11}$

6. $x = 10$, $y = 8$

8. (i) Alternate angles

9. (i) Lengths of sides may be different

10. (i) Both equal $90° + |\angle CBG|$

11. $\sqrt{105}$

12. $\angle DEA$

13. Proof

Exercise 6.2

1. (i) $36\,cm^2$ (ii) $6\,cm$

2. (i) $4.8\,cm$ (ii) $10.5\,cm$ (iii) $21.6\,cm$

3. (i) $96\,cm^2$ (ii) $126\,cm^2$ (iii) $143\,cm^2$

4. $308\,cm^2$; $17\frac{1}{9}\,cm$

5. (i) Largest is $\angle BAC$; smallest is $\angle ACB$;

     $|AC| > 5\,cm$ and $< 15\,cm$

6. (i) $5\,cm$ (iii) $8\,cm$

7. (i) $30\,cm^2$ (ii) $30\,cm^2$

    (iii) $45\,cm^2$ (iv) $4\,cm$

8. (ii) 150 sq. units

9. (i) $3(a + 2)$; $7a$ (ii) $a = 1.5$

10. (i) $5(2x + 1)$; $12x$ (ii) $x = 2.5$

11. $76\,cm^2$

Exercise 6.3

1. (i) 2.5   (ii) 9   (iii) $5\frac{5}{6}$

2. $x = 8.4$, $y = 2.8$; $a = 6$, $b = 8.4$

3. 14.4

4. 4.8

5. $|BC| = 4.2$; $|BP| = 1.6$

6. (i) $20\,cm$ (ii) $2:3$ (iii) $20\,cm$

7. (i) $8\,cm$ (ii) $7\,cm$

8. $\dfrac{12}{x}$

9. (i) Triangles equiangular

    (ii) [DF]   (iii) $x = \frac{96}{7}$, $y = \frac{64}{7}$

10. $x = 4.5$, $y = 4$

11. (i) [XY]   (ii) $x = 9$, $y = 13.5$

12. (i) $x = 16\frac{2}{3}$, $y = 10$ (ii) $x = 8$, $y = 5\frac{1}{3}$

13. (i) 9   (ii) 18

14. (ii) 6

15. $|BD| = 11.25$; $|AB| = 9$

16. (i) $\triangle ABC$ and $\triangle DBC$ (ii) $m = 6$, $n = 6$

17. $x = 5$

18. (i) $\triangle WXZ$ (ii) $w = 6\frac{2}{3}$, $v = 5\frac{1}{3}$

19. $x = 0.618$; $1 : 1.618$

20. $\dfrac{\sqrt{2}}{1}$

21. $10.8\,m$

Exercise 6.4

1. $a = 96°, b = 88°, c = 136°, d = 84°, e = 48°$
2. $a = 52°, b = 44°, c = 45°, d = 20°$
3. $a = 47°, b = 94°, c = 43°$
4. $f = 40°, g = h = 55°$
5. $a = 42°, b = 48°, c = 40°, d = 55°, e = 35°$
6. $a = 95°, b = 75°, c = 43°, d = 116°, e = 64°$
7. $60°, 54°, 66°$
8. (i) $90°$ (ii) $50°$ (iii) $50°$ (iv) $80°$
9. $a = 55°, b = 90°, c = 49°, d = 49°, e = 67°$
10. (i) $62°$ (ii) $44°$
12. $20°$
13. (i) $146°$ (ii) $17°$
15. (i) $\triangle$'s XRZ, YQZ and PYX
    (ii) $61°$ (iii) $|\angle XZY| = 61°; |\angle ZYX| = 61°$ and $|\angle ZXY| = 58°$
16. (i) $106°$ (ii) $74°$ (iii) $53°$
17. (i) $48°$ (ii) $48°$
18. Proof

Revision Exercise 6 (Core)

1. $3, 6$
2. $a° = 100°$
3. 16 cm
4. $b° = 29°$
5. $|BE| = 7.2$ cm, $|FC| = \frac{10}{3}$ cm
6. $48\ u^2$
7. $x = 2y$
8. $x = 1.5$
9. (i) 4.8 (ii) 6.4 (iii) 3.6
10. $|AB| = 3$

Revision Exercise 6 (Advanced)

1. $\frac{5\sqrt{5}}{2}$
2. Proof
3. (i) $120°$ (ii) $108°$ (iii) $\frac{(n-2)180}{n}, 144°$
4. $68°$
5. $x = 20$
6. $x = 28$
7. $x = 50°, y = 68°, c = 63°, d = 54°$
8. Proof
9. Proof

Revision Exercise 6 (Extended Response Questions)

1. Theory
2. (a) 105.8 cm (b) 122.5 cm
3. (ii) (b) is not always true

4. (i) $\frac{14 + \sqrt{115}}{2}$ m (ii) (a) $h = \frac{2 + 7\sqrt{2}}{4}$ m
   (b) $x = \frac{7\sqrt{2} - 4}{2}$ m
5. (i) Proof (ii) $v = 131°, x = 228°, y = 78°$
   (iii) $\angle BED = 70°, \angle 110°$ (iv) Proof
6. (i) Proof (ii) 50.6 cm (iii) $2:1$ (iv) Proof
7. (i) $r = 8$ cm, $h = 16\sqrt{2}$ cm (ii) $8\sqrt{2}$ cm
   (iii) $\frac{1}{8}$ (iv) 11.11 cm (from top)
8. (i) Proof (ii) $x = 22$ cm

Chapter 7: Differential Calculus

Exercise 7.1

1. (i) 4 (ii) 1 (iii) -3
2. $\frac{16}{7}$
3. (i) $-\frac{25}{7}$ (ii) 4
4. $\frac{25}{8}$
5. (i) 8 years (approx.) (ii) 12 cm per year
6. (i) $S(x) = 6x^2$ (ii) 42 cm² per cm
7. (i) 5 (ii) 4.5 (iii) 4.1 (iv) 4

Exercise 7.2

1. (i) $x = 0$ (ii) $x = 3$ (iii) $x = -2$
   (iv) $x = 2$ (v) $x = -3$
   (vi) $x = -\frac{\pi}{2}$ and $x = \frac{\pi}{2}$
2. (i) $x = 0$ (ii) $\frac{2}{0}$ is not defined
3. $\tan \frac{\pi}{2} = \frac{k}{0}$, which is not defined
4. (i) $x = 4$ (ii) $x = -5$ or $x = 5$
   (iii) $x = -1$ or $x = 4$
5. (i) $\frac{5}{4}$ (ii) -4 (iii) $\frac{3}{4}$
6. (i) -1 (ii) $-\frac{3}{2}$ (iii) $\frac{2}{3}$
7. (i) 2 (ii) 4 (iii) 10
   (iv) -1 (v) 3 (vi) $-\frac{1}{7}$
8. 6
9. (i) 0 (ii) 0 (iii) 0 (iv) 0
10. (i) $\frac{3}{2}$ (ii) $\frac{4}{7}$ (iii) $-\frac{3}{4}$
11. (i) $\frac{1}{3}$ (ii) $\frac{5}{2}$ (iii) $\frac{1}{3}$
12. (i) 2 (ii) $2x$ (iii) $2x$
13. $\frac{1}{27}$

n	1	2	5	10	100	1000	10000
$f(n)$	2	2.25	2.488	2.594	2.705	2.717	2.718

$e = 2.718$

Exercise 7.3

1. (i) 5   (ii) 3   (iii) -4
2. (i) $2x$ (ii) $4x + 9$ (iii) $6x - 4$
3. (i) $2x - 2$ (ii) 2
   (iii) $2x - y + 1 = 0$
5. (i) $-2x$ (ii) $4 - 2x$ (iii) $-1 - 6x$
6. $4x - 3$; (i) 9   (ii) $9x - y - 20 = 0$
7. $2\pi r$
8. $f'(x) = 2x - 3$; $\left(1\frac{1}{2}, -1\frac{1}{4}\right)$

Exercise 7.4

1. (i) $25x^4$ (ii) $10x - 4$
  (iii) $12x + 5$ (iv) $3x^2 - 8$
  (v) $2x + 2 - \dfrac{1}{x^2}$ (vi) $6x^2 + 2x - \dfrac{2}{x^3}$

2. (i) $14x + \dfrac{3}{x^2}$ (ii) $\dfrac{3}{2\sqrt{x}}$
  (iii) $\dfrac{1}{\sqrt{x}} - \dfrac{4}{x^3}$ (iv) $2x - \dfrac{5}{2\sqrt{x}}$
  (v) $\dfrac{-3}{2\sqrt{x^3}}$ (vi) $\dfrac{-6}{x^3} - \dfrac{1}{4\sqrt{x^3}}$

3. $x^2 + x - 6$

4. (i) $\dfrac{1}{3\sqrt[3]{x^2}}$ (ii) $\dfrac{3}{2\sqrt{x}} + \dfrac{2}{x^3}$
  (iii) $-\dfrac{4}{x^2} - \dfrac{3}{2\sqrt{x^3}}$ (iv) $\dfrac{3}{x^2}$
  (v) $\dfrac{1}{\sqrt{x}} + \dfrac{1}{3\sqrt[3]{x^2}}$ (vi) $-6x$

5. $\dfrac{1}{2\sqrt{x}} + 1$; $1\frac{1}{4}$

6. $3x^2 + \dfrac{1}{\sqrt{x}}$; $48\frac{1}{2}$

7. $-\dfrac{1}{16}$

8. $\dfrac{5}{2}\sqrt{x^3}$; $p = 5$

9. $k = 5$
11. 2
12. 1; $x - y + 2 = 0$
13. -3; $3x + y - 10 = 0$
14. $x = -2$
15. $(1, 0)$
16. $(1, -3)$
17. $a = 5$

18. Slope $= 0 \Rightarrow$ parallel to x-axis
19. $(3, -3)$
20. $\left(-\dfrac{3}{4}, -\dfrac{9}{8}\right)$
21. $a = 12$, $b = -18$
22. 6 sq. units

Exercise 7.5

1. (i) $6x - 2$ (ii) $24x - 1$
  (iii) $3x^2 - 2x + 2$ (iv) $6x^2 - 2x - 4$
  (v) $3x^2 - 2x - 2$ (vi) $8x^3 + 3x^2 - 2$

2. (i) $\dfrac{18}{(2x + 6)^2}$ (ii) $\dfrac{-5}{(x - 1)^2}$
  (iii) $\dfrac{2x^2 + 6x}{(2x + 3)^2}$ (iv) $\dfrac{4x^2 - 12x + 2}{(2x - 3)^2}$
  (v) $\dfrac{-8x^3 + 6x^2}{(1 - 2x)^2}$ (vi) $\dfrac{-3x^2 - 4x - 9}{(x^2 - 3)^2}$

3. -3

4. $\dfrac{6x - 1}{2\sqrt{x}}$

7. (i) $2(x + 4)$ (ii) $6(2x - 1)^2$
  (iii) $9(3x + 5)^2$ (iv) $4x(x^2 - 1)$
  (v) $16x(2x^2 + 3)^3$ (vi) $-15(1 - 3x)^4$

8. (i) $\dfrac{2}{\sqrt{4x + 1}}$ (ii) $\dfrac{x}{\sqrt{x^2 - 4}}$
  (iii) $\dfrac{3x^2 - 2}{2\sqrt{x^3 - 2x}}$

9. (i) $2(2x + 5)^3 + 12x(2x + 5)^2$
  (ii) $2x(3x + 2)^2 + 6(3x + 2)(x^2 - 1)$
  (iii) $2(x + 4)(x - 2) + (x + 4)^2$

10. 24
11. $-\dfrac{19}{16}$
12. -28

13. $\dfrac{3x + 2}{2\sqrt{x + 1}}$

14. $\dfrac{-4x^2 - 5}{2x^2}$

15. $\dfrac{\sqrt{x} + 2}{2(\sqrt{x} + 1)^2}$; $\dfrac{3}{8}$

16. $\dfrac{5}{(1 - 2x)^2}$

17. 3
19. $a = 2$, $b = 1\frac{1}{2}$, $c = -2$
20. $\dfrac{3}{8}$
21. A
22. (a) (i) $3x^2 - 5$ (ii) $9x^2 + 6x - 1$
  (b) $x = -\dfrac{1}{2}$

Exercise 7.6

1. $6x + 4$
2. $12x^2 - 6$
3. $\dfrac{2}{x^3}$
4. $\dfrac{6}{x^4} + 6$
5. $\dfrac{2}{x^3}$
6. $-\dfrac{1}{4\sqrt{x^3}}$
7. $\dfrac{-1}{\sqrt{(2x + 3)^3}}$
8. $54(3x - 2)$
9. $\dfrac{2}{(x + 4)^3}$
10. $12x^2 - 6x \,;\, x = 0, \dfrac{1}{2}$
14. $\dfrac{dy}{dx} = -\dfrac{1}{2\sqrt{x^3}} \,;\, \dfrac{d^2y}{dx^2} = \dfrac{3}{4\sqrt{x^5}}$

Exercise 7.7

1. (i) $2 \cos 2x$ (ii) $-6 \sin 6x$
   (iii) $4 \sec^2 4x$ (iv) $2 \cos(2x + 3)$
   (v) $-3 \sin(3x - 1)$ (vi) $2x \sec^2(x^2)$
   (vii) $\dfrac{1}{2} \cos \dfrac{1}{2}x$ (viii) $-2x \sin(x^2 - 1)$
   (ix) $2 \cos 2x - 4 \sin 4x$
2. (i) $2 \sin x \cos x$ (ii) $-3 \sin x \cos^2 x$
   (iii) $4 \tan^3 x \sec^2 x$ (iv) $12 \sin^2 4x \cos 4x$
   (v) $-4 \sin(2x + 1) \cos(2x + 1)$
   (vi) $12 \tan^2(4x + 3) \sec^2(4x + 3)$
3. (i) $6 \cos 3\theta - 2 \sin 2\theta$
   (ii) $2 \tan \theta \sec^2 \theta + 2 \sec^2 2\theta$
   (iii) $-4 \sin 4\theta + \dfrac{1}{4} \sin \dfrac{\theta}{4}$
   (iv) $3 \tan^2 \theta \sec^2 \theta$
4. (i) $\sin 2x + 2x \cos 2x$
   (ii) $2x \cos x - x^2 \sin x$
   (iii) $\sin x + (x + 3) \cos x$
7. (i) 2 (ii) -1 (iii) 0
9. $\dfrac{3\sqrt{3}}{2}$
10. $\cos x - 3 \sin x$
11. $-4 \sin^2 x$
12. 0
13. $-\dfrac{3\sqrt{3}}{4}$
14. (i) $-2 \sin 2x$ (ii) $4 \sin x \cos x$
17. $k = \dfrac{1}{2}$
18. $a = 1, b = 2$

Exercise 7.8

1. (i) $\dfrac{6}{\sqrt{1 - 36x^2}}$ (ii) $\dfrac{3}{1 + 9x^2}$
   (iii) $\dfrac{2}{\sqrt{-4x^2 - 4x}}$ (iv) $\dfrac{2x}{1 + x^4}$
3. (i) 2 (ii) 2
4. (i) $\dfrac{-3}{x\sqrt{x^2 - 9}}$ (ii) $\dfrac{4}{x^2 + 16}$
5. (i) $\dfrac{x}{\sqrt{1 - x^2}} + \sin^{-1} x$
   (ii) $2 \tan^{-1} x + \dfrac{2x}{1 + x^2}$
7. $k = -1$
8. $-\dfrac{2}{7}$
9. $-\dfrac{1}{2}$
10. $\dfrac{9}{5}$

Exercise 7.9

1. (i) $4e^{4x}$ (ii) $-3e^{-3x}$
   (iii) $2xe^{x^2}$ (iv) $2e^{2x + 4}$
   (v) $(2x + 3)e^{x^2 + 3x}$ (vi) $\cos x(e^{\sin x})$
2. (i) $\dfrac{1}{2}e^{\frac{x}{2}}$
   (ii) $2 \sin x \cos x(e^{\sin^2 x})$
   (iii) $e^{2x}(1 + 2x)$
3. (i) $e^{2x}(2 \sin x + \cos x)$
   (ii) $2e^x(e^x - 1)$
   (iii) $e^{x + 1}$
4. (i) $2e^{2x} + 3e^{3x}$
   (ii) $\dfrac{e^{2x}(2x - 1)}{x^2}$
   (iii) $xe^{\cos x}(2 - x \sin x)$
5. $-\pi e^3$
6. $\dfrac{d^2y}{dx^2} = 4e^{2x}$
10. $\dfrac{d^2y}{dx^2} = m^2 e^{mx} \,;\, m = -1, 4$
12. $y = 2x + 8$

Exercise 7.10

1. $\dfrac{1}{x}$
2. $\dfrac{2}{2x + 3}$
3. $\dfrac{2}{x}$
4. $\cot an\, x$
5. $\dfrac{2(x - 3)}{x^2 - 6x}$

6. $-3 \tan 3x$

7. $\log_e x + 1$

8. $2x \log_e 3x + x$

9. $\dfrac{1 - \log_e x}{x^2}$

10. (i) $\dfrac{9}{3x + 1}$ (ii) $\dfrac{5}{(2x + 1)(1 - 3x)}$

     (iii) $\dfrac{x}{1 + x^2}$ (iv) $\dfrac{1}{2} \cotan x$

     (v) $\dfrac{4x}{x^2 + 4}$ (vi) $\dfrac{1}{2x(x + 1)}$

11. $-\dfrac{4}{x^2}$

13. $\dfrac{1}{x}$

14. $\dfrac{5}{2}$

15. $\dfrac{2}{e}$

16. $\dfrac{\cos t}{1 + \sin t}; k = 1$

Revision Exercise 7 (Core)

1. (i) $2x - \dfrac{1}{x^2}$ (ii) $6(2x + 3)^2$

     (iii) $\dfrac{3}{2\sqrt{1 + 3x}}$

2. $\dfrac{dy}{dx} = 2x + 3$

3. (i) $(x + 2)^2$ (ii) $\dfrac{2}{(x + 1)^2}$

4. (i) $4x + \dfrac{6}{x^3}$ (ii) $24 \cos 6x$

     (iii) $6xe^{x^2}$

5. -11

6. (i) 2 (ii) $12x - y - 8 = 0$

7. (i) $6x - 1 - \dfrac{3}{x^2}$ (ii) $\dfrac{3x^2 - 6x}{(x - 1)^2}$

     (iii) $-8 \cos 4x \sin 4x$

8. $4 - \dfrac{6}{x^2}$

9. $-\dfrac{2}{3}$

10. $-\dfrac{\pi}{3} + \dfrac{\sqrt{3}}{2}$

11. $2x + y - 4 = 0$

12. $\dfrac{7}{32}$

13. (i) 10 (ii) 16

14. $\dfrac{5}{1 + 25x^2}$

15. $2x - y + 1 = 0$

16. $k = 11$

Revision Exercise 7 (Advanced)

1. 1

2. π

3. $(1, 1), \left(\dfrac{1}{2}, \dfrac{1}{4} - \ln 2 \right)$

4. $x = 0, 2$

5. (i) $\dfrac{4}{x}$ (ii) $-\dfrac{1}{2}x$

6. $\dfrac{dy}{dx} = ne^{nx}$; $\dfrac{d^2y}{dx^2} = n^2 e^{nx}$; $n = 2, 3$

7. $(-1, 11), (3, -5)$

8. $a = 8, b = 11$

9. (i) $(0, 2160000), (30, 0)$;

     Full tank $= 2160000 \,\text{m}^3$;

     Empty tank after 30 mins

     (ii) $640000 \,\text{m}^3$

     (iii) $152000 \,\text{m}^3/\text{min}$

     (iv) $96000 \,\text{m}^3/\text{min}$

10. $k = \dfrac{3}{2}$

11. $-\dfrac{1}{2}$

12. $y = 0$

13. $k = -\dfrac{3}{2}$

14. $\dfrac{4}{5}$

16. (ii) $2 - 3h + h^2$

     (iii) As h approaches zero, the slope of the chord will approximate to the slope of the tangent at A; gradient $= 2$

Revision Exercise 7 (Extended Response Questions)

1. (i) $(0, 0), (2, 0)$

     (ii) Slopes are -2 and 2

     (iii) $2x + y = 0$ and $2x - y - 4 = 0$

     (iv) $53°$

     (v) $p = 10, q = -6, r = 15$

2. (i) $k = 2$

     (ii) $y = 3x + \ln 2 - 3$

3. (i) $2x - 4y - 9 = 0$

     (ii) $A = (-2, 3)$

     (iii) $C = \left(\dfrac{1}{2}, -2 \right)$

4. (a) $\dfrac{h^3 + 6h^2 + 11h}{h}$

(b) (i) 14.25   (ii) 11.61
     (iii) 11.0601   (iv) 11.006001

(c) 11

(d) 11

(e) $3a^2 + 3ah + h^2 - 1$

(f) $3a^2 - 1$

6. (a) $\dfrac{dD}{dt} = k.50e^{kt} = kD =$ a constant times D

(b) 20 cm/year

7. (i) -1

(ii) $2nx(x^2 - 1)^{n-1}$

(iii) $3(x - 2)^2$ is always positive

8. (i) $(x - k)(3x - k)$

(ii) $(k, 0), \left(\dfrac{k}{3}, \dfrac{4k^3}{27}\right)$

(iv) Midpoint $= \left(\dfrac{2k}{3}, \dfrac{2k^3}{27}\right)$; show that the curve contains this midpoint

Chapter 8: Trigonometry 2

Exercise 8.1
Questions 1 – 26 Proofs

Exercise 8.2

1. (i) $\dfrac{\sqrt{3} + 1}{2\sqrt{2}}$ (ii) $\dfrac{\sqrt{3} + 1}{2\sqrt{2}}$ (iii) $\dfrac{1 - \sqrt{3}}{2\sqrt{2}}$

2. (i) $\dfrac{\sqrt{3} - 1}{\sqrt{3} + 1}$ (ii) $\dfrac{1}{\sqrt{2}}$ (iii) $\dfrac{\sqrt{3} + 1}{\sqrt{3} - 1}$

3. (i) $\dfrac{33}{65}$ (ii) $\dfrac{16}{63}$

4. (i) $\dfrac{\sqrt{3}}{2}$ (ii) 0   (iii) $\dfrac{1}{2}$ (iv) 1

5. (i) $\tan 3A$ (ii) $\sin 3\theta$

7. $4\dfrac{1}{2}$

8. $\dfrac{\pi}{4}$ (or 45°)

9. $\dfrac{1}{2}$

10. $\dfrac{1 + \sqrt{3}}{2\sqrt{2}}$

11. $\dfrac{\sqrt{3} - 1}{\sqrt{3} + 1}$; $7 - 4\sqrt{3}$

14. $h = 6$ m

17. $h = 2$ m or 3 m

Exercise 8.3

1. (i) $\dfrac{24}{25}$ (ii) $\dfrac{7}{25}$ (iii) $\dfrac{24}{7}$

2. (i) $\dfrac{4}{3}$ (ii) $\dfrac{4}{5}$

3. $\dfrac{7}{9}$

4. $\dfrac{\sqrt{5}}{4}; \dfrac{\sqrt{11}}{4}$

5. (i) $\dfrac{1}{2}$ (ii) $\dfrac{1}{2}$ (iii) $\dfrac{1}{\sqrt{2}}$

6. 1

10. $\dfrac{4}{3}$

11. (i) $\dfrac{24}{25}$ (ii) $-\dfrac{7}{25}$

14. $\dfrac{1}{2}$ or -2

15. (i) $\dfrac{5}{3}\sin \beta$ (ii) $\dfrac{\sqrt{11}}{5}$

16. (ii) $\dfrac{7}{25}$

18. (i) $1 - 2\sin^2 2A$ (ii) $2\cos^2 2A - 1$

19. (ii) $\dfrac{1}{4}$

Exercise 8.4

1. (i) $2\sin 4x \cos x$ (ii) $2\cos 3x \sin x$

(iii) $2\cos 2x \cos x$ (iv) $-2\sin 6\theta \sin \theta$

(v) $-2\sin 2\theta \sin \theta$ (vi) $-2\cos 5\theta \sin 2\theta$

2. (i) $\cos 20°$ (ii) 0   (iii) $-\dfrac{1}{\sqrt{2}}$

4. (i) $\sqrt{2}\cos x$ (ii) $-\sqrt{3}\sin x$

5. (i) $\sin 5A + \sin A$ (ii) $\sin 5x - \sin 3x$

(iii) $\cos 7A + \cos 3A$ (iv) $\cos 8A - \cos 4A$

(v) $-\dfrac{1}{2}[\cos 3A - \cos A]$

(vi) $\dfrac{1}{2}[\sin 6x - \sin 4x]$

6. (i) $\dfrac{1}{2}(\sqrt{3} + 1)$ (ii) $\dfrac{5\sqrt{2}}{2}$

12. 2

Exercise 8.5

1. (i) 45°   (ii) 60°   (iii) 45°   (iv) 30°

(v) $-60°$ (vi) $-45°$ (vii) 120° (viii) $-30°$

3. (i) x (ii) $\sqrt{1 - x^2}$ (iii) $\dfrac{x}{\sqrt{1 + x^2}}$

4. (i) $\dfrac{4}{5}$ (ii) $\dfrac{1}{\sqrt{2}}$ (iii) $\dfrac{8}{17}$

5. (i) $\dfrac{24}{25}$ (ii) $\dfrac{119}{169}$

7. $\dfrac{56}{33}$

8. Both $\dfrac{24}{25}$

Revision Exercise 8 (Core)

1. $\frac{12}{13}$

2. $\frac{63}{65}$

4. $\frac{24}{7}$

6. (i) $\frac{15}{17}$ (ii) $\frac{240}{289}$

7. (i) $\frac{\sqrt{3}}{2}$

8. $a = 2, b = 1$

9. (ii) $\frac{120}{169}$

10. (i) $k = 2$ (ii) $\sqrt{3}$

Revision Exercise 8 (Advanced)

1. (ii) $\frac{\sqrt{3}}{2}$

2. (i) $-\frac{7}{25}$

3. (i) $\sin 6\theta + \sin 2\theta$ (ii)   2

5. (i) $\frac{\sqrt{3}}{2}$

8. $\tan A = \dfrac{1 - \tan B}{1 + \tan B}$

9. $\frac{\sqrt{2}}{2}$

10. $\theta = \dfrac{\pi}{6}$

Revision Exercise 8 (Extended Response Questions)

3. (ii) $k = 25$

4. (i) Proof   (ii) Proof

    (iii) (a) $\frac{\sqrt{3}}{2}$ (b) $\frac{1}{2}$ (iv) Proof

5. (ii) $a = 2, b = 1$

6. $41.4°; 55.8°; 55.8° > 41.4° \Rightarrow |AB| > 2$, as bigger side is opposite greater angle

7. (i) (a) $\frac{1}{\sqrt{2}}$ (b) 1

8. (ii) $x = \sqrt{6}$

9. (i) 4θ radians

    (ii) $2 \sin 2\theta; \theta = \dfrac{\pi}{6}$ radians

10. (i) $|AC| = 2r \cos \alpha$

Chapter 9: Sequences – Series – Patterns

Exercise 9.1

1.   (i) 30, 36, 42   (ii) 27, 32, 37
    (iii) 9.5, 10.7, 11.9   (iv) $-10, -13, -16$
    (v) 38, 51, 66   (vi) 46, 38, 30
    (vii) $-15, -20, -25$ (viii) $-28, -19, -10$
    (ix) 54, 162, 486   (x) 30, 42, 56
    (xi) $-\frac{3}{4}, -1\frac{1}{4}, -1\frac{3}{4}$ (xii) 16, 22, 29
    (xiii) 35, 48, 63   (xiv) $48, -96, 192$
    (xv) $\frac{1}{30}, \frac{1}{42}, \frac{1}{56}$

2.   (i) 2, 6, 10, 14   (ii) 4, 9, 16, 25
    (iii) $-1, 0, 3, 8$ (iv) 8, 15, 24, 35
    (v) 0, 7, 26, 63   (vi) $\frac{1}{3}, \frac{2}{4}, \frac{3}{5}, \frac{4}{6}$
    (vii) 2, 4, 8, 16   (viii) $-3, 9, -27, 81$
    (ix) 2, 8, 24, 64

3.   (i) 5, 9, 13, 17   (ii) 21 cm

4.   (i) 1, 2, 4, 7, 11, 16 (ii) 8

5. $u_1 = 1, u_5 = 17, u_{10} = 37$

6. $u_1 = 4, u_6 = -128, u_{11} = 4096$

7.   (i) 5, 9, 13, 17, 21, 25
    (ii) 1, 5, 10, 17, 26, 37
    (iii) 2, 4, 8, 16, 32, 64

8.   (i) C (ii) B (iii) D (iv) A

9.   (i) $n + 4$ (ii) $2n$ (iii) $3n - 1$
    (iv) n^2 (v) $n^2 + 1$ (vi) $(-1)^n$
    (vii) $4n - 3$ (viii) $\frac{1}{n}$ (ix) $\dfrac{n + 1}{n + 2}$
    (x) $(n + 1)(n + 2)$

10. Sequence is formed by adding the previous two terms; 34, 55, 89, 144

11.   1   5   10   10   5   1
         1   6   15   20   15   6   1
      1   7   21   35   35   21   7   1
   1   8   28   56   70   56   28   8   1

    (i) 1, 2, 3, 4, 5, ... $T_n = n$

    (ii) 1, 3, 6, 10, 15, ... $T_n = \dfrac{n(n + 1)}{2}$

    (iii) 1, 2, 4, 8, 16, ... $T_n = 2^{n - 1}$

    (iv) 3, 6, 10, 15, 21, ... $T_n = \dfrac{(n + 1)(n + 2)}{2}$

Exercise 9.2

1.   (i) $T_n = 5n + 3, T_{22} = 113$
    (ii) $T_n = 20n - 4, T_{22} = 436$
    (iii) $T_n = 13 - 3n, T_{22} = -53$

2. 3, 8, 13, 18

3. (i) 21   (ii) 20   (iii) 32

4. (i) $a = 4, d = 3$

    (ii) 4, 7, 10, 13, 16

    (iii) $T_{20} = 61$

5. (i) 8 red and 22 orange

    (ii) No since $T_n = 3n + 6 \neq 38$

6. $a = 3, d = 2$; 3, 5, 7, 9, 11, 13

7. (i) $k = 4$

    (ii) $p = -2$

8. (i) 12, 20, 28; $T_n = 8n + 4$

    (ii) 124

    (iii) shape 20

9. $d = 4$ a constant $\Rightarrow$ sequence is arithmetic

10. $d = 2n + 3$ $\therefore$ not constant

11. (i) 8

    (ii) 49

    (iii) $T_n = n^2 + 8$

12. (i) No, since $T_n = 4n + 2 \neq 87$

    (ii) $T_n - T_{n-1}$ is not constant

    (iii) 5 completed levels and 32 left over

13. 9 weeks

Exercise 9.3

1. (i) $S_n = 2n^2 - n$; $S_{20} = 780$

    (ii) $S_n = 51n - n^2$; $S_{20} = 620$

    (iii) $S_n = \dfrac{n^2 + 19n}{20}$; $S_{20} = 39$

    (iv) $S_n = 2n^2 - 9n$; $S_{20} = 620$

2. (i) $n = 12, S_{12} = 336$

    (ii) $n = 100, S_{100} = 5050$

    (iii) $n = 20, S_{20} = 460$

3. 7 terms

4. $a = 2, d = -3$; $S_{10} = -115$

5. 10 weeks

6. (i) 69   (ii) 54   (iii) 5050

7. (i) $\displaystyle\sum_{n=1}^{31} 4n$ (ii) $\displaystyle\sum_{n=1}^{29} \dfrac{n-21}{2}$

    (iii) $\displaystyle\sum_{n=1}^{401} \dfrac{n+99}{10}$

8. 3, 7, 11, 15, 19

9. $S_{33} = 1980$

10. (i) 51 rings

    (ii) 101 rings; $S_{20} = 1070$

11. 14 terms; $d = 4$

12. 4950

13. $a = 3.5, d = 0.1$; $S_{30} = 148.5$

14. 60

Exercise 9.4

1. (i) $r = 3$; 243, 729

    (ii) $r = \dfrac{1}{3}$; $\dfrac{1}{81}, \dfrac{1}{243}$

    (iii) $r = -2$; $-16, 32$

    (iv) $r = -1$; $1, -1$

    (v) not geometric

    (vi) $r = a$; a^5, a^6

    (vii) $r = 1.1$; 1.4641, 1.61051

    (viii) not geometric

    (ix) not geometric

    (x) $r = 6$; 972, 5832

2. (i) $a = 5, r = 2$; $T_{11} = 5120$

    (ii) $a = 10, r = 2.5$; $T_7 = 2441.41$

    (iii) $a = 1.1, r = 1.1$; $T_8 = 2.1436$

    (iv) $a = 24, r = -0.5$; $T_{10} = -0.046875 \left(-\dfrac{3}{64} \right)$

3. $a = 4, r = 3$; 4, 12, 36, 108, 324, ...

4. $r = 3$

5. $-16, 4, -1, \dfrac{1}{4}, -\dfrac{1}{16}$

6. A and C are geometric

    B and D are not geometric

7. $n = 6$; 4, 6, 9, 13.5

8. $a = -7, r = -3$; $T_n = -7(-3)^{n-1}$

9. 6.75

10. 1, 3, 9, 27 or 9, 3, 1, $\dfrac{1}{3}$

11. 3, 6, 12, 24, 48

12. $6, 4\dfrac{1}{2}, 3\dfrac{3}{8}, 2\dfrac{17}{32}$

13. 40, -20, 10, -5

14. (i) $x = -1\dfrac{1}{2}$; $-4\dfrac{1}{2}, -1\dfrac{1}{2}, -\dfrac{1}{2}$ or

       $x = 4$; 1, 4, 16

    (ii) $x = 3\dfrac{1}{2}$; $4\dfrac{1}{2}, 7\dfrac{1}{2}, 12\dfrac{1}{2}$ or

       $x = -2$; $-1, 2, -4$

    (iii) $x = 6$; 4, 6, 9

    (iv) $x = 10$; 4, 20, 100

15. Proof

16. No

17. (i) $n = 7$ (ii) $n = 6$

18. (i) 18, 12, 8, $\dfrac{16}{3}$ (ii) $T_n = 27\left(\dfrac{2}{3}\right)^n$

    (iii) 0.21 m

19. (i) €4000

    (ii) €4120, €4243.6, €4370.91, €4502.04

    (iii) €5375.67

    (iv) 23 years

20. $r = 2\%$

Exercise 9.5

1. (i) $\frac{1}{3}$ (ii) 5 (iii) 1

2. (i) $\frac{1}{2}$ (ii) 0 (iii) 1

3. (i) No limit (ii) 4 (iii) 0

4. (i) 9 (ii) $\frac{1}{6}$ (iii) ∞

5. (i) 0 (ii) ∞ (iii) ∞

6. $\left(\frac{a}{b}\right)$

Exercise 9.6

1. $S_{10} = 59\,048$

2. $n = 6$; $S_6 = 2016$

3. $S_8 = 255$

4. $S_{10} = 63.94$

5. -728

6. 8 terms; $S_8 = 546\frac{2}{3}$

7. 4, 16, 64; $S_6 = 5460$

8. $S_8 = 19\,680$

9. $S_{10} = 5.994$

10. (i) $\frac{7}{9}$ (ii) $\frac{35}{99}$ (iii) $\frac{7}{30}$

(iv) $\frac{10}{27}$ (v) $\frac{161}{990}$ (vi) $\frac{53}{165}$

11. $S_n = 2 - \dfrac{1}{2^{n-1}}$; $S_\infty = 2$, $n = 11$

Exercise 9.7

1. 2, 8, 32, 128, 512

2. (i) 2, 8, 26, 80, 242 (ii) 1, 3, 7, 17, 41
(iii) 0, 1, 3, 8, 21

3. 6, 8, 10, 12, 14

4. $T_n = T_{n-1} + T_{n-2}$, 0, 1, 1, 2, 3, 5, 8, 13

5. (i) 21 (ii) -1

6. 2, 0, 4, 4, 4

7. (a) (i) 7, 9, 11 (ii) 15, 19, 23
(b) Proof (c) $a = 4$, $b = -1$ (d) 79

Exercise 9.8

1. (i) $T_n = 4n + 1$ (ii) $T_n = 3n - 2$
(iii) $T_n = 5n + 6$

2. (i) $T_n = 3 - n$ (ii) $T_n = 2 - 2n$
(iii) $T_n = 2n - 8$

3. (i) $10\,150\,\text{mm}^2$ (ii) $560\,\text{mm}$

4. (i) $900\,\text{cm}^2$ (ii) 21st design

5. (i) $10\,100\,\text{cm}^2$ (ii) 15th triangle

6. (i) $T_n = 2n^3 + n^2 + 4n - 1$
(ii) $T_n = n^3 - 4n^2 + n + 5$
(iii) $T_n = n^3 - 4n + 2$

7. (a) $T_n = n^2 - 1$; 575 bright, 1 dark
(b) $T_n = n^2 - 2$; 574 bright, 2 dark
(c) $T_n = n^2 - n$; 552 bright, 24 dark

8. (i) $T_n = 3n^2 + 4$
(ii) $T_n = 2n - n^2$
(iii) $T_n = 2n^3 + n - 4$
(iv) $T_n = 4n - 6$
(v) $T_n = 3n^3 + 2n^2 - 1$

Revision Exercise 9 (Core)

1. (i) 7, 10, 13, 16 (ii) 5, 11, 17, 23
(iii) 1, 2, 4, 8 (iv) 20, 30, 42, 56
(v) 2, 9, 28, 65

2. $a = 79$, $d = -4$

3. $r = \frac{2}{3}$

4. (i) $r = -2$; $T_n = (-2)^n$
(ii) $r = \frac{1}{2}$; $T_n = \left(\frac{1}{2}\right)^{n-1}$
(iii) $r = -3$; $T_n = 2(-3)^{n-1}$

5. (i) $T_n = 8n + 4$ (ii) 250 cubes

6. (i) $r = -3$ (ii) $a = -7$

7. Explanation

8. $19\,900$

9. 195

10. 280

Revision Exercise 9 (Advanced)

1. (i) 12 lumens (ii) $T_n = 2000\left(\frac{3}{5}\right)^n$
(iii) 5th mirror

2. (i) $t = \dfrac{\ln 2}{\ln(1 + i)}$
(ii) (a) 35 years
(b) 14.2 years
(c) 7.3 years

3. (i) $10 + 2(6 + 3.6 + 2.16 + \ldots)$
(ii) Infinite geometric series
(iii) $40\,\text{m}$

4. (i) $T_n = 3(2)^{n-1}$
(ii) 20th term

5. (i) €2.1×10^7
(ii) €9.2×10^{16}

6. 5, 11, 17

7. (i) $V = P(1 - i)^a$
(ii) €14 953
(iii) end of 12th year

8. (i) $1, \frac{1}{3}, -\frac{1}{9}$
(iii) $k = -1$

9. (ii) $T_n = 6n - 2$

(iii) $2n(6n^2 + 3n - 1)$

10. $\frac{1}{2}\log_2 x$; $r = \frac{1}{2}$; $k = 2$

Revision Exercise 9 (Extended Response Questions)

1. (i) $T_2 = 4a + 2b + c$; $T_3 = 9a + 3b + c$;

$T_4 = 16a + 4b + c$

First difference $= 3a + b$; $5a + b$; $7a + b$

Second difference $= 2a$, $2a$

(ii) (a) $2a$ (a constant)

(b) $3a + b$

(iii) First difference $= 7, 13, 19$

Second difference $= 2$

(iv) $T_n = 3n^2 - 2n + 4$

(v) $T_{20} = 1164$

2. (i) $T_n = 40(0.69)^n$

(ii) 69%

(iii) 27.6, 19.04, 13.14, 9.07, 6.26

(v) 9 bounces

(vi) 9 bounces

3. (i) Scheme 1: $S_n = n(n + 19)$

(ii) Scheme 2: $S_n = 400\left[\left(\frac{21}{20}\right)^n - 1\right]$

(ii) Scheme 1

(iii) 16th week

4. (i) 136 litres (ii) Proof

(iii) 872 litres

5. (i) Proof (ii) 2020

(iii) €22 657 (iv) 2.8%

Chapter 10: Statistics 1

Exercise 10.1

1. (i) Numerical (ii) Categorical

(iii) Numerical (iv) Categorical

2. (i) Discrete (ii) Discrete

(iii) Continuous (iv) Discrete

(v) Continuous (vi) Discrete

(vii) Discrete (viii) Discrete

3. (i) Categorical (ii) Numerical

(iii) Numerical; (ii) is discrete

4. Race time is continuous; Number on bib is discrete

5. (i) No (ii) Yes

(iii) Yes (iv) No

6. (i) Contains two pieces of information

(ii) No. of eggs

(iii) Amount of flour

7. (i) Categorical (ii) Numerical

(iii) Numerical

(iv) Categorical; Part (iii) is discrete;

Bivariate continuous numerical

8. (i) True (ii) True

(iii) False (iv) False

(v) True (vi) True

(vii) True (viii) True

9. Small, medium, large; 1-bed house, 2-bed, 3-bed; Poor, fair, good, very good.

10. (i) Primary (ii) Secondary

(iii) Primary (iv) Secondary

11. (i) Secondary

(ii) Roy's; they are more recent

12. (i) No. of bedrooms in family home and number of children in the family

(ii) An athlete's height and his distance in a long-jump competition.

Exercise 10.2

1. (i) Too personal (it identifies respondent)

(ii) Too vague/subjective

2. (i) Too personal (ii) Too leading

(iii) Overlapping

3. QA: Judgemental and subjective

QB: Leading and biased

4. Not suitable; too vague, not specific enough

6. B and D are biased; B gives an opinion;

D is a leading question

7. (i) Do you have a part-time job?

(ii) Are you male or female?

8. Explanatory variable: Length of legs

Response variable: Time recorded in sprint

9. Explanatory variable:

Number of operating theatres

Response variable:

Number of operations per day

10. (i) Group B (ii) The new drug

(iii) Blood-pressure

(iv) Designed experiment

Exercise 10.3

1. Census – all members of the population surveyed.

Sample – only part of the population surveyed.

A sample is more convenient and cheaper.

2. Any sample of size n which has an equal chance of being selected.

3. (i) Likely biased   (ii) Random
    (iii) Random   (iv) Random
    (v) Random
4. Selecting a sample in the easiest way;
    (i) Convenience sampling
    (ii) High level of bias likely;
    unrepresentative of population
5. (i) Convenience sampling
    (ii) Systematic   (iii) Stratified
6. (i) Very small sample; not random and not
    representative
    (ii) Each member of the local population
    should have an equal chance of being
    asked. The sample shouldn't be too
    small. Sample should be stratified to
    ensure all age and class groups are
    represented.
7. (i) Convenience
    (ii) Her street may not be representative of
    the whole population.
    (iii) Systematic random sampling from a
    directory **or** Cluster sampling of travel
    agents' clients, i.e., pick one travel agent
    at random and survey them about all
    their clients.
8. (i) Assign a number to each student and
    then use a random number generator to
    pick n numbers.
    (ii) (a) 23   (b) 8
9. (i) Quota sampling
    (ii) Convenient as no sampling frame
    required.
    Left to the discretion of the interviewer
    so possible bias.
10. (i) Cost and time, without a great loss in
    accuracy.
    (ii) A list of all items that could be included
    in the survey.
11. (i) 52 Junior; 48 Senior
    (ii) Stratified sampling is better if there
    are different identifiable groups with
    different views in the population.
12. (i) Cluster sampling (ii) Convenience
    (iii) Systematic

Exercise 10.4

1. (a) (i) 8   (ii) 7
    (b) (i) 7   (ii) 7
2. (i) 41 km/hr (ii) 39.45 km/hr

3. (i) 14   (ii) 14   (iii) 17
4. 14   **5.** 4, 6
6. (i) 25.857   (ii) 15; Median
7. (i) 195   (ii) 19
8. 79.2%
9. Median, since 50% of the marks will be
    above the median mark.
10. (i) 16.2   (ii) $x = 35$
11. (i) 25 (ii) 6 (iii) 5.6 (iv) 14 (v) 6
12. (i) 4   (ii) 4   (iii) 4.25
13. (i) 32 years (ii) (30–40) years
14. (i) 42.7   (ii) Mean will increase
15. (i) (a) B   (b) C
    (ii) Categorical data is not numerical
16. (i) 4.3 mm
    (ii) 26.5 hours
    (iii) 3 mm; 15 hours
    (iv) 2.5 mm; 16.5 hours
    (v) median rainfall and mean sunshine
    (least rainfall and highest sunshine)
17. 3.36 or 3.48

Exercise 10.5

1. (i) 8   (ii) 57
2. (i) 33   (ii) 29
    (iii) (a) $Q_1 = 27$ (b) $Q_3 = 34$ (c) 7
3. (i) 13   (ii) 8
    (iii) 15   (iv) 7
4. (i) 5 marks   (ii) 14.5 marks
    (iii) On average, the girls didn't do as well
    as the boys. The girls' marks were more
    dispersed.
5. (i) 25   (ii) 50
    (iii) 65   (iv) 15
6. (i) $Q_1 = 3.2$; $Q_3 = 4.0$;
    Interquartile range $= 0.8$
    (ii) 5.5
7. (i) 3.5   (ii) 2.7   (iii) 3.9
8. 1.414; 1.414
    (i) New set is $x + 10$
    (ii) Both the same
    (iii) If all the numbers are increased by the
    same amount, the standard deviation
    does not change.
10. (i) 14; 14   (ii) Route 1: 2; Route 2: 2.3
    (iii) Route 1, as times are less dispersed
11. 1.6   **12.** 0.84
13. 1.9   **14.** 11; 4.36

15. (i) 25   (ii) 5.3
     (iii) 30.3 and 19.7   (iv) 3
16. (i) $\bar{x} = a + 2$ (ii) $a = 5$
17. (i) 80%   (ii) 20%
18. (i) No, as it does not tell you what
     percentage did worse than Elaine.
     (ii) 480
19. (i) 53.5   (ii) 74.5
     (iii) 10.5   (iv) 4 students
     (v) 40th percentile
20. (i) €55   (ii) €32
     (iii) 13   (iv) €59; 7
     (v) 53rd to 56th percentile
21. $a = 10 - b; a = 6, b = 4$

Exercise 10.6

1. (i) 4   (ii) 27   (iii) 8   (iv) 36
2. (ii) 8   (iii) 16
3. (i) 6   (ii) 4.3 sec
     (iii) 3.25 sec   (iv) 3.5 sec
4. (i) 62   (ii) 47   (iii) 67   (iv) 20
5. (i) 41   (ii) 32   (iii) 47   (iv) 15
     (v) 47
6. (i) 19   (ii) (a) 66   (b) 49
     (iii) 55   (iv) 26
7. (i) 76; 27   (ii) 68; 38
     (iii) Those who didn't smoke; lower median
8. (ii) 55   (iii) 66.5
     (iv) English; Higher median
9. (i) 31 mins   (ii) 17.5 mins
     (iii) 15 mins   (iv) 0.75
     (v) Both have median 17.5, similar ranges; hence no significant difference
10. (i) 52 mins
     (ii) (a) 52 mins   (b) 69 mins
     (iii) (a) 31 mins   (b) 55 mins
     (iv) Women in the survey have a higher median and a wider range.

Exercise 10.7

1. (ii) 12   (iii) (20–40) km
     (iv) 40%
2. (i) 10   (ii) (40–50) years
     (iii) 12   (iv) 60
     (v) (50–60) years   (vi) (40–50) years
3. (ii) 38   (iii) (12–16) mins
     (iv) (12–16) mins   (v) 30
     (vi) 8

4. (i) 19   (ii) 54
     (iii) (10–15) sec   (iv) (10–15) sec
     (v) 20   (vi) 20
5. (ii) (25–35) mins   (iii) (25–35) mins
     (iv) (15–25) mins   (v) 48 people
     (vi) 29 mins

Exercise 10.8

1. Symmetrical;
     (i) Normal   (ii) Peoples' heights
2. Positively skewed; Age at which people start third-level education
3. (i) c   (ii) a   (iii) b   (iv) b   (v) c
4. Negatively skewed;
     (i) Mean   (ii) Mode
5. More of the data is closer to the mean in Ⓐ.
6. (i) B   (ii) B
7. (i) A   (ii) Equal
8. (i) B   (ii) A
9. (i) A   (ii) B
10. (i)

A	B	C	D
✗	✗	✓	✗
✓	✗	✗	✗
✗	✓	✗	✓
✓	✗	✗	✗
✓	✓	✓	✗

     (ii) D, as more of the data is located further from the mean.

Revision Exercise 10 (Core)

1. (i) Primary   (ii) Secondary
     (iii) Primary   (iv) Secondary
     (v) Secondary
2. (i) 13   (ii) 8   (iii) 15   (iv) 7
3. 10; 3.7
4. (i) Census surveys entire population; sample surveys only part of the population
     (ii) 25 students
5. (i) 32   (ii) €48   (iii) €25
     (iv) €29   (v) Males, higher median
6. (i) (b) because it has the greater spread
     (ii) 2; 1.14
7. (i) Stratified, then simple random sampling
     (ii) 20 students
     (iii) Give each student a number and then select 10, using random button on calculator.

8. (i) Yes. May not be representative as there is no random element to the survey.
(ii) Use stratified sampling based on gender, age, marital status, income levels, etc. and then use simple random sampling.

9. See definitions in textbook.

10. (ii) 4.7 mins   (iii) 4.05 mins; 1.2 mins

Revision Exercise 10 (Advanced)

1. David as standard deviation of his marks is smaller.

2. (i) $P_{40} = 57\%$ (ii) 75th percentile

3. (i) A, D   (ii) C, A   (iii) B
(iv) A   (v) A

4. 2.3

5. (i) Negatively skewed as most of the data occurs at the higher values.
(ii) A = mode; B = median; C = mean
(iii) Age when people retire

6. Large, 15; Medium, 25; Small, 20

7. (i) Mean = 3.74   (ii) $\sigma = 2.37$
(iii) In the later study, the average number of accidents has increased. The spread has also increased as the standard deviation is higher.

8. (i) Explanatory: Fertilizer; Response: Wheat yield.
(ii) Explanatory: Habitat; Response: Species.
(iii) Explanatory: Amount of water; Response: Time to cool.
(iv) Explanatory: Size of engine; Response: Petrol consumption.

9. A: Systematic; B: Convenience; C: Simple random; D: Stratified; E: Quota

10. (i) Median = 40; Interquartile range = 50
(ii) (a) Because zero would not be a typical average
(b) It would be distorted by the zeros or very high values.

Revision Exercise 10 (Extended Response Questions)

1. (i) (a) Median = 2 goals; Interquartile range = 3 goals
(b) Mean = 2.56 goals; $\sigma = 1.66$
(ii) The mean is higher in the 2008/09 season and the standard deviation is also higher. The wider spread in the 2008/09 season suggests more open games. However, the median number of goals per game is the same for both seasons. Overall, there is little significant difference between the two seasons.

2. (i) 22   (ii) $X = 11, Y = 27, Z = 22.5$
(iii) Strand Road as the median is higher.

3. (i) Driver: Positively skewed as a lot of the data is clustered to the left in the (20–30) year age-group.
Passenger: From ages (0–40) years, it is a symmetrical distribution with a mean of approximately 20 years. The values fall away as you move away from the centre.
(ii) (a) Driver: 20 years
(b) Passenger: 18 years
(iii) A uniform distribution, suggesting casualties equally likely at all ages with moderate peak from (15–25) years.
(iv) The (17–25) years age-group. Most of the casualties among both drivers and passengers occur in this group.

4. (ii) **Similarity:** Both have the same mode (3). **Difference:** Girls distribution resembles a normal distribution. For the boys, most of the data is concentrated at the lower values (1–3).
(iii) Though the medians are the same, the girls' distribution has a greater spread. The samples are sufficiently different to suggest that this could not happen by chance.
(iv) They could include more boys and girls who are not in GAA clubs. Include both urban and rural children so the sample would be less biased. Also, be more precise about what 'playing sport' means.

5. (i) A – run; B – cycle; C – swim
(ii) 25 mins   (iii) Approx. 3 mins
(iv) It would be very unusual for two or more athletes to have the same time as it is continuous numerical data (times were to the nearest 1000th of a second).

6. (i) Histogram – ensure that the class intervals are equal.
(ii) The distribution has a positive skew (tail to the right). Median = **225** days.

(iii) It is not a normal distribution and so z-scores are not appropriate. The distribution has a positive skew and hence it is not a normal distribution.

(iv) $\frac{24}{115}$ (or 0.21). This is the relative frequency of the next earthquake occurring between 100 and 200 days later.

(v) The idea of 1000 deaths is very subjective as earthquakes occur in areas of low population also. An earthquake relatively low on the Richter Scale could result in a lot of deaths in a densely-populated area. So the size of the earthquake, as measured on the Richter Scale, may be more relevant to a future analysis than the number of deaths. Finally, the data may be divided by region and the frequency plotted against the size of the earthquake.

Chapter 11: Coordinate Geometry: The Circle

Exercise 11.1

1. (i) $x^2 + y^2 = 4$ (ii) $x^2 + y^2 = 25$
    (iii) $x^2 + y^2 = 2$ (iv) $x^2 + y^2 = 18$
    (v) $16x^2 + 16y^2 = 9$ (vi) $4x^2 + 4y^2 = 25$
2. $x^2 + y^2 = 25$
3. $x^2 + y^2 = 17$
4. (i) $(0, 0)$ (ii) 5   (iii) $x^2 + y^2 = 25$
5. $x^2 + y^2 = 17$
6. (i) 3   (ii) 1   (iii) $3\sqrt{3}$
    (iv) $\frac{5}{2}$ (v) $\frac{2}{3}$ (vi) $\frac{7}{4}$
7. (i) $\sqrt{5}$ (ii) $x^2 + y^2 = 5$
8. $x^2 + y^2 = 25$
9. $x^2 + y^2 = 10$
10. $x^2 + y^2 = 20$; t is a tangent

Exercise 11.2

1. (i) $(x - 3)^2 + (y - 1)^2 = 4$
    (ii) $(x - 1)^2 + (y + 4)^2 = 8$
    (iii) $(x - 4)^2 + y^2 = 12$
    (iv) $x^2 + (y + 5)^2 = 18$
2. $(x - 2)^2 + (y - 2)^2 = 10$
3. (i) $(1, 3)$
    (ii) $(x - 1)^2 + (y - 3)^2 = 8$

4. (i) $(3, 2); r = 4$ (ii) $(-2, 6); r = 2\sqrt{2}$
    (iii) $(3, 0); r = \sqrt{5}$ (iv) $(0, -2); r = \sqrt{10}$
5. $(x + 2)^2 + (y - 5)^2 = 72$
6. $(3, 3); (x - 3)^2 + (y - 3)^2 = 9$
7. (i) $(2, -4); r = 5$ (ii) $(1, 3); r = 5$
    (iii) $(4, 0); r = 2\sqrt{6}$ (iv) $(-2\frac{1}{2}, 3); r = \frac{9}{2}$
    (v) $(1, -\frac{3}{4}); r = \frac{5}{4}$ (vi) $(0, 3\frac{1}{2}); r = 2$
10. Inside
11. Outside
12. $k = -8$
13. (ii) 4   (iii) $(x + 4)^2 + (y - 3)^2 = 16$
14. (i) 2   (ii) $(4, -4)$
    (iii) $(x - 4)^2 + (y + 4)^2 = 4$
    (iv) k_4
15. $(x + 4)^2 + (y - 4)^2 = 16$
16. (i) $(2, 6)$
17. $(x - 2)^2 + (y - 2)^2 = 1$
18. (i) A: $(-7, -1); r = 10$;
    B: $(3, -1); r = 10$;
    C: $(-2, -1); r = 5$
    (ii) $(x + 7)^2 + (y + 1)^2 = 100$

Exercise 11.3

1. Centre $= (0, 0)$; radius $= \sqrt{10}$
2. $(3, -4); r = 5\sqrt{2}$
3. Not a tangent
4. $(x + 1)^2 + (y - 2)^2 = 13$
5. $(x - 2)^2 + (y - 1)^2 = 18$
6. (i) $(1, 1)$
    (ii) 1
    (iv) $|-g|$ and $|-f|$ equal to radius length
7. $(x - 2)^2 + (y - 2)^2 = 4$
8. $(x - 2)^2 + (y - 3)^2 = 4$
9. (i) $(2, -3); r = 5$ (ii) $-31, 19$
10. (i) $2x + 8y - 1 = 0$ (ii) $8x - 2y - 21 = 0$
    (iii) $\left(\frac{5}{2}, -\frac{1}{2}\right)$ (iv) $\sqrt{\frac{17}{2}}$
    (v) $\left(x - \frac{5}{2}\right)^2 + \left(y + \frac{1}{2}\right)^2 = \frac{17}{2}$
11. $x^2 + y^2 - 2x + 4y = 0$
12. $x^2 + y^2 - 6x - 8y = 0$
13. $-g - 2f = 6; 6g + 10f + c = -34$;
    $2g - 6f - c = 10; x^2 + y^2 - 4x - 4y - 2 = 0$
14. $f = 0; 3x^2 + 3y^2 - 14x - 67 = 0$
15. (i) $r = 3$
    (ii) $k = 4; T = (2, 0)$
16. (i) $g = f$ and $g, f < 0$
    (ii) $x^2 + y^2 - 6x - 6y + 9 = 0$

17. (ii) $2x - 3y - 8 = 0$

(iii) $x + 5y + 9 = 0$

(iv) $(1, -2); r = \sqrt{13}$

(v) $x^2 + y^2 - 2x + 4y - 8 = 0$

18. $x^2 + y^2 - 8x - 12y + 27 = 0$

19. $x^2 + y^2 + 10x - 10y + 30 = 0;$
$x^2 + y^2 - 2x + 2y - 18 = 0$

20. (i) $y = 1$

(ii) $(x - 15)^2 + (y - 7)^2 = 36$

(iii) $(x - 13)^2 + (y - 7)^2 = 36$

Exercise 11.4

1. $x + y = 4$

2. $3x - y + 10 = 0$

3. $4x - y - 17 = 0$

4. (ii) $(1, -2)$

(iii) $x + 2y - 7 = 0$

5. $4x - y + 2 = 0$

6. $(2, -5); r = \sqrt{37}; x + 6y - 9 = 0$

7. 5

8. $(3, 2); r = \sqrt{5}$

9. $(3, 1), r = 5; c = -38, 12$

10. $k = 3, \dfrac{1}{9}$

12. $(x - 2)^2 + (y + 1)^2 = \dfrac{5}{2}$

(or $2x^2 + 2y^2 - 8x + 4y + 5 = 0$)

13. $mx - y = 0; y = 0; 4x - 3y = 0$

14. $mx - y - 3m + 5 = 0; y - 5 = 0;$
$24x - 7y - 37 = 0$

15. $3x + 4y + c = 0; 3x + 4y + 8 = 0;$
$3x + 4y - 22 = 0$

16. (i) $\sqrt{5}$

(ii) $(x - 3)^2 + (y - 5)^2 = 5$

(iii) $2x + y - 6 = 0$

17. (i) $(5k, -3)$ (ii) $k = 2$ (iii) $d = -53$

18. (i) $r = 3$ (iii) 4

19. $(7, 1); r = 4; 5$

20. $\sqrt{10}$

21. $3\sqrt{2}$

22. $c = 12$

Exercise 11.5

1. $(-1, 2)$ and $(-2, -1)$

2. $(1, -3)$

3. $(2, -1)$

4. (i) $(4, 2)$ and $(-1, 7)$

(ii) $(-1, 4)$ and $(3, -4)$

(iii) $(2, 1)$ and $(0, -5)$

5. $(-2, 5)$

6. (i) $(3, 1)$ and $(-1, -1)$

(ii) $(1, 0)$

(iii) $(x - 1)^2 + y^2 = 5$

7. $(6, 0)$ and $(-2, 0)$; 8 units

8. $(0, -7)$ and $(0, 1)$; 8 units

9. $a = 6, b = 1$

10. 6 units

11. $2x - y - 3 = 0; (2, 1)$ and $(-1, -5)$

12. $3x - 4y - 9 = 0; (-1, -3)$

13. $(-3, 4)$ and $(-5, 2)$

14. (i) $(-1, 4)$

(ii) Rising: $(-3, 1)$; Setting: $(1, 1)$

Exercise 11.6

1. $s_1: (1, 0); r = 4; s_2: (7, 8); r = 6$

3. $(2, 1); r = 5; (8, 9); r = 5; |c_1 c_2| = 10$

4. Externally

5. (ii) $x + y - 9 = 0$ (iii) $(4, 5)$

6. (i) $r = 5$

(ii) $(x - 3)^2 + (y - 0)^2 = 5^2$

7. (iii) $2\sqrt{7}$ units

8. (i) $(4, 5)$

(ii) $x^2 + y^2 - 8x - 10y + 16 = 0$

9. $\left(x - \dfrac{5}{2}\right)^2 + (y - 2)^2 = \left(\dfrac{5}{2}\right)^2$

[or $x^2 + y^2 - 5x - 4y + 4 = 0$]

10. (i) $r = \sqrt{30}$

(ii) $(x + 1)^2 + (y + 4)^2 = 30$

11. (i) $(3, 4)$

(ii) $(x - 3)^2 + (y - 4)^2 = 25$

12. $(3, -2); r = 5; k = 36$

Exercise 11.7

1. $(x - 3)^2 + (y + 4)^2 = 16$

2. $(x + 3)^2 + (y - 2)^2 = 9$

3. (i) $y = 5$

(ii) $(x - 5)^2 + (y - 5)^2 = 25$

(iii) $x = 10$

4. (ii) $r = 4$

(iii) $(6, 4)$

(iv) $(x - 6)^2 + (y - 4)^2 = 16$

5. (i) $r = 4$

(ii) $(4, 5)$

(iii) $(x - 4)^2 + (y - 5)^2 = 16$

6. $x^2 + y^2 - 8x - 6y + 16 = 0$

7. $x^2 + y^2 - 8x + 6y + 9 = 0$

8. $(x - 6)^2 + (y - 5)^2 = 25; (x + 4)^2 + (y - 5)^2 = 25$

Revision Exercise 11 (Core)

1. (i) $\sqrt{13}$ (ii) $(x + 1)^2 + (y - 5)^2 = 13$
2. $(1, 2); r = \sqrt{14}; x^2 + y^2 = 14$
3. $(x - 2)^2 + (y - 3)^2 = 9$
5. $(x - 1)^2 + (y + 1)^2 = 8$
6. $P = (11, 0); Q = (-1, 0)$
7. $(1, -2); r = 1; k = 0, 2$
8. 4
10. $(x - 6)^2 + (y - 8)^2 = 29$
11. 1257 km

Revision Exercise 11 (Advanced)

1. $(3, 1); r = \sqrt{13}; 2x + 3y - 22 = 0$
2. (ii) $p = 0$ or $p = -\dfrac{12}{35}$
3. $k = -25, 48$
4. (i) $p = -6$ (ii) $(4, 3)$ and $(1, 0)$
5. (ii) $(x - 2)^2 + (y - 1)^2 = 64$
6. (i) $C = (0, 5)$ (ii) $\sqrt{5}$ (iii) $(2, 4)$
7. $(0, 0); r = 2$ and $(4, 3); r = 3; 4x + 3y - 10 = 0$
8. (i) $2g + 5f = -18; 2g - f = 6$
    (ii) $g = 1, f = -4$
    (iii) $x^2 + y^2 + 2x - 8y + 7 = 0; (-1, 4); r = \sqrt{10}$
9. $(x - 4)^2 + (y + 3)^2 = 25$
10. (i) $C = (-3, 2)$ (ii) $r = 5$ (iii) 4
11. $(x - 7)^2 + (y - 3)^2 = 9$ or
    $x^2 + y^2 - 14x - 6y + 49 = 0$
12. (i) $(x - 6)^2 + (y - 5 - 2\sqrt{3})^2 = 1$
    (ii) $0.645 \, u^2$

Revision Exercise 11 (Extended Response Questions)

1. (i) 1 unit   (ii) $\sqrt{11}$
    (iii) $4x^2 + 4y^2 - 64x + 191 = 0$
2. $3x - 4y + c = 0; 3x - 4y + 9 = 0;$
    $3x - 4y - 41 = 0$
3. (i) $C = (8, 1); D = (2, 1)$
    (ii) $(5, 4)$
    (iii) $(x - 5)^2 + (y - 4)^2 = 9$
4. (i) Proof
    (ii) $x^2 + y^2 + 6x - 6y + 9 = 0;$
       $x^2 + y^2 + 30x - 30y + 225 = 0$
    (iii) Proof   (iv) $k = 5$ (v) Proof
5. $(x - 8)^2 + (y - 2)^2 = 16$
    or $(x - 32)^2 + (y - 2)^2 = 16$

6. (iii) $(x - 4.5)^2 + (y - 2.5)^2 = 2.5$
    (iv) $(x - 1.5)^2 + (y - 3.5)^2 = 2.5$

7. (i) $(x - 3)^2 + (y - 5)^2 = 25$
    (ii) $3x - 4y + 36 = 0; (-12, 0)$
    (iii) $4x + 3y - 52 = 0; (13, 0)$
    (iv) 60
8. (i) $(a, b); r = a$
    (ii) $(x - 1)^2 + (y - 3)^2 = 1$
       or $(x - 5)^2 + (y + 1)^2 = 25$
    (iii) $4\sqrt{2}$

Chapter 12: Algebra 3

Exercise 12.1

1. (i) $x > 4$ (ii) $x \leqslant 1$ (iii) $x < -3$
2. (i) $x < 10$ (ii) $x \leqslant 7$ (iii) $x < 8$
3. (i) $x < 4$ (ii) $x \leqslant -\dfrac{1}{2}$ (iii) $x > -7$
4. (i) $-3 \leqslant x \leqslant 2$ (ii) $-4 \leqslant x \leqslant -2$
    (iii) $-\dfrac{1}{2} < x \leqslant \dfrac{1}{2}$
5. (i) $2 < x < 7$ (ii) $-\dfrac{1}{2} \leqslant x \leqslant 3\dfrac{2}{3}$
    (iii) $-14 \leqslant x \leqslant -7$
6. $x > 2.5$
7. (i) $x < 4$ (ii) $x > 2$ (iii) $2 < x < 4$
8. (i) $x > 2\dfrac{1}{2}$ (ii) $x < 3$ (iii) $2\dfrac{1}{2} < x < 3$
9. (i) $x < 7$ (ii) $x > 8$ (iii) Null set
10. (i) $x \leqslant 4$ (ii) $x \geqslant 4$ (iii) $x = 4$
11. Length $= 10$ m, width $= 9$ m
12. $a = 6.645, b = 7.645, n = 7$
13. (i) $a^n < b^n$ (ii) $a^n > b^n$ (iii) $a^n > b^n$
    (iv) $a^n < b^n$
14. $x = 6$

Exercise 12.2

1. (i) $-2 \geqslant x \geqslant 3$ (ii) $-5 \leqslant x \leqslant 2$
    (iii) $\dfrac{1}{2} < x < 2$
2. (i) $-3 \leqslant x \leqslant 2$ (ii) $-4 < x < 1\dfrac{1}{2}$
    (iii) $-3\dfrac{1}{2} \leqslant x \leqslant 0$
3. (i) $-1\dfrac{1}{2} > x > 1\dfrac{2}{3}$ (ii) $-4 \geqslant x \geqslant 4$
    (iii) $-1\dfrac{1}{2} \geqslant x \geqslant 4$
4. $-1 < x < 7$
5. Proof
6. $-3 \geqslant k \geqslant 1$
7. $-4 \leqslant k \leqslant 1$
8. $-1 \leqslant p \leqslant 3; p = 2$
9. (i) $-2 > x > -1$ (ii) $x > 3$
    (iii) $-10 < x < -3$

10. (i) $-14 > x > 5$ (ii) $-\frac{1}{2} < x < -\frac{3}{10}$

     (iii) $\frac{1}{5} < x < \frac{6}{11}$

11. (i) $1\frac{1}{2} > x \geq 3$ (ii) $1 < x < 3$

     (iii) $-1 \geq x > 1$

12. (i) $-3 < x < 10$ (ii) $-9 < x < 5$

     (iii) $1 > x \geq 2\frac{1}{2}$

13. $-3 > x > -2$

14. No real roots

15. (i) $1\frac{1}{2} \geq t \geq 5$ (ii) $2 \leq t \leq 4.5$

     (iii) $1\frac{1}{2} < t < 2$ and $4.5 < t < 5$

16. (i) $-3 > x > -\frac{1}{2}$ (ii) $1 \geq x \geq 3$

     (iii) $-1\frac{1}{2} \leq x \leq 0.5$ (iv) $-1 < x < 5$

17. (i) Length > 3.75 (ii) width > 0.75

18. $-2 < p < 3$

19. (i) $x < 10$

     (ii) $x > 1$

     (iii) $1 < x < 10$

20. $x = 2\,\text{m}$ or $3\,\text{m}$

Exercise 12.3

1. (i) $(-4, -2)$ (ii) $(-2, 6)$ (iii) $(-2, 3)$

     (iv) $(\frac{1}{2}, 1)$ (v) $(2, 4)$ (vi) 2

2. $-1, 2\frac{1}{3}$

3. $f(x) = |x|$, $g(x) = |x - 4|$, $h(x) = |x + 3|$,
     $f(-2) = 2$, $g(2) = 2$, $h(-5) = 2$

4. $f(x) = |x + 1|$, $g(x) = |2x + 2|$, $h(x) = |3x + 3|$

5. 4

6. (i) $4 < x < 8$ (ii) $-6 \leq x \leq 2$

     (iii) $x \leq -2$ or $x \geq 3$ (iv) $x \leq -5$ or $x \geq 6$

     (v) $-3 < x < -\frac{1}{3}$ (vi) $1 < x < 7$

7. (i) $-3 \geq x \geq 4$ (ii) $-1\frac{1}{2} \leq x \leq -1$

     (iii) $-\frac{1}{3} \leq x \leq 5$

8. $-2\frac{2}{3} \leq x \leq 8$

9. $x \leq -24$ or $x \geq 0$

10. $-1 < x < 1$

11. $x = -1, 0; -1 > x > 0$

12. (i) $-4 < x < 2$ (ii) $x < -4$ or $x > 2$

     (iii) $1\frac{1}{4} < x < 3\frac{1}{2}$ (iv) $2 < x < 3$

     (v) $1\frac{1}{4} < x < 2$ (vi) $2 < x < 3$

     (vii) $3 < x < 3\frac{1}{2}$

13. (i) $\frac{2}{5} < x < \frac{1}{2}$ (ii) $x = -1, 1\frac{2}{3}$

     (iii) $-2 < x < 0$

Exercise 12.4

1. Proof   **2.** Proof   **3.** Proof

4. Proof   **5.** Proof   **6.** Proof

7. Proof   **8.** Proof

Exercise 12.5

1. Proof   **2.** Proof   **3.** Proof

4. Proof   **5.** Proof   **6.** Proof

7. Proof   **8.** Proof

9. $(a + b)(a^2 - ab + b^2)$; proof

10. Proof   **11.** Proof   **12.** Proof

13. Proof   **14.** Proof   **15.** Proof

16. (i) $(a - b)(a + b)(a^2 + b^2)$

     (ii) $(a - b)^2(a + b)(a^2 + b^2)$

17. Proof   **18.** Proof   **19.** Proof

20. Multiply both sides by $d(b + d)$; then divide both sides by bd

21. Proof

Exercise 12.6

1. (i) a^5 (ii) x^4 (iii) $6x^6$ (iv) x^3

     (v) x^{-1} (vi) 1 (vii) 3 (viii) a^6

     (ix) x^3 (x) $9a^2b^2$

2. (i) 4 (ii) $\frac{1}{9}$ (iii) 8

     (iv) $\frac{9}{4}$ (v) 2

3. (i) 4 (ii) 8 (iii) 9

     (iv) 27 (v) 25

4. (i) $\frac{9}{4}$ (ii) $\frac{3}{2}$ (iii) $\frac{125}{27}$

     (iv) $\frac{25}{9}$ (v) $\frac{3}{2}$

5. 4^{-2}

6. $\frac{11}{12}$

7. (i) $\frac{y^3}{x^2}$ (ii) $\frac{p^{12}}{q^8}$ (iii) $\frac{1}{a}$

     (iv) $y^{\frac{2}{3}}$ (v) $\dfrac{1}{a^{\frac{9}{2}}b^2}$ (vi) $x^{\frac{1}{4}}$

8. (i) $\frac{x + 1}{x}$ (ii) $x^2 - x$ (iii) $1 + x$

9. $\frac{x}{x - 1}$

10. $k = \frac{1}{2}$

11. $262\,\text{Hz}$

12. $\frac{9}{16}$

13. $k = 24$

14. $k = 28$

Exercise 12.7

1. (i) 5   (ii) $\frac{3}{2}$ (iii) $\frac{3}{2}$ (iv) -3
2. (i) $-\frac{3}{2}$ (ii) $-\frac{5}{2}$ (iii) 3   (iv) $-\frac{3}{2}$
3. (i) $-\frac{1}{2}$ (ii) $\frac{5}{4}$ (iii) $-\frac{1}{6}$ (iv) $-\frac{1}{3}$
4. $2^{\frac{5}{2}}; \frac{15}{8}$
5. $x = \frac{2}{3}, y = -\frac{16}{3}$
6. $4.2^x; 2.2^x; c = \frac{5}{2}$
7. $x = 1, 2$
8. $x = 2$
9. (i) $x = 0, 3$ (ii) $x = 0, 2$
10. (i) y^2 (ii) $2y^2$
    (iii) $8y; x = -1, 2$
11. $x = -1, 0$ 12. $x = -\frac{1}{2}, 0$
13. $x = 0, 3$ 14. $x = \pm 1$
15. $x = 1, 3$

Exercise 12.8

1. (i) B   (ii) A   (iii) D   (iv) C
2. (i) 1000 ha
   (ii) (a) 4000 ha   (b) 5278 ha
   (iii) A(ha) graph
   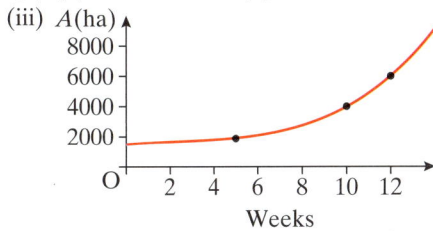
   (iv) 5 weeks
3. (i) decreasing   (ii) decreasing
   (iii) increasing   (iv) decreasing
4. (i) 0.6   (ii) 3   (iii) 8   (iv) 6
5. (iv) $-2 \leqslant x < 0$ (v) $0 < x \leqslant 4$
   (vi) $x = 0$ (vii) $0 < x \leqslant 4$
6. (i) Decay
   (ii) (a) 3 days
        (b) 9 days
        (c) 18 days
   (iii) 3.9°C
7. (a) (i) 97.6%   (ii) 94.2%
   (b) 5780 years
   (c) 1964 years
8. (i) 1000 ha
   (ii) (a) 2000 ha   (b) 4000 ha   (c) 5278 ha

9. (i) R(t) graph
   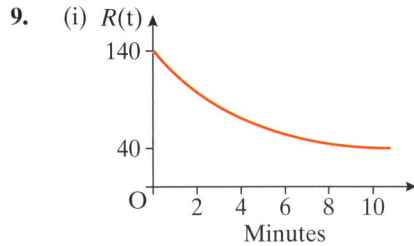
   (ii) 140 beats per minute
   (iii) (a) 5.5 minutes
         (b) 10.5 minutes
   (iv) 50 beats per minute
10. 1000
11. (i) 40
    (ii) $b = 1.2; b > 1$ $\therefore$ the number of flies is increasing

Exercise 12.9

1. (i) 2   (ii) 4   (iii) 3   (iv) 6
2. (i) $\frac{4}{3}$ (ii) $\frac{3}{2}$ (iii) $\frac{5}{4}$ (iv) -3
   (v) -4
3. (i) -3 (ii) 4   (iii) 64   (iv) 8
4. (i) $\frac{1}{2}$ (ii) $\frac{3}{2}$ (iii) $\sqrt{2}$ (iv) -1
5. (i) 3   (ii) 2   (iii) 2
6. (i) 0   (ii) 2
7. (i) $a + 1$ (ii) $a - 1$ (iii) $2a - 1$
   (iv) $2a - 3$ (v) $2a + 1$
8. (i) 7.64   (ii) 3.86   (iii) 1.93
   (iv) -0.279
9. (i) $x = 1 + \dfrac{\log(y - 3)}{\log 2}$
   (ii) $x = 3.3219$
10. Proof
11. Proof
12. (i) 13   (ii) 10   (iii) -3
13. Proof
14. (i) 0.602   (ii) 1.43   (iii) 2.55
    (iv) 3.75   (v) 4.46   (vi) 5.54
    (vii) 6.59
15. Minimum $= 10^3 = 1000$
    Maximum $= 10^4 = 10\,000$
16. (i) 0.143   (ii) 5.28   (iii) 0.504
17. (i) $\frac{4}{3}$ (ii) $\frac{3}{5}$
18. Proof   19. Proof
20. $p = 2q^3$ 21. $a = \sqrt{3}$
22. 5.66   23. $x = 4$
24. $x = \pm\frac{4}{3}$ 25. $x = 21$

26. $x = 3$

27. $x = \frac{2}{3}, 5$

28. $x = -2, 6$

29. $x = \frac{1}{8}$

30. $x = 3, y = 2$, or $x = \frac{2}{5}, y = 15$

31. (i) $x = \frac{1}{16}, 2$ (ii) $x = \frac{1}{4}, 2$

Exercise 12.10

3. (i)

x	$\frac{1}{9}$	$\frac{1}{3}$	1	3	9
$y = \log_3 x$	-2	-1	0	1	2

(iii) 0.8 (iv) 0.834

4. One graph is the inverse of the other

5. Graph

6. Graph

7. (i) $x = \dfrac{\log(y + 5)}{\log 3} - 2$ or $\log_3(y + 5) - 2$

(ii) 1.236

8. Graph

9. Graph

10. Graph

Exercise 12.11

1. (i) (a) €5030 (b) €5060.18 (c) €5090.54

(ii) €5000 $(1.006)^t$

(iii) 116 months

2. 0.25

3. (ii) 8.8 minutes (iii) 15°

4. (i) $0.1\,\mathrm{Wm}^{-2}$ and $0.01\,\mathrm{Wm}^{-2}$

(ii) 130 dB

5. Proof $[E = A^{1.5}.10^{4.8}]$

6. (i) €100 $(1.045)^t$ (ii) €155.30

(iii) €80.25

7. (i) 0.6 kg (ii) 15% (iii) 5 months

8. (i) $M_0 = 10\,\mathrm{g}, k = 0.00495$

(ii) 7 g

(iii) 325 days

Exercise 12.12A

1. Proof **2.** Proof **3.** Proof

4. Proof **5.** Proof **6.** Proof

7. Proof **8.** Proof

Exercise 12.12B

1. Proof **2.** Proof **3.** Proof

4. Proof **5.** Proof **6.** Proof

7. Proof **8.** Proof **9.** Proof

10. Proof **11.** Proof **12.** Proof

Exercise 12.12C

1. Proof **2.** Proof **3.** Proof

4. Proof **5.** Proof **6.** Proof

7. Proof

Revision Exercise 12 (Core)

1. $-3.5 \leqslant x \leqslant 1$

2. (a) (i) 3162 (ii) 0.65

(iii) 1.32 (iv) 2.7

(b) (i) 30 (ii) 6.38

(iii) 0.00823 (iv) 0.99

3. (i) $a = \frac{1}{2}$ (ii) $b = \frac{3}{2}$

4. $x = 5, x = 11$

5. (i) $n = 1$ (ii) $n = -\frac{10}{3}$

6. (i) $a + b = 2.5, 4a + b = 4$

(ii) $a = 0.5, b = 2$

7. $C = \ln x, A = \ln x + 1, B = \ln(x + 1)$

8. $x = 2, 3$

9. $A = \frac{9}{2}, b = \ln\frac{4}{3}$

10. $k = \dfrac{4}{\ln 3}$

11. $a = 2, b = 3$

12. $x = 1.96$

Revision Exercise 12 (Advanced)

1. (i) $x < -2$ or $x > 5$ (ii) $-5 < x < 3$

(iii) $-5 < x < -2$

2. (i) 30 g (ii) 1585 years (iii) 6644 years

3. (i) 1000 (ii) 20

4. $125, \frac{1}{25}$

5. $x \leqslant 3.38$

6. (ii) $x = -1$ (iii) $-3, \leqslant x < 0$

7. $x = \mathrm{e}^y + 3$

8. $-24 \geqslant x \geqslant 0$

9. $x + 1$

10. Proof

12. (i) $-3 \leqslant k \leqslant 4\frac{1}{2}$

(ii) $-\frac{1}{2} < k < \frac{1}{2}$

14. $u_{n+1} = (n - 19)2^{n+1}, u_{n+2} = (n - 18)2^{n+2}$

15. $x = \frac{1}{2}, y = 1$

16. (i) An exponential function

(ii) 57 030

(iii) 40 000

(iv) 23.5 years

17. (i) $P = A\mathrm{e}^{kt}$, where $k = 0.078576$ and

t = number of years and $A = 8000$

(ii) 17 553

(iii) 2016

Revision Exercise 12 (Extended Response Questions)

1. (i) $t = 0$, $N = 5000$; $t = 5$, $N = 2362$; claim
   is valid

   (ii) 1115.65

   (iii) 5000

   (iv) 26.1 days

2. (i) $0.02 (0.92)^{\frac{x}{10}}$

   (ii) $0.0197 \, \text{mm}^2$

   (iii) $0.02 (0.92)^{(10 - 2.9x)}$

   (iv) $x > 2.59$

3. (i) $A = (0.83)^n I$; $B = (0.66) (0.89)^n I$

   (ii) 6 stations

4. (i) $A(1.11)^t$ (ii) $10A(0.95)^t$

   (iii) 14.8 years   (iv) 29.6 years

   (v) Graphs

5. (i) Growth   (ii) Proof

   (iii) Proof   (iv) $a = 1, \frac{1}{2}$

   (v) $a = 1, b = 0$; $a = \frac{1}{2}, b = \frac{1}{2} \ln 2$

   (vi) $A = 20\,000$

   (vii) 6.64 hours